SPOON

Phaidon Press Limited
Regent's Wharf
All Saints Street
London N1 9PA

Phaidon Press Inc.
180 Varick Street
New York, NY 10014

www.phaidon.com

First published 2002
Reprinted in paperback 2004, 2005
© 2002 Phaidon Press Limited

Images © the designers unless otherwise stated

ISBN 0 7148 4455 1

A CIP catalogue record for this book is available from the British Library.

Project Editor: Emilia Terragni
Editorial Manager: Victoria Clarke
Senior Editor: Julia MacKenzie
Editorial Assistants: Verena Merli, Emily Winter
Designer: Mark Diaper, Eggers + Diaper, Berlin
Production Manager: Paul Hammond

Printed in China

ACKNOWLEDGEMENTS

Special thanks are due to the 100 designers in *Spoon* and the ten curators:
Ron Arad, Giulio Cappellini, Ultan Guilfoyle, Brooke Hodge, Laura Houseley,
Hansjerg Maier-Aichen, Ryu Niimi, Ramón Ubeda, Lisa White, Stefan Ytterborn.
Thanks are also due to Helena Attlee for copyediting and Imogen Forster,
Graham Thomson and Shaun Whiteside for translations.

The publishers would also like to thank the following for their assistance
in providing the images for the design classics: Apple, for the i-sub by
Apple Design Team; Bd Ediciones de Diseño for the Banco Catalano by
Óscar Tusquets Blanca and Lluís Clotet; Cappellini for the Tavolo '64 by AG
Fronzoni; Citroën for the Citroën DS by Flaminio Bertoni; Salvatore Licitra
for the Superleggera Chair by Gio Ponti; Museum of Finnish Architecture for
Savoy Vase by Alvar Aalto; Piaggio for the Vespa by Corradino d'Ascanio;
United Publishers for the Heineken WOBO by Alfred Heineken and John
Habraken; Wilhelm Wagenfeld Museum, Bremen for Max and Moritz salt
and pepper shakers by Wilhelm Wagenfeld; Wright Gallery, Chicago for Flag
Halyard Lounge Chair by Hans Wegner.
Text by Roland Barthes reproduced courtesy of Hill and Wang, New York.

PREFACE

Spoon provides a global overview of contemporary product design. It presents the work of 100 designers who have broken new ground internationally in the last five years. The designers have been selected by ten curators, who are all highly respected for their knowledge of the contemporary design scene worldwide. The ten curators work in different countries and hold a variety of positions in the design field: they are designers, critics, museum curators, educators and entrepreneurs. Deeply involved in innovative developments in contemporary design, they have chosen those who, in their opinion, are the most interesting designers of today. The result is a wide range of recent design projects: from furniture to kitchen utensils, from lamps to motorcycles.

The selected designers are presented in alphabetical order with an introductory text written by the curators who chose them. The curators were also requested to pick a 'design classic', which they think best exemplifies the concept of 'good design'. These 'classics' are illustrated at the end of the book and are accompanied by a text in which the curators discuss these icons of design.

The designers featured in *Spoon* cover every field of industrial design and come from a wide variety of countries and backgrounds. Some are very young and have just started to have projects manufactured industrially. Others have worked in related disciplines and have only recently started to do product design. Working in a field that explores new technologies but at the same time renews established techniques, the designers have very different approaches to their projects: some draw sketches that the manufacturer transforms into products, others supply precise technical drawings and computer renderings, while still others work only with three-dimensional models. The final object is the last stage of a long process that starts with the designer's creativity and is developed in the manufacturer's workshop through trial and error. *Spoon* illustrates some of the drawings or prototypes, together with the finished products, to give an idea of that production process. All of the designers selected have had products industrially manufactured.

Certain common themes emerge in the work of the selected designers. For example, many of the designers are concerned about ecology and the benefits of recycling. Some of them have chosen to use materials and techniques that are non-polluting, while others have created objects with components that can be easily dismantled for recycling, or they have designed products that are intended to help us behave in a more ecologically friendly way.

One of the recent developments in the design world that is highlighted here is the expansion in the kind of products industrial designers work on. For a long time the industrial production of furniture and lighting has sought an aesthetic combination of form and function, but it is only in the last few years that the leading manufacturers of high-tech products such as computers or telephones have started to concern themselves with the look of their products and to seek designers to lead their internal design teams. These teams, some of whose work is illustrated in *Spoon*, represent new and interesting phenomena in the industrial design field.

Spoon is a comprehensive view of contemporary industrial design, showing not only a huge range of products and materials but also something of the design method, revealing the fascinating and complicated process of designing an object such as a simple spoon. EMILIA TERRAGNI

RON ARAD is a designer and co-founder of both the design and production studio One Off (1981) and of the Associates architecture and design practice (1989). He is currently Professor of Design Products at the Royal College of Art in London. He designs for many leading companies, including Alessi, Cassina, Cappellini, Fiam, Kartell, Moroso and Vitra. His architectural projects include the Tel Aviv Opera House, the Adidas Sport Café in Toulon, the new Technology Hall at Selfridges, London and various gallery and exhibition designs. Arad has exhibited at many major museums and galleries throughout the world and his work is in many public collections.

GIULIO CAPPELLINI was a founder member of the furniture manufacturer Cappellini, where he worked with young designers from all over the world and exhibited Cappellini products in some of the most important museums in the world. Since 1997 he has been involved in the opening of Cappellini single-branded shops; to date they have opened in Milan, Vienna, New York, Moscow, São Paolo and, most recently, in Paris. He has had work published in magazines internationally and has given lessons to the architectural faculty of Milan Polytechnic, to the Domus Academy, and to the European Institute of Design, and has been visiting professor at the universities of Montreal and Valencia.

ULTAN GUILFOYLE is a documentary film-maker by profession and has worked in London and New York. He is Director of Film & Video Production at the Solomon R Guggenheim Museum in New York. His films have appeared on the BBC and Channel 4 in Britain and CBS, HBO, Bravo and PBS in the United States. He is currently producing Sydney Pollack's first feature documentary on the California architect Frank Gehry, which will be released in the spring of 2003. He writes on industrial design and architecture in Britain and the United States. In 1995, Guilfoyle was invited by the Guggenheim Museum in New York to organize what became the landmark exhibition, 'The Art of the Motorcycle'. The exhibition was inaugurated in New York and then travelled.

BROOKE HODGE is the Curator of Architecture and Design at the Museum of Contemporary Art in Los Angeles. Formerly Director of Exhibitions and Publications at Harvard University Graduate School of Design she has also held the position of Adjunct Curator of Architecture at the Fogg Art Museum, Harvard. Hodge has curated exhibitions of the work of architects, theatre designers, artists and fashion designers. She is currently working on an exhibition of the work of car designer J Mays, scheduled to open in Los Angeles in November 2002, and an exhibition of Frank Gehry's newest projects, which will open in conjunction with the Disney Concert Hall in 2003.

LAURA HOUSELEY was the Architecture and Design Editor of the international lifestyle magazine *Wallpaper**. For over four years she scoured the globe in search of new, innovative and well-crafted designs with which to fill the pages of this celebrated publication. She also revisits and documents iconic or forgotten designers.

HANSJERG MAIER-AICHEN is the founder of the design brand Authentics, a leading international design company of plastic products for everyday use, which received the European design prize in 1987. His work has been exhibited all over Europe and has received many prestigious awards. Between 1974 and 1984 he worked as a cultural consultant for the European Community. He is now a member of the board of directors of the German Design Council and of the Design Labor Bremerhaven. Since 1998 he has been a visiting professor at Central Saint Martins College of Art & Design, London and has recently been made Professor for Product Design at the Hochschule für Gestaltung, Karlsruhe.

RYU NIIMI is a curator, writer and critic. Professor of Arts Policy and Management at Musashino Art University, he has also worked as curatorial adviser to the Isamu Noguchi Garden Museum of Japan. For seventeen years, from 1982 to 1999, he was curator at Sezon Museum of Art, Tokyo, where he curated several exhibitions of design and architecture, including 'Bauhaus' (1995), 'Isamu Noguchi and Kitaoji Rosanjin' (1996), 'De Stijl' (1997) and 'Design of Sori Yanagi' (1998). He is author of *Essays on Modern Architecture, Design and Gardens* (2000).

RAMÓN UBEDA is a writer on architecture and design and was Editor-in-Chief of the magazines *De Diseño* and *Ardi*. He is currently contributor to *El Pais* weekly and to various architecture and design magazines including *Diseño Interior*, DMP, *Domus* and *Frame*. Together with the editorial work he is active in the graphic and industrial design fields and is artistic director of Bd Ediciones de Diseño. He is art director of various companies, including ArtQuitect, Bd and Jean Pierre Bua.

LISA WHITE is a 'diplomat' with a drive for design and a passion for publishing. Beginning at the trend-forecasting offices of Studio Edelkoort, Lisa helped found and develop the magazines *View on Colour*, *INview* and *Bloom*, as well as the *Materi-Colour* card, an annual trend and material library-in-a-box. Currently Editor-in-Chief of these publications, and director of United Publishers, Lisa also develops new books and catalogues. She organizes design shows and seminars in Paris, Milan, Cologne and New York and curated the design show 'En Quête d'Objets' at the Centre Pompidou in Paris (2000). She is currently working with the *Bloom* team on product development projects of a horticultural nature.

STEFAN YTTERBORN founded C&Bi Interior in 1986 and led the way in the distribution of international contemporary design in Scandinavian markets. In the same year he started another company with the ambition to export Swedish contemporary design internationally. In 1993 he convinced IKEA to develop a more dynamic line, which became IKEA PS; he managed and directed it until its launch in Milan two years later. Since then he has worked as design manager in his own company Ytterborn & Fuentes Corporate Design whose client list includes Hackman, iittala, Absolut and SAAB. Ytterborn has curated exhibitions of designs from around the world.

ONTENTS

SPOON

A Piece Of Cloth (A-POC): for me this is not only the most impressive achievement of a young designer, but also one of the most significant events in industrial design in recent years. By no stretch of a definition can Issey Miyake be called an up-and-coming young creator, but he is included here with his young partner, Dai Fujiwara.

Inspiration, wisdom and huge generosity led Issey Miyake to hand over the design of the Issey Miyake label to his protégé in the year 2000. 'I took off on an adventure. The voyage we have undertaken is to a planet we have named A-POC. My companions and partners on this journey are Dai Fujiwara and several other young people …'. Dai is a 'post-digital-revolution textile scientist'. (*A-POC Making, Issey Miyake and Dai Fujiwara*, Vitra Design Museum, Berlin, 2001).

A-POC is produced in endless spools of computer-controlled machine cloth. The cloth contains 'information for endless options that can be cut out of it'. The fabric itself does not fray when cut and there are hidden seams marking different patterns. The length of a piece of cloth can be separated to make say a dress, a bag, a hat, etc. It is like extruding an infinity of quantity and quality. This is yet another proof that the more advanced the machine and its 'brain' are, the less machine-like its product becomes. The more sophisticated the industrial production – from the thread to the spools of cloth – the greater the diversity and the easier it is to adapt to individual needs and whims.

Dai talks about nano- and bio-technologies, hybrids of silk worms and spiders, polyester extracted from rice, and artificial intelligence. At the same time, he can look at an ancient piece of cloth that has been excavated, attribute computer theory intuition to the engineers of its time, and recognize that 'so far as making cloth and the use of thread are concerned, there is no difference between ancient times and the information that is whirring in engineers' heads today'.

The A-POC project is evolving. It is hard to tell where this amazing partnership between the grand master and the young master of technologies is going to take us. With the first phase of A-POC running and rolling beautifully, they have now zoomed in on the threads that make up the fabrics and I can say, without the slightest risk of exaggeration, that they are the most fascinating pieces of cloth I have ever seen. A-POC's influence will spread beyond fashion. It cannot not. RON ARAD

1 **Zoo**, A-POC, 2001, silk/cotton/nylon stretch material, Miyake Design Studio.
› A-POC (A Piece Of Cloth) is based on the possibility of producing endless lengths of new fabric with the help of computer-programmed machines. Patterns can be worked into the textile, and a sophisticated system of links and holes between the two sides of the tube of cloth allows the user to cut out seamless clothing from the fabric in different variations. Instead of the strict matrix of warp and weft that must be sewn in the shape of the human body, a seamless continuum emerges which comes closer to the human form than ever before. Just like in a pop-up picture book, unique animals appear from the tip of the scissors. This group of knits includes Panther, Teddy Bear, Monkey, Turtle and Octopus.

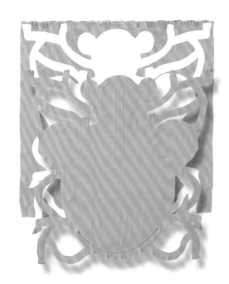

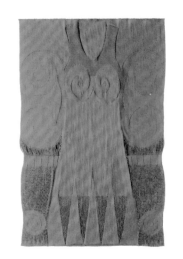
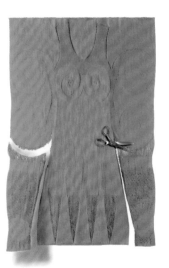

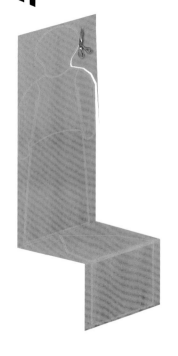

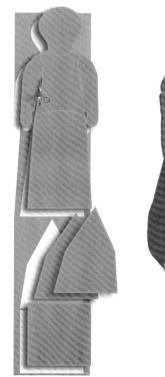

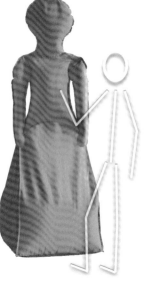

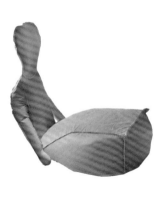

A.POC

1 One Piece, A-POC, 2001, silk/cotton/nylon stretch material, Miyake Design Studio.
› The computer can be used to define characteristics at different points of the fabric, and some of the fabrics can be cut at any point. Here a dress is born from a machine with just one thread. A swirl of tape is cut out from the cloth along its perforated lines, to be worn tied using the tapes, or loose.

2 Midas, A-POC, 2000, silk/cotton/nylon stretch material, Miyake Design Studio.
› This is a mobile, interior object. Here A-POC has come away from the body and gone into the living area. When you sit on it, it is a cushion, when you cuddle it, it is a doll, and when you go to sleep it is a bed. It receives you with the same soft feeling as clothing material.

| 1 | 2 |

VOLKER ALBUS FRANKFURT

It is unusual to find anyone as vehemently committed in so many different areas as Volker Albus. There are three parts to his working life: his high-profile output as an author, his role as a product designer and his exemplary work as a university teacher. As an author on design in its broadest sense, Albus champions progress. In recent years he has also developed some very striking and autonomous products, many of them made by teams of students working under him.

Albus is determined to extend the cultural boundaries of design. He believes that it is the designer's duty to expand into new areas, such as the service industries, exhibition architecture and event management. His work reflects a very dry sense of humour, but never degenerates into kitsch or obvious commercialism.

As a teacher, Albus works with the younger generation, and this makes him particularly responsive to current trends. His awareness of the demands that design will face in the future, and the radical changes in store, brings a highly contemporary spirit to his own work, which is uncompromising and modern in the best sense of the word.

Trained as an architect, Albus applies an architectural understanding of light, space and material to his work. In his hands, decorative detail is not merely superficial, it becomes a means of communication.

Volker Albus taught himself and then his students to distance themselves from 'secure knowledge'. Instead of following a pragmatic routine, they must ask themselves this question: 'How would it be if things were different'? He does not see accumulated experience as progress, quite the reverse.

Within his overall idea of design, Albus uses a kind of 'childlike curiosity' as the basis of his attempt to do things differently. 'Do we always want to sit up straight on a chair?' he asks. This and similar questions symbolize his complex understanding of design. He also develops arguments against too much similarity between products, a stance that takes on great importance in our global era when design should produce distinctive products.

The most recent example of his rather spare work as a designer is the floor light, Downlight (2000). The light can be carried on a stick equipped with a switch to wherever it is needed. A functional light without unnecessary decorative features, it displays a quality that is both humorous and aesthetic – something that cannot be said of many lights. HANSJERG MAIER-AICHEN

1 **Squarelight**, 2001, polyethylene, light stand 150 cm, shell 28 x 28 x 10 cm, prototype.
> These lampshades are made of two identical square half-shells that stay together thanks to a positive-negative lap-joint. The shells are available in various colours and look good positioned either alone or with numerous others as a collection. The very thin stand combined with the simple shape of the shade is reminiscent of traffic signals. The design is also very powerful when seen from the birds-eye view.

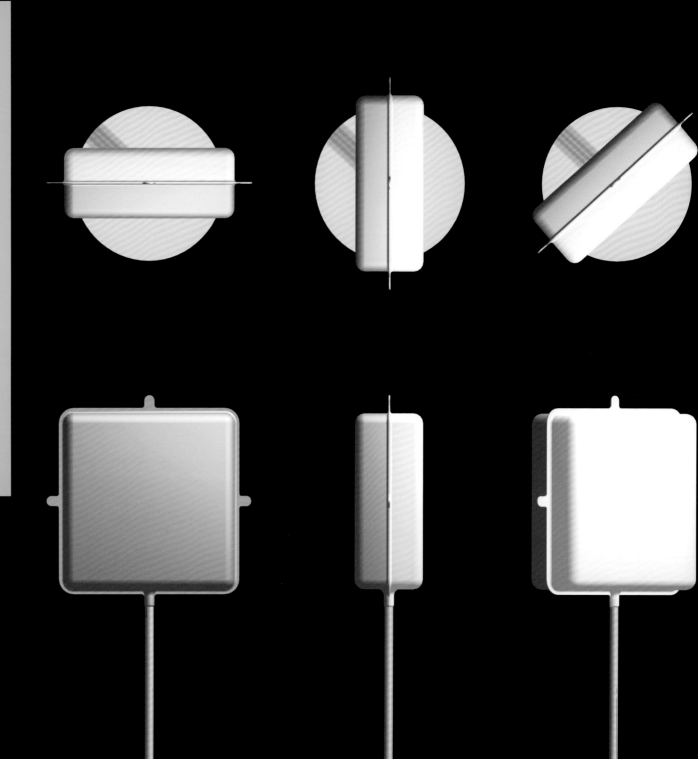

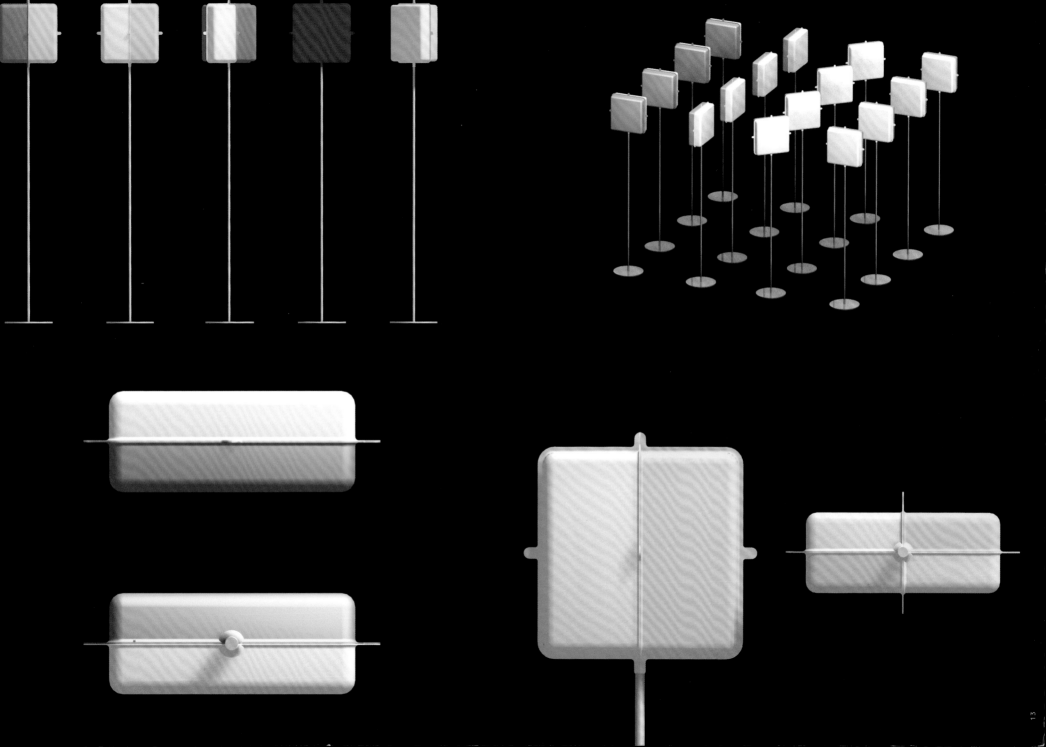

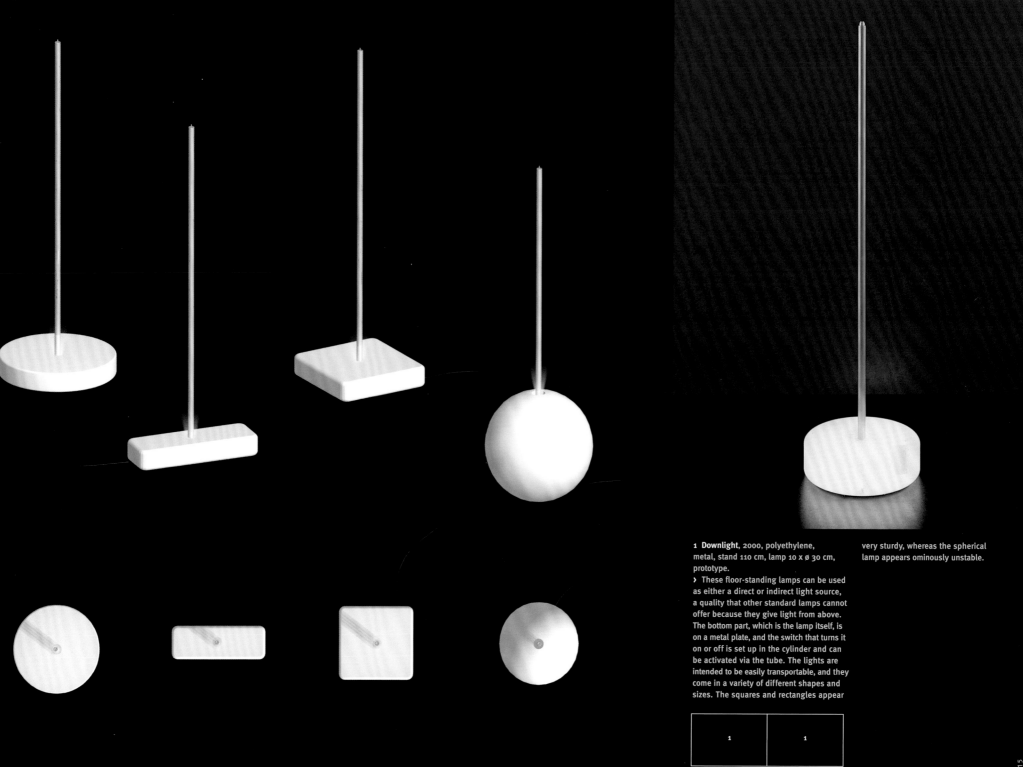

1 Downlight, 2000, polyethylene, metal, stand 110 cm, lamp 10 x ø 30 cm, prototype.
> These floor-standing lamps can be used as either a direct or indirect light source, a quality that other standard lamps cannot offer because they give light from above. The bottom part, which is the lamp itself, is on a metal plate, and the switch that turns it on or off is set up in the cylinder and can be activated via the tube. The lights are intended to be easily transportable, and they come in a variety of different shapes and sizes. The squares and rectangles appear very sturdy, whereas the spherical lamp appears ominously unstable.

1	1

MICHAEL ANASTASSIADES LONDON

Imagine a bedside table that doubles as an alarm clock: it rattles and vibrates, making everything on it shake (but not break) until the noise eventually wakes you up. There is also a 'weekend' version of the table, which has a removable felt muffler. Or how about a social light? It will glow only when spoken to and stays alight only when there is noise nearby. Or its counterpart, the anti-social light? This lamp will glow only when there is silence around it. These inventive designs are not the product of some experimental workshop, but the work of the London-based Greek designer Michael Anastassiades.

A graduate in civil engineering, Anastassiades studied industrial design at the Royal College of Art in London from 1991 to 1993. He then spent some years working for the innovative fashion designer Hussein Chalayan, as director of set design for his catwalk shows, before embarking on a career in product design in 1997. Predominantly an ideas man, he has devoted his talent to messing about with the function of furniture. Nothing in his collection is what it seems.

'It is very difficult to describe or sum up a particular style that represents me,' Anastassiades says, 'especially when a style's primary function is to serve the ideas behind an object.' This is Anastassiades' starting point: process and materials may be important, but their primary function is to express the concept. Symbiotic relationships between the object and the user are also a crucial part of his designs. When talking about the Social Light he explains that 'the user has to respect the Light's behaviour to receive its glow. It therefore becomes more like a companion.'

Although Anastassiades manufactures much of his work himself, he also works with London-based Babylon Design for the production of some pieces. His ambition is to mass-produce some of his key products. Among these is Message Cup (1998), an apparently simple cup that conceals a secret recording device. The cups can be used to exchange messages in the domestic environment. Each individual has his or her own cup in which other people can leave voice messages.

A collection of corner mirrors (2001) represents Anastassiades' latest foray into the world of unexpected design. Here he intentionally confuses and disorientates the viewer by wrapping the looking glass around walls and ceilings, thereby distorting the reflection. LAURA HOUSELEY

1 **Corner Mirror**, 2001, silvered glass, wood, 114 x 40 x 4 cm, edition of five pieces.
› This mirror is a deliberate exercise in distortion; two flat materials have been curved to fit the shape of a 90-degree angle. The image of the surroundings that is projected is therefore distorted by the curvature in the glass, and the mirror becomes a source of intrigue rather than simply a functional object.

2 **Ball Vases**, 2001, silvered glass, 50 x ø 25 cm, Babylon Design.
› In this design, the traditional vase shape has been inverted and the reflective

qualities of the surface are used to enhance the illusion.

3 **Message Cups**, 1998, laminated birch ply, styrene, electronics, 6 x ø 8 cm, prototype.
› These cups are used to exchange messages in a domestic environment. They are fitted with voice recording and playback equipment, allowing people to store messages for each other. The cups are activated by turning them from an upright to a face-down position.

4 **Mirror Chair**, 1998, English oak, mirror, 90 x 45 x 45 cm, prototype.
› This whimsical design consists of two mutually exclusive functions: the mirror becomes redundant as soon as someone sits on the chair, and the chair cannot be used when someone is looking in the mirror.

| 1 | 2 | 3 | 4 |

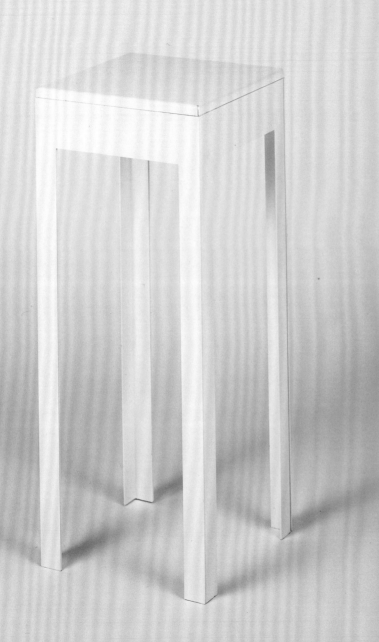

1 **Alarm Clock**, 1998, enamelled metal, vibrating device, 45 x 20 x 20 cm, prototype. This is simultaneously a bedside table and an alarm clock with a difference. When the timing device situated beneath the tabletop goes off, instead of a conventional ringing alarm, the whole table starts vibrating, rocking on its two uneven pairs of legs.

2 **Weekend**, table, 1998, tubular metal frame, removable felt suit, 45 x 35 x 35 cm, prototype.
> This bedside table is a progression from the alarm-table design; the felt cover

muffles the vibration of the table, allowing a good night's sleep.

3 **Sitooteries**, 2000, fibreglass, resin, fountain 160 x ø 35 cm, stool 42 x ø 40 cm, prototype for Belsay Hall, Northumberland.
> The taller of these two white columns is a fountain. The adjacent stool is positioned so that the sitter's eyes capture the perfect view of the veil of water brimming over the concave bowl. The simplicity of these designs provides a great contrast to the ornamental garden.

4 **Box Light**, 1998, acrylic fitting, silvered bulb, 15 x 23 x 23 cm, Babylon Design.
> This is a light within a box. The silver-tipped bulb peeping out at the top spreads light through the main body of the design, creating an even, gentle glow.

1	2	3	4

ED ANNINK THE HAGUE

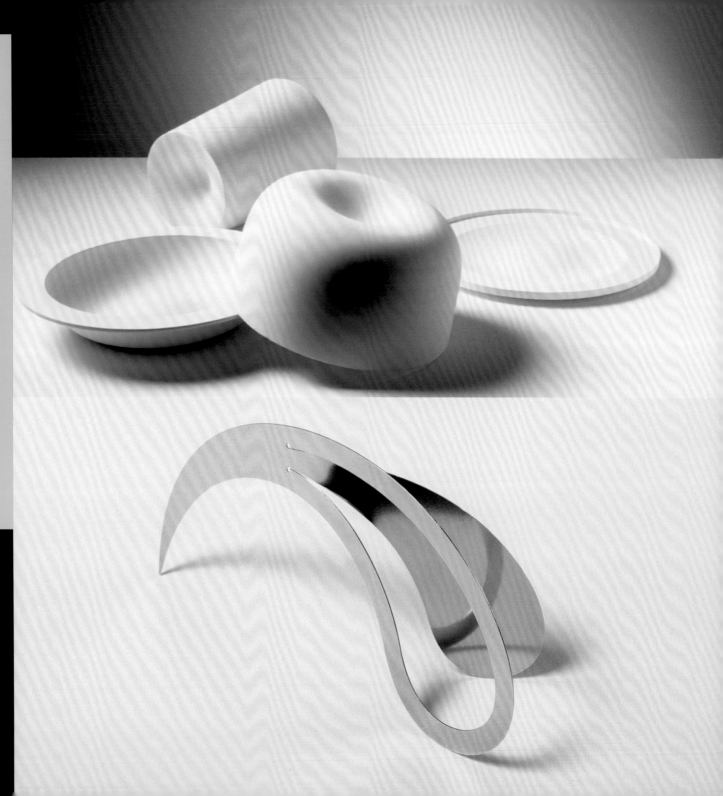

The development of Droog, the well-known group of Dutch designers, would have been unthinkable without Ed Annink as product designer, creative co-ordinator and exhibition designer. From very early on, Annink was interested in the interaction between the product and its presentation in a spatial environment. He conceived and staged the first Droog exhibition at the Salone del Mobile in Milan in 1996, where it attracted considerable attention. The collection included two memorable Annink products: a soft wardrobe knob in polyurethane foam, and a coconut-fibre mat in the shape of a darting hare.

As a character, Annink is rather reticent and watchful. His projects are often inter-disciplinary, as he has a particular interest in extending the boundaries of design work and staking out new areas of activity. He seeks design solutions that are in dialogue with elementary sensory perceptions and an authentic formal language.

Annink is a Dutchman with an innate sense of curiosity, coming from a country with a globally open and multi-layered cultural tradition. In Holland, students of design are brought together with manufacturers and businessmen. During this early phase of a student's training, they swap conceptual and innovative designs and product plans for practical advice on implementation and production methods. Popular exchange programmes with colleges in other European countries encourage cultural interaction. Today, Annink is himself a teacher, dealing with the designer's cultural-political role in a world of increasingly rapid communication.

Annink's work is shaped both by his innovative way of teaching and by the recent tradition of art and design in his native country. Rietveld and the De Stijl artists are also obvious examples of designers who sought to re-think the applied arts, and to engage critically with their surroundings. Following in the footsteps of these role models, Annink is developing distinctive products, expanding his capacity for analysis and his curiosity about technical achievements and new materials. His ability to make quick decisions enables him to get rapidly to the heart of whatever design tasks he is set, and to do so with great attention to detail.

The 'poetry of material' is often apparent in Annink's work, particularly in products whose quality and charm lie in the juxtaposition of different materials. Annink is one of a new generation of designers attracted to a combination of simplicity with new and surprising materials.

HANSJERG MAIER-AICHEN

1 Sisters Set of Bowls, 1999, plaster, 35 x ø 26 cm (stacked), prototype.
› This design was part of the Dutch Room, a project in which Annink reproduced the setting of a painting by Jan Steen. This set of bowls was based on household objects, translated into plaster models.

2 Bird Letter Opener, 2001, stainless steel, 8 x 17.5 x 4.5 cm, Ontwerpwerk.
› This letter opener is not intended to be just another knife, but an interpretation of a cat's nail.

3 Multipurpose Clothes Hanger, 2001, Gaudi, soft polyurethane, 8.5 x 7.5 cm, Luna, white porcelain, mirror, 5.5 x 4 cm, Jons, stainless steel, 12.5 x 13.5 cm, Cleverline.
› The soft-knob feature of Gaudi is inspired by button mushrooms. It is a total contrast to Luna, which is a white porcelain hanger with a small mirror. Jons' shape provides a useful hanger for numerous objects.

4 Double Vase, 2000, ceramic, 38.5 x 18.5 x 18.5 cm, Driade.
› This stack of two vases enables different kinds of flowers to be put together.

5 Single Ashtray, 1997, silicone, 3.8 x ø 7 cm, Authentics.
› The silicone has been chosen for its heat-resistant properties and lightness.

1		4
	3	
2		5

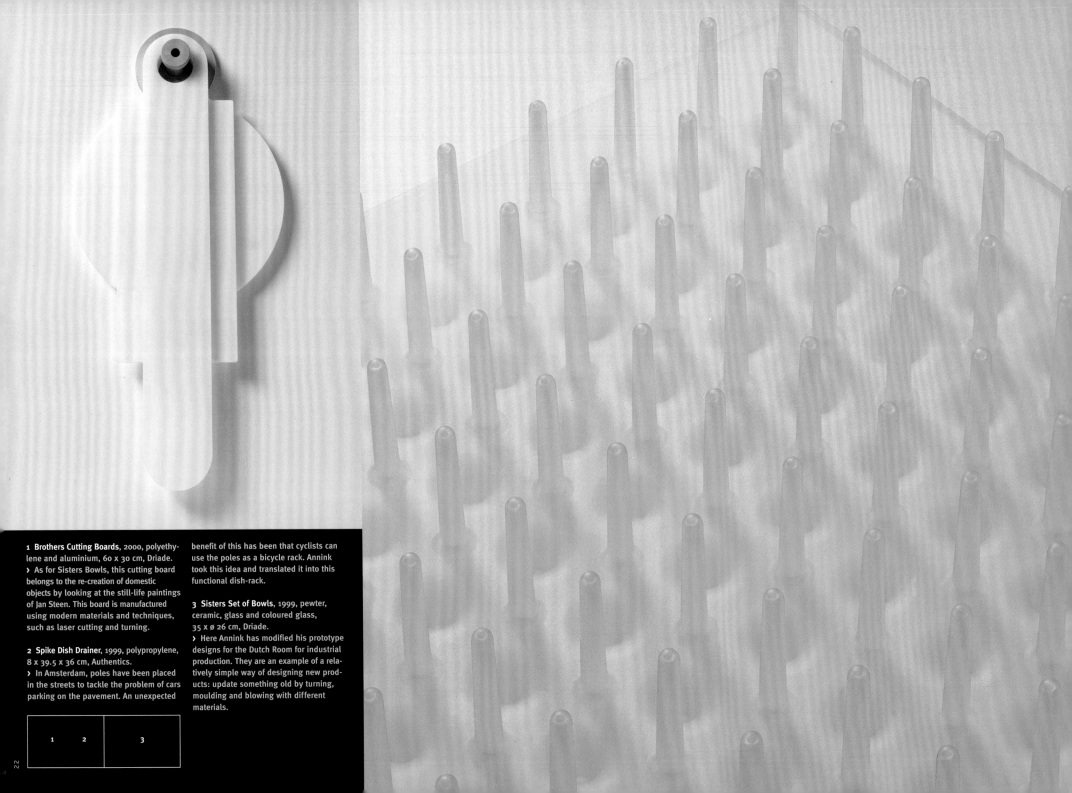

1 Brothers Cutting Boards, 2000, polyethylene and aluminium, 60 x 30 cm, Driade.
› As for Sisters Bowls, this cutting board belongs to the re-creation of domestic objects by looking at the still-life paintings of Jan Steen. This board is manufactured using modern materials and techniques, such as laser cutting and turning.

2 Spike Dish Drainer, 1999, polypropylene, 8 x 39.5 x 36 cm, Authentics.
› In Amsterdam, poles have been placed in the streets to tackle the problem of cars parking on the pavement. An unexpected benefit of this has been that cyclists can use the poles as a bicycle rack. Annink took this idea and translated it into this functional dish-rack.

3 Sisters Set of Bowls, 1999, pewter, ceramic, glass and coloured glass, 35 x ø 26 cm, Driade.
› Here Annink has modified his prototype designs for the Dutch Room for industrial production. They are an example of a relatively simple way of designing new products: update something old by turning, moulding and blowing with different materials.

| 1 | 2 | 3 |

The Apple computer has changed the way an entire industry sees itself and presents its wares. Much of the credit for this change must go to Jonathan Ive, Apple's young British director of design. Apple itself is not inclined to credit him too highly – the ever-vigilant PR people always take pains to stress team effort. Fine. No great designer works in complete isolation and some of the best make great managers. Nevertheless, Ive's accomplishments are too great to bury beneath corporate collective responsibility. Apple has always understood the ability of great design to draw an audience. Never has this been more striking than in the past year, with the introduction of two signature Ive designs.

Ive's iMac, with its adjustable flat screen and delightfully concealed hardware, breaks the mould of the personal computer. It strides so confidently off in another direction that the entire computer industry is left looking like a flat-footed dolt. The iMac is a wonderful visual joke with a very serious intention. Its clever flat screen mimics a model's make-up mirror, and the working heart of the computer is squeezed into its base. This design addresses the critical issue of space in the work environment, where new machines proliferate. Suddenly, the user does not have to worry whether the computer will fit. And if the information on screen is boring, just look at the thing itself – it will make you laugh.

The iPod is a gloriously simple MP3 player which can hold 1,000 songs, providing a marketing line as brilliant as the design itself. The design is a coup for Ive and for Apple. While all other MP3 players chase colours and functions in a vain search for 'hi-techness', Ive goes in the opposite direction. This is the sleekest, coolest little machine to hit the consumer since Sony designed its first Walkman. The control panel on the iPod is a study in simplicity and functionality. Only one word appears on the face: Menu. It is all that is needed – the rest is obvious. The true brilliance is in the little finger wheel that doubles as cursor and volume control. You do not notice it until you have to use it, but once you swirl it under your fingers and enjoy its tactile quality, you want to do it again and again.

It is understood that both of these machines exceed expectations – a prerequisite in the critical high-tech world, where one mistake can kill a company. The fact that they look and function so much better than anything else is owing to Ive and his team of engineers and fellow designers. Ive's work at Apple is now the biggest influence on the entire computer industry.

ULTAN GUILFOYLE

1 iBook, laptop computer, 2001, polycarbonate die-cast magnesium, 3.4 x 28.5 x 23 cm, Apple.
> Apple's 12.1-inch iBook is the lightest and smallest full-featured notebook on the market. Weighing just 2.22 kg, the iBook fits perfectly into today's active digital lifestyle, with all the tools needed to share digital photos, build a music library, burn CDs and edit movies.

2 iMac, computer, 2002, polycarbonate, ABS, stainless steel, aluminium, 32.9/ 50.9 x 38.3/ 41.5 x 27/ 41.5 cm, base: ø 27 cm, Apple.
> The new iMac is designed around a stunning 15-inch LCD flat screen that floats in mid-air – allowing users to adjust its height or angle with just a touch. The new iMac also features a powerful G4 processor and Apple's revolutionary SuperDrive for playing and burning CDs and DVDs.

1	2

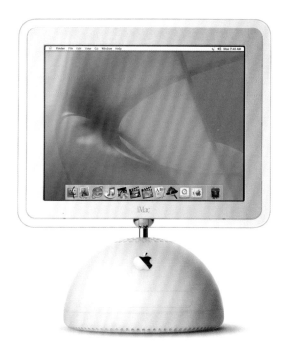

1 iPod, MP3 music player, 2001, polycarbonate, stamped stainless steel, 10.2 x 6.18 x 1.99 cm, Apple.
› iPod is a breakthrough MP3 music player that packs up to 1,000 CD-quality songs into an ultra-portable, 140-gram design that fits in the pocket. iPod's high-capacity 5GB or 10GB hard drives double as portable FireWire hard drives for storing presentations, large documents, images and digital movies.

2 Titanium PowerBook G4, 2001, polycarbonate, stamped stainless steel, 2.6 x 34.1 x 24.1 cm, Apple.

› With a sleek titanium enclosure, a 15.2-inch megawide display, and speeds of up to 800 MHz, this portable computer sets new standards for portable design and performance. The elegantly engineered slot-loading Combo drive lets you watch DVDs and burn CDs anywhere.

3 Apple Flat Panel Displays, 23-inch Apple Cinema HD Display, 2002; 22-inch Apple Cinema Display, 1999; 17-inch Apple Studio Display, 2001; 15-inch Apple Studio Display, 1999, moulded polycarbonate plastic and form sheetmetal, Apple.
› Apple's flat panel displays are digitally driven from the computer to provide razor-sharp images, deeply saturated colours and lightning-fast pixel response, all in an elegant industrial design.

1	2	3

MIDORI ARAKI TOKYO

Among the many unusual things about Midori Araki is the fact that her first career was as editor of *Elle Deco* magazine. However, her interest in design also comes from her passion for art installation. Her highly sensitive and unusual presentation of her objects draws both on her experience as an editor and her knowledge of contemporary art.

It is Araki's unique attitude to design that has made her something of a cult figure among the younger generation. Like a Surrealist, she loves to work with 'found objects' and to confound the viewer. Her ceramic Bottle Lights (1999) moulded from plastic detergent bottles are an example of this way of working. Araki's desire to surprise can be seen in her book *Junk Sweets* (2000), a compilation of cakes created in the disturbing forms of toilet paper, soap, etc. She chooses artifacts that express her desire to be 'selfishly herself', as she puts it. They represent a fragment of daily human existence and her aim is to encourage the user, in a thousand ways, to promote and cultivate his or her unique sense of personal identity.

Essentially, Araki's design is both open ended and open minded, acting as a performance which resembles the purity of a Japanese tea ceremony. Her products work like a personal invitation into her own home, offering us a welcome that is both hospitable and highly sophisticated. Her designs have their own poetry and are imbued with the atmosphere of a theatrical performance.

Araki's range of organic furniture also takes its inspiration from the shapes of plants and animals, such as the Polar Bear Table (1999). In this case, she draws on the tradition of bear-shaped playthings which adorn the parks of Tokyo to create an object for the home. Another product which uses an organic form is the Stump Chair (2000), recalling the tree stump which Araki imagines to have been the first chair used by humans.

Adopting the ephemeral, challenging spirit of installation art, Araki works to deconstruct the design process. From this position, she confronts the crisis of the globalized, high-speed society, and seeks to evoke a very personal and imaginative response from the users of her products. She pursues an individual path, taking her inspiration from a primitive, archaic time when design lay at the heart of ritual and communication. RYU NIIMI

1 Bottle Light, 1999, ceramic, various dimensions, E&Y.
› Midori Araki's philosophy is based on freedom from preconception and common sense. Her first product was a series of ceramic lights which have been moulded from detergent bottles. This expresses the idea of defending the environment from an overwhelming amount of rubbish.

2 Polar Bear Table, 1999, FRP, acrylic, 61 x 120 x 55 cm, E&Y.
› Bear-shaped playthings are widespread in the parks of Tokyo. In this design Midori Araki imagined bringing a public form into the private house. On the bear's back there is a hole in which you can place a plant. The tabletop is detachable.

| 1 | 1 | 2 |

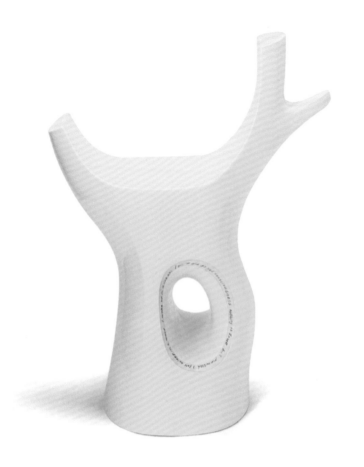

sit here
close you eyes
using fully 7 senese,
you caught
what is real?

1 Stump Chair, 2000, FRP,
81 x 65 x 30 cm, E&Y.
› Midori Araki has engraved a fragment
of a poem on each of the 20 stump chairs.
Each person has their individual piece, so
that when 20 people are together, they
can share the pleasure of the whole poem.
Stump is a piece that challenges modern
design by recalling what Midori Araki
imagines to be the first chair used by
humans, a tree stump. The message is
that furniture is not simply a tool, but
rather a means of expressing an idea.

2 Junk Sweets, Cake Sculpture Art Book,
2000, paper, Aspect.
› This is the cover for the book *Junk Sweets*,
in which Midori Araki presents a series of
concept cakes, baked and decorated in
the unlikeliest of forms: toilet paper, soap,
and also dentures.

3 Church-less Chair, 1999, wood, acrylic,
82 x 37 x 44 cm, E&Y.
› As the name suggests, this is a disused
church chair. Midori Araki has changed its
wooden seat into an acrylic one, and where
you might expect to see hymn or prayer
books, she has placed glossy magazines.
Her intention is to collect discarded chairs
from churches all around the world.

1	
	3
1	2

31

Italian designer Miki Astori began his career as a product designer for the prestigious Driade company. He is now a prominent figure among a new generation of Italian and European designers. His work represents a unique step towards creating a new school of design to serve the lifestyles of the twenty-first century.

The newness of Astori's work, and the breathtaking freshness of his design, comes from the delicate balance that he strikes between the post-war Italian tradition, so full of gestures and theatrical effects, and a brand new, revitalized approach. A lightness of outlook and of design is the defining feature of Astori's work. He sets out to find a middle way between elegance and the functional lightness of contemporary forms and materials. The results of this process are quite unique.

Astori always takes function as the starting point of his work. As a typical Italian, he conceals the essential nature of the design behind light, tactile materials, creating products that are ideally suited to the younger generation.

Produced by Driade, the Galoppino (1997) is one of Astori's most beguiling designs. It is a trolley with colourful, translucent plastic shelves, tubular chrome supports and free-moving wheels. The trolley shelves consist of trays that can be removed for washing and adjusted to various heights, making this a very functional product. As with so many of Astori's products, the trolley is designed to inspire the user's imagination as to how it should be used. The shelves are adjustable, turning it into an office trolley for transporting and storing documents. Adjusted again, the trolley turns into a bookcase, useful in the home, or a trolley for transporting food between the kitchen and the dining room.

The extraordinary range of Astori's work is mainly devoted to making the kitchen more functional. It encompasses products such as the fantastic and yet functional Plug In kitchen storage system (1997) and the Thali tables (2001), which combine a stainless-steel frame with a wide variety of tops. Taken together, his work represents a new form of elegance that is still intrinsically Italian. RYU NIIMI

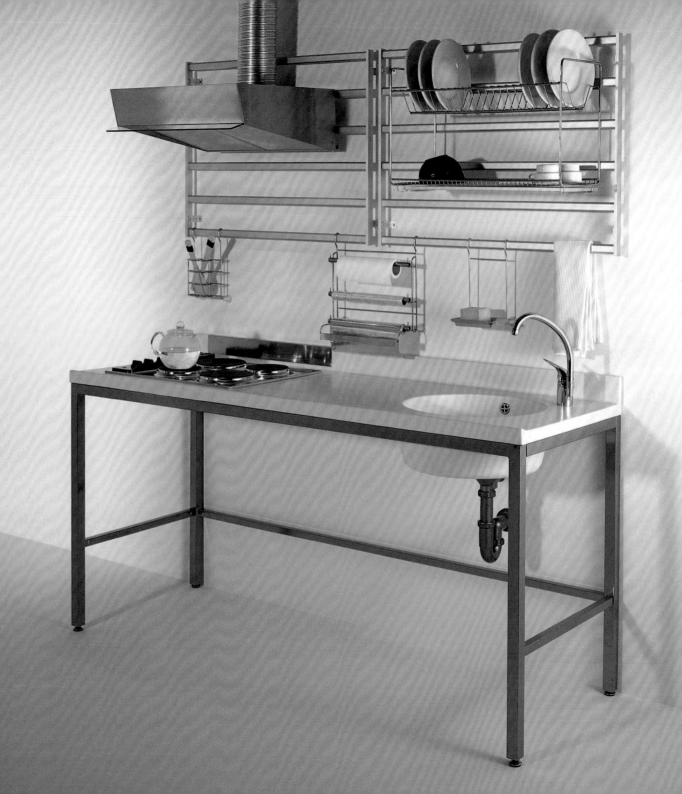

1 Fucina, kitchen unit, 1999, steel, EKOTEK (polyester resin), 90/197 x 180 x 64.5 cm, Driade.
› The wall frame is a kitchen unit which provides simple fittings to hold equipment that might otherwise clutter the work surface. The material used has a high resistance to heat and mechanical shock.

2 Galoppino, trolley, 1997, chrome-plated steel, polypropylene, various dimensions, Driade.
› These trolleys come in different colours and dimensions, and could have a remov-able tray fitted on the top. The structure is a combination of shelves and steel tubes linked by simple screws. The construction is fast and the form of the plastic shelves enables them to support heavy loads.

3 Plug In, kitchen fittings, 1997, plastic, beech wood, aluminium, glass, various dimensions, Driade.
› These are complementary fittings for Fucina, and permit functional organization in the cooking area. The plastic spacers make contact with, and protect, the wall.

4 Satori, lamp, 1998, anodized aluminium, galvanized steel, stylo-bulb, polypropylene, 90/120/180 x 15 cm, Driade.
› This lamp shelf is a multiple-function object: a shelf, a light and a tool holder.

1	2
	3	4

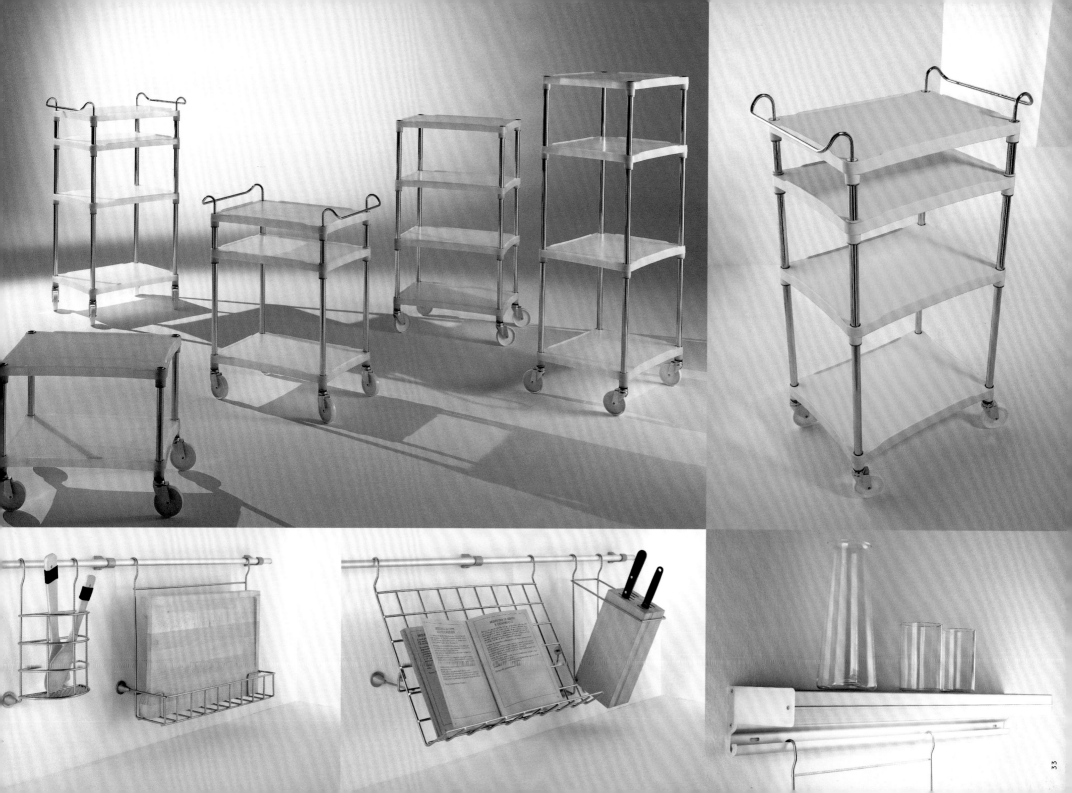

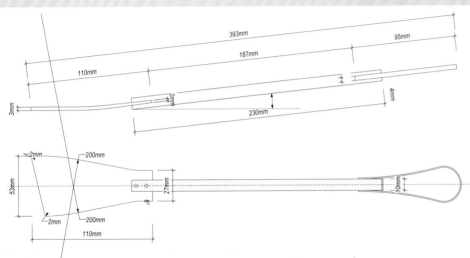

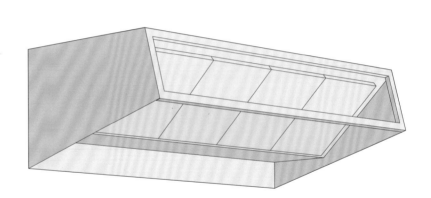

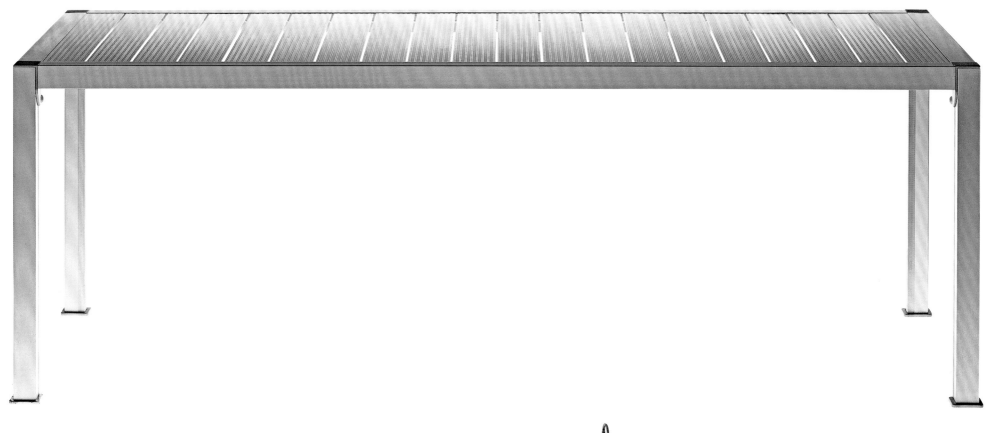

	2	4	
1			
	3	3	4

ASYMPTOTE NEW YORK

Lise Anne Couture and Hani Rashid work together under the name of Asymptote in New York. They are famous within the design community as the architects who anticipated and then worked with the digital design tools that proliferated in the 1990s. Their speciality, which almost amounts to a mission, is virtual architecture, a world of imagined spaces and volumes that owes nothing to the 'first reality' imperatives of concrete, steel, wood and stone. Such was their influence that they were chosen, along with Greg Lynn, to represent the United States at the Venice Architecture Biennale in 2000.

Even architectural theorists have to put bread on the table, and Asymptote's plunge into the world of fully realized buildings and objects was marked by two important projects. First was the opening of the Hydra Pier in April 2002. This small, breathtaking pavilion is built on a lake outside Amsterdam. Although reminiscent of Eero Saarinen's TWA terminal at Kennedy Airport, New York, the Pier bears the distinctively fluid and organic hallmarks of Asymptote's design.

The second project was a less obvious departure from Asymptote's former role. Commissioned by Knoll, the A3 is a new concept in office organization. Andrew Cogan, Knoll's chief executive, wanted Couture and Rashid precisely because they were not furniture designers. As an industrialist, Cogan was attracted by the way Couture and Rashid disassembled the very concept of a working environment and started afresh, taking their new version direct from computer to production.

An adaptable, modular office system, the A3 is both beautiful to behold and practical in a very thoughtful way. Hani Rashid found inspiration in the experience of working on an aeroplane, with luggage overhead, and a laptop computer on his lap. Lise Anne Couture was determined to design the space first, rather than creating a set of components that add up to a system. A virtual womb of curved, translucent fabric and amoeba-shaped work surfaces, filing cabinets, shelves and overhead bins surrounds the worker. Each self-contained workspace kaleidoscopes together, creating a small group. In this way the system can offer both privacy and a sense of team membership. Our preconceptions about the way we work were only slightly dented by the dot.com boom – and subsequent bust – of the 1990s. The A3 is a far greater challenge to our attitudes. Rashid and Couture are moving fast along the road to a success that they certainly deserve. ULTAN GUILFOYLE

Knoll A3, office system, 2002, steel tubing, MDF, form injected moulded ABS, Knoll tensile fabrics, die-cast zinc, 182 x 175 x 274 cm, Knoll International.

1 Frame and Screen
› In addition to establishing feelings of wellbeing, the workspace must also respond to the need for privacy and community. The deliberate gaps in the A3 enclosure and the use of semi-transparent screens help to achieve this response to a variety of needs.

2 Components
› Many new manufacturing techniques and materials were used in the project, including injection-moulded plastics and newly engineered textiles. By streamlining the quantity of materials used in the workstation, using a high percentage of recycled material, and facilitating the separation of materials for future recycling, Asymptote was able to create not only a more humane and functional work environment but also one that better respects the natural environment.

| 1 | 2 |

36

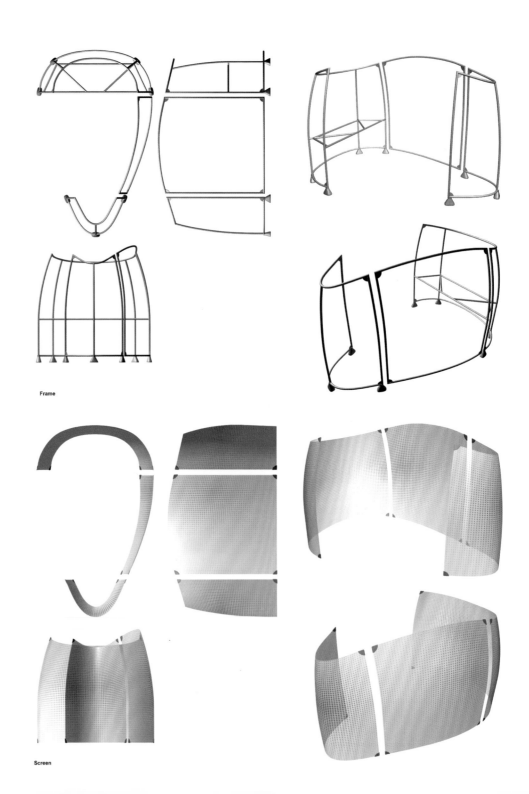

Frame

Screen

A3 frame

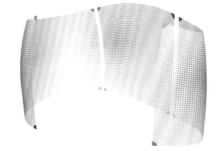

screen

pad

Flipp lamp

Arc work surface

Surf return

Slipp work surface

Slipp table

Filez file pedestal

Tript pedestal

small Aerial overhead

large Aerial overhead

power module

Visor

Orbit cups

Scoop

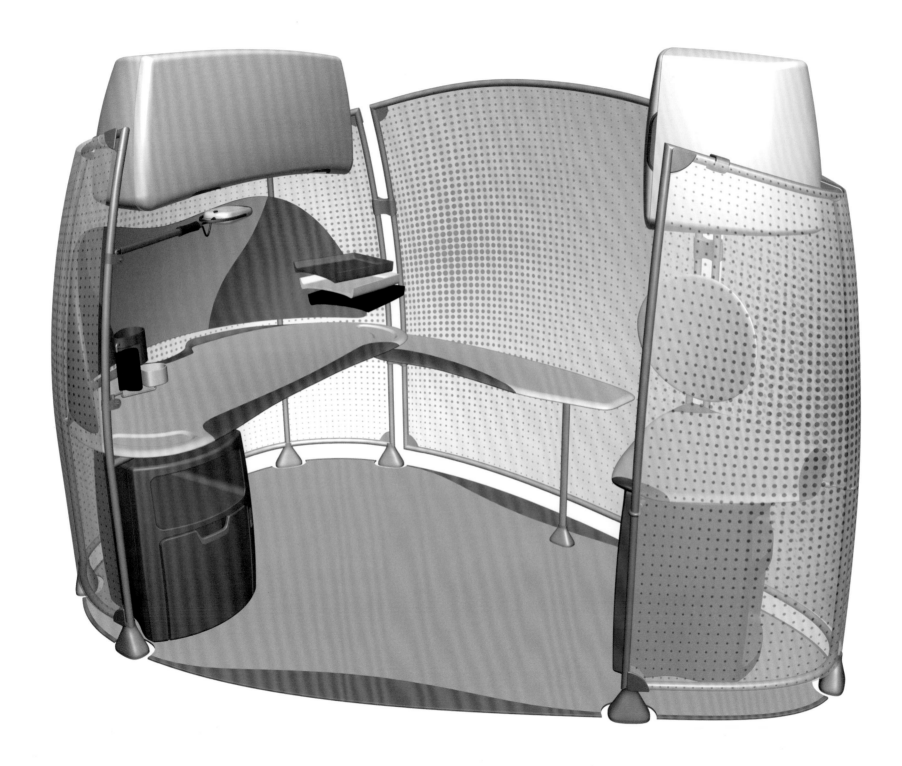

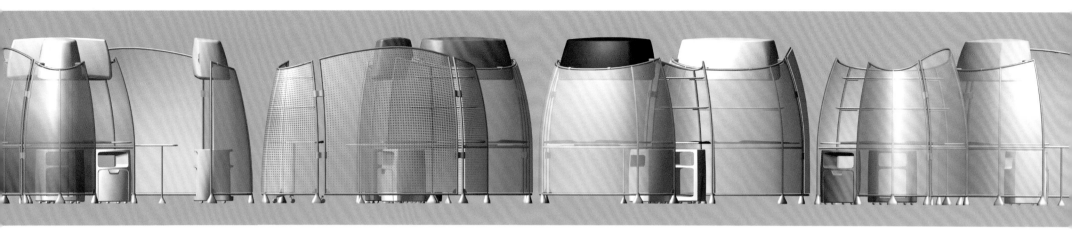

   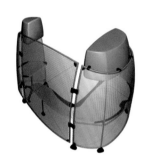 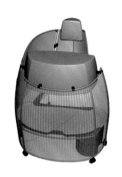 

 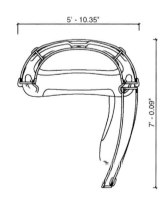 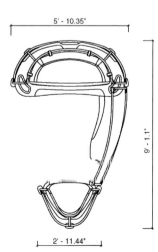 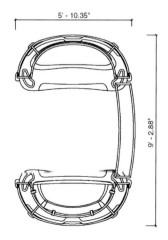

5' - 10.35"   5' - 10.35"   5' - 10.35"   5' - 10.35"

2' - 8.43"   7' - 0.09"   9' - 1.1"   9' - 2.88"

2' - 11.44"

1 Knoll A3, office system, 2002, steel tubing, MDF, form injected moulded ABS, Knoll tensile fabrics, die-cast zinc, 182 x 175 x 274 cm, Knoll International.
> The Knoll A3 project was seen as a valuable opportunity to rethink the dynamics of the office landscape. With a background in architecture as opposed to industrial design, Asymptote was predisposed to take an initial approach that was spatial and environmental rather than primarily object driven. The overall planning scale creates a new antidote to the usual rigid, rectilinear and monotonous interiors. One of the most important skills of architectural design is the ability to think on multiple scales simultaneously. Here this meant considering space from the scale of the individual to the group cluster arrangements of the entire workspace.

JAMES AUGER LONDON

'At 16, I was to start a trade, a trade that would consume the next five years of my life. These five years were to leave a nasty rash of boredom on my world, and I went in search of an ulterior motive for life. The answer: product design, where my wildest dream can become reality and from the quagmire that is my brain can spring forth objects of innate beauty', writes James Auger to accompany his graduation pieces at the Glasgow School of Art in 1995. After which James goes on to start a ... trade that would consume the next four years of his life. He takes employment with a firm of model makers, turning himself into one of the most accomplished and clever members of his trade. Making models of innate beauty, has boredom (the mother of creation) kicked in again? The search for an ulterior motive for life goes on. This time the answer is Design Products at the Royal College of Art. More than any of his fellow students (or tutors), James, with his Midas modeller's touch, was totally free from worrying about how to process and make his objects.

There is something unsettling about the acting out of Gibsonesque objects (referring to William Gibson, the well-known science-fiction writer). It is not like the sci-fi pages, where the objects are props serving the narrative. When you look at or try on James' real, immaculately engineered and beautifully made working things, you have to write the narratives yourself. The poker-faced presentation does not reveal whether the Audio Tooth Implant (2000), an artificial tooth which is planted as a secret hearing device in a human mouth, is 'look at my wonderful device' or 'this might happen if you are not careful', or even 'this is what is going to happen, happening already'. Nor do we get clues as to which is the real use of the telepresence contraption (2001). Is it the horrific slave scenario, where one person is the blind body of a sighted person, or is it a caring invention to help housebound grandpa take a virtual walk outdoors with the help of the family dog?

I think James is still delaying the revealing of his hand. We know it to be a brilliant one, and the longer it is kept off the table the more possibilities it will entertain. In the meantime, we can look at the wonderful image of the dog wagging its pixel tail to spell 'I love you', totally believe it, and forget that it was us that just typed the message. RON ARAD

All the projects in these pages form part of an exploration into the convergence of technology with nature. The projects are not intended to be manufactured, but as props to engage the viewer.

1 Social Telepresence, 2001.
> The remote hardware of the Social Telepresence consists of a small camera and a binaural microphone. Telepresence is the experience of being fully present at a live (i.e. non-virtual) location which is remote from one's physical location. It has long been used for military and exploratory purposes, but in this project it is used in a social context, and is seen as an alternative to the extreme nature of implantation.

2 Ear-Lid Helmet, 2000.
> Wearing the Ear-Lid Helmet enables the user to switch off all sounds coming into the head. This simple but desirable feature is made possible by the implantation of a digital inner ear.

3 Artificial Horizon, 2000.
> Through a head-mounted gyroscope, with 2 degrees of freedom and cross hairs, a constant view of true horizontal is achieved. It re-aligns the sensory disorientation which can manifest itself as travel sickness when the body is moved by external forces.

1	2	3

1 LED Tail Light, from the 'Augmented Animals' book, 2000.
> This is a device to enhance the relationship between pet and owner. LED flashes at various frequencies and a pre-programmed message is spelled out when the tail passes through the air. This can be altered depending on the WPM rate, allowing the owner to imagine and 'translate' what the dog is saying.

2 Dog Telepresence, 2001.
> By attaching the camera belt to the dog, the user can go window-shopping or for a walk in the country.

3 Audio Tooth Implant, 2000, project in collaboration with Jimmy Loizeau.
> The Audio Tooth Implant enables a form of telepathy to take place. Thanks to a micro-vibration device, sound information is transferred from the tooth into the inner ear by bone resonance.

4 People Blind Dates, 2001.
> This rent-a-body service allows users to borrow an alternate body which is then used at the temporary owner's discretion. A contract is drawn up between the user and the rented body regarding liability if a crime is committed in the remote space. This product is an example of technology as a modifier of behaviour.

| 1 | 2 | 3 | 4 |

MASAYO AVE MILAN

Masayo Ave's work radiates vital energy born of a combination of innovative design and new materials. Born in Japan, but now living in Italy, she combines the eastern Zen tradition – an almost austere reduction of means – with western enlightenment. Her work, which is both unusual and intensely personal, occupies a position in an intermediate cultural zone. She has been invited to take her designs to many international exhibitions and fairs, and over the past three years her felt and foam products have provoked a great deal of interest in both the East and the West.

Trained as an architect in Japan, Ave focused her attention on engineering. Her work reflects an advanced understanding of technology – both old and new – and she has a high level of discipline and an unlimited determination to pursue a given goal with great urgency. The products born of this combination are independent and uncompromising in character.

Ave gained her master's degree at the Domus Academy in Milan, and her love of European, and particularly Italian, design is unmistakable. By choosing Italy as her new home, Ave has brought a duality to her work, which now appears to be suspended between rational engineering and the poetry of design solutions.

Italy offers a great diversity of working environments to the designer. Workshops range from family factories to technologically advanced, large-scale industries. This diversity fuels the country's flow of design ideas, which are always surprising and innovative. Masayo Ave lives in the highly industrialized environment of Lombardy, and her work develops in the atmosphere emanating from Milan, the undisputed Mecca of new design. She combines intensive research into new materials, manufacturers and resources with very high standards of production, which may be technical or craft based. Working on the spot with technicians in their factories and testing out new or alternative techniques, Ave has sometimes produced startling solutions. She has made various products from different kinds of foam and plastic, reinterpreting them both formally and by using new technology. Both Genesi (1998) and Cool Cushion (2000) are examples of her innovative use of foam, while the Arca table basket, which she produced in 2000, uses industrial felt in an imaginative way. Altered perceptions of new materials combined with a crossing of boundaries and the use of surprising working methods gives Ave's work the freshness and character of authentic design. HANSJERG MAIER-AICHEN

1 Ad Hook Family, 1998, PVC, stainless steel, hook and brush holder 8 x 3 cm, tumbler holder 8 x 9.5 cm, Authentics.
› One of the smallest items in the Authentics collection, the Ad Hook Family has a unity of design across bathroom items such as towel, toothbrush and tumbler holders. The stainless-steel wire structures are stripped to the absolute minimum and are secured simply with big suction pads, which express Authentic's logo and serve as ad-hoc decorations on empty surfaces such as mirror and window glass.

2 Duet Magazine Rack, 2000, industrial wool felt, wood, ABS screws, iron wire, 28 x ø 27 cm, MasayoAve creation.
› Two sheets of differently coloured wool felt are curved around a wooden base, creating a wonderfully simple yet functional design.

3 Arca Table Basket, 2000, industrial wool felt, wood, ABS screws, large 30 x 40 x 30 cm, small 20 x 30 x 25 cm, MasayoAve creation.
› This innovative tablebasket comes in two sizes and a selection of colours. The screws are a very powerful motif in the design.

1	2	3

44

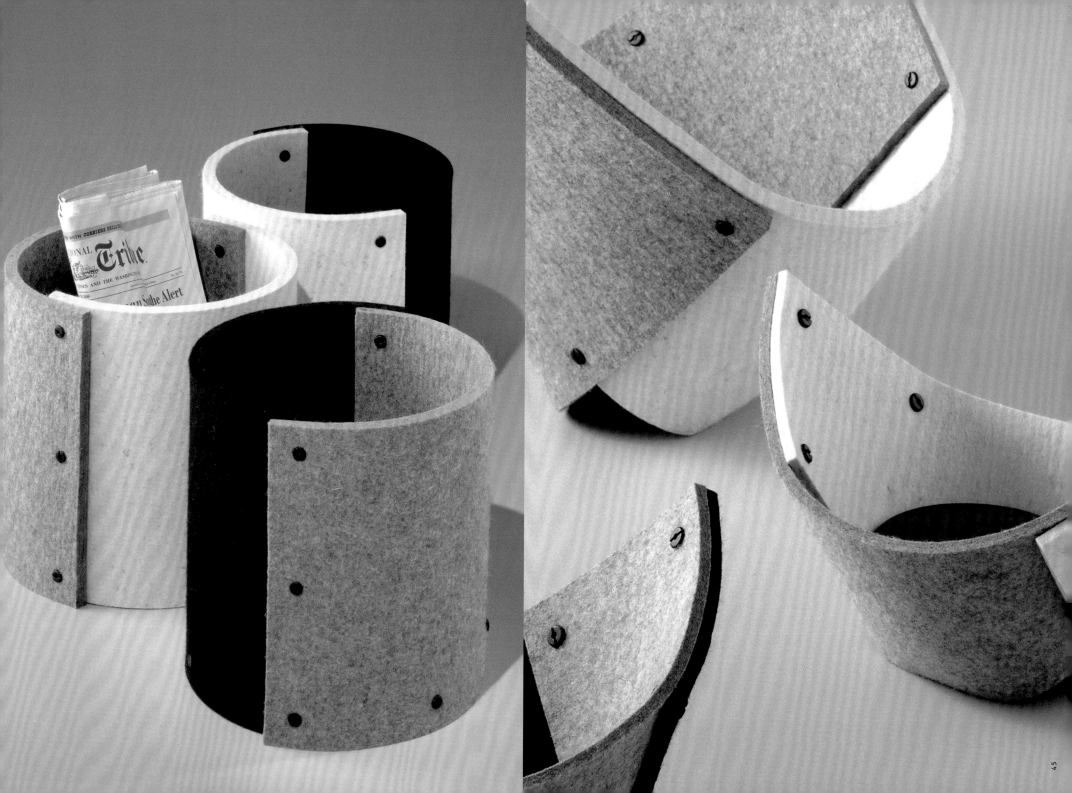

Masayo Ave creation

1 Block Modular Sofa Bed, 2000, CFC-free foam, polyester, antiflame protection on FMVSS 302, block 60 45 x 60 x 60 cm, block 120 45 x 60 x 120 cm, block 180 45 x 60 x 180 cm, MasayoAve creation.
❯ This sofa has been made out of the highest quality industrial foam, using CFC-free polyester. The large open-cell structure is firm enough for seating and soft enough for relaxing. It is suitable for both interior and exterior use, and is washable and recyclable.

2 Cool Cushion, 2000, CFC-free foam, polyester, 42/32 x 42/32 cm, MasayoAve creation.

❯ These cushions consist of black foam chips packed in translucent black tulle sacks. There are endless variations of differently shaped pieces. Cool cushions are the perfect companions for Block.

3 Genesi, lamp, 1998, CFC-free foam in polyester, polypropylene, chromed metal, fluorescent compact bulb, large 35 x ø 50 cm, small 28 x ø 30 cm, MasayoAve creation.
❯ The diffuser for this tablelight is made of washable open-celled polyester foam that snaps directly onto the polypropylene body. Simply by choosing how the snaps are fastened, it is possible to create a variety of rounded organic forms. The unique cell-structure softens the cold glare of the fluorescent light, creating a mystical and peaceful glow.

| 1 | 2 | 3 |

47

SHIN + TOMOKO AZUMI LONDON

Partners in life and work, Japanese designers Shin and Tomoko Azumi attracted attention a few years ago with their eye-catching tableware. Snowman (1999) is a salt and pepper shaker set, produced with a crafts-man-like attention to detail, and distinguished by its simple but pronounced design. Among countless interchangeable shaking devices, Snowman is distinctive because of its suggestion of a stylized snowman – its face formed from the tiny holes in the shaker. This gives it an almost iconic quality and makes it instantly recognizable.

Training at the Royal College of Art in London, combined with time spent in countries such as Italy, Germany and Holland, soon taught these Japanese designers to understand the mentality and character of European design and its markets. The team swiftly produced a furniture collection. An intense reduction in materials and form brings a figurative quality to these pieces that is typical of their work. Big Arm (2000), an upholstered chair, or hm30 (2001), an asymmetrical sofa, demonstrate this principle of deliberate figuration, which contrasts to earlier, almost minimalist simplifi-cations and repetitions in their work.

After a successful phase of 'New Simplicity' lasting more than a decade, an interest in the 'figuration of a product', or what might be called 'soft associative forms', has become apparent in the Azumis' designs. Over the past two years, Shin and Tomoko Azumi have also been trying their hand at designing exhibitions and events, putting their treatment of space and product presentation to the test. In the future, we might also imagine examples of virtual design entering their repertoire.

It is precisely because we do not know much about how Shin and Tomoko work together, for example how they divide their labour, whether each phase of development is discussed or who influences and informs their work, that we can speculate about it being a very private communal achievement – perhaps a typical Japanese working method. The Azumi team is an example of successful co-operation, and their products are a tribute to a permanent interplay of ideas. Shin and Tomoko do not dumb down their product ideas or adapt them to the market. Within a very short space of time, the Azumis have taken their place among the foremost young international designers, drawing their strength from a unique combination of professionalism and concrete design ideas. HANSJERG MAIER-AICHEN

1 hm30, sofa, chair and table, 2001, upholstered on wooden frame, single seater 68 x 92 x 81 cm, two seater 68 x 152 x 81 cm, three seater 68 x 212 x 81 cm, Hitch Mylius.
› The hm30 range comprises asymmetric seat units with sofas that can be used alone, or combined with a corner ottoman to cre-ate larger seating arrangements. Moveable armrests and low tables with etched-glass tops complete the collection. This clever lop-sided design means that when installed individually, the sofa looks as if it is defy-ing gravity by standing on one leg.

2 Snowman, salt and pepper shakers, 1999, fine ceramic, 6.7 x ø 5.8 cm Authentics.
› Rather than positioning the holes on the top of these salt and pepper shakers, they have been placed on the side, a very minor detail that makes a big difference in the interaction between the object and the user. Although the combination of the shapes is abstract, people recognize them as figures. The idea was to explore the bound-ary between 'abstract' and 'cartoon' with this design.

1	1
2	

48

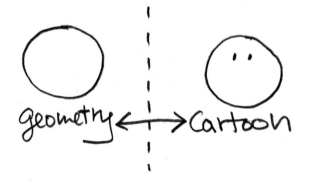

geometry ←—→ cartoon

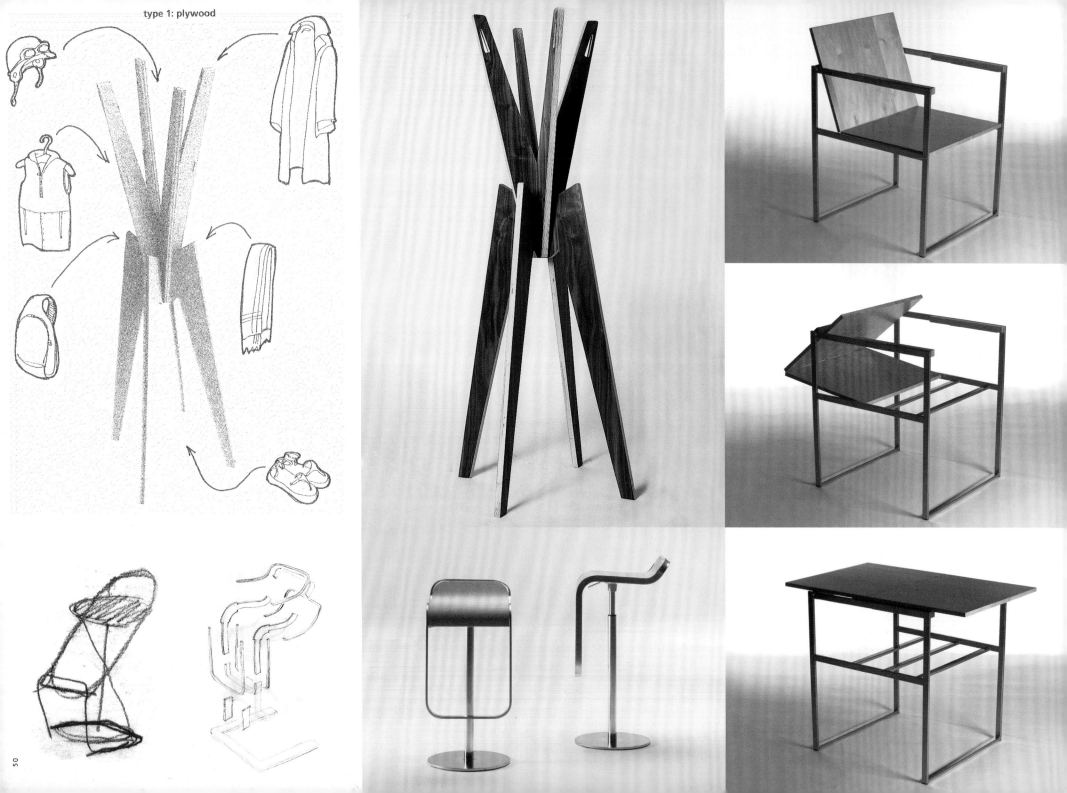

type 1: plywood

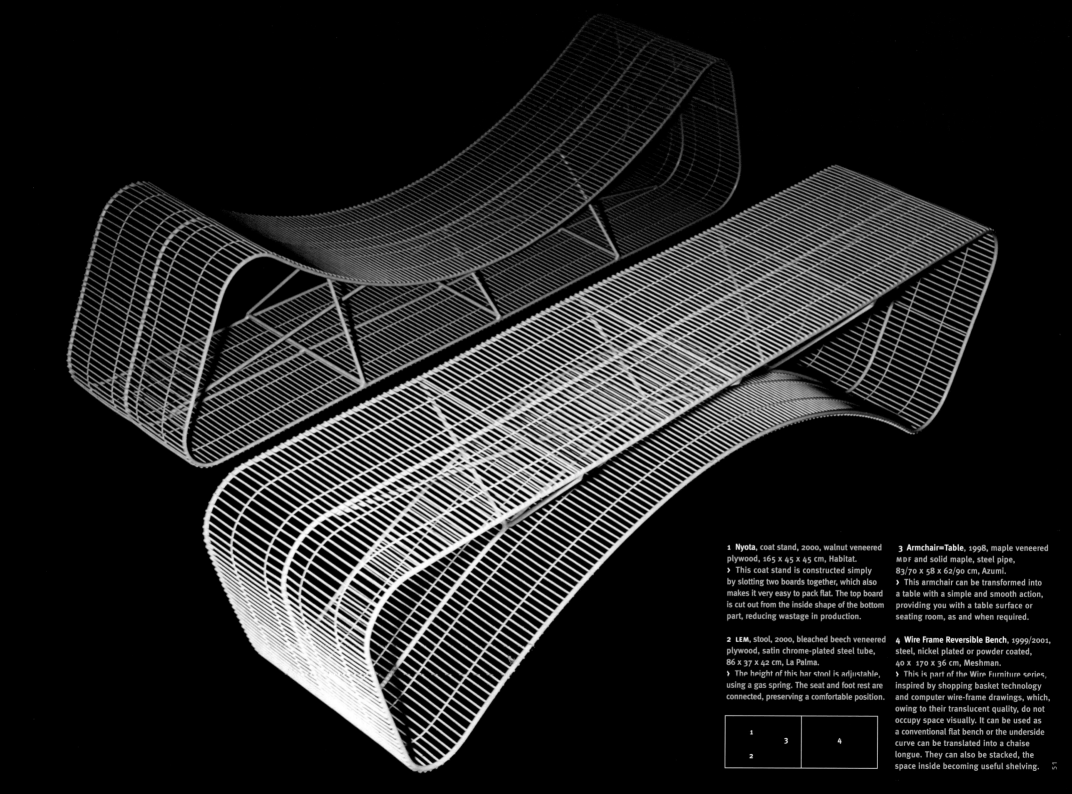

1 Nyota, coat stand, 2000, walnut veneered plywood, 165 x 45 x 45 cm, Habitat.
> This coat stand is constructed simply by slotting two boards together, which also makes it very easy to pack flat. The top board is cut out from the inside shape of the bottom part, reducing wastage in production.

2 LEM, stool, 2000, bleached beech veneered plywood, satin chrome-plated steel tube, 86 x 37 x 42 cm, La Palma.
> The height of this bar stool is adjustable, using a gas spring. The seat and foot rest are connected, preserving a comfortable position.

3 Armchair=Table, 1998, maple veneered MDF and solid maple, steel pipe, 83/70 x 58 x 62/90 cm, Azumi.
> This armchair can be transformed into a table with a simple and smooth action, providing you with a table surface or seating room, as and when required.

4 Wire Frame Reversible Bench, 1999/2001, steel, nickel plated or powder coated, 40 x 170 x 36 cm, Meshman.
> This is part of the Wire Furniture series, inspired by shopping basket technology and computer wire-frame drawings, which, owing to their translucent quality, do not occupy space visually. It can be used as a conventional flat bench or the underside curve can be translated into a chaise longue. They can also be stacked, the space inside becoming useful shelving.

1	3	4
2		

BARBER OSGERBY LONDON

England has probably produced more successful designers than any other country, and since many of them work abroad they dominate the international design scene. Part of the English success may be because there is not something easily identifiable as typical English style; it is quite eclectic. There is, however, a consistent emphasis on good quality. The design partnership Barber Osgerby is evidence of the English ability to keep on producing outstanding designers. Edward Barber and Jay Osgerby met when they were studying at the Royal College of Art in London and started working together in 1996. They quickly established themselves and by 1998 were doing work for Cappellini, the leading company in contemporary furniture.

One of their early pieces for Cappellini was the chaise longue (1999). This is a very strong design with no fuss about it or unnecessary detailing. The dimensions are perfect so that it is comfortable to lie on, relaxing and gives a sense of wellbeing. The pleasure of physical contact with the piece is important to the designers, and this is also manifest in their wooden Hula stool (2000), made for Cappellini. The partners work across a wide range of products, however. They created two moulded hangers to be used in all Levi Strauss shops when the Engineered range was launched in 1999. Designed to display the jackets and jeans to the best advantage, the hangers are unobtrusive and very functional. They are made of a semi-translucent blend of Styrene, using the minimum amount of material, and can be stacked easily. When the jeans are hung by loops from the notches in the trouser hanger, their three-dimensional form is revealed; the jacket hanger has a slight curve along the top edge, hinting at the shape of human shoulders.

A more ambitious project has been the Cross Bathmodule (2002). Barber Osgerby have created a bathroom that is a self-contained unit: it could be placed in a living or work space to divide up a large open area such as in a loft or it could be located outside to be a changing/shower room by a pool or a lake. The cross shape evolved from the four main bathroom functions – each one taking place in its own semi-private area – and the glass walls can be made of clear or opaque glass depending on the unit's location. It is a wonderful example of how to organize a bathroom in a more rational way. STEFAN YTTERBORN

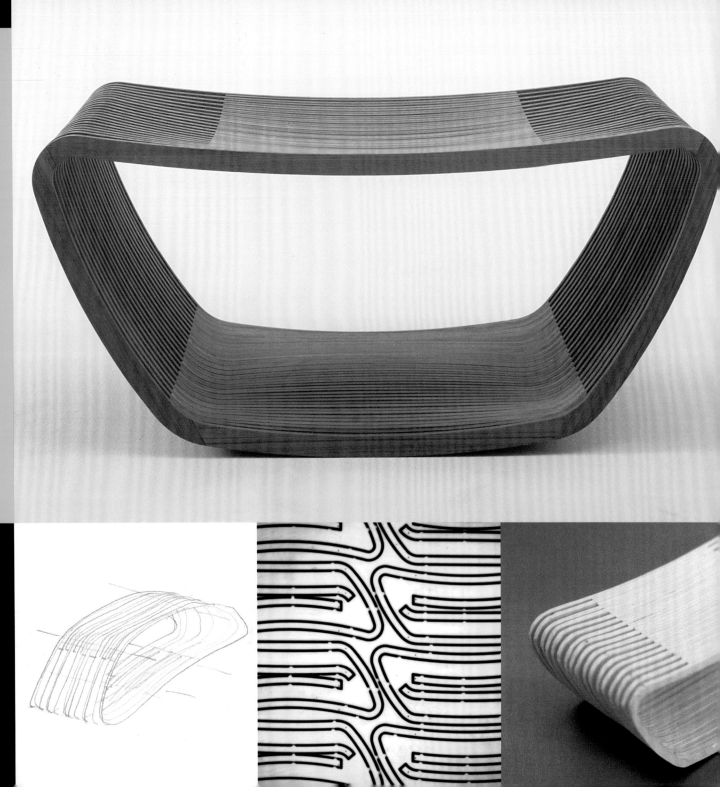

1 Hula Stool, 2000, available in a range of solid wood, 32 x 75 x 45.5 cm, Cappellini.
› This stool was the result of a competition for which the designers were invited to produce a piece of furniture from a single sheet of plywood. The stool can either sit solid or be inverted to form a rocking stool. Hula is now made of hardwood and constructed with mechanical fixings, ensuring the stool's longevity by permitting necessary movement in the joints.

2 Stencil, screen, 2002, transparent perspex, 170 x 272 x 12 cm, Cappellini.
› An experiment into the number of elements required to display clothing resulted in this wonderfully simple screen, proving the answer to be one. Designed to hold six pieces of clothing, this screen is either a night stand for an open-plan space or a distinctive display system for a retail environment.

1	2

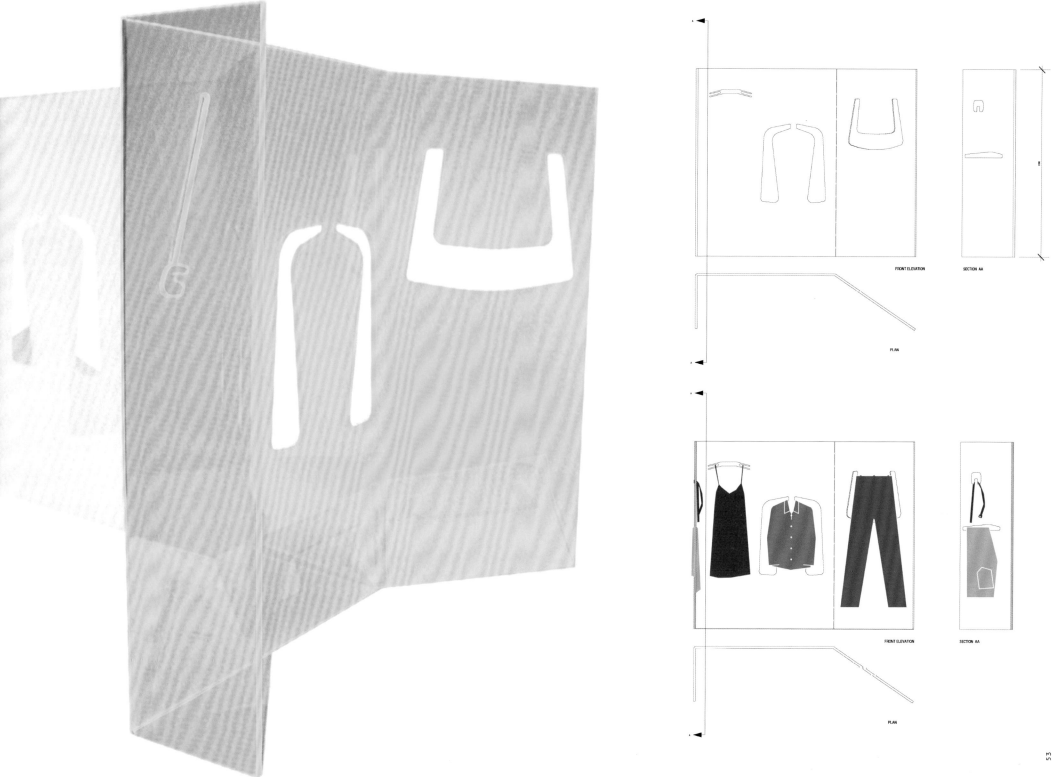

FRONT ELEVATION

SECTION AA

PLAN

FRONT ELEVATION

SECTION AA

PLAN

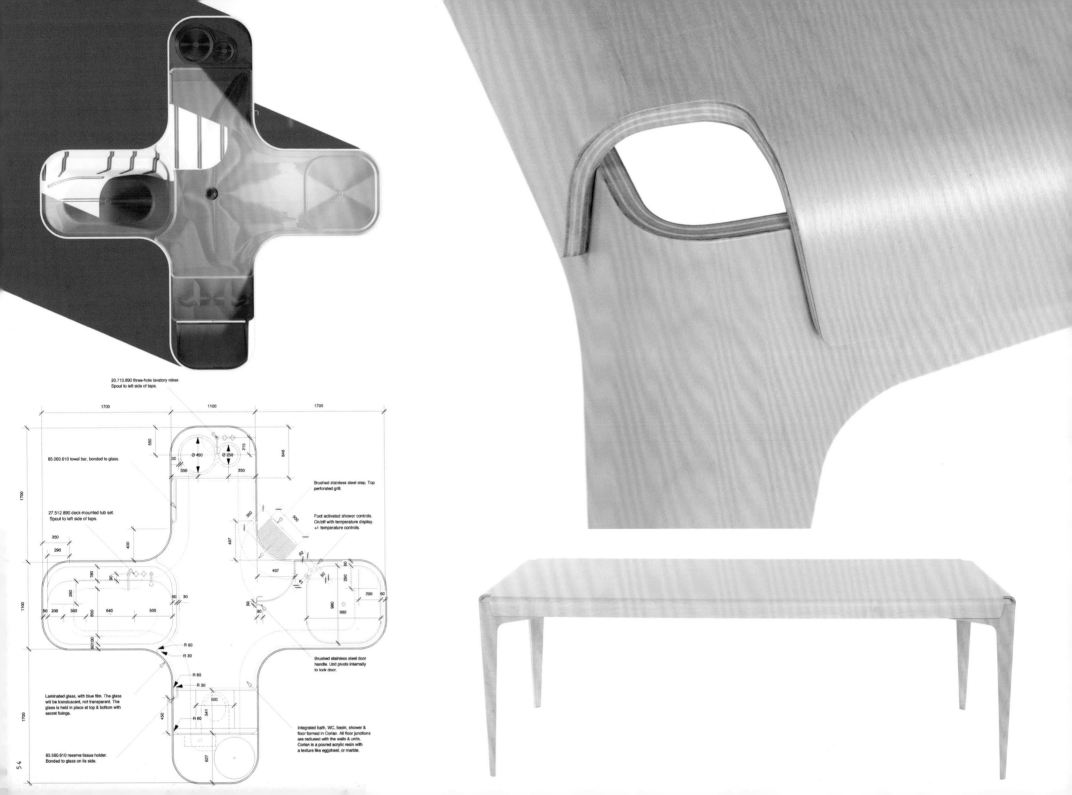

20.713.890 three-hole lavatory mixer.
Spout to left side of taps.

83.060.610 towel bar, bonded to glass.

27.512.890 deck-mounted tub set.
Spout to left side of taps.

Brushed stainless steel step. Top perforated grill.

Foot activated shower controls. On/off with temperature display. +/- temperature controls.

Brushed stainless steel door handle. Unit pivots internally to lock door.

Laminated glass, with blue film. The glass will be translucent, not transparent. The glass is held in place at top & bottom with secret fixings.

Integrated bath, WC, basin, shower & floor formed in Corian. All floor junctions are radiused with the walls & units. Corian is a poured acrylic resin with a texture like eggshell, or marble.

83.590.610 reserve tissue holder.
Bonded to glass on its side.

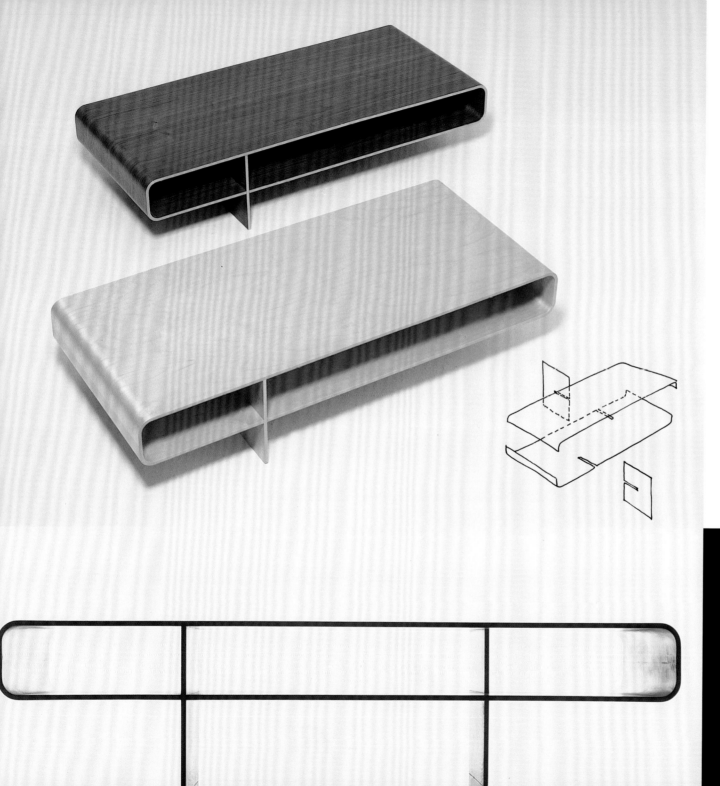

1 The Cross Bathmodule, 2002, glass and cast Corian, 400 x 450 x 450 cm, prototype for Dornbracht.
> In the bathmodule the role of the conventional bathroom has been dissected into four separate functions. All sanitary-ware extrudes from the floor, eliminating junctions and facilitating maintenance. It can be positioned in any number of locations and doubles as a sculptural installation.

2 Shell Table, 2001, lacquered plywood, 35 x 180 x 90 cm, Cappellini.
> The objective in designing this table was to produce something with a minimum number of components that can be assembled easily. The result is a table with a light ply structure which takes its strength from its folded edges.

3 Loop Table, 1997, laminated birch plywood, 29 x 135 x 60 cm, Isokon Plus/Cappellini.
> The distinctive feature of this table is the offset legs, creating the illusion of mass floating off the ground.

4 Shirt and Jeans Hangers, 1999, injection moulded translucent plastic, 16 x 47 x 8 cm, Levi Strauss.
> The curved shirt hanger mimics the broad shape of the human shoulder yet uses only the same amount of material as a conventional hanger. The unique shape means that many hangers can be stacked together to minimize the volume of storage and delivery.

			4
1	2	3	

A circular bar of glycerine soap with a big hole in the middle and a plastic hook developed specifically for it was the first project that I developed with the young English designer Sebastian Bergne. Since then formal aesthetic certainty, technical curiosity and the quest for the right production processes have lain at the heart of all his designs.

Bergne works quickly, creating products distinguished by a simple and unambiguous clarity that permits no alternatives. He demonstrates a surprising certainty in his work and a tendency not to ask too many questions about the way things are. Nevertheless, his designs are always dominated by the convincing solutions that he has found to formal and technical problems. Bergne's catch-phrase could be 'always a bit less', and this constant striving seems to spark a purification process in the course of designing domestic objects. His efforts are directed in such a way that they always maintain contact with the possibility of serial production.

Sebastian Bergne is a practised industrial designer and a convincing communicator about his own products. This is an ability that many more successful designers sorely lack. Their failure to communicate is not the result of inadequate theoretical training, but simply a preference for visual rather than verbal language. Much of the quality of a product depends on the nature of the communication between the designer and the manufacturer. The latter is generally better able to respond to models and drawings than to verbal explanations. Sebastian Bergne is a fine example of a designer who can also communicate effectively verbally with the manufacturers who will eventually produce his work.

Bergne was born in Iran and spent his childhood and adolescence in many very different countries. As a consequence of this international experience, he has a highly trained eye for multi-layered cultures, and he is familiar with much that is still strange to others. This training of his senses and cultural values has given Bergne a great deal of multicultural certainty and a healthy self-confidence. His works are expressions of a clearly ordered, organized and structured imagination, and they do not have any decorative details. It is this cool clarity that gives them their very individual charm, and a personality that is sometimes stunning and often surprising. 'Less is less' would be a simple interpretation of what we see: less than we are used to, an absolute reduction to the essential.

HANSJERG MAIER-AICHEN

1 Dr Spock, lamp, 1999, porcelain shade, chrome-plated stem, ceiling lamp 50 x ø 26/ 29 cm, floor lamp 150/ 192 x 50 x ø 26/ 29 cm, wall lamp 22/32 x 50 x ø 26/ 29 cm, Oluce.
> Designed as a family of lamps, the bicone form of the shade allows the structural and electrical connections to be separated and swapped in different models. The floor lamp includes a dimmer for atmospheric effect, whereas the reading lamp is more suited to a stronger more direct light. The wall-mounted version is capable of both, and its enamelled porcelain reflector is able to rotate 360 degrees. The result is a highly flexible family of typologies, conceived as such from the outset rather than as an afterthought. The material is pure and utterly alluring.

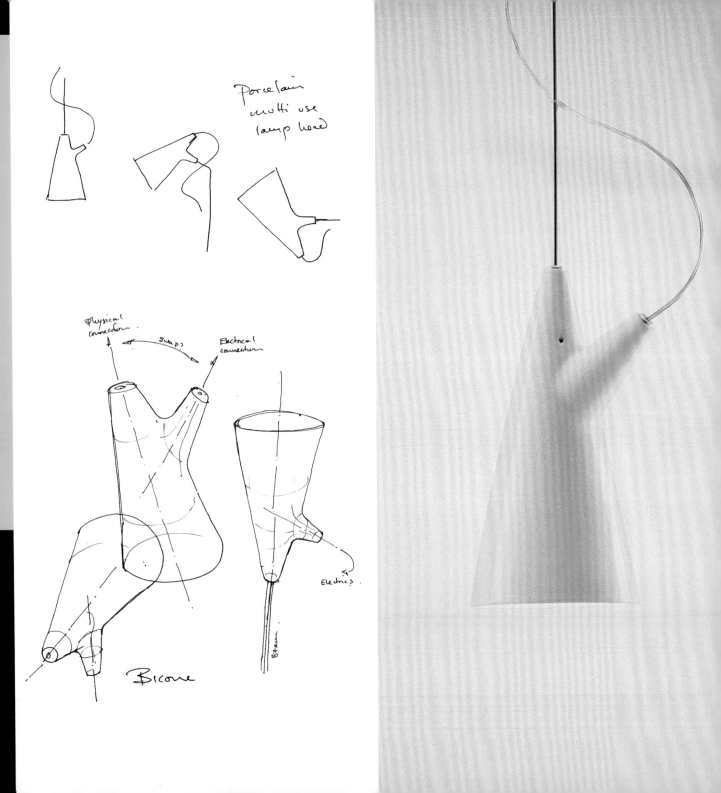

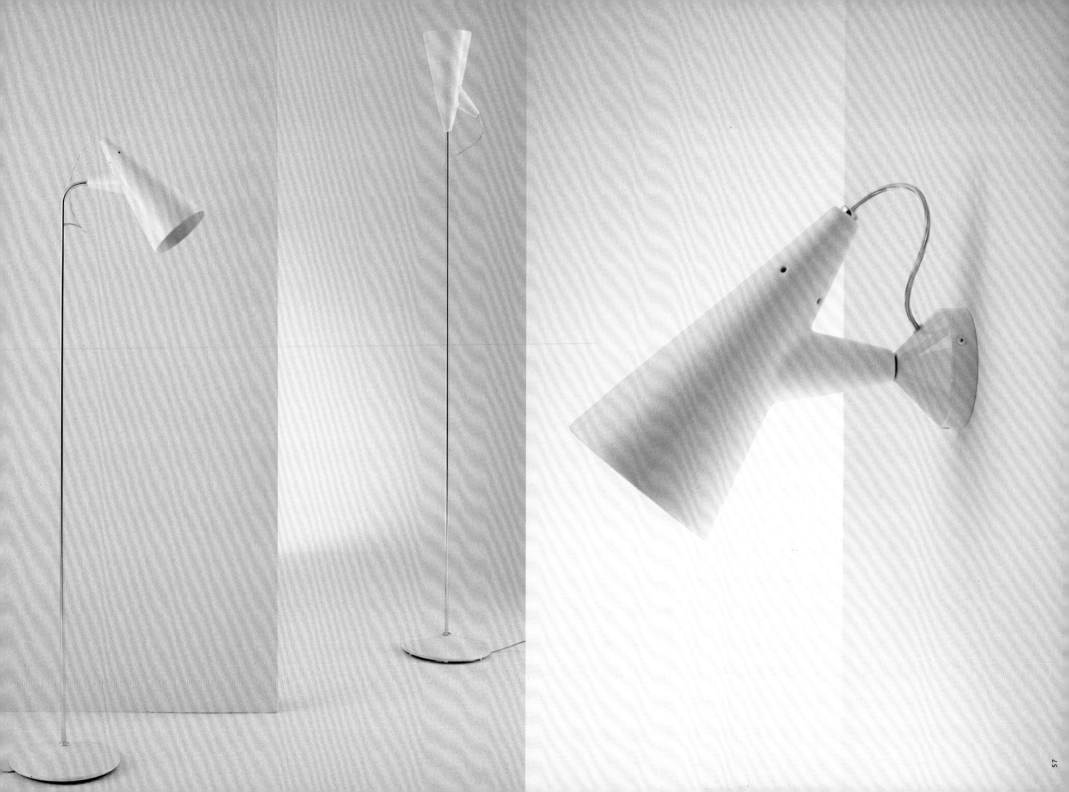

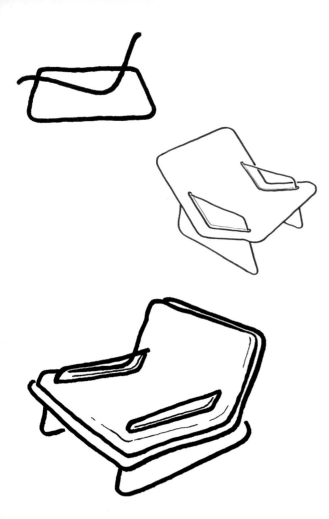

1 **Slot Low Chair and Stool**, 2000, stainless steel, plywood shell covered with zebrano veneer or cowhide in various colours, chair 70 x 80 x 80 cm, stool 30 x 80 x 40 cm, View.

> The Slot Low Chair and Stool are made of two simple elements. Two trapezoidal stainless-steel frames create the structure of the chair. The seat itself is a plywood shell covered with zebrano veneer and/or cowhide, creating an unusual effect. The chair frame cuts through the seat and back, securing the two parts and in so doing creates arm rests. By applying the same principle to the stool, the double-sided top can be removed and used as a tray.

1	1

LENA BERGSTRÖM STOCKHOLM

What Lena Bergström admires most in a design is simplicity, but being humorous and beautiful to look at come a close second. These qualities can certainly be found in her glasswork, for which she has gained international recognition. Since 1994 Bergström's name has been synonymous with that of Orrefors, the acclaimed Swedish glass manufacturers, and most of her work has been produced exclusively for them.

Bergström claims to admire designers that know a material well. She also extends her praise to those who master many disciplines with equal success. The discipline that she first became familiar with herself was textile design. It was this that she studied in Britain and Japan, before working with interior designers in her home country of Sweden.

Bergström's work was already becoming more architectural and graphic when she undertook a trial placement with Orrefors to try her hand at glass design. As Bergström is now one of the world's most celebrated contemporary glass designers, it goes without saying that the experiment was successful. She has produced many objects for the company, often preferring to thrash out the possibilities of a production-line piece than playing around in the limited-edition sector.

It is Bergström's dedication to pushing the boundaries of mass production that has made her designs so widely available. She cites Squeeze (2000) as the piece most representative of her style. The design is the product of a truly open-minded approach. 'When I first began designing glass, I wondered how I would ever be able to invent something new', she says, but with Squeeze she broke all of the usual boundaries by abandoning the glass-blowing process halfway through and hand squeezing the vase. Slitz (1998) is another innovative collection. The glass is cut and then reheated so that the sides of the vessel open like a petal.

The three collections, Planet (2000–2), Pastill and Flovers (2002), demonstrate Bergström's true affinity with colour. Pastill is a dynamic and energetic form with rainbow layers achieved through a technique of under- and over-layering. Designed for a position on the floor, the piece is the closest that Bergström has come to creating a piece of furniture.

Although her glass-blowing techniques are sometimes complicated, Bergström's finished products often appear simple. Similarly, the most obtuse of her pieces will often be produced by a very simple method. Furniture and architectural designs may be the next disciplines that she explores. LAURA HOUSELEY

1 Slitz, vase, 1998, crystal, 52 x ø 20 cm, 53 x ø 29 cm, Orrefors.
The slits cut into the surface of the glass are created by cutting and polishing the surface and then returning it to the furnace where, aided by the heat, the tube flares out creating a surprising new effect.

2 Pastill, bowl, 2002, crystal, 29 x ø 32 cm, 16 x ø 17 cm, Orrefors.
› These large, vibrant bowls are intended to be placed on the floor. With their red, green and blue insides and white exterior, the larger bowls make eye-catching solitaires, while the smaller versions are more functional.

3 Planet, bowl, 2000, crystal, 14 x ø 17 cm, 11 x ø 17 cm, Orrefors.
› These sculptures are made by hand, using an under- and over-layering technique. The glass is then allowed to cool, cut in half, and an invisible layer of milky white glass is revealed.

1	2	3

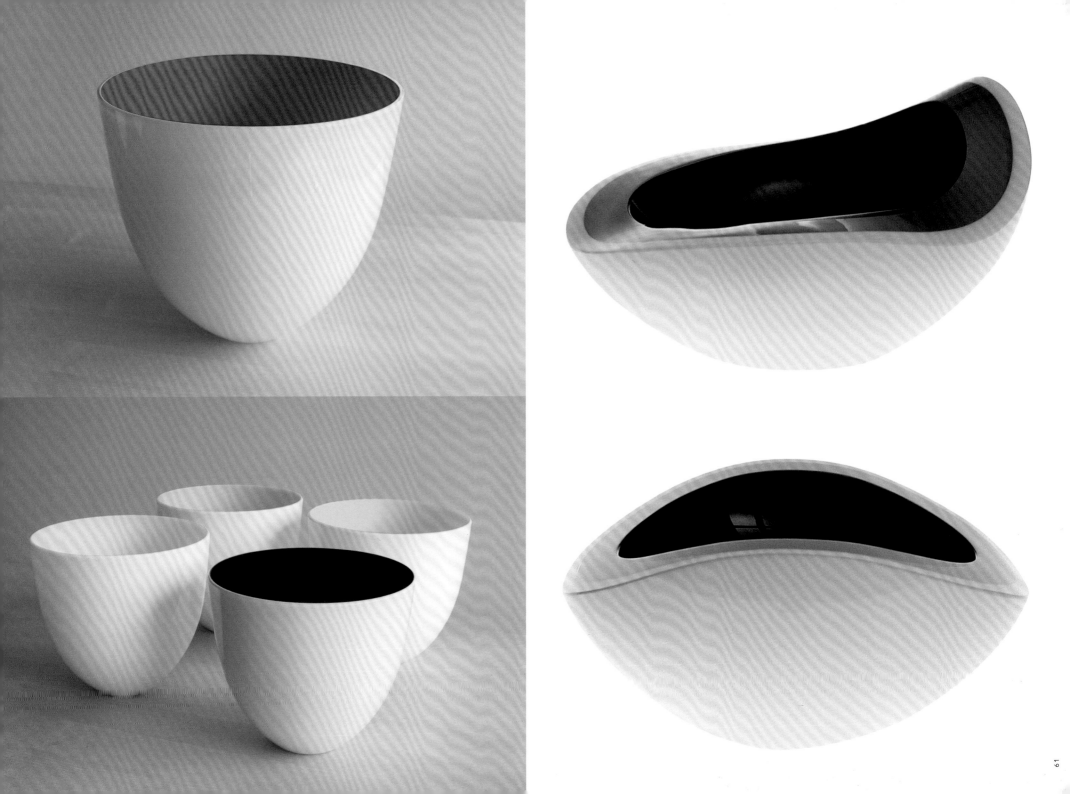

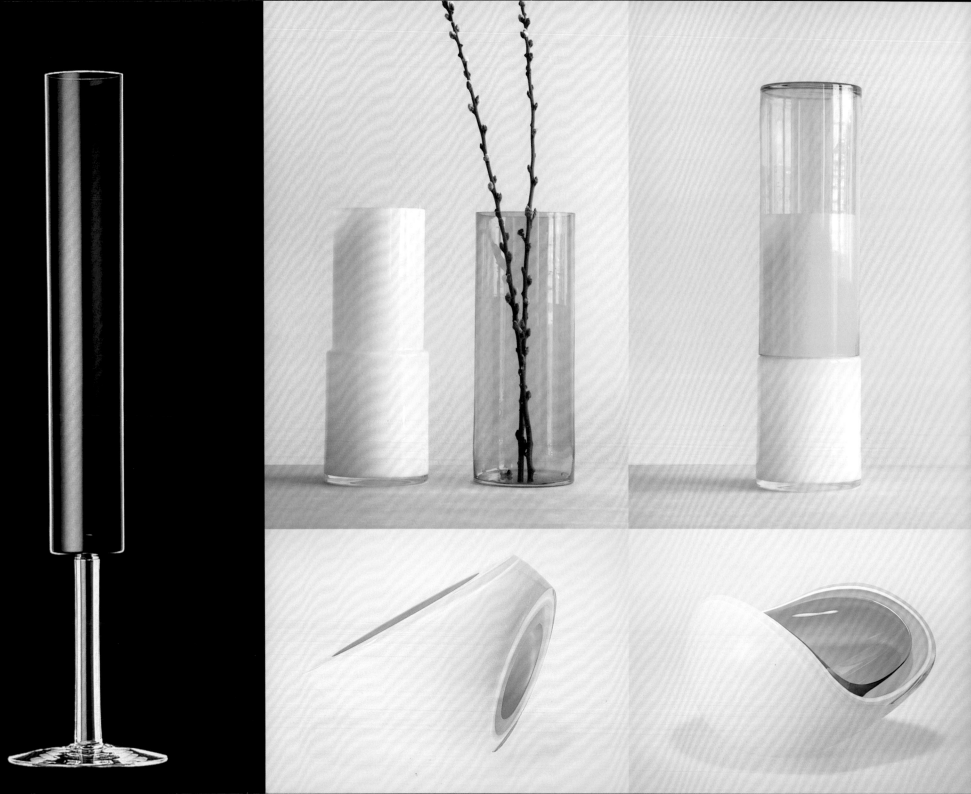

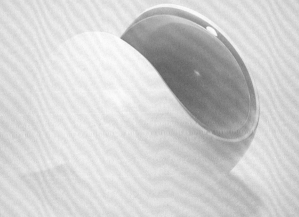

1 Cyrano, vase, 1999, crystal,
37 x ø 6 cm, Orrefors.
> This has a topaz-smoked body and a thin
stem that rests upon a clear circular base.

2 Flovers, vase, 2002, crystal,
60 x ø 16 cm, Orrefors.
> The name Flovers is a fusion of flowers
and lovers. The vases appear to cling to
each other and also work as a sculpture.

3 Planet, bowl, 2000, crystal,
10/20 x 20 x 25 cm, 18 x 19 x 25 cm, Orrefors.

4 Roll, 1998, felted wool, polyester wadding,
130 x 45/65 cm, Designers eye Sweden.
> Roll is a felted-wool mattress for chairs,
floors, benches or pillows.

5 Wall, screen, 2002, MDF board, felted
wool, polyester wadding, 145 x 125 cm,
Designers eye Sweden.
> Wall is a flexible screen system with
sound-absorbing wadding, covered with
felted wool. It can be rolled up or coupled
together with magnets.

6 Squeeze, vase, 2000, crystal,
34 x ø 15 cm, Orrefors.
> This vase stayed in the furnace just
a second too long, with stunning results.

7 Cyclop, bowl, 2002, crystal,
19 x ø 18 cm, Orrefors.

	2		4	5	6
1					
	3		7	3	

JEFFREY BERNETT NEW YORK

It was his minor design projects for an Italian manufacturer that first drew my attention to New York designer Jeffrey Bernett. A modest young American from Illinois in the Midwest, he came regularly to Italy, looked into the state of furniture production, saw global developments at the Salone del Mobile in Milan, and met interested Italian manufacturers. At that time, there were huge numbers of young and innovative designers, and media and digital technology were cutting down global travel so that the time factor was measured down to the nearest second. Every time a new invention appeared, however unimportant, the press held its breath for a moment. In this turmoil of media and design, Jeffrey Bernett went his own steady way with clear goals in mind and without haste.

He has kept on with this style of working in an orderly, organized and, to my mind, by no means American way. His work is in the tradition of European design. Without knowledge of the Bauhaus and many other protagonists in the history of European design, his products would be neither explicable nor plausible. For this very reason, Bernett's designs are distinguished by their extreme simplicity. Each detail is logical and understandable, and yet the products are not boring. They have the charm of simplicity, unaided by any kind of decoration or formal flourishes.

Bernett's chaise longue (2001) for B&B Italia clearly demonstrates his simple solutions to form and function. Seeing the 'special in the normal' is one of the constants – apparent early on – running through all of Bernett's work.

If we consider the state of American design over the past ten years, we see very little autonomous design culture – a stark contrast to developments in architecture, graphic design, art or music. Perhaps the great American craft tradition acts as a hindrance to the development of design in the US. Even the new generation of cutting-edge consumer establishments, such as Murray Moss's incomparable design store in New York, clearly reveal the dominance of European designers. Despite the fact that Moss is highly committed to involving American designers in his concept, even his store is still very much focused on the Italians. Given this situation, and bearing in mind the tendency to produce rather neo-baroque and figurative design in the US, Jeffrey Bernett's works have a greater significance within the European tradition. HANSJERG MAIER-AICHEN

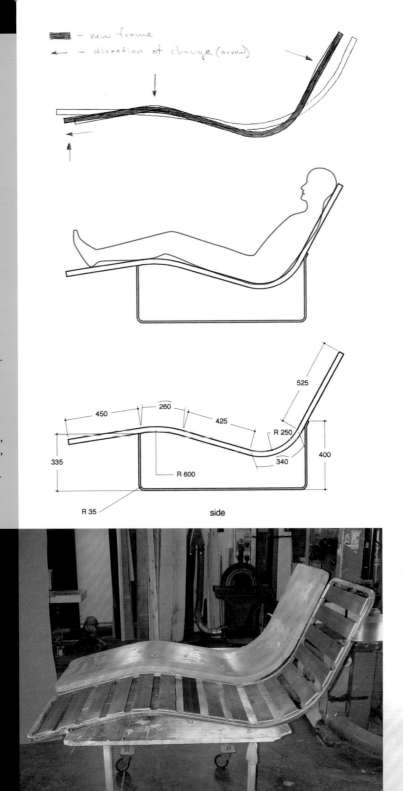

1 **Landscape**, chaise longue, 2001, stainless steel, polyurethane foam, leather or upholstery, 79 x 161 x 61 cm, B&B Italia.
> B&B Italia pioneered the first injection-moulded polyurethane foam seating. This chaise longue was developed to push the limits of this technology with fresh and innovative details. A cantilevered structure placed on a nickel or graphite varnished metal base creates this minimalist and light design. The sparing use of cushioning made the correct relation of the seating planes especially critical for seating comfort. The headrest is secured to the chaise with magnets and it is upholstered in felt or leather sewn in segments. Seams around the edges accentuate the overall design.

2 **House Project**, 1998, concept, living and dining room.
> The House Project is an affordable housing concept that could be sold as a kit and erected in a fraction of the time of a conventional building. All of the utilities (electricity, plumbing, gas, etc.) are consolidated for maximum efficiency in a unit in the middle of the floor plan.

| 1 | 2 |

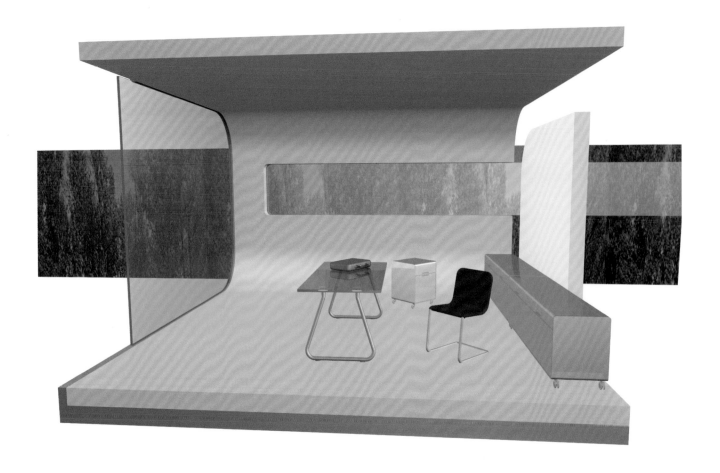

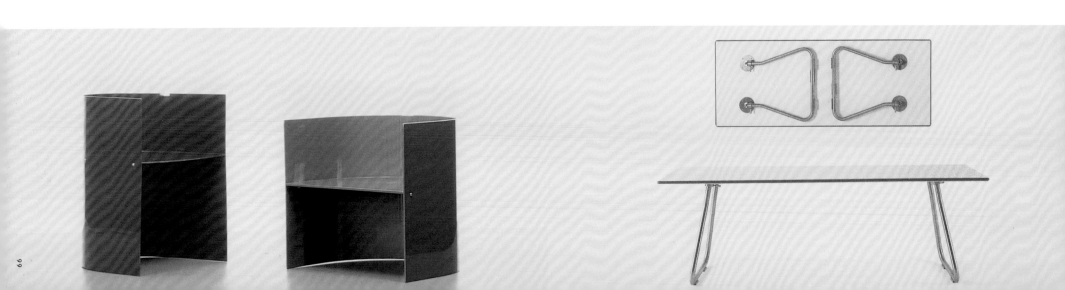

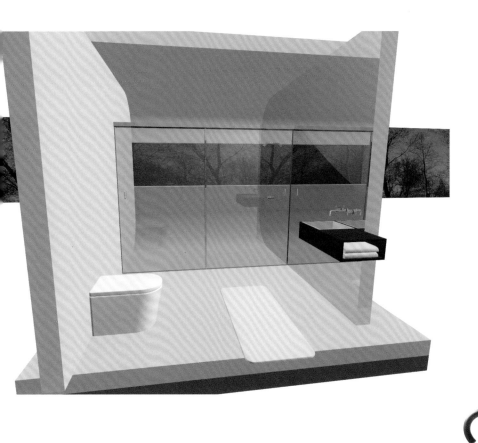

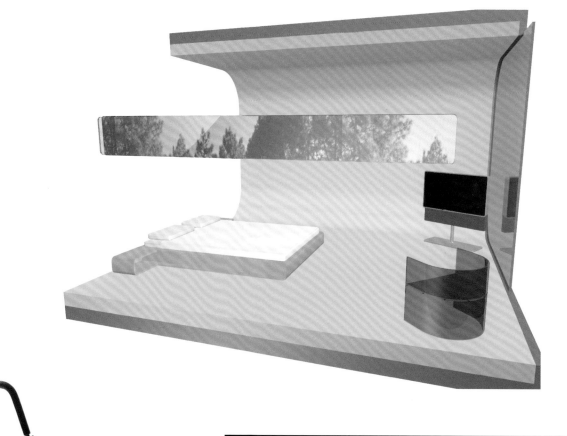

House Project, 1998, concept.
1 Home Office, **2** Bathroom, **3** Bedroom.
> All of the rooms and appliances in the house are powered by solar energy. Further energy could be obtained from a window containing a light-reflective element that shades the interior during the hot summer months and permits the sun's warmth to penetrate during the winter.

4 Monza, chair, 1999, powder-coated steel, low 60 x 65 x 55 cm, high 70 x 53 x 50 cm, Cappellini.
> Cold-rolled steel was chosen because

the project could then be easily realized using existing rolling and bending machines, thus requiring no new investment.

5 Urban, table, 2001, stainless steel, glass or laminated MDF, 70 x 80 x 180/210 cm, Cappellini.
> Conceived as either a worktable or retail store fixture, there are two versions of this multi-use table: one has folding legs for storage when not in use, the other version has legs fixed in the open position.

6 Umbrella Stand, 1999, stainless steel, 60 x ø 35 cm, Cappellini.
> The functional design of this object has also a fairly strong sculptural identity. Stainless steel was the only material used in this project because of its strong anti-corrosion properties.

1		2	3
4	5	6	

Thomas Bernstrand captured the interest of the design world in 1999 when he was in his last year at Konstfack, the University College of Arts, Crafts and Design in Stockholm. His graduation pieces, which can be described as 'party' furniture, burst upon the design scene in Scandinavia with a freshness and wit that was both remarkable and welcome. For, after an initial boom in Swedish design in the 1990s, much of what was being produced was predictable and uniform. The design world was debating how to renew itself and Bernstrand's pieces were a significant contribution to that debate. All his graduation products are about having fun: the Do Swing which is a hanging lamp designed so that you can also swing on it; a wall lamp which you can box with, made of silicon that covers the actual lamp bulb so it can withstand the punches; a stepped sofa to enable a group of people to sit together either as an audience or in a sociable way. These projects brought Bernstrand a lot of local recognition very quickly and broke the status quo of typical Swedish design. After graduation he went on to establish his own business, Bernstrand & Co, which also works in a collaborative way with other designers.

In 2000 the Dutch group Droog Design invited Bernstrand to exhibit with them at the Salone del Mobile in Milan. They are now producing the Do Swing commercially. Another product that has been developed from his party furniture is an outdoor version of his stepped-sofa design with wooden slats replacing the soft covering. One of Bernstrand's most intriguing pieces to date is the Tablelighttable (1999), which has an almost physical presence thanks to its animal-like character with its four legs and lamp growing out of the top of the table. Even the flex, often an intrusion on a light design, seems in place because it is reminiscent of a tail. The table is a wonderful mismatch of design languages – the light itself is almost baroque while the legs have a very simple, minimalist structure. The whole object has a witty personality that you can chat with when alone!

What characterizes Bernstrand's pieces is humour, the quality that is probably most lacking in Swedish design. But humour is difficult to carry off – it needs to be perfectly balanced, smart and meaningful – and Bernstrand does this with great confidence. His playful approach to the appearance of the object is part of what makes his pieces so unique.

STEFAN YTTERBORN

1 **Tablelighttable**, 1999, steel, coloured MDF board, lampshade, 62 x 64 x 42 cm, Bernstrand & Co.
› Tablelighttable has been likened to a small animal. The positioning of the various components is paramount; the lamp is perfectly balanced with the electric flex, as are the spindly legs with the sturdy tabletop.

2 **Do Swing**, lamp, 1998, stainless steel, second-hand lampshades, 10 x 46 x 50 cm, Droog Design.

› This is no ordinary chandelier: Do Swing has been designed to withstand an adult's weight, is easy to grab hold of, has no sharp edges and is as durable as it looks. The lights at either end of the crossbar are working lights – handy while swinging and for lighting the hallway.

3 **Sugar Ray**, lamp, 1998, stainless steel, fibre optics, silicone rubber, 22 x 42 x 42 cm.
› Another example of adventurous lighting, this boxing wall lamp offers the perfect opportunity to work off your frustration. When you are in a more tranquil state of mind, Sugar Ray lights up the hallway.

| 1 | 2 | 3 |

1 Sluk, clothes hanger, 2001, chromed steel, hooks, stretchable cord, 200 x 96 x 96 cm, Bernstrand & Co.
> This coat stand does not take up any space when not in use, but when needed, it looks as happy carrying one solitary jacket as it does piled up with eighty anoraks – and a couple of hats.

2 Olympic, bench, 2001, steel, wood, 72 x 175 x 110 cm, Nola Industrier AB.
> This stair-shaped bench is intended for schoolyards or public parks. The design is derived from the traditional slatted benches, but Olympic takes into account a growing population.

3 Wembley, sofa, 1998, stainless steel, plywood, polyester, cloth, 74 x 160 x 30 cm, Bernstrand & Co.
> This sofa has three rungs which provide ample sitting space for up to nine people. It is brilliant for viewing any sporting event, and two placed facing each other provide a perfect setting for light hearted debate. They are economical with space, which is pertinent in a retail or office setting.

1	2
	3

JURGEN BEY ROTTERDAM

With discreet determination, Jurgen Bey is modifying the definition of design. His is not a practice of form following function, of marketing or commerce. He is slowly but surely changing the landscape of contemporary design, through evolution rather than revolution.

Above all, concept is the key for Bey. A case in point is his Kokon series (2001), which developed from the Dutch word for cocoon. He realized that cocoons are skins, giving coherent shape to lumpy and evolving organic interiors beneath a smooth exterior. Building on this, Bey assembled an eclectic collection of furniture under a stretchy synthetic skin, which allowed their original shapes to show through, while unifying them in one pristine casing. In a similar way, Bey produced the Lightshade-shade (1999), consisting of a vintage chandelier surrounded by an additional shade of see-through mirror foil. When off, the light looks like a sleek grey lampshade; when on, the effect is spectacular, with the old lamp glowing through eerily.

Bey's work is also a form of contemporary fairytale, where the sitter or user becomes an integral part of his storytelling. Walking through the forest, he conceived the Tree Trunk Bench (1999), which has become a landmark in contemporary design. He combined a felled tree trunk with bronze-cast archetypal chair backrests, planting them in the middle of the trunk. The result seems self-evident, if slightly unsettling.

Finally, Bey asks for mental and physical efforts on the part of the user. Although he often works with old objects that take on new meaning in his designs, he also seeks to recondition damaged objects, transforming them into ingenious new products. He sets out to prove that what is considered a disadvantaging handicap for some is an advantage for others. In his Healing series (2000), he began by sawing off one leg of a chair and propping it up with a stack of books, transforming the leg into a wooden toy for the child of the house. Putting stacks of books to work when not in use then became a part of his Do Add project (2000) for the Do Create label, producing chairs that become usable only when the user integrates a propping element from his environment. In such a subtle, even subversive, way Bey asks us questions and makes us conscious of our surroundings, rehabilitating not just objects but our relationships to them. LISA WHITE

1 **Healing Chair-Toy**, 2000, armchair, cotton embroidery, 80 x 50 x 50 cm, Jurgen Bey.
2 **Healing Table-Oven**, 2000, dark beech, enamelled steel, 75 x 70 x 80 cm, Jurgen Bey.
3 **Healing Cupboard-Storage**, 2000, laminated wood, wallpaper, 185 x 100 x 35 cm, Jurgen Bey.
› The starting point for the Healing series was the idea of changing familiar furniture. By removing and adding elements, the designer creates new and unexpected functions.

4 **Tree Trunk Bench**, 1999, tree trunk, brass, 75 x 400 x 45 cm, Jurgen Bey.
› The woods of Oranienbaum are scattered with felled trees which can serve as giant benches, providing an interesting interaction between culture and nature. The tree trunk provides a ready-made seat, and casts of existing chair backs transform the log into a proper piece of furniture.

1	2	3
	4	

72

1 Gardening Bench+Container, wood, dried grass, bench 75 x 50 x 200 cm, container 150 x 75 x 90 cm, Jurgen Bey.
> Extrusion containers press garden waste into endless non-durable benches which can be shortened to any length; it is up to nature to decide when to reclaim them.

2 do add, 2000, laminate wood, chromium-plated, chair 83 x 45 x 45 cm, bench 83 x 45 x 110 cm, Jurgen Bey.
> One leg of this chair is shorter than the others. By adding whatever seems appropriate, the user transforms what appears to be a broken chair into something new and characterful. The bench is for two or more people to enjoy each other's company, but it relies on trust. If one person stands up, the balance is disrupted.

3 Kokon, 2001, existing furniture, PVC coating, Jurgen Bey. **Lightshade-shade**, 1999, chandelier, polyester film with see-through mirror coating, 83 x ø 39 cm, Moooi.
> These products have been wrapped in an elastic synthetic fibre. The material shrinks tightly round the furniture, forming a smooth elastic skin. Any piece of furniture can be given a new lease of life in this design. When turned off, Lightshade-shade is a mirror which reflects its environment. When the light is on, the chandelier is revealed through the mirror in its old garments, giving comfort and character.

1		2
	2	
2		3

BIGERT + BERGSTRÖM STOCKHOLM

Mats Bigert and Lars Bergström are two Swedish artists who met while studying at the Royal Academy of Fine Arts in Stockholm and have collaborated since 1986. They are included in this book because they give a glimpse of the future, of how the design industry has to draw on talent from other disciplines if it is going to continue to be innovative. With their art-oriented approach they can see possibilities that those in the industry do not see. And yet, combined with their ideas, there is a tremendous knowledge of construction techniques and the practicalities of how things are made because of the quality and type of installations that they have produced.

From the beginning they had a desire to create artificial worlds. In their Climatic Chambers 2, exhibited at the Swedish Pavilion at EXPO 98 in Lisbon, they wanted the public to experience a variety of climates within a succession of 'rooms'. The four structures' egg-shape, which they said 'fell on us like an apple', was perfect for exploring ideas about climate and how it has created unique cultures. The humidity, heat, storm and freeze chambers were made of material inside and out with the correct associations. For example, copper was used for the heat chamber and aluminium for the freeze chamber, which also had a white exterior reminiscent of a fridge. When walking through the chambers people have a complex art experience: they feel they are on the inside of a sculpture, and the extreme climates stimulate the senses.

Temperature and people's expectations of materials also play an important role in the artists' 'hot and cold' mug and glass. In this case they play on the associations of hot and cold: red and blue, soft and hard, etc., and they build these into the form, pattern and materials of the receptacles. So the mug has red trim with a pattern of 'soft' semicircles and is made of white china suitable for hot drinks, while the glass has a blue, 'hard' triangle pattern and is ideal for an ice-cold drink in summer.

The egg shape of the Climatic Chambers continues to appeal to them. In 2000 they made a white egg-shaped rug suitable for one person to lie down on.

One of the basic elements of design is communication and, ironically, it is Bigert + Bergström, artists not designers, who are the best communicators I know. STEFAN YTTERBORN

1 **Climatic Chambers 2**, 1998, 8.5 x 12 x 36 m, Swedish Pavilion, EXPO 98, Lisbon.
> The essential idea here was to frame physical climates in rooms. The egg shape creates a perfect 'think-tank' structure in which one can hatch specific ideas related to the climate inside. All the materials used in the eggs reflect associations connected to the different climates. As you walk through the chambers, you are meant to have the sense of passing through the intestines of a series of sculptures.

2 **Humidity Chamber**, 1998, iron-powder-coated fibreglass, 7 x ø 5 m.
> This chamber includes glass circuit-board floors and dripping sound-studio sponge-walls, and is coated with rust.

3 **Storm Chamber**, 1998, aluminium, PVC, 5 x ø 7 m.
> Just like a storm, this chamber twists itself into a spiral.

4 **Heat Chamber**, 1998, polycarbonate, mirror foil, 7 x ø 5 m.
> The heat chamber has been built like a tropical greenhouse.

5 **Freeze Chamber**, 1998, fibreglass, gel coat, 7 x ø 5 cm.
> To create the effect of shimmering whiteness, the designers used the idea of a shiny fridge.

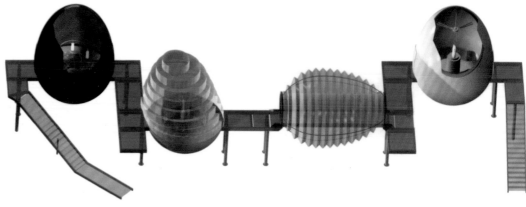

1 Storm Chamber, 1998.

2 Freeze Chamber, 1998.

3 Hotfront Mug, 2001, porcelain, 11 x ø 7 cm.
4 Coldfront Glass, 2001, glass, 13 x ø 6 cm.
> The Hotfront Mug was designed along-
side the Coldfront Glass, as one of the features for the third issue of the cultural magazine *Cabinet*, which was about the weather.
They are abstract representations of the two
climatic extremes. By placing the symbols on
the 'lip level' of the mug or glass, the concept
and the experience of drinking is reinforced.

5 Egg Carpet, 2000, cotton, 200 x 120 cm,
Asplund.
> The Egg Carpet was designed as a spin-off
from the installation Climatic Chambers 2. The
size of the carpet is designed to accommodate
a person lying down. It becomes an elevated
plan drawing of our first habitat – the egg.

6 The Waiting Room, 2002, photos, glass
globes, light, electric motors, various
dimensions, installation at Zinc Gallery,
Stockholm.
> From a suspended 'office' ceiling hang
nine spherical photographic lamps depicting the room in negative, yet the figures
populating the images are represented in
positive. The globes rotate slowly on their
own axis, giving the visitors the cinematic
effect of a fish-eye lens panning the room.

1	2	3	4	5
		6		

Blu Dot's philosophy centres on affordable design, an approach that permeates not only the collective's finished products, but also its design thinking and witty catalogue copy. Founded in 1996 by John Christakos, a sculptor with an MBA, and Charlie Lazor and Maurice Blanks, both architects, Blu Dot has grown into a design and manufacturing company that produces several lines of furniture as well as smaller objects, such as CD racks and letter holders.

In order to fulfil its low-cost mission, Blu Dot developed a list of parameters: they decided to use veneers instead of hardwoods, powder-coated steel rather than stainless, and they were determined to pack every piece flat, so that they would never be paying to transport empty space. Such stringent guidelines might have led to work that was banal, simplistic or utilitarian, but Blu Dot added a healthy dose of wit and intelligence to the recipe, a love of modern design, and a respect for the relationship between user and product. The result is clean, elegant, sophisticated, smart, strong and timeless. Blu Dot's pieces never look as if saving money was the primary objective.

Chicago (1997) was the first furniture series. Typifying Blu Dot's straightforward approach to design and assembly, this shelving system consists of cherry or maple boxes slung on steel tubes in multiple configurations. As for the name, the catalogue says: 'Just because we like Chicago.' Modu-licious (1999), as its clever name suggests, is a modular system of maple-veneer cabinets that can be mixed and matched in almost infinite possibilities. Blu Dot has subverted the traditional notion of wooden drawers and doors, substituting bullet-proof painted steel in a range of colours including 'Frank Lloyd Wright red'. Both Chicago and Modu-licious reflect the influence of modernist designers such as Charlotte Perriand and Charles and Ray Eames, and even the minimalist furniture designs of Donald Judd.

The 2D:3D series, started in 1998, consists of smaller products made from powder-coated steel in a range of colours. These are the most popular of Blu Dot's products. Sheets of metal are cleverly perforated and can be tucked and folded into CD racks, coat hooks or magazine holders – 'fold along dotted line' the catalogue instructs. With its consumer participation and creative packaging, the series typifies Blu Dot's mission to offer utility, affordability and modernity. Although very serious, the delight that this team takes in its work is obvious. BROOKE HODGE

1 Li'l Buddy, side table, 2001, powder-coated steel, bent ply, chrome steel wire, 78.5 x 86.5 x 50.5 cm, Blu Dot.
› This compact table is clearly based on traditional writing desks. It has a pull-out front, now more likely to hold a keyboard than a pen and paper, and the flat tabletop is ideally suited to holding a computer.

2 Feltup Chair, 2000, tube steel, felt, nylon backing, 61 x 68.5 x 96.5 cm, Blu Dot.
› This chair, reminiscent of the traditional deckchair, is well suited to be an inexpensive lounge chair or a chair for nomadic living. Industrial felt was chosen for its surface quality and its ability to act as a cushion, almost like upholstery compressed in sheet form. The chair was commissioned by the Walker Art Center in Minneapolis.

3 Chicago Low Boy, wall unit, 1997, cherry veneer, tubular steel legs, 91 x 152 x 33 cm, Blu Dot.

4 Chicago 8 Box, wall unit, 1997, cherry veneer, tubular steel legs, 190 x 236 x 29 cm, Blu Dot.
› The Chicago series is based upon an efficient principle: a structural box or box beam and steel legs that pass through two or more panels. The legs are attached with a minimal, socket-type connection for clean and easy assembly and disassembly. The boxes are proportioned and divided to function as desk, bookshelf or table.

1	2	3
		4

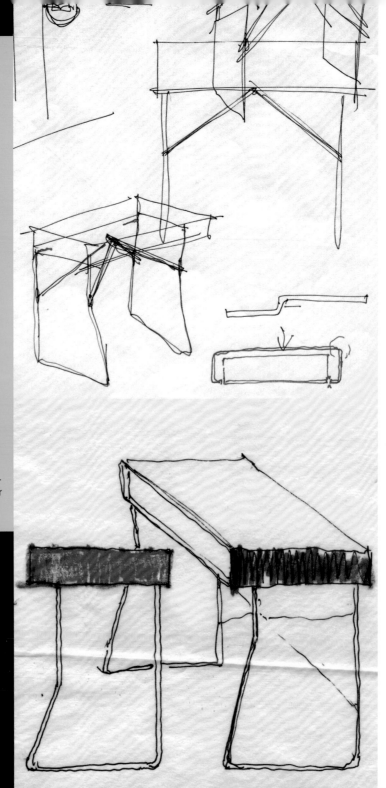

OPEN CUBE

CUBE w/ SHELF

CUBE w/ DOOR

CUBE w/ DRAWERS

OPEN DOUBLE CUBE

OPEN w/ SHELF

DOUBLE CUBE
w/ DOORS

DOUBLE CUBE
w/ DRAWERS

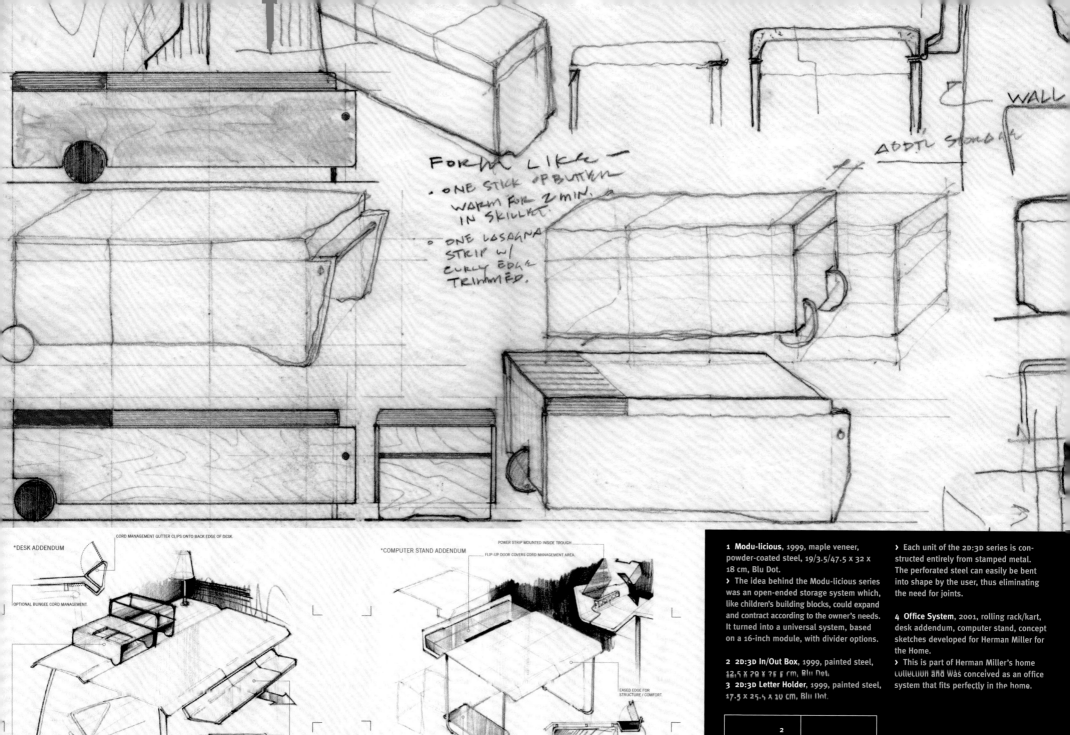

FORM LIKE —
- ONE STICK OF BUTTER WARM FOR 2 MIN. IN SKILLET.
- ONE LASAGNA STRIP w/ CURLY EDGE TRIMMED.

WALL

ADD'L STORAGE

*DESK ADDENDUM

CORD MANAGEMENT GUTTER CLIPS ONTO BACK EDGE OF DESK.

OPTIONAL BUNGEE CORD MANAGEMENT.

ADDITIONAL DESK ACCESSORIES PLUG INTO HORIZONTAL GROOVE.

GENEROUSLY SIZED KEYBOARD SLIDE.

*COMPUTER STAND ADDENDUM

POWER STRIP MOUNTED INSIDE TROUGH

FLIP-UP DOOR COVERS CORD MANAGEMENT AREA.

EASED EDGE FOR STRUCTURE / COMFORT.

OPTIONAL CPU, PRINTER, AND OTHER PERIPHERAL STANDS ATTACH TO BACK BRACE.

1 **Modu-licious**, 1999, maple veneer, powder-coated steel, 19/3.5/47.5 x 32 x 18 cm, Blu Dot.
› The idea behind the Modu-licious series was an open-ended storage system which, like children's building blocks, could expand and contract according to the owner's needs. It turned into a universal system, based on a 16-inch module, with divider options.

2 **2D:3D In/Out Box**, 1999, painted steel, 12.5 x 29 x 25.5 cm, Blu Dot.
3 **2D:3D Letter Holder**, 1999, painted steel, 17.5 x 25.4 x 10 cm, Blu Dot.

› Each unit of the 2D:3D series is constructed entirely from stamped metal. The perforated steel can easily be bent into shape by the user, thus eliminating the need for joints.

4 **Office System**, 2001, rolling rack/kart, desk addendum, computer stand, concept sketches developed for Herman Miller for the Home.
› This is part of Herman Miller's home collection and was conceived as an office system that fits perfectly in the home.

| 1 | 2 | 4 |
| | 3 | |

TORD BOONTJE LONDON

In his project Rough & Ready (1998), Tord Boontje distributes free instructions for making his furniture out of found, and slightly searched for, objects and materials. The project is all about, and nothing but about, the author's creativity. The 12,000 instruction drawings issued (how many were actually used?) are the artefact, not unlike Christo's drawings for his Valley Curtain. True, by this free-issuing act, Tord might be protesting against the culture of mass production. However, I doubt if it's driven by communal, social motives, but by an unstoppable designer-creator-crafts-man-poet. Even though Tord claims it's a positive thing, offering people the information to make their own furniture, I still think it's 'his' own furniture, not 'their' own.

It would be easy to brand Tord an Artist, but we won't. This is not just because he sometimes wears the industrial designer's hat, or should I say designer's eye-wear (from fashion designer Alexander McQueen), but mainly because, through all his poetic layers, the preoccupations of a designer are clearly at the centre.

Ever since Adolf Loos declared it a crime, designers have had a restless approach-avoid relationship with ornament. Tord just grabs the ornament and makes it his subject matter. He does oversized embroidery of rabbits and horses on fabrics, he photo-etches floral patterns on thin stainless-steel foil to produce lampshades, but best of all, he punches decoration on distorted, Loosian-style straight-sided glass tumblers (Bunny and Horse Vase, 2001). Loos was the first person ever to convince a glass manufacturer to produce straight-sided tumblers. It is very difficult to grasp how revolutionary this was at the time. Tord seems to be saying to Loos, 'is ornament really a crime – if it is, let's have more of it, let's make a feature out of it'. The twist is that Tord's glasses are not decorated by a craftsman, but industrially produced by Dartington Glass and Salviati.

Tord's memorable cut reclaimed wine bottles (1997) are another take on industrial production and industrial augmentation. In most of the writings about this project you read things such as, 'tranSglass is concerned with issues of recycling, developing, and owning one's own production process', but I think it's about something else. Isn't it all about taking a mass-produced industrial object and then exposing a beautiful section, completely hidden and non-existent until Tord cut at his angle of choice? Doesn't the pleasure of design come from producing something that did not exist before? RON ARAD

1 **Rough and Ready Chair**, 1998, wood, blankets, plastic sheeting, fluorescent lights, tape, screws, various sizes, prototype.
› These pieces of furniture have been designed in such a way that anyone can construct them, anywhere, with materials found lying around. Diagrams that explain the making process can be downloaded from the internet for free.

2 **Red Bunny Chair**, 2001, wood, wool blanket, embroidery, 85 x 55 x 40 cm, prototype.
› Part of the Wednesday collection, this timber-framed chair has been upholstered with a woollen blanket and embroidered with a simplistic bunny motif.

1	2

1 Wednesday Light, 2001, stainless steel, 40 x 20 x 20 cm, prototype.
> A floral garland has been wrapped around a light bulb which creates the effect of light shining through leaves. The light can be extended and freely formed to any scale.

2 Blossom Table, 2001, aluminium, coloured resin, wood, 110 x 45 x 90 cm, prototype.
> A blossom motif decorates the CNC (Computer Numerical Controlled) punched metal top of the table. Colour is added by pouring on resin.

3 Bunny Vase, 2001, glass, 30 x ø 15 cm, Salviati.

4 Horse Vase, 2001, glass, 30 x ø 15 cm, Salviati.
> A pattern of small dots is imprinted in the hot glass of these vases, creating a distortion in form and an endearing image.

5 Jug, 1997, glass, 27 x ø 7 cm, in collaboration with Emma Woffenden, tranSglass.
> This jug is part of a collection of vases and glasses made by cutting up and recycling wine and beer bottles.

1	2	3	4	5

FABIO BORTOLANI MODENA

My first impressions of the work of Fabio Bortolani came in the form of delicate watercolours with the charm of narrative still lifes. For all their lightness, the paintings were very precise and expressive, communicating an unmistakable personal style, and showing that the 'language of the hand' is still far ahead of any digital techniques.

Fabio Bortolani is 100 per cent Italian, but he is not part of the 'lifestyle capital' of Milan. Born in a little village near Modena, he trained as an architect in Florence before retreating back into his familiar realm. Although he is always within shouting distance of Milan, his work is focused on simple people and everyday household objects. Close contact with elementary objects and practical materials has determined the clear, unambiguous style of his design work. For some years his products have been characterized by startlingly simple design solutions and a high level of innovation. Examples of this are the Bucatini accessories (1998), where simple steel tubing, covered in plastic, is used to support the different bathroom items.

Bortolani makes his sketches and watercolours by seeking a definitive form among countless variations. He develops his palette of products in a similar fashion, passing through the individual steps in a quite intelligent way, analysing and improvising, polarizing, integrating and sometimes provoking us with the pure simplicity of his results. It is in this setting that he achieves his goals, a long way from high culture and urban sophistication.

Fabio Bortolani is not part of the mainstream 'design circus' but is nonetheless very up to date with what is going on. In utter seclusion, he creates products that are both distinctive and viable on the mass market. These 'products of the everyday', with their strong design identity, such as the Professional series of combs (2001), are highly convincing, and reveal his realistic understanding of production processes.

Within a few years Fabio Bortolani has made a name for himself within Italy's design landscape. He has been represented in the high-profile collections of Italian and European companies, and his products stand out from the great majority of mediocre design solutions. He stands apart, an 'author-designer' among many industrial designers who are distinguished more by their big offices than by their extraordinary achievements. I am convinced that the secret of Bortolani's success lies in the meditative equilibrium of his life, his almost childlike curiosity and his freedom from prejudice.

HANSJERG MAIER-AICHEN

1 Gerba, soap dispenser, 1998, EVA recycleable material for medical tools, stainless steel, 35 x 13.5 x 0.45 cm, Agape.
› These liquid-soap dispensers are recycleable and easy to use. When the soap runs out, the new one is hung onto the pin valve. They resemble medical drips.

2 Staccami, dish, 2000, Materbi recycleable organic material from corn, double plate ø 32 cm, single plate ø 28 cm, Pandora.
› The only decorative feature on this plate is the fine stencil effect around the edge. Although intended to be abstract, the shape is evocative of pieces of cutlery.

3 Triangle, candle, 1999, wax, 20 x 20 x 3 cm, Authentics.
› To overcome the old frustration of candles burning asymmetrically, this one can be turned over and lit from the other end.

4 Professional Combs, 2001, stainless steel, ruler 0.15 x 2 x 20 cm, square 0.15 x 7 x 7 cm, double 0.15 x 2 x 18.5 cm, with mirror 0.15 x 7 x 14 cm, in collaboration with Donata Paruccini, virtuallydesign.com.
› This is a set of four combs for professional use, and each one has its own specific function. The cutting of the steel prongs was done by an innovative chemical technique.

	2	
1		4
	3	

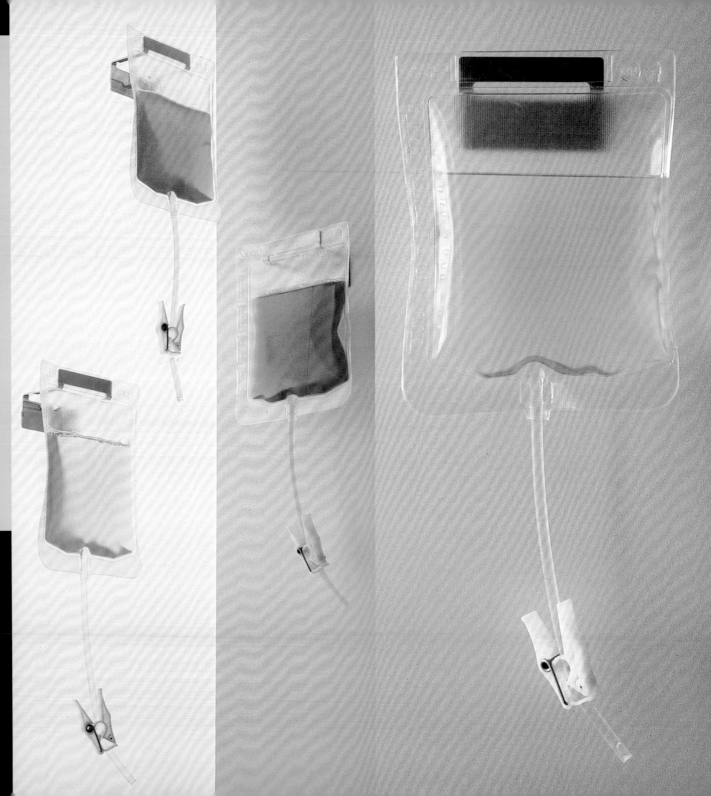

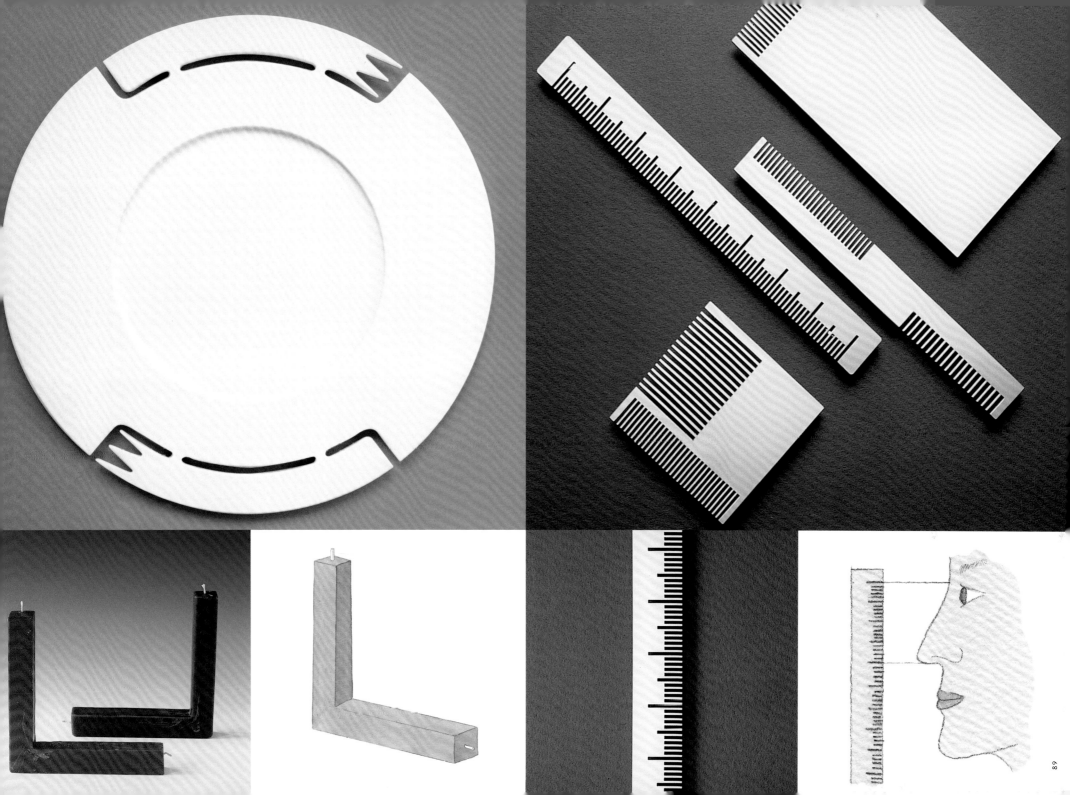

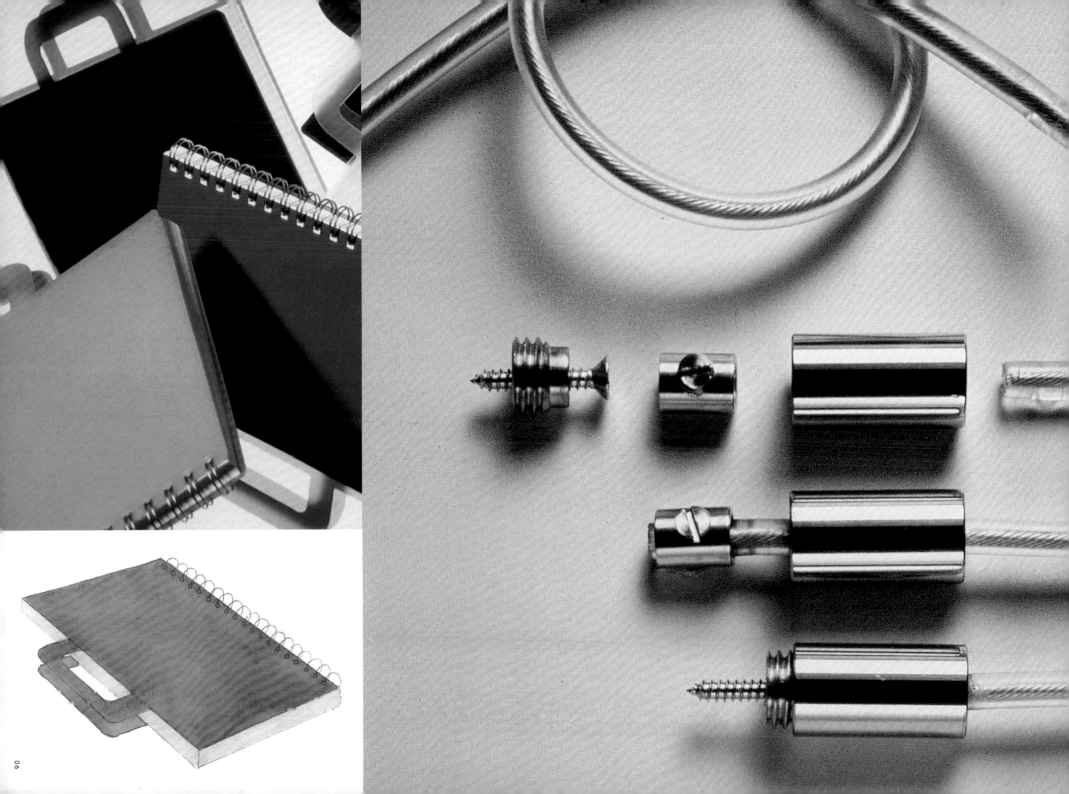

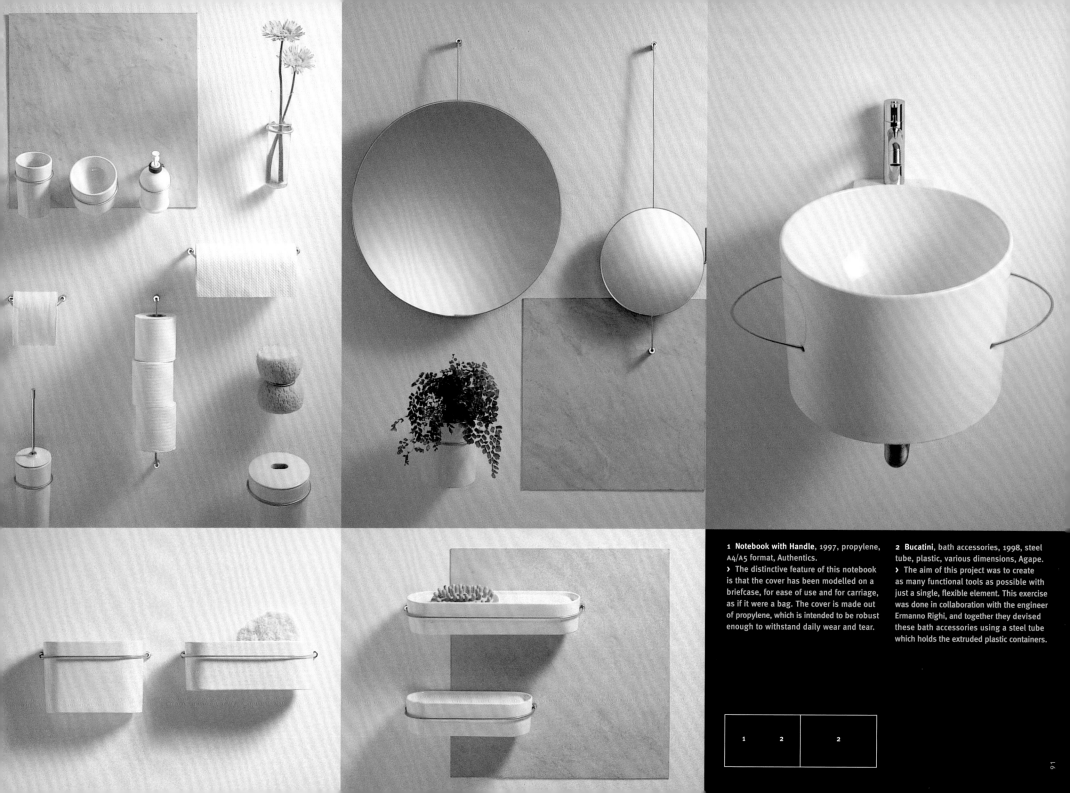

1 **Notebook with Handle**, 1997, propylene, A4/A5 format, Authentics.
> The distinctive feature of this notebook is that the cover has been modelled on a briefcase, for ease of use and for carriage, as if it were a bag. The cover is made out of propylene, which is intended to be robust enough to withstand daily wear and tear.

2 **Bucatini**, bath accessories, 1998, steel tube, plastic, various dimensions, Agape.
> The aim of this project was to create as many functional tools as possible with just a single, flexible element. This exercise was done in collaboration with the engineer Ermanno Righi, and together they devised these bath accessories using a steel tube which holds the extruded plastic containers.

| 1 | 2 | 2 |

RONAN + ERWAN BOUROULLEC PARIS

The confidence and sophistication of Ronan and Erwan Bouroullec's work belies the youth of these French brothers, who have worked as partners only since 1999. The Bouroullecs describe their objects as tools which make their own solutions, and as open questions on ways to live. While their practice is characterized by the quest for practical perfection, it is also marked by a responsiveness to the human body and the materials of their craft. To them, the most important element of design is an awareness of the dialogue between object and user.

Rigorous research informs the Bouroullecs' design. Their work is drawn from an intimate understanding of objects, their development, their history, and the way in which they can help us to manage the vicissitudes of daily life. They seek a return of feeling to the relationship between humans and the material world, aiming for an effect that is enduring rather than ephemeral, a compromise between 'macro' and 'micro'. They achieve this through methods that seek to reconcile the traditional know-how of the artisan with industrial production processes.

A tautness and flattening out of surfaces marks the Bouroullecs' production, which includes chairs, beds, shelving, lamps and vases for clients ranging from high-end manufacturers such as Cappellini to mass-market outlets such as Habitat, as well as an interior for fashion designer Issey Miyake's A-POC shop in Paris. Their materials range from common styrofoam, to luxurious, lacquered wood. While their work is clever (a small dent on a saucer holds a cube of sugar) it is not gimmicky. Both elegant and beautiful, it is devoid of empty flourishes and embellishments.

Before Ronan Bouroullec, the elder of the brothers, was offered the opportunity to develop ceramic work by the city of Vallauris in the South of France, he had not looked beyond industrial production, a process that does not encourage unpredictability, spontaneity or intuition at the manufacturing stage. During his stay at Vallauris he discovered an interest in the artisan tradition. He saw the value of maintaining traditional techniques, while continuing to evolve one's own work. The new objects he produced – a necklace, vases, a coat hook/mirror, trays, carafes – are simple and without ornamentation, and yet their forms and uses are inventive. They are 'open' objects that are anchored in the everyday, but they can be adapted or transformed by each person who uses them. Their sensual surfaces are monochromatic and endlessly smooth, their enigmatic forms are at once beautiful and functional. BROOKE HODGE

1 Parasol Lumineux, 2001, painted polyester resin, metal and neon bulb, 200 x 186 x 186 cm; **Grape Carpet**, 2001, wool, 12 pieces ø 30 cm each, limited edition, Galerie Kréo.
› The lamp with its canopy's exaggerated dimensions and the strong neon light defines a space within a room, while the irregularly shaped Grape carpet enters and leaves the 'lightspace'.

2 Honda Vase, 2001, fibreglass painted with car body paint, 100 x 55 x 30 cm, Galerie Kréo.

› The seductive beauty of this vase is created by its unusual proportions and shape. It has a glossy, reflective finish that contrasts with its matt interior.

3 Square Vase, 2001, polyester resin painted with car body paint, and neon bulb, 52 x 66 x 15 cm, Galerie Kréo.
› This rather surreal piece looks at first glance like a television or an aquarium but is actually an internally illuminated vase.

4 Objets Lumineux, 1999, birch plywood, heat-formed perspex and fluorescent bulb, H 120/160/240 cm, ø 50 cm each, Cappellini.
› The sculptural presence of these ceiling lights means they both populate a room and provide a source of light.

	2	
1		4
	3	

92

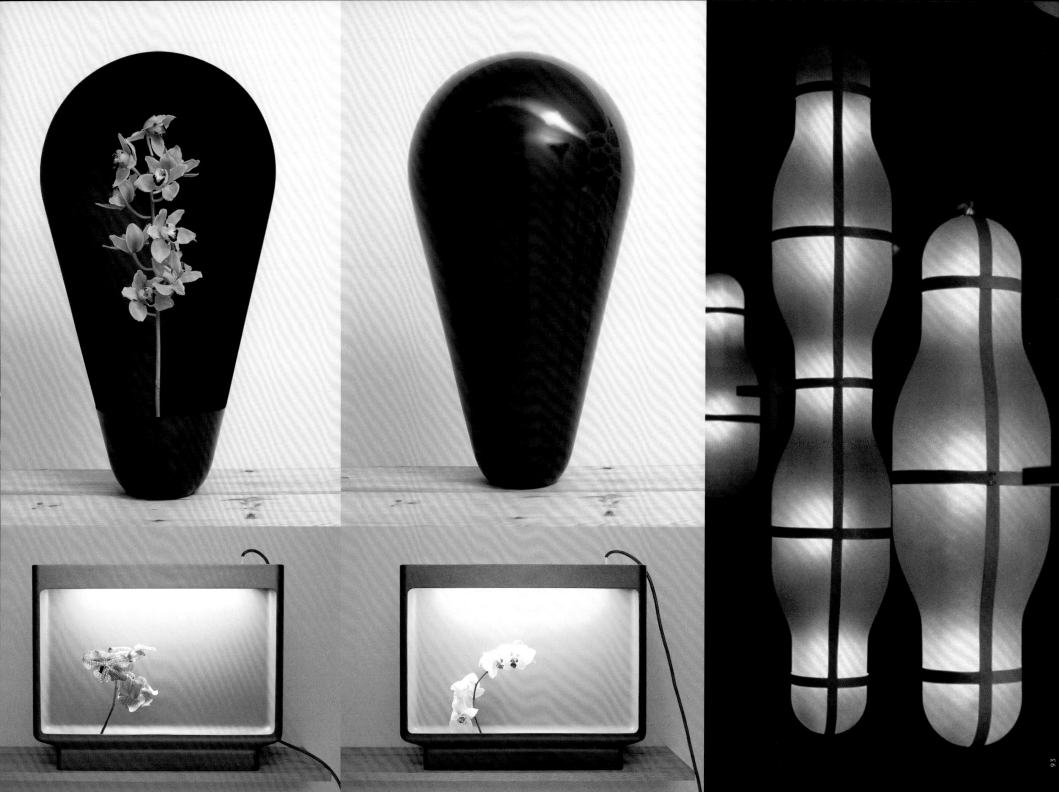

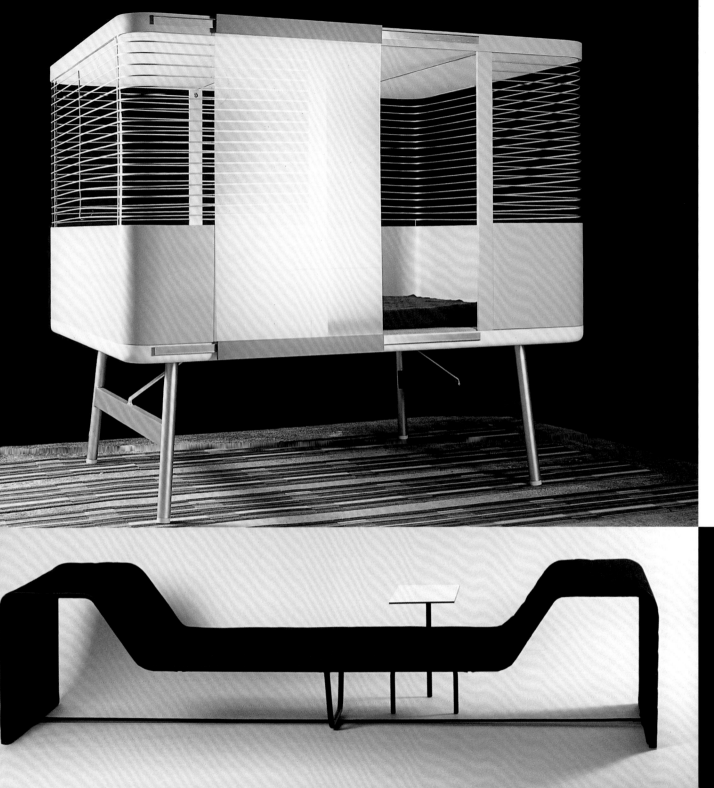

1 **Cabane**, 2001, plastic and metal structure, wool fabric, 200 x 230 x 200 cm, Galerie Kréo.
› This flexible structure can be used to create a porous room-like space within a larger area such as a loft.

2 **Hole Chair**, 2000, lacquered aluminium, 73 x 45 x 45 cm, Cappellini.
› This chair shows the brothers' extraordinary ability to reinvent traditional furniture types, by recreating them in ways peculiarly appropriate to our time.

3 **Spring Armchair**, 1999, polyurethane shell, foam, stainless steel, wool fabric, 45 x 240 x 80 cm, Cappellini.
› The elegance and formal control of this chair is an example of how the archetypes of international design can be re-invented.

4 **Lit Clos Bed**, 2000, lacquered birch plywood, steel, aluminium, perspex, fabric, 215/325 x 200 x 240 cm, Cappellini.
› The bed is inspired by the traditional enclosed bed used by Breton peasants to create an intimate space within a communal room. The drawings are from the video *Motion Notebook* made by Fulguro.

5 **Safe Rest Day Bed**, 1999, wool, foam, cotton, steel, zip, 54 x 230 x 73 cm, Domeau & Pérès.
› A spare wafer–thin elongated day bed on which one or two people can read and relax.

	1		4	
2		3		5

BOYM PARTNERS NEW YORK

New York designers Constantin and Laurene Boym are among the most radical protagonists on the contemporary design scene. Constantin is an architect who grew up in Russia, emigrated at an early age to the US and struck out on a path of his own. Laurene, the lively, curious and charming young American, is unspoilt, naïve, emancipated and bent on change. The studio that they share was set up in 1994, although Constantin produced work individually before then, and together they present an explosive combination of determination and power. Distinctive in the early works, in which Constantin's influence predominates, is the tradition of Russian Constructivism.

In all their work, considerations of function are restricted to the essential, and the formal quality of the work is austere, almost chilly. There is no decoration or emotion. We face the bare scaffolding of an outline awaiting further additions. When I commissioned Constantin Boym to design three shop windows in downtown New York, for the major American retail chain Bed, Bath and Beyond (BB&B), he produced a series of roughly drawn, sticky-tape architectural models. A concentrated knowledge of design had come into play to produce this unbeatably radical response, and the retail chain had never seen a more uncompromising display of goods in its shops.

It has always been obvious that neither Laurene nor Constantin Boym intended to fulfil normal expectations of the industrial or product designer, and now these two extreme forces have been combined. Some of the Boym Partners' ideas, demanding high quality and costly skills, are realized with international manufacturers, such as the plastic accessories for Authentics, while others are almost independent productions. The partners create small editions that are very production-intensive, involving high overheads, which make the involvement of middlemen almost impossible. The working principle is very similar to that of an independent artist. The work of the studio occupies the intermediate space between handcraft and industrial production.

The solid training behind these two design warriors enables them to accomplish almost any task in the field of design in its broadest sense, and stamp their own hallmark on their products. The charm of their concepts lies in the combination of two distinctly different personalities from very different cultural backgrounds. Together, they form one of the most radical teams in the world of European and American design. HANSJERG MAIER-AICHEN

1 The Menagerie, rug, 2001–2, wool, 75 x 75 cm, Handy.
> These small rugs and pillow covers, with their bright graphics, serve as ideal accessories for children's playrooms or bedrooms. The drawings were generated by computer but are executed manually, with a high degree of craftsmanship.

2 Glow, carpet, 2001, wool and phosphorescent fibres, 180 x 180 cm, Handy.
> After exposure to light, the pattern on these carpets gently glows in the dark

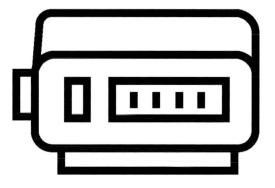

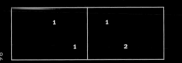

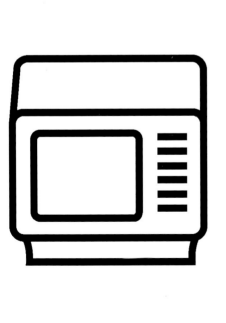

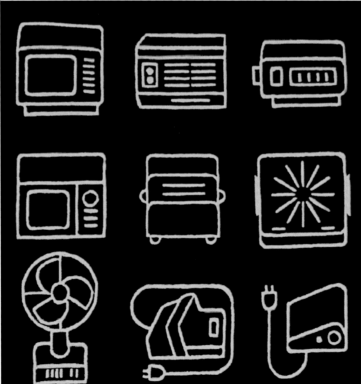

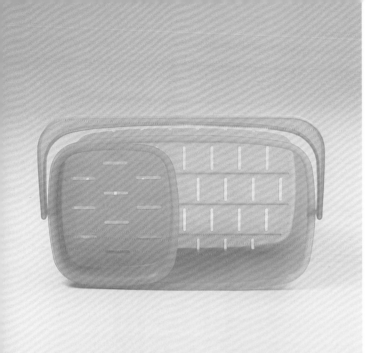

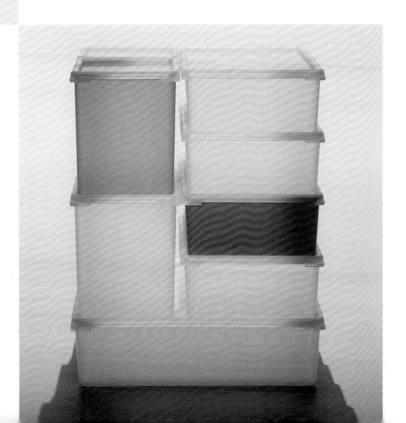

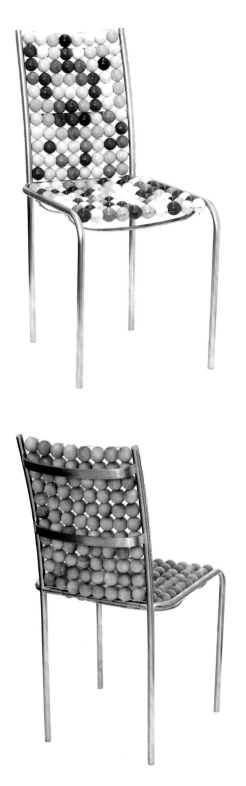

1 Wet/Dry, bath fitting, 1998, polypropylene, 14 x 20 x 8 cm, Authentics.
› This shower caddy alludes to the shape of traditional woven Shaker baskets. A small removable tray is provided for display and storage of bath accessories.

2 Loop Mirror, 1997, polypropylene, ø 40 cm, Authentics.
› This simple yet practical mirror is suspended on a polypropylene loop, an ironic reference to what is considered the 'classy' way of hanging mirrors on a silk ribbon.

3 Use It, boxes, 1995, polypropylene, various sizes, Authentics.
› The series was one of the first to use translucent polypropylene.

4 Salvation, 2002, second-hand ceramic pieces and adhesive, various sizes, Moooi.
› This project attempts to give a new and eternal life to objects that have been discarded. Mismatched ceramic pieces from thrift shops are assembled into sumptuous new objects, using a high-tech adhesive.

5 Taxi Cab, chair, 2001, steel frame, with wooden balls, 100 x 40 x 45 cm, prototype.
› This chair was inspired by the wooden seat covers often used by taxi-cab drivers to ease back pain. Instead of being placed on a seat, the cover becomes a chair.

1	4	5
2	3	

TODD BRACHER MILAN

American-born designer Todd Bracher first came to the attention of the design world with Open Privacy, a thought-provoking project produced in 2001. A beautifully sculptural installation of plywood, carton and steel tubing, Open Privacy is essentially a framed arrangement of a table and chairs designed for public use in cafés. The steel tubing is reminiscent of a tent frame but its function is at first unclear – where is the canopy that should surely enclose it? The project was designed to examine the limits of perceived privacy. This, Bracher's first work, is subtly academic, questioning our comfort about dining in public spaces, but delightfully sculptural and tectonic too. Bracher says of this experimental piece: 'Inspiration came from the intimacy of this most personal event, dining, and the codes and rules that are underlying it. In addition I considered how this furniture might relate to the architectural environment.'

The analytical approach that Bracher takes to his work makes it unique. He sums up his own style as 'respectful, patient and understated'. Ideas either come to him haphazardly or after a period of analysis and experimentation. Nothing, it seems, is forced.

Bracher's designs are without precedent – perhaps this is because he has not been around long enough for tradition to stick. He has had four homes, first in America, then Denmark, France and finally Italy, where he now lives and works. The most important element of his designs is the 'respectful dialogue with the user'. Bracher is intent on exploring this dialogue further in To22 (2002). A collaboration or a discourse between himself, the designer Mark Goetz and the designer/film-maker Efe Buluc, the project focuses on the thought processes behind design decisions, rather than the end products.

The products that embody Bracher's provocative theories are certainly easy on the eye. Bloom (2001) is another café installation, produced at the same time as Open Privacy. A pressed-ash veneer table and stools fit together, puzzle-like, when not in use. The Chairing Project (2001) is Bracher's latest foray into the world of dining. It makes experimental use of the various postures that people take when seated at a table. The table itself has no legs, but the backs of the chairs slot into holes in its top, lending it their support. More recently, Bracher has worked on Freud (2002), a sofa design for Zanotta, which is destined for mass production, a collection of wool rugs for Urban Outfitters, and several hanging-lamp concepts. LAURA HOUSELEY

1 Open Privacy, 2001, steel tubing, plywood, cartoon, 150 x 160 x 160 cm, Zanotta.
› Open Privacy seeks to enhance the patrons' privacy while dining in a public eatery. The frame of the table delineates a space that isolates it from the outside world.

2 Penumbra, lamp, 1998, ceramic, steel, coated fibreglass, 35 x 170 x 35 cm.
› Bracher's intention here was to design a light fixture where the quality of the light could be physically adjusted instead of using an electronic device such as a dimmer switch. As the shade is raised or lowered, it achieves a myriad of different lighting effects.

| 1 | 1 | 2 |

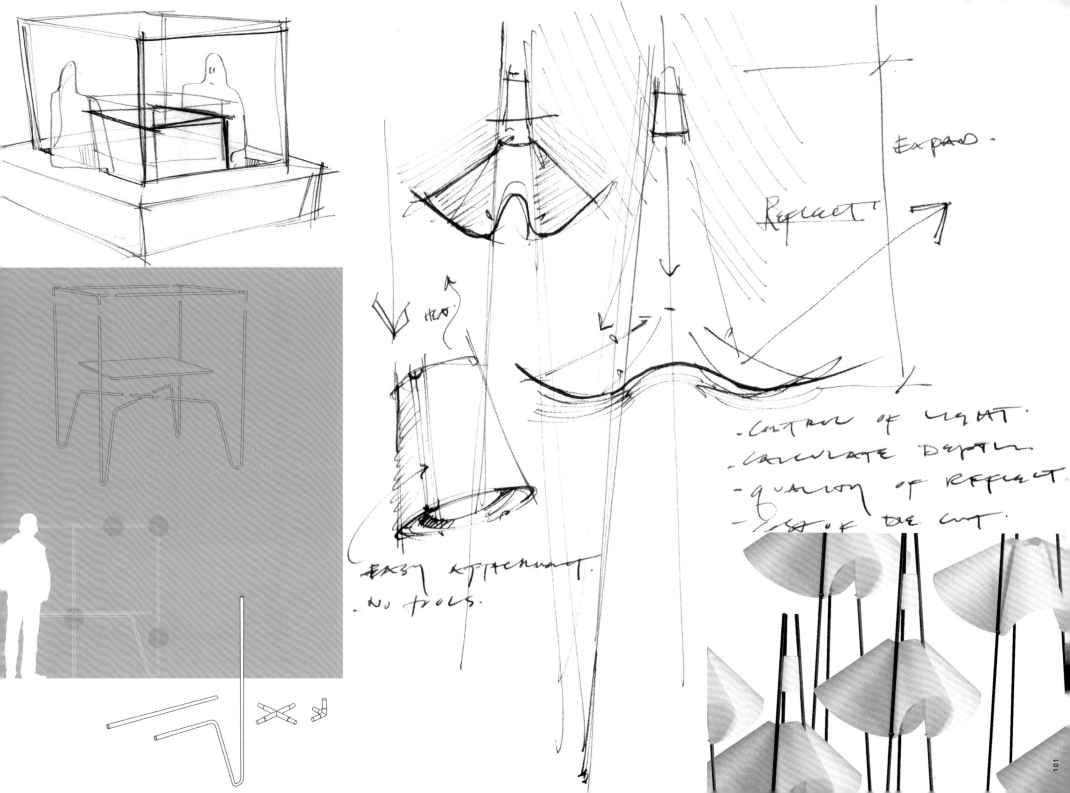

EXPAND.

REFLECT

- CONTROL OF LIGHT.
- CALCULATE DEPTH.
- QUALITY OF REFLECT
- EASY OF DIE CUT.

HEAT?

EASY ATTACHMENT.
NO TOOLS.

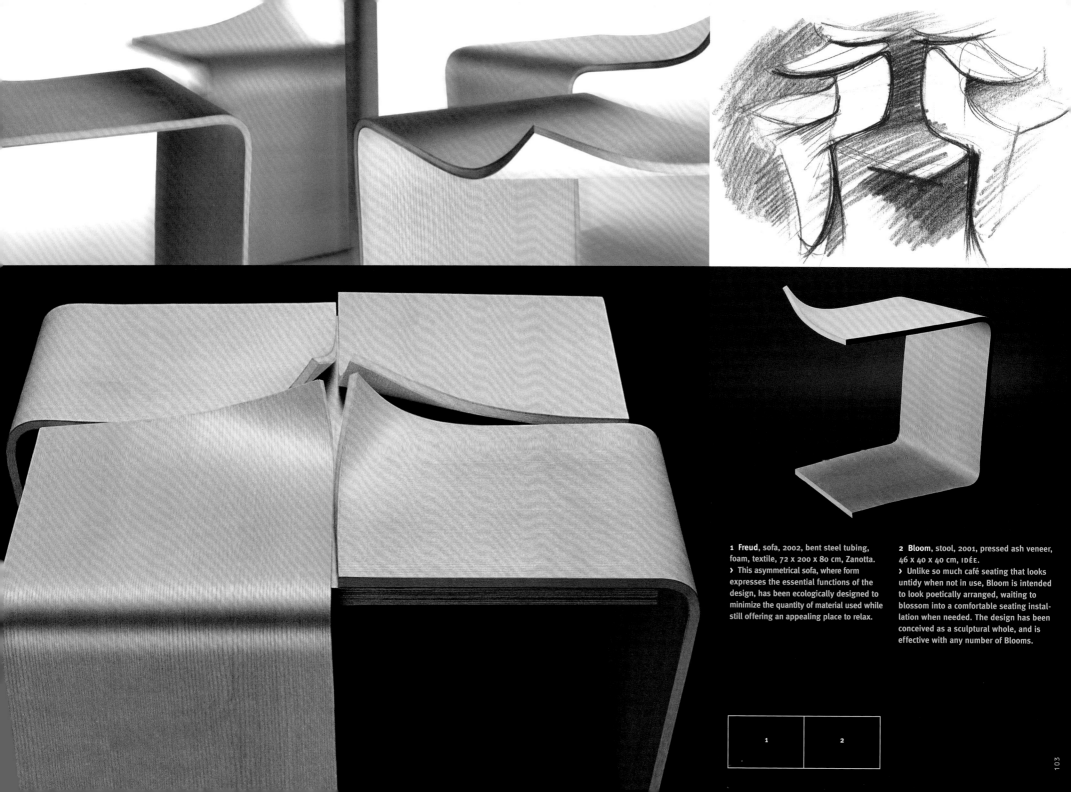

1 Freud, sofa, 2002, bent steel tubing, foam, textile, 72 x 200 x 80 cm, Zanotta.
› This asymmetrical sofa, where form expresses the essential functions of the design, has been ecologically designed to minimize the quantity of material used while still offering an appealing place to relax.

2 Bloom, stool, 2001, pressed ash veneer, 46 x 40 x 40 cm, IDÉE.
› Unlike so much café seating that looks untidy when not in use, Bloom is intended to look poetically arranged, waiting to blossom into a comfortable seating installation when needed. The design has been conceived as a sculptural whole, and is effective with any number of Blooms.

1	2

THE CAMPANA BROTHERS SÃO PAULO

In the history of design, as in the world of entertainment, there have been double acts of all kinds, and some of them prove to be inimitable one-offs. The most frequent partnerships are purely professional – like that of Óscar Tusquets and Lluís Clotet. Others, like Charles and Ray Eames, were also husband and wife. Brothers also form partnerships, but these are less common. One of the most recent examples is that of the Campana brothers.

Fernando and Humberto Campana are Brazilian, and Brazil is a huge country with a great tradition of exporting soccer, Samba and carnival, but very little design. Strictly speaking, the brothers are not really designers. Fernando is an architect and Humberto studied law, although he has the soul of a sculptor. In 1983 they decided to form a design partnership. They presented their first designs to the São Paulo Museum of Art in 1989, in a show that was more like a manifesto than a furniture collection.

One of the characteristic features of the Campanas' work is their use of 'poor' or humble materials such as string, cardboard or packaging plastic. When handled with skill, these materials can be more beautiful than noble wood, polished metal or the finest leather. The exquisite skill with which they used their materials gained them entrance to the European market. By the mid-1990s they were exhibiting at trade fairs in Verona and Milan, and before long, they were designing for Italian firms such as Edra.

In 1997 the Campanas astonished us all with designs such as the Cone Chair and the Inflating Table, included by Philippe Starck in the 1997 Design Yearbook. In 1998 MoMA in New York put on an exhibition of their work.

Not since Shiro Kuramata died has anybody put so much poetry into a simple piece of furniture. By way of example we have the trilogy of string chairs, Azul, Vermelha and Verde, which they designed (1998) for Edra, a company that is always open to experimental design. Before they started working for European firms, Fernando and Humberto produced their own designs under the name Campana Objetos. These included pieces such as the Bubble Wrap Chair (1995) and the Cardboard Sofa (1998, produced by Edra in 2001), made from packing materials, or the Garden-hose Chair (1998) assembled, as its name suggests, from lengths of ordinary garden hose; designs that seem to have been transported from the *favelas* of Brazil to astonish the world. RAMÓN UBEDA

1 **Vermelha**, chair, 1998, enamelled steel, dyed-cotton-cord upholstery, 80 x 80 x 60 cm, Edra.
2 **Verde**, chair, 1998, enamelled steel, dyed-cotton-cord upholstery, 88 x 45 x 54 cm, Edra.
3 **Azul**, chair, 1998, enamelled steel, dyed-cotton-cord upholstery, 78 x 98 x 84 cm, Edra.
› These three chairs were designed for the Italian firm Edra. About 400 m of thick, dyed cotton cord is carefully wound around a steel frame. The chairs are a visual shock: the Campana brothers' intention is to stim-

ulate interest in a project that uses basic and redundant materials, as well as recovering the traditional skills of the manual arts.

4 **Batuque Vase**, 2000, glass, 47 x 43 x 50 cm, Cappellini.
› This arrangement of glass tubes makes a highly individual vase; despite their fragility the tubes are balanced with such precision that no additional support is necessary. Even without the flowers, it is a powerful and engaging object, so it is perhaps not surprising that a firm of such exquisite taste as Cappellini adopted this design.

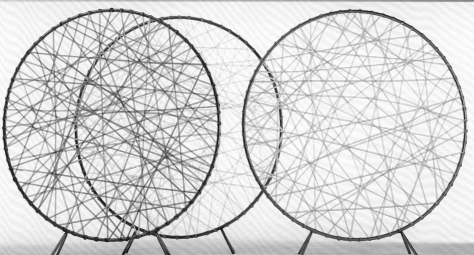

1 Cardboard Collection, 2001, corrugated cardboard, metal, screen 180 x 50 x 5 cm, table 44 x 136 x 50 cm, sofa 80 x 160 x 70 cm, Edra.
› This collection of hard-wearing furniture consists of layer upon layer of cardboard packaging, built up from a sleek metal frame. The original designs were manufactured by the brothers' own company, but have subsequently been incorporated into the Edra catalogue.

2 Anemona Chair, 2001, stainless steel, dyed-cotton-cord upholstery, 78 x 60 x 84 cm, Edra.
› This organic design, where a cord seems to be arbitrarily wound around the most basic metal structure, exudes comfort. The choice of material strikes a perfect balance between strength and elasticity.

3 Zig Zag Screen, 2001, stainless steel, plastic string, PVC, 200 x 90 x 60 cm, Edra.
› This modesty screen consists of a simple frame wrapped liberally in sheets of transparent PVC. It is a prime example of the brothers' concern with using materials that are both inexpensive and readily available.

4 Sushi, chair, 2002, various textiles, 90 x ø 110 cm, Edra.
› Textiles of different types – felts, wools, carpets, rubberized – are rolled together and pushed into a tube of elasticized cloth. There is no structure, the object is formed from the textiles, skilfully manipulated.

	2	4
1	3	

CLAESSON KOIVISTO RUNE STOCKHOLM

Marten Claesson, Eero Koivisto and Ola Rune began to work together in 1995 in Stockholm, specializing in interiors and conversions. The spaces they create are simple, delicate and luminous. Their minimalist approach means that anything superfluous is eliminated, leaving only objects that are strong and memorable.

Following these early ventures, the trio turned to industrial design, working on a range of products that immediately won them international acclaim. The roots of their design philosophy are clearly visible. They do not conceive of objects in isolation, but create genuine domestic 'landscapes'. Their products are modular and adaptable, and they often include stacking systems. For example, they designed Scoop (2001), a light, modular seating system that can be combined in an infinity of ways, defining whole areas of a home or a public space. With a few simple movements, both their form and their function can be altered. This flexibility encourages a strong bond between the design objects and their users.

The strong, vivid and basic use that Marten Claesson, Eero Koivisto and Ola Rune make of colour, such as in Pebbles (2001), is a reflection of their Nordic origins. After some research, they now use a wide variety of materials, including glass, wood, fabric and metal, such as the Fruit Bowl (2000) made out of wood or the Criss Cross coffee table (2001) with the top made out of rattan. They do not design products for their own personal satisfaction, but try to create beautiful objects that will attract and intrigue the public, while also meeting its needs.

The products made by this group often take the form of small-scale, architectural pieces. If handled correctly, the change in scale from architecture to design can produce extraordinary results. Another important aspect of their approach is a refusal to think of the house as divided into rigidly separate areas. Claesson, Koivisto and Rune create useful, easy objects that fit naturally into the home or office, finding their proper place in a whole variety of rooms. It is clear that the three have learned an enormous amount from the great designers of northern Europe, without ever becoming excessively knowing, or making clichéd references to the past. Coming from diverse backgrounds and viewpoints, Claesson, Koivisto and Rune are united in their determination to create striking designs to which they all contribute. GIULIO CAPPELLINI

1 Pebbles, sofa, 2001, fabric upholstery, metal, 65 x 207/232 x 155/178 cm, Cappellini.
› The top and bottom units of these seats are interchangeable and in total there are nine possible combinations. The top unit can also swivel. This system is intended to fulfil many seating requirements, be it waiting, lying down, working or playing.

2 Fruit Bowl, 2000, laminated wood, 30 x ø 29 cm, Cappellini.
› The objective in designing this bowl was to develop a fruit bowl with minimal points of contact between the fruit and the bowl, thereby contributing to the freshness and long life of the products.

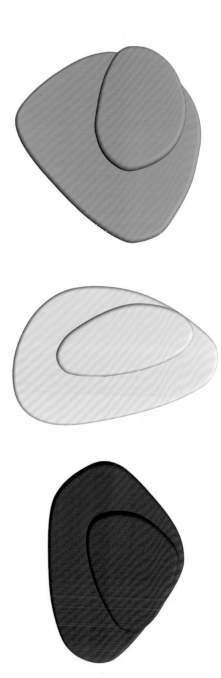

| 1 | 2 |

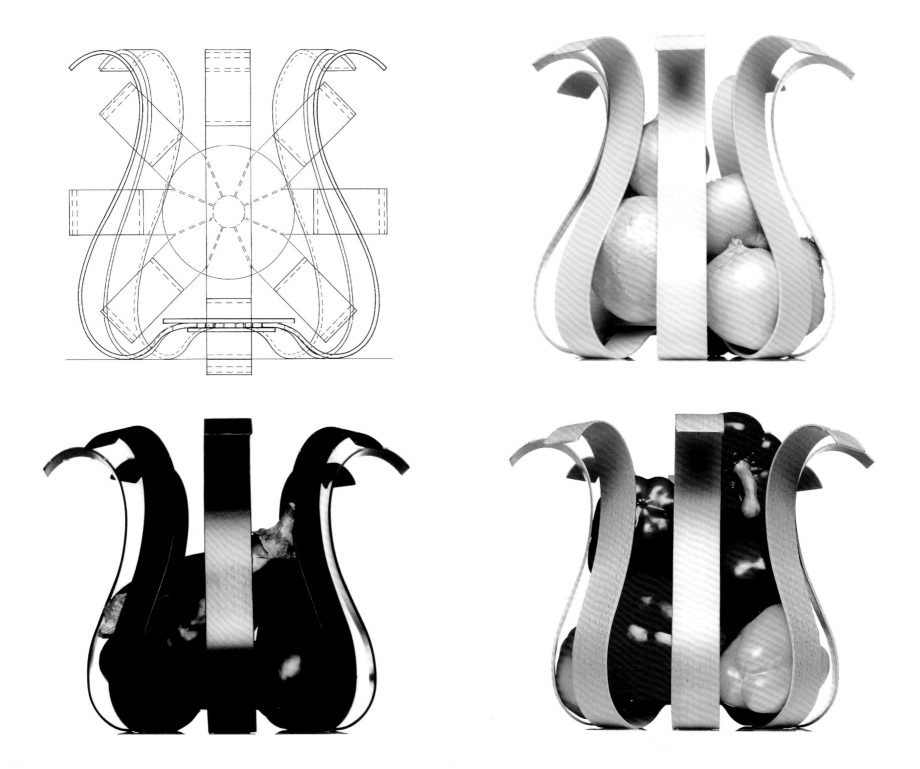

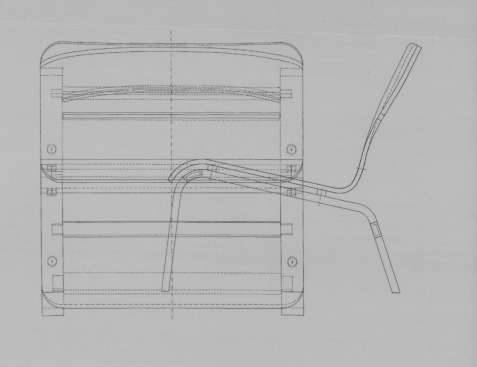

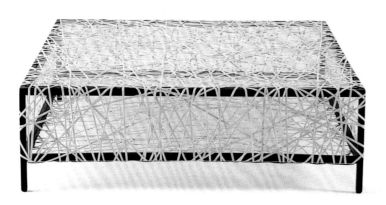

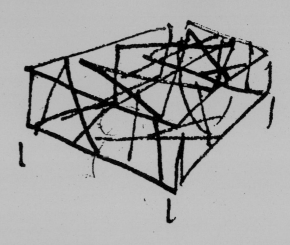

1 Bowie, chair, 1998, laminated wood (possible upholstered seat), 68 x 72 x 69 cm, David Design.
› The simple slit in this chair not only gives it a defining characteristic, it also permits greater flexibility and comfort in an otherwise solid seat.

2 Scoop, seats, 2001, upholstery, metal, 64 x 180/90 x 85 cm, Living Divani.
› The lines of these sofas and chairs are reminiscent of a tennis ball, consequently the volumes and surfaces take on a dynamic relationship.

3 Arc, table, 2000, wood, 72/40 cm, various dimensions, Asplund.
› The distinctive detail of these solid wooden tables is the line of the curve which extends from the leg right up to the surface of the tabletop. This creates the illusion that the top is extremely thin when viewed from certain angles.

4 Criss Cross, table, 2001, metal, rattan, glass, 34 x 100 x 100 cm, Cappellini.
› Traditional materials and techniques are given a new purpose in this coffee table design.

| 1 | 3 |
| 2 | 4 |

It is not easy to guess where Curro Claret will end up in the future. Somebody who recycles shoeboxes to make shoe-stands or creates pens from the pages of old magazines Is not considered to be 'good for business' by the manufacturers. Claret is the antithesis of the smug designer, despite his years at the Escola Elisava in Barcelona and Central Saint Martins College of Art & Design in London, two of the most prestigious colleges in the world.

Reusing is better than recycling – that is Curro Claret's motto. He is attracted to paper, cardboard and other readily available materials that do not require complex industrial transformation. For example, Claret noticed the mess made by people buying hot chestnuts from street vendors and throwing the shells on the ground. He hit on a solution to this problem while he was playing with a sheet of the paper used by chestnut vendors. Turning and folding it in his hands, he made a double container, which could hold the hot chestnuts on one side and the shells on the other. It was an instant solution that did not involve any industrial processes.

To make a shoe-stand Claret needs nothing but a shoebox and an articulated metal support. The support holds the shoe while it is being brushed and also serves as a handle for transporting the box. If he needs a pen, Claret tears a page out of an old magazine and twists it around an ink cartridge. He likes the user to play an active part in the definition of an object, and he enjoys the casual aesthetic that comes from this participation. For example, the pen will be quite different if it is made from the page of a women's magazine rather than an ironmonger's catalogue.

Curro Claret prefers to dispense with unnecessary decoration. At most, he will give a blackboard finish to one end of a storage box, enabling the owner of the box to label it. Asked to design a fruit bowl for oranges, Claret produced four metal rods and suspended the net bag containing the oranges from it. It would be good if this designer, whose talent is as sharp and fresh as those oranges, found a place in our industrial culture, reminding the rest of us that the humbler side of the profession can be as brilliant as any other. RAMÓN UBEDA

1 Chestnut Holder, 1999, newspaper, 14 x 14 x 6 cm, prototype.
> This simple adaptation of the traditional chestnut bag accommodates not only the hot chestnuts, but also the empty shells which are otherwise dropped on the ground. Folded out of old newspaper, this design requires no extra expense and can be adopted by any chestnut seller, anywhere. The design is part of a project to recycle left-over and thrown-away things.

2 Orange Mesh Fruit Bowl, 2000, metal rods, plastic netting, 10 x ø 25 cm, prototype.
> This simple fruit bowl is made from bent metal rods and the same plastic netting that supermarkets use for the packaging of fruit and vegetables. The fruit is suspended in the netting, which serves as an elegant bowl, but also enables air to circulate freely around the contents.

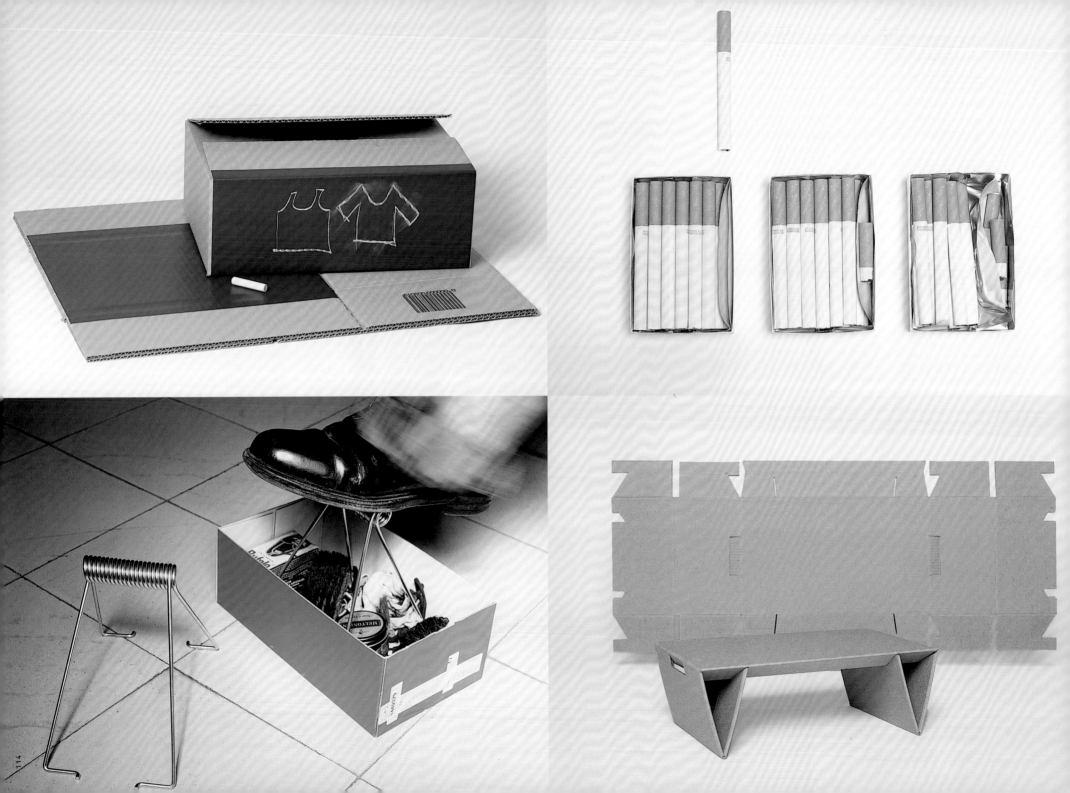

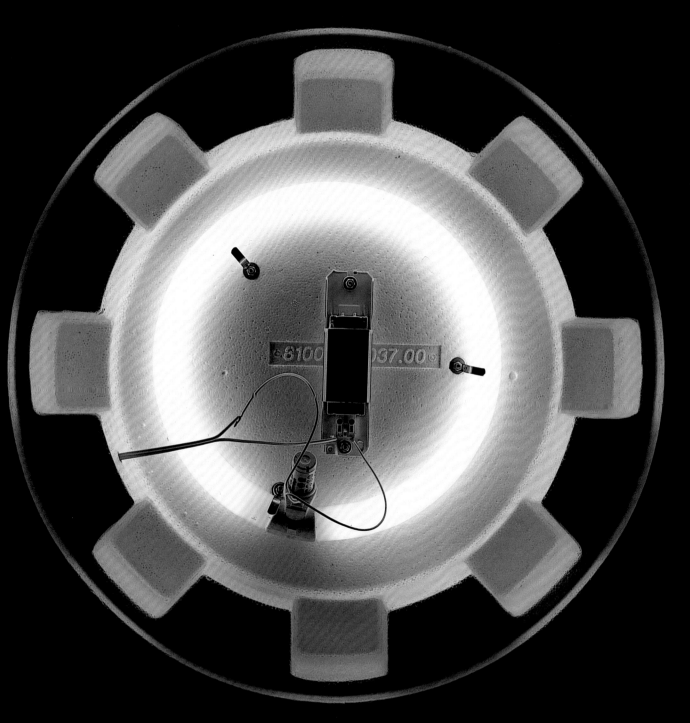

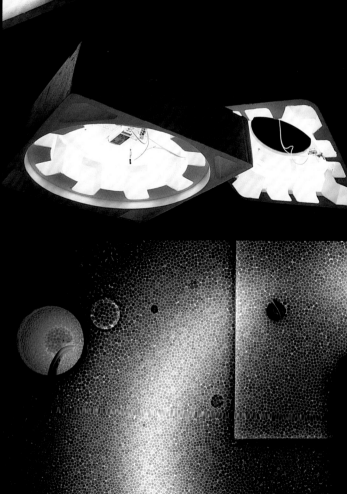

1 Wardrobe Box, 1997, cardboard, slate paint, chalk, variable dimensions.
› The original idea was to adapt cardboard boxes into wardrobe space. The design has since been refined to feature a blackboard, on which it is possible to write or draw the box's contents in chalk.

2 Cigarette Pack, 1997, fireproof paper, variable dimensions, prototype.
› The packet consists of two parts: as the cigarettes are removed, a section of fire-proof paper unfurls which keeps the butts totally separate and contains the smell.

3 Cleaning Shoe Box, 1999, cardboard box, metal rod, 18 x 14 x 16 cm, Opos Gallery.
› This structure consists of a pair of metal rods, articulated like a clothes peg, which supports the shoe while it is being brushed. The support doubles up as a handle for carrying the box.

4 Cardboard Tray, 1999, cardboard, 25 x 60 x 40 cm, prototype.
› This tray is formed out of a disused card-board box. When folded up it can be stored in very little space.

5 Recycled Porexpan Lighting, 2001, reused porexpan packaging, 14 x 53 x 53 cm, prototype.
› Porexpan is good at reflecting light and is frequently used by photographers to obtain indirect lighting.

1	2	
		5
3	4	

CLAUDIO COLUCCI PARIS – TOKYO

Claudio Colucci's work combines lightness with tactile sensuality and a sensibility for organic forms. His approach is quite casual, and as a result his products are never over-designed. This attitude could be interpreted as a direct result of his multicultural background. An Italian born in Switzerland, he studied in Geneva and Paris. Subsequently, he has worked in London, Paris and Tokyo.

As a European, he is powerfully attracted to Japan's unique recognition of space and form, and in particular he is interested in the concept of *sukima*, which in Japanese means the vacant space between objects. His admiration of the Japanese culture is also evident in products such as Dolce Vita (1997), in which he has shaped the traditional tatami (mat) into a modern chair.

In 1998, Colucci worked for a time as an assistant to the distinguished French designer Philippe Starck, designing miscellaneous goods such as pens, tape dispensers, toothbrushes and hairbrushes for Seven-Eleven, the grocery chain. In this area, Colucci is one of the successors to Starck's design concept, aimed at creating 'non-products' for the 'non-consumer'. Starck's intention was to combat the consumer lethargy which has resulted from the constant bombardment by marketing-oriented products. He did this by involving consumers in the design process, and calling on them to put the finishing touches to the design (see 'Interview with Philippe Starck' by Kozo Fujimoto in *Kyu-Plus*, no.4, 1999).

Humorous designs are also to be found among Colucci's work. He likes to work in dough, using the bubbly forms of the bread as inspiration for various product designs. This playful attitude is evident in objects such as the colourful Fisholino toilet brush (2000), where the handle of the brush is in the shape of a diving fish, or in heart-shaped armchair Joly Coeur (1997).

Another witty example of a Colucci design is Sumo (2001). Looking something like a car tyre, the form was inspired by the body of a Sumo wrestler, where the strength of the muscle is hidden within the soft, white flesh. It can stand upright and serve as a shelf, or lie down and be used as a round table. There is something very Japanese in this duality of purpose, which is also evident in the Solo armchair and the Duo sofa (2001). These very successful products can be rapidly transformed from seats into beds. RYU NIIMI

1 Squeeze, lamp, 2002, corian, 178 x ø 47 cm, VIA, Du Pont de Nemours.
› This lamp has a unique corian shade and a sensual, slender silhouette. Switched off, it is a sculptural object on the scale of an average human. Switched on, designs which have been etched on its frosted surface appear, projecting shadows into the space.

2 Sumo, table, 2001, fibreglass, glass, 75 x 90 x 35 cm, Claudio Colucci Design.
› This can be either a low table or a shelf. The round shape enables it to be quickly transformed from a table to a shelf.

3 Dolce Vita, chair, 1997, tatami, aluminium painted steel, 78.5 x 62 x 103.5 cm, prototype for IDÉE.
› Tatami is the traditional Japanese mat made of woven dried grass. Here it is set out on a modern-shaped chair.

4 Fisholino, toilet brush, 2000, polypropylene, plastic, 40.6 ø 11.7 cm, Marna.
› Visually this is a fun object. The underlying message, however, is that as the water on earth gets dirtier, it is harder for fish to live. The hope is that eventually toilets will be cleaned without the chemicals that kill the fish.

5 Joly Coeur, chair, 1997, wool fabric, aluminium painted steel, 80 x 90 x 90 cm, IDÉE.
› This heart-shaped sofa represents *kawaii*, the Japanese word for pretty and sweet.

	2	2	2	
1				3
1		4	5	

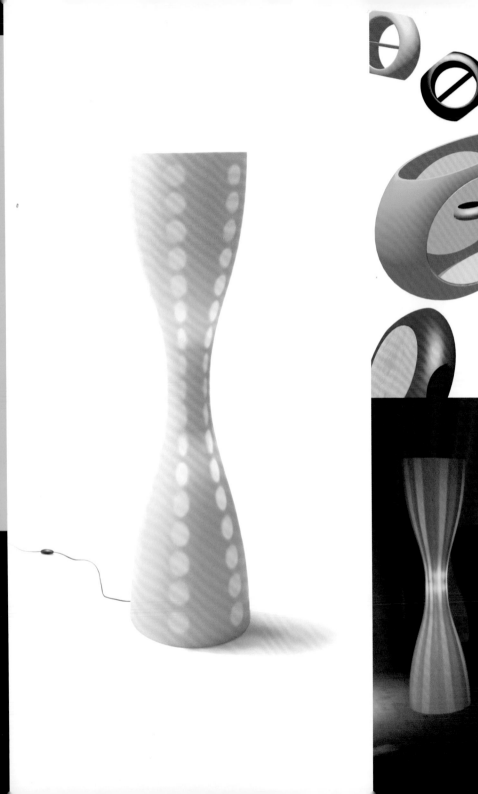

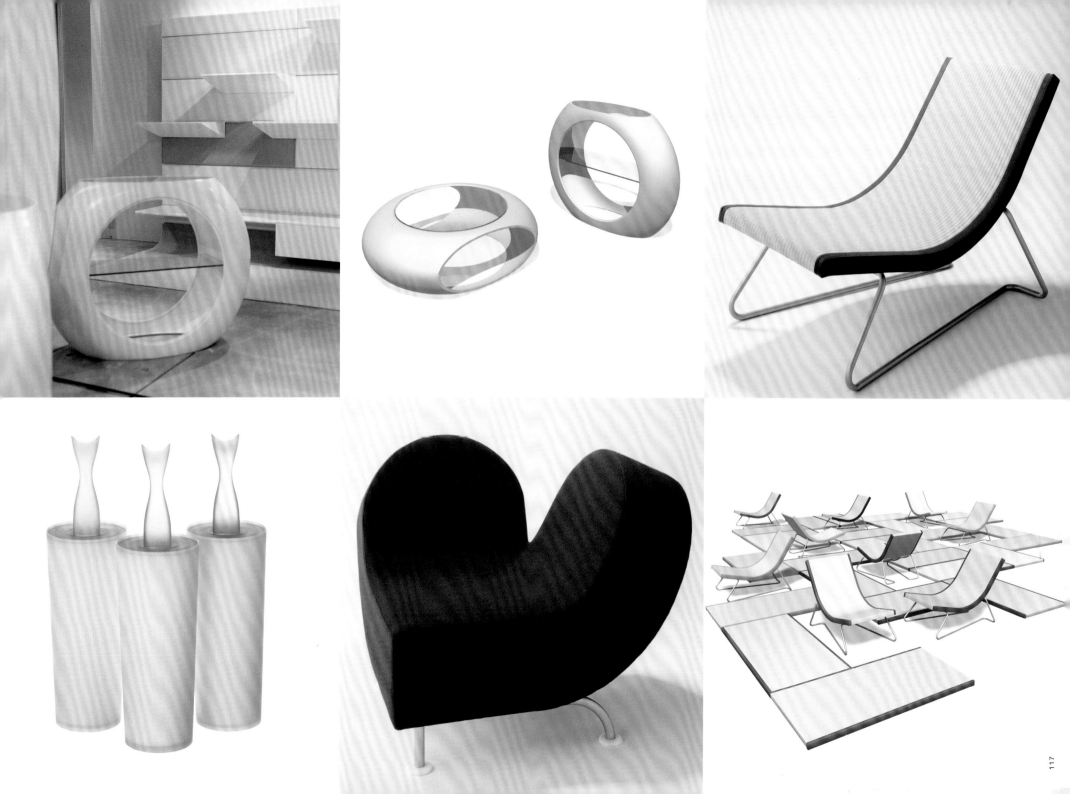

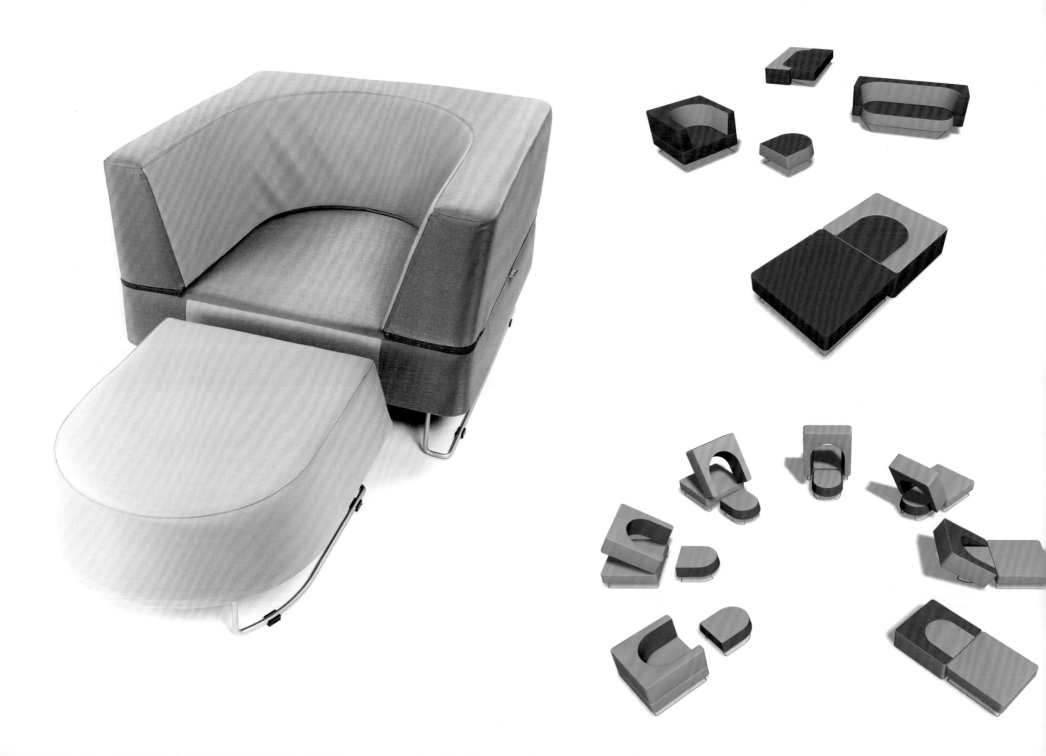

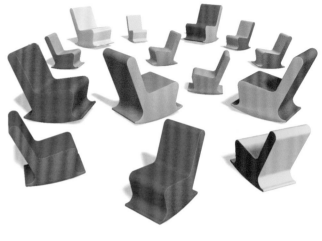

1 Solo, armchair/bed, 2001, cotton, steel, armchair 70 x 95 x 95 cm, bed 35 x 95 x 190 cm, Habitat.

2 Duo, sofa/bed, 2001, cotton, steel, sofa 70 x 198 x 95, bed 35 x 198 x 190, Habitat.
› Part of the Colucci series, these sofas and beds originated in the relationship between two people who meet and make love. The designer has created a very simple way to transform an upright seat into a comfortable bed, simply by turning the back upside down.

3 Dada, chair, 1997, wool fabric, Dada 82 x 83 x 55 cm, Mini Dada 57.5 x 57.5 x 35 cm, IDÉE.
› The design of this rocking chair is the height of simplicity. Seen from the front, all you can see is a wavy, abstract shape; seen from the side, the rocking chair reveals a different colour.

1	2	
	1	3

MATALI CRASSET PARIS

Matali Crasset is generally seen as an up-and-coming designer who will shortly be famous. Ironic and laid-back, but acutely aware of new developments, she offers designs that are always innovative and full of surprises. Her approach is interesting because it reflects the radical changes wrought by society on the role of the contemporary designer. We see in her work a response to new forms of consumer behaviour, and her products are only one component in a much broader design for the human environment.

Matali built up her experience as a designer by working in major studios, such as those of Denys Santachiara and Philippe Starck. There she learned that a finished product is not the result of improvisation, but of careful study that does not overlook a single detail. She has made a close study of today's world but does not offer us products to meet our daily needs. Instead, she tries to map out future scenarios, demonstrating the possibility of creating a profoundly different relationship with the environment, without neglecting human nature.

Her designs are fascinating and her objects beautiful, although more to the touch than to the eye. With their extraordinary power and vitality, Matali's designs are a perfect reflection of her enthusiastic nature. They are not pure exercises in style, but well-thought out, carefully considered surprises. Her whole world revolves around colour, new and different ways of using natural and artificial materials, and a profound link with nature in all its manifestations. Some of her products are huge and some tiny. Their size is always designed to give dignity to every element in the furnishing of a home.

As a young mother, she is accustomed to telling stories. She incorporates these stories into her designs, which often give the impression of having been created for personal pleasure. In the long list of her products or prototypes, we cannot omit to mention the Orangina Glass (2000) and Permis de Construire (2000), which is both a seating system and a children's game, and expresses Matali's ideas to the full.

We often see elements of the world around us in Matali's work, picked up and put together in a new way. Her style is contemporary because it offers us a new approach to habitats and lifestyles that exist outside established bourgeois conventions. Her work reflects a particularly sharp observation of the liberated behaviour of young people today. GIULIO CAPPELLINI

1 Birdhouse, 1998, recycled polypropylene, 13 x 11 x 12.5 cm, Authentics.

2 Digestion, sofa, 1998–2000, foam, bag, 30 x 53 x 53 cm, Edra.
> The large, square, plastic bags used by Arab immigrants are here turned into furniture. The message is political and ecological, provoking a new outlook on the world.

3 Artican, basket, 2000, aluminium, polypropylene, 60 x ø 50 cm, Gilles Peyroulet.
> This wastepaper basket is made of brushes picked up by street sweepers.

4 Homewax, candle, 2000, wax, wicks, 16.5 x 11.5 x 2 cm, Gandy Gallery, Prague.
> This natural candle has two wicks. It was designed in 2000 as a prototype for Authentics, but from 2002 it has been produced by the Gandy Gallery.

5 Quand Jim Monte à Paris, sleeping system, 1995–8, foam, cotton, 190 x 34 x 34 cm, Domeau & Pérès.
> When opened, this column is transformed into a screen or bed.

6 Permis de Construire, seating system, 2000, high-resilience foam, cotton, 72 x 180 x 70 cm, Domeau & Pérès.
> This couch/children's game consists of 2 armrests and 20 bars.

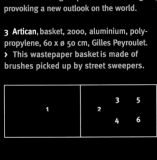

1	2	3	5
		4	6

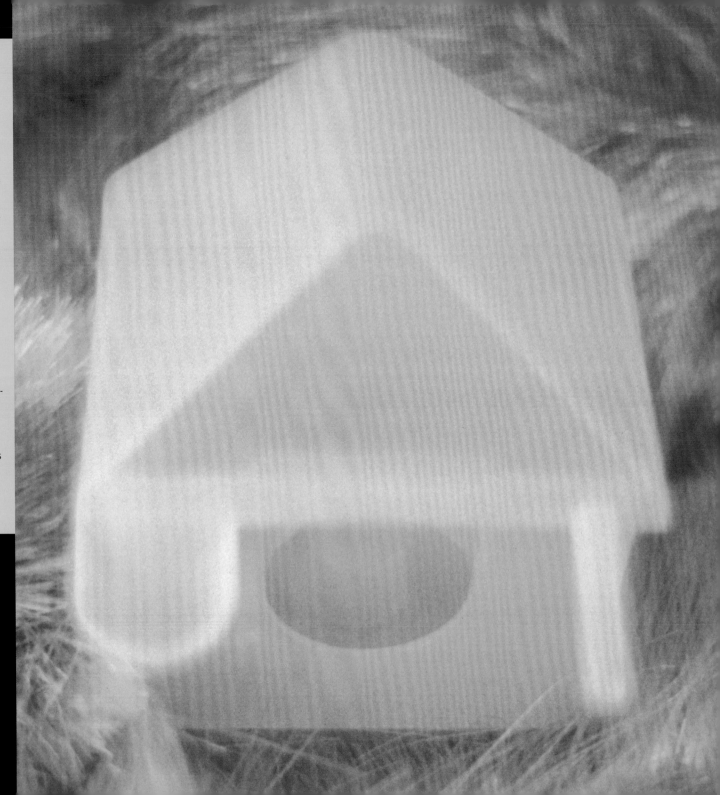

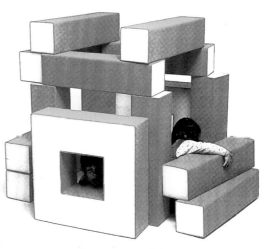

1 Bebox, 2000, wood and brush, 2 parts, 4 x 13.5 x 7 cm, Dim.
› This is a jewellery box for valuable or secret possessions, described as a 'box for love and to be loved'.

2 Spongeman & Spongewoman, 2000, bicolour natural sponge, 17 x 10 x 3 cm, 17 x 12 x 3 cm, Authentics.
› These sponges are part of a collection that was aimed at converting trivial things into objects that are capable of living a new life.

3 Together, glasses, 1999, machine-blown glass, 16.7 x ø 5.7 cm, Authentics.
› This is a totally functional pair of drinking glasses that have been turned into something special and personal. It is an example of how the traditional systems of design intervene in everyday life with slight or gradual changes on merchandising.

4 Mobiwork, 2001, metal, epoxy paint, plastic, 140 x 90 x 70 cm, Domeau & Pérès.
› The idea behind Mobiwork was to create a real workspace by integrating the computer and its additional elements within something the size of a wardrobe.

5 Verres, 2000, glass, 12 x ø 7 cm, Orangina.
› A glass for the very famous French soft drink.

	2		5
1		4	
	3		

123

Imagine skiing down a steep slope somewhere. Suddenly, as so often happens to pros and amateurs alike, some instinct tells you that you are going to fall. Down you go, sliding, sliding. And hurting, hurting. Or, more dangerously still, you are rounding a bend on a fast motorcycle, and you get that sickening realization that you are about to fall.

Now imagine that in the short time between your loss of control and your body hitting packed snow and ice, or more unforgiving tarmac, an air bag popped open and enveloped you in a cocoon, saving you from the worst of the impact. The D-Air jacket (2001–2) can do just that – it protects those parts of your body that are most vulnerable to injury: the upper body, neck and head. This is no longer the stuff of imagination. This is the future for adventurous, if accident-prone, skiers and bikers.

The D-Air jacket is the brainchild of Lino Dainese. An Italian designer and inventor, Dainese is the presiding genius of equipment design for what he calls the 'dynamic sports': motorcycling, mountain biking, skiing and snowboarding. Developed first for motorcycling, the most dangerous sport of all, the D-Air jacket, with the breathtaking simplicity of all great ideas, takes the technology of automobile airbags and marries it to Dainese's legendary safety clothing.

Curiously, the automobile airbag is something we are not actually very familiar with, even though it has saved countless thousands of lives in Europe and the United States, where it is a standard safety feature in cars. It is one of those 'gizmos' that we hope never to see put to the test. The same may well be said about the D-Air jacket, whose introduction is, nevertheless, eagerly awaited by motorcycle riders and skiers alike.

A self-taught designer and avid motorcyclist, Dainese's first designs were motocross trousers – a natural crossover from the leather industry where he first worked. In the years since he first branched out on his own, Dainese's brilliant, intuitive designs for safety clothing, including the BAP, a back protector for motorcyclists, have evolved further than could have been imagined. His motorcycle and ski suits are now distinguished by a unique Dainese style: part fighter pilot or astronaut, part comic book Ninja Turtle. His aesthetic imprint on the world of motorcycle racing is profound. Expect the same in skiing and snowboarding. ULTAN GUILFOYLE

1 **D-Air, Airbag for Motorcyclists**, 2001–2, vest: textile and net + PE, gas generator: metal, bags: textile, Dainese, in collaboration with Merhav A.A.P.
› The strongest point of D-Air is the sophisticated system that protects the parts of the body that are most vulnerable to traumas: the upper part of the chest, the neck and the head. It is capable of inflating in 30 milliseconds, and of maintaining an appreciable pressure in the sacks for twenty seconds after activation. The electronic control system, known as STM (Sensing, Triggering and Memory), is managed by a CPU that monitors data collected by sensors and decides to inflate depending on particular conditions. The three airbags were designed with an appropriate ergonomic shape and with technical characteristics for D-Air to cover the back, hips and chest of the rider.

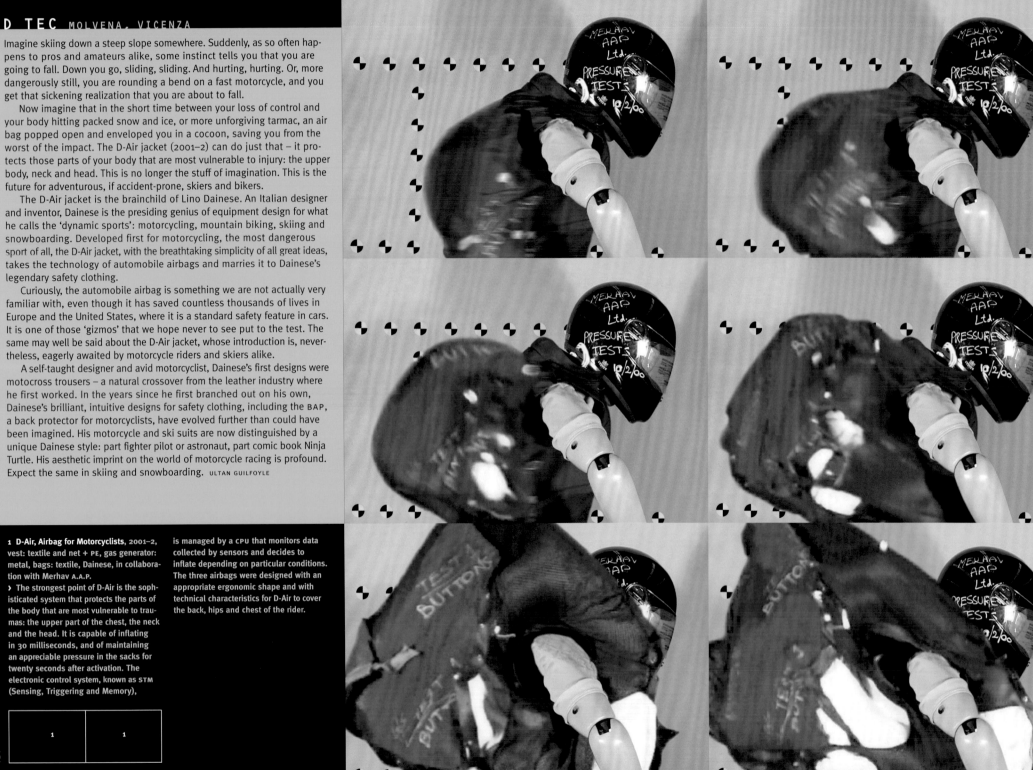

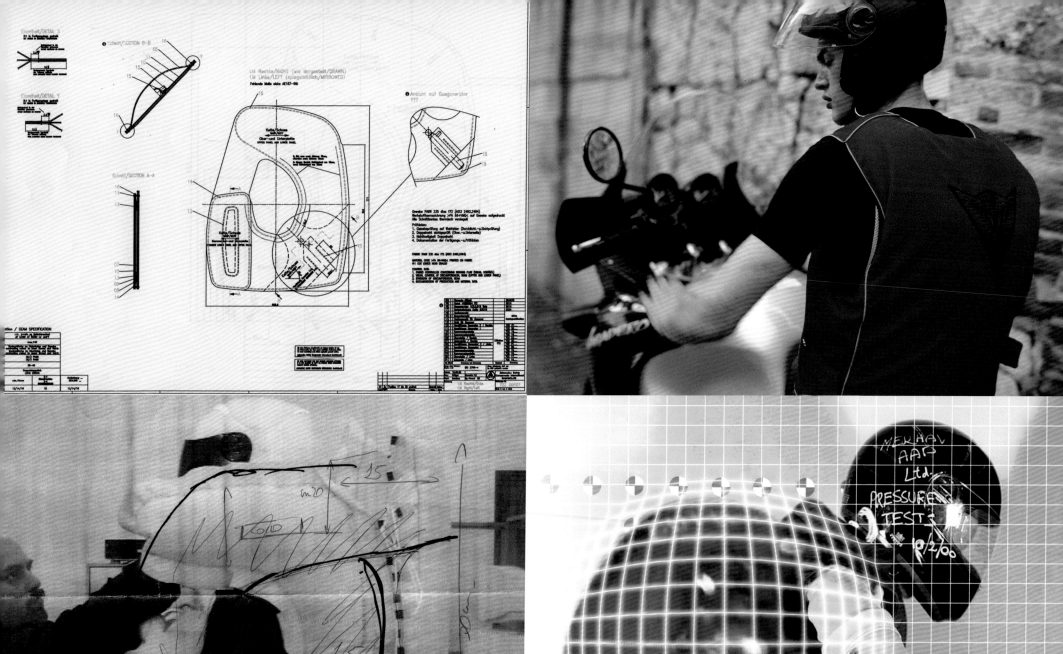

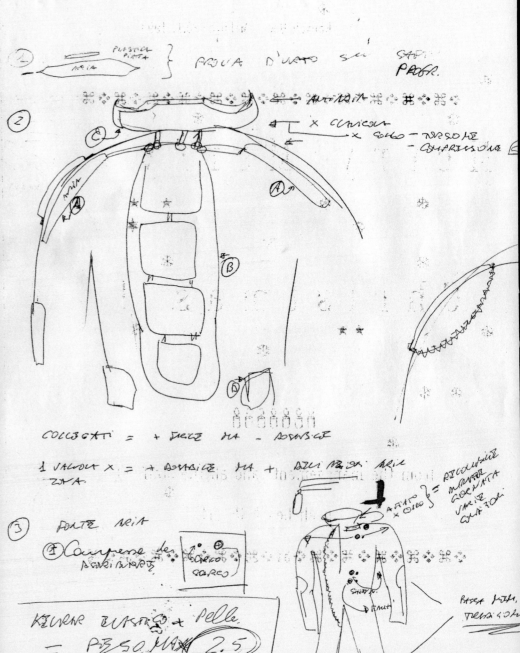

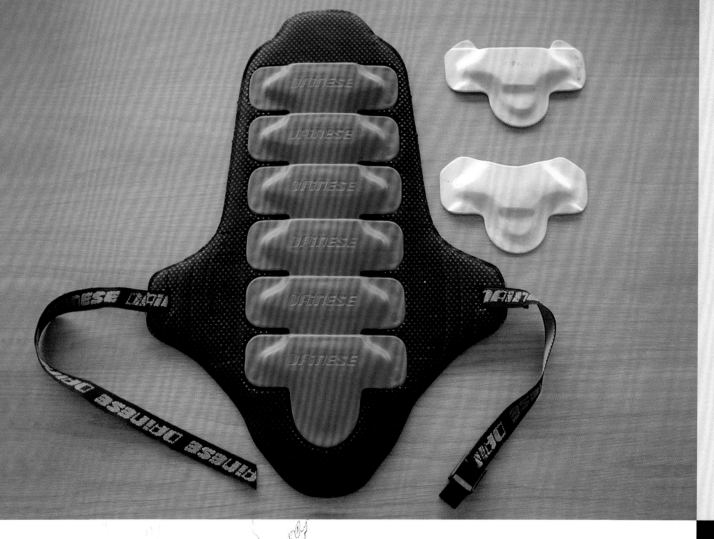

CODICE	ANCOREGE *(solo 7 placche)*	
IMPIEGO	*IN ABBINAMENTO A GIACCA*	
ATTACCO	*CINGHIETTE CON AUTOMATICI*	
MATERIALI	**DESCRIZIONE**	
11	*CORDELLA MARCATA DAINESE ALTEZZA 2,5*	
13	*FEMMINA DI BOTTONE AUTOMATICA MISURA 8*	
14	*MASCHIO DI BOTTONE AUTOMATICO MISURA 8*	
P1, P3, P5	*VEDI PARTICOLARE P1, P3, P5*	

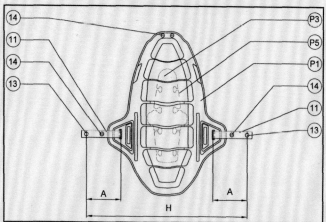

TAGLIA	H	A
S	56	10
M	56	10
L	56	10
XL	56	10

DPI 6	06/02/96	rev. 00

1 Safety Jacket, 1997, Net, PE cushions with holes, composite protective material, 72 x 60 x 12 cm, in collaboration with Marc Sadler, Dainese.

> The Safety Jacket is probably the garment that best expresses the protective concepts developed by Dainese for application to a wide array of sports. It has been constantly developed in order to ensure its technical characteristics stay at the forefront of the market. Sketches, schemes and a prototype show the process of creating the Safety Jacket for motorbiking. It has been adapted for mountain biking, skiing and snowboarding.

1	1

LORENZO DAMIANI MILAN

Lorenzo Damiani was born in Brianza, northern Italy, the centre of Italy's furniture industry. In his work there is a strong link both with his region and with the industrial and craft traditions of his native city.

Even as a very young man, Damiani paid great attention to the function of objects. He was always trying to find different ways of using materials and experimenting with new means of expression. Today, his products always have extremely elegant lines and, although they are always simple, they cannot be described as dull. The product of a young man's imagination, Damiani's work also embodies the skill of someone who has been accustomed to dealing with technical issues and production problems ever since he was a child.

At present, Damiani is in transition between a purely experimental phase and the more practical business of making finished products. With the instincts and energies natural to a young designer, Damiani conceives many designs. However, he always checks their feasibility against the actual needs of the market, and then has the strength of mind to abandon any project that fails the test. He often creates his design prototypes by hand, to test for himself all the messages that they convey.

His products are designed to go straight into people's homes. Far from being facile or predictable, however, they reach their target by making a consistently strong visual and tactile impact. He likes to experiment with a wide variety of materials, both natural and artificial, and tries to allow each one its proper dignity. He is thorough, decisive, meticulous and determined only to design products that will make an impact. The user of Damiani's designs will never be allowed to be passive. His products demand interaction, and the user is called on to move them around, sometimes changing their original form, such as with the Tavolante (1999), where the lamp can be opened and the top pulled up.

Damiani likes to use advanced industrial techniques in his work. However, he never underestimates the quality that comes from a craftsman's detail, applied with a personal touch. Mirror-Table (2001), which is a light table that can also be hung on the wall as a mirror, is among the objects that give the clearest insight into Damiani's approach: the variety of its uses intrigues us and the materials used are in perfect harmony.

GIULIO CAPPELLINI

1 Mirror-Table, 2001, aluminium, rubber, mirror, 75 x 160 x 180 cm, prototype.
› The mirror can be taken off the wall and 'opened' to become a table with a reflecting top. The table's main feature is its lightness. The mirror top is rectangular with rounded corners, and because it is made from aluminium, there is rigidity. The table edge has both a practical and an aesthetic function.

2 Shelf-Salver Tray, 2001, fluorescent acrylic, 7 x 27 x 80 cm, prototype.
› The shelf-tray hangs on the wall by means of a simple plastic bayonet system, made to

hold the shelf up safely. To use the shelf as a tray, you unhook it from the wall. Rectangular openings on both sides form handles and the corner edges form useful supports for the tray.

3 W Doppio Tray Box, 2001, thermoformed fluorescent and transparent acrylic, 8 x 27 x 35 cm, prototype.
› The box can be used to contain food while the cover can also be used as a tray.

4 Filocontinuo Lamp, 2001, bulbs, electrics, 15 x 20 x 10 cm, prototype.
› The transparent cable forms part of the lamp and can be installed in a variety of shapes on the wall. The bulb hangs from the wall by a blown-glass hook, but it can also stand upright as a floor lamp on its transparent feet.

	2	
1		4
	3	

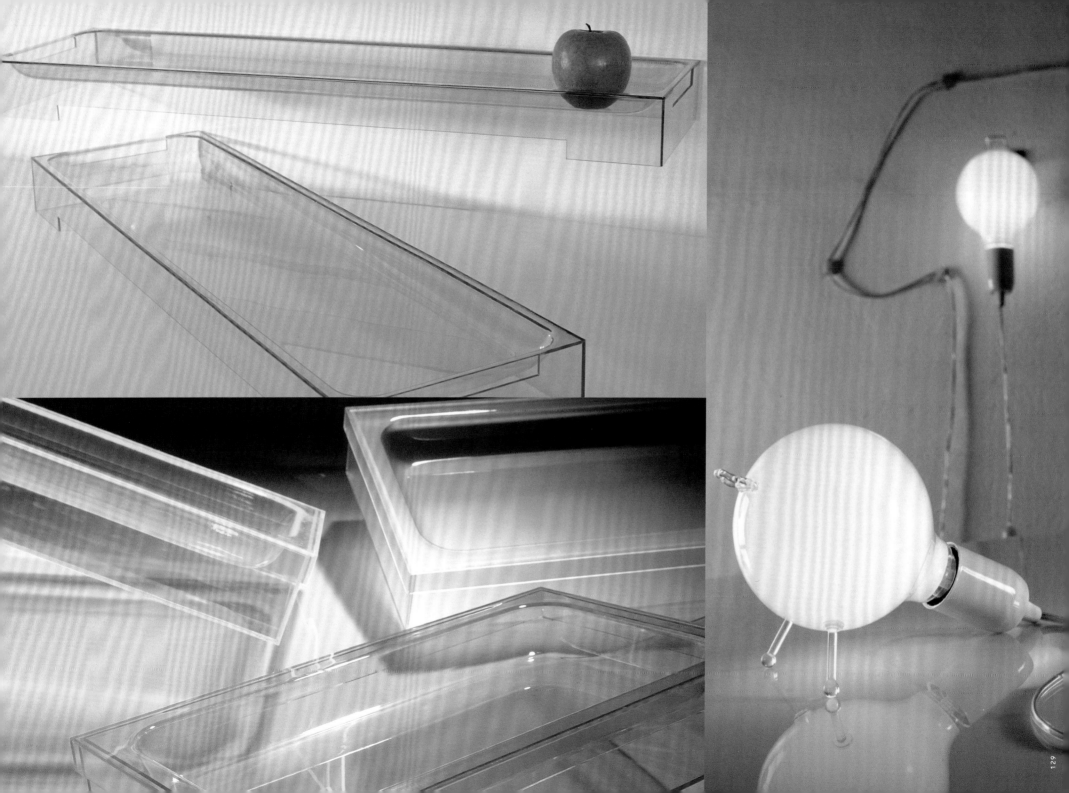

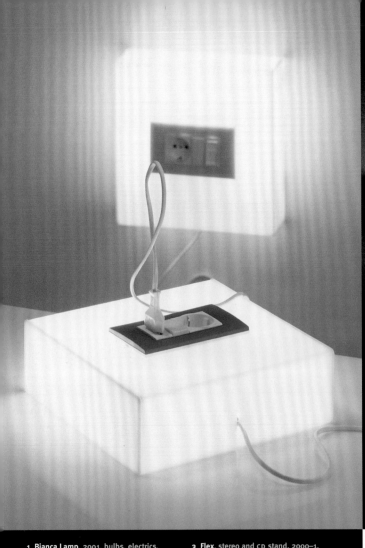

1 Bianca Lamp, 2001, bulbs, electrics,
9 x 26 x 26 cm, prototype.
› This is both a floor and a counter-top
lamp. On its upper part, it hosts a socket,
either for mains current or for the phone
and the on/off switch.

2 Packlight Collection, 1997, Osram Dulux
bulb, 18 x 10 x 6 cm, prototype.
› An Osram light bulb is packed in a
commercial plastic wrapping and can be
used in a conventional lampshade or left
in its packaging, whereby it becomes an
illuminating apparatus in its own right.

3 Flex, stereo and CD stand, 2000–1,
90 x 50 x 155 cm, structural coverflex
and steel, Montina.
› The wood panel can be bent harmoniously
and hung on the wall. The CDS can be
stored either vertically or horizontally.

4 Tavolante Table and Light, 1999, polyte-
len, steel, 30 x 120 x 200 cm, prototype.
› A chandelier-table provides a solution
midway between two different furnishing
styles. The light diffuser consists of two
semi-spheres (ø 60 cm); through a system
of pulleys, the upper sphere can be moved
to various heights above the table.

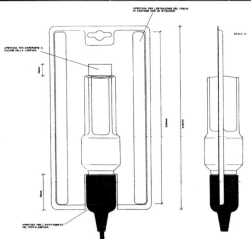

Largely unknown outside the world of motorcycle design and manufacture, Willie G Davidson has created a social and design phenomenon unparalleled in the history of American industrial design. To Harley-Davidson fanatics around the world Willie G, as he is affectionately known, personifies Harley-Davidson.

In the post-Vietnam era of the mid-1970s, many war veterans felt disenfranchised by the society to which they had returned. Their reaction was to reject comfortable, middle-class values, in favour of the blue-collar values of times past. And in the mythology of the American blue-collar male, the motorcycle ranks high as a symbol of freedom. This was fertile ground for the genius of Willie G Davidson.

After graduating from the Art Center College of Design in Pasadena, California, Willie G returned to the family business, co-founded by his great-grandfather in 1903. Brilliantly alive to the social conditions of the day, Willie saw a desperate need for revival. This was the beginning of a 30-year design project, not only to create a series of signature motor-cycles, but also to feed the Harley rider, and his hyper-American sensibilities, with the clothing, equipment and insignia that would identify him as the proto-individual of his time. The fact that one Harley-riding individualist ended up looking exactly like every other Harley rider is an irony not lost on Willie G. He believes that anyone nursing a desire for separateness is better off if he resembles a group of like-minded loners.

All went well until the mid-1990s, when the average age of the Harley owner was creeping into the upper forties. A market demographic of ageing rebels (now practising as doctors and lawyers, it must be stressed) is not good for business. Davidson had to find a younger, wider and more inclusive audience. He had to find a way to turn the heads of Honda riders, used to Japanese performance, or Ducati riders, used to Italian style. With the V-Rod (2001), unquestionably his greatest design, Willie G simultaneously reinvented himself and Harley-Davidson. Sleek and powerful, the V-Rod looks fast even when it is standing still. More important from a designer's point of view, it is uniquely modern. The aesthetics and the technology (much of it from Porsche) owe nothing to cowboy movies, the Ho Chi Minh trail, or to a generation of rebels without a cause. This may well turn out to be Willie G Davidson's true design legacy.

ULTAN GUILFOYLE

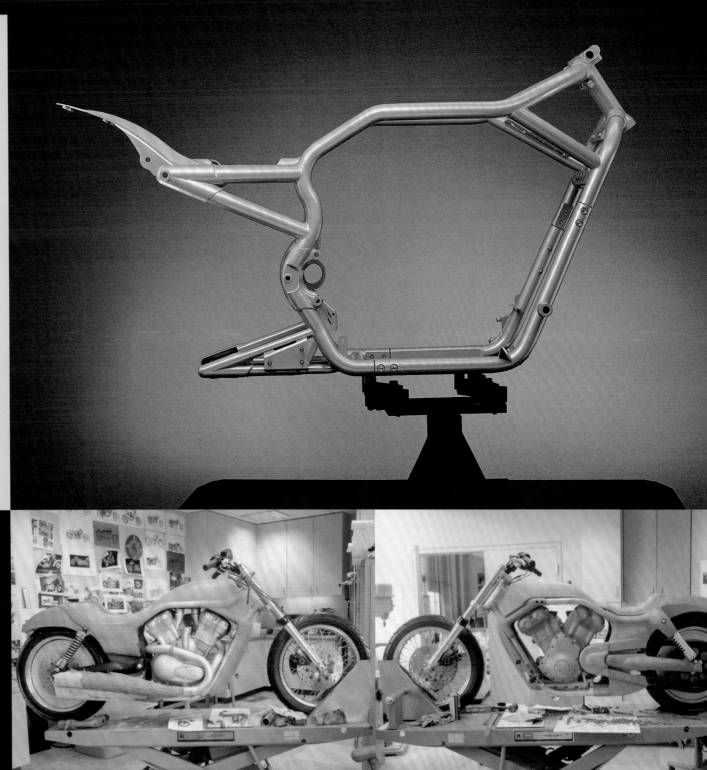

1 V-Rod, 2001, 1130 cc, Harley-Davidson.
> A high-pressure water-moulding process is used to create the frame components of the V-Rod. The seamless, complex shapes eliminate the need for much of the welding on traditional frame manufacture.

2 V-Rod, 2001, 1130 cc, Harley-Davidson.
> These two clay mock-ups show the hands-on working style of Davidson's young and talented design team.

3 V-Rod, 2001, 1130 cc, Harley-Davidson.
> The liquid-cooled, Porsche-designed engine is perhaps the most radical and non-traditional element of the V-Rod. Despite this departure, the engine compartment retains unmistakable Harley-Davidson lines. Finding a workable radiator shape to provide adequate airflow for the liquid-cooled engine dogged Harley-Davidson's designers and engineers – the solution came from an adapted FedEx box.

	1	3
	2	

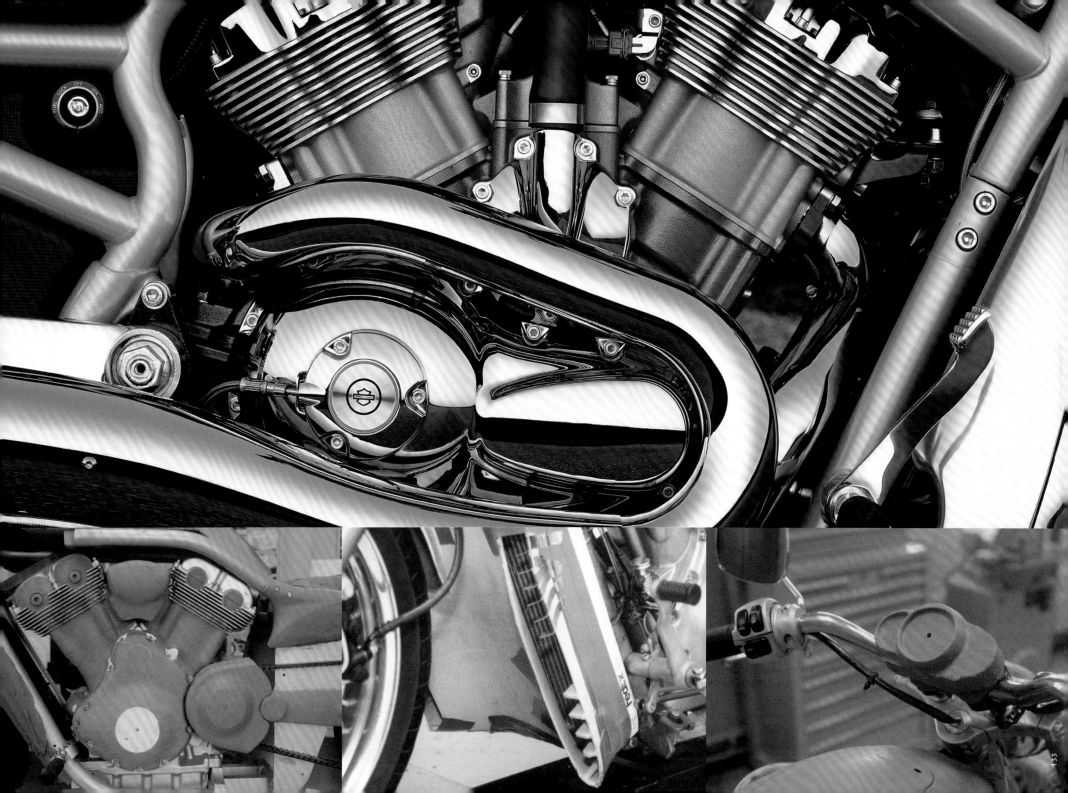

1 V-Rod, 2001, 1130 cc, Harley-Davidson.
› The bends of the silver-dipped frame are achieved through a hydroform process and are accentuated by bolt-on lower-frame rails. Tucked tightly inside the frame, an underseat fuel tank not only gives the V-Rod a more customized look, but also facilitates improved handling. Such styling is even more evident with the new integrated instrument panel, which features the speedometer, tachometer, fuel gauge and warning lights. There is also a start-up self-diagnostic check, multiple trip meters and a fuel range indicator.

2 V-Rod, 2001, 1130 cc, Harley-Davidson.
› The V-Rod, a traditional, feet-forward power cruiser, is thoroughly modern in every way. It is the perfect evocation of a Western horse in twenty-first-century mechanical form.

| 1 | 2 |

DUNNE + RABY LONDON

For some reason I left writing about Tony and Fiona to last. Maybe I was not sure how I was going to convey my admiration for the clarity of their ideas, their commitment to their uncompromising independence from anything near mainstream, their teaching, their writing and their following. I also needed to consider their design as the carrier for their ideas about 'relationships between people and objects, about what electronics actually does, about the hidden magnetic fields surrounding us, the electronic information hanging in the air', and the feeling that the visual language, form and choice of materials embrace too readily a prevailing formal genre, well ... minimalism. It is easy to understand the choice (if it is one) that nothing should upstage the purity of the ideas, that the design of a table, for example, is like a white gallery containing the exhibits (i.e. ideas) without competing with them. I am sure they know that there is no such thing as No Style, No Design. It is difficult for me to accept that the physical form of a piece could not play a bigger role than just being neutral.

I thought a little break from writing might be a good idea, so I walked to the Camden Art Centre in north London to see the 'Atelier Van Lieshout' exhibition. Sunday, midday, not a soul in the gallery but Dunne and Raby. Of course, it is a show that they would visit, but still, how incredible. 'I need to talk to you, I am in the middle of writing about you':

Q – People when looking at your work tend to either 'praise' it as Art or 'dismiss' it as Art?

A – We think it is just research, exploring ideas about the way we live today in relation to technology. We use products, sometimes furniture, as our medium. It is interesting that people either dismiss or praise it as art but it does not really affect the way we think of it.

Q – Most of your pieces seem to be more comments about things rather than designs for the things themselves. The table with the compasses or the GPS are not there as your proposition for a new design for a table so why insist on playing in the design field and not art?

A – Because if it becomes art it seems to be on the edges of everyday life, a special category of objects in galleries and museums. And even if the piece ends there, it is not our intention, whereas if we present it as design then we think people interpret it in a different way.

This year for the first time, a Dunne + Raby piece, the Compass Table, was put in production, no longer a mere exhibit but a product available to all.

RON ARAD

Weeds, 1998, English oak, prototypes in collaboration with Michael Anastassiades.
› Weeds are a series of issues revolving around nature and its life. People can learn to observe nature through bizarre tools that enhance the senses in a poetic way. These objects stimulate conversations between humans and plants.
1 Garden Horn, 22 x 160 x 5 cm.
› A device for speaking to plants that otherwise might be neglected.
2 Intensive Care, 110 x 30 x 30 cm.
› This allows communication with demanding plants, anywhere, anytime.

3 Talking Tabs, 1998, 26.5 x 9 x 1 cm.
› These are labels that recite poems or recipes to plants.
4 Meeting, 85 x 85 x 85 cm.
› A piece of indoor furniture to grow and look after. A place to meet and make up when lovers become neighbours.

Placebo Furniture, 2001, prototypes.
5 Loft, MDF, lead, 238 x 80 x 112 cm.
› This lead-clad box on top of a ladder is a place to store precious magnetic mementoes away from potentially harmful electromagnetic fields.
6 Phone Table, MDF, high-frequency electromagnetic field sensor, microcontroller, lamp, 110 x 23 x 29 cm.
› A mobile phone is placed inside the table; the table top gently glows green when the phone receives a call.

1	2		
3	4	5	6

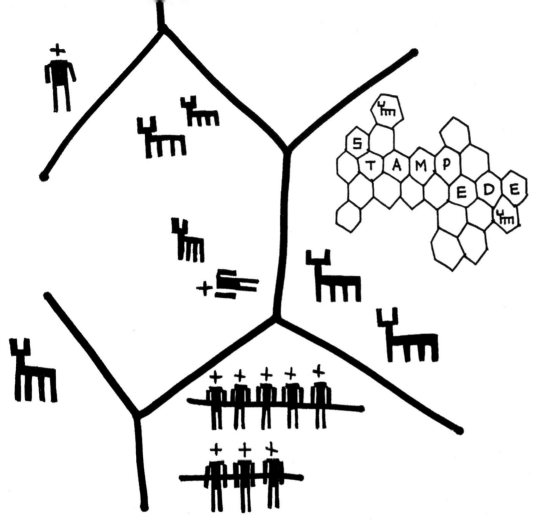

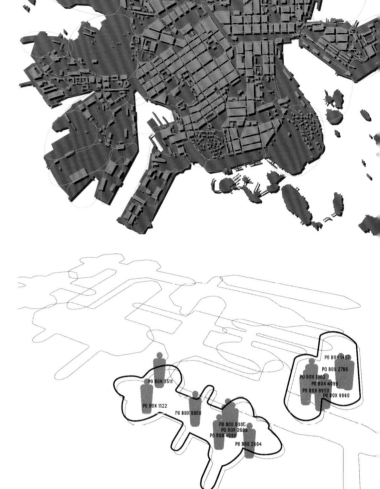

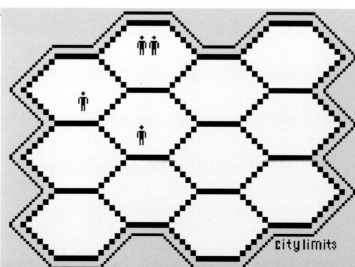

Placebo Furniture, 2001, prototypes.

1 Compass Table, MDF, glass, compass needles, steel, plastic, 75 x 75 x 75 cm, Hidden.
> The 25 compasses set into the table twitch and spin when devices like mobile phones or laptop computers are placed on it.

2 Nipple Chair, MDF, low-frequency electro-magnetic field sensor, micro-controller, 94.5 x 45 x 69 cm.
> When the chair is placed in an electro-magnetic field the nipples set into its back start to vibrate and the sitter is made aware of the radio waves penetrating his body.

3 Electro-Draught Excluder, MDF, conductive foam, stainless steel, 57.5 x 52 x 13 cm.
> Though the draught excluder uses conductive foam, it is not grounded and therefore does not really absorb radiation.

4 Parasite Light, 2001, 25 x 121 x 15 cm, prototype.
> The light works when placed near an electronic product. It uses an electromagnetic sensor to relate the intensity of its function to the strength of the field it senses.

5 Flirt Pics, 2001.
> The name stands for Flexible Information and Recreation for mobile users. It is an EC research project on the development of digital structures, and aims to investigate the potential of location specific information, both as a resource and as a medium for social interaction.

1	2	
3	4	5

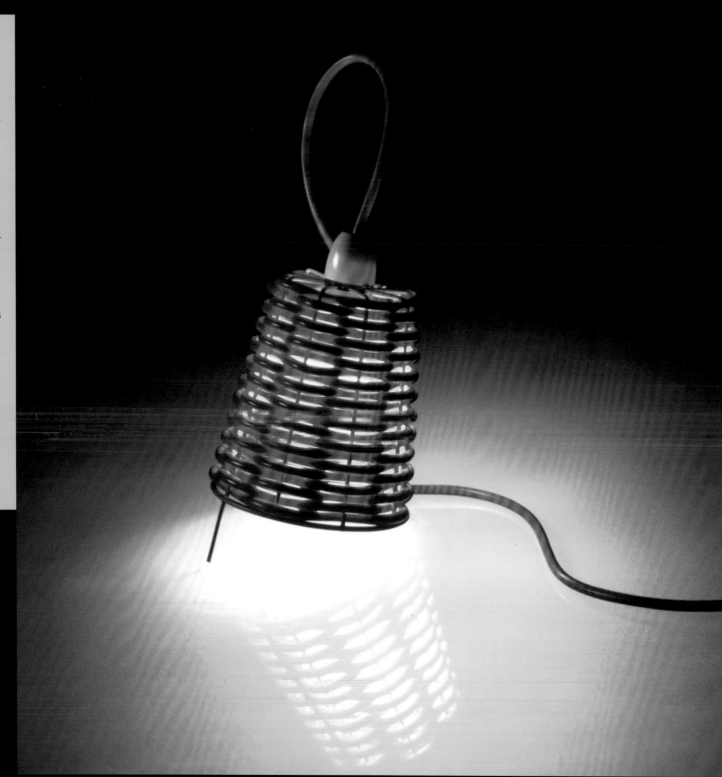

Only a few people manage to establish themselves as designers without being sucked into the compromise and jargon orgy of the commercial world. A lot of new designers concede that they have to concede, but in none of El Ultimo Grito's projects can you spot submission to what most other people are happy to accept as unquestionable requirements.

It is the humour that makes Roberto Feo's and Rosario Urtato's journey a delight to follow. The journey, in El Ultimo Grito's case, was an almost impossible one. Rather than knocking on company doors, they started producing and marketing their products themselves. Is there a gentler word than marketing? Maybe exhibiting and selling, maybe winning awards for their stands year after year. Why did they come to London, where it is all so difficult? Why not Spain, where they enjoy the love that is showered on local heroes? Maybe because the challenge of London is a healthy fuel for their creativity.

I know from my early days that producing your own designs, as well as being an important developmental stage, also affects the scope of the products you design and their nature. I remember the first time I was commissioned to design by an outside company. I came back from visiting the factory of the mighty Vitra, with its 2,000-strong workforce and its state-of-the-art manufacturing facilities, and all I felt able to do for them was design something that I could have produced myself, in my bucket-and-spade workshop. Looking back, I would not have the Well Tempered Chair designed in any other way, and I would not have any of El Ultimo Grito's projects designed and produced differently from the current, charming way that they are produced now.

Roberto and Rosario reveal not only the process of designing a product, but also the process of starting a practice. Each and every one of their projects, from its conception to its witty christening, with names such as Ego Club (2001) for a disco cubicle designed for one person, and What Goes Down Must Come Up (2000) for a self-rising laundry basket, confirms this attitude.

Recently, the inevitable started happening: Roberto and Rosario found themselves in demand by other companies, some of which presented new El Ultimo Grito projects at the 2002 Milan Salone del Mobile, but the bulk of this new development is yet to come. We can absolutely trust them to lose none of their vitality and never to sell out. RON ARAD

1 **La Lu**, lamp, 1999, flex, wire structure, 20 x ∅ 12 cm, EUG.
› The shade of this lamp has been made by long-established basket-weaving techniques, but instead of using traditional reed, it is the electric flex which is woven.

2 **Mind the Gap**, table, 1998, steel, synthetic rubber, 35 x 80 x 60 cm, Punt Mobles.
› The top of this table creates its own shape, the synthetic rubber simply falls through into the gap and shapes itself into a useful pocket.

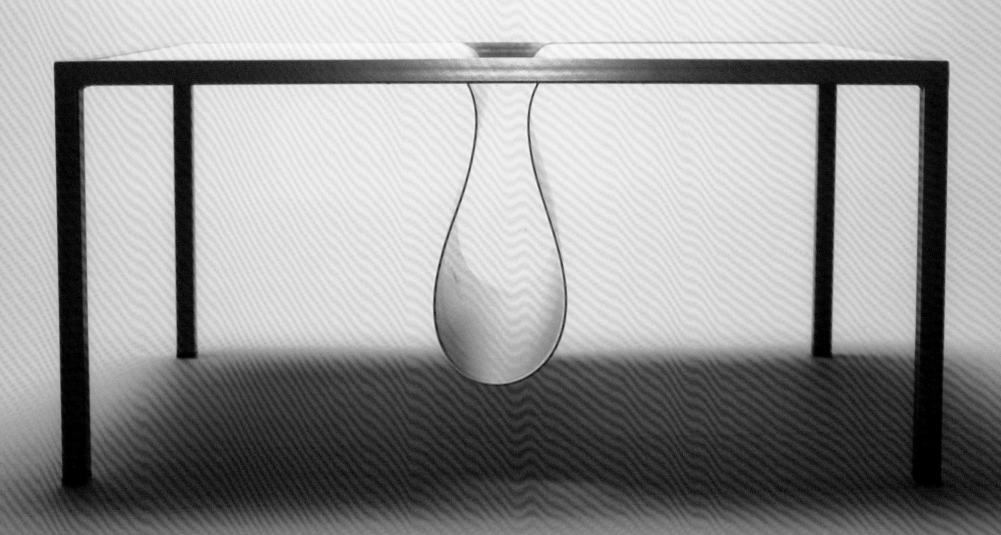

EGO CLUB

ENTER AND PRESS RED BUTTON ON/OFF

WARNING! STROBE LIGHTING INSIDE

CAMILA FIX SÃO PAULO

Thanks to the Campana brothers, we know that Brazilian design does exist. In their wake a new generation of younger talents has emerged, dedicated to stimulating design culture and revitalizing the design industry in Brazil. A number of these designers trained in Rio de Janeiro, where Carmen Portinho set up the Escola Superior de Desenho Industrial in the 1960s. The other centre of new design in Brazil is São Paulo, and Camila Fix is one of its most distinguished members.

Camila Fix studied architecture and then worked for two years in the design department of the Contemporary Art Museum (MAC) in São Paulo. This work nurtured her interest in the design of objects, and in 1995 she launched Fix Design, with the aim of producing furniture, objects and accessories. Like the Campana brothers, Fix uses wood, aluminium and stainless steel, the standard materials of industrial manufacture, as well as other, less common materials such as Corian.

Using Corian, a remarkable material, she developed the Rio Line collection (2001). This is a series of pieces that focus on frequently neglected details, such as the ergonomics of the human hand. Other designs reveal a special interest in the manufacturing process. The Poli Jug (1997), for example, is made up of three parts that are fitted together without screws or welds. A playful attitude is also evident in other projects, such as the Magnetico Bench (2000), made of seating modules that are held together by magnets, making it possible to arrange them in a variety of different ways.

Mobility and versatility are two qualities in which Camila Fix takes a special interest. Her Rótula Table (2000) shows this to perfection. The design offers an attractive solution to the problem of how to convert a low, auxiliary table into a higher table with quite different features. Fix meets the challenge by giving the table articulated stainless-steel legs. These fold out, raising the top to the height of a conventional dining-room table.

The Ripa Screen (1999) is mobile, versatile, and modular into the bargain. The basic design subsequently gave rise to an elegant range of garden furniture with an ingenious system of moving hinges that make it easier to store, transport and assemble. Practicality is as important in a piece of furniture as the production process. Aesthetics is not the only consideration, as Camila Fix, designer and producer, knows very well.

RAMÓN UBEDA

1 Ripa Furniture, 2001–2, anodized aluminium, injected polypropylene or wood, seat 44 x 37 x 34 cm, long seat 44 x 153 x 34 cm, side table 50 x 53 x 50 cm, dining table 74 x 81 x 78 cm, Fix Design.
> This outdoor furniture is an assembly of various types of industrially produced standard aluminium bars. Each object is composed of square section tubes, with circular tubes as spacers and rods as structural elements. The assembly system and mobile hinging allow for easy transport and storage.

2 Ripa Screen, 1999, anodized aluminium, injected polypropylene, two-module screen 170 x 115 x 3.5 cm, three-module screen 170 x 172.5 x 3.5 cm, Fix Design.
> Each screen module is composed of a sequence of closing bars (square section tubes) alternating with spacers (circular tubes), mounted horizontally on the vertical structural elements (rods) through circular holes drilled at the ends of the square tubes. The number of closing bars and the height of the spacers can be altered to produce different levels of visibility.

1	1	2

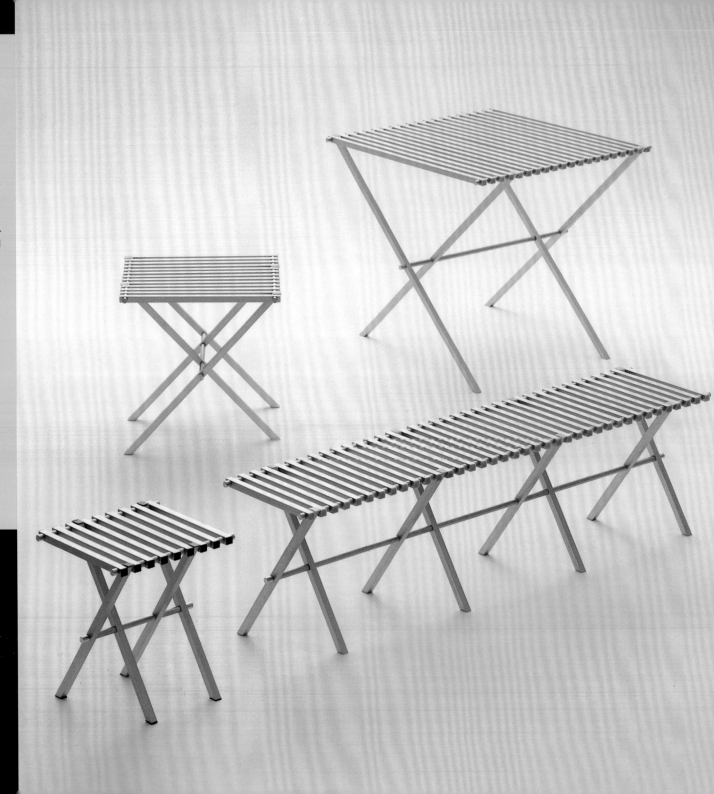

144

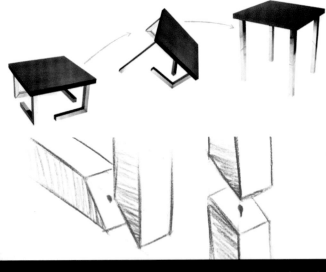

1 Rótula Table, 2000, stainless steel, wood, 76/40 x 80 x 80 cm, Fix Design.
› The mobile hinges on the table legs enable it to function in two ways: as a coffee table and as a dining table.

2 Poli Jug, 1997, anodized aluminium, chrome, small H 25 cm, large H 31 cm, Polimold.
› The Poli jug comprises three different elements – body, support and handle – which are fixed together by pressure, thus avoiding the use of welding or screws. Each piece is assembled through a cryogenic process. The body is made of a standard aluminium tube with a slanted top, which effectively replaces the jug's lip and facilitates the flow of liquids. The brass handle with a chrome finish is fixed only at the base.

3 Rio Line, 2001, Corian, bed tray 30 x 56 x 30 cm, rectangular tray 5 x 40 x 20 cm, Fix Design.
› The Rio houseware line is the result of careful moulding of Corian board, made in a way that fits the human hand ergonomically.

1	2	
		3

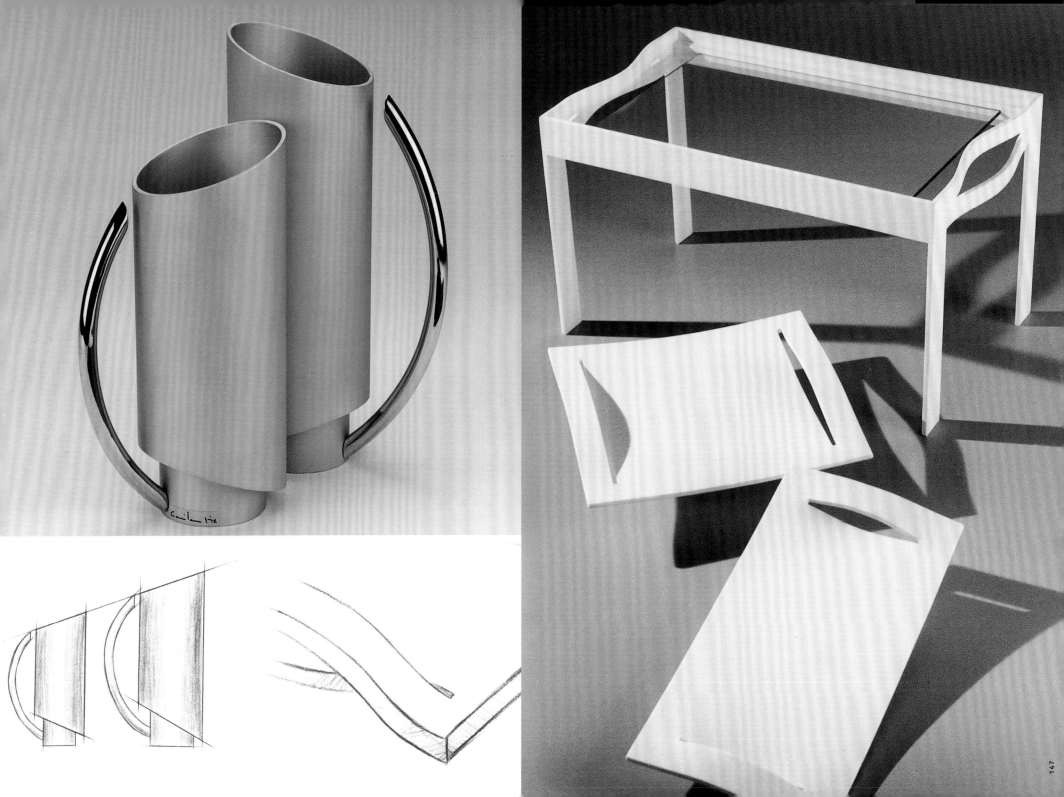

JOZEPH FORAKIS MILAN – NEW YORK

Beyond designing a product, Jozeph Forakis is intent on designing gestures. Form follows experience in what he defines as the 'aesthetics of behaviour'. Whether designing a mobile sound hood, a watch-phone or a toilet brush, he is concerned above all with the way that a user will move, bond with and enjoy a product. Even if the end product is almost virtual, the experience is not.

As European design director for Motorola from 1999, Forakis has been a designer of strategies. He heads the company's research, design and development of their smart communications products, such as the Other's Eyes (2001) shared experience system, which allows one to see through someone else's eyes, using a hand-held miniature camera. The mood hood (2001), a wearable music environment, allows friends scattered throughout the city to listen to music together, and to speak via a 'buddy' network. These two products both create new gestures – hand to eye, head to hood – that are instantly recognizable, whether or not one can identify the product itself.

The focus on subject rather than object was already apparent in CopyWriter, developed for Forakis' master's thesis at the Domus Academy in Milan in 1992, before the Palm Pilot generation. Working from the belief that the personal computer, while designed for everyone, suits no one, his aim was to create a computer system for writers. The CopyWriter can record, scan, hand-write or type, and it incorporates various accessories, which can be worn, carried or left behind, as required.

Forakis' behaviour-oriented design extends to more mundane objects, designed at Studio Forakis, which he set up in 1993 in Milan. The Ballo toilet brush (2002), produced by Magis, is a study in ease and playfulness. Carefully weighted, it can move in any direction, and wobbles when placed on the floor, without falling over. Materials are just as important in Forakis' own range of products as those he designs for Motorola. The Vela home and office screen (2002), for example, is made from an extruded plastic that allows it to be infinitely long. It can be used to create an intimate space, even in the busy, impersonal environment of a trade fair.

Forakis has also designed the Swatch Talk (2001), the first watch with a GSM dual-band mobile phone. It is very similar to the Motorola V70 (2002), an industry icon and currently the smallest mobile phone on the market. The aesthetics may be similar, and the functions, too, but for Forakis the difference lies in user behaviour. LISA WHITE

1 Vela, screen, 2002, extruded PMMA, co-extruded Polyurethane, ABS, 170 x 200 x 12 cm, Magis.
> Two simple extrusions, for the panel and connector, make a modular screen system which would be just as suitable for a home, an open-plan office or a tradeshow.

2 Ballo, toilet brush, 2002, gas-moulded polypropylene, nylon bristles, steel, 50 x 20 x 20 cm, Magis.
> The simple curved design of this toilet brush allows it to wobble, but ensures that it always returns upright, ready for use.

3 CopyWriter, 1992, tyvek-type waterproof, tearproof paper envelope with padding, textiles, ABS, silicon rubber, steel, 1 x 30 x 21 cm, prototype.
> This design was part of some independent research Forakis carried out for Smart-Tools. CopyWriter is a flexible system which is designed to support the unique and unpredictable working habits of a writer.

4 mood hood, 2001, textiles, aluminium, silicon rubber, ABS, various modular sizes, prototype for Motorola.
> The mood hood is part of the Wearable Communication Experience. It gives the wearer the sense that they are completely surrounded by sound. This is achieved by the use of 3-dimensional directional sound imaging.

1	3	
		4
2	4	

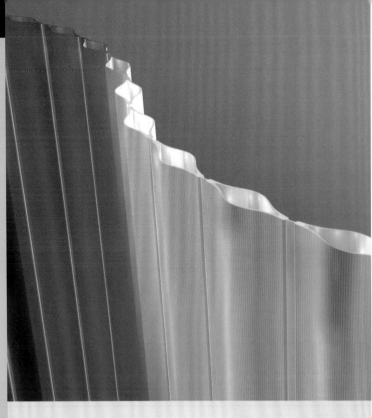

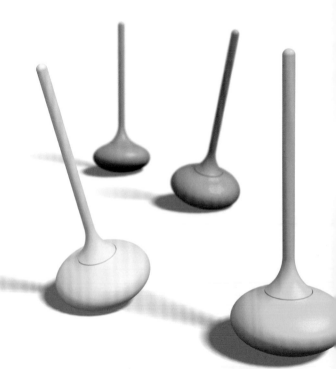

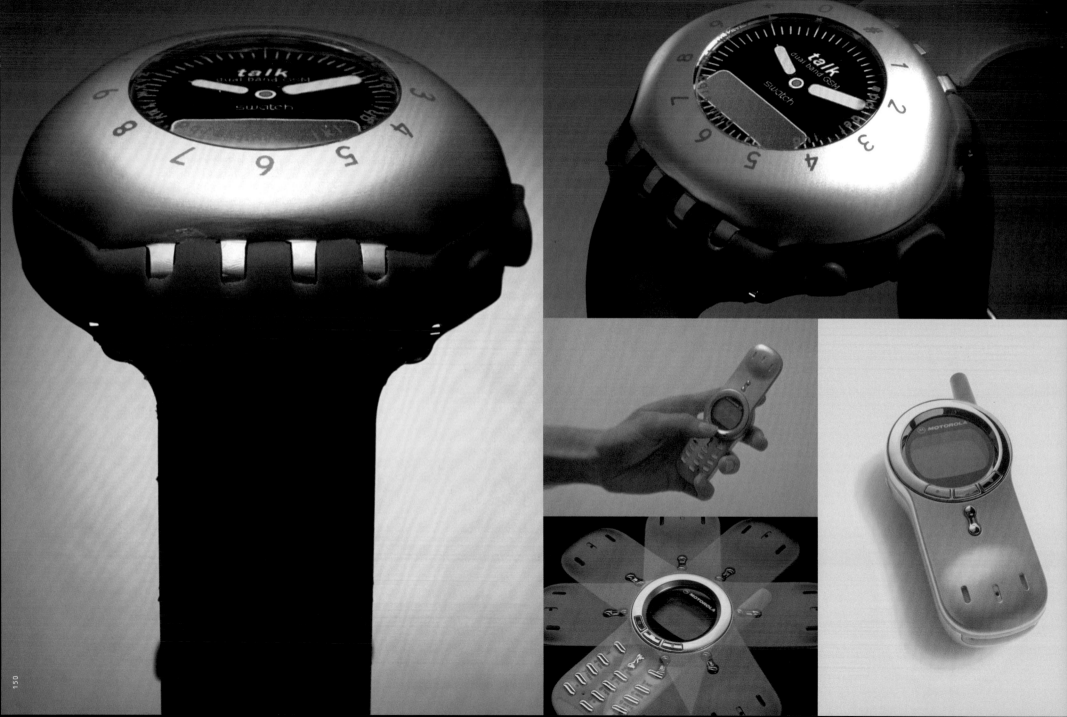

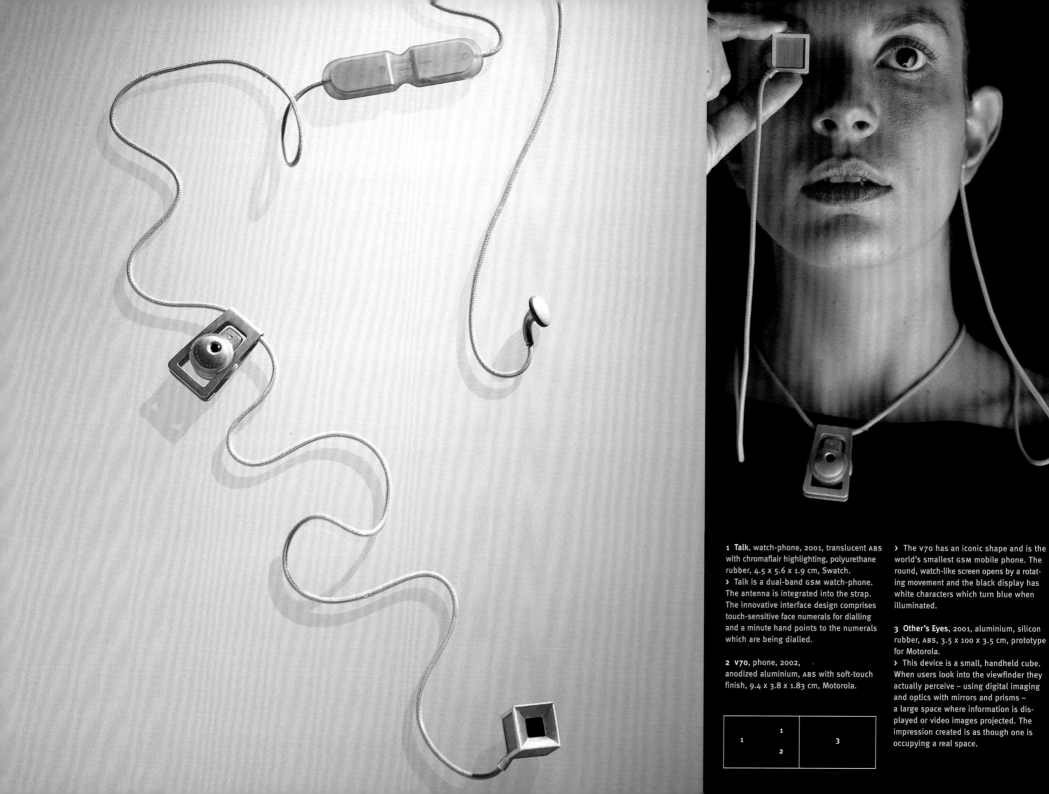

1 Talk, watch-phone, 2001, translucent ABS with chromaflair highlighting, polyurethane rubber, 4.5 x 5.6 x 1.9 cm, Swatch.
› Talk is a dual-band GSM watch-phone. The antenna is integrated into the strap. The innovative interface design comprises touch-sensitive face numerals for dialling and a minute hand points to the numerals which are being dialled.

2 V70, phone, 2002,
anodized aluminium, ABS with soft-touch finish, 9.4 x 3.8 x 1.83 cm, Motorola.

› The V70 has an iconic shape and is the world's smallest GSM mobile phone. The round, watch-like screen opens by a rotating movement and the black display has white characters which turn blue when illuminated.

3 Other's Eyes, 2001, aluminium, silicon rubber, ABS, 3.5 x 100 x 3.5 cm, prototype for Motorola.
› This device is a small, handheld cube. When users look into the viewfinder they actually perceive – using digital imaging and optics with mirrors and prisms – a large space where information is displayed or video images projected. The impression created is as though one is occupying a real space.

	1	
1	2	3

FRANCÈS + POLICAR PARIS

Elsa Francès and Jean-Michel Policar have been inseparable design partners since they met at Thomson Multimedia's European design team, Tim Thom, in 1993. Though each is now design manager of a different department – Francès directs Strategic Design Research and Policar directs Colour and Material Innovation – and though each has a separate personal life, they work in such symbiosis that in conversation one will often finish the phrase of the other, to perfection.

The Radio Porcelain that Francès developed for Thomson in 1998 looks like a mortar and pestle. She has combined the newest digital technology with an ancient design archetype, encouraging a gesture that brings us back to our primitive selves, while simultaneously permitting greater finesse of station selection. In 1999, Policar developed Smiling Orange, the Thomson portable TV with a soft surface akin to a sports-shoe sole. The user 'dynamizes' his or her relationship with this ergonomically designed TV, moving it actively about the house and garden.

Francès brings an intellectual rigour to the partnership, while Policar is more intuitive and 'thinks with his hands'. The design process begins with a 'desire for a new state of being' which is followed by a flurry of drawings, each designer explaining the drawing of the other and building on it with a sketched response until the final concept emerges. Clarity is one of the key elements to their design, but their style is also characterized by invisible technology, which imparts an element of magic and physical discovery to each item. Their first personal project, Dé-Lumineux, produced by Ligne Roset (1999), initially appears to be an empty translucent cup placed on a side table. When the cup is turned upside down, creating a lampshade form, it offers a light to accompany a conversation, a film or a meal, without being overpowering. The On Air lamp (1999), functions as a bowl of light, the intensity changing as one rubs a finger along its glass rim. Francès and Policar's latest light, La Conic (2002), seems at first glance to be an ordinary lamp. Upon closer inspection, one discovers that the light emanates not from a bulb in the centre of the lampshade, but from the lampshade itself through the use of a very thin, circular neon light hidden from view. In proposing such discreet objects for everyday life, Francès and Policar free the user from the mindless options of 'on' or 'off', and open up new dimensions. Their lights function as subtle passages between different states of being. LISA WHITE

1 Radio Porcelain, 1998, porcelain, 13.5 x ∅ 19 cm, Thomson.
› This radio is an object that combines technology with 'table art'. The sound comes from the interior of the porcelain bowl and the frequency is changed by turning the 'pestle'.

2 Videosender, 2001, transmitter 4 x ∅ 10 cm, receiver 4 x 13 x 10.5 cm, Thomson.
› This home-entertainment set allows images and sound to be sent wirelessly from a video source to other TV monitors within the house. The two matching sender/receiver units are equipped with small parabolic antennae (for audio and video) and mini-rod aerials (to relay infrared commands). An infrared extender can also be placed alongside the three different devices, working almost like an unlit string of Christmas tree lights.

3 Smiling Orange, 1999, 36 x 36 x 36 cm, Thomson.
› This portable TV is all about attitude. It illustrates the designers' determination to introduce colour into technological devices, so that they will enhance, rather than blend into, the living space.

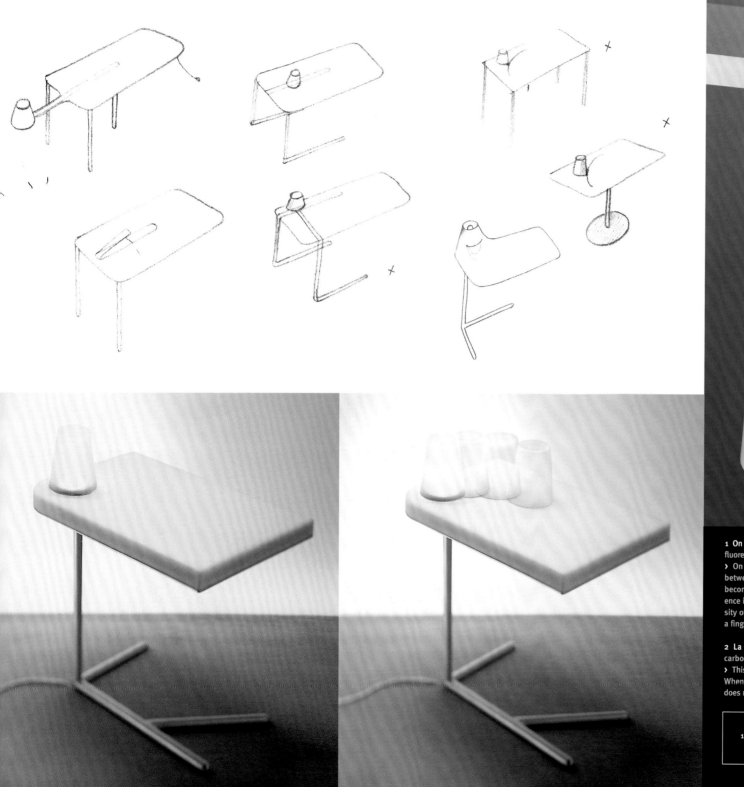

1 On Air, lamp, 1999, polycarbonate, steel, fluorescent tube, 130 x ø 35 cm, prototype.
› On Air suggests a gentle relationship between light and space. Technology has become invisible, while the tactile experience is made much more relevant. The intensity of the light can be adjusted by sliding a finger along the top edge of the bowl.

2 La Conic, lamp, 2002, metal, polycarbonate sheet, 34 x ø 35 cm, Ligne Roset.
› This is a lamp that can be hung anywhere. When observed from underneath, the light does not originate from a central bulb, but from a very thin circular neon light placed in the thickness of the cone.

3 Dé-Lumineux, 1999, aluminium, polycarbonate, 55 x 42 x 60 cm, Ligne Roset.
› This is a table and a lampshade without either wire or bulb. When the lamp is upside down, it is 'empty' of light, but by inverting it, it magically shines. It can be moved around the table to give different lighting effects.

4 So Watt, lamp, 2002, lacquered metal, 36 x ø 21 cm, Ligne Roset.
› This lamp can be placed either upright on a table or suspended from a shelf since the weight of the base makes the light stable in any position. It is possible to modulate the light simply by sliding the lamp up and down the stand.

1	2	3	4

The years 1998–2000 spent at London's Royal College of Art gave form to Thorsten Franck's furniture collections. The quirky approach to home decoration in Britain inspired him to develop a system of furniture that, though not traditionally British, retained what he calls 'the sweetness' of British interiors. Un-furnished (2001) consists of household items such as mirrors, clothes pegs and clocks that we would normally expect to be wall-mounted; instead they are attached to poles and leant against a wall. 'Un-furnished has the spirit of nomadic life and contemporary living', says Franck. The pieces are moveable both within an interior and if the user moves house. Franck took his thinking on the subject further with Lamp for White Rooms (2000), a standard lamp that actually has wallpaper pasted to it.

Plywood (1999–2000) was also formulated while Franck was studying in London. He built a family of furniture essentials around one three-point joint. 'I made a profile', he says, 'and then applied it in as many ways as I could.' The joint allows Franck to use exceptionally thin plywood with a surprising load-bearing capacity. The objects are simple to construct. With only four wing nuts to tackle on most pieces, even the biggest DIY-phobe could get to grips with Franck's designs. Most pieces carry the functional/decorative detail of a cut-out handle, an idea that Franck lifted from the humble banana box.

Long before he went to the RCA, Franck explored the possibilities of traditional German woodwork. This craft background helped him to formulate his oeuvre, although now everything that he designs is conceived on a computer. Those early works seem far removed from his most recent adventure in design, the Build in a Minute series (2001). Working with the manufacturers Möbelbau Kaether & Weise's CNC (Computer Numerical Control) machine, Franck developed a form that could be laser cut in only four minutes, and then pushed into shape by a metal wire. After years of devoting weeks or even months to creating individual pieces, this was a revelation to Franck. The new form could then be assembled into the support for a trestle table, a bookshelf or a wardrobe. The possibilities were infinite. The products take only a minute to build and use board only 6 mm thick. Minimizing material and maximizing support is the key to this collection. It seems that Franck's penchant for relaxed and easy design is a successful formula. LAURA HOUSELEY

1 **Un-furnished**, 2001, maple dowels, plywood, PVC coated hooks, mirror, metal, H 185 cm, Nils Holger Moormann.
› This is a collection of domestic accessories, such as pegs and a clock, which, instead of being attached to the wall in the usual way, have been put on long wooden poles. This means they can be easily moved or hidden away.

2 **Stacking Stool**, 2000, alludibond (aluminium sandwich material), 44 x 32 x 26 cm, prototype.

› This simple stool is formed out of two sheets of alludibond glued together and its construction shapes its form. The bent edge brings stability to the thin material. Several stools can be piled up to create a system of shelves.

3 **Plywood Chair and Table**, 2001, maple dowels, bent plywood, chair 70 x 37 x 52 cm, table 75 x 160 x 70 cm, prototype.
› This collection consists of easily built essential furniture for the home; each piece is constructed out of plywood and uses a triangular joint.

1	2	3

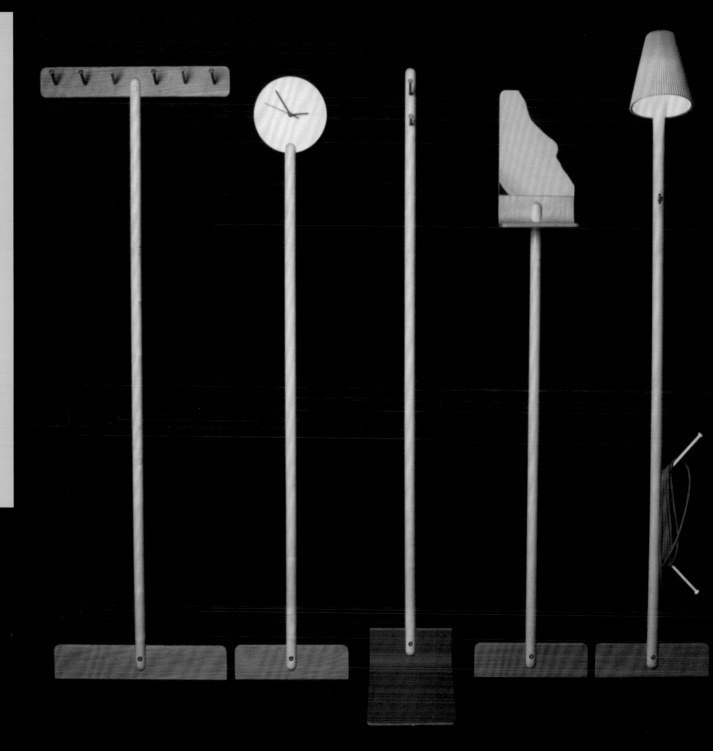

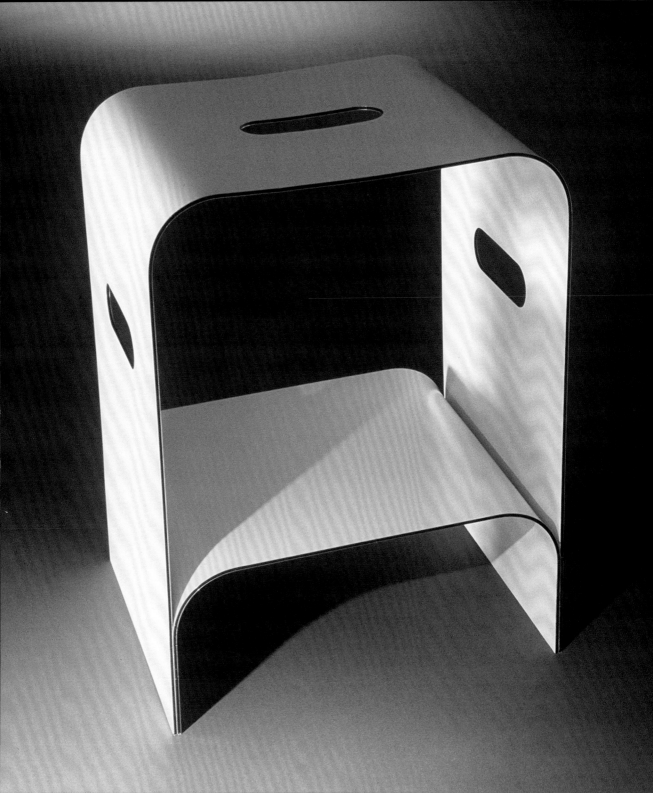

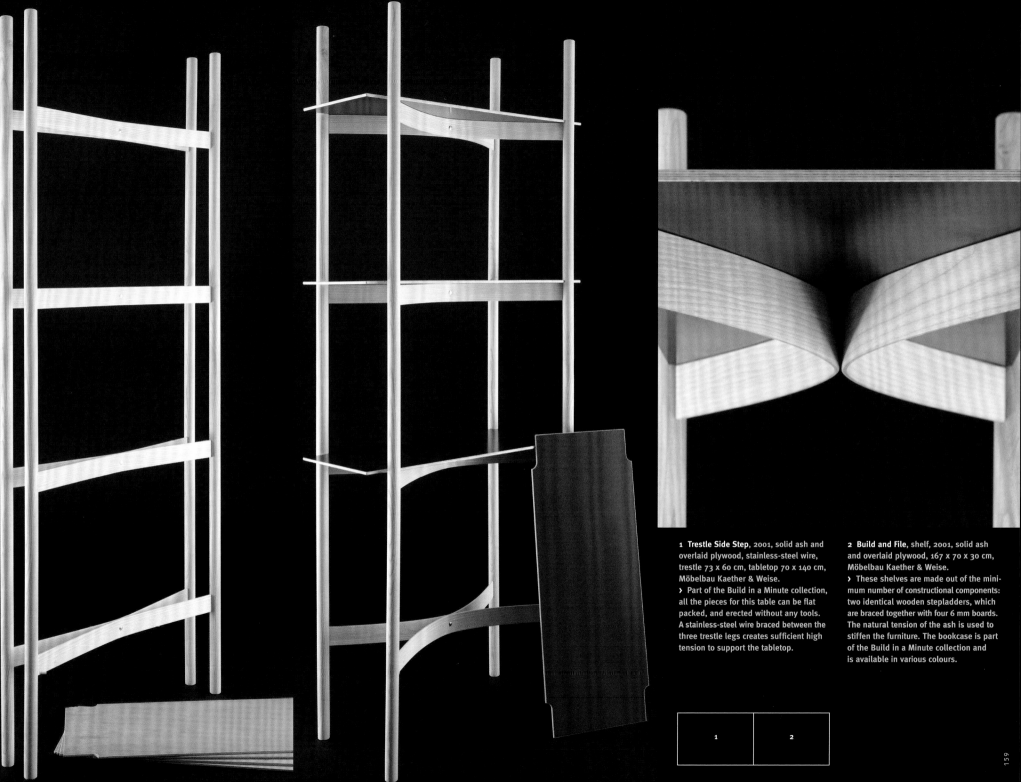

1 Trestle Side Step, 2001, solid ash and overlaid plywood, stainless-steel wire, trestle 73 x 60 cm, tabletop 70 x 140 cm, Möbelbau Kaether & Weise.

› Part of the Build in a Minute collection, all the pieces for this table can be flat packed, and erected without any tools. A stainless-steel wire braced between the three trestle legs creates sufficient high tension to support the tabletop.

2 Build and File, shelf, 2001, solid ash and overlaid plywood, 167 x 70 x 30 cm, Möbelbau Kaether & Weise.

› These shelves are made out of the minimum number of constructional components: two identical wooden stepladders, which are braced together with four 6 mm boards. The natural tension of the ash is used to stiffen the furniture. The bookcase is part of the Build in a Minute collection and is available in various colours.

1	2

JOAN GASPAR BARCELONA

Joan Gaspar learned design the old-fashioned way. After studying at the Escuela de Artes y Oficios (School of Applied Arts) in Barcelona, he served his apprenticeship with Lluís Porqueras in the Barcelona lighting firm Vapor. From Porqueras, a master of lamp design, Gaspar learned two important things: that good design 'tries to be simple, without showiness' and that 'a product's true value is only appreciated with the passage of time'.

In the early 1990s, Vapor was taken over by Marset Illumination. Fortunately for the firm, Gaspar was included in the deal. Having learned the lesson of the creative craftsman well, Gaspar began another training process, this time in industrial design. His new boss at Marset had the courage and intelligence to allow him some freedom, and he soon began to show what he could achieve with the new resources at his disposal.

Gaspar made his début with the Sac (1996), a soft and squashy silicone lamp that can be bounced off the wall like a toy. He then took on a more serious and complex exercise, the design of an adjustable, flexible desk lamp. The Atila (1998) was a strong design with very convincing lines and ingenious articulations. It also had a slightly retro-look, a characteristic that was to become more evident in Gaspar's subsequent projects. The Atlas lamp (1999), for example, is nothing more than a reinvention of the spotlight. It has all the usual features, but it is dressed in a new, transparent outfit. Putting a classic Par-30 bulb inside a suit of injected polycarbonate, Gaspar achieved a beautiful effect of transparency and weightlessness, simultaneously creating a sharply technological image. His solution for the rotation system consists here of two pulleys of injected acetyl resin held in place by a double spring. This simple and ingenious solution earned him plenty of points with the ADI FAD (Asociación de Diseño Industrial del Fomento de las Artes Decorativas) jury which awarded him a Silver Delta Prize in 2001. Gaspar continued to work the retro-revival seam with Flash (2001). Bored by light sources so small that they can hardly be seen, he dared to pay tribute to the groups of spotlights that were all the rage back in the 1980s.

Among all these lamps, there are also other designs, such as the Sydney Table (2000). Gaspar is the perfect example of a young designer who has managed to integrate himself successfully into the industry. Having got his postgraduate diploma in lighting, he now wants to study in other areas. RAMÓN UBEDA

1 **Olivia**, pendant lamp, 2001, glass and metal, 34 x ø 54 cm, Marset.
› These half-sphere pendant lamps made of hand-blown glass combine tradition with innovation. An adjustable counter-balancing device sustains the lamp's centre of gravity, which varies because of the imperfections of hand-blown glass. The opaque inner core effectively funnels the light directly downwards.

2 **Sac Lamp**, 1996, silicone, polycarbonate, glass, 12 x ø 15 cm, in collaboration with Cristian Díez, Marset.

› This silicon-filled light can be mounted directly on the wall. The silicon is soft and squashy which protects the bulb if the light is thrown against a wall. The lamp comes with a long cable so it can be easily moved to a new location.

3 **Sydney**, table, 2000, aluminium, 30 x 150 x 75 cm, prototype.
› The upper surface of this aluminium coffee table slides smoothly from one side to the other. The elegance of the design derives from its apparent simplicity; the mechanism is sleek and minimal, and no attempt has been made to disguise it. The two-tier format means objects are easily accessible but do not take up valuable table space.

1	2	3

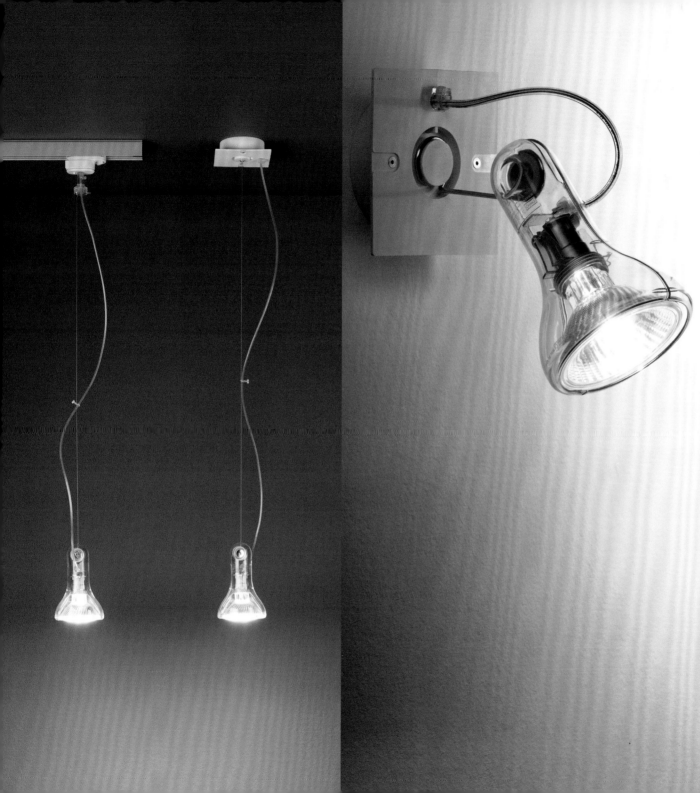

1 Atila, lamp, 1998, aluminium, polycarbonate, light shade ø 15 cm, arm 90.5 cm, Marset.
> Atila is an articulated desk lamp. Gaspar set himself two objectives in this design: one was aesthetic, that it should have a decidedly retro look; the other functional, that the second arm should be able to rotate around the same axis as the first. The light can be wall-mounted or freestanding.

2 Flash, lamp, 2001, polycarbonate, glass and metal, 10 x ø 15 cm, Marset.
> This design is based on an old-fashioned ceiling light. To create a really bright retro-look, any number of lights can be arranged together in a group. This revival of 1980s lighting is in defiance of the current trend to minimize light sources and to hide them out of sight.

3 Atlas, lamp, 1999, transparent polycarbonate, Par-30 light bulb, lighting 23 x ø 11 cm, wall support 10 x 10 cm, Marset.
> Gaspar designed a new transparent suit of clothes for the classic Par-30 bulb. The weightlessness is exaggerated by the complex system of pulleys and springs which enables the light to be moved up and down effortlessly, and the direction of the spotlight can be fine tuned.

1	3
2	

JOHANNA GRAWUNDER MILAN/SAN FRANCISCO

Johanna Grawunder is an architect who trained in California before emigrating to Italy. Since 1985 she has been a partner in the prestigious Sottsass Associati architectural practice in Milan. She also has her own studio, the Studio Grawunder, established in 1995, which operates in Milan and San Francisco.

Lowriders, customized cars with lowered suspension and elaborate interiors, have cult status in parts of America. They were the inspiration for Johanna Grawunder's furniture collection (2001) of the same name. 'Lowriders are about complete Individualism', she explains. The collection was a move away from her previous experiments in abstract design – particularly light installations – and an attempt to produce substantial pieces of furniture. She dedicated herself to achieving comfortable proportions and to using high-tech upholstery fabric, combined with a splash of chrome. Each piece is named after a real lowrider. Juan's Slammed Monte, for example, is a beautifully proportioned and worked chair in the International style. The twist is that the upholstery is rubber and the traditional bolster cushions are made from reflective material. There is also a high-beam headlight mounted in the back of the seat. Hot Impala boasts a green neon light shining from beneath a brushed-steel frame. Grawunder's use of unusual materials is also evident in the use of kitsch disco-ball tiling on a curved, wall-mounted mini-bar called Sweet '55 Effie (2001).

Grawunder seeks to celebrate in her work the forms created by Modernist architects such as Le Corbusier and Eileen Gray. She refers to this practice as 'first quality perception'. The Grawunder magic begins to operate when she 'works over' these forms, focusing on the 'second quality perceptions' of colour, texture and materials. Personal idiosyncrasy is the 'third perception', and this manifests itself in accessories and oddball additions. Remember the headlight?

Grawunder's interpretation of Modernism is fascinating. When all around her are mimicking the forms of the Modernist movement, and the current interest in the Scandinavian tradition has spawned a billion blonde wood units, Grawunder has brought something new to the table. As she says: 'When I see the thousandth version of a chic and minimal sofa or chair, I want to be nihilistic and take it to the chop shop.'

Grawunder's inspiration is drawn from myriad sources, including contemporary culture and technical disciplines such as architecture and heavy machinery. She is currently working on new collections for Italian manufacturers Flos and Salviati. LAURA HOUSELEY

1 **Loco '64**, table, 2001, liquid-rubber-painted wood, spotlight, transparent cord, 60 x 40 x 40 cm, Post Design Gallery.
> Part of the 2001: Lowrider collection, this is intended to be an ironic design. It consists of three simple components: a black table, a light bulb and a chunky electric flex. The bulb is fastened underneath the table, giving off a curious, almost demonic, dim red glow. That the bulb and flex are not obscured is pivotal to the whole design.

2 **Juan's Slammed Monte**, bench, 2001, liquid-rubber-painted wood, polyester upholstery, reflective silver ribbons, fluorescent light, bench 35 x 180 x 80 cm, cushions ø 22 cm, Post Design Gallery.
> In this design the clever use of lighting transforms an unremarkable bench into a striking object: a fluorescent spotlight has been built into the top; cylindrical, reflective cushions emit a subtle glow; and the main light shines out from a concealed source beneath the bench.

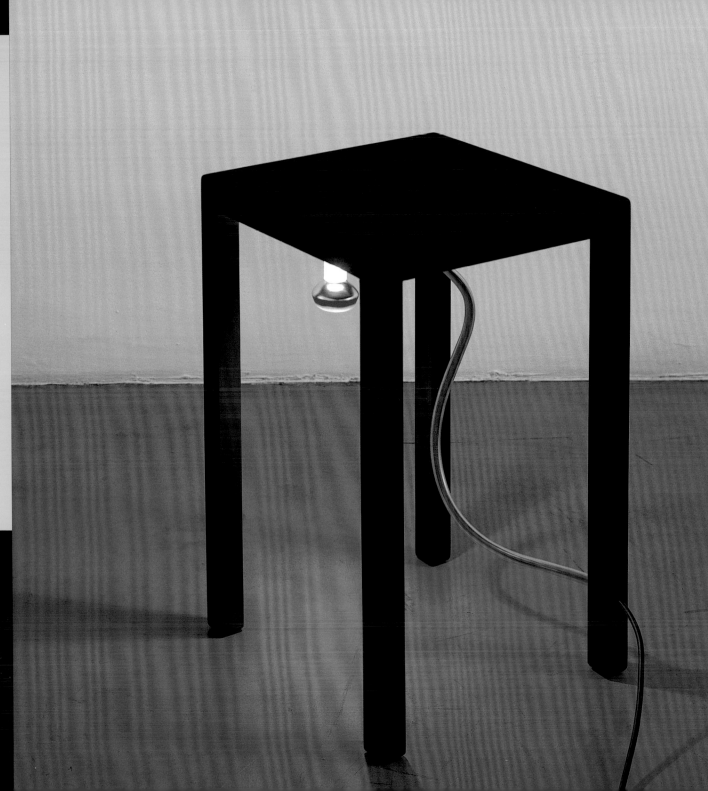

1	2

1 **Hot Impala**, sofa, 2001, steel frame, foam cushion, polyester upholstery, green fluorescent light, 62 x 120 x 82 cm, Post Design Gallery.
› This sofa consists of a sturdy steel frame and a dense foam cushion. A green neon light under the sofa gives it an effect of hovering.

2 **Art 02**, lamp, 1997, mirror, fluorescent light, 80 x 120 x 15 cm, Post Design Gallery.
› The dazzling effect of this light is achieved by a myriad of narrow mirror strips arranged at slightly different angles, thereby amplifying and deflecting the light in all directions.

3 **F4**, lamp, 1999, aluminium, fluorescent and halogen light, 100 x 169 x 34 cm, Post Design Gallery.
› This light consists of a rectangular sheet of formed aluminium painted exactly the same shade as the walls.

| 1 | 2 | 3 |

KONSTANTIN GRCIC MUNICH

Among the younger generation of German designers, Konstantin Grcic is in every respect an exception. Neither he nor his design attitude fit in with the norms of German training or any template for German product-development. Grcic studied at the Royal College of Art in London. All of his work to date has been characterized by a craftsman-like seriousness, meticulous research into the recent history of design and architecture, and a deep interest in technology. From the beginning of his first independent works, and running through to the present day, his product-developments represent associations with familiar everyday objects, with a clear typology.

Although the compulsive quest for invention in design generally leads to very mediocre variations on already familiar solutions, Konstantin Grcic does careful research before putting his stamp on his design solutions, having carefully weighed up many components, such as the choice of material, technology and dimension. He looks for 'the extraordinary in the everyday', making functional products with a subtle aesthetic component, such as Mayday (1998). Sometimes the products are simply practical and beautiful, but these obvious qualities often conceal complex technical innovations. In the Relations Glasses (1999), he stacks a series of glasses in a simple and unexpected way, using a step inside each glass.

The industry has not yet reached a point where such innovative ideas can translate into mass production. As a result, many of Grcic's designs, although conceived as large editions, end up being realized by high-class manufacturers or small workshops. Grcic's work tends to be better represented in the press than on the factory floor, giving an insight into the complex state of affairs that is holding back the development of design. There is a great distance between an actual idea and its industrial realization. With few exceptions, industry tends to pursue the adaptation of successful products, keeping risk to a minimum. This way, manufacturers may implement technical developments but are likely to ignore creative innovations.

Konstantin Grcic is also an enthusiastic planner of spatial concepts. Over the years he has developed a subtle sense of sophisticated architecture for product presentation, attracting attention by altering our perceptions about the display of commodities. The result is always simple, almost austere.

Grcic's 'design actions' are works in progress, always striving piece by piece for greater authenticity and knowledge. The phrase 'it's not the road you walk it's the walking' comes to mind when I see his work. HANSJERG MAIER-AICHEN

1 Chaos Side Chair, 2001, polyurethane foam, leather or fabric, steel, 74 x 66 x 90 cm, ClassiCon.
> This was Grcic's first piece of upholstered furniture. The seat is narrow in profile, yet opulent in the front and rear views. It is a sort of magical throne, which ennobles everyday situations, such as sitting, waiting or observing, and gives them an aura of something special. The frame is made out of steel tubing with rubber webbing, and the upholstery is available in a selection of fabrics or leather.

2 Relations Glasses, 1999, pressed glass, decanter 52cl, goblet 32cl, whiskey 30cl, universal 23cl, cocktail 12cl, tray ø 34 cm, bowls ø 5.8/7.5/9/12 cm, iittala.
> The design of these glasses came from a subtle detail: taking a classic, cone-shaped glass, Grcic changed the internal wall thickness from thin to thick to create a small step on the inside of the glass. This step acts as the stop for stacking the next glass and it is also a detail that can only be produced in pressed glass.

1-27

1 Chef Microwave, 2000, stainless steel, field 40 x 50 cm, small pot ø 19, medium pot ø 29.5, large pot ø 33 cm, Whirlpool Europe.
› Chef tries to make the microwave become a more natural cooking device. All the technical components are discreetly hidden beneath the top of the cooking station. The pots have big cylindrical handles.

2 H2O, bucket with lid, 1997, polypropylene, 32 x ø 32 cm, Authentics.
› Authentics stand for a functional simplicity in design. H2O is just a bucket.

3 Mayday, lamp, 1998, polypropylene, 55 x ø 21 cm, Flos.
› This portable lamp is a practical tool that comes in handy in all sorts of expected and unexpected situations. It has a practical handle, which incorporates the on/off switch, two spikes to wind up the 5-metre-long cable, and a big hook to install the lamp wherever needed.

4 ONE, chair, 2002, die-cast aluminium, 82 x 60 x 60 cm, Magis.
› The cast aluminium body of this stackable chair is as pure as a graphic illustration. It is composed of lines and planes in space, almost like a constructivist sculpture. It is a timeless design that seems immune to the vagaries of fashion.

	1		4
1		3	
	2		

MARTÍ GUIXÉ BARCELONA

Martí Guixé is an extraordinary character – one of those people who seem capable of reinventing the world. His first designs revolved around food. He made his debut in 1997 with the SPAMT montage in the H2O gallery in Barcelona. In essence, SPAMT was simply a reinvention of a traditional Catalan snack. In Guixé's modernized, universal version, traditional bread spread with tomatoes and olive oil became a snack for the times we live in. You could even eat it while you surfed the Web, without dripping oil all over the keyboard. After SPAMT came the Techno-Tapas (1997) and many other creative exercises with food.

Guixé studied interior design in Barcelona and industrial design in Milan, but when it comes to introductions, he defines himself as a 'Technograph', a 'MultiTalent' or, more recently, as an 'Ex-designer' – the word that appears on his business card. For those that do not know Guixé, such a presentation might seem somewhat affected, to say the least. People familiar with him, however, feel that if such a character did not exist it would be necessary to invent him, immediately.

Guixé has managed to stake out a territory of his own within the design world, a profession that is increasingly uniform and in thrall to industry. His work consists of constructing ideas, and he works within parameters that do not conform to the conventional norms of consumer society. Guixé uses his own formula, the Mandorla, which he describes as his own particular way of thinking. It can be visited at www.guixe.com. The Mandorla is composed of equal parts of fun, magic and iconography, with a dash of functionality. It is a method that has nothing to do with inspiration, a more or less mechanical process that handles abstract concepts capable of providing solutions to specific commissions. Take the Flamp (1997), for instance: a phosphorescent lamp conceived as an emergency light; or the Galería H2O chair (2000), which can be adapted to the size of the user by simply piling books on the seat.

These designs, a lamp and a chair, are at first sight two of the most conventional projects from a creative talent who can even extract a host of surprises from a roll of adhesive tape, transforming it into a soccer ball (Football Tape, 2000), a baroque frame (do frame, 2000) or a stretch of motorway (Autoband, 1999). RAMÓN UBEDA

1 Aprons, 1998, cotton, full apron 110 x 82 cm, waisted apron 82 x 75 cm, Authentics.
> The inspiration for these aprons was drawn from origami. Each apron is made from a single piece of fabric and instead of using conventional ribbons or fasteners the aprons are secured by an ingenious system of folding and geometry.

2 Autoband, 1999, polypropylene with adhesive, 15 x ø 10 cm, Galería H2O.
> In Autoband adhesive tape has been reborn as a children's game. Decorated with a pattern that evokes a three-lane motorway, Autoband can be attached to any surface, enabling children to race their cars on an infinite number of routes. Instructions for the toy are in the form of a comic strip.

3 do frame, 2000, adhesive tape, 5 x ø 10 cm, presented in the international exhibition 'do+Droog Design=do create'.
> This adhesive tape has been printed with an ornate, baroque pattern. The idea is that people should stick the tape around the sides of posters, to imitate real paintings in frames.

172

1	2	3

AUTOBAND KIT

OPEN IT.

2 CARS
SCALE 1:250

15 Km 3way
High Way
SCALE 1:250

parental advice:

WARNING!

playing with **autoband,** children learn
abstract concepts such as "lobbing" "politics"
"ecology" "public opinion" "territory".

HOW TO PLAY:

STICK Autoband
on any SURFACE

DO TRUMPETS...

CLOVERLEAFS

* ID FRAME *
MARTI GUIXE * IROOG DESIGN *
VINYL TAPE * 50 M *
I AM A TENANT IN A BUILDING HE
OWNS. THE BUILDING MANAGER HE
HAS HIRED IS NOT COMMUNICATING
IMPORTANT INFORMATION TO HIM *

AUTOBAND
Design: Marti Guixé
Editor: Galería H₂O Barcelona

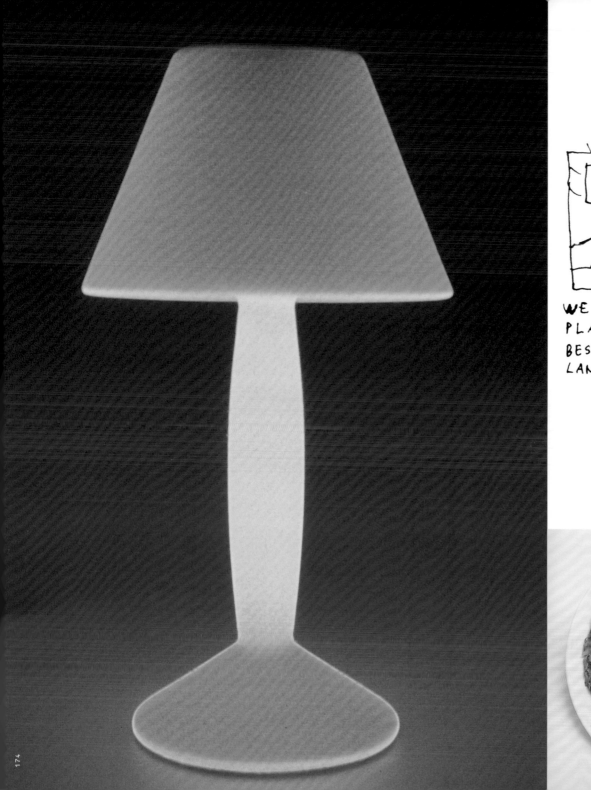

WE RECOMEND YOU
PLACE FLAMP
BESIDE A CONVENTIONAL
LAMP

LIGHT IS ON

TURN OFF!

YOU HAVE 20 MIN.
TIME BEFORE YOU
ARE IN DARK.

ENJOY THE SHADOW

GALERIA H₂O CHAIR

AT 3

AT 6

AT 13

AT 25 ₁₁₁

AT 90

GUIXÉ 2000

A CHAIR FOR YOUR WHOLE LIFE

1 Flamp, lamp, 1997, painted resin, 15 x 8 x 8 cm, Galería H2O.
> Instead of being powered by electricity, this innovative and energy-saving lamp is recharged from natural light and can provide illumination in complete darkness for up to 20 minutes.

2 Sponsored Food, 1997, edible material, Galería H2O.
> Printing logos on foodstuffs as diverse as beans or potato omelettes is a new and highly effective means of communication. It is thought that the impact brand logos have while literally being eaten is much greater than that achieved through conventional advertising.

3 Galería H2O Chair, 2000, painted resin, 45 x 80 x 20 cm, Galería H2O.
> This chair was commissioned by the gallery-owner, publisher and writer, Joaquim Ruiz Millet. His brief stipulated simply that the design should be closely related to books. Guixé interpreted this literally and designed a disproportionate chair frame, on which real books are piled. The height is adjustable by means of adding or removing books, a system which is ideal for children as the chair can be adapted as they grow.

1	3
2	

175

ALFREDO HÄBERLI ZURICH

Häberli's Swiss family ran a restaurant in Argentina but it was the cars on the nearby racing track that first sparked his interest in design. And it was his experience of his sister's Golf GTI after the family moved back to Switzerland when he was 13 that made him realize that there is a whole industry in designing objects. Finally, when Häberli saw an exhibition of the work of the leading Italian designer Achille Castiglioni he became clear about his own career path. After graduating in industrial design from the Hohere Schule für Gestaltung in Zurich in 1991, where he was awarded the Diploma Prize, Häberli first set up in partnership with Christophe Marchand and then in 2000 established his own company, Alfredo Häberli Design Development Atelier.

Häberli's work is characterized by its breadth – he is interested in architecture, curating exhibitions, making books as well as products – and quality. And his designs have that elusive 'ah ha' element – simple, clever and obvious solutions to a problem that make you wonder why nobody has thought of them before. Ginger (2001), a barstool with a shelf under the seat to store your bag or papers Is one such product. The stools were part of a whole design concept that Häberli did for the Ginger – more than sushi restaurant in Zurich. Häberli also thinks about how we use an object from a practical point of view. This has led to the Solitaire low chair with integrated table (2001) and the work in progress Hang by Hand coat hanger with handle. Both these projects show the influence of the Italian modernist designers of the 1950s and 1960s, even down to the use of the coloured plastic for the coat hanger. Häberli is not, however, a retro-romantic – he is inspired by the designers of the past such at Castiglioni but filters their aesthetic and comes up with something new.

The Origo table service (2000), made for the Swedish manufacturer Rörstrand, was the result of Häberli examing how people spend time at home. The china is stackable so it can be carried from the kitchen to the living/dining room in one go and is meant for use when you are in a hurry and do not wish to set the table properly. The informality of its use is underlined in the design – the striped elements mixed with the white china makes the whole ensemble swing. STEFAN YTTERBORN

1 **Ginger Stool**, 2001, upholstery and stainless steel, 80 x 39 x 37 cm, 54 x 36 x 32 cm, 40 x 38 x 34 cm, Bd Ediciones de Diseño.
> This range of stools was designed for a restaurant. The upholstery cover of the high barstool has been used to provide a shelf immediately beneath the seat, which is ideal for the storage of personal belongings.

2 **Solitaire**, chair, 2001, upholstery and metal, 65 x 93 x 62 cm, Offecct.
> Solitaire is an evolution of the auditorium chair; it consists of a low seat combined with a small table, but unlike the majority of auditorium chairs, Solitaire is irresistibly comfortable. The chair is freestanding and can face any direction

| 1 | 1 | 2 |

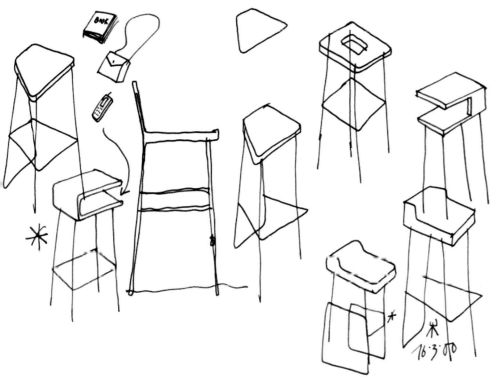

16·3·00

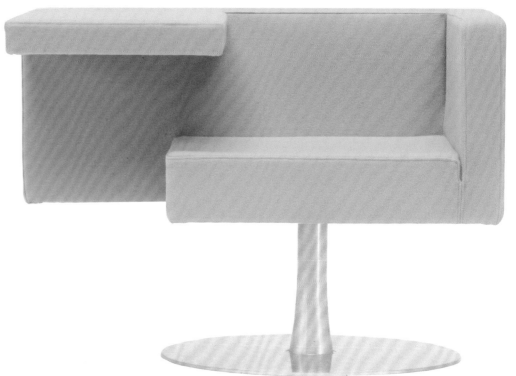

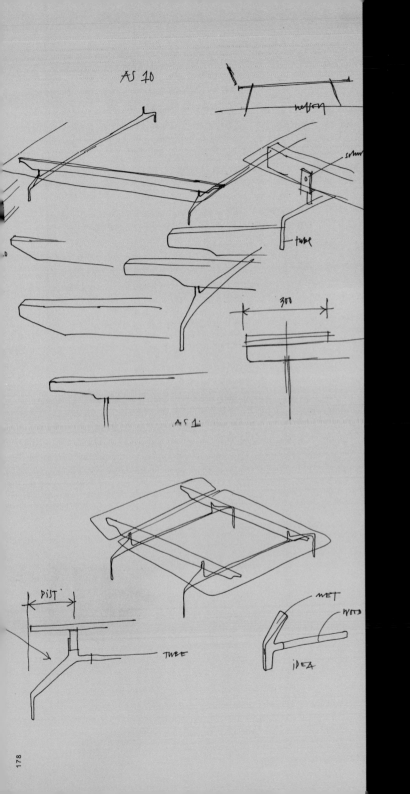

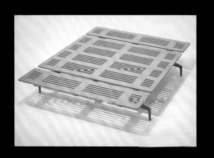

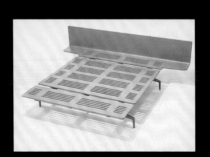

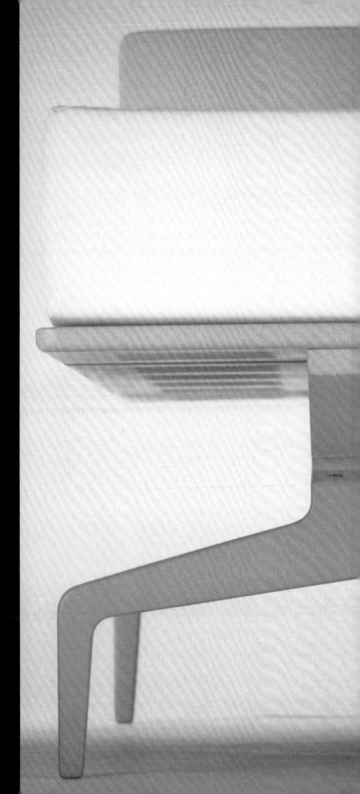

1 **LegnoLetto**, bed, 2001, wood and aluminium, 52 x 160 x 180 cm, Alias.
› This modular wooden bed has no frame and the legs are not attached to the corners. It has a large number of components, which allows for easy transportation and different choices when assembling.

2 **Hang by Hand**, coathanger, 1999, poly-carbonate, 30 x 42 x 1,5 cm, prototype.
› The novelty of this product is the incorporated handle, which enables the hanger to be held without touching the item of clothing.

3 **Essence**, glasses, 2000–2, clear glass, red wine 45cl 23 cm, white wine 33cl 23 cm, sweet wine 15cl 19cm, water 35cl 10 cm, jug 100cl 30 cm, iittala.
› The challenge here was to create a balance between modernity and tradition, shape and function. The 'essence' has been found in details such as the conical stem, the completely flat bottom plate and the trapeze shape of the bowl. The pink carafe evokes the colour of a drop of wine.

4 **Origo**, table service, 2000, porcelain, biggest plate ø 26 cm, Rörstrand.
› The aim was to create everyday table-ware which is both portable and has a variety of applications. There are stacking rings on the bottom of the plates for fixing cups and bowls, and the decorative elements are uncomplicated.

	2	
1		
	3	4

THOMAS HEATHERWICK LONDON

An amazing window installation at Harvey Nichols, Knightsbridge, 1997: Dr Caligari-type structures completely ignoring the window panes. I can't remember the merchandise displayed in the windows, if any, but the building embraced by these structures is still a vivid memory. Who did it? What did it take to convince a department store to go for it? How much control do you need to realize it? What has he done before? I had to find out and that is how I became aware of Thomas Heatherwick, an ex-furniture graduate from the Royal College of Art in London.

Materials House (1999) at the Science Museum in London was another big 'who-done-it'. From that point on, Thomas Heatherwick had to live up to great expectations, and he did. Each of his projects celebrates a big idea, and achieves some great impossibility, be it in materials, geometry or structure. The pleasure of creation is equal to the delight rendered to viewers.

Although Thomas' work is largely on an architectural scale, you would never for one minute mistake it for the work of an architect. The work comes from a different discourse. Materials are pushed to their limits. For example, miles and miles of clingfilm are used, proving that clingfilm can be both a structural material and an expressive medium (Identity Crisis, Glasgow, 1999).

Twisting a wall as if it were a timber slat, thus forcing it to transform into a roof, is an obvious example of scale shifting by someone who has previously enjoyed twisting a timber slat. The rolling bridge proposal (Berkshire, 2001) is another example of a micro-mechanism going big, having a delightful presence whether rolled or spread out.

When you look at Thomas' projects you can trace most of them back to geometry and the materiality of small things. Plank (2000) is a lonely example, but I have no doubt that it will be followed by lots of new, and in Thomas' case seriously new, small things. In the same way that the big things benefited enormously from their small origins, so will the small things enjoy the reduction process.

Thomas' latest work is the spectacular Blue Carpet (2002) in Newcastle upon Tyne. It is a public square on a vast scale, made of tiles cast with minute chips of recycled blue bottles. The small here is inseparable from the big. RON ARAD

1 Materials House, 1999, mixed media, 6 x 3 m, Science Museum, London.
> A tactile sandwich of 213 different materials, which contains 'everything that anything can be made of', builds up a stripy 3-dimensional form that resembles a contour map. Materials have been donated by 80 companies from all over the world, and their properties have been studied to avoid decay or adverse chemical reactions.

2 Autumn Intrusion, 1997, birch aero-ply, polystyrene, 1 x 20 m, Harvey Nichols.
> The project aimed to relate the shop windows to the grand architecture of the building, and to integrate them in one idea that unifies the entire façade. A single element twists its way through the shop-front, weaving in and out and climbing up the windows. The project exploits the inherent lightness and tensile strength of the mixed media.

3 Identity Crisis, 1999, clingfilm, galvanized steel, Glasgow 1999.
> For an exhibition of contemporary product design, the gallery space at the Lighthouse was arranged so that the 400 exhibits were placed in simple galvanized steel boxes suspended by clingfilm between cast-iron columns.

1	2	3

180

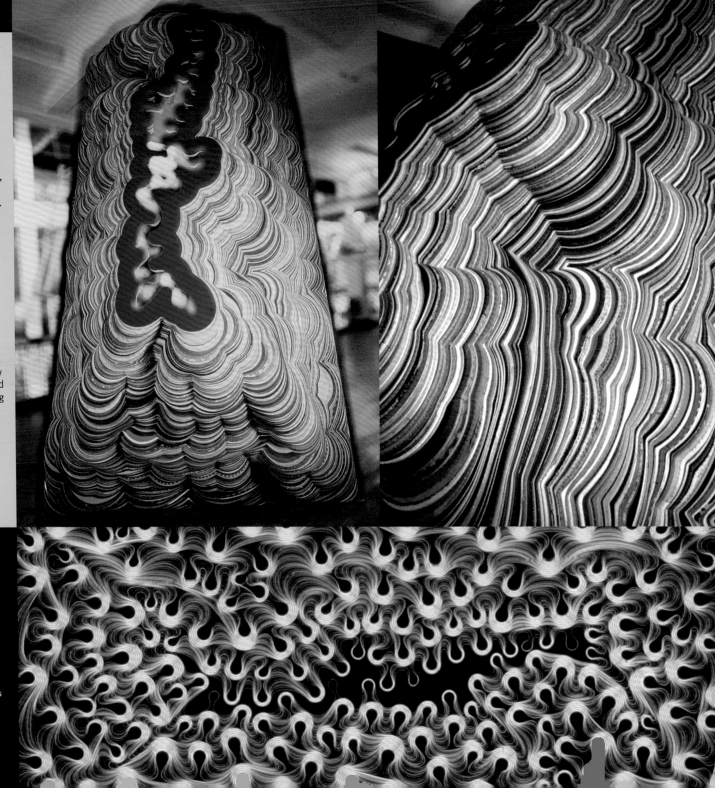

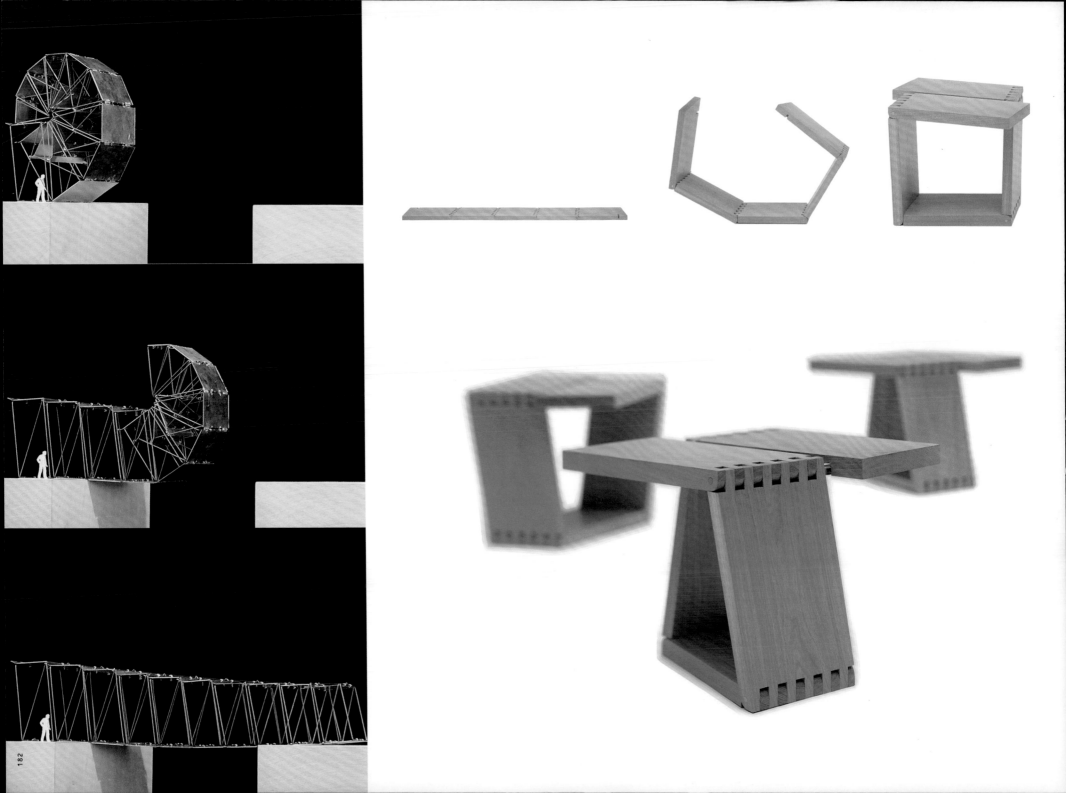

1 Rolling Bridge, 2001, 200 x 20 x 20 m, structural engineering: Packman Lucas Consulting Engineers.
> This bridge is a covered pedestrian walkway with a roof that gets progressively lower towards one end. As the bridge closes, each section lifts up and over its neighbour until the whole walkway has been rolled up, allowing boats to pass. The bridge has a 20-metre span and is operated by a single cable without complex electronics or hydraulics. In its upright position, the bridge has a sculptural, shell-like, form.

2 Plank, furniture, 2000, wood, 30.5 x 182.9 cm, Keen.
> People have been turning planks into furniture for centuries. Here the plank is the furniture, it functions as either a side table or a stool. Five folds are set at slight angles, causing the plank to make a spiral as it folds. The joints must be engineered to extremely high tolerances in order to fit perfectly together and fold well.

3 Blue Carpet Square, 2002, mixed media, Newcastle upon Tyne.
> The square is a rethinking of a pedestrian site, where art could play a part. It has a colourful surface into which fragments of recycled glass have been pressed into resin-based paving blocks. Benches are formed by peeling back the tiles, revealing a pattern of coloured neon lights.

1	2	3

SAM HECHT LONDON

Discreet, thoughtful, ever polished and professional, Sam Hecht's designs seem as effortless as his manner. In the space of six years Hecht has progressed from design student to Head of Industrial Design at IDEO, London. Since his appointment in 1999, he has produced new typologies in computing and printing, prototypes for cross-cultural breakfasting, soft computer hardware, and in-store design choreography.

No matter how complex the project, Hecht achieves results that are smooth, quiet and visually restful. His high-tech products take advantage of the most recent technology and acknowledge the latest evolutions in human behaviour. Fabrications, produced for Eleksen in 2001, use smart textiles to weave design and technology into soft machines. The keyboard, for example, responds to stroking rather than typing, and the Conference Telephone is designed to sit at the centre of the table, a receptacle which words drop into and emerge from. These products are not sci-fi inventions; they use technology to fulfil real needs without going overboard into fiction. For example, the watch-phone made with Elektex (2001) has two distinct modes: when wrapped around the wrist it functions as a watch, when unwrapped it becomes a flat phone. One of Hecht's most recent sets of products has been the range of items developed for the Prada stores (2002). There are hand-held staff devices, clips and customer cards that locate the products in the building, making the enormous boutique more easily accessible. Information flows seamlessly from the staff device to ensure, for example, the delivery of clothes from stock room to dressing room. When a client enters the store with his/her card, data is automatically transmitted to the staff so they can offer a fully personalized service.

Hecht's lower-tech products are characterized by an easy evidence and aesthetics. In designing the world's smallest two-slice toaster for Matsushita (1998) he confronted the problems of bringing English toast into the Japanese home. The toaster is a new hybrid, adapted to limited space and different bread sizes.

One of Hecht's latest projects is a no-frills, polyurethane lampshade, called 12 Light Years (2002). Hecht has created a shade like an elastic skin that slips effortlessly over an ungainly long-life bulb, giving it a traditional round shape and a friendly glow.

In 2002 he opened the Sam Hecht Studio in collaboration with IDEO, and he looks set to take his simple, straightforward and efficient style to new levels. LISA WHITE

1 Conference Telephone, 2001, methacrylate, ABS, pressure-formed Elektex, 8 x 21 x 21 cm, Eleksen.
› The microphone in this conference telephone can detect voices at long range so only one device is needed on a table. The lid is removed and placed underneath to create the back-volume for the speaker, thus transforming a neutral desktop product into a communications device.

2 Soft Keyboard, 2001, pressure-formed Elektex, foamed silicone, 2.8 x 30.2 x 14 cm, Eleksen.

› This keyboard rests either on the lap or on a table and connects directly to a computer or a television set.

3 Soft Phone, 2001, siliconized rubber, Elektex, 21.5 x 4.6 x 1.8 cm, Eleksen.
› This mobile phone has a squeezable and bendable body. The phone module migrates easily between the soft phone and the wrist phone. It uses a mirroring LCD interface, controlled from the back by the forefinger. Access to the phonebook is by stroking the graphic scale on the front.

4 Soft Remote Control, 2001, pressure-formed Elektex, foamed silicone, 14 x 6.2 x 2.8 cm, Eleksen.
› Using Elektex allows both sides of the remote to be used. One keypad is for text input for web TV, the other for TV control.

	2
1	
	3	4

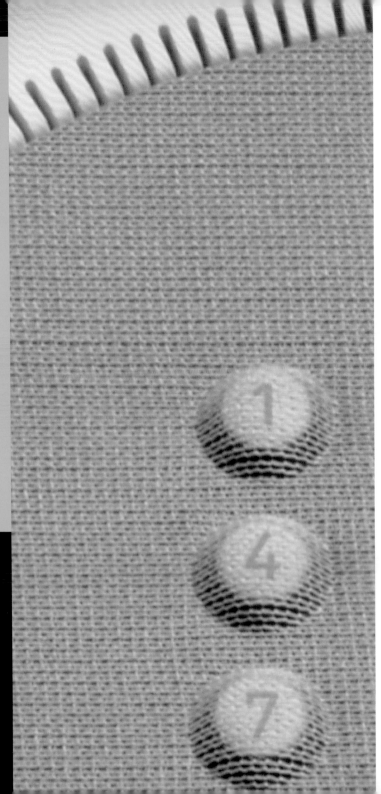

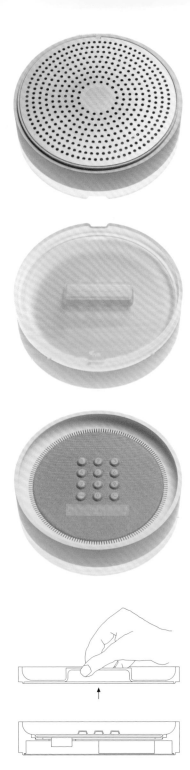

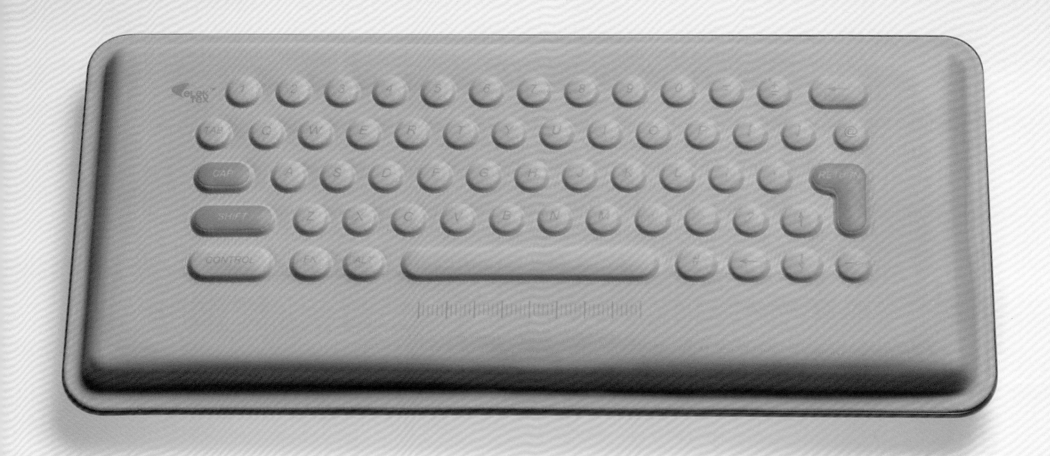

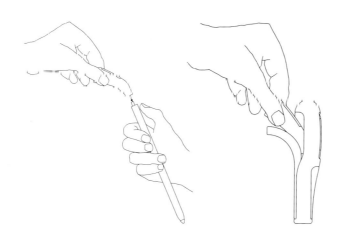

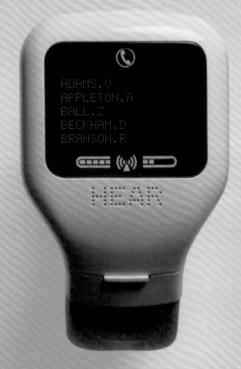

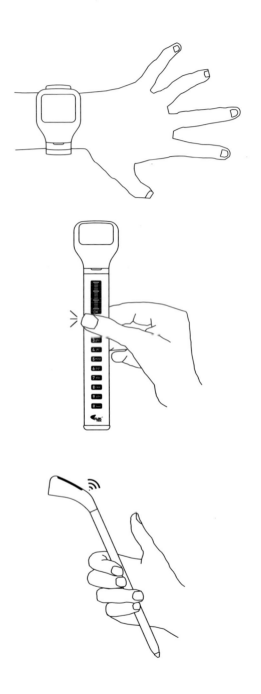

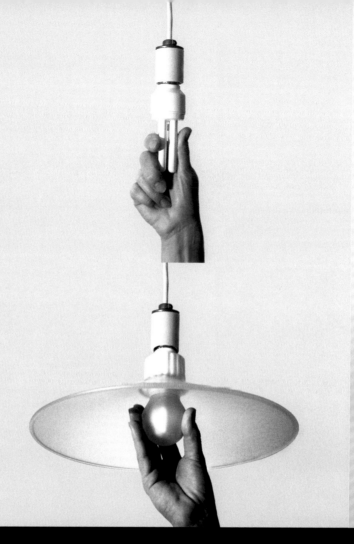

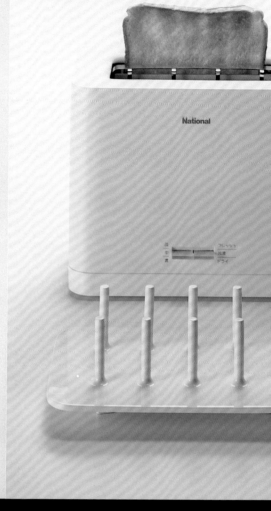

1 Soft Wrist Phone, 2001, aluminium die-casting, painted/anodized finish, 11.2 x 6 x 2.5 cm, Eleksen.
> This is a telehone/watch. To use the phone the user has to take off the wrist watch and to unroll the band.

2 Working Lunch, 2001, epoxy coated MDF silkstrate/glass, polycarbonate, anodized aluminium alloy, 220 x 340 x 300 cm, Steelcase Strafor.
> The restaurant is such an effective location to do business that the designer has taken it as a model for this new office system.

3 Prada Staff Devices, 2002, staff device, polycarbonate, silicone, acrylic, acetyl, 20 x 10.7 x 6.5 cm, charging block, ABS, PET, 20 x 14.4 x 10 cm, Prada.
> Designed to be used in Prada stores, these choreographic devices allow the staff to pay closer attention to customers' needs.

4 12 Light Years, 2002, UV stabilized polyurethane, 14 x 30 x 30 cm, Proverb.
> Made from a single polyurethane moulding that slips over an ecologically sound bulb, the light will last for up to 12 years.

5 XY Toaster, 1998, polypropylene, tin plate, ceramic, 18 x 15 x 12 cm, Matsushita.
> This is the smallest two-slice toaster on the market, yet it has a large toasting capacity. The ceramic lid keeps the product clean and serves as a toast rack.

| 1 | 2 | 5 |
| | 3 | 4 |

It is impossible to consider the many successes of Richard Hutten without acknowledging the phenomenon of contemporary Dutch design. Droog Design, a collective of Dutch designers of which Hutten was a founder member, exhibited for the first time at Milan's Salone del Mobile in 1993. Hutten, who had graduated from the Design Academy in Eindhoven only two years earlier, and had just established his own studio, was part of the show. International acclaim followed.

Asked to describe the style that has brought him so much success, Hutten refers to Gerrit Rietveld and Mart Stam, Holland's greatest modernist designers. 'My conceptual and minimal approach is similar to Rietveld. What I add is humour. The result is Happy-Modernism.' On the same subject, he says: 'Styleless is my style. For me style refers to shape and form. If possible, I don't make a form, I take a form. By transforming, repeating, stacking, changing the material, etc., a new design is made.' If neither materials nor form dictate Hutten's style, then how does he measure a successful design? In his own words, 'When a design is good you don't question the size, material and all the other elements – you simply enjoy.'

Hutten believes Table-chair (1995) to be one of his most influential pieces. The chair is divided into two parts, then stacked. Not only did Table-chair effectively launch Hutten's career and serve as a signature piece, it is also his most collected piece to date. And the now famous form has spawned a family of equally inspired designs from Hutten.

Sexy Relaxy (2000) was a chair designed for the Tokyo furniture manufacturer E&Y. The aesthetic differences between this and Table-chair are adequate proof of Hutten's stance on 'styleless' design. Sexy Relaxy is a provocative design in white moulded plastic, with a split base that encourages the sitter to sit with legs wide apart – hence the product's name.

Hutten's client list reads like a *Who's Who* of contemporary furniture manufacturing. Despite this prestigious profile, he has many ambitions yet to fulfil. He would like to design a one-shot, injection-moulded chair and work on a concept for a hotel. Products such as cutlery and crockery have yet to make it into his repertoire, and even a house is not beyond his imagination.

After a decade of success, Hutten remains one of the freshest talents on the design circuit, and the taste for Dutch design shows no signs of abating. LAURA HOUSELEY

1 Coattrunk, coatstand, 2000, steel, 200 x ø 45 cm, Pure Design.
› This coat stand has been conceived like a tree, with 'branches' of different lengths and heights that act as hooks. Each one projects from the 'trunk' at different angles, selected at random. The outline of Coattrunk resembles the shape of a leaf.

2 The Cross, table and benches, 1994, maple, PU-coated soft-foam, 75 x 120 x 200 cm, Droog Design.
› The Cross is a signature piece which was designed for an exhibition 'Abitare il tempo' in Verona, Italy, in which 15 designers were asked to make a piece on the theme 'a journey to Italy'. Hutten took the symbol of the Catholic Church and transformed it into a table and benches.

3 Sexy Relaxy, chair, 2000, polyester, 80 x 70 x 60 cm, E&Y, Tokyo.
› This chair was designed for an exhibition organized by E&Y for which the theme was 'relax, clean, sexy'. The original piece was designed in a numbered, limited edition, but is now being mass-produced in a wooden and upholstered version.

1	2
	3

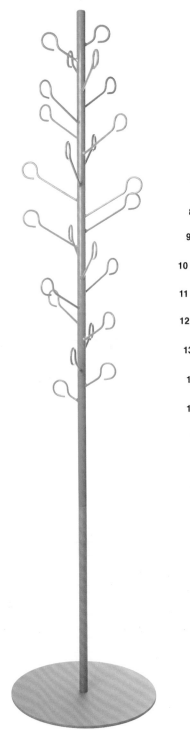

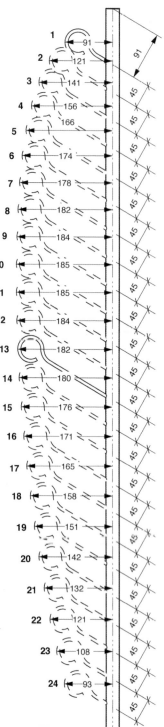

1 91
2 121
3 141
4 156
166
5
6 174
7 178
8 182
9 184
10 185
11 185
12 184
13 182
14 180
15 176
16 171
17 165
18 158
19 151
20 142
21 132
22 121
23 108
24 93

91
45

2000
125

something soft to protect the floor

ø 450

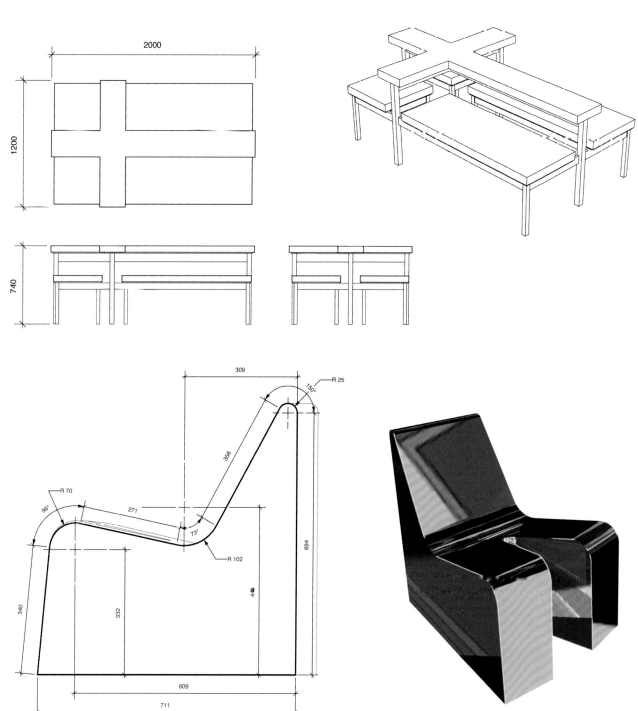

2000

1200

740

309

R 25

150°

356

R 70

96°

271

73°

R 102

694

340

332

609

711

1 **3 Minus 1**, desk and table, 1996–7, laminate birch, 110 x 160 x 60 cm, Studio Richard Hutten.
› In this furniture, the top becomes the leg and the leg becomes the beam without any visible division.

2 **Who's the Boss?**, chair, 1999, beech, plywood, 76 x 140 x 80 cm, Studio Richard Hutten.
› Here the inspiration was Hutten's young son, who believed he owned the world.

3 **What Happened?**, vases, 2001, Murano glass, various sizes, Smash by Covo.
› Hutten slashed the liquid glass on a glassblower's pipe. As he blew, the vase grew and the wound healed.

4 **One of a Kind**, 1999, Alucabond, chair 75 x 75 x 50 cm, table 76 x 100 x 70 cm, Hidden.
› The One of a Kind series was the result of a commission to create a chair out of this lightweight composite material.

5 **Zzzidt-Object 2000**, LDPE rotation-moulded, 47 x ø 55 cm, Studio Richard Hutten.
› Designed for the garden of the Central Museum, Rotterdam, this table or stool was based on a 'jumping ball'. It can be moved around the garden and the handle can also be used to hold your glass.

1	2		4	
1	3		3	5

Hisae Igarashi has a style that sets her apart from other Japanese contemporary designers. She is not driven by nostalgia for artisan skills, but is interested in using a wide range of materials, from wood, which is her favourite, to high tech such as titanium. Her products are imbued with intimacy and tranquil elegance.

In an interview with Masaya Yamamoto, published in *Comfort* magazine in December 2000, Igarashi stated that her standpoint as a designer is the one of a daily user. This is based on *seiri seiton*, which in Japanese means to arrange things and to put them in the right order. This has been the traditional task of the housekeeper, who must tidy and clean the house. This practice, which can sometimes become an obsession, is the starting point for Igarashi's design. It brings a tremendous tactile smoothness to her work and a gracious balance between absolute purity and something much more practical.

Igarashi's famous wooden chest, Tango (1997), was designed in response to an initiative by the city of Shizuoka, which was intended to reinvigorate the manufacture of traditional wooden furniture. The chest is made from maple, worked to look as though it were woven. Its curved form is soft and organic. The design has since been developed, and a cabinet and side-table have been added to the collection, using a variation on the woven pattern. The juxtaposition of mass and void is reminiscent of the work of the Arts and Crafts designer Edward William Godwin (1833–86), whose work shows Japanese influences.

Igarashi has observed that her style differs greatly from that of Shiro Kuramata, with whom she has worked for many years. However, when we consider humorous and ironic pieces such as Modern Times (1997), a laminated table shaped like a cog, or her bent titanium chair Sunny Side Up (2001), it is obvious that she will be his successor in the world of contemporary Japanese design.

Finally, I would like to mention Igarashi's interior design. A fine example is the Royal restaurant in Tokyo (2001), in which she has used wood to recreate the warm, intimate atmosphere of a mid-twentieth-century interior. Like so much of her work, the restaurant evokes a sense of nostalgia, and simultaneously expresses a unique mix of the global and the local, creating the perfect expression of our times. RYU NIIMI

1 Astral M1, mirror, 1997, screen print on maple and glass, 40 x 40 x 2.5 cm, Matsunaga.
› A geometrical pattern has been printed on the surface of this mirror; to exaggerate the illusion, the pattern has been extended to the frame, making it difficult to distinguish where the frame stops and the mirror starts.

2 Massage Chair, 2000, polyurethane foam, vinyl, 113.2 x 98.7 x 71 cm, Yudai Tachikawa.
› This chair was developed to add comfort and relaxation to massage sessions. The design supports the entire body, but the parts are arranged so that the function of the chair becomes ambiguous and far from looking like a massage chair.

3 Modern Times, tables, 1997, melanin board, Japanese line plywood, bearing, 40 x ø 30/55 cm, Igarashi Design Studio.
› These tables, available in various dimensions, are shaped as mechanical cogs and, true to their appearance, can be rotated and interconnected. The balance of these tables is critical to their success.

	2
1	3

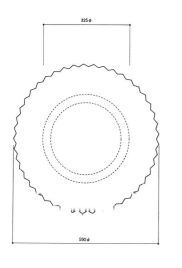

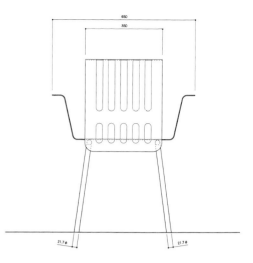

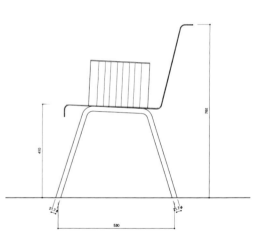

1 Tango Chest 120, 1997, maple,
100 x 120 x 45 cm, Horizumi.
> The bowed front of the drawers together
with their configuration like a brick wall
create a natural means of pulling out the
drawers.

2 Tango Cabinet 165, 1997, maple,
165 x 165 x 45 cm, Horizumi.
> This cabinet is composed of 9 boxes whose
handles are discreetly located behind the
square doors. The alternating orientation
of the boxes creates a woven effect.

3 Pure+Pure Display Shelves, 1999,
camphor wood, Pure 1 60 x 42 x 92 cm,
Pure 2 150 x 42 x 35 cm, Hashizume.
> Pure+Pure is a series of furniture that
was conceived to make use of very small
pieces of camphor wood, and in so doing
provide a space to store objects. The
round sections have been laboriously
cut and shaved with a fine-edged tool.

4 Sunny Side Up Chair, 2001, titanium,
76.2 x 65 x 62.4 cm, Ishimaru.
> This design looks more like a big titani-
um spatula than an outdoor chair. The technique used exploits the natural graduation
of titanium colours. Despite the material,
the designer has taken every precaution
to ensure that the chair is both comfortable and can withstand the elements.

1	2	
		4
3		

HELLA JONGERIUS ROTTERDAM

Working more like an artist or a scientist than an industrial designer, Hella Jongerius' hands are perpetually 'dirty'. She refers to her studio, Jongeriuslab, as a space where she experiments 'like a hyper-modern alchemist'. It contains a mass of trial pieces, rejects and retrials – but very few finished objects. In 2002 she moved her entire lab to the Vivid Gallery for two months so that visitors were able to witness the process of trial-and-error that precedes her final designs. She insists that the end result is only a moment and that it is the process itself that makes break-throughs in design, guiding her to the finished product and beyond.

Jongerius has been a key member of the Dutch company Droog Design since it was founded, when her groundbreaking Soft Vases (1994–9) in colourful polyurethane gave a subtle new twist to the concept of hardware. Her Kasese Foam Chair (1999) takes a traditional wooden African model and translates it into a high-tech folding chair in knitted carbon fibre and neoprene.

Mixing the industrial and the artisanal, Jongerius takes fragments from the past and turns them into something contemporary. When she was given some fourteenth-century pottery shards by the Boijmans Van Beuningen Museum in Rotterdam, she designed four new pots to industrial standards, and then cut a piece out of each one to correspond to the shape of a par-ticular shard. This done, she cemented the shards into the modern pots and covered them with paint generally used on the bodywork of cars, thus uniting old and new.

In 2001 Jongerius was curator of an exhibition about Delft porcelain at the Gemeentemuseum in The Hague. On this occasion she mixed price-less antiques with broken shards and contemporary pieces that were either designed by her, or by a selected group of artists and designers.

Jongerius has also moved into the world of technology. In 2001 she was commissioned by MoMA in New York to create a project for the 'Workspheres' exhibition. My Soft Office took the concept of the home office to extremes, introducing high technology in low-tech, domestic forms. Her lazy, comfort-able office included a fully articulated and wired bed, with a computer integrated in the footboard, speakers in the mattress corners and a pillow-keyboard. Jongerius' own office is in the heart of busy Rotterdam, but she is now setting up a 'no-tech' country office where she will take time to think and read, demanding a slower pace of life. LISA WHITE

1 Bed in Business, 2001, 200 x 260 cm, prototype for My Soft Office, realized for the 'Workspheres' exhibition at MoMA, New York.
› This project reconciles extreme opposites, work and rest. A large computer screen has been included in the foot of this extra-long bed, and the keyboard and mouse ball can be found in the touch pillow. Bed in Business is the ultimate symbol of relaxation and rapid modernity.

2 Embroidered Tablecloth, 2000, linen, cotton, porcelain plate, 2 x 150 x 80 cm, JongeriusLab.
› Ceramic decorations are closely related to textile techniques, such as embroidery. In this design the two become almost indis-tinguishable, as the design embroidered into the tablecloth continues uninterrupted-ly onto the surface of the ceramics.

3 Kasese Foam Chair, 1999, carbon fibre, neoprene foam, 75 x 50 x 65 cm, Cappellini.
› This folding chair is the product of com-bining a traditional African wooden chair with Western industrial design techniques. It is a new interpretation of our sensitivity towards handmade products, yet allowances are made for the prevailing attraction of things technical.

| 1 | 3 |
| 2 | |

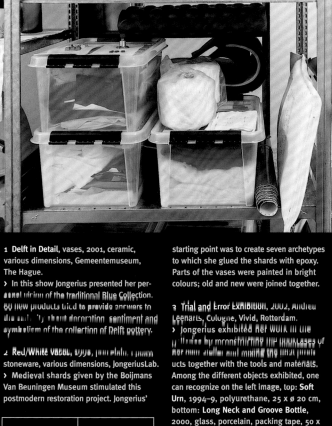

1 **Delft in Detail**, vases, 2001, ceramic, various dimensions, Gemeentemuseum, The Hague.
› In this show Jongerius presented her personal vision of the traditional Blue Collection. 60 new products tried to provide answers to the questions about decoration, sentiment and symbolism of the collection of Delft pottery.

2 **Red/White Vases**, 2000, porcelain, stoneware, various dimensions, JongeriusLab.
› Medieval shards given by the Boijmans Van Beuningen Museum stimulated this postmodern restoration project. Jongerius'

starting point was to create seven archetypes to which she glued the shards with epoxy. Parts of the vases were painted in bright colours; old and new were joined together.

3 **Trial and Error Exhibition**, 2002, Andreu Leenarts, Cologne, Vivid, Rotterdam.
› Jongerius exhibited her work in the atelier by reconstructing the showcases of her own atelier and mixing the final products together with the tools and materials. Among the different objects exhibited, one can recognize on the left image, top: **Soft Urn**, 1994–9, polyurethane, 25 x ø 20 cm, bottom: **Long Neck and Groove Bottle**, 2000, glass, porcelain, packing tape, 50 x ø 15 cm, JongeriusLab; on the right image: **B-Set Dinner Service**, range of plates, cups and pitcher, 1998, porcelain, various dimensions, DMD.

1	2	3	3

199

IOSHIKO KAWAGUCHI TOKYO

Kawaguchi's work is a rare and marvellous example of Japanese, multicultural, new-age design. She is an architect-designer capable of bringing a contemporary twist to traditional Japanese furniture, architecture, woodwork and fabrics.

Kawaguchi spent time in Vienna, and *fin-de-siècle* Viennese artists such as Otto Wagner, Josef Hofmann and Kolo Moser have been one of her main sources of inspiration and her work expresses an appreciation of the delicacy of Viennese handicraft of that period. Nonetheless, Kawaguchi treads a fine line between the Viennese Jugendstil, with its intricate surfaces, and the colourful humour of Italian design. This balance was particularly apparent in her work on an Italian restaurant in Hagi (1997). Here, she designed furniture with complex, organic forms in cast iron. There may also be a tongue-in-cheek allusion to the interior design work of Hans Hollein, with whom she worked in Vienna.

Kawaguchi has now begun to produce her own pieces, inspired by traditional Japanese materials, woodworking techniques and furniture designs. In the recent period of economic difficulty, her interest in working with local craftsmen is interpreted as a sign of social commitment.

Kawaguchi's Escargot shelves (1997), which can be folded up and moved, form part of the Paulownia furniture collection. The paulownia wood, which has been used for the traditional Japanese kimono wardrobe, is famous for its smooth, luxurious surface and for its lightness. The shelves, which are based on the golden section, recall the traditional Japanese square space but also fit into a contemporary interior.

The Nautilus (1998) is a spiral bench which is also made of paulownia. Thanks to the lightness of the wood, it is easy to open up the bench into different positions.

More recently, in 2001, Kawaguchi has designed a series of screens and partition walls, called Washi because of their use of washi, the traditional Japanese paper. Once again she calls on Japanese tradition but makes something that is very contemporary.

When we consider the icons of Japanese design, with their simplicity and sharpness, we realize that their influence is still active in the world of contemporary design, producing a unique combination of form and function.

RYU NIIMI

1 Nautilus Bench, 1998, paulownia wood, steel, 38 x 124 x 77 cm, Kuriyama Bussan.
› Part of the Kiri series, this bench, made of paulownia wood, is designed as a spiral. The wheels enable it to be easily opened out to become a sequence of seats in a variety of positions.

2 Washi Fitting & Partition, 2001, handmade paper, fitting 210 x 180 x 95 cm, partion 145 x 85 x 180 cm, Adachi Shiki Kogyo.
› These modern-looking screens and partitions were made out of a handmade paper called minokami, a particular version of the Japanese traditional paper, washi. Instead of the conventional sliding mechanism of Japanese partition walls, these works can be put in a variety of positions, thanks to the wheels. The minokami paper was made by Tadashi Sawamura and Satoshi Hasegawa.

1	2

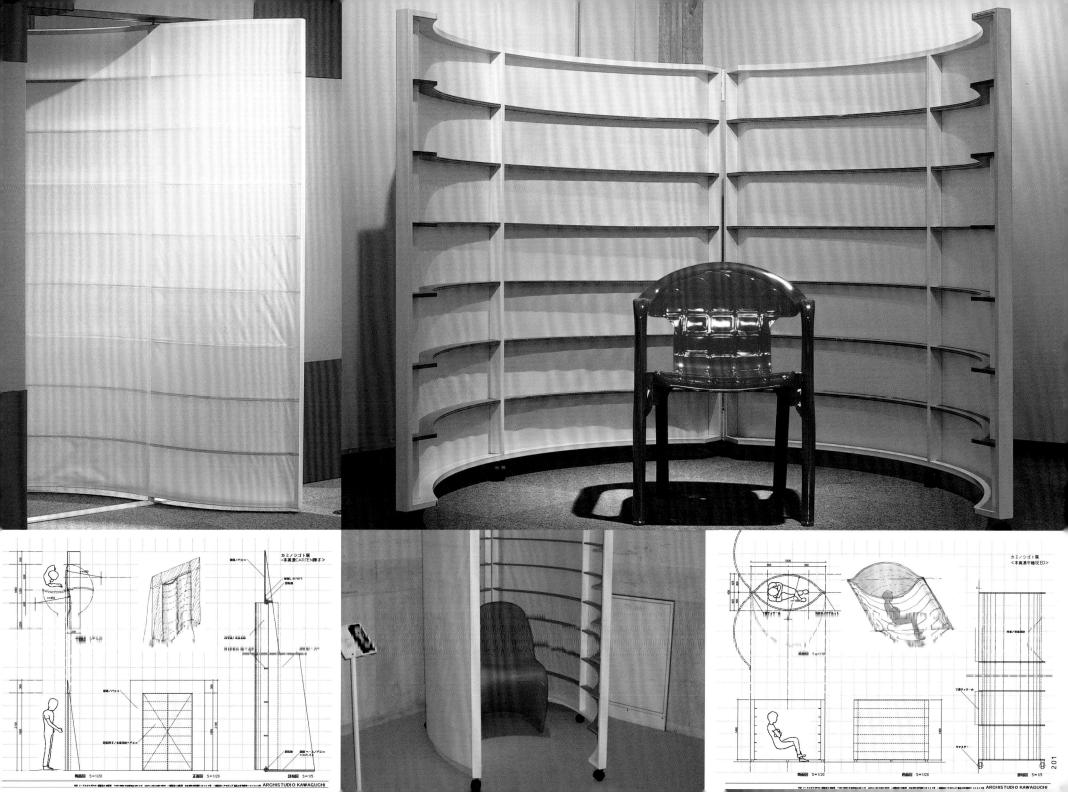

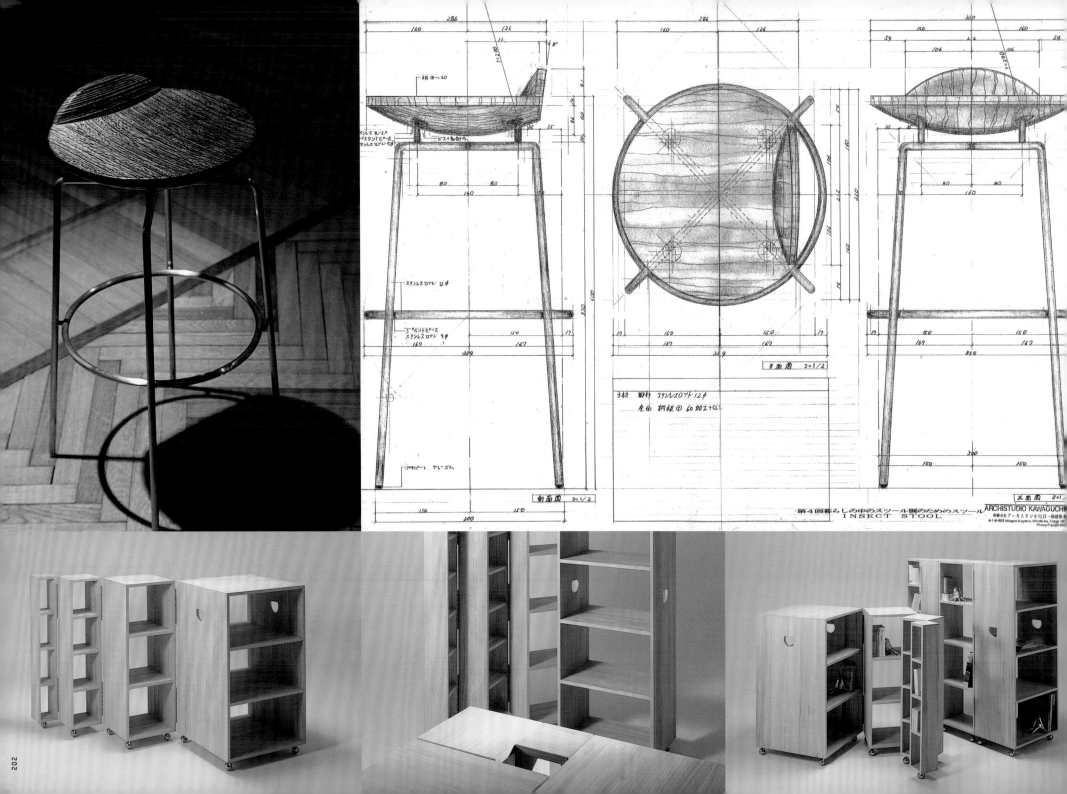

第4回暮らしの中のスツール展のためのスツール
INSECT STOOL

ARCHISTUDIO KAWAGUCHI
有限会社アーキスタジオ川口一級建築士事務所
6-1-6-609 Minami Aoyama, Minato-ku, Tokyo 10
Phone/Fax 03-54

側面図 S=1/2
平面図 S=1/2
正面図 S=1

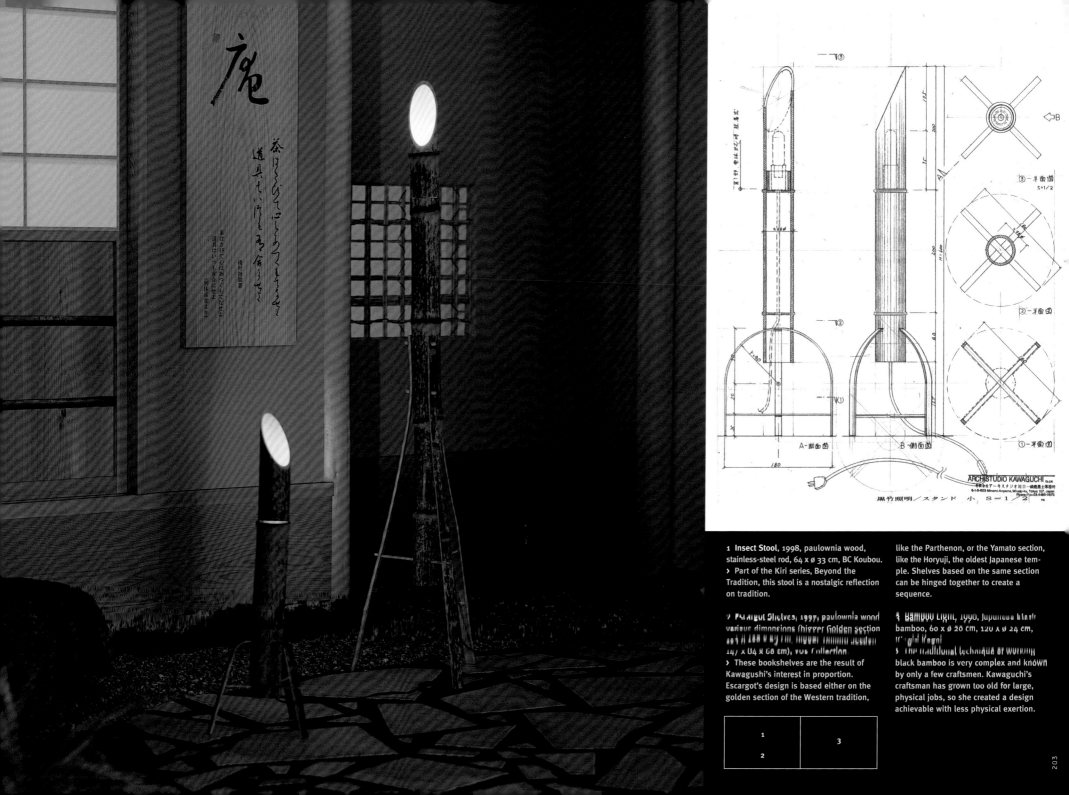

ARCHISTUDIO KAWAGUCHI

黒竹照明／スタンド　小　S=1／2

1 Insect Stool, 1998, paulownia wood, stainless-steel rod, 64 x ø 33 cm, BC Koubou.
› Part of the Kiri series, Beyond the Tradition, this stool is a nostalgic reflection on tradition.

2 Escargot Shelves, 1997, paulownia wood, various dimensions (bigger Golden section 161 x 188 x 69 cm, bigger Yamato section 147 x 64 x 68 cm), VOS Collection.
› These bookshelves are the result of Kawagushi's interest in proportion. Escargot's design is based either on the golden section of the Western tradition,

like the Parthenon, or the Yamato section, like the Horyuji, the oldest Japanese temple. Shelves based on the same section can be hinged together to create a sequence.

3 Bamboo Light, 1998, Japanese black bamboo, 60 x ø 20 cm, 120 x ø 24 cm, Knight Kogei.
› The traditional technique of working black bamboo is very complex and known by only a few craftsmen. Kawaguchi's craftsman has grown too old for large, physical jobs, so she created a design achievable with less physical exertion.

1		3
2		

203

Arash Kaynama came to the interview for a place at the Royal College of Art with a portfolio of projects that he had worked on at Central Saint Martins College of Art & Design. The portfolio demonstrated some sort of reluctant compliance with an educational system that Arash never accepted. The things that upstaged all the completed projects were his little books of cartoons, all on the subject of industrial design. As well as being highly amusing and witty in their own right, and drawn with a delightful lightness, they were also a very comprehensive declaration of intentions. One could trace any of his projects at the college back to pages of his cartoons.

Some designers look back with longing at their *magnum opus* from college days, seeing it as their most exciting piece of work, done before the responsibilities of what they perceive as professional life took their toll. Not Arash.

As a student, he did not put all of his (enormous) energy into polishing and packaging the 'big idea'. Instead, he juggled and played with lots of ideas. Some of these turned into a stream of delightfully witty products: for example, a series of experimental projects with a light sign, which can be read only when the light is switched off, or a map that you can read only by obscuring the light. Another series explored shifting functions by altering scale. In Genius (1999), post-it notes grow to become a table, and in Big Clip (1999) paperclips are blown up to clip bigger, heavier things without compromising their formal appearance.

Arash is not joining the profession in a hurry. His research project Off-the-Wall (2001) – including the Missing Office and the Nearly Tetris Office – which was arranging the transformable workplace for the global office-supplies manufacturer Esselte, showed no attempt to blend or even to co-exist with the company's product landscape. Instead, he proposes projects that create an environment capable of shifting from order to chaos and everything in between.

The big ideas? They are coming. I see Arash, who has tried out various creative partnerships, incessantly trying new ideas, new materials. His current collaborator is Kelly Sant, a fellow graduate from the RCA, who comes to design from involvement with resins and fabrics. It has been said that most of the pleasure in Arash's projects comes from encountering them for the first time, rather than living with them long term. Maybe this is because the projects he tackles are still part of marking and mapping in preparation for the great works of the future. RON ARAD

1 **Loving McDonald's**, containers, 1998, unglazed bone china, ashtray 1 x ø 7 cm, sundae container 5 x ø 8 cm, in collaboration with Jennie Idrizi.
> This ashtray and junk-food container, which were intended to be used only once, have been transformed into permanent, precious objects.

2 **Eurobowls**, 2000, plywood, resin, paint, 120 x 120 cm, in collaboration with Pascal Anson.
> European countries are here turned into bowls; the western countries are finished in skin-tones, whereas the northern countries are much paler tan than those in the south.

3 **Bic Candle Lighter**, 1999, wax, 10 x 2 x 1 cm.
> In this witty design the usual Bic disposable lighter has been cast in wax, as a candle.

4 **Lemon Squeezer**, 1997, stainless-steel mesh, chromed mild-steel rod, 5 x 9 x 15 cm.
> The wire mesh has been stamped to form the shape of a squeezer and has become rigid. The forming process dictates the shape of the edge.

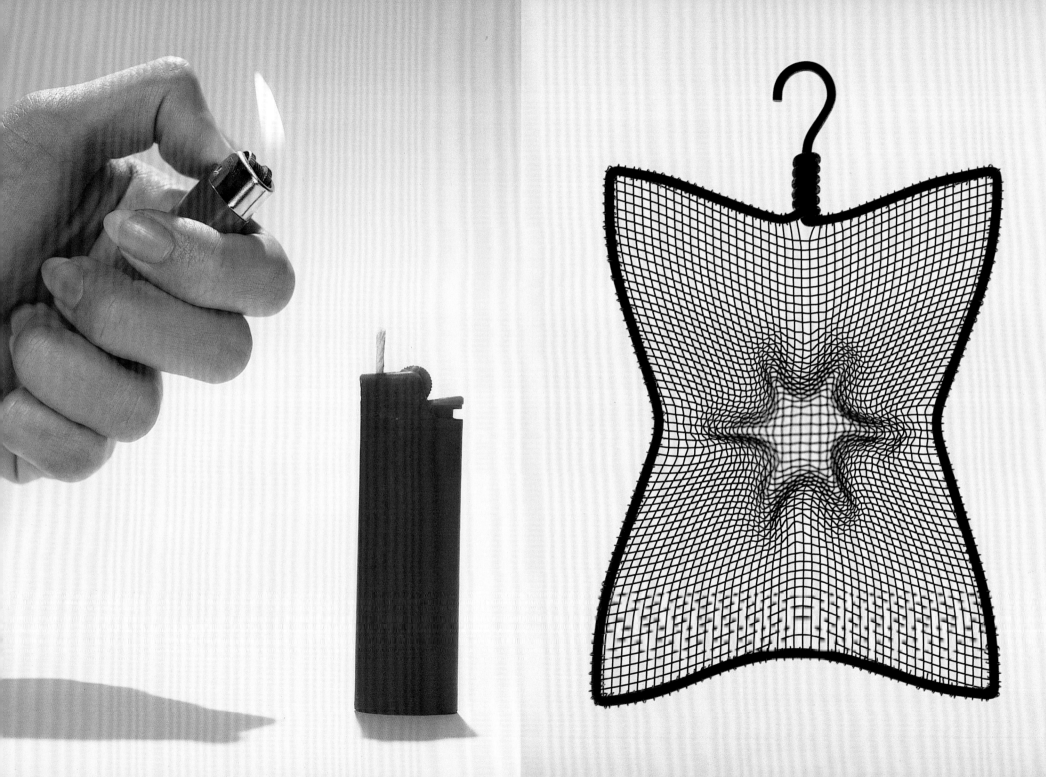

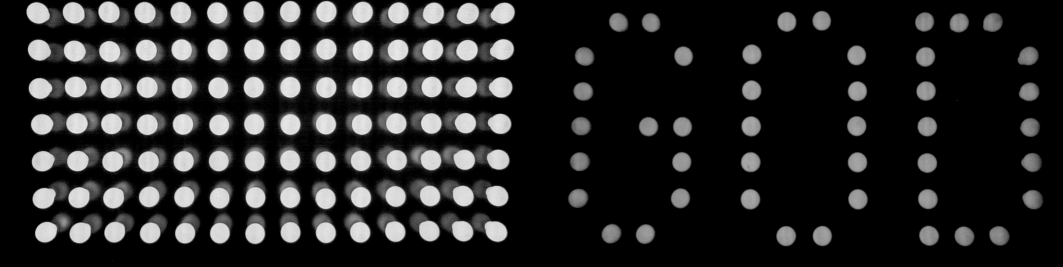

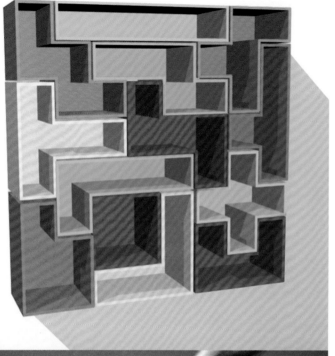

1 **God Light**, 1999, aluminium, light bulbs, photoluminiscent paint, 15 x 180 x 80 cm.
› The light flashes on and off thanks to a time switch. In the dark some of the bulbs reveal the word GOD.

2 **The Empire Strikes Back**, flag, 2000, silk-screened print, fabric, 200 x 80 cm.
› The us flag has been recreated in red and yellow. This turns the symbol of capitalism, choice and freedom into the symbol of communism, dogma and oppression.

3 **The Missing Office**, storage system, 2001, MDF, steel rod, rubber bands, 30 x 30 x 2 cm.
› This system allows products to be stored on the wall and shows when items are missing.

4 **The Nearly Tetris Office**, storage system, 2001, cardboard, steel, 180 x 180 x 30 cm
› This interlocking system enhances the ability to recall and find information through shape, colour and position.

5 **Genius**, table, 1999, paper pad, mild-steel frame, 45 x 30 x 30 cm, Hidden.
› The tabletop is a writing surface that, like the post-it, can be stuck anywhere.

6 **Big Clip**, coathook, 1999, chromed mild-steel bar, 28 x 8 x 5 cm.
› Paperclips have been blown up to form an object on which clothes can be hung.

1		4	6
			4
2	3	5	

HELEN KERR TORONTO

Like most industrial designers, Helen Kerr's practice, known as Kerr & Co, encompasses a range of domestic product types – from dustpans to dish racks and laundry hampers to ladles. Recently, her work has focused most closely on the development of a collection of cutlery for the Toronto-based manufacturer Gourmet Settings. Together with her client, Kerr has set out to create strong, beautiful and resolutely modern designs made of the highest quality stainless steel. What makes Kerr different is that these collections are destined for the mass-market, even though their quality and beauty matches that of cutlery sold for three times the price elsewhere. For the design-conscious consumer, finding the perfect cutlery pattern can involve either a lifetime of searching or a major investment. When has such a thing ever been available at the price of Kerr & Co's products for Target? And they are beautifully packaged as well.

Educated at the Ontario College of Art and Design in Toronto (with a first degree in environmental design), Kerr has a Utopian vision of 'good design for the masses', a legacy of modernism, which is fused with a *modus operandi* that is more akin to that of an anthropologist than a designer. Kerr likes to be thought of as an interpreter of culture and says, 'What you're doing is interpreting human need and giving life to objects that people are going to use in their everyday lives. It requires perception, empathy, and physicality.'

Kerr and her team begin the process by carefully studying the task that an object will fulfil, spending time asking consumers questions and testing other, similar products. Returning to the studio, they use computer modelling to explore variations, taking into account the subtle nuances that will improve, for example, the design of a fork. Foam sketch models are then made so that they can experience how the product will work and look in three dimensions and on a real scale.

Kerr's practice is also driven by a socially conscious approach to design. She believes in designing responsibly, getting the most from her materials and processes. She is as excited by the finished product as she is by the fact that, through their involvement in the manufacturing process, she and her clients have been able to affect positive change in both the conditions for the workers and production standards in the factories in eastern China where the cutlery is made. BROOKE HODGE

1 **Oval Measuring Cups**, 1998, stainless steel, 1/4 cup 18.7 x 4.8 x 3 cm, 1/3 cup 19.3 x 5.2 x 3 cm, 1/2 cup 20 x 6.6 x 3, 1 cup 20.5 x 7.5 x 4.6 cm, Browne & Co.
› The use of heavyweight stainless steel means that even if heated these cups will not dent or warp.

2 **Silicone Spatulas**, 2000, silicone heads on brushed stainless steel handles, large 29.7 x 6.5 x 1.5 cm, medium 29.7 x 5 x 1.5 cm, small 28 x 4.2 x 1.5 cm, Browne & Co.
› Interchangeable spatula heads (available in six colours) allow for easy cleaning.

The silicone heads are heat resistant up to 345°C and are dishwasher safe.

3 **Balance Cutlery**, 2001, brushed stainless steel, small fork 18.8 x 0.25 cm, large fork 21.6 x 0.28 cm, knife 24.6 x 0.28 cm, large spoon 20.8 x 0.55 cm, small spoon 18.1 x 0.48 cm, Gourmet Settings.
› The distinct form of this cutlery is rooted in sculptural detailing rather than surface patterns.

4 **Balance Cutlery**, 2001, foam prototypes.

5 **Flow Cutlery**, 2001, foam prototypes.

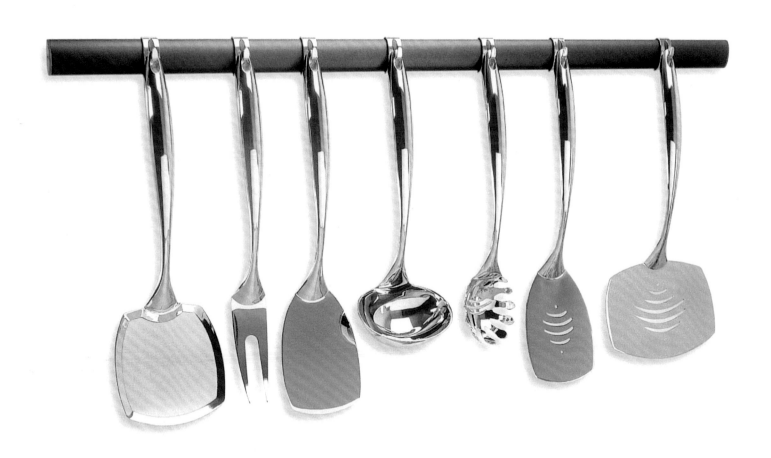
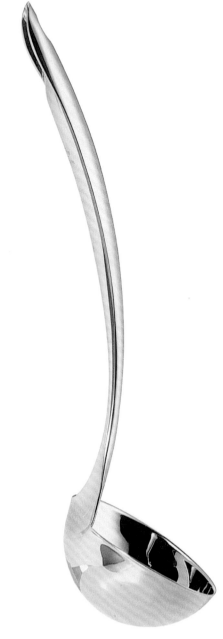

1 Tempo Tools Collection, 2000, 18/10 mirror-finish stainless steel, skimmer 36 x 11.6 cm, fork 34.8 x 0.3 cm, spatula 36.9 x 4.5 cm, ladle 32.7 x 10.2 cm, spaghetti server 32.5 x 6.6 cm, slotted spatula 36.9 x 4.5 cm, fish turner 36.5 x 16.5 cm, Browne & Co.
> Elegant, lightweight and durable, these kitchen utensils were designed to withstand the rigours of daily use. The slim and timeless line of the implements makes them functional for cooking yet sufficiently elegant for serving.

> The rubber strips on this mat are both elegant and functional. They are both non-slip and heat resistant so that the mat can also be used as a trivet. It has been designed for easy assembly and disassembly for recycling.

3 Coffee Grinder Brushes, 2000, brushed stainless steel, nylon, natural bristles, 10.5 / 8.5 x 1.2 cm, Browne & Co.
> Shape and material transform these simple but functional kitchen utensils into appealing objects. Part of the Cuisipro Café Line.

2 Non-slip Base, 1998, brushed stainless steel, silicone rubber, ø 21 cm, Browne & Co.

4 Coffee Bag Clip, 1999, brushed stainless steel, 12.5 x 2.4 x 3.2 cm, Browne & Co.
> By providing a tight seal on the coffee bag, the clip preserves the aroma of fresh coffee.

5 Coffee Bag Clip, 1999, foam prototypes.

1	2	5
	3	4

HARRI KOSKINEN HELSINKI

If Harri Koskinen were simply to design glassware for the rest of his life, his legacy would be secure. But this talented designer has also worked on a rich variety of outstanding products ranging from furniture to cutlery, such as the barbecue set he designed for Hackman, the famous Swedish kitchen-ware company. Trained entirely in Finland, Koskinen's repertoire of techniques is dazzling, as is his joyful use of colour, shape and form (is it a candle holder or is it a tumbler, or both?).

One of his first designs to arouse public attention was a light, the DHS Block (1996). It is funny, simple and brilliant, all at the same time. A block of rough, sculptural glass is cut in half and carved so that a light bulb with its flex can be placed in the middle. It could be a piece of contemporary art if it was not so practical and such a deft and playful design. This blurring of the line between artistic form and practicality is one of the most entrancing things about Koskinen's work.

His talent shines from the various glasses, tumblers and candle holders that he has designed for the iittala glass company. His amoebic shapes nod a little to Alvar Aalto, but that is inevitable, given Aalto's towering influence in both Finland and in the wider design world. But Koskinen has not a derivative molecule in his body. His studio speaker (2001), designed for the up-market audio company Genelec, bears this out. Neatly incorporating speaker and stand, Koskinen's instincts for curves and the experience of his work with glass combine to create a seductive object.

Koskinen's versatility is revealed by the diverse set of international clients with whom he works, including Issey Miyake. This is curious because Miyake, the king of the hard-edge pleat, seems a strange home for Koskinen's sensuous aesthetic. Nonetheless, the collaboration was a great success.

Other Koskinen designs, such as his sofa bed (2000) are characterized by their sleight-of-hand simplicity. These words apply also to Koskinen's prototype shelf system (2000) in which long, simple planks of wood are held in suspension by two pieces of curved glass. It is the kind of shelf that demands nothing be placed on it – if only life were that simple.

To call Koskinnen the best Finnish designer since Alvar Aalto and Tapio Wirkkala underlines the strength of contemporary Finnish design and the deep tradition in which it flourishes. ULTAN GUILFOYLE

1 **Outdoor Cooking**, barbecue set, 2002, 18/10 stainless steel, various dimensions, Hackman.
› This elegant kitchen utensil set consists of a carving fork, tongs, spatula, steak knife and fork, all intended to be used for outdoor eating or for barbecues. The set exemplifies the practical and aesthetic qualities of great Scandinavian design: perfectly balanced functional objects. The looped handles have been devised to enable cutlery to be put down without dirtying the surface.

1	1

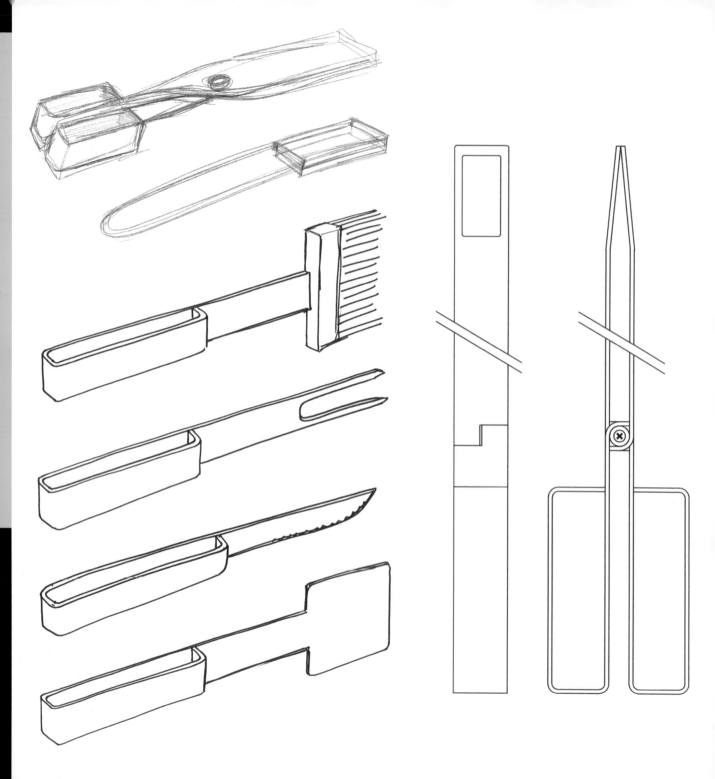

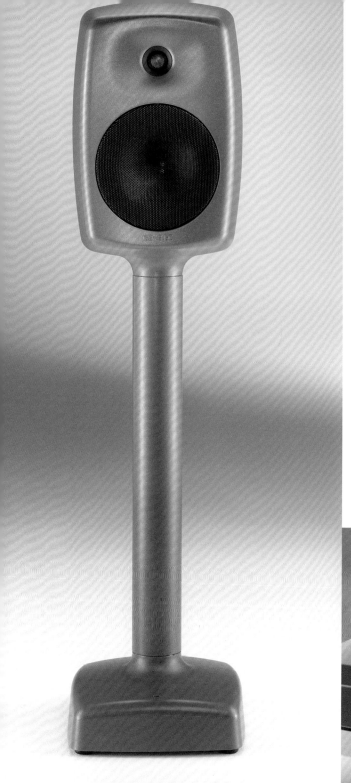

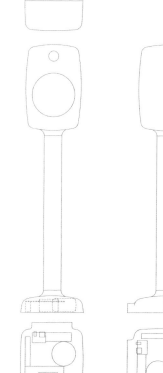

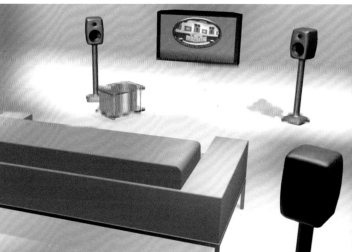

1 Air, container, 2001, plastic, 7 x 17 x 11 cm, 8 x 22 x 17 cm, 6 x 33 x 17 cm, Arabia.
> These practical air-tight food containers come in three sizes, and can be used to serve or preserve food, or be heated up in a microwave or oven.

2 Shelf System, 2000, oak shelf 4 x 48 x 250 cm, glass (or acrylic) element 50 x 48 x 48 cm, 3 shelves with elements 150 x 48 x 250 cm, self-produced.
> This wood and glass shelf system is a triumph, combining two great materials into a light and effective modern whole.

3 Sofa Bed, 2000, stainless steel, upholstery, 50 x 250 x 110 cm, self-produced.
> In Koskinen's effortless design, the cushion backrest simply flips down for a bed and back up for a sofa.

4 Block Lamp, 1996, cast glass, 11 x 10 x 16 cm, Design House Stockholm.
> The Block Lamp is a simple, practical lamp; it can be used in a wide range of places – the floor, a table, etc.

5 6040A, active speakers with built-in amplifiers, 2002, aluminium, 100 x 30 x 30 cm, Genelec.
> The new generation of surround-sound speakers is exemplified by the curvaceous and compact 6040A speaker with stand and the 6040A sub-woofer.

1	2	
3	4	5

TSUTOMU KUROKAWA TOKYO

Kurokawa's work represents the cutting edge of contemporary product and interior design in Tokyo. The key to understanding his unique style is the knowledge that he has his roots in the Punk Rock generation. Refusing to be satisfied with the superficial effects that can be created by adopting high-tech materials, Kurokawa works with the stamina and physical sensitivity of an athlete to create products that harness the pure strength of materials drawn from different ages and cultures. The results of this process have their own unique personality and rhythm. Kurokawa's designs take us far beyond the mere sophistication of a multicultural, urban style. Echoes of his ex-maestro, Takashi Sugimoto, are especially obvious in designs so hard edged that they sometimes look nihilistic.

Kurokawa's interior designs are simply astonishing. Some of his boutique designs make us particularly aware of his confrontational style. One of his trademarks is the challenging use of case-style shelves in a variety of materials. This gives a strange solidity to the space. By using futuristic materials, such as acrylic resin, he imbues the space with an odd ambivalence. For example, the interior of Underpass x Private Room, with its illuminated entrance, is very like the entrance to a spaceship, turning a mere shopping trip into a space odyssey. Kurokawa plays on this atmosphere by using striking, black iron cross-supports that run from the ceiling to the walls. While creating a harsh and breathtaking division of space, the supports also serve as rails on which the clothes can be hung.

The sense of urban solitude so vividly expressed by Underpass x Private Room is again apparent in his product design. Much of this work takes the form of unique prototypes for made-to-order furniture. Fal (2000), a chair with seat and legs stretched from a single piece of polypropylene, encapsulates the essence of his cutting-edge style. Like Fal, the Papina chair (2001) is an intrinsically organic design in which Kurokawa has developed the same approach to space and solitude.

Lastly, I must mention Kurokawa's collaborative interior-design project with Yoichi Nagasawa. Together they are creating Self+Service, a new type of store selling clothes, stationery and toiletries whose production is based on recycling and is environmentally friendly. RYU NIIMI

1 Fal, chair, 2000, polypropylene, stainless steel, 77 x 62.5 x 54.5 cm, OUT.DeSIGN.
› Fal was designed to furnish a high-school lecture room. Since stacking was needed, Kurokawa designed a chair with a hole and an inverted V-type leg structure.

2 Papina, chair, 2001, chromed steel, fabric, 73.5 x 61.5 x 58.5 cm, OUT.DeSIGN.
› The challenge in this design was to create the frame of the chair out of one bent pipe. Papina's steel tube is welded only in one place, and the capability of modern machines means that complicated 3-dimen-

sional designs can now be mass-produced.

3 Mapell, chair, 2000, polycarbonate, fabric, 85.5 x 54 x 44 cm, OUT.DeSIGN.
› The idea of combining a structure of four detachable legs came from the desire to produce stools and chairs which could be easily assembled. By the process of injection moulding, Kurokawa achieves an easy and convenient design. The coloured and clear legs suggest lightness and convey a wonderful feeling of floating.

4 Olberi, table, 2000, acrylic resin, wood, 72 x 150/180 x 90 cm, OUT.DeSIGN.
› One of Kurokawa's main subjects is to explore the potential of acrylics in furniture design, specifically when combined with natural materials such as wood. This table shows the charming, soft result of this synthesis.

		3
1	2	4

216

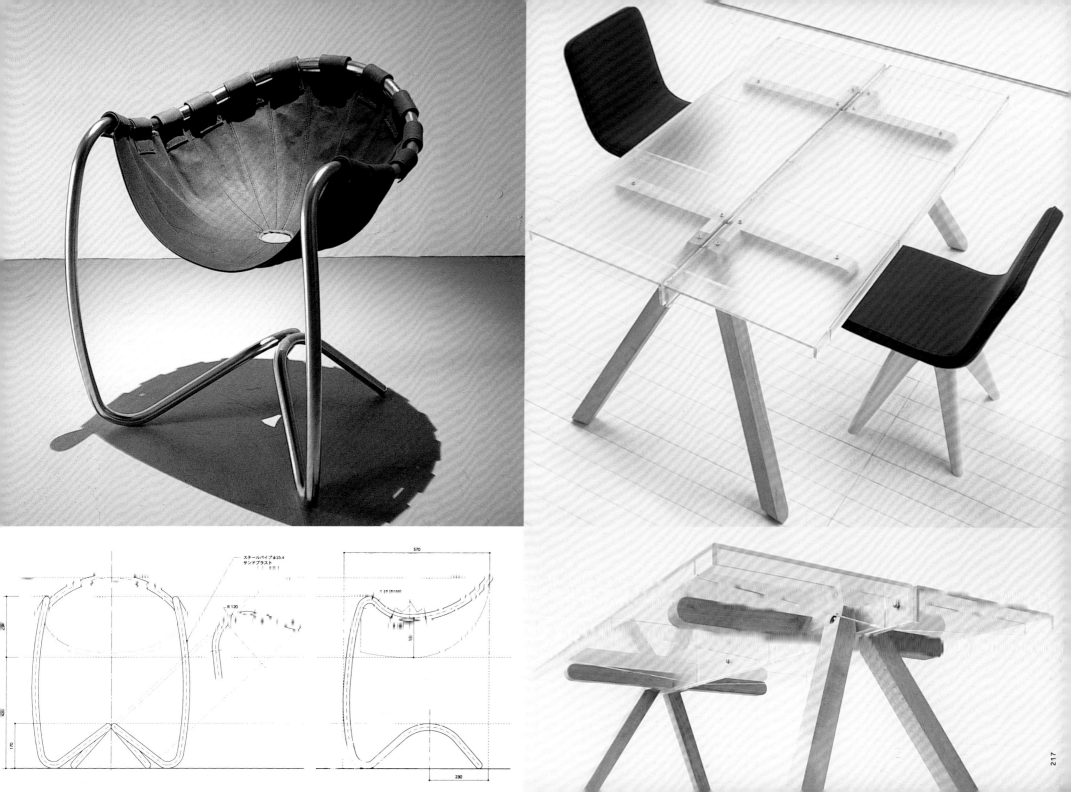

スチールパイプ φ25.4
サンドブラスト

570

R 120

R (R120)

170

230

217

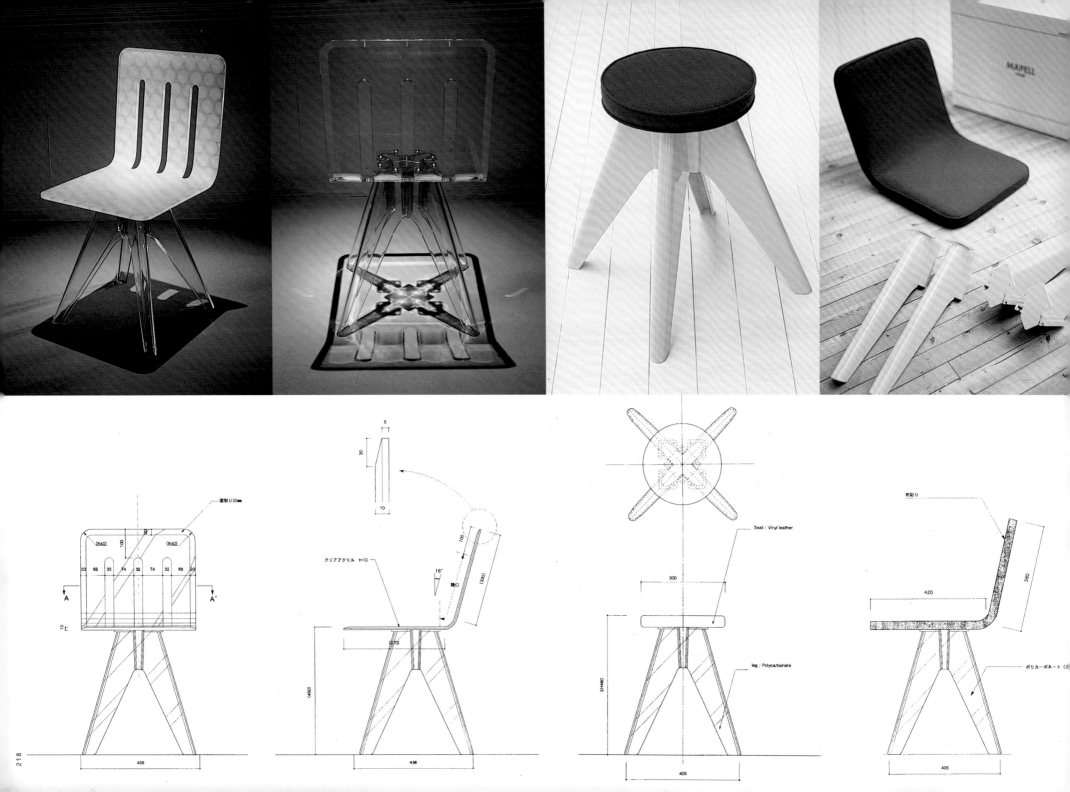

面取り20mm

(R40) (R40)

100

20 68 32 74 32 74 32 68 20

A ———— A'

10

436

5

20

10

クリアアクリル t=10

100

(350)

16°

開口

(370)

(450)

436

Seat : Vinyl leather

300

SH480

leg : Polycarbonate

405

布貼り

380

420

ポリカーボネート

405

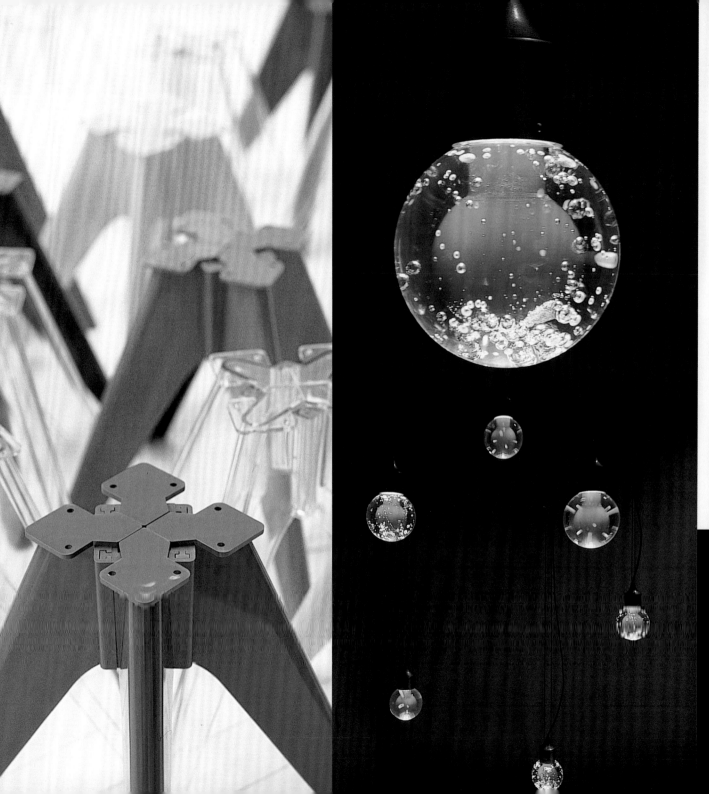

1 Mapell, chair, 2001, polycarbonate, acrylic resin, 84 x 51 x 42 cm, OUT.DeSIGN.
> After the upholstered versions, this chair was designed to be made in acrylic and the use of this material was a challenge. Numerous prototypes were made to test both clear and patterned acrylic seats.

2 Mapell, stool, 2000, polycarbonate, fabric, 40 x 44 (seat Ø 10) cm, OUT.DeSIGN.

3 Mapell, chair, 2000, polycarbonate, fabric, 85.5 x 54 x 44 cm, OUT.DeSIGN.

4 Maty, lamp, 2001, acrylic resin, aluminium, LED, 17 x Ø 10 cm, OUT.DeSIGN.
> A fluorescent green bulb is wrapped up in a transparent ball. The Light Emitting Diode source does not conduct heat, which enables the acrylics to expand and adjust, emitting a wonderful indirect light.

5 Kalfa, chair, 2001, aluminium, plywood, 71 x 51 x 49 cm, OUT.DeSIGN.
> The design for this chair was motivated by the observation that chairs are normally seen from the back. The curve of the aluminium expresses a light rhythm and increases the perception of space when many chairs are put together.

1	2	3	4	5

MARTIN LOTTI PORTLAND OR

Portland, Oregon, on the rugged, rain-drenched northwest coast of the United States, seems an unlikely place to find a Swiss product designer, much less a sports-shoe designer who is, by wide acclaim, one of the most gifted designers of his generation. But then, nothing is predictable about 27-year-old Martin Lotti, the creative director of the Nike Women's Footwear Division. Nor, for that matter, is there anything very predictable about his employers, except that they consistently clothe the world's top athletes.

There are visual analogies in Lotti's designs with those of contemporary architects such as Frank Gehry or Santiago Calatrava. For example, the lower ribs of Calatrava's sublime pedestrian bridge in Bilbao are replicated in the soles of Lotti's Air Max Specter shoes (2001). Lotti is the son of an architect and consequently his understanding of architecture is deep and informed. He is not a glib, pop designer, quoting Gehry simply because he thinks it is cool. He looks to architecture for the volumes, structures and functionality that he needs to apply to his own work.

Lotti draws inspiration from an impressive range of sources. The Ovidian reversible shoe (2000) was the result of conversations with fashion-addicted school kids who told him that they just had to wear something different every day. And what if that was not possible? They would just turn their clothes inside out. This information sparked a two-year search for the technology and materials that would allow Lotti to create reversible outer shoes around an inner booty. And the name? Well, Ovid's *Metamorphoses* does not feature on the reading list of the average American teenager, but Lotti used it, and included a random Ovidian quote in the shoe for good measure.

Air Visi Havocs are a range of sling-back running shoes inspired by a trip to South Beach, the epicentre of Florida's clubland. Lotti was struck by the open-air cafés, the summer clothes and the women's sling-back sandals. Sling-back running shoes? It is hard to imagine, but Lotti was determined to challenge the uniformity of women's sporting footwear. He decided that sports shoes should be seasonal, just like every other fashion design. As a result of this breakthrough, Lotti has moved from designing individual shoes to designing ever-changing collections.

Sitting in the far northwest of the United States, Lotti's designer's gaze is cast far and wide. But he does allow himself one little Swiss idiosyncrasy: a Swiss flag stamped on the soles of all his designs. ULTAN GUILFOYLE

1 Ovidian, sports shoe, 2000, split suede, canvas, Nike.
> The first reversible athletic footwear, Ovidian challenges the status quo of the traditional athletic shoe. The name comes from the Roman poet Ovid who wrote the *Metamorphoses*, which are stories of mythical changes. A quotation from Ovid – 'palace by the purple light' – was integrated into the midsole of the shoe. The project took over two years owing to the very specific rubber compound that needed to be developed for it.

2 Air Visi Havoc, sports shoe, 2001, upper: various materials including full-grain leathers and stretch synthetics, midsole: phylon with full-length air bag, outsole: solid rubber, Nike.
> Air Visi Havoc incorporates a new silhouette, which is a breakthrough for women's athletic footwear. This is a refreshing and distinctive women's only design, with an innovative heel-fit system.

| 1 | 2 |

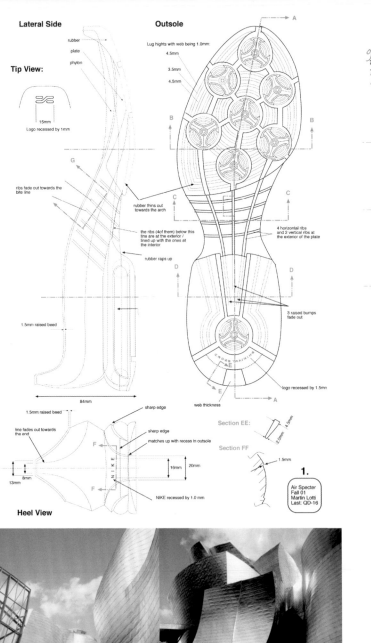

Lateral Side

Tip View:

rubber
plate
phylon

15mm

Logo recessed by 1mm

Outsole

Lug hights with web being 1.0mm:

4.5mm
3.5mm
4.5mm

A

B — B

ribs fade out towards the bite line

rubber thins out towards the arch

the ribs (4 of them) below this line are at the exterior / lined up with the ones at the interior

rubber raps up

1.5mm raised beed

C — C

D — D

4 horizontal ribs and 2 vertical ribs at the exterior of the plate

3 raised bumps fade out

E — E

84mm

logo recessed by 1.5mm

web thickness

A

1.5mm raised beed

sharp edge

line fades out towards the end

sharp edge

matches up with recess in outsole

Section EE:

4.5mm
2.0mm

Section FF:

1.5mm

16mm 20mm

13mm
8mm

NIKE recessed by 1.0 mm

1.

Air Specter
Fall 01
Martin Lotti
Last: QD-16

Heel View

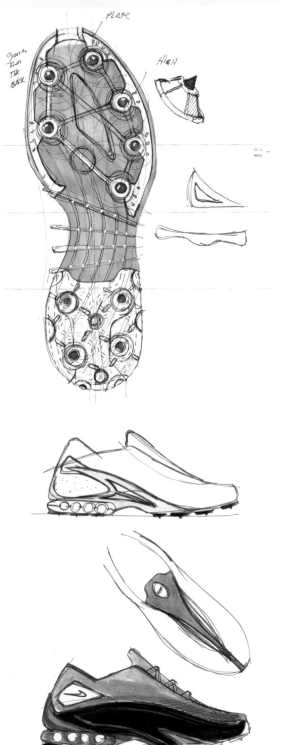

PLATE

grooves from the back

HIGH

10.0
BALL

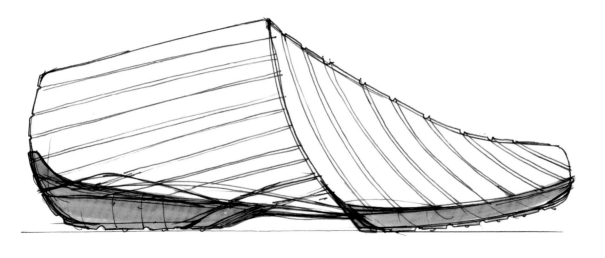

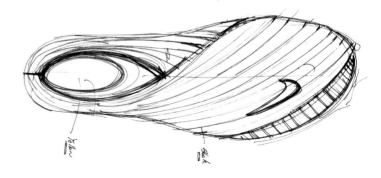

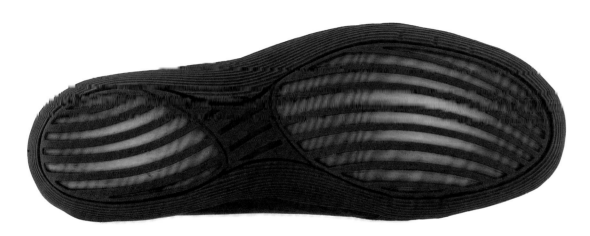

1 Air Max Specter, sports shoe, 2001, upper: synthetic leather and mesh combination, midsole: phylon, outsole: rubber, plate: TPU, Nike.

› Air Max Specter is a cross-training shoe inspired by the Guggenheim Museum in Bilbao, Spain. It is a hybrid product between a track and field spike shoe and a trail runner. The main feature is the full-length TPU plate technology for added support and stability.

2 The Kyoto, sports shoe, 2002, upper: rubber and stretch material, midsole: double-lasted phylon, outsole: rubber combination, Nike.

› The Kyoto is a comfortable, stylish shoe to wear to and from yoga. The stretch material offers a snug and comfortable fit with styling inspired by the kimono and Nike's own heritage. Relevant technical points are the double-lasted phylon midsole for cushioning low to the ground, and outsole in a solid and clear rubber combination for versatile traction.

1	2

JEAN-MARIE MASSAUD PARIS

Undoubtedly one of the foremost names on the current French design scene, Jean-Marie Massaud works in many different areas. As he moves from art installation to interior decoration, from graphic design and packaging to sophisticated furnishings, his work as a designer is constantly maturing. There is evidence in all that he does of a heartfelt belief in the importance of both quality and elegance.

Massaud's work is characterized by meticulous attention to detail and a determination to reveal the full potential of every material used. His products resemble miniature architectural constructions rather than design objects, and in each case the structural element is reduced to a minimum. He always works with simple volumes, and their rounded forms lend his designs both a remarkable lightness and a sensuous quality. Massaud has studied with some of France's leading contemporary designers, including Marc Berthier. From them he learnt that attention to detail and constant fine-tuning are needed to make a successful product. Despite their input, however, Massaud's own design language has remained unique.

Often alternating opaque and translucent surfaces, Massaud makes extraordinary use of materials. His first aim is always to find the optimum use of the material that he has chosen to use, and this forms the basis of his working methods. Whether his materials are new, or already in common use, he explores their potential to the full. He tries to operate freely, experimenting in different fields and transferring techniques and production methods from one discipline to another.

Massaud never sees a product as an end in itself; he always tries to imagine it as part of a more complex project. He is always searching for new ways of using and handling familiar household objects. This approach results in work that is truly contemporary, and products that meet both the needs and the expectations of his consumers. Works such as In-Out (2001), a bench that can be used inside or outside, and Green Colony (2002), a living sculpture, share Massaud's creative input, demonstrating how objects with very different functions, appearance and materials can all reflect a distinctive vision. GIULIO CAPPELLINI

1 **Net Shelf**, 2000, polypropylene, 4 x 116 x 4 cm, Liv'it.
> These modular, self-standing shelves help in displaying and storing depending on your own archiving method. The Net is a visual quotation of ideas and abstractions, reminiscent of the diffusion of information.

2 **Loft Unit**, 2002, lava, corian, wood, glass, cloth, leather, project for Cappellini.
> This is a collection of units that can be used to subdivide an open-plan living place. The three principle furnished spaces are: Dream Unit (bedroom), Pure Unit (bathroom) and Flavour Unit (kitchen). This project is currently being developed.

1	2

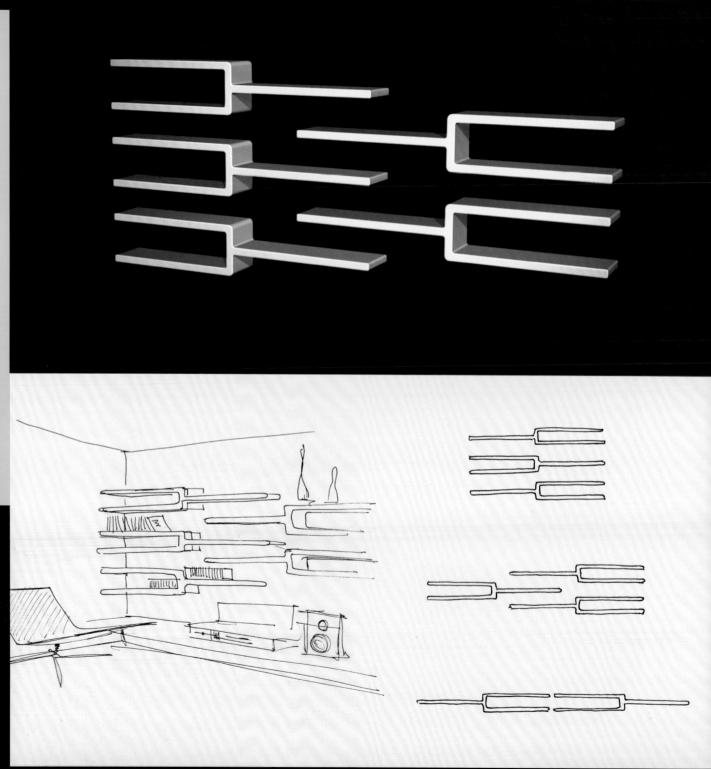

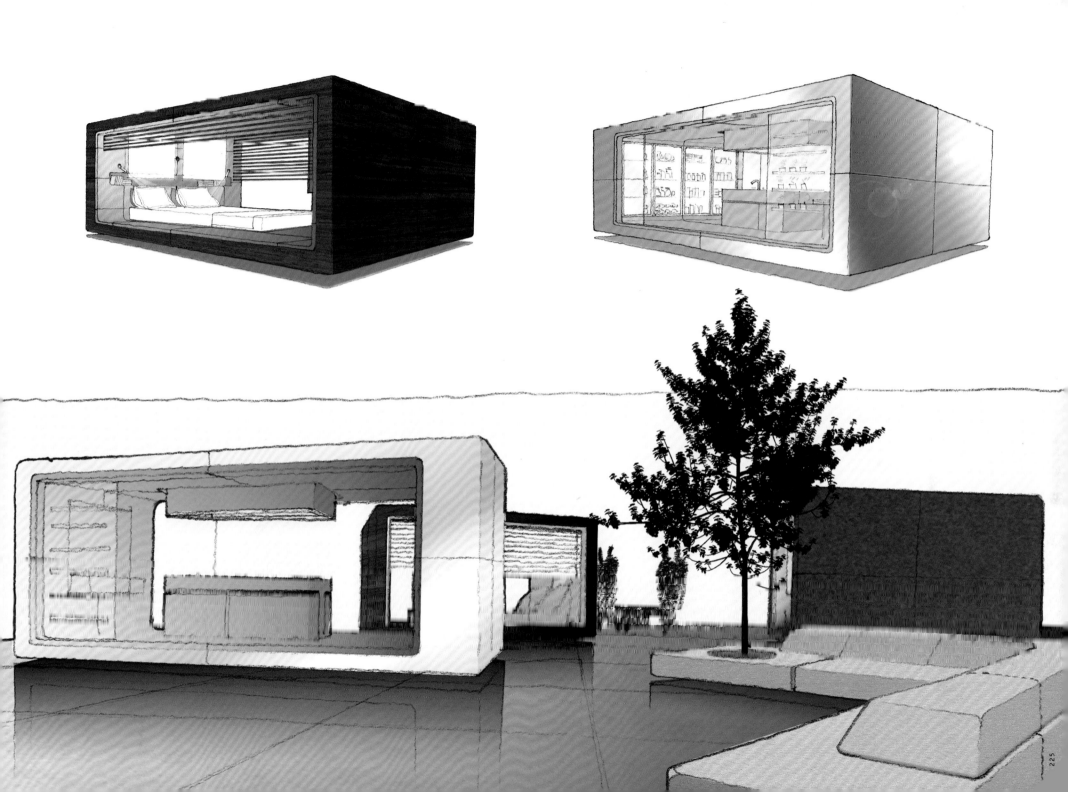

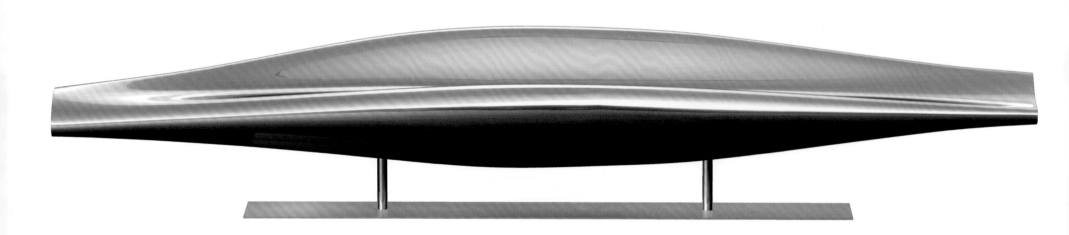

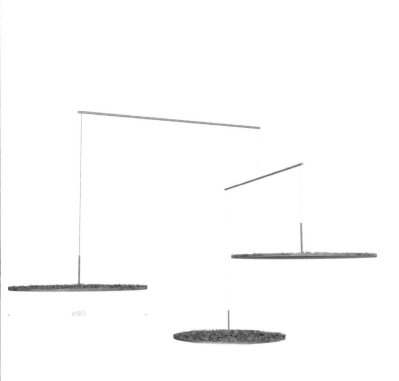

ø50

85

190

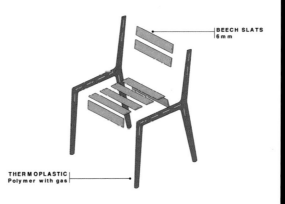

BEECH SLATS
6 mm

THERMOPLASTIC
Polymer with gas

$2 X \sqcap + 8 X \diagdown = 1,6 \ kg$

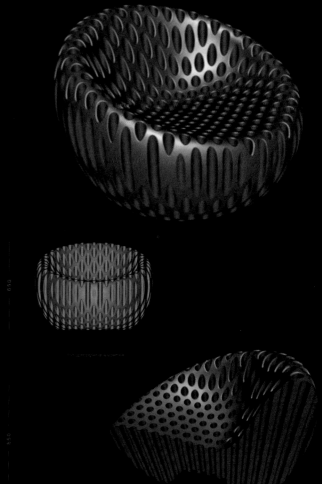

1 **Outline**, sofa, 2001, polyurethane, leather/cloth, stainless steel, 64 x 210 x 93 cm, Cappellini.
1 The design of this sofa is not just about making a statement, it is also a useable and comfortable design whose form expresses its function.

2 In-Out, sofa, 2001, polyurethane, leather/cloth, gel coat finish, stainless steel, 53 x 305 x 60 cm, Cappellini.
> In-Out is either a sofa for internal use or a bench for use outside. Its minimal form is almost biomorphic and alludes to some-

thing organic, such as a muscle, verging on the abstract.

3 **Green Colony**, 2002, microplants and lava, Heaven.
> This is a living sculpture; it consists of microplants growing on lava places.

4 **O'Hazard**, chair, 1998, polypropylene, aluminium, rubber 80 x 60.5 x 78.5 cm, Magis.
> This is an archetypal chair. Its extremely light features replicate the lines of the designer's drawing.

5 **Projet 000.1**, chair, 2002.
> The chair will be developed in extended polypropylene, which is extremely light, hollowed out to economise on material.

1			
	3	4	5
2			

MAT Studio is the name adopted by a group of four young designers – Antonio Brizzi, Babette Riefenstahl, Carla Crosina and Marco Bellomo – all of whom are Italian except Babette, who was born in Germany. Although they come from different professional backgrounds, they have one thing in common: a desire to design high-quality, mass-produced objects. This does not mean that their creative impulses have been stifled, they are simply focused on making distinctive products that will fit comfortably into people's homes.

Like so many of the most talented young designers today, MAT Studio gives great attention to detail and to the production process. This approach has won MAT's designs a prominent position on the contemporary scene. Its aim is to create products for all, trying not to work for a small niche market, but for a wider public drawn into design by its light-hearted, engaging products.

MAT's products are honest and tailored to the needs of the public. In this respect they can be seen as the true heirs of the great masters of Italian and international design. A serious and professional approach means that its designs must be tested exhaustively. As a result, its products often have a very long period of gestation. It also puts great emphasis on the search for the expressive potential of different materials, and on their industrial application.

MAT's agenda is not to create works of art, but to produce restrained designs of high quality, intended to last. Like many young designers, they take a great interest in colour and new colour ranges, demonstrating that it is possible to make products that are both useful and beautiful, pleasing to contemplate and to touch. The different personalities of the members of the group add great strength to their designs, producing the best fruits of a dialogue between professionalism and enthusiasm, seriousness and energy. When we look at MAT's work we really have the feeling that we are on the threshold of an important new phase in Italian design, a successor to its past glories.

The Extra Shelf (2001) is a perfect example of MAT's work. It responds perfectly to the user's needs by providing storage, but at the same time it is a high-tech object with strong visual impact. The Due (2000–2) sink, on the other hand, is an example of its unusual approach to the use of materials, in the search to create a captivating and arresting object.

GIULIO CAPPELLINI

1 Sitting System, 1999, polyurethane covered by textile, 96 x 120 x 70 cm, prototype.
› These modular seats are aimed to be as curvaceous as the human body. They are covered with a high-tech soft resin whose liquidity makes the plastic resemble velvet.

2 Libreria Gialla, shelf, 1999, expanded polystyrene, polyurethanic resin, 200 x 100 x 40 cm, prototype in collaboration with M Baldini.
› This is an experiment into unusual technology. Once sprayed with polyurethanic resin the expanded polystyrene becomes very resistant but preserves its dimensional qualities and its lightness.

3 Extra Shelf, 2001, aluminium, various dimensions, prototype.
› This shelf is intended as a functional design, economical in material but striking in its simplicity. The design consists of an outline of a more conventional shelf; the single sheet of formed aluminium slides into the adjustable track.

1	2	2
		3

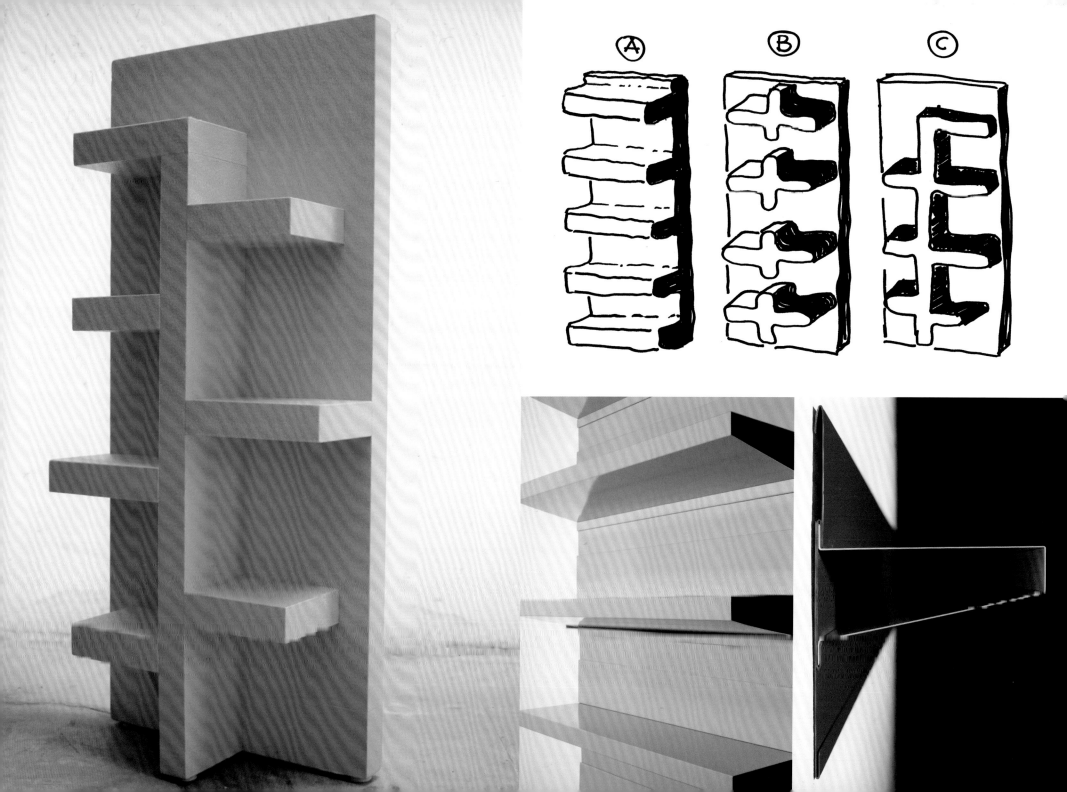

A   B   C

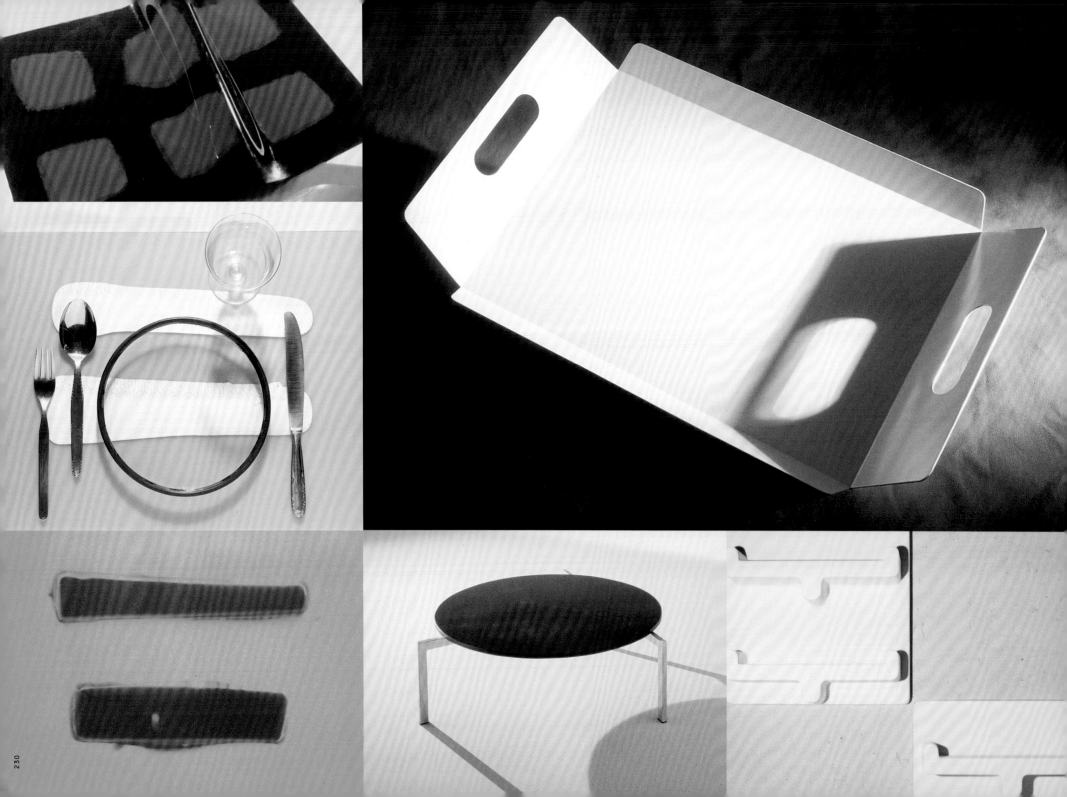

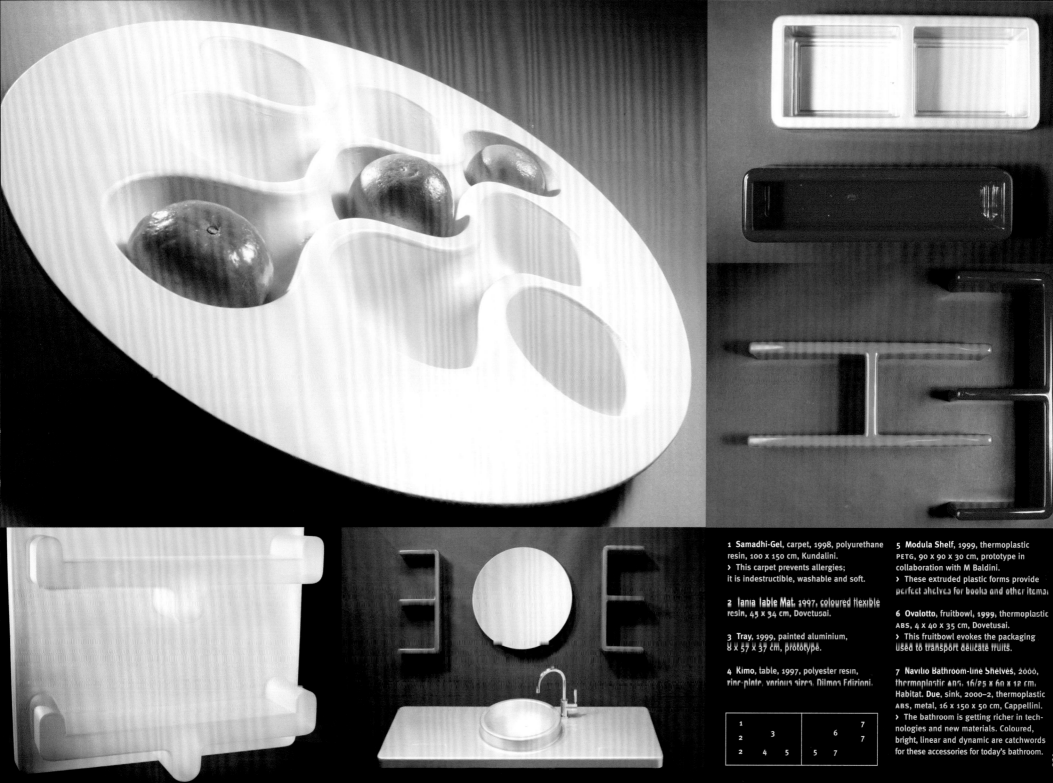

1 **Samadhi-Gel**, carpet, 1998, polyurethane resin, 100 x 150 cm, Kundalini.
› This carpet prevents allergies; it is indestructible, washable and soft.

2 **Tania Table Mat**, 1997, coloured flexible resin, 45 x 34 cm, Dovetusai.

3 **Tray**, 1999, painted aluminium, 8 x 57 x 37 cm, prototype.

4 **Kimo**, table, 1997, polyester resin, ring-plate, various sizes, Dilmos Edizioni.

5 **Modula Shelf**, 1999, thermoplastic PETG, 90 x 90 x 30 cm, prototype in collaboration with M Baldini.
› These extruded plastic forms provide perfect shelves for books and other items.

6 **Ovalotto**, fruitbowl, 1999, thermoplastic ABS, 4 x 40 x 35 cm, Dovetusai.
› This fruitbowl evokes the packaging used to transport delicate fruits.

7 **Navilio Bathroom-line Shelves**, 2000, thermoplastic ABS, 16/25 x 60 x 12 cm, Habitat. **Due**, sink, 2000–2, thermoplastic ABS, metal, 16 x 150 x 50 cm, Cappellini.
› The bathroom is getting richer in technologies and new materials. Coloured, bright, linear and dynamic are catchwords for these accessories for today's bathroom.

1				7
2	3		6	7
2	4	5	5	7

231

As Vice-President of Global Design for Ford Motor Company, J Mays oversees the design of an enormous range of vehicles, but he also gets directly involved in the design process. At Ford Mays' mission has been to develop a design strategy that operates at a conceptual level. 'What it really comes down to is how a car engages you emotionally, pulls you in and connects naturally, hopefully umbilically, with your lifestyle and your life stage', he explained in a speech to the International Motor Press Association in November 1998. 'Lust', 'desire' and 'aspiration' are words Mays often uses to describe the feelings that cars should evoke in consumers.

After graduating in 1980 from the Transportation Design programme at Pasadena's Art Center College of Design, Mays worked in Germany for Audi AG for 14 years. The Teutonic approach to design, based on an attention to precision, function and the rigour of geometric form, that he absorbed at Audi is the basis of his own design thinking. But Mays also approaches design holistically and believes that branding and identity play as important a role as the actual design of the vehicle. He constantly looks at fashion, architecture, industrial design, film and graphic design as source material to inform his design choices.

In 1990, Mays returned to America to open the Southern California design studio for Audi–Volkswagen where he developed the first concept for the new VW Beetle (first shown to the public in 1994). The key to the new Beetle's success is a witty design that is remarkably contemporary but that maintains a strong visual and emotional association with the well-loved original. The circle is the overriding shape of the new car, even down to the headlights and speedometer. Anything added to that basic vocabulary would have muddied the message of simplicity and honesty that Mays wanted to convey.

Mays should be credited with the current craze for retro-design in cars, as it was sparked off by the design for the new Beetle. He does not consider his work as 'retro', preferring instead the term 'retrofuturism'. This describes his way of taking an iconic car from the past, which evokes strong feelings and cultural associations, and rethinking it for a contemporary market. Mays' recent work includes the redesigned Thunderbird, the Ford Forty-Nine concept, which is based on the 1949 Ford, and the new GT40, which is slated to go into production in 2003. BROOKE HODGE

1 Ford Thunderbird, 2002, Ford Motor Company.

> The modern Thunderbird borrows classic styling but retains a modern look. Among other details, the car's two-seat configuration, scoop in the bonnet, round headlights and egg-crate grille pay homage to the past but with 21st-century materials, technology and design language.

2 24.7 Pickup and Wagon Concept, 2000, Ford Motor Company.

> This boxy concept car comes in three versions, each designed for different lifestyles. Its dashboard is almost entirely a computer screen that features highly advanced communications technologies, including voice commands. These allow the driver to access e-mail, a hands-free mobile phone, real-time route assistance and weather reports.

1	2

1 24.7 Coupe Concept, 2000,
Ford Motor Company.
> The vehicle's exterior design features
simple geometric shapes and machined
surfaces that provide a technical look and
feel. These complement the advanced
communications technologies inside.

2 Forty-Nine Concept, 2001,
Ford Motor Company.
> This coupe concept car is inspired by
the '49 Ford, which was the first postwar
Ford design. The new Forty-Nine's smooth
appearance is achieved by an all-glass

upper body, velvety black finish, chrome
detailing, concealed windscreen wipers
and wrap-around tail lights. The car's
main gauges – the analogue tachometer
and electronic speedometer – are in a
single round instrument binnacle, similar
to the hot rods of the era.

3 GT40 Concept, 2002,
Ford Motor Company.
> The new high-performance concept car
is inspired by the legendary GT40 created
by Henry Ford II during the 1960s. Essential
elements of the original, such as the low
profile, sleek silhouette and V-8 engine,
have been retained, but every dimension
has been changed. The sweeping cowl,
subtle accent lines and fibre-optic headlights give the car a contemporary look.

1	2	3

There has long been a connection between the two design worlds of Scandinavia and the West Coast of America. It is partly, perhaps, the mutual heritage of liberal ideas that unites the two regions. Eero Saarinen and Charles Eames' collaboration is evidence of the association in the past, and today the Swedish-born industrial designer Thomas Meyerhoffer carries on the interaction between the two cultures by working in San Francisco.

After working for Porsche, IDEO and Apple, Meyerhoffer founded his own studio in 1999. He is now bringing his experience of industrial design to domestic products, such as the Cappellini m2 Chair (2002). Moving across the disciplines in this way is quite unusual and the more craft-based European domestic product business will gain from what Meyerhoffer has learnt in the world of us high-tech industrial design.

Meyerhoffer first came to prominence as part of the design team that designed the Apple eMate computer in 1998. This was Apple's first translucent computer, produced as part of Steve Jobs' repositioning of the company after a period in the doldrums. It took courage, but suddenly here was a laptop computer that was not for business people but for a young audience who wanted to have fun. The colour and organic shape, together with the translucency and clever features such as the integrated handle, brought a playfulness into computer design that has both taken the industry by storm and improved Apple's standing.

The studio's work now covers a wide spectrum: furniture, glass, sport and technology objects, and in part this is a reflection of Meyerhoffer's personality. He is an urban, sporty person interested in the latest technology. Designing sportswear is demanding because there are so many needs that have to be met: for example, the item has to be comfortable, aerodynamic and look good. Very interesting work comes from operating within these constraints. The goggles that Meyerhoffer has produced for Smith (2000) are both innovative and successful: he has designed a new kind of strap to be used specifically with helmets.

Meyerhoffer has developed a wearable combined computer/telephone for Ericsson called the m03. This prototype arose from thinking about which services are necessary to carry with you and how they can be tailored to suit an individual's need. The computer is a wrist device which uses the latest bluetooth (wireless) technology, and the personal phone comes as a clip with detachable earbuds. The m03 shows yet again Meyerhoffer's imaginative use of new materials. STEFAN YTTERBORN

1 eMate, laptop computer, 1998, translucent polycarbonate, 4.6 x 30.4 x 28.8 cm, Apple Computer.
› This design has been credited not only with numerous design awards, but was also the first stage in a dramatic reversal of Apple's fortunes. It was the first of their translucent computers, which are now integral to their identity. It incorporates innovative features such as the integrated handle and the tilted keyboard.

2 m2 Chair, 2002, plastic, aluminium, rubber, leather and nylon, 101 x 71.5 x 73.6 cm, Cappellini.
› This chair has brought together two styles – Californian surf culture mixed with Scandinavian simplicity – to produce something very original but with universal appeal.

1	2

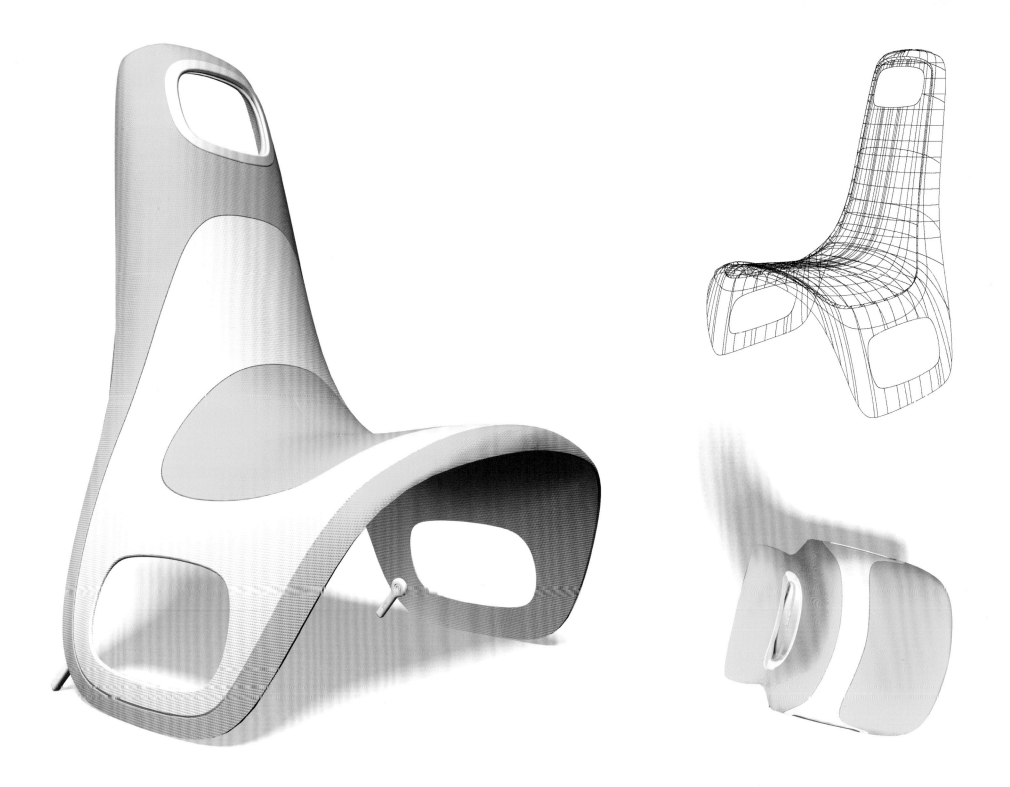

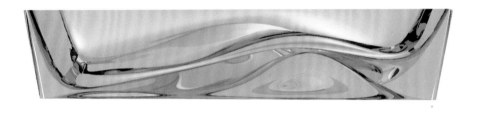

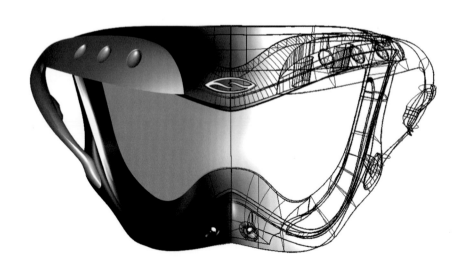

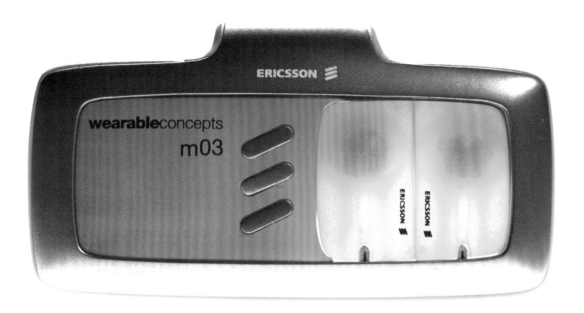

1 **Swell**, bowl, 2002, glass, silicon rubber, 8 x 3.6 x 17.6 cm, Danese.
› The design gives the bowl an unstable appearance, almost as though it were moving. The surface is created by a digital process, and each bowl is minutely different. The bowl is accompanied by a small personal pod in soft silicon, which is intended to hold your most valuable possessions.

2 **Warp Goggles**, 2000, rubber, polycarbonate, 9.2 x 20.2 x 6.8 cm, Smith Sports.
› Outrigger is a revolutionary strap attachment designed specifically for use with helmets in motorcars and skiing; it creates even pressure and helps position the frame on the user. The goggles have been highly acclaimed and have been worn by numerous world champions.

3 **m03**, phone, 2000, aluminium, rubber, injection-moulded plastic, body clip 3.2 x 7.2 x 7.2 cm, wrist computer 6 x 5.3 x 0.65 cm, camera 2.8 x 2.4 x 4.8 cm, concept for Ericsson.
› This phone is part of a series of wearable technology. It has three separate components: a detachable earphone in the aluminium frame, a wrist computer which is the input device and information display; and a small camera, placed on one's finger, for true 'point and shoot' action.

| 1 | 2 | 3 |

239

ANA MIR BARCELONA

Ana Mir, a Spaniard from Valencia, has a strong artistic streak that neither can nor should be concealed. She studied first at the Universidad de Bellas Artes in her native city, where she specialized in drawing. She then trained in industrial design, initially at Central Saint Martins College of Art & Design in London, and later in the Barcelona studio of Óscar Tusquets, with whom she worked for a couple of years.

In 1996, Mir launched her own studio in Barcelona in partnership with Emili Padrós. Mir first met Padrós when they were both studying at Central Saint Martins in London and the partnership has proved highly successful. Together they have designed a series of modest but highly ingenious objects, such as the Slástic Hanger (1997) and the Open 24 Hours Medicine Cabinet (1997).

In 1999, Mir took part in Futur Compost, meaning 'composite future' in Catalan, a competition staged during the Primavera del Diseño (spring design event) in Barcelona. Her entry represented a new concept for the bathroom. She used 'Gelapeutic', a jelly-like substance containing an active bacterium that feeds on dirt, has an in-built ability to cleanse itself and either a relaxing or a stimulating action on the user, depending on its temperature. Science fiction? Perhaps. The entry earned Mir a Ciutat de Barcelona (City of Barcelona) prize, along with all the credentials necessary to start her career.

When Mir and Padrós took part in a competition organized by *Domus* magazine they carried off the first prize, defeating big, international names such as Richard Sapper and Toyo Ito. The brief was to design the interior of the new Boeing 737-700. The jury was impressed by the Flying Carpet (2000) that Mir and Padrós developed in conjunction with Bernat Cuní, Susana Zarco and industrial engineer Ramón Camps. They did not present a project for the interior of an aeroplane, but a whole new concept of transport. Their design included areas for communal activities among passengers, such as a 'chill-out' space, a steam room and a kitchen.

Ingenuity and invention are Ana Mir's trademarks. Her products are designed to give pleasure to the whole body – not just the eyes. The Mininanicuña carpet or the fun-filled Pillow Play cushions beautifully illustrate this aspect of her work. If you are seeking a fuller understanding of sensory design, however, I must recommend making love between Mir's Kleensex sheets, after a glass of Cava, drunk while eating chocolate!

RAMÓN UBEDA

1 Flying Carpet, 2000, prototype in collaboration with Emili Padrós. Co-authors Bernat Cuní, Susana Zarco and Ramón Camps.
› This design won the *Domus* competition for the interior of the new Boeing 737-700 business jet. The project offers passengers the chance to make good use of their flying time by providing space for 'chilling out' and a steam room. It also gives them the opportunity to 'absorb' the journey, thanks to the chameleon-like ability of the cabin interior to take on the changing colour of the territory the plane is flying over.

2 Kleensex, sheets, 2001, tyvek, within packet 18 x 14 x 1.5 cm, unfolded 214 x 116 cm, prototype.
› Kleensex are disposable sheets that are especially suitable for the sex industry because they are clean, hygienic and come ready-folded to tuck away in a pocket or handbag. They are made of a light, thin and pleasant-to-touch material (tyvek, a derivative of polyethylene), and come in a variety of colours.

1	2

240

kleensex®
clean contact

1
disposable
pocket
sheet

100% polyethyl[...]

clean contact·kleensex·c[...]

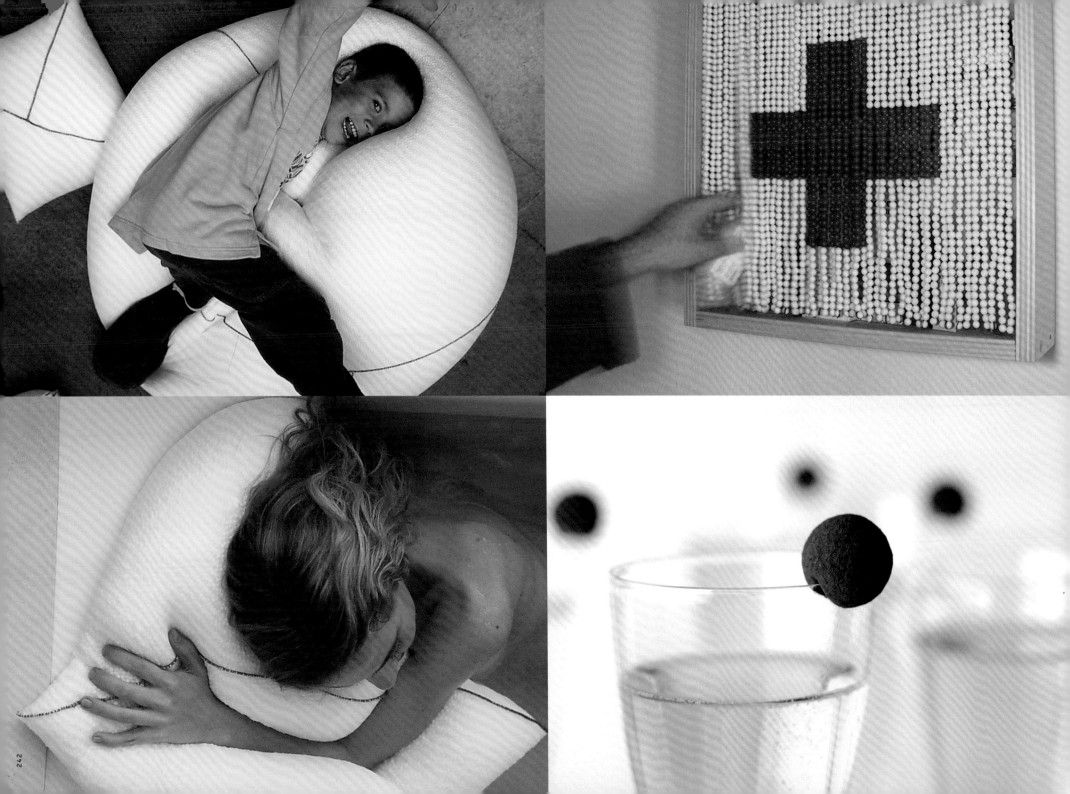

espacio
colectivo
repercute

1 Pillow Play, 1999, lycra, polystyrene,
5 sizes: 35 x 35 / 40 x 40 / 50 x 50 / 70 x 70 /
90 x 90 cm, prototype.
› These cushions are made from just one
piece of material and because they are filled
with little polystyrene balls weigh next to
nothing. The elastic fabric is as soft and yield
ing as skin and the texture is very therapeu-
tic. The cushions are easy to wash and you
can even take them into the bath with you.

2 Open 24 Hours Medicine Cabinet, 1997,
plywood, plastic balls, glass, 44 x 44 x 10 cm,
prototype in collaboration with Emili Padrós.

› This is designed to take the mystery out
of the traditional medicine cabinet by providing easy access via the curtain, which
also allows for ventilation.

3 Chocolate Accents, 2000, chocolate,
ø 2 cm, Enric Rovira.
› The chocolate ball has a slit that holds it,
like a cocktail olive, on the rim of a glass of
cava. This commission was from chocolate-
maker Enric Rovira for sweetening night visits
to the roof of Antonio Gaudí's celebrated
La Pedrera building in Barcelona.

4 Gelapeutic Bath, 1999, foam, silicone,
280 x 280 cm, prototype.
› This is a bath where water is replaced by
a special gel that has all the hygienic properties necessary for cleaning the body and
protecting and toning up the skin.

	2	4
1	3	

243

MARRE MOEREL NEW YORK

Marre Moerel is a young designer who has established herself as one of very few new figures on the American design scene. She belongs to a group of young people who have taken lessons from the great American design tradition of the 1950s, and this has brought new force and energy to their work.

For many years, designers in the United States have been divided into two groups. One group gives greater emphasis to the object's function than to its formal or sensuous qualities. The other group, to which Moerel naturally belongs, produces small collections of their own work. The artisan character of their products is often coupled with very high prices. Moerel started her career as a craftswoman and designer. She created her first products with enormous respect for her materials, great attention to detail, and a lively curiosity about production methods. These products, such as the Anatomy Series of glasses (2001), are simple, small, delicate and shaped with the skilful hand of someone with a deep love of their work.

Although Moerel's designs are both surprising and forceful, they are never loud or strident. Her materials are delicate, her colours bright, and her surfaces often translucent or opalescent. This combination makes her products seductive and pleasing to the touch. She is constantly searching for new forms, materials and functions, and often thinking of contemporary variations on the ways objects were used in the past. Her designs always have a profound simplicity that never becomes hackneyed.

Moerel lives in a big city, but she works with all the calm and serenity of someone living in an oasis of tranquillity, allowing her to think deeply and to contemplate at length her approach to a design project. Her style is feminine, gentle, rounded, but it shows great energy and determination. She does not fret about having constantly to create new designs, but works steadily, always striving to improve the products she makes and to find new, expressive effects. Given her tenacity, she will certainly succeed in carving out an increasingly distinctive position for herself on the international scene. Her designs have a timeless quality and will not easily become dated. For example, the Grow storage unit (1998), based on the structure of crystals, is an astonishing object that combines function with an extraordinary sculptural presence and a well-judged use of materials.

GIULIO CAPPELLINI

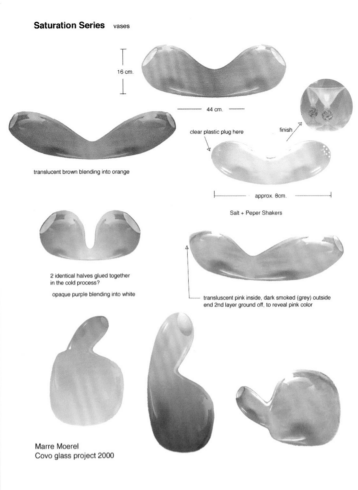

Saturation Series vases

16 cm.

44 cm.

clear plastic plug here   finish

translucent brown blending into orange

approx. 8cm.

Salt + Peper Shakers

2 identical halves glued together
in the cold process?

opaque purple blending into white

transluscent pink inside, dark smoked (grey) outside
end 2nd layer ground off, to reveal pink color

Marre Moerel
Covo glass project 2000

1 **Anatomy Series**, vases, 2001, Murano glass, various sizes, Smash for Covo.
› In this collection forms based on the human body were blown in Murano glass. The result is a series of unpredictable, sensuous glassware which has been manipulated into playful, organic forms.

2 **Soft Box MS2**, electric table lamp, 1998, earthenware ceramic, 40 x 15 x 15 cm, Cappellini.

3 **Soft Box Series**, candle holders, 1998, earthenware ceramic, various sizes, Cappellini.

4 **Spores and Colony**, candle holders, 2000, earthenware ceramic, various sizes, Cappellini.
› These collections exploit the fascinating way in which incandescent light is absorbed by unglazed ceramics.

5 **Perfume Bottle**, 1997, silicon implant, rubber nipple, 6 x ø 15 cm, concept prototype.
› This perfume bottle was conceived as a new concept for cosmetic packaging, soft and flexible with the feel and scent of a real human being.

6 **Small Models for Coral Lamp**, 2000, earthenware ceramic, various sizes, prototype.
› Many of Moerel's collections are inspired by her fascination with the origin of things: from molecular cell division, to skin tissue, to fully-grown organisms.

| 1 | 2 | 3 | 4 |
| 1 | | 5 | 6 |

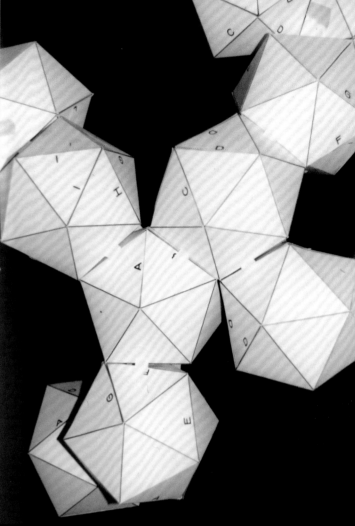

1 Gem, stool and table, 1998, plywood vinyl, various dimensions, prototype.
2 Grow Cabinet, 1998, works in progress.
› The Gem stool and table and the Grow Cabinet were developed simultaneously and were inspired by growing crystals.

3 Palette of Seductions I, lamp, 1996, ceramics, electric lights, 30 x 46 x 23 cm, Marre Moerel.
› This lighting fixture consists of 10 wall-mounted ceramic clogs. The installation marked a turning point in Moerel's work, when she started looking back to her own heritage and rediscovered her personal and cultural identity.

4 Lightweight Stool, 2001, insulation foam, laminate, 43 x 38 x 33 cm, Marre Moerel.
› By using simple construction techniques a series of knock-down furniture is developed. It is super lightweight and easy to produce, assemble and ship.

5 Grow, storage system, 1998, painted MDF, 157 x 71 x 61 cm, Marre Moerel.
› This modular storage unit is designed to accommodate chaos: things can just be thrown in without careful arranging or folding. This cabinet consists of six poly-hedral units that are randomly stacked on top of each other.

1		4	5
	3		5
2			

TED MUEHLING NEW YORK

Ted Muehling first attracted attention with his elegant jewellery, recognizable both for its sculptural simplicity and economy of materials. He uses fine metal and precious and semiprecious stones, and is inspired by found objects, both natural and artificial, from locations as diverse as the seashore and the flea market.

Muehling introduced his first tableware line in 2000, commissioned by Nymphenburg, the legendary 200-year-old German porcelain factory. His exquisite bowls, cups and spoons seem a natural extension of his work with jewellery. The 17-piece collection is inspired by the forms and colours of eggs and sea shells which, like porcelain, have a fragility that belies their inherent strength. 'What I do', he said in 2000, 'is simplify the natural object. I make it easier to see the beauty of it, the soft, smooth shape of it.' Muehling's work is not a direct quotation from nature, but rather a delicate recasting of it. His pieces are man-made, yet they remain immersed in nature.

Salviati, the revered Venetian glass house, asked Muehling to create a collection and several of these pieces were shown during the Salone del Mobile in Milan in 2001. A set of delicate, amber-coloured glass bowls with increasingly tapered forms nest inside one another, looking like an unusual flower – a protea perhaps, or a lotus.

Despite the variety of his materials, Muehling describes his work as a continuum, evolving as he is exposed to new materials, techniques and collaborators. His fascination with the organic forms and textures of the natural world is always evident. Certain forms are refined and transformed over time, or developed in new ways for new materials. The twig, which appears in both porcelain and metal, is one such example. Eggs crafted from semiprecious stones appeared as door knobs early on, and later as bowls and cups made in porcelain.

An incurable collector, Muehling's studio is filled with twigs, eggs, coral, nests, bone and pieces of bark. His work is not about the latest technology or the newest materials; it is about the creation of beautiful, enduring pieces from the traditional materials of the artisan. As he says, 'My design embodies a combination of craftsmanship and intuition, a tracing of the invisible forms that exist between nature and our perceptions of it.' His unique vision and imagination render the pieces both timeless and original.

BROOKE HODGE

1 Sconce, candle holder, 1998, sterling silver, 28 x 10 x 11 cm, Ted Muehling.
› Sconce has been made out of a single piece of hand-hammered and formed sterling silver. The flickering light of the candle is reflected by the shiny metal, creating a glowing yet serene source of light.

2 Ginkgo Hairpin, 1976, silver, 14 x 5 cm, Ted Muehling.
› One of Muehling's earliest designs, these hand-hammered silver hairpins epitomize elegance. They are extremely delicate without having fussy detail and they are simple without being primitive.

3 Coral Vase, 1999, porcelain, 29 x ø 13 cm, Porzellan-Manufaktur Nymphenburg.
4 Coral Lantern, 1999, porcelain, 15 x ø 10 cm, Porzellan-Manufaktur Nymphenburg.
› The intricately perforated porcelain sparkles like the night sky when the lantern is lit with a candle. As with all Muehling's porcelain pieces, each item has been thrown, formed and painted by hand.

5 Lotus Bowls, 2001, glass, large plate 14 x ø 54 cm, wide bowl 17 x ø 33 cm, narrow bowl 28 x ø 18 cm, tall vase 39 x ø 9 cm, Salviati.
› The Lotus set of bowls consists of four nesting amber-coloured glass pieces. They are part of a limited edition of 15, all of which are hand blown.

| 1 | 2 | 3 | 5 |
| | | 4 | |

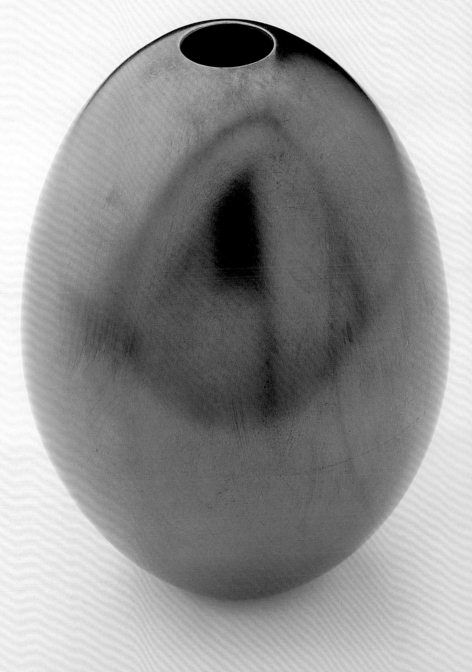

1 **Lotus Dish**, 1998, sterling silver,
4 x ø 10 cm, Ted Muehling.
2 **Silver Shell Dish**, 1998, sterling silver,
4 x ø 10 cm, Ted Muehling.
3 **Egg Vase**, 1999, oxidized bronze,
11 x ø 7.5 cm, Ted Muehling.
› Many of Muehling's designs are inspired
by beautiful natural forms.

4 **Coral Spoons**, 1999, white bisque and red
glazed porcelain, 14/15 x 3 cm, Porzellan-
Manufaktur Nymphenburg.
› The textured white spoon was inspired
by bleached shards of coral found on a

Caribbean beach, while the rich red-orange
colour and branch shape of the caviar spoon
resembles the coral of the Mediterranean.

5 **Concave Cup**, 1999, bisque porcelain,
9 x ø 8 cm, Porzellan-Manufaktur
Nymphenburg, with **Queen Anne's Lace
Tea Strainer**, 1999, sterling silver, ø 7 cm,
Ted Muehling.
› The delicate tea strainer is inspired by
the Queen Anne's Lace flower, a form
Muehling has also used in jewellery design.

6 **Bone Cufflink**, 1998, 18k white gold,
2.6 x 1.6 x 1.3 cm, Ted Muehling.
› The shape of these solid cufflinks
is inspired by small animal bones.

7 View of Ted Muehling's studio.

1		5	7
	3	4	
2		6	

I don't know anything about Yugo Nakamura, I don't know his age, his day-time job or where he appeared from. I don't even know if he really exists, but I do own one of his clocks. Actually, I don't exactly own it, rather I down-loaded his product. The clock is made of ever-stacking building blocks that form six towers. Each tower represents a digit, and when they reach ten high they topple. I shouldn't be describing it to you really, just go to Yugo Nakamura's website: http://surface.yugop.com and see for yourself; I think it is called Clockblock.

While you are on the site, I recommend you also go to the Industrious Clock which, incidentally, I prefer. But the Clockblock makes the point bet-ter – the point being that while we designers spend our computer time on rendering representations of our objects or building CAD models to be trans-lated into real objects, Yugo's (can I call you Yugo?) virtual reality is the object, not depicting anything else, not giving instructions for anything else.

If we believe that design and objects are there to render pleasure and delight while performing a function, Yugo's products can be identified as doing just that, and doing it beautifully. Although mouse-clicking is a very lonely activity, at http://surface.yugop.com other people's loneliness is right there with you!

Fingertracks is a good example. When, fuelled by human curiosity and Pavlovian instinct, you follow opaque dots on a matrix with your cursor, each revealing 'nothing', you can then see the traces of your quest for some-thing, finding nothing, and also many other people's equally fruitless trails. Identical quests but infinitely diverse routes – aren't we all individuals?

By the time this book goes to print I am sure that Yugo Nakamura's website will have a lot more products, and if anyone is anxious about virtual reality taking over from tangible reality, a visit here could only enhance the anxiety! But on the other hand, it might provide a reassuring relief from it. RON ARAD

http://surfac

1 Yugo Nakamura website address.

2 **Clockblock**, 2001, website, Yugo Nakamura.
› When the user opens this 'clock' on the website, six displays appear containing the hour, minute and second. The time is constantly updated by a hand putting little wooden cubes one on top of another; when they reach the number ten the hand knocks the pile down and starts again from one.

| 1 | 2 |

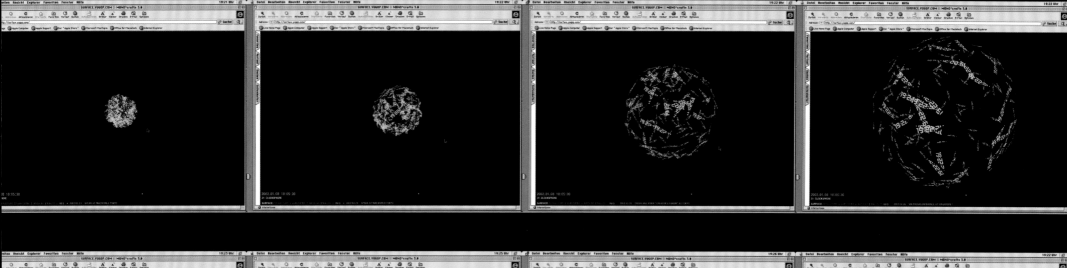

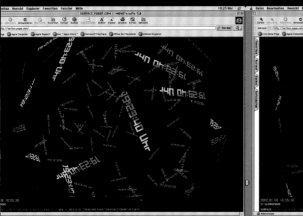  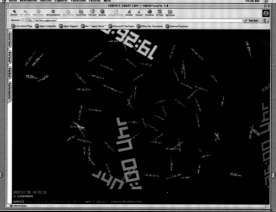 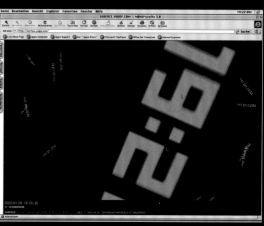

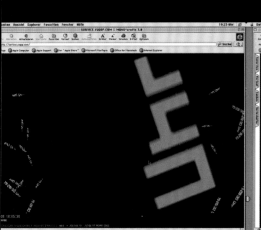 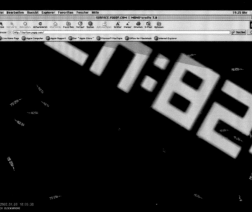

1 Industrious Clock, 2001, website,
Yugo Nakamura.
> In this clock-calendar the six displays
contain the year, month, day, hour, minute
and second, all the numbers for which are
written in pencil, by hand. The data is constantly updated in real time: the old number is erased and the new one written in
the space.

2 Clocksphere, 2002, website,
Yugo Nakamura.
> In a video loop, the digital numbers
indicating the hour, minute and second
appear and start floating in the computer
screen until the moment they come
together to form a sphere, and then they
again start to divide. The clock is adapted
to the country and time zone of the computer user.

1	2

Although Marc Newson's name is known among *cognoscenti*, it is only recently that his products have become familiar to a wider, less exclusive, international audience. Newson's ideas have developed along a clear trajectory ever since his earliest do-it-yourself projects. Among these are his use of organic forms and his interest in biomorphism and streamlined, 1950s design.

Having worked for a number of years in Tokyo with Idée – a Japanese furniture and design company under the direction of Teruo Kurosaki – Newson was little known on the international scene. It was not until about 1997, when he produced the Dish Doctor dish rack, that Newson became a feature of the American design scene. The Dish Doctor, manufactured by Magis, was designed when Newson moved to London, formed a partnership with architect Benjamin de Haan, and began to work with advanced, computer-aided design software. His use of rapid prototyping enabled him to go straight from the computer screen to tooling, so he could produce the piece in large quantities at a low price. But this was not the only reason for the product's success: dish racks had never been seen in such brilliant colours and his ingenious design did away with the need for a separate tray. Suddenly, consumers realized that such an everyday object could be both useful and dashing. Newson's work has since come to be identified by his use of bright, almost fluorescent, oranges and greens. He has developed other household items, such as doorstops and soap dishes, using the same production methods.

A recent line of hair-care appliances for Vidal Sassoon represents an expansion in Newson's range of product types. It reveals his ability to examine an everyday object and give it a twist that reinvigorates it, making it inherently more functional. This can be seen in the flattening out of the hair-dryer's head, which allows it to rest on a sink edge without falling off. These new appliances are infinitely more stylish than anything comparable on the market.

By refusing to limit his practice to one type or line of product, Newson has been able to chart new territory and try his hand at assignments as varied as a bicycle for Biomega, a concept car for Ford and the interior of a private jet. His desire to push boundaries and to experiment with new production methods has invested his work with unexpected strength and vigour.

BROOKE HODGE

1 Dish Doctor, dish rack, 1997, injection-moulded polyethylene, 10.5 x 39 x 45.5 cm, Magis.
> The dish rack is a stylish accessory that no longer needs to be hidden under the sink; it is simple, attractive and available in a range of colours. In manufacturing this product, the designer used rapid prototyping technology to go from screen to production with few modifications.

2 Apollo Torch, 1997, aluminium, 24 x ø 5.6 cm, Flos.
> The sleek silver design was inspired by Apollo, the god of light. Made of anodized aluminium and resting in an orange plastic case, Apollo dispels the notion that a torch must look utilitarian.

3 Bumper Bed, 1997, polyurethane, webbing strap, 45 x 252 x 192 cm, Cappellini.
> The bed structure comprises upholstered segments held in place with an elasticated webbing strap.

4 Hair Care Appliances, 1999–2000, injection-moulded plastic, Vidal Sassoon.
> These hair-care appliances have been transformed from banal objects into trendy accessories. The hair dryer is especially well designed: its flat head allows it to rest on a countertop or sink so the user need not worry about breakage or electrocution.

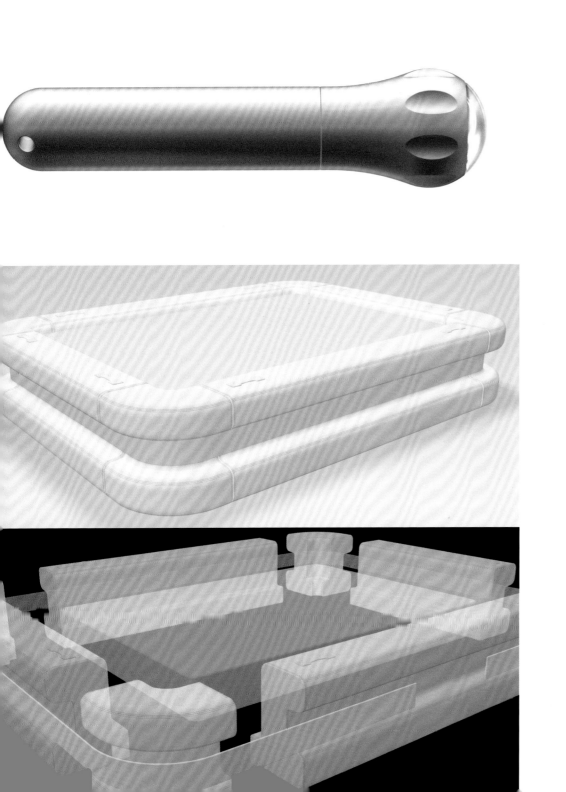
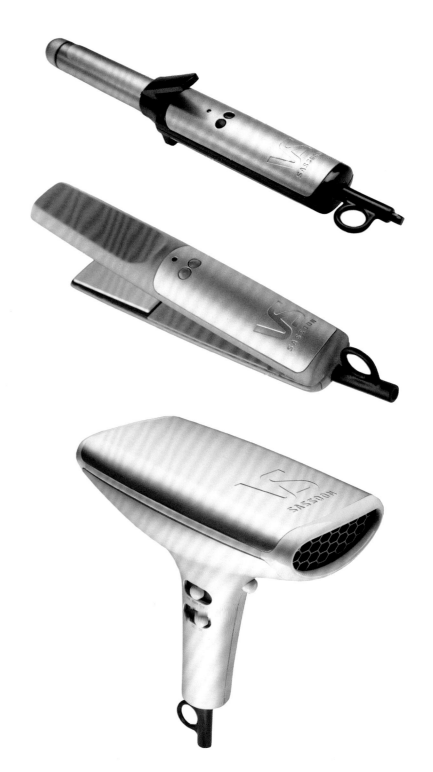

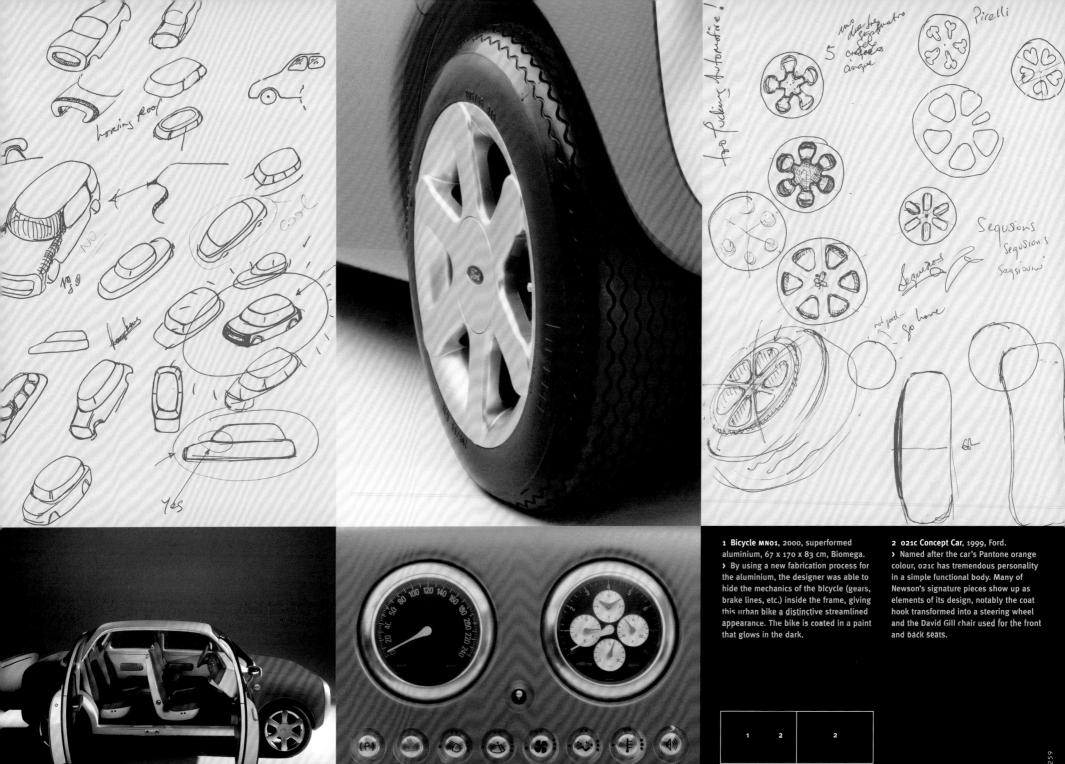

1 **Bicycle MN01**, 2000, superformed aluminium, 67 x 170 x 83 cm, Biomega.
> By using a new fabrication process for the aluminium, the designer was able to hide the mechanics of the bicycle (gears, brake lines, etc.) inside the frame, giving this urban bike a distinctive streamlined appearance. The bike is coated in a paint that glows in the dark.

2 **021c Concept Car**, 1999, Ford.
> Named after the car's Pantone orange colour, 021c has tremendous personality in a simple functional body. Many of Newson's signature pieces show up as elements of its design, notably the coat hook transformed into a steering wheel and the David Gill chair used for the front and back seats.

1	2	2

SHIN NISHIBORI KYOTO

I am particularly enamoured of Nishibori's Sponge Chair (1999), which is known and loved by a wide public. It is a sensual object, and when it was installed in Elfish, the café that Nishibori designed in Kyoto, it made a great impact. The chair derives its effect from a combination of strange shapes, bright colours and its unusual, spongy material, reminiscent both of the sponges used for washing up and the sheet sponge sometimes used to line interior walls. Thus, like so many of Nishibori's designs, the chair evokes many layers of association and many different levels of response. This multi-layered aspect of the work means that it sits as well in a cutting-edge, futuristic café as in the warm, intimate interior of a mid-century revival café, where wood is the dominant material. In its dual nature it combines references to the warm, domestic intimacy of the kitchen with the large, impersonal spaces of the factory floor. Beyond both of these references is the chair's eccentricity, which evokes images of a futuristic space odyssey.

Nishibori's designs are no simple reflection of contemporary style in Japan. After working as an in-house designer for a large manufacturer of domestic electrical goods, he has developed a style that is uniquely his own. His working environment has brought a severe professionalism to his work, which has evolved in a landscape dominated by business theory, market research and consumerism.

During his time with Panasonic, Nishibori designed the P-case (1996), a revolutionary casing for a CD player. This piece was seen as a funda-mental challenge to the normal criteria applied to the design of household electric goods, as in Japan it was rare that really good design emerged in this field. But the overwhelming response to the P-case, with its witty but essentially functional design, proved that this is no longer true (see Tomoko Ishiguro's article on Nishibori in *Axis*, no.7/8, 1999). The P-case is profoundly simple. It is slim, its surface is smooth, and it is presented in a white box. The simplicity of the design, so typical of Nishibori, has powerful appeal.

In the *Axis* magazine article Nishibori said that the designer must be self-critical and must mount a protest against the consumerism and conspicuous consumption that has filled the environment with industrial waste and superfluous goods. In this Nishibori is truly contemporary.

RYU NIIMI

1 **P-case**, CD player, 1996, ABS, aluminium, 17.7 x 46 x 7 cm, Panasonic.
› This is a portable CD player. The striking look is achieved by keeping the few lines of the design clear and to a minimum. The durable, plain appearance is enhanced by the use of aluminium.

1 **Cokmok Series**, 2002, stainless steel, wood, potato peeler 1.4 x 15 x 5.5 cm, bottle opener 1.4 x 14.5 x 3.5, Covo.
› These tools are sleek, practical pieces of cutlery, intended for everyday use. The material has been carefully selected for its strength and water-resistance.

2 **Kyorokyoro Speakers**, 1999, maple wood, 26.4 x 70 x 30, Shin Products.
› The pair of eye-shaped speakers are finely balanced instead of lying flat on a surface. This allows them to rock sideways.

3 **Tongpoo**, rug, 1999, wool, small 132 x 75 cm, medium 192 x 102 cm, large 252 x 130 cm, Shin Products.
› Nishibori has named this cloud-shaped rug Tongpoo, Japanese for eastern wind

4 **ring*ring**, dishware, 2000, ceramic, various dimensions, Ricordy and Sfela.
› Plain but not ordinary, this set of dishware has the decoration integrated into the form. Each object has a sequence of contours that is unique to the item, but unites them all as a set.

5 **Sponge Chair**, 1999, polyurethane, steel, 70 x 38 x 50 cm, Sogo.
› By cutting a single polyurethane mattress into a wavelike form, Nishibori has revived comfort and style. The colours of this chair were chosen to evoke the tail of a goldfish.

	1		5
			4
2	3		

PATRICK NORGUET PARIS

Patrick Norguet belongs to the young generation of French designers. He came to industrial design after working for many years as a dress designer with some of the top French fashion houses. There he experienced the pleasure of working on designs of the highest calibre, and learned that quality is to be looked for in the way a product is actually made, rather than in superficial glamour. This has been the guiding idea behind Patrick Norguet's creative development. He loves to experiment with different materials and forms, often combining them in new and unusual ways. Working with materials in this way does not compel him to create craft objects. His aim is always to make products with a solid grounding in industrial culture. He is constantly developing that aspect of his work, since he firmly believes that modern techniques can often match or even improve on the quality of products that were once exclusively handmade.

Norguet's forms are never angular or rigid, but rounded and appealing, and the materials that he uses never conflict. To the casual glance, his pieces look like art works, but on closer examination they reveal themselves as genuine and innovative design objects. His cultural background means that he works completely independently, uninfluenced by the great designers, and without any reference to France's leading contemporary architects.

Colour and decoration are constants in Norguet's work, but they are used to enhance form and function, never to conceal it. His designs are strong, clear and striking, but at the same time they fit easily into domestic interiors of all kinds, proof that, while they are utterly contemporary, they have strong traditional roots.

Patrick Norguet's design style could be called glamorous in the best sense of the word, a sign of its modernity and individuality. His Rainbow Chair (2001) is one of his most characteristic works, combining advanced industrial techniques with a sculptural form to produce a multicoloured chair with a strong visual impact. The Rive Droite Collection (2001) of furniture, on the other hand, shows how a good design can be clothed in the fabrics of a great stylist such as Emilio Pucci, without losing its own identity. GIULIO CAPPELLINI

1 Hold On, tray, 2002, stamped silver-plated tray, 5 x 27 x 42.5 cm, De Vecchi.
› This design seeks to demonstrate that a minimalistic object is interesting as long as it continues to express modernity.

2 Ancolie, vase, 1998, ceramic, 5 x 24 x 10 cm, Musée des Arts Decoratifs, Paris.
› This vase is an organic design which evokes a highly stylized form of nature. It is able to transform a few flowers into a blooming coronet.

3 Glove, bowl, 2001, ceramic, 15 x ø 30 cm, Artoria.
› This fruit basket has a perfectly semi-spherical bowl, which is supported by an arcaded rim.

4 Element, dish, 2001, ceramic, 12.5 x ø 33 cm, Artoria.
› This table centre could serve as anything from a plant pot to a bread basket. The design is simple but endearing. The central disk is stacked on a crown, which doubles as a suppport.

	2	
1	3	4

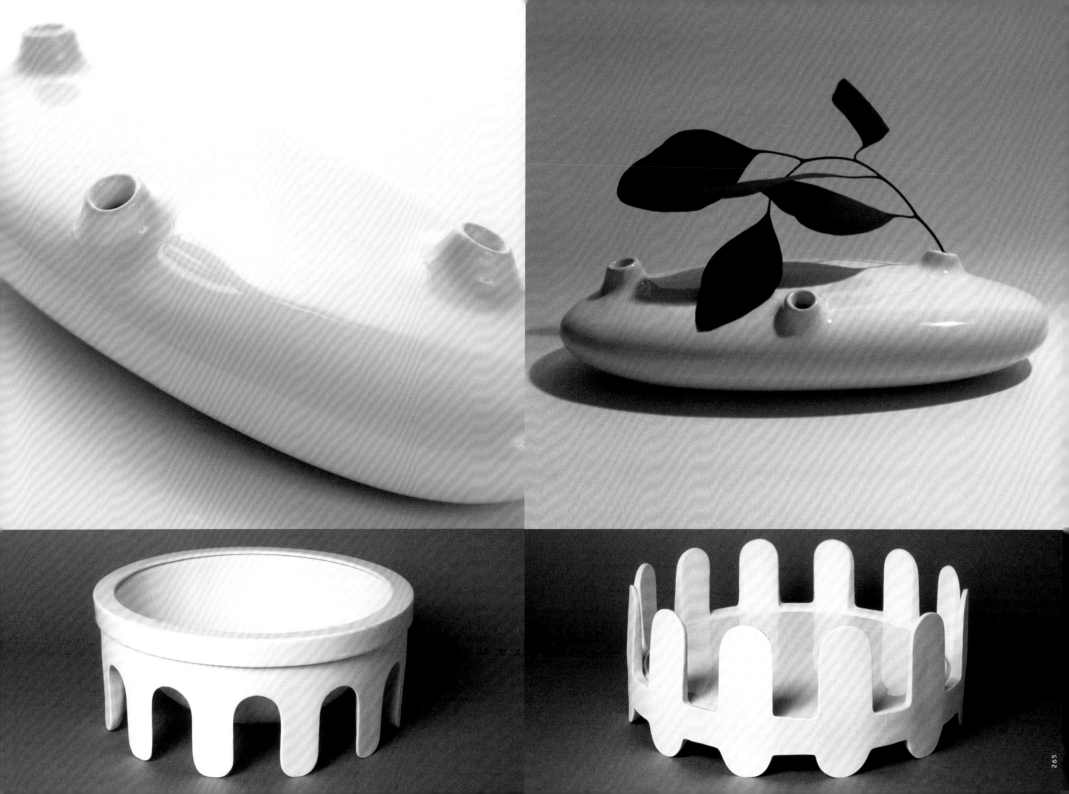

1 Seo Table, 2002, thermoformed wood, lacquered finish, stainless steel, 40 x 110 x 55 cm, Liv'it.

2 Empty Table, 2001, metal, injected polyurethane foam, coloured glass, 50 x ø 60 cm, Cappellini.
› In this table transparent and opaque disks float on tube legs. A dish can be inserted in the central opening.

3 Rainbow Chair, 2001, PMMA resin sandwich, plexiglass, 85 x 50 x 42 cm, Cappellini.

› This chair is made of an innovative PMMA sandwich in which several coloured sheets are cut and glued together.

4 Rive Droite Collection, 2001, injected polyurethane foam, Emilio Pucci fabric, sofa 76 x 180 x 68.5 cm, armchair 66 x 90 x 68.5 cm, Cappellini.
› The interaction of graphic and fashion design creates hybrids that are more than contemplative objects.

5 Apollo, chair, 2002, injected polyurethane foam, fabric, 66 x 90 x 53 cm, Artifort.
6 What's Up, sofa, 2002, injected polyurethane foam, fabric, 53 x 180 x 68.5 cm, Artifort.
› Although industrially produced, these seats have a personal touch that so many mass-produced objects lack.

1			5
	3	4	6
2			

267

NORWAY SAYS

The Norway Says collective exhibited together for the first time in 2000 at Milan's Salone del Mobile. The five members, Andreas Engesvik, Torbjørn Anderssen, Frode Myhr, Tore Borgersen and Espen Voll, were united by a desire to overcome the lack of a design tradition in Norway. When the collective was first formed, its members presented their prototypes together, but they always worked separately. As mutual respect has grown, some of the group have started to collaborate on individual projects. They work to a calendar dictated by the annual round of design fairs, which they are dedicated to attending.

When asked to justify their collective style, which is craft-based, warm, considered, and human in scale, with unabashed modernist overtones, Norway Says refers to the lack of a national style that has characterized Norwegian design in recent years. Given this situation, the group has a blank sheet of paper to work on. 'We have no national heroes like Aalto in Finland or Jacobsen in Denmark,' they explain, 'we can interpret Norwegian design in any way we see fit.'

Norway Says does not deny that craftsmanship and hard work are built into its collective character, but inspiration comes from every corner of the globe. All the members have chosen to stay in Norway for the time being. 'If you can't produce nice stuff when surrounded by peace in Norway,' they explain, 'then you won't do it by changing your address to New York, London or Milan.'

And nice stuff is indeed what Norway Says produces. The Konrad Chair (2001) by Torbjørn Anderssen is assembled from four laminated oak components, making it incredibly simple to manufacture. Anderssen's intention is to paraphrase Scandinavian design traditions, while giving the construction an open aesthetic and a fresh edge. The chair has a wonderfully individual character. Anderssen's most recent adventure, however, uses a completely different kind of material. An outdoor/indoor chair called Backyard Accessory (2001), it is made from polypropylene. Storage units, such as Hiawatha (2001) by Frode Myhr, or Mer shelving (2000) by Tore Borgersen are functional and discreet. Engesvik's slick, slim, wall-mounted bureau, PS (2000), is typical of the collective's considered reworkings of the usual furniture types.

Norway Says is the antithesis of the celebrity designers who attract so much attention today. Its honest and hard-working approach to design is something for which we should be grateful. LAURA HOUSELEY

1 **Konrad Chair**, 2001, laminated oak, 32 x 70 x 45 cm, designed by Torbjørn Anderssen.
› Konrad is a low seat constructed from traditional Scandinavian furniture types.

2 **Mer**, shelf, 2000, laquered plywood, 180 x 90 x 7 cm, designed by Tore Borgersen.
› This system enables shelves to be positioned easily on the vertical support. Each horizontal slot provides ample support for the shelves.

3 **PS**, desk, 2000, oak veneer, 50 x 80 x 6 cm, designed by Andreas Engesvik.
› This compact desk is fixed to the wall, the work surface folds down and objects can be stored as shown for ease of use.

4 **Playmo**, table, 2001, MDF, 50 x 45 x 130 cm, designed by Torbjørn Anderssen.
› This table pays homage to plastic toys.

5 **Hole**, table, 2000, laminated plywood, veneered in teak, 35 x 80 x 30 cm, designed by Espen Voll.
› Hole's wheels function on a ball-bearing mechanism developed by the designer.

6 **Crème & Choco**, 2001, cotton canvas, wool fabric, varnished steel, table 72 x 130 x 130 cm, chair 72 x 60 x 45 cm, designed by Frode Myhr.
› The table has two surfaces: one for eating, the other for trays and dishes. The wide seats provide the comfort needed while eating.

1	2	3
	4	5	6

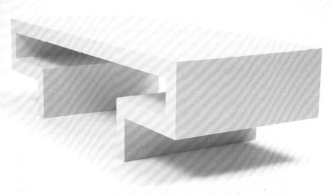
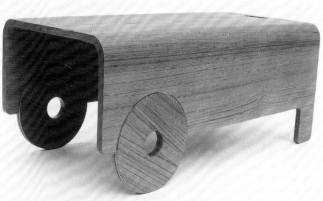

1 Hiawatha, storage system, 2001, epoxy, foam, veneer, aluminium, 50 x 240 x 50 cm, designed by Frode Myhr, prototype.
› This storage system can store almost anything and can also be used as a bench. Each shell has its own track and slides beneath the next one.

2 Backyard Accessory, chair, 2001, stainless steel, polypropylene, 85 x 40 x 66 cm, designed by Torbjørn Anderssen in collaboration with Myrna Becker and Merethe Strømmen.
› The outdoor/indoor chair shows the group's willingness to experiment with materials other than traditional wood. Backyard has plug-in accessories which enable the user to customize the chair for their comfort and convenience.

3 Dock High, chair, 2000, laminated wood, steel, 73 x 50 x 45 cm, designed by Tore Borgersen and Espen Voll, Globe.
› This light dining chair is built up of single, curved, laminated slats into a stable double-curved shape. The chair is stackable and can be separated from its legs for ease of transport. The Dock chair family consists of five chairs: the high version with and without armrests; a lounge version; a stool and a barstool.

		3
1	2	

FABIO NOVEMBRE MILAN

Fabio Novembre belongs to the new generation of Italian designers, and in the space of a few years he has acquired both prestige and a high public profile. Although his style has evolved in the design environment of Milan, his approach is individual, bold and ironic. He has never been 'one of the pack', and this has allowed him to make surprising and entirely unexpected designs, which seem at first sight to have no commercial rationale.

Before moving into industrial design, Novembre built up a solid body of work as an interior designer, specializing in restaurants and discotheques, where the element of spectacle is fundamental. He then transferred the idea of the 'logical surprise' to articles for everyday use. It is often difficult to retain the same powers of expression when changing scale from interiors to individual objects. In Novembre's case, the transition has been entirely successful. His curiosity about new forms and materials, whether those of the craftsman or the more technologically sophisticated practitioner, is always evident in his designs.

Novembre does not wish merely to make useful objects. He aims above all to create things that we can live with, play with and enjoy. His own personality combines the professionalism of a designer with the enthusiasm of a man who believes deeply in his work, and most of all he tries to give joy and pleasure. Although they are industrial products, his designs are like works of sculpture, at home in the most varied settings. Often monumental, they always have a strong appeal for the user. Their sensuous shapes, so unlike the rigid models often imposed by industrial design, make them hard to resist. It is never enough simply to admire Novembre's work, you are always drawn into a deeper relationship with it.

Novembre seems to inhabit a fairytale world, a place in which we would all like to take refuge. We cannot think of the ORG table (2001) or the NET carpet (2001) as purely practical objects, but as a stage on which to perform, or a toy to amuse ourselves with.

In design terms, AND (2002) situates itself midway between architecture and object. Far from being passive observers of the product, we immediately find ourselves trying to interact with it. AND shows us that a large, imposing object can capture our attention and take us by surprise.

GIULIO CAPPELLINI

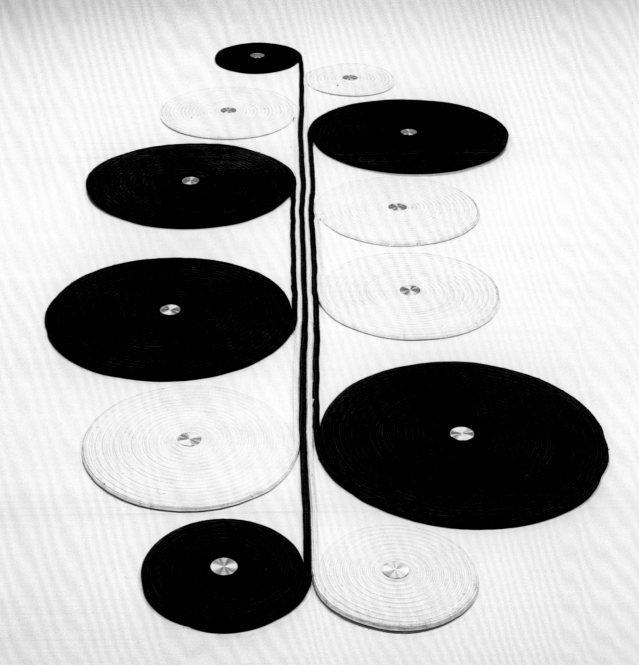

1 NET, carpet, 2001, woven polypropylene rope, stainless steel, 300 x 150 cm/600 x 200 cm, Cappellini.
> NET is a carpet generated by whorls of rope all flowing from a central, connecting spine. The composition allows for movement of the different whorls to create a changing pattern on the floor.

2 ORG, table, 2001, flexible polypropylene rope, brushed stainless steel, glass, 72 x 100 x 200 cm, 72 x ø 120 cm, 110 x ø 60 cm, Cappellini.
> ORG is a table worried about what is going to happen under it. In the largest version, the 175 legs, of which only six are for support, create a sort of ORGanism which floats in space. The table's soft rope legs interact with the legs of the people sitting around it and create an unexpected environment for those who want a different experience.

| 1 | 2 |

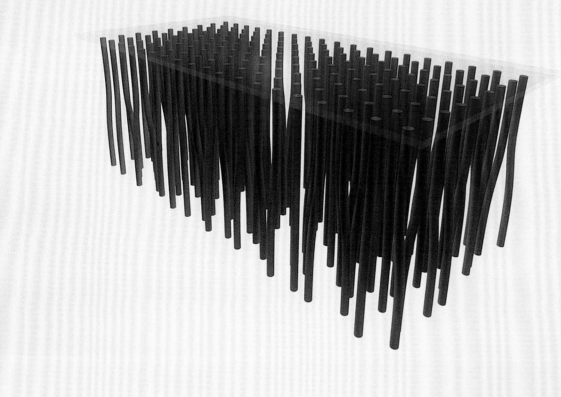

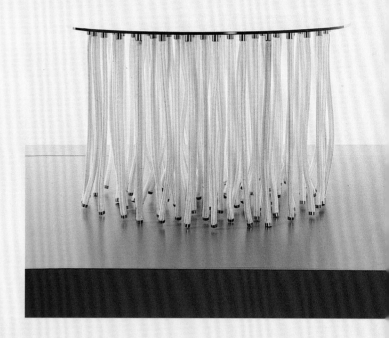

1 NET, carpet, 2001, woven polypropylene rope, stainless steel, 300 x 150 cm/600 x 200 cm, **ORG**, table, 2001, flexible polypropylene rope, brushed stainless steel, glass, 72 x 100 x 200 cm, Cappellini.

2 AND – Time for Conjunction, sofa system, 2002, wood, metal structure, multi-density-polyurethane foam, fabric or leather, 45/230 x 160 x 175 cm, Cappellini.
> AND is an asymmetrical, spiral, vis à vis sofa that can be joined in an endless system to become a metaphorical DNA for people who want to get together. This is a new generation spatial seating system after Verner Panton's Visiona '70.

1	2

FRANK NUOVO LOS ANGELES

Frank Nuovo is Nokia's Vice President and its chief designer. As the company is the world's largest producer of mobile communication devices, his designs are ubiquitous. An industrial design graduate of Pasadena's Art Center College of Design, Nuovo began his career at Designworks/USA, a California design consultancy that is now an in-house studio for BMW. There he worked on a wide range of products, including car interiors, air-traffic controls, and patio furniture for Samsonite. In 1992 Nuovo designed the Nokia 101, the design that is now so closely identified with the company. He joined the company officially in 1995 and since then he has been responsible for the design of all their phones.

Nuovo is quick to point out that his is not a sole enterprise. Like his design colleagues at large corporations, such as J Mays at Ford Motor Company or Tom Ford at Gucci, he oversees the design of several product lines. Working with a team of other designers and technicians, his role is that of a creative director. Nevertheless, Nuovo has a hands-on approach – he constantly sketches new ideas for phones. His design team then works them up into wax or digital models.

When Nuovo began to do work for Nokia, mobile phones were still something of a novelty. His vision was a combination of cutting-edge technology (function) and design (beauty) that made the mobile phone into more than a calling device. With Nokia, he has introduced a number of innovations: the changeable colour faceplates of the Nokia 5100 (1998); the emphasis on a larger screen display area; and the elliptical design theme of the Nokia 2100 (1994) and 6100 series (1997), which softened the sharp corners that tore at the linings of pockets and handbags. Nuovo also introduced luxurious finishes, using materials such as chrome, stainless steel, matt aluminium and titanium.

Early in 2002, Frank Nuovo announced the formation of Vertu, a separate company and brand under the Nokia umbrella, and launched a new line of personal communication devices. More than just mobile phones, Vertu products combine the highest levels of design and craftsmanship with precision engineering. They are billed as the world's first luxury communication instruments, offering multi-language text input, text messaging and a large user memory, among other features. This is Frank Nuovo's brainchild and he sees Vertu as raising the standard of mobile communications to a whole new level. BROOKE HODGE

1 8810, 1998, ABS, metallic plating, 7 x 4.6 x 1.8 cm, Nokia.
> Clear lines and sophisticated technology make the Nokia 8810 a premium phone, not just as a personal communications tool, but as a truly exquisite accessory. It weighs only about 100 grams and has a distinctive metallic coating.

2 101, early 1990s, PC/ABS coloured resin, 19 x 5.7 x 2.7 cm, Nokia.
> The 101 was the first mobile phone to have easy one-touch dialling, available in a variety of colours.

3 8110, 1997, PC/ABS resin, 14.1 x 4.8 x 2.5 cm, Nokia.
> The revolutionary curved design of the 8110 fits the natural shape of the face and has a unique sliding mouthpiece for maximum voice quality. This is the first Nokia phone with dot matrix full-graphic display, which changes the text size automatically for easy viewing.

4 5100, 1998, PC/ABS coloured resin, 13.2 x 4.7 x 3.1 cm, Nokia.
> The first mobile phone with interchangeable covers, the 5100 was designed to appeal to the mass-market as a fashion accessory. This product established Nokia as the industry leader in personal and leisure communications.

	2	
1		4
	3	

1 8910, 2002, titanium,
10.3 x 4.6 x 2 cm, Nokia.
> This sophisticated and elegant mobile
phone combines fine mechanics and materials with GPRS (general packet radio services)
and Bluetooth (wireless) capabilities.

2 9210, 2002, PC/ABS resin,
15.8 x 5.6 x 2.7 cm, Nokia.
> This pioneering product showcases the
key elements in future mobile communications, such as easy navigation, high quality
colour display, and mobile messaging with
high-speed data transmission.

3 7210, 2002, PC/ABS resin,
10.6 x 4.5 x 1.8 cm, Nokia.
> The 7210 exudes urban trendiness with
a daring design, including a new keypad
layout and a 4-way scroll. It features a high-
resolution colour screen and an FM radio.

4 6100 series, 1997, PC/ABS coloured
resin, 13 x 4.7 x 2.8 cm, Nokia.
> This stylish and ergonomical design
features three chameleon covers which
change colour according to the light and
the phone's position.

5 Vertu, 2002, platinum,
12.2 x 4.2 x 1.5 cm, Nokia.
> The Vertu combines the highest levels
of design, craftsmanship, precision engineering and personal service. It has a full
sapphire face and solid metal detailing.

| 1 | 2 | 3 | 5 |
| | | 4 | |

ORA-ÏTO PARIS

It is quite difficult to find a precise location for Ora-Ïto on the map of contemporary design. He could be described as a graphic artist, a designer, a visionary, an illustrator or an inventor of 'impossible' designs that have created huge public interest in his work.

As a very young man, convinced that he would not find a production company willing to take him seriously, Ora-Ïto began to create designs based upon the theme of Utopia. He devised a series of virtual products that could have fitted into the collections of any number of great fashion or design houses such as Nike or Louis Vuitton. The designs were meant to be ironic and iconoclastic, but in the event they proved feasible, further increasing interest in Ora-Ïto. The designer would now have us know that his hypothetical products were in fact the result of a careful design process and a close analysis of the demands of the market. As a designer, Ora-Ïto may seem to live on another planet, but actually he has his feet firmly on the ground. He is a most attentive observer, aware of the demands of the market and of everything going on around him. Having always designed imaginary products, he has been able to express himself freely and independently. Now his products are popular and he has to position himself carefully in the real world of a market led by the major manufacturers.

With true brilliance, Ora-Ïto has moved nimbly from the world of dreams to reality, incorporating his characteristic irony and originality into products that are designed to be made. Another interesting aspect of Ora-Ïto's work is his emphasis on communication. He believes that any product can succeed if it is presented in the right way, and that we should not be afraid to use new advertising media to excite public interest.

Ora-Ïto stands at the forefront of the latest generation of designers. More familiar with the computer than the drawing board, they are capable of using new technology to create objects of poetic beauty. It is difficult to pick out key examples of Ora-Ïto's design work, since they are all equally arresting for one reason or another. However, his Louis Vuitton Back Up (1999), and his Apple hack-Mac (1999) express to the full the free-and-easy approach of a designer who creates remarkable objects with a great sense of irony. They were part of a piracy campaign launched without any agreement from the brand concerned. The scheme consisted of a fake advertising campaign presenting this virtual product through full-page advertisements in magazines. GIULIO CAPPELLINI

1 **Petal**, lounge chair, 2002, fibreglass, foam rubber, fabrics or leather, 76 x 104 x 182 cm, Cappellini.
› When you lie inside Petal you can discover a cocoon-like atmosphere. The sounds are smoother and you feel protected like a foetus in the womb. The flower-shaped seat can also support two people who wish to be more intimately curled up.

2 **Swing Pod**, 2002, fibreglass, iron cables, fabrics, 210 x 165 x 70 cm, Cappellini.
› Taken from childhood imagery, Swing Pod was designed for those adults who have decided not to grow up too fast. Supported by iron cables on a stable axle, the seat is just like an open cradle solidly fastened to the structure.

3 **Cappellini's Roulotte**, 2001, virtual prototype.
› This mobile home refreshes the old-fashioned caravan to satisfy the most demanding travellers, and is imagined as a seductive 'camping de luxe'. When moving, it occupies the minimum of space, but once it is stationary its inside surface can be extended from 20 m to 70 m. Hydraulic jacks enable the external walls to be opened and transformed into terraces.

1		
		3
	2	

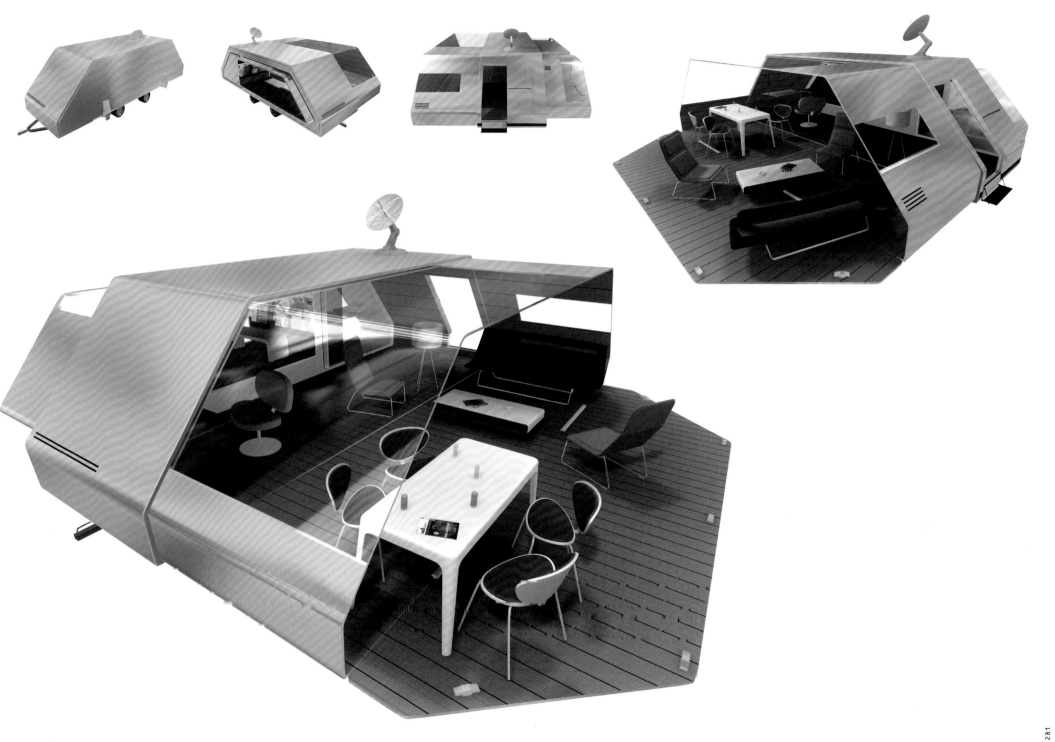

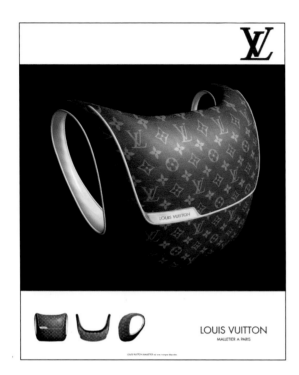

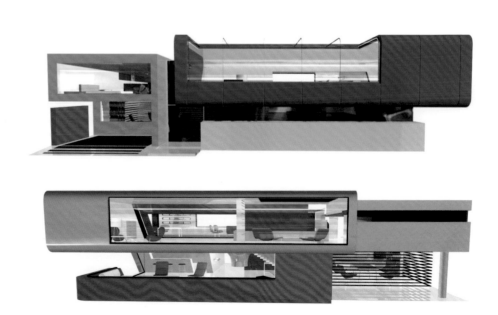

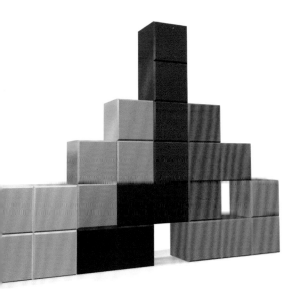

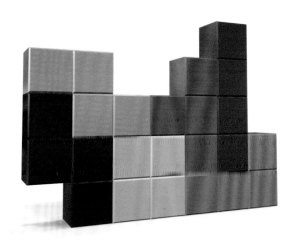

1 **Back Up**, backpack, 1999, leather,
25 x 30 x 15 cm, 3D virtual prototype.
› Ora-Ïto pirated Louis Vuitton's graphic
identity for this virtual backpack.

2 **hack-Mac**, laptop computer, 1999,
vulcanized titanium, 25 x 34 x 8.5 cm,
3D virtual prototype.
› This virtual model was launched without
Apple's agreement and it was a success.

3 Heineken Collection, 2000, **Gelulo Fresh**,
plastic, 23 x ø 6 cm, **Aluminium Bottle**, 100%
aluminium, 19 x ø 6 cm, **Carry & Open**,

aluminium and rubber, 45 x 6 x 7 cm,
Heineken.
› Gelulo-Fresh is an isotherm capsule
designed to keep the new, luxury aluminium bottle fresh. Carry & Open is a combined carrier and bottle opener.

4 **Casa Cappellini**, 2001, advertising campaign conceived with Giulio Cappellini.

5 **Hi-Bliss**, watch, 2000, rubber, steel,
Swatch conceptual projects.
› Ora-Ïto was consulted by Swatch to mod-
ernize their range of digital watches.

6 **Tetris Furniture System**, 2002, wood,
rubber, 40 x 40 x 40 cm, Cappellini.
› Inspired by the electronic game, this
system allows architectural, not virtual,
constructions.

1	3	3	5
2	4	6	

283

EMILI PADRÓS BARCELONA

I first heard of Emili Padrós when he hatched the idea of removing the handle from a broom and hanging the broom-head on the wall, bristles upward. Put into production by Cha-Chá, it proved the perfect place to put cards, a flower, keys or any of the things that we take out of our pockets when we come home. I have since learned that Padrós was born in Barcelona and studied industrial design at the Escola Elisava. He rounded off his education at Central Saint Martins College of Art & Design in London. One of his fellow students was Ana Mir, with whom he has shared a studio since 1996.

Like Ana Mir, Padrós proved that imagination is the greatest asset of a young designer at the beginning of his career, when resources are scarce. With nothing but a sketchbook and a bit of metal, Mir and Padrós came up with the idea for a range of bathroom accessories that they called Anónimo's Family. Starting with two supports, a piece of elastic, some hooks and some coloured pencils, they also created the Slástic Hanger, the first clothes hanger in the world with a graphic memory.

After this initial period of working ingeniously with the materials that he could find in hardware stores, Padrós was invited to take part in Futur Compost – meaning 'composite future' in Catalan – during Barcelona's Primavera del Diseño (spring design event) in 1999. He did not waste this opportunity. His reflections on how we will relate to technology in the future, his experimental projects for the TOU computer and his Soft Human Energy project were striking enough to win him a Ciutat de Barcelona (City of Barcelona) prize.

Soft Human Energy is a meditation on a future in which we are self-sufficient in terms of our energy needs. Padrós designed products that make use of energy generated by the users themselves during their every-day lives. For example, the N-S-S – or Non-Stop-Shoes charge with energy as you walk. When you get home, you can use that energy to power a lamp, a fan or other domestic appliance.

The professional careers of Emili Padrós and Ana Mir have two trajec-tories, one separate and one combined. Their individual talents are highly complementary – a fact beautifully illustrated by their work on the Shadow Play Programme, a whole new idiom for the furniture in our city parks, falling somewhere between an interactive game and urban sculpture.

RAMÓN UBEDA

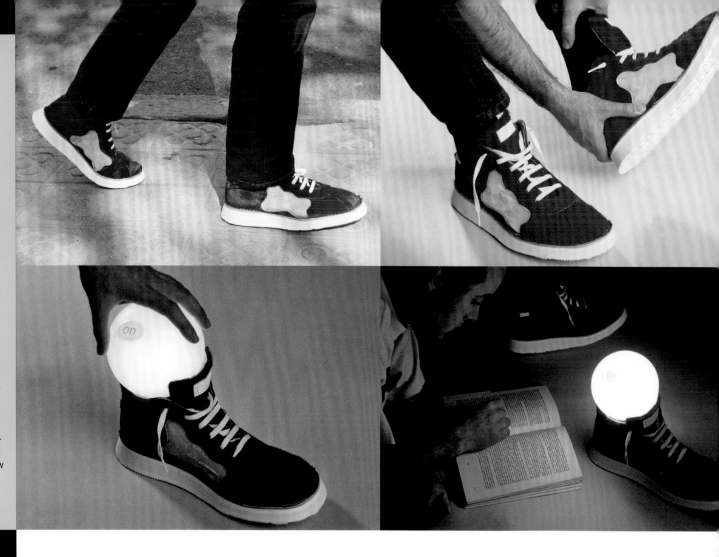

1 N-S-S, Non-Stop-Shoes, 1999, shoes, bulbs, rubber, experimental project presented in the exhibition 'Futur Compost' in Barcelona in collaboration wtith Camper.
› These shoes charge with energy during the day: the more the wearer walks, the more energy they create. On returning home this energy can be used to power lights and other electrical appliances.

2 Slástic Hanger, 1997, steel, elastic band, coloured pencils, 15 x 150 x 7 cm, prototype, in collaboration with Ana Mir.
› The Slástic Hanger consists of a length of elastic stretched between two wall-mounted supports with a metal clothes hook attached to it, which in turn has a coloured pencil attached. When you hang a handbag or a jacket on the hook, its weight pulls the elastic downward and the pencil draws a mark on the wall.

3 Anónimo, toilet-roll holder, 1998–9, stainless steel, 13 x 10 x 5 cm, prototype in collaboration with Ana Mir.
› Part of a series of ideas for bathroom accessories, the design for this toilet-roll holder derives from the fact that there is somebody in every family who has a habit of reading a book or a newspaper in the bathroom. Anónimo provides a space for the reading matter.

1	2
	3

option A: hang the paper holder after fixing the screws on to the wall.

option B: screw the paper holder directly on to the wall.

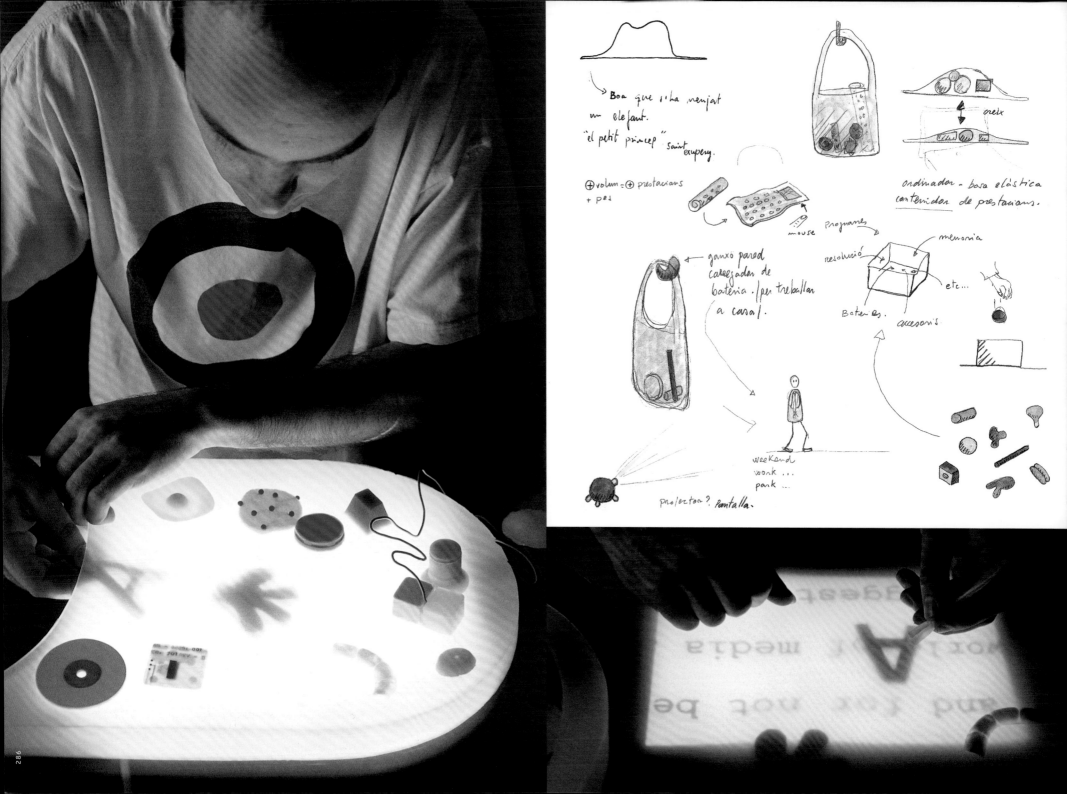

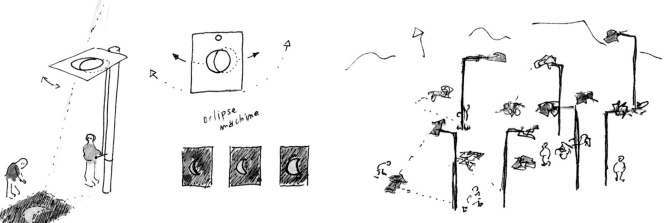

1 TOU Soft Portable Computer, 1999, silicone, rubber, 90 x 30 x 2 cm, experimental project presented at the 'Futur Compost' exhibition in Barcelona.
> The most personal computer yet, the TOU is in the form of a soft, elastic, translucent bag. The components are configured in small packages of different textures and colours which can be put in or taken out of the bag according to the user's specific needs at that moment. An imaginative exercise on how we might relate to technology in the future.

2 Shadow Play, urban sculpture, 2001, stainless steel, coloured perspex, H 400 cm, Richter Spielgeräte, in collaboration with Ana Mir.
> This is an urban sculpture that is also an interactive game of shadows for children and adults alike. The central mast rotates the screen so the sun casts a composition of patterns and colours on the ground. Shadow Play can also change with the weather, the time of day and the season of the year.

1	2

SATYENDRA PAKHALÉ AMSTERDAM

Born in India, educated in Bombay, Switzerland and France, and based in Holland, Satyendra Pakhalé has successfully designed his own cultural identity. The multicultural nomadism of contemporary life readily embraces this unique yet universal identity, expressed in unusual pieces that connect life with art, craft with industry, human warmth with cool technology.

Pakhalé takes archaic and archetypal forms and interprets them with contemporary sleekness. Yet this sleekness contains a symbolic, emotional and sensory charge that make his objects globally appealing and accessible. He claims that 'the form of an object should have a content, a universal thought'. For example, the Horse Chair (2001) and Flower Chair (2002) bring chairs back into the realm of the ceremonial. The Horse Chair, which came from 'somewhere between flesh and object, between folk art and contemporary form' offers a generously sized and shaped seat reminiscent of a horse's back. The Flower Chair, made in clay of 'pots and parts', has hollow backrests that are intended to receive flower offerings for the sitter.

Working with Indian artisans, Dutch high-tech companies and Italian industrialists has given Pakhalé new views on the relationship between the handmade and the serially produced and he points out that almost every industrial product started out as a handcrafted prototype. He continues to blur these borders, for example using the traditional Indian bell-metal lost-wax technique to create vases, hangers and bowls, as well as large objects. Pakhalé claims: 'I am interested in the new craftsmanship, which allies modernity with tradition and daily folklore with advanced technology in the eclecticism of its methods.' Within this process, he has experimented with numerous materials, creating several versions of the Horse Chair in bell metal, fibreglass, ceramic, natural cord and roto-moulded plastic.

Pakhalé seeks to ensure that old designs will have new significance in the coming century. His Surya Calendar (2000) takes the concept of a sundial and translates it into a playful object that physically connects us to time as we manipulate the wooden dice to set the date and observe the hour indicated by the sun on the aluminium dial. His version of this low-tech product looks high-tech, bringing the sundial distinctly into the realm of twenty-first century design and illustrating Pakhalé's statement, 'I come from a culture of object making ... I was surrounded by a thousand years of history of object making. So design for me is an ancient historic activity which also makes a meaningful contribution to contemporary culture.'

LISA WHITE

1 B M (Bell Metal) Object Making Process, 1996.
› B M is a mixture of recycled brass, bronze and copper. This process of metal casting is known as 'lost wax' and has been practised in the central regions of India for several thousand years. By refining and further developing this ancient craft, a series of contemporary design objects are made, each one cast from a fresh mould.

2 B M Vase, 2000, bell metal, 33 x ø 17.6 cm, Cappellini.
› This project, initially developed as a craft design object, is now being evolved into industrial production for the Progetto Oggetto Collection, but it retains the textural warmth and surface finish of the initial prototype.

3 B M Hanger, 2000, bell metal, 19 x 42 x 4.7 cm, Satyendra Pakhalé.
› This hanger is now being evolved into an industrial version using state-of-the-art gas-injection moulding manufacturing processes.

4 B M Fruitbowl, 2000, bell metal, base 9 x ø 31 cm, basket 10 x ø 19 cm, Cappellini.
› This fruitbowl set consists of two parts: a base with three legs and an upper basket which serves many functions.

| 1 | 2 |
| | 3 | 4 |

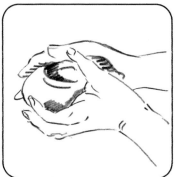

A core is made with a mixture of fine clean sand and fine clay collected either from the riverside or from ant-hills.

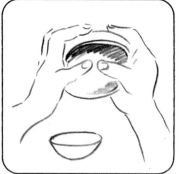

Goat-dung is soaked in water and then ground and mixed with clay in equal propertion. This soft mixture is used to create the base mould- later when it is dry, it is used to create a wax pattern on it.

A special natural wax (found in jungle terrian in abundant quantity collected from trees) is melted over an open fire and strained through a fine cloth into a basin of cold water, where it becomes solid.

A great care is taken to keep the wax absolutely clean and free of impurities. It is next squeezed through a sieve syringe and recovered in the form of wax wires- thick or thin as desired

Each wax thread is single wound around the core one after another, until the whole surface is covered. The working craftsman sits in the sun to let the clay core and wax coating warm up uniformly.

Now the whole model is covered with a thick layer of a mixture of equal parts of clay, sand and cow-dung. This covered model becomes ready for firing.

Then a crap metal- piceces of brass,

Finish product is ready after cleaning

This technique is an ancient metal casting technique- which is practiced in the Bastar region of India for several thousand years now. We have refined this ancient process to create a contemporary design product.

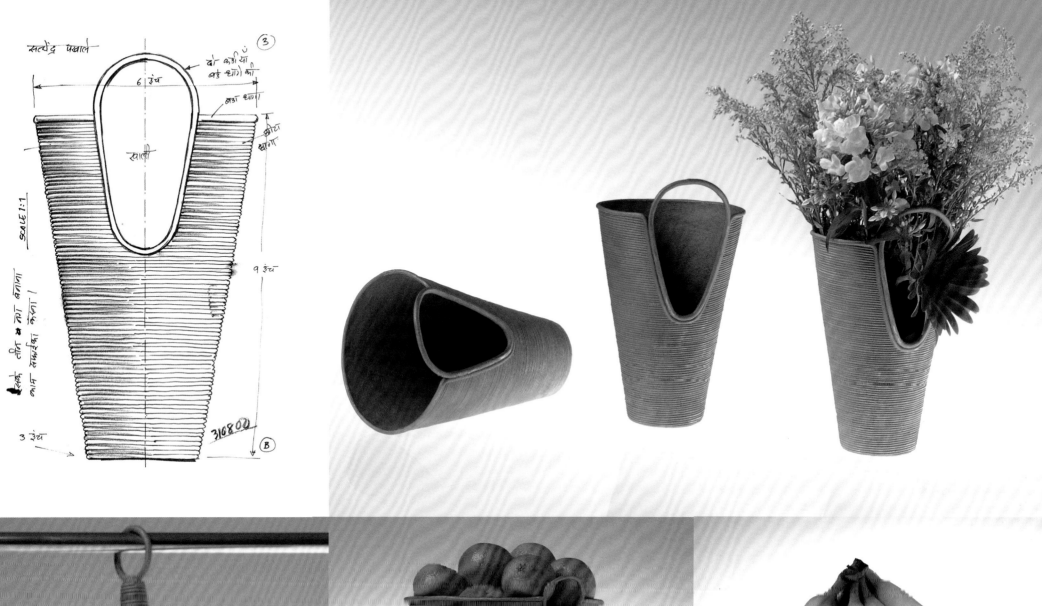
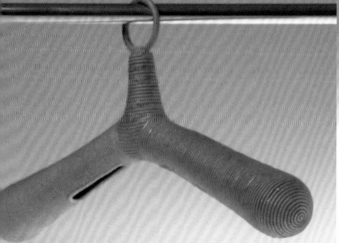

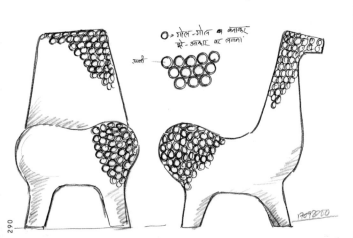

○ » गोल-गोल क बेलाकर
घे-आकार वट लगाना

खाली

17098010

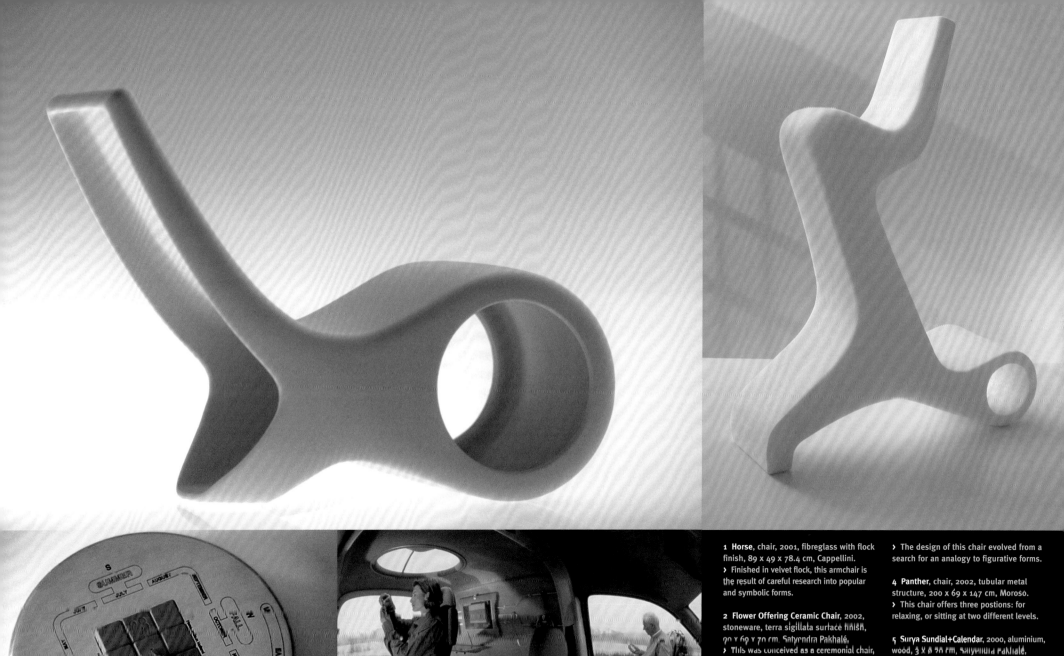

1 **Horse**, chair, 2001, fibreglass with flock
finish, 89 x 49 x 78.4 cm, Cappellini.
› Finished in velvet flock, this armchair is
the result of careful research into popular
and symbolic forms.

2 **Flower Offering Ceramic Chair**, 2002,
stoneware, terra sigillata surface finish,
90 x 62 x 70 cm, Satyendra Pakhalé.
› This was conceived as a ceremonial chair,
with flower holders in the backrest.

3 **Fish**, chair, 1997, 2002, tubular metal
structure, 71 x 46 x 85 cm, Cappellini.

› The design of this chair evolved from a
search for an analogy to figurative forms.

4 **Panther**, chair, 2002, tubular metal
structure, 200 x 69 x 147 cm, Moroso.
› This chair offers three postions: for
relaxing, or sitting at two different levels.

5 **Surya Sundial+Calendar**, 2000, aluminium,
wood, 3 x 8 x 70 cm, Satyendra Pakhalé.
› In adjusting the components of this sundial and calendar, the user becomes more
aware of their relationship with the seasons.

6 **Pangéa Concept Car**, 1997, in collaboration with Udo Hischke, Renault and Philips.
› A concept interior for an electric car to
do environmental field research, Pangéa
is equipped with a turbine generator and
a satellite for worldwide communication.

1	2		3	4
1			5	6

JORGE PARDO LOS ANGELES CA

By choosing to include Jorge Pardo in a book devoted to industrial design, I am intentionally placing him in a context with which he has flirted for some time. Pardo is an artist by training and profession, with a practice that is squarely situated in the art world. However, he straddles the two worlds of art and design by addressing many of the issues and problems faced by designers. Pardo is clearly conscious of this dichotomy and uses it to question both the nature of his own work and the nature of work located in a museum.

Pardo achieved widespread recognition in 1998 with the design of his own house, which also served as an off-site exhibition for the Museum of Contemporary Art in Los Angeles. With this project he was able to explore, on a real scale and in a real domestic situation, the relationships between design and art that have come to characterize his work. This project led to his design for the lobby/bookstore of the Dia Center for the Arts in New York, and to the production of furniture and lights for gallery shows and eventually for private residences. Why are these projects classified as 'installations' and not 'design commissions'? When does Pardo's furniture cease to be sculpture and become design? These are the questions that Pardo encourages and engages with, and it is for this reason that his work is intriguing.

Pardo's work is not really a hybrid, lying somewhere between art and design, but it is often seen as such. Although it is relatively easy for an artist such as Pardo to have his work accepted by a museum, the same can never be said of a designer. Pardo's work draws attention to this contradiction, and helps to erode the boundaries between art and design.

When placed in an art gallery or museum, Pardo's work is stripped of its functional nature, and its meaning becomes the important thing. We cannot sit in his chairs or sleep in his beds, and the beautiful glass lights are not really there to illuminate anything. When placed in a house, the nature of the pieces changes completely and becomes functional once again. Pardo's work allows us to reconsider design from a purely aesthetic position, without having to worry whether it works or not. Unsurprisingly, it does work, both as art and as design. BROOKE HODGE

1 Untitled, light, 1998, steel, paint, variable dimensions.
› Installation view of Pardo's *Wool, Cotton, Latex, Wax and Steel* at Friedrich Petzel Gallery in New York.

2 Untitled (Blue #781), light, 1998, steel, paint, 142.2 x 61 cm.
› This piece was created at the same time as the *Wool, Cotton, Latex, Wax and Steel* installation, but it was not exhibited in the same exhibition.

3 Untitled, chair, 2000, birch plywood, wood veneer, 71.1 x 43.2 x 59.1 cm.
› Pardo's chair is characteristic of his use of the bright colours and spare forms of modernism.

| 1 | 2 | 3 |

1 **Untitled (set of 6 lamps)**, 1998, glass, electrical wires, dimensions variable.
2 **Untitled, 80 glass lamps**, 1999, dimensions variable.
3 **Untitled (set of 21 lamps)**, 2001, poplar plywood, PVC, glass, electrical wiring, commissioned by Sotheby's for 'Art in Autumn', organized by the Art Production Fund.
4 **Untitled (set of 7 lamps)**, 2001, acrylic, electrical wiring, 54.6 x 58.4 cm.
› Pardo has often created suites or series of lamps for his installations in galleries and museums. Made as art objects, the lamps

may be acquired by collectors and used by them as functional light fixtures.

5 **Project, lobby, bookshop, gallery**, 2000, 36.3 x 36.3 m.
› A view of Pardo's redesign of the lobby, bookstore and ground-floor gallery at New York's Dia Center for the Arts.

6 **Untitled**, 1998, mixed media, dimensions variable.
› Installation view featuring vanity unit with stool and a painting by Laura Owens at Patrick Painter, a Santa Monica art gallery.

1	2		6
		5	
3	4		

Looking at Stephen Peart's output it is tempting to place him as one of the great techno-designers of the computer era. And he is, or was, just that. He spent the early part of his career with Frog Design, the legendary German design company that more or less defined Silicon Valley aesthetics in the 1980s. During that period he made some of the early designs for Apple, among others.

In a way, Peart has now become, if not an *éminence grise*, then something of a conscience for industrial design and production. 'A designed object is not a sculpture, for my pleasure alone. My designs have to involve the people that commission them, I have to be aware that I'm supplying into people's livelihoods', he says.

Any changes that Peart has wrought in his personal philosophy have not affected his prodigious ability to interact with the livelihoods of the people for whom he works. He wants his designs to work for both parties. Like several other designers, Peart is looking hard at the office environment as a place to start a quiet revolution.

The Panel Floor System (1999), designed for Herman Miller, combines Peart's philosophy of freedom for the individual with a strong loyalty to his client. He seeks to change the concept of office design by allowing data and power to be delivered to any part of an office, thereby setting the worker free from the dreaded 'cubicle'. This represents a huge leap for the office planner. Peart's system, which needs no special assembly or installation tools, allows workstations to be placed at random. They no longer need to be anchored to conduits or fixed data and power supplies, and can be reconfigured at will.

Peart's imagination is that of a schoolboy, untrammelled by limits of any kind. Were he not such a forward-looking modernist, he might be from a lost, nineteenth-century England of refined, curious, romantic adventurers and explorers. Two of his current projects are straight out of Ian Fleming: a flying car, and a small, personal helicopter-cum-flying machine. In perfect tune with current thinking in aviation, both machines are powered by large, ducted fans. Stylistically, the designs are part James Bond, part Thunderbirds, quintessential English icons of mechanical ingenuity.

It is this curiosity and desire to change the world, this wonderful Englishness, which Peart carries with him so successfully to twenty-first century California. ULTAN GUILFOYLE

1 Persona, answering machine, 1998, Sun Microsystems.
> Peart has, as much as anyone, shaped the aesthetics of the computer industry. This Internet Answering Machine, breaking away from the black box, is typical of Peart's mission to apply humanist, organic forms to the binary, machine-age aesthetic of computers.

2 Solotrek, flying machine, 2001–2, prototype.
3 Air Car, flying machine, 2001–2, prototype.
> These amazing flying machines show the playful, comic-book side of Peart's nature. They are no mere fantasies, however. The ducted fans which propel, lift and direct these machines are very much part of current aeronautical design thinking.

	2
1	
	3

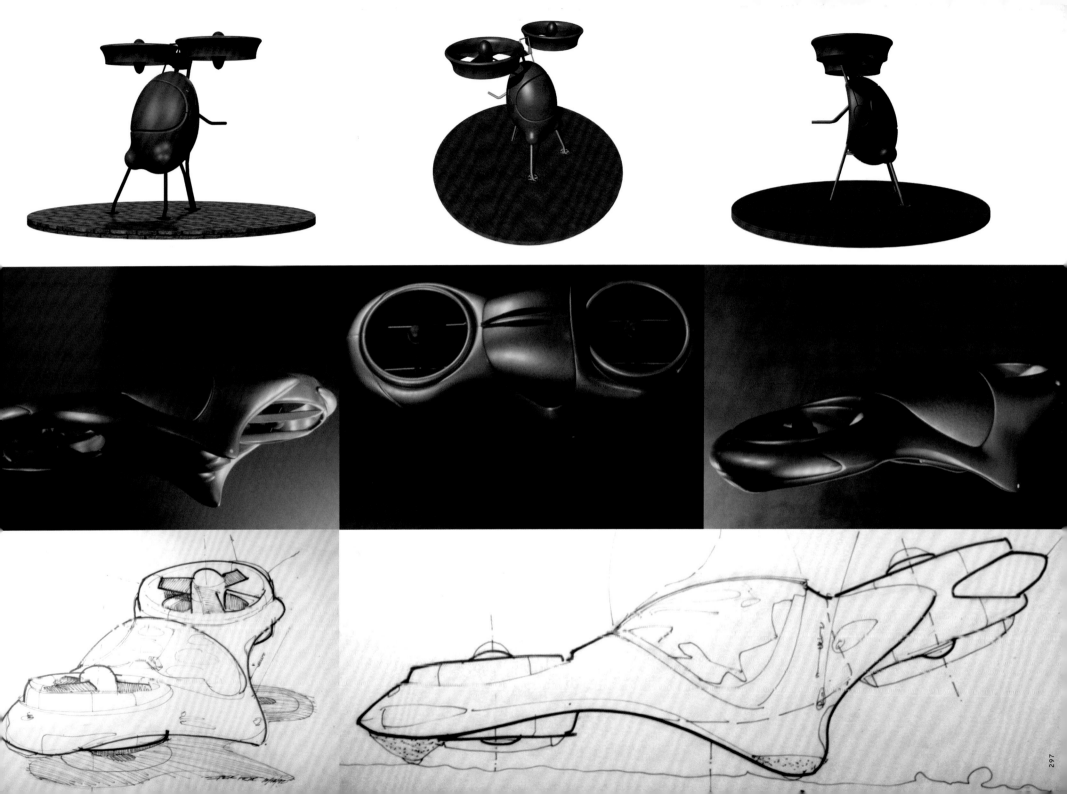

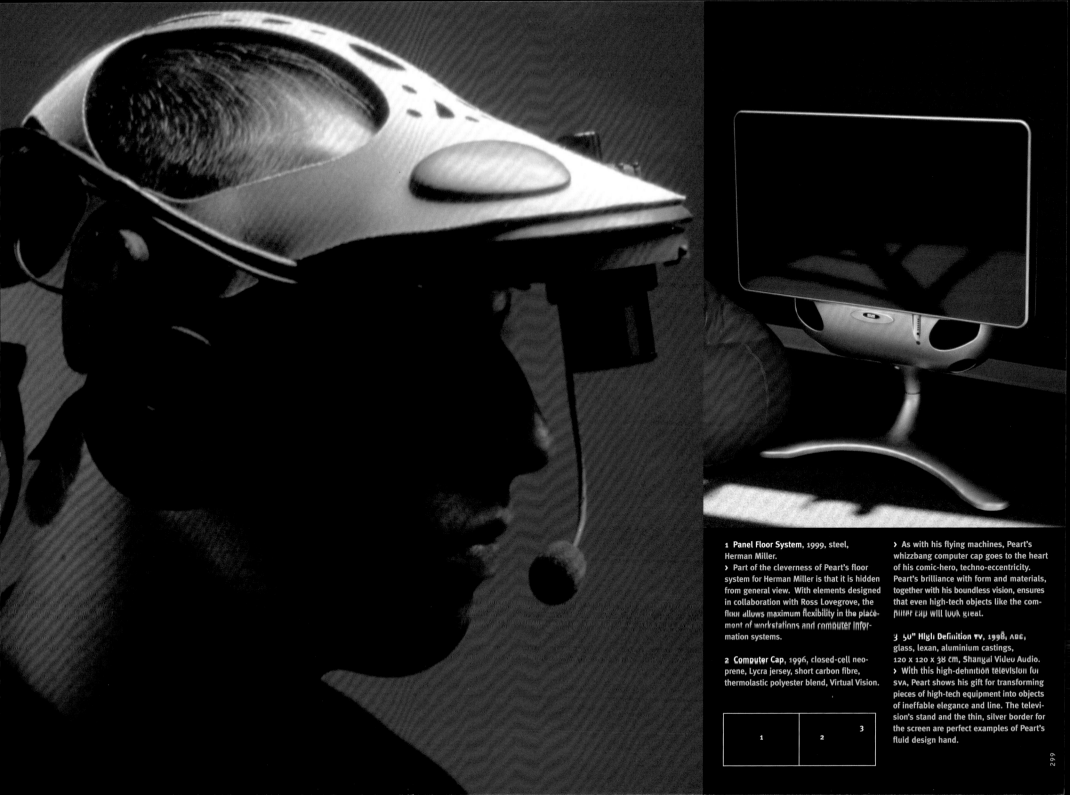

1 **Panel Floor System**, 1999, steel, Herman Miller.
› Part of the cleverness of Peart's floor system for Herman Miller is that it is hidden from general view. With elements designed in collaboration with Ross Lovegrove, the floor allows maximum flexibility in the placement of workstations and computer information systems.

2 **Computer Cap**, 1996, closed-cell neoprene, Lycra jersey, short carbon fibre, thermolastic polyester blend, Virtual Vision.

› As with his flying machines, Peart's whizzbang computer cap goes to the heart of his comic-hero, techno-eccentricity. Peart's brilliance with form and materials, together with his boundless vision, ensures that even high-tech objects like the computer cap will look great.

3 **50" High Definition TV**, 1998, ADG, glass, lexan, aluminium castings, 120 x 120 x 38 cm, Shangai Video Audio.
› With this high-definition television for SVA, Peart shows his gift for transforming pieces of high-tech equipment into objects of ineffable elegance and line. The television's stand and the thin, silver border for the screen are perfect examples of Peart's fluid design hand.

1	2	3

OLIVIER PEYRICOT PARIS

Olivier Peyricot is a design guerrilla, working both inside and outside the system. He encourages us to rethink our habits as well as our habitats, deconstructing and reconstructing the design landscape, experimenting with stackable, tiered couches, tent-like apartment walls or coffee cups with integrated saucers. His Double Siège (1999) made out of metal and clingwrap takes up little physical and visual space, and supple fabric extensions make the most of whatever chair you have, whether you are in sleeping, playing or reading mode. Peyricot seeks to offer items that bridge the gap between the demand generated by changing consumer behaviour and the supply offered by the design industry.

For several years Peyricot has created domestic objects that are manufactured by Axis, such as Tasses 200% (1999) and the Verre Poisson Rouge (1998). Now he is taking on the heavyweight furniture sector, not with a couch or a chair but with a space filler. The Body Props human support system (2000) is composed of coloured foam and gel shapes. It is designed to soften the space between our surroundings and our bodies, whether in the usually uncomfortable position of lying on one's stomach to read, kneeling, or lying on one's side. Manufactured by Edra, these pieces are playful, surreptitious propositions that literally fill a design void.

In 2000, Peyricot founded the Idsland design agency, with offices in Paris and Toulouse. Here, he has brought graphic artists and architects into his brainstorming space. This has allowed him to branch out, developing tyre patterns for Michelin, store concepts for Mandarina Duck, scenography for the Musée d'Art Moderne de la Ville de Paris, posters and websites – such as www.base-design.com. As a reaction against car designers who do nothing but styling, in 2000 Idsland proposed a series of cars based on slow or no movement. The engine has been cut out of one model, making room for a couch. Another has been fitted out as a slow-moving, float-like platform useful for other urban activities. These ideas obviously inspired Renault, who have hired Peyricot and Idsland to work on interior elements for a future concept car.

Peyricot also began his own underground design magazine, *Mobile*, (with Cédric Scandella and Chlöe Braunstein), which analyses such subjects as 'stock', 'free time' and 'proximity' from angles that are political and social as well as historic and aesthetic. A toolbox for designers, it also serves as a glimpse inside the brain and the design agenda of this multi-talented individual. LISA WHITE

1 Tasses 200%, cups, 1999, porcelain, 10.5 x ø 10 cm, Axis.
› Tasses 200% is an all-in-one cup and saucer. Although the components are fixed, it is possible to manipulate the vessel from the rim of the saucer.

2 Verre Poisson Rouge, glass, 1998, glass, 9 x ø 8.5 cm, Axis.
› When you fill this glass with water the fish appears to grow very large. It has been conceived to bring fun to children's dinners.

3 Double Siège, chair, 1999, metal,

polyethylene, 120 x 120 x 45 cm, Idsland.
› This double seat offers the possibility of twin occupation, which reinforces its structure. The strong 'plastic wrap' material offers a light, almost invisible aesthetic.

4 Pioneer Wagon, 2000, Low PAO, various dimensions, Idsland.
› Powered by a lawn-mower engine, this car has a limited speed and excellent visibility. Passengers observe traffic and are able to leap out at the first sign of danger.

5 Scream, sofa, 1999, metal, foam, 120 x 140 x 120 cm, Domeau & Pérès.
› This seat encourages a new panoramic viewpoint in the home.

6 Salt and Pepper Vessels, 1999, porcelain, 2.5 x 8.5 x 4.5 cm, Axis.

	2		4
1		3	5
	1		6

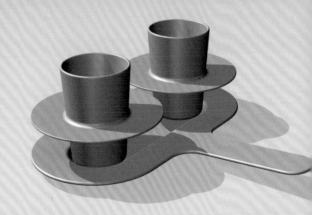

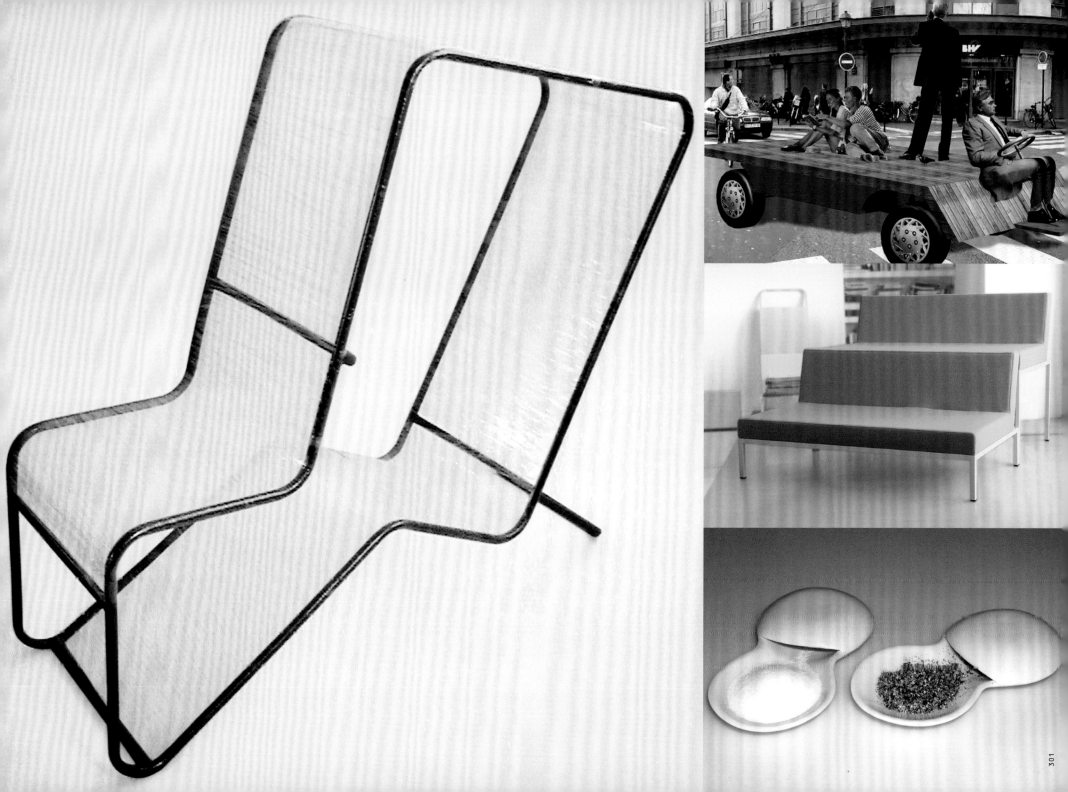

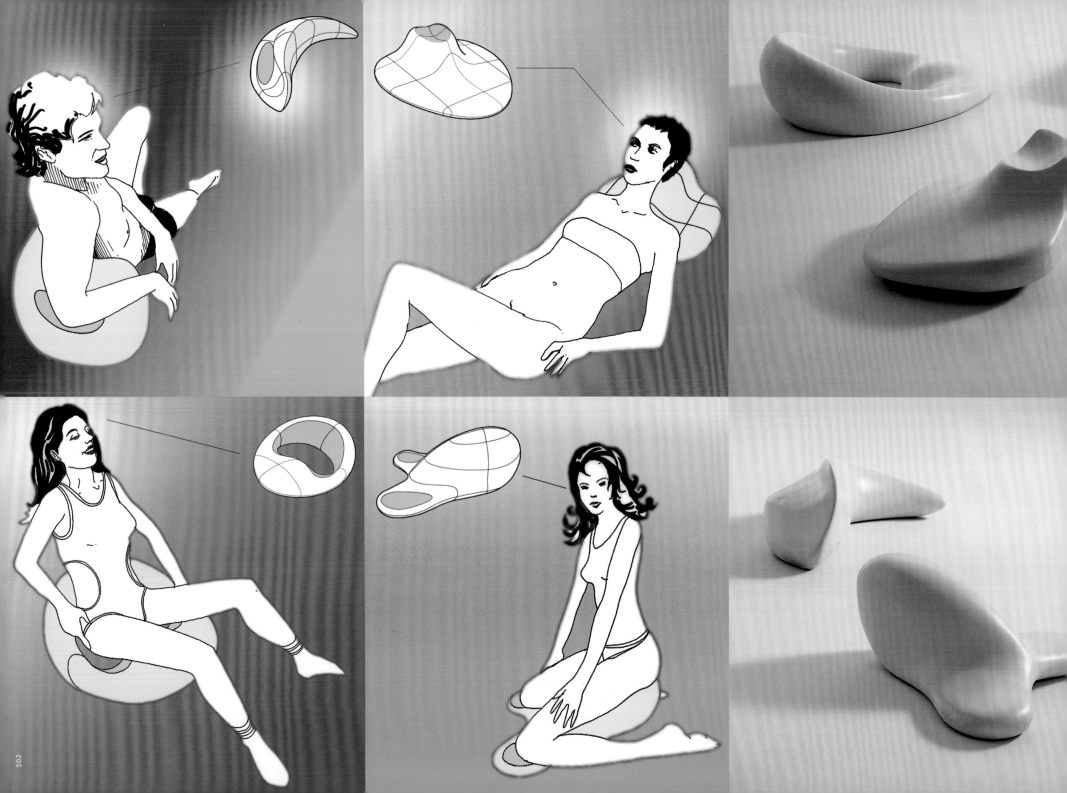

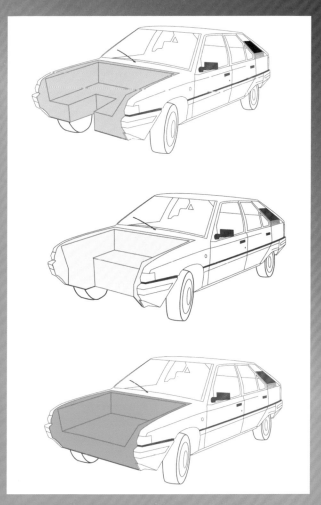

1 Body Props, 2000, polyurethane, various dimensions, Edra.

› There are five variations of the body props. They are soft forms, moulded in expanded polyurethane, with elastic varnish finish. They are intended as an extension of the body in its different postures: lying on the ground, propped up on one elbow or relieving the pressure on the spine while kneeling.

2 Slow Rider, 2000, used car, wood, various sizes, Idsland.

› The idea in this design was to strip a used car of all of its superfluous accessories, replacing the car engine with a refrigerator motor. The driver can then be comfortably installed in the front or back, and drive at a maximum speed of 15 km/h.

1	1	2

CHRISTOPHE PILLET PARIS

Like many designers of his generation, Christophe Pillet prides himself on his versatility. 'A designer is like an actor,' he says, 'he can play lots of different roles.' Whether Pillet is designing furniture, interiors, theatre sets or products, all of his projects display the same playful approach.

After graduating from the Domus Academy in Milan in 1986, Pillet worked for five years with the renowned contemporary French designer, Philippe Starck. Like his former employer, Pillet clearly believes in design's dual role of bringing pleasure and fulfilling a function. He claims to find inspiration both everywhere and nowhere, and refuses to be romantic about his work: 'We designers are about creating chairs, salt and pepper pots, everyday objects – nothing you would dream about.'

Pillet's Elysée seating system, designed for Edra in 2001, consists of upholstered square modules with a large surface area, low back rests and rounded corners. The generous dimensions encourage the user to sprawl across them in a way not usually suggested by formal sofas. The elaborate floral prints and 1970s throwback styling – the sofa was launched in Milan amid a cloud of dry ice and neon lights – exemplify the humour Pillet likes to apply to his work.

Pillet describes himself as using a 'soft' style. His work seduces rather than confronts the user, and comfort is always a key component. To this end, Pillet prefers to use simple, often curvaceous, shapes. For Domeau & Pérès, for example, he designed another sofa, Nath's (2000), with its loop-like, fluid form appears to be pressed from a single mould, and seems to enclose the body. It is one of Pillet's favourite pieces.

Pillet's preferred materials are usually pliable. Latex and polyurethane are favourites. If he does use metal, it is often hidden or given a brushed, less abrasive finish. The lozenge-shaped Extra Light (1998), designed for FontanaArte, sheds a gentle light that is diffused by opaque glass. There is nothing exceptionally provocative about Extra Light, it is simply an amusing object that fulfils its function perfectly.

People fall for Pillet's products, and this is a gift that is making him increasingly popular with manufacturers. Among the giants he has worked for are the Italian manufacturers Cappellini and Moroso, and Whirlpool, producer of technical goods. As with much of the most admired contemporary French design, his work has a democratic touch and is whimsical, without descending into novelty. LAURA HOUSELEY

1 **Elysée Modular Seating System**, 2001, wood, polyurethane upholstery, cotton, various dimensions, Edra.
2 **Elysée Low Table**, 2001, lacquered wood, metal, 35 x 135 x 85 cm, Edra
› This giant sofa system gives more than a nod to the lobby furniture of the 1970s: it is grand in scale, brash in its upholstery.

3 **Beach Table**, 2001, silk-screened fibreglass, 50 x 140 x 40 cm, Cappellini.
› This two-tier table is decorated with an orange flower motif on a grey background.

4 **Nath's**, sofa, 2000, wool, metal, 70 x 243 x 76 cm, Domeau & Pérès.
› This sofa is a continuous loop of upholstered foam. The emphasis is on a strong, unbroken, fluid horizontal line.

5 **Video Lounge**, 1999, metal base, structure in foam and wood, wool cloth, chair 55 x 63 x 98 cm, stool 35 x 55 x 45 cm, Domeau & Pérès.
› This is a simple, elegant lounge chair for everyday use.

6 **Chaise Longue**, 2002, plastic, structure in foam, cloth, 40 x 54 x 150 cm, Moroso.
› Fluidity of form is a repetitive element in Pillet style. This chaise is a winning example of it.

1	4
2	
3	5 6

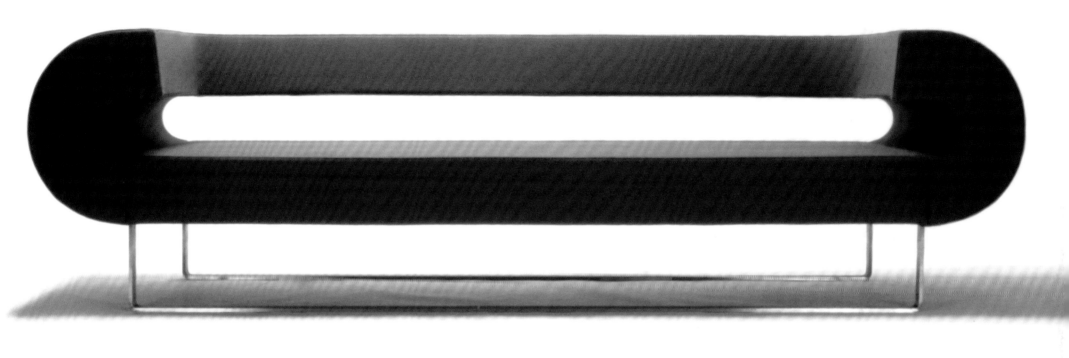

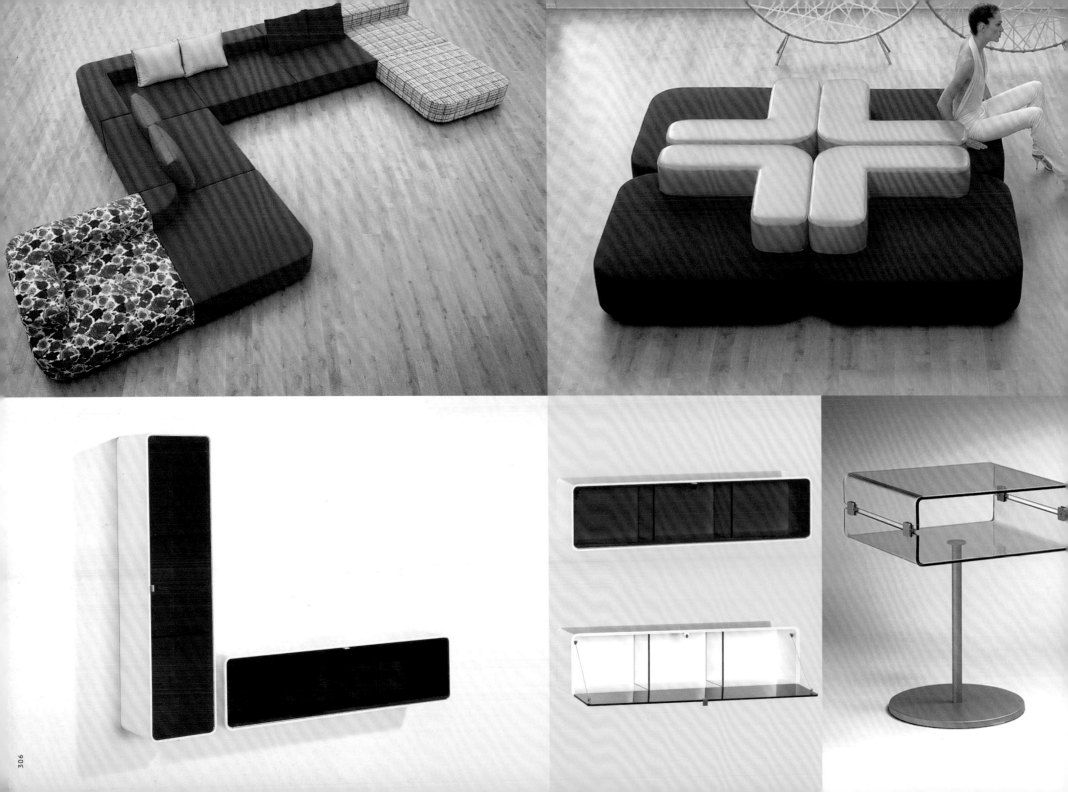

1 **Elysée Modular Seating System**, 2001, wood, polyurethane upholstery, cotton, various dimensions, Edra.
› In one of these configuration, the seats encircle a central space intended for a plant.

2 **Sport Bar**, storage system, aeea, plastic, plexiglass, 80 x 25 x 20 cm, Dornbracht.
› Pillet used colour as ornament to enliven these functional storage units.

3 **ç&c Night Table**, 2002, glass, steel, 70 x 120 x 50 cm, Fiam.

› An occasional table designed to slot into ambiguous interior spaces.

4 **After Hours**, table, 1999, metal, glass, 35 x 120 x 120 cm, FontanaArte.
› This slender and elegant table is typical of Pillet's work. The delicate metal frame looks almost too fragile to support the mass of heavy sheet glass.

5 **Extra Light**, 2000, lacquered metal, 130 cm, FontanaArte.
› Pillet's favourite form, the lozenge, is here applied to a light. The standard lamp is an ambiguous design that could be a reference to either industrial lighting or to curvaceous product designs of the 1970s.

1	1	1	5
	2	3	4

CANDELA REYMUNDO BARCELONA

Candela Reymundo is in no hurry to make it to the top. She does not even seem sure that she wants to make it at all. She works in Barcelona, but her origins and her culture are those of southern Spain. Born in the Andalusian city of Cordoba, she studied industrial design at the Escola Massana in Barcelona. The Massana has never been regarded as the most fashionable school, but Reymundo was attracted by its links with the art world and its broad outlook.

After completing her course, Reymundo stayed on at the Massana as a tutor, and she is still there, snug within the building's ancient stone walls, refusing to be dragged into the vortex of industrial production. She prefers the culture of quality to that of quantity and consumerism. She allows objects to go through the natural cycle of birth, growth and death. Reymundo is committed to rediscovering the quality of slowness, what she calls 'the culture of the snail'. She is interested in designs that grow out of memories, sparking a sense of recognition or a series of associations.

Reymundo does not have a backward-looking stance. She is more than willing to make use of all the technological resources at her disposal. If she is interested in an object's soul, she is also interested in its anatomy. Out of that curiosity came her first well-known design: the Lolaluna weighing scales (1997). She was stripping down some conventional bathroom scales when she was struck by the beauty of the dynamometer and the system of levers hidden inside it. She decided to design her own transparent scales, making a feature of the mechanism. Her idea appealed to the Rapsel company, who started producing it, but it also attracted the interest of other manufacturers, who lost no time in copying it. Perhaps this is why Reymundo has taken so long to design another scales, electronic this time. This is pure technology domesticated by the designer in her hand-coloured drawings.

Reymundo has no wish to attach more importance to the idea than the actual use of the object. Nor will she confuse symbolism with fashion and consumerist styling. Her romantic interpretation of the designer's calling is all too rare these days, but Reymundo knows, too, how difficult it is for an imagined object to remain intact and unsullied as it is realized and then adapted for mass production. RAMÓN UBEDA

1 **Lolaluna**, scales, 1997, wood, glass and inox, 8 x 30 x 28.5 cm, Rapsel.
> On taking apart some ordinary bathroom scales, Reymundo was struck by the mechanical beauty of the components. These scales are traditional in form, but the transparent casing allows the individual components to be admired.

2 **Guayaba**, scales, 2000, plastic, 7 x 78 x 9.5 cm, prototype.
> These bathroom scales have been totally remodelled to accommodate the notion that things do not have to work the same way for every user. The precision electronic system of the Guayaba gives the exact weight whichever way the scales are configured, and objects of all shapes and sizes can be weighed without difficulty.

1	2

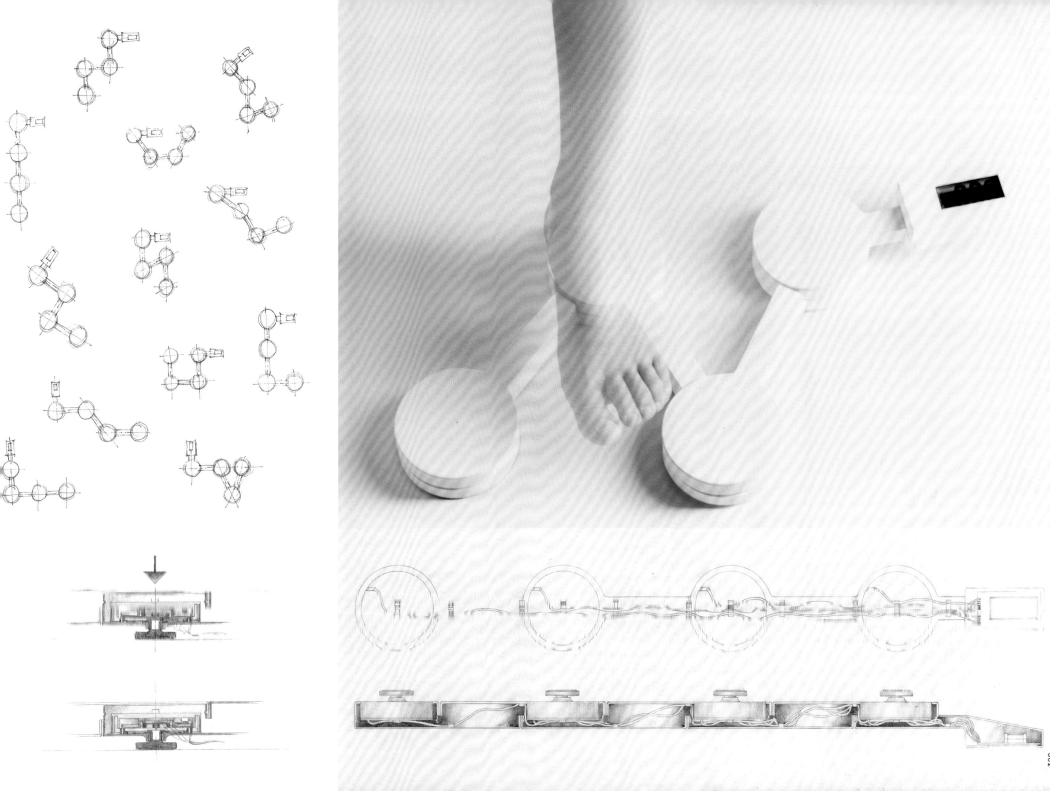

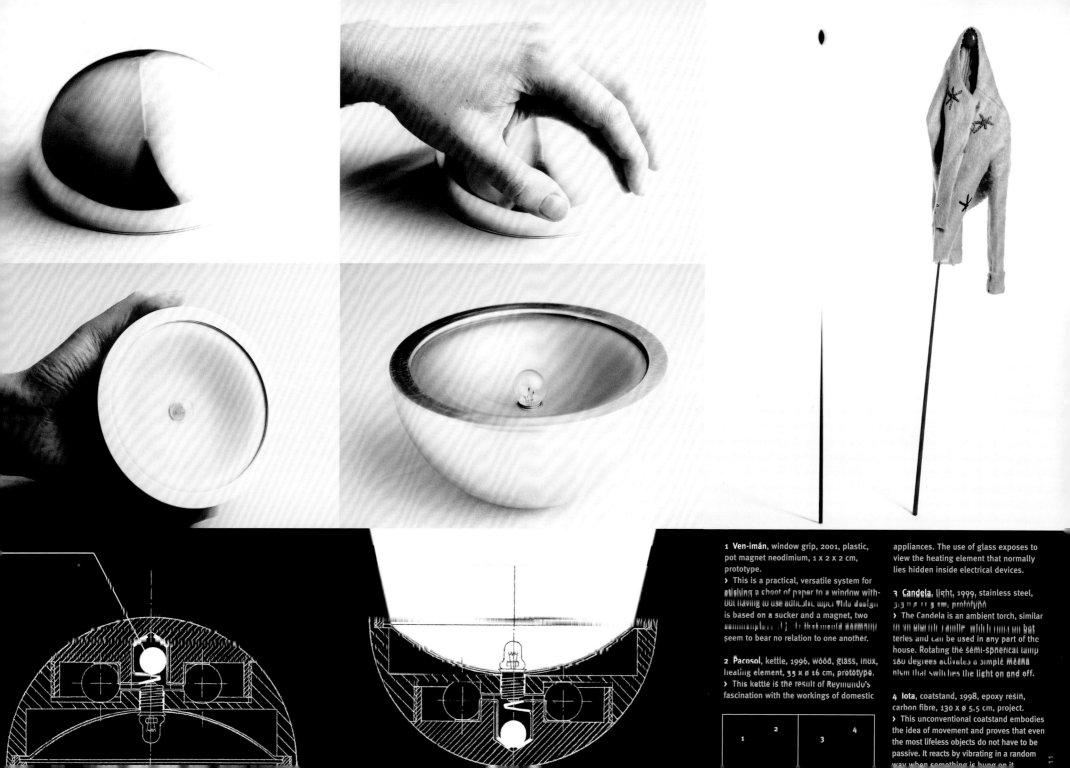

1 Ven-imán, window grip, 2001, plastic, pot magnet neodimium, 1 x 2 x 2 cm, prototype.
> This is a practical, versatile system for sticking a sheet of paper to a window without having to use adhesive tape. This design is based on a sucker and a magnet, two components that at first would normally seem to bear no relation to one another.

2 Pacosol, kettle, 1996, wood, glass, inox, heating element, 35 x ø 16 cm, prototype.
> This kettle is the result of Reymundo's fascination with the workings of domestic appliances. The use of glass exposes to view the heating element that normally lies hidden inside electrical devices.

3 Candela, light, 1999, stainless steel, 35 x ø 11.5 cm, prototype.
> The Candela is an ambient torch, similar to an electric candle, which runs on batteries and can be used in any part of the house. Rotating the semi-spherical lamp 180 degrees activates a simple mechanism that switches the light on and off.

4 Iota, coatstand, 1998, epoxy resin, carbon fibre, 130 x ø 5.5 cm, project.
> This unconventional coatstand embodies the idea of movement and proves that even the most lifeless objects do not have to be passive. It reacts by vibrating in a random way when something is hung on it.

	2		4
1		3	

DAVID ROBB MUNICH

By the time David Robb arrived in Munich, BMW motorcycles had acquired a strictly utilitarian character. They were reliable, solid, honourable and distinctly Teutonic. But no one ever described a Ferrari or a Ducati as reliable or honourable, and this was BMW's big problem. Their bikes needed flair and style. In short, they needed to be 'designed' as they once had been, many decades before.

A graduate of the Art Center College of Design in Pasadena, California, which has become one of the automotive-design incubators of the world, Robb's brilliance was soon spotted by his bosses at BMW. He was working in the car division, but everyone knew he was a passionate motorcyclist.

Robb was quickly appointed to revamp the entire BMW motorcycle range. His first task was to design a cruiser – the quintessential American motorbike. If BMW was to enter the booming American cruiser market, Robb had some problems to solve. The most obvious of these was to avoid the inevitable comparisons with Harley-Davidson, whose bikes traditionally define cruiser style. The other problems facing Robb were more subtle. He had to wean his bosses off their notions of what a BMW should be. Then he had to design an American bike that was still recognizable as a BMW. The result was the R1200C, BMW's first cruiser. It was an instant success, and sales outstripped all expectations in both America and Europe when it was launched in 1997.

The bike's success on the American market came as no surprise to those familiar with Robb. His style has always been deeply rooted in the American tradition. As a young graduate, Robb interned with the elderly Raymond Loewy, and worked briefly with Larry Shinoda, designer of that seminal 1960s car, the Corvette Stingray. So his career is replete with powerful and positive influences, which show clearly in the R1200C. The use of chrome and brushed aluminium are very American characteristics, as is the feet forward, laid-back riding position. The soft, flowing lines of the bike and its intrinsic sportiness are the hallmarks of Robb's design. The R1200 series' seductive appearance is coupled with technology that is pure BMW: reliable, solid, honourable, distinctly Teutonic, but no longer boring. ULTAN GUILFOYLE

1 **R1200C**, 1997, 1170 cc, BMW.
> The R1200C is BMW's first cruiser motorcycle. Robb's sketches for the prototype show just how far he strayed from the traditional, Bauhaus-inspired design tradition of BMW. Picking up styling cues from the 1950s heyday of American cars – air intakes and cylinder-heads – Robb's modernist take on the traditional American boulevard cruiser is anything but future-retro.

2 **F650CS**, 2002, 650 cc, BMW.
> For his F650CS, Robb has again played tricks with past designs, echoing such features as the fairing/tank shape of Hans Muth's Suzuki Katana, but at the same time, he has taken bold steps in a new direction, for example in his adaptable luggage-carrying tank-top.

1	2

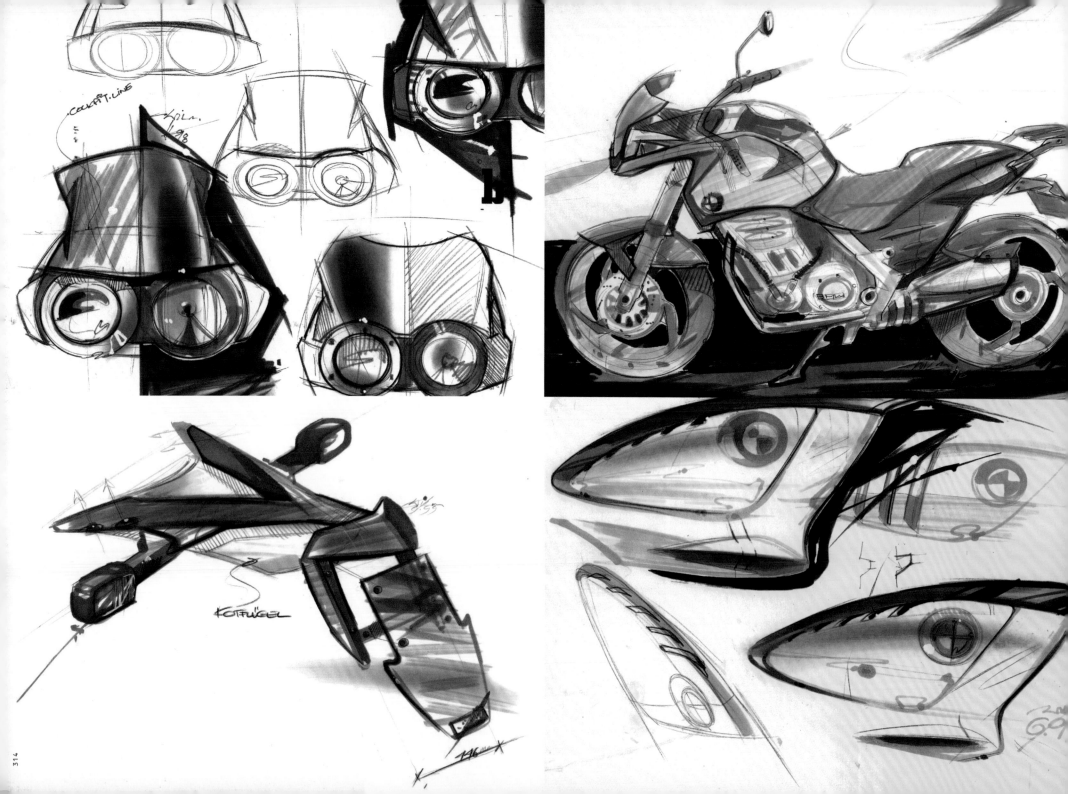

COCKPIT.LINE

KOTFLÜGEL

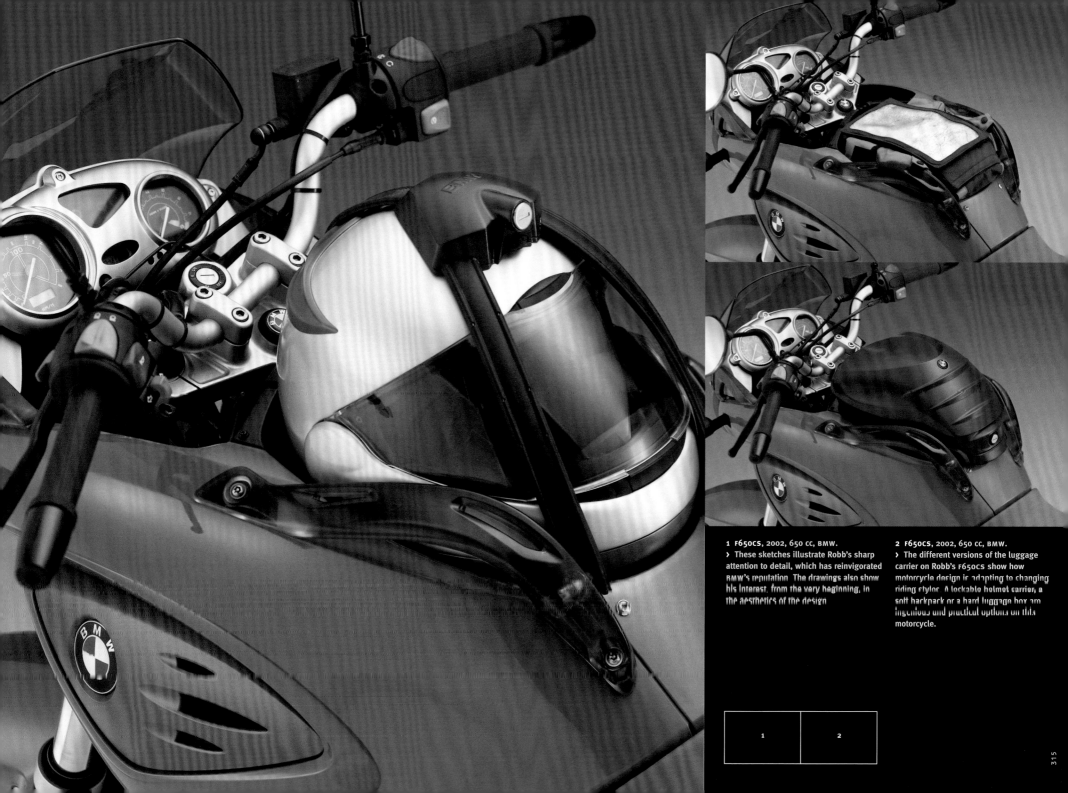

1 F650CS, 2002, 650 cc, BMW.
› These sketches illustrate Robb's sharp attention to detail, which has reinvigorated BMW's reputation. The drawings also show his interest, from the very beginning, in the aesthetics of the design

2 F650CS, 2002, 650 cc, BMW.
› The different versions of the luggage carrier on Robb's F650CS show how motorcycle design is adapting to changing riding styles. A lockable helmet carrier, a soft backpack or a hard luggage box are ingenious and practical options on this motorcycle.

1	2

MARTÍN RUIZ DE AZÚA BARCELONA

Martín Ruiz de Azúa was born in the Basque country in the north of Spain but moved to Catalonia to study fine art at the Universitat de Barcelona, an education he later rounded off at the ETSAB School of Architecture in Barcelona with a postgraduate diploma.

Ruiz de Azúa's Basic House project (1999) is the creation of a designer with a vivid imagination, a concern for the environment and an interest in the world of objects. The Basic House is a response to an environment dominated by the demand for more and more products to satisfy artificially created needs. Ruiz de Azúa invites us to learn from other cultures that live with the bare essentials, but this is not a return to the cave. The Basic House takes full advantage of modern technology. It is a shelter that can be folded up and carried in a pocket, to be taken out when it is needed, and inflated by heat – either from the sun or the human body. A large, cubic balloon, the Basic House is so light that it floats, and yet its metallic, polyester walls protect against extremes of cold or heat. It is the ideal home for the person who dreams of a life unencumbered by material possessions.

The Basic House aims to satisfy the user's primary needs, not only for shelter but for food and social relationships as well. Ruiz de Azúa's stance is summed up in his proposal to make the 'equals' sign (=) the new symbol of the International Red Cross. The sign implies a change of values and a future in which discrimination will have made way for equality of opportunities and rights, with a move from humanitarian aid to genuine social justice. Design can contribute to this vision with products such as the Rebotijo Water Jug (2000) or the Universal Plate (2001), which seek to re-establish the social aspect of food as something entirely natural – an idea that is lost to our society.

Ruiz de Azúa is at home in the realms of Utopia and experimentation. He hardly seems to mind waiting a year to see how nature will decorate his plant pots in the wonderful underwater Tache Naturelle (1999). Other designs, such as the Interactive Cushions (2000), are conceived with a view to promoting social consciousness and stimulating communication between people by physically demonstrating that every movement we make has repercussions on others. RAMÓN UBEDA

1 **Tache Naturelle**, vases, 1999, ceramic, 30 x 20 x 20 cm, an assignment at the Ecole des Beaux Arts de Saint-Etienne.
› Fascinated by nature's capacity to appropriate the artifical, Ruiz de Azúa submerged several very porous, white, ceramic plant-pots in water and left them, undisturbed, for a year. The mosses and lichens that grew on their surface emerged as totally unique designs that could never be replicated.

2 **Basic House**, 1999, polyester metal finish, 2 sq. m, Païbe Thio.
› This pocket-size house takes the form of an inflatable cube. The metallized polyester is reversible and acts as a thermostat: the gold interior insulates the occupant from extremes of cold weather while the silver deflects extreme heat. The difference in air temperature between the inside and out ensures that the cube remains upright. It is extremely light, weighing only 200 grams, and is easy to fold and carry.

1	1	2

1 **Universal Plate**, 2001, plastic and moulded polypropylene, 25 x 50 x 0.2 cm, Paï Thio.
> This plate is designed to facilitate eating standing up. Made from a sheet of moulded polypropylene, it has a hole for a glass or cup and a support for cutlery or chopsticks. The plate bends up at the end around the thumb-hole but easily unfolds for cleaning or storing.

2 **Interactive Cushions**, 2000, plastic, 160 x 90 x 45 cm, Paï Thio.
> A valve between these two air-filled cushions means that a change in pressure on one has an immediate effect on the other.

The design was intended to promote social consciousness, illustrating the impact one human has on another.

3 **Screen Chair**, 1999, EVA (ethylene vinyl acetate), 140 x 70 x 1 cm, prototype.
> As an alternative to projecting images on a flat surface in the conventional way, this screen has been designed to fit the curvature of a standard chair. Life-size recorded images of people are projected onto it, emulating real people in real space.

4 **Rebotijo Water Jug**, 2000, clay, 31 x 15 x 10 cm, Aguadé Ceramic.
> Ruiz de Azúa has retained the functional aspects of the earthenware water jug, while modernizing the appearance to resemble a hybrid between a bottle and a tetra pak.

1	2
	4
3	

TIMO SALLI HELSINKI

When considering the work of designers it is important to look at the context in which they operate. Timo Salli cannot be divorced from his Finnish background. Finland is different from its Scandinavian neighbours in many respects: its language, its relationship with Russia and its status as a republic, for example. These factors have led to a Finnish attitude that can be characterized as proud, serious, independent and having great integrity. The Finns also have a very direct way of looking at things. Consequently, Finnish design has a drama, strength and courage that cannot be found in neighbouring countries and all these traits can be seen in the work of designers such as Timo Salli.

Finnish design has undergone a regeneration in the last five years, after a relatively lean period that began in the 1970s, and Salli belongs to the new generation of designers which has been instrumental in bringing about this renewal. After taking a degree in furniture design, he founded his own company, Muotoilutoimisto Salli Ltd, in 1993 and he was one of the founder members of Snowcrash, a design group that made a big impression when they first exhibited at the Salone del Mobile in Milan in 1999. Salli's Firecase (2000) and long Firebox (2001) are characteristic of his work. They are incredibly daring and dramatic products. Salli's use of the reflective properties of steel and glass to enhance the impact of the fire is also very clever. And it is perhaps only a Finn who could come up with the idea of having a fire as a piece of furniture that can be moved about instead of being an integrated architectural feature.

The fire products show that Salli has an ability to produce objects that confound the viewer's expectations. Lamplamp, which he created in 2001 for the Spy Club in Dublin, is also an example of this. It is a wall lamp but it is also a mirror, with the hidden bulb providing a halo of light around the mirror. Salli's exploration of what is a lamp is also evident in his TimoTimo lamp (1999), which although it has an unfinished look is actually extremely well thought through and very consciously assembled. Salli enjoys finding and using unusual materials and transforming them into products. This is part of his desire to provoke and to question.

STEFAN YTTERBORN

1 L, exhibition furniture, 2001, steel, acrylic, 9 x 20 x 15 m, Innovation Forum, Lume, Helsinki.
› Because of the enormous open space of the Lume exhibition centre, Salli's idea was to try displaying objects of different sizes and contrasting functions and thereby to build a metaphorical red carpet in the middle of the space. The different heights and sizes of the platforms are very apparent from a distance and the effect is intended to welcome and draw people into the exhibition.

2 LampLamp, 2001, glass, stainless steel, 49 x 68 x 15 cm, Muotoilutoimisto Salli.
› This light-cum-mirror is a testimony to multi-functionalism and double meanings in design. By day Lamplamp is a mirror, which reflects the sunlight; in the evenings a conventional electric light is employed to enable the mirror to become a window through which it is possible to see and to be seen.

1	2

320

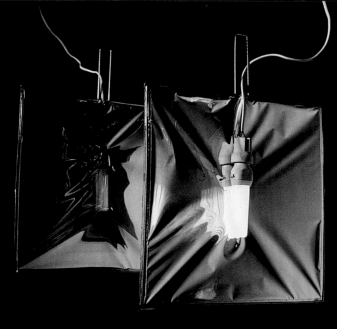

1 Firecase, 2000, ceramic glass, stainless steel, stones, 50 x 40 x 40 cm, prototype for Snowcrash.

2 Firebox-long, 2001, ceramic glass, stainless steel, 40 x 250 x 25 cm, Muotoilutoimisto Salli.

1 Fire is one of the most mesmerising phenomena. Yet even with the new generation of gas fires, where flues are no longer necessary, the fireplace has stuck rigidly to its original form. In these fireboxes, Salli has reinvented the representation of fire in the living space in a new and exciting way. On the top of Firecase is a 2 kg filter made predominantly of stones; toxic waste sticks to the stones and they can be easily washed if they start to discolour.

3 TimoTimo, lamp, 1999, transparent and semi-transparent metallic polyester foil, 30 x 30 x 3 cm, Kierketjar für e kieletleyer.

3 TimoTimo is just a plastic bag with a light. The idea was to make a simple, multifunctional, mass produced piece by using techniques that are normally confined to the packaging industry. The lamp has a transparent reflector and can be wall mounted or placed on the floor, seat or bed.

		3
1	2	

KAZUYO SEJIMA

There can be little doubt that Sejima will become one of the most important architects of the twenty-first century. For now, she is best known for having adopted the Superflat concept in architecture. The Superflat concept was promoted by the artist Takashi Murakami, who curated an exhibition of Superflat works which toured the United States in 2001. The concept is based on an anti-hierarchical philosophy, and involves an accessible approach to the use of space, in terms of structure and materials as well as from a social point of view. It is a user-friendly, open-ended, unstructured system, reminiscent of the truly democratic architecture and design championed by Alvar Aalto himself. Sejima concentrates on deconstructing the rules and restrictions that inhibit the work of other architects, with results that are smooth, smart and relaxed.

Flatness, smoothness and simplicity are the key words to define Sejima's designs. It was inevitable that she should be chosen by MoMA in New York as one of the two architects to work on their 1995 'Light Construction' exhibition. Their other choice was Toyo Ito, who Sejima had worked alongside before she built her own studio.

Sejima has the same open-minded, purist attitude to product design as she does to architecture. She never regards her designs as objects in the normal sense, but as part of an organic system akin to nature itself. The designs follow their own evolutionary paths, growing or fading away like living organisms. It must always be remembered, however, that these designs are not just poetic concepts, they are functional products. The practical nature of Sejima's work was particularly apparent in work commissioned in 2000 by Driade.

The Sofa-chair represents a wonderfully theatrical gesture. The metal chair has a removable air cushion and looks like a chair 'wearing' a sofa or a sofa with a chair hidden inside its body. The concept is reminiscent of Named Platform, one Sejima's early architectural projects, consisting of a series of houses that symbolized a new approach to architecture. They could be interpreted as non-functional, or as multi-functional spaces with the potential to be used in different ways. They were user-oriented, neutral spaces, accessible to anyone for any purpose. This open-ended approach, resulting in buildings or products that can be infinitely transformed, crops up regularly in the history of design and architecture. So, Sejima should not be seen as the inventor of this idea, but simply the architect and designer with the technology to express this concept in the spirit of our time. RYU NIIMI

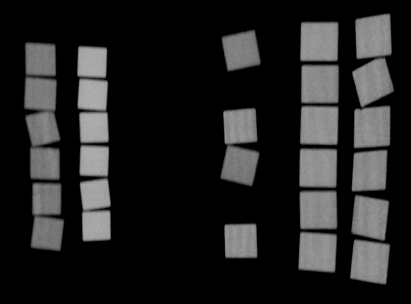

1 Floor Stand Light, 1990, glowing surface sheet frame, acrylic pipe, Nippon Electric Glass.
› This lamp provides an unusual light owing to the coloured material of its square components.

2 Flower Chair, 2001, polyurethane, PVA coating, 39 x 104 x 113.5 cm, IDÉE.
› The Flower Chair was designed for the Information Corner of the Sendai Mediatheque in Japan, which was built by Toyo Ito. The Information Corne is a place where people can hold discussions, meet friends, do research or browse through magazines. This large 50 x 50 metre space is filled with Flower Chairs, which can be arranged and rearranged to resemble an endless field of flowers.

630

373

1135

390

1040

1040

325

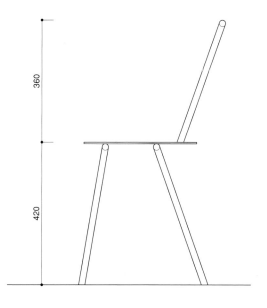

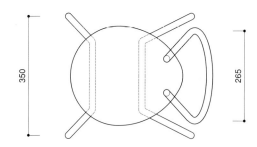

1 Marumaru, chair, 2000, steel tubular inner frame, moulded polyurethane foam shell, satin stainless-steel legs, 56.8 x ø 73 cm, Driade.
› This chair is a doughnut-shaped cushion wrapped in elastic fabric. By placing the hole off-centre, the cushion becomes a comfortable shape for sitting.

2 Hanahana, flower stand, 2000, stainless-steel frame and base, 160 x 92 x 25 cm, Driade.
› This flower stand, shaped like a tree, was designed so the user could create his favourite flower arrangement. In this way, a mixture of of nature and an artificial counterpart can be enjoyed at the same time. It is also suitable for outdoors.

3 Café Chain, 1990, steel, 36 x 73 x 73 cm, in collaboration with Ryue Nishizawa SANAA, Device Co.
› The Café Chair was designed for a small café built by Kazuyo Sejima and Ryue Nishizawa in a park in Koga in Japan. It can be used both indoors and outdoors because of the materials employed.

1	**2**	**3**

HÉCTOR SERRANO LONDON

Most young Spaniards who set their sights on a career in design dream of training in Barcelona. But not so the Valencians. With its own, distinctive school of design, Valencia has no need to look to Catalonia. And if young Valencian designers want to continue their studies, they usually go to the Royal College of Art in London, where they work under Ron Arad.

Héctor Serrano went to London in 1998 when he was barely 20, and there he stayed. At the Royal College he met his fellow Valencians Alberto and Raky Martínez, with whom he designed the Aiberia table (2000) and the Siesta jug (2000). These two works betray a certain degree of nostalgia for the students' country of origin. La Siesta is a jar that has the look of a plastic water bottle and the characteristics of the traditional Spanish earthenware jug, capable of keeping the water inside it cool even in the middle of August, when it is 40 degrees centigrade in the shade.

Nostalgia disappeared completely from Serrano's work when he fell under the spell of remarkable, modern designers such as Snowcrash and Droog Design. One of his designs, the Superpatata lamp (2000), ultimately ended up in the Droog Design catalogue – something all young designers must dream about. The Superpatata is a simple yet ingenious product. A lamp made of latex and filled with salt, it can also be used as a pillow, providing light, colour and heat.

After this early success, Serrano continued to work with light, designing products such as the Playboy lamp (2001), which can be personalized with its own clothes, or the Top Secret lamp (2001), made from polyester film that has been passed through a document shredder. The fine strips that come out the other end are packed into a net of transparent nylon, like the bags used to pack oranges – a passing reference to Serrano's country of origin.

Manolo is Gonna Have Fun (2002) is a project that Serrano developed with Lola Llorca, another Valencian drawn by the cultural pull of the English capital. Manolo is a middle-aged man, serious and a little boring, the stereotype of the average Spaniard. The project focuses on transforming all the humdrum objects in his and every other house into amusing toys. With a little imagination the coffee table can be turned into an improvised trampoline, the lamp becomes a stupendous ball and a dinner plate makes a great Frisbee. RAMÓN UBEDA

1 La Siesta, jug, 2000, white terracotta, 32 x ø 10 cm, La Mediterránea, in collaboration with Alberto Martínez and Raky Martínez.
> This hybrid between a plastic water bottle and a traditional earthenware jug has been craft-manufactured from a special white clay.

2 From Infinity to Beyond, 2001, steel, rubber, foam, fabric, 30 x 120 x 100 cm.
> This table is part of the Manolo is Gonna Have Fun collection which demonstrates how everyday objects can be transformed into fun toys. When not being used as a coffee table, this exhibit can be used as a trampoline.

3 I like Football on Sunday Afternoon, 2001, silicon, PVC, compact fluorescent light bulb, ø 70 cm.
> Part of the Manolo is Gonna Have Fun collection, this lamp can be played with as though it were a large ball – kicked, thrown or bounced – yet it simultaneously lights up the room.

4 Don't Play With Your Food, 2001, polystyrene, 3 x ø 30 cm.
> Part of the Manolo is Gonna Have Fun collection. This photograph catches the moment when a polystyrene plate, with all its contents, is tossed into the air like a Frisbee.

	2		
1			4
	3		

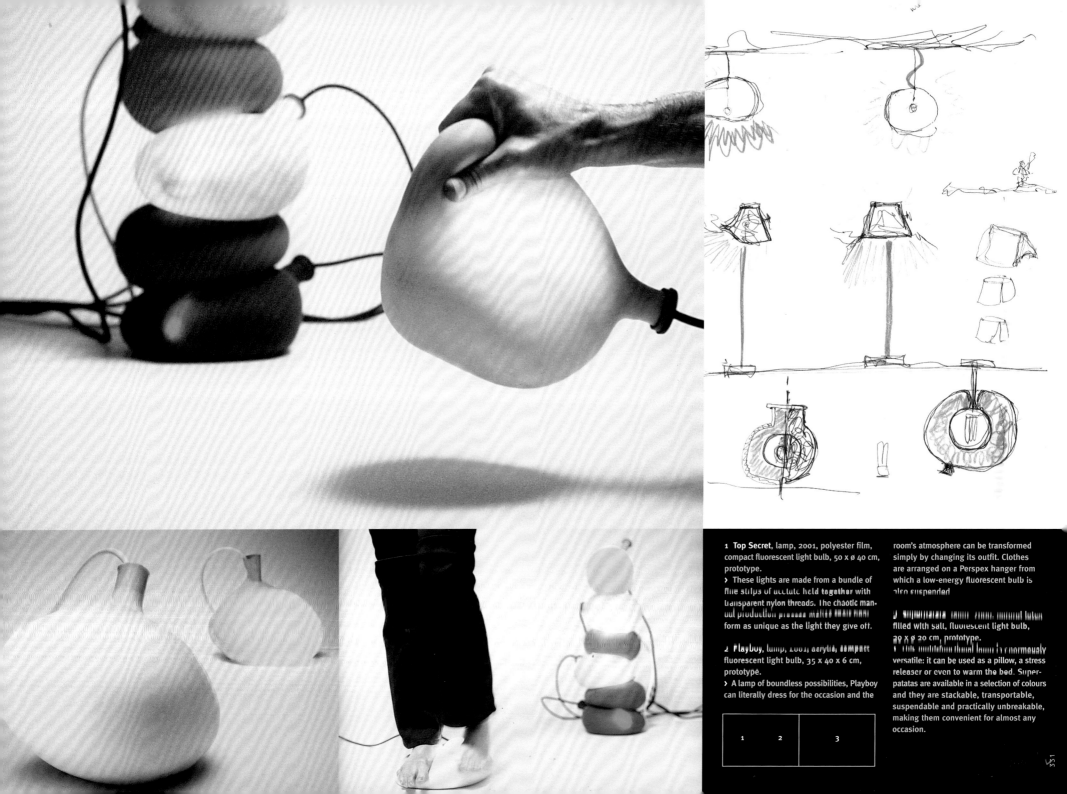

1 **Top Secret**, lamp, 2001, polyester film, compact fluorescent light bulb, 50 x ø 40 cm, prototype.
> These lights are made from a bundle of fine strips of acetate held together with transparent nylon threads. The chaotic manual production process makes each final form as unique as the light they give off.

2 **Playboy**, lamp, 2001, acrylic, compact fluorescent light bulb, 35 x 40 x 6 cm, prototype.
> A lamp of boundless possibilities, Playboy can literally dress for the occasion and the room's atmosphere can be transformed simply by changing its outfit. Clothes are arranged on a Perspex hanger from which a low-energy fluorescent bulb is also suspended.

3 **Superpatata**, lamp, 2001, mineral lotex filled with salt, fluorescent light bulb, 20 x ø 20 cm, prototype.
> This multifunctional lamp is enormously versatile: it can be used as a pillow, a stress releaser or even to warm the bed. Superpatatas are available in a selection of colours and they are stackable, transportable, suspendable and practically unbreakable, making them convenient for almost any occasion.

1	2	3

331

CARINA SETH ANDERSSON STOCKHOLM

Carina Seth Andersson searches for and reaches perfection in the simple and this demands both discipline and time. Her work has a confidence and vital elegance of expression that is refreshing and will establish her as one of the classic Scandinavian designers of our time. She trained initially in glass and ceramic ware at Konstfack, the University College of Arts, Crafts and Design in Stockholm, graduating in 1983, and went on to win a scholarship at the Orrefors Glass School in 1986. She then set up her own company. After an exhibition of her mouth-blown pieces, the cbi company approached her to do stacking glass cylinders which were a great success. Each cylinder can handle everything from goldfish to flowers.

A common element in her work is her desire to satisfy a number of needs in the same object. The work she did in 1998 for the Finnish company Hackman is an example of this. She designed two double-walled stainless-steel serving bowls. They are just perfect in their size and shape, ideal for all kinds of food, work well on their own and also relate to each other very beautifully. By using double-walled stainless steel she not only increases the insulating capacity of the bowls but also adds to the character of the pieces. The accompanying wooden spoons contrast nicely in texture with the bowls. These are the kind of products that everyone should possess.

Seth Andersson has also designed glassware for Swedish and Finnish companies. She has used the constraints imposed by working with manufactured glass as a creative impetus and is sensible about the amount of material being used. This is in keeping with the traditions of Scandinavian design: simplicity of form evolved because of limited resources and the antipathy to unnecessary labour and cost. Seth Andersson is working within and renewing that heritage.

Seth Andersson is full of ideas. When she has decided what she wants to produce, she acts decisively. Her form of expression, however, moves between the spontaneous and the machine-operated: at times these are combined in the same product, at other times they are separate. She appears to be very unhurried and calm during the creative process and it never seems to bother her that the outside world moves faster than she does. Seth Andersson has great integrity and does not seem to need to fulfil herself through her products. There is something pure about her which is reflected in her work. STEFAN YTTERBORN

1 Balja, glasses, 2001, clear glass, water glass 7.5 x ø 9 cm, wine glass 15 x ø 9 cm, carafe 15 x ø19 cm, Skruf.
› Balja is a series of mouthblown glasses. The set of only three pieces is meant to cover all possible needs and situations.

2 Salad Cutlery, 1997, wood, 35 cm, Hackman.
› The cutlery was developed simultaneously with the stainless-steel bowls. The heat-treated Scandinavian wood is intended to give a warm and tactile experience to balance the cold character of the bowl.

3 Bowls, 1997, stainless steel, 10/14 x ø 26/34.5 cm, Hackman.
› The bowls have a double body made of mat polished 18/10 stainless steel. The two bowl sizes are meant to meet every need.

1	2
	3

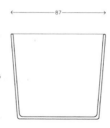

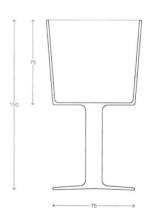

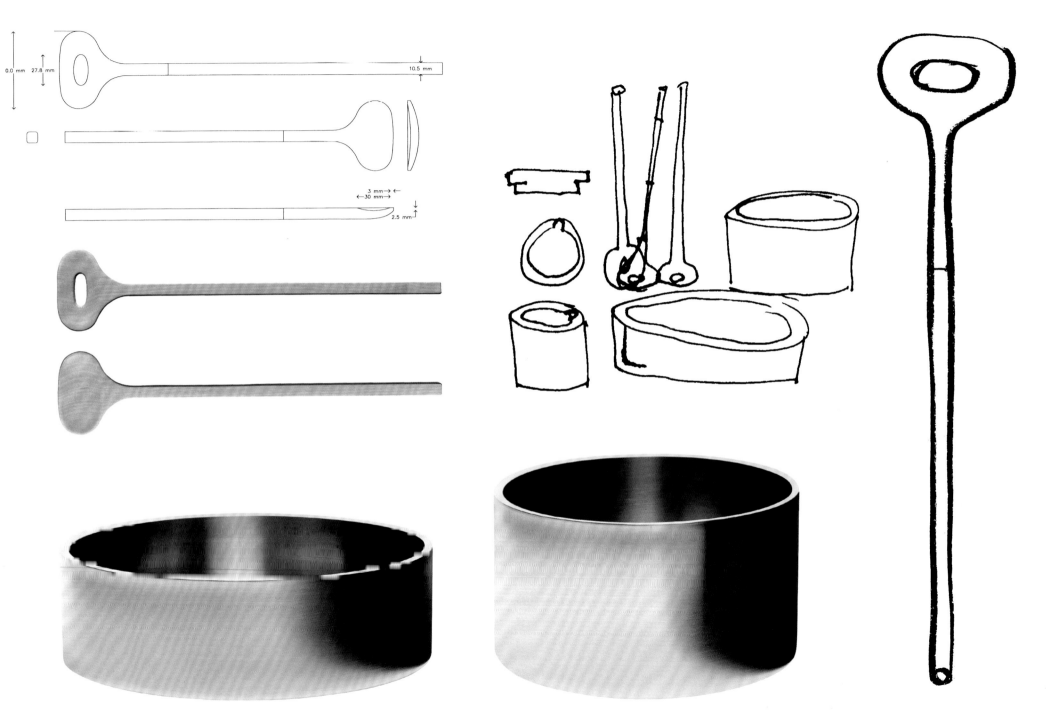

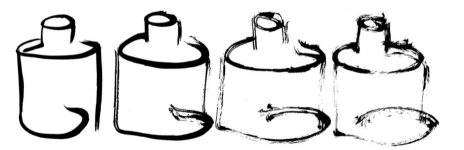

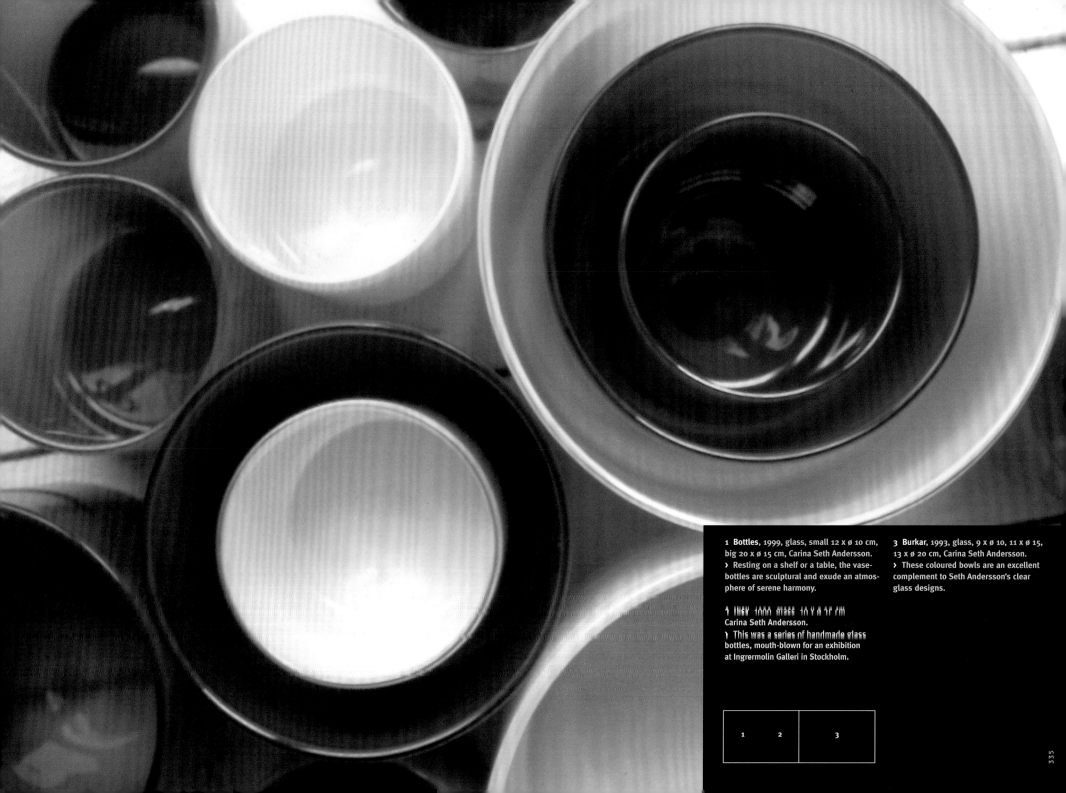

1 Bottles, 1999, glass, small 12 x ø 10 cm, big 20 x ø 15 cm, Carina Seth Andersson.
› Resting on a shelf or a table, the vase-bottles are sculptural and exude an atmosphere of serene harmony.

3 Burkar, 1993, glass, 9 x ø 10, 11 x ø 15, 13 x ø 20 cm, Carina Seth Andersson.
› These coloured bowls are an excellent complement to Seth Andersson's clear glass designs.

2 IHSK 1000 glass 10 x ø 15 cm
Carina Seth Andersson.
› This was a series of handmade glass bottles, mouth-blown for an exhibition at Ingrermolin Galleri in Stockholm.

1	2	3

MATT SINDALL PARIS

In a business where you are increasingly pushed to create and produce at a fashion designer's pace, Matt Sindall is not afraid to work slowly and thoughtfully, designing questions – not answers – in the form of objects.

Open-minded and as curious as a child, Sindall asks questions that seem simple but often prove to be metaphysical. 'Why can't a chair change colour?' or 'At what point is an object an object?' Instead of leaving these questions dangling, he sets about probing them, computer mouse in one hand and saw in the other, first creating a perfect, virtual design and then realizing it with his hands.

Sindall has recently solved the problem of instilling animated information into an inert surface. His celebrated Chromatic Chair was shown in 2001 by VIA (Valorisation de l'Innovation dans l'Ameublement) in France, where this Englishman has lived and worked for just over a decade. This chair turns sitting into a technicolour experience. Its colour is dependent on the light, and the angle from which it is seen. Lenticular film takes the surface through shades of green, blue, red, orange and yellow and back to green. The concept of Chromatic Chair came before Sindall's choice of material as he avoids making the medium the central concept of his work. He believes in taking existing materials in new directions and takes full advantage of the innovative ones that are available.

Engaged in a battle between form and surface, Sindall says: 'I try to keep forms stupidly simple.' He describes his Whole Table (1998) as an exercise in pure form. The shape of his Red Bed/Black Bed (2000) is more complex. Created from foam with a high-frequency saw, it incorporates pockets of air to keep the body cool and make the bed easy to roll up.

Having set up his own company, Sindall makes a distinction between 'personal' projects, divorced from commercial pressure or constraint, and professional projects, such as designing urban lighting or fire hydrants. Many of his lighting systems are somewhat magical. In Biarritz, for example, his streetlights on the promenade have an aerial, seagull-like quality and the fibre-optic lamps give off a light that seems to emanate from everywhere and nowhere in particular. Sindall's personal projects are also entering the professional realm, with the production in 2001 of his memory-foam chair, Niel, manufactured by Sawaya & Moroni. Through questions and discoveries he will undoubtedly leave his mark on the design world. LISA WHITE

1 **Chromatic Chair**, 2000, wood, lenticular film, 85 x 48 x 45 cm, prototype.
› Lenticular film has been used to play with the colour spectrum in the design of this striking chair. The spectrum effect has been achieved by juxtaposing several different layers of the film that are visible depending on the viewing angle.

2 **Niel**, seat, 2001, chromed steel, memory foam, 34 x 90 x 90 cm, Sawaya & Moroni.
› Memory foam is used in hospitals to prevent bed sores when patients have been lying in one position for long periods of time. This characteristic of leaving imprints for short periods of time is used as the distinguishing feature of this bench.

3 **A Little Light Reading**, 2000, 34 x 28 x 3 cm, prototype.
› The book has a fluorescent bulb integrated into the main body of the object. The design originated from the idea that the user can be enlightened by reading.

4 **Scarabée**, table, 2000, silk-screened polycarbonate, steel, 40 x 71 x 34 cm, prototype.
› These tables/stools were made during a workshop at the school of St Etienne and were the result of research on how it is possible to incorporate a fictive 3-dimensional surface into the top of a seat.

1	2	3
		4

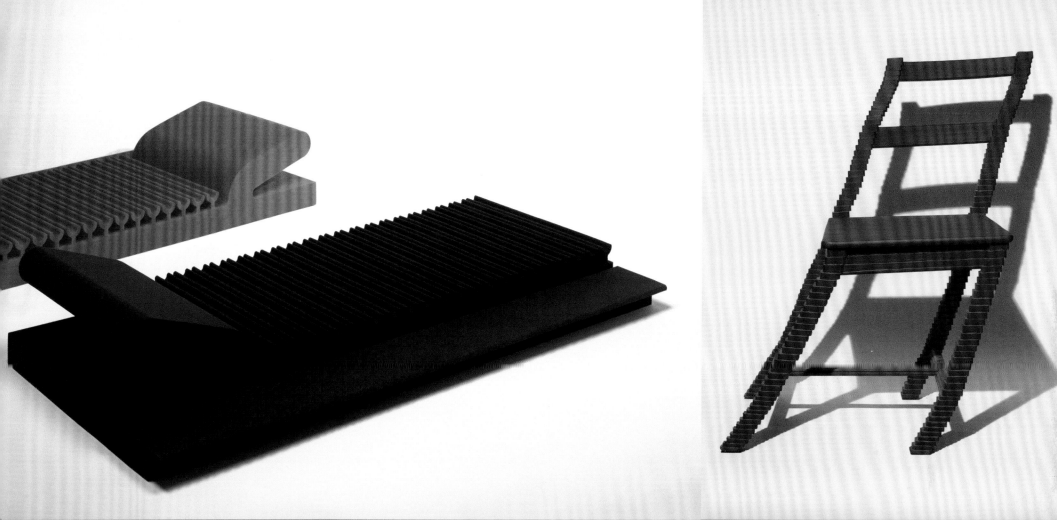

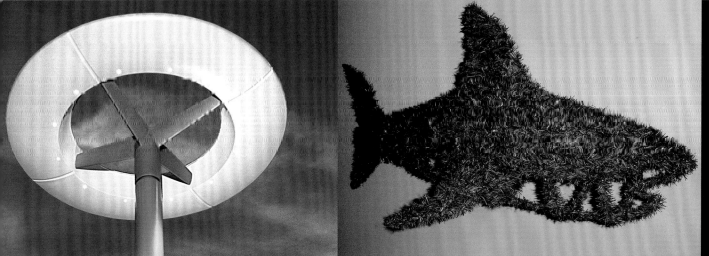

1 **Whole**, table, 1998, fibreglass, PVC tube, lead, 73 x ø 130 cm, prototype.
> This table eliminates all straight edges or the notion of wall thickness, which is usually inherent in plastic furniture.

2 **Red Bed/Black Bed**, 2000, foam, 35 x 90 x 180 cm, prototype.
> These simple foam block beds have been cut with a high frequency saw creating a profile almost impossible to make by hand. The 'V' profile create air pockets reducing the problems of perspiration which are normally associated with foam mattresses.

3 **Chair Under the Influence**, 2000, wood, 85 x 50 x 70 cm, prototype.
> This IKEA chair was sliced up and reconstructed at an angle of 45 degrees, transforming it to the point where it no longer serves its original purpose but still remains a chair. It is also a manifestation of physically introducing interference into a 3-dimensional object, like a TV with bad reception.

4 **Street Lamp**, 2000, optic fibres, metal, 450 cm, related.
> This street lamp uses optic fibres to transmit the light which is situated at the base of the mast. This idea can save time and money because the source is changed and repaired at the base, eliminating the need for a lift.

5 **Shark Christmas Tree**, 2001, artificial tree, 40 x 100 x 30 cm, Exhibition Paris Mode.

		3
	2	
1		
	4	5

JOB SMEETS ANTWERP

Continually striving to break free from the perceived constraints of industrial design, Job Smeets sees the ideal role of the designer as a 'poetic moralist', whose work holds meaning beyond function. Strong in his belief that 'design has been at the mercy of functionalism', Smeets seeks to make function irrelevant.

Smeets refers to the work at Studio Job as 'Post-craft'. His designs are inspired by the one-off nature of art, the craftsmanship of the Wiener Werkstätte, the intuitive and elaborate character of haute couture, and the plastic modularity of his Playmobile-dominated childhood. He describes his pieces as 'extreme unique', and they are indeed singular and eccentric. His Communication Unit (2000) was created from 300 kg of aluminium. The massive control panel serves as an intercom system for an audiovisual office complex in Rotterdam. For the same building, he created a Hall Cabinet (2000) that denies common furniture styles, incorporating over 50 doors and storage spaces, all coated in lacquered layers of shiny polyurethane.

For Smeets, the material is the mood. His smooth, organically shaped, veneer-covered Modular Furniture (2000) is made from perfectly assembled puzzle pieces. Together, they ask a question: 'When does form become function?' He also made the heavy, bronze-cast Extrème Unique home appliances that mock our throwaway society (2001).

Concept, form, material and production processes are inextricably linked in Job's mind. They must be carefully and cleverly associated in order to maximize the message. Most of the designs are made manually by quality furniture makers or by Studio Job. Production processes include the kneading of the wax moulds for the Elements archetypes (2000), ensuring that fingerprints and palette-knife marks are visible in the final result.

Though Smeets elevates the status of craft, casting it in a contemporary mood, the conceptual nature of his work seems to belong to the realm of art. He claims that 'theory is the only reason to design at all', and his intellectual, intuitive working processes are similar to those of an artist. He points out the paradox: 'If a designer manages to sell a thousand copies of a product, he is immediately hailed as a truly wonderful designer. Yet a work of art is venerated because it is unique.' Indeed, with Studio Job, Smeets has created his own realm outside the common definitions of designer and artist, appropriately defining his position as that of an 'intimate architect'.
LISA WHITE

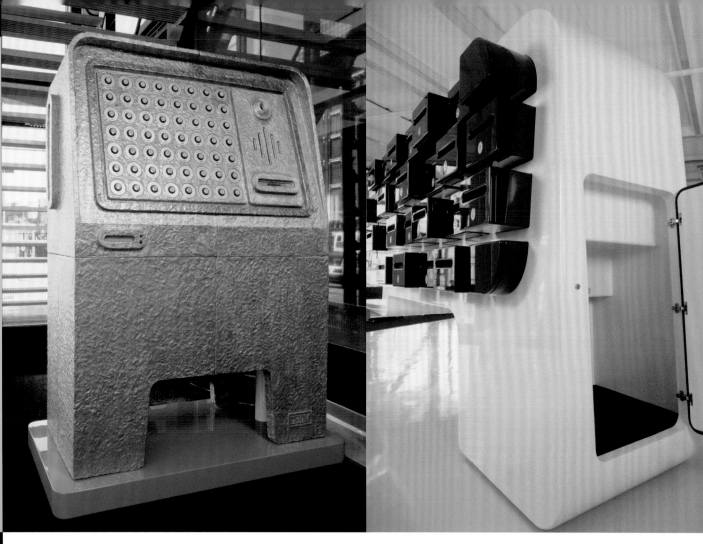

1 Communication Unit, 2000, aluminium, electric elements, 180 x 120 x 60 cm, 25 kV building, Rotterdam.
> This unit was produced using the lost-wax method but it is filled with a high-tech communication network.

2 Hall Cabinet, 2000, multi-ply board, glossy coating, 210 x 390 x 460 cm.
> The cabinet contains more than 50 doors and two big lids behind which are hidden a functional work space and chair storage.

3 Modular Cabinet, 2000, multi-ply board, oak veneer, 250 x 350 x 120 cm, Studio Job.
> The development stages of this work aim to be a comment on, and a contribution to, the discourse on design. Smeets chooses his materials for their suitability to support his philosophical or theoretical notions.

4 Moulding Grey, 1999, cast aluminium, 150 x 600 x 200 cm, Marantz-Audio.
> This design uses music to explain the shaping process. Form and colour can shape feelings in design similar to the emotions one might feel listening to a song.

5 Curved Cabinet, 1999, CNC, PU, Perspex, 250 x 950 cm, Studio Job.
> The choice of material depends on the designer's state of mind or the character he wants to establish for a piece or collection.

1	2	4
3		5

1 **Craft**, 2001, cast bronze, clockworks, oak, various dimensions, Studio Job.
> Smeets works with bronze in a free way to set new trends. His inventive 'craft series' consists of utensils and containers cast in bronze, using traditional kitchenware such as a coffee pot and pressure cooker as moulds.

2 **Drawings**, 1999.
> Expressive and subjective, Job pushes his inspiration to the extremes in his Pièces Uniques project, where the uniqueness of one object or piece of furniture calls for an outspoken, haute-couture touch.

3 **Elements**, 2000, mixed media, PU, various sizes, Studio Job.
> This design is a means of researching, developing and realizing a certain mood. Attracted to the adventure of the creative process, Smeets is fascinated by the abstractions of the mood in the final result.

4 **De Chair**, 2001, multi-ply board, oak verneer 83 x 44 x 40 cm, Centraal Museum, Utrecht.
5 **Be Sofa**, 2001, multi-ply board, oak verneer, 83 x 80 x 58 cm, Centraal Museum, Utrecht.
> The use of veneer throughout the collection allows Smeets to avoid, as much as possible, standard solutions to shape a form (nails, hinges) which disturb the organic flow of the design.

6 **Alpha China**, cups, 2001, pressed porcelain, Royal Makkum Tichelaar.

		3	6
1	2		
		4	5

REIKO SUDO / NUNO TOKYO

In the work of Japanese textile designer Reiko Sudo, hand and machine are given equal importance. Each possesses its own inherent beauty. Sudo believes that design must find a balance between the human touch and mechanization, and this informs all of her work. She is the chief designer at the NUNO Corporation, which she helped to establish in 1984, but it was not until 'Structure and Surface', an exhibition of Japanese textiles at MoMA, New York in 1998, that her work became known to a wider, international audience.

With her intense creativity and love of experimentation, Sudo is a pioneer in her field. She explores new technologies and appropriates processes developed for other industries, which become radical when applied to the design and production of textiles. While it is clear that she draws inspiration from the rich textile traditions and weaving culture of Japan, her fabrics are industrially milled, not hand-loomed, one-of-a-kind pieces.

NUNO's textiles have been used by architects such as Toyo Ito, Itsuko Hasegawa and Kazuyo Sejima. The textiles have such a strong presence, however, that they stand alone as objects in their own right. Pattern is structurally embedded in the work and is always a direct result of process, never the determining factor behind the appearance of a piece.

An interest in natural forces, such as weathering and decay, has led Sudo to explore recycled materials such as rusted nails, metal plates and barbed wire. These are used to overlay both surface and pattern on a fabric base. Textiles have also been created by stitching fibres to a water-soluble base, which ultimately dissolves, as in Paper Roll (2001), leaving an intricate pattern of fibres that has a lacy, perforated or openwork quality. By working with technicians in the car industry, Sudo learnt to coat fabric with a smooth, stainless-steel finish. Her Origami Pleats (1997) combine a machine process with a hand-pleating process, enabling the fabric to open out into a three-dimensional construction, and to collapse completely flat. As the cloth has been sandwiched between forms that are vacuum set in a high-temperature press, the works have a memory and always return to their original, angular shapes even when the folds are pulled open. NUNO's Burner Dye (2000) combines an ultra-fine, high-tech, stainless-steel fibre with the primitive technique of flame tempering to create a beautiful, iridescent fabric. BROOKE HODGE

1 Origami Pleat, 1997, polyester, 44 x 150 cm, Reiko Sudo, Mizue Okada/ NUNO Corporation.
> This fabric is folded repeatedly at sharp angles, dyed in three separate colours, then permanently pressed in a special pleating process, for which the patent is pending. The resulting pattern is abstract, yet suggestive of innumerable shapes.

2 Paper Roll, 2001, nylon, 83 cm, Reiko Sudo/NUNO Corporation.
> Rolled-up papers, viewed in spiralling cross-section, provided the inspiration for this textile.

3 Burner Dye, 2000, stainless steel, 118 cm, Reiko Sudo/NUNO Corporation.
> This complex fabric is made of stainless steel. By taking a burner to it, an effect is created similar to the way that steel kitchen utensils become iridescent from the flames on a stove.

4 Tsumami Shibori, 1997, polyester, 115 x 115 cm, Reiko Sudo, Hiroko Suwa/ NUNO Corporation.
> Another unusual pleated fabric which employs a highly unorthodox tie-dyeing process.

| 1 | 2 | 3 | 4 |

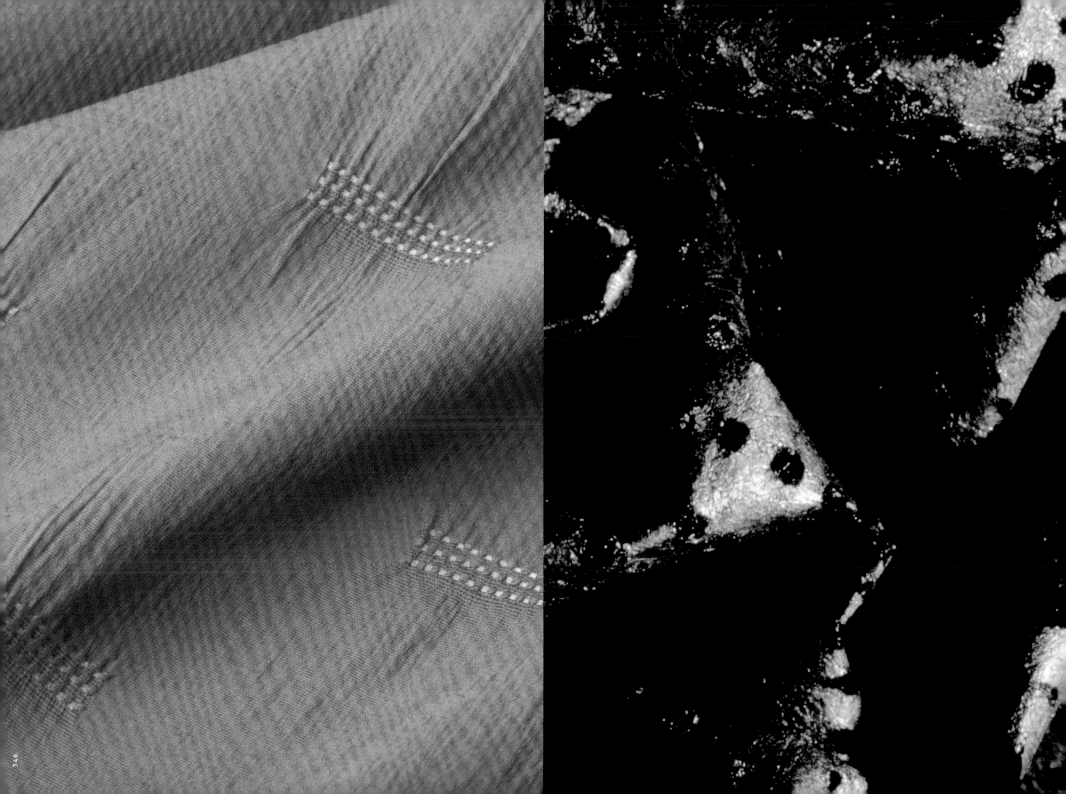

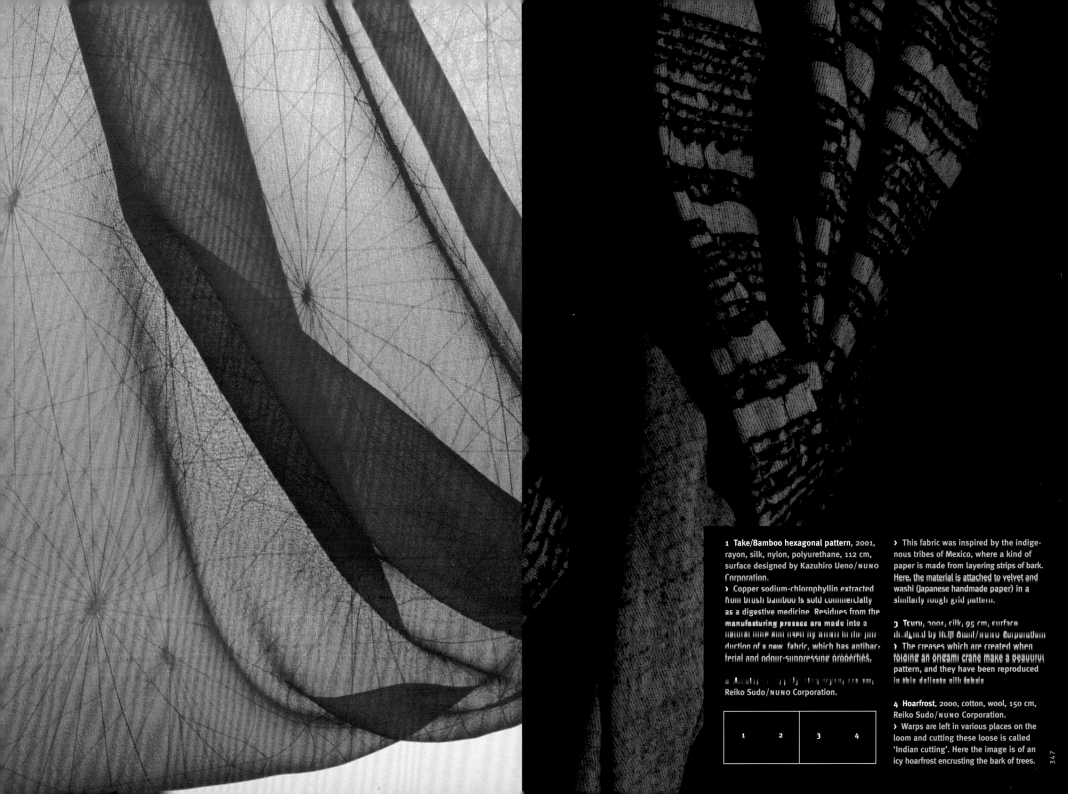

1 **Take/Bamboo hexagonal pattern**, 2001, rayon, silk, nylon, polyurethane, 112 cm, surface designed by Kazuhiro Ueno/NUNO Corporation.
› Copper sodium-chlorophyllin extracted from brush bamboo is sold commercially as a digestive medicine. Residues from the manufacturing process are made into a natural dye and used by NUNO in the production of a new fabric, which has antibacterial and odour-suppressing properties.

2 **Amate**, 2001, polyester, nylon, 112 cm, Reiko Sudo/NUNO Corporation.
› This fabric was inspired by the indigenous tribes of Mexico, where a kind of paper is made from layering strips of bark. Here, the material is attached to velvet and washi (Japanese handmade paper) in a similarly rough grid pattern.

3 **Tsuru**, 2001, silk, 95 cm, surface designed by Reiko Sudo/NUNO Corporation.
› The creases which are created when folding an origami crane make a beautiful pattern, and they have been reproduced in this delicate silk fabric.

4 **Hoarfrost**, 2000, cotton, wool, 150 cm, Reiko Sudo/NUNO Corporation.
› Warps are left in various places on the loom and cutting these loose is called 'Indian cutting'. Here the image is of an icy hoarfrost encrusting the bark of trees.

1	2	3	4

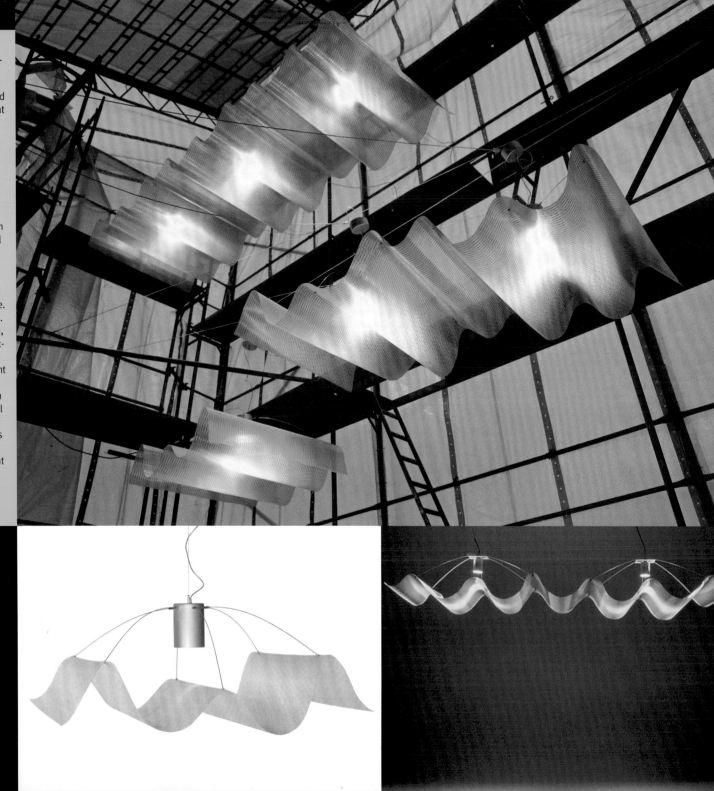

ILKKA SUPPANEN HELSINKI

A subtle manifesto of lightness, Ilkka Suppanen's work moves seamlessly between archaic, nomadic concepts and high-tech contemporary lifestyles. He is the designer of the iconic Flying Carpet (1998), a sofa made of thick felt, one of the most ancient of fabrics, and metal poles that can be easily disassembled and moved, like a traditional, nomadic tent. The felt suspended on the metal frame creates supple slopes, expressing an easy freedom that made it an instant design classic.

'I think rationally in order to express myself emotionally' explains Suppanen, whose degree in architecture gave him the intellectual rigour to examine a project from a practical point of view when beginning the design process. When he first began developing the Hiwave Light in 1998, his starting point was a suspended ceiling. Many loft spaces, both private and public, leave wires, cables, plumbing and other infrastructures exposed, creating a need for visual calm. Accordingly, the Hiwave was conceived to cover maximum ceiling space while offering a light source. Once the function was determined, Suppanen became fascinated with the high-tech material used in making sails, and incorporated this material in his light. The pull of gravity on the material itself created the softly undulating forms, offering poetry in a practical light, one that is both architecture and object.

Suppanen's work expresses what he calls an 'ecological lightness' as he concentrates on using the least amount of material and moving parts possible. In developing this lightness, he crosses the borders between disciplines. When he created the Airbag Chair in 1997, with fellow Finn Pasi Kolhonen, the idea was to create a combined chair and mattress inspired by the functionality of sports equipment. Adjustable straps adjust the angle of the seat back, and curved seams are needed in order to give the final product a straight appearance. Furthermore, like clothing, the Airbag can be folded away or hung up when not in use. The Airbag, as well as designs by other Finnish architects and designers, spawned the 'Snowcrash' show at the Salone del Mobile in Milan in 1997. Its success has inspired an entire movement, and a company of the same name, whose goal is to foster experimental products to equip contemporary life better.

Using materials that evoke sails, feathers or water, such as Frozen Light (1997), Suppanen's visual lightness offers a cool version of design that is grounded in architectural precision yet soars with creativity and clarity.

LISA WHITE

1 Hiwave Lamp, 1998, polyester fabric, aluminium, 100 x 14/27/40 x 14 cm, Snowcrash.
> This is a suspended ceiling light which floats overhead like a radiant carpet; the textile shade extends to make a gently undulating path of light that can transform interior spaces and can be adjusted to vary the effect to suit the occasion or location. Hiwave is available in one, two or three units.

2 Nomad Chair, 1997, steel, felt, 52 x 48 x 72 cm, prototype.
> This lightweight chair consists of a slim steel base, four spring-steel rods and a piece

of felt, yet it appears solid and enduring. It can be easily dismantled and carried – it has been devised to fit in with the lifestyle of the urban nomad.

3 Flying Carpet, sofa, 1998, steel, felt, 160 x 85 x 82 cm, Cappellini.
> This sofa has a flexible spring-steel structure which reiterates the notion of movement also implicit in the asymmetrical line of the seat. Suppanen has made this design appear ominously unstable.

4 Game, shelf, 1999, composite textile of polymer fibres, aluminium. 45 x 140 x 35 cm, Snowcrash
> An aluminium sheet has been bent to create a modular shelf and bench. The shelf can be rearranged into different configurations according to one's individual needs.

		3
1	2	
		4

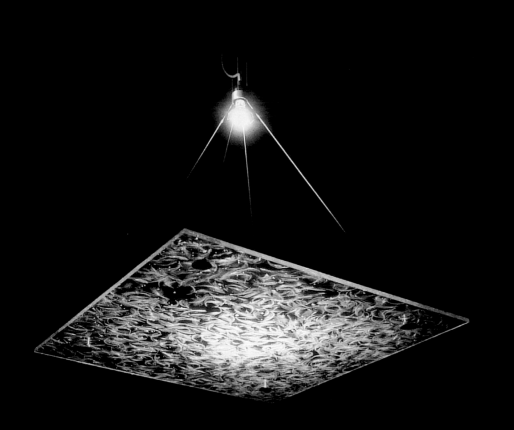

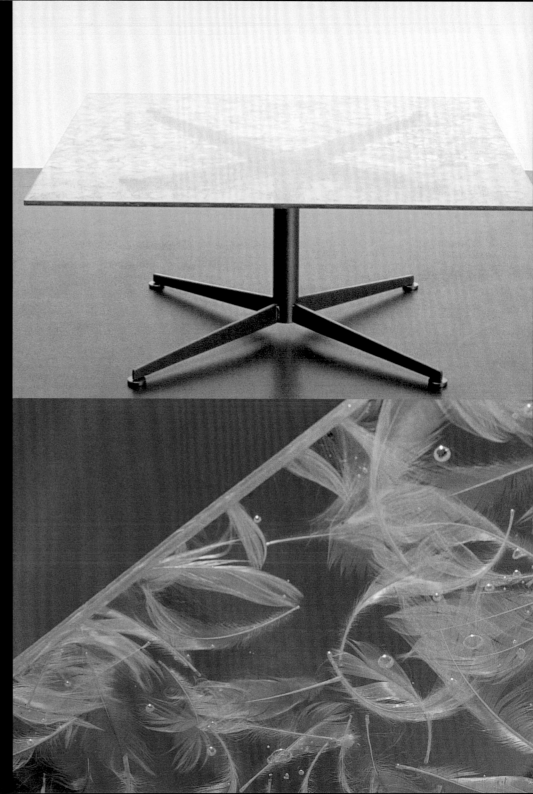

1 Frozen Light, 1997, glass, halogen bulb, 80 x 80 x 80 cm, prototype.
› A glass reflector has been constructed using special lamination techniques, whereby feathers are laminated inside the pieces of glass· this gives a unique light quality, and even when not illuminated it is a very intriguing and attractive object.

2 Frozen Table, 1999, laminated glass, steel, 45 x 90 x 90 cm
› Based on the same idea as the Frozen Light, this table was developed in a variety of different sizes. The feathers embedded in

the glass give an unusual quality to the tabletop.

3 Airbag Chair, 1997, nylon upholstery, polyester straps, polystyrene filling, 80 x 90 x 85 cm, Snowcrash.
› This is a combined chair-cum-mattress that can be used either indoors or outside. When not in use it folds away into a compact package or can be hung up. The carrying straps double up as adjusters for varying the angle of the back of the seat.

TARTARINI DESIGN TEAM MODENA

Motorcycle design has rarely commanded any attention. Indeed, it is only in the last ten years that the motorcycle has even been recognized as a designed object. The situation was greatly improved by 'The Art of the Motorcycle' exhibition at the Guggenheim Museum in New York. A paean to motorcycle design, the show brought wide critical and popular attention to the subject. The exceptional work of designers such as Leopoldo and Alessandro Tartarini also does much to focus public attention. The Tartarinis are a father and son team working at Italjet, where they mount a continuous challenge to the most sacred shibboleths of bike design.

Leopoldo Tartarini has been something of a maverick among motorcycle designers for over 30 years, working with Ducati among others. He founded Italjet in the 1960s, and for many years the company was deemed eccentric. This is certainly not the case today. Alessandro has teamed up with his father at the head of a young and talented design group, producing work characterized as much by technical innovation as aesthetic flair.

Two of Italjet's most popular designs are the Dragster and Formula 50 scooters (1997). The Tartarinis identified a market for new scooter designs among Italian teenagers who dismissed the venerable Vespas and Lambrettas as the scooters ridden by their parents. While keeping to the small-wheel, small-displacement rules of the scooter, the team reinvented the genre. They incorporated technical innovations not seen on motorcycles far bigger and more expensive. For example, the Formula 50 has a liquid-cooled engine, independent, hydraulically operated, disc brakes as standard, and a unique steering and suspension system that neutralizes some of the more heart-stopping handling quirks of the traditional small-wheeled scooter. Italjet's motorbikes are not only functional, they are also extremely handsome, but without any concessions to retro-styling, the current scourge of automative design.

Having conquered the scooter market, the Tartarinis are now heading off in a completely different direction with the three-wheeled Scooop (2002). Part scooter, part car, its three wheels give it much greater braking power than a scooter, with cornering ability that is also a huge improvement over traditional scooter design. But is it a scooter or ... a snowmobile? It is both, a challenging idea, and who knows if the world will respond with open arms. But that has always been the Tartarini style. ULTAN GUILFOYLE

1 Dragster, 1997, 50 cc, Italjet.
> The Tartarinis create small scooters with technology and value not found in much more expensive motorcycles. The Dragster has technological marvels such as the cantilevered front suspension and the truss frame. Every part of the Dragster has been created to combine the best technology with visual impact: the aggressive nose, the wide, low headlight, the sleek black undercarriage, the neat chassis and the suspension system with a dazzling silver finish.

2 Formula 50, 1997, 50 cc, Italjet.
> The Formula 50, a sinuous, elegant take on the traditional Italian scooter, is making a strong impact in the hitherto scooter-unfriendly market of the United States. Typical of the Tartarinis' design is the abundance of high-tech details, such as the centre-hub steering regulated by a single liquid-air shock absorber, differentiated tyres and dual disk brakes, which ensures perfect roadholding at all times. Looking closer at it, the design and characteristics of this scooter exceed all the existing standards.

1	2

353

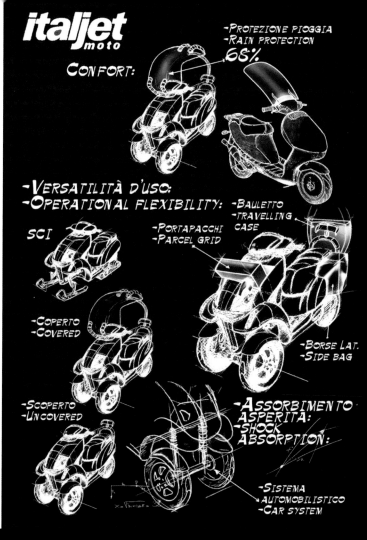

italjet moto

CONFORT:

−PROTEZIONE PIOGGIA
−RAIN PROTECTION
68%

−VERSATILITÀ D'USO:
−OPERATIONAL FLEXIBILITY:

SCI

−COPERTO
−COVERED

−SCOPERTO
−UNCOVERED

−PORTAPACCHI
−PARCEL GRID

−BAULETTO
−TRAVELLING CASE

−BORSE LAT.
−SIDE BAG

−ASSORBIMENTO ASPERITA:
−SHOCK ABSORPTION:

−SISTEMA AUTOMOBILISTICO
−CAR SYSTEM

1 Scooop, 2002, 50 cc, Italjet.
› The Tartarinis have invented a new hybrid vehicle, which while maintaining the great advantage of moving on a scooter is a improvement in terms of safety and comfort. Compared to traditional scooters, the two wheels on the forecarriage facilitate a huge reduction in the braking distance without being risked. Turning is governed by a system of two independent wheels at the front that maximize the roadholding. The scooter can be seen in the illustrated road trials. Motorcycle fans have laughed off previous attempts at three-wheelers, but the industry is now taking seriously the Tartarini concept called the Scooop.

1	2

ALI TAYAR NEW YORK

Ali Tayar received his master's degree in architecture from MIT in 1986, an institution that places almost as much importance on technology as design. He set up Parallel Design Partnership in 1991. His design and architecture practice represents a sustained investigation into the relationship of design to mechanical reproduction, and a firm belief that problems are better solved by acknowledging industrial production in the design process. Despite this approach, there is a playful elegance to his work, which is not strictly functional or overly industrial in character.

Tayar's work ranges from furniture to restaurant design. His pleasure in the industrial is manifest in his choice of materials and his exploration of the manufacturing process. Whenever possible, Tayar will find a generic solution to individual design problems, developing them into something suited to mass production. Ellen's Brackets (1994) began as a one-off commission for a New York City loft conversion and evolved into the prototype for a system of mass-produced, wall-mounted shelving hardware.

Ellen's Brackets consist of vertical or horizontal aluminium tracks, brackets of extruded and milled anodized aluminium, and stainless-steel pins that attach the brackets to the track. The brackets feel substantial and luxurious in the hand, but their shape was not designed solely to give pleasure, it was the result of a careful study of load-bearing capacity. Tayar drew as many as 15 variations of the bracket before he got the shape and formula just right. Subsequent projects, such as the Spider shelving system for Magis (2001), are clear extensions of Tayar's thinking about Ellen's Brackets.

Tayar's interest in combining off-the-shelf materials with computer-controlled technology is evident in his Elephant Table (2001). In this piece a plane of MDF (medium density fibreboard) is intersected with a series of four, off-the-shelf plywood tubes. A CNC (Computer Numerical Control) machine has been programmed to mill out the intersection of the plane and the tube. The supports, which are identical, are laminated to the tabletop, their positions depending on the location of the cutout. The use of CNC technology allows Tayar to achieve infinite variations in the design of the table, effectively producing a mass-customized object.

Recent work, such as Roy's TV Table and the Icon Work/Wall system, reflects Tayar's continued exploration of new technology and materials. He aims for small production runs and pieces that are machine-made but unique. The rigour of his work is admirable and his designs are consistently desirable.

BROOKE HODGE

1 Ellen's Brackets, wall-mounted shelving system, 1994, aluminium, glass, 145 x 25 cm, Parallel Design Partnership.
> This shelving system consists of extruded and milled anodized aluminium tracks and brackets.

2 Spider, shelf system, 2001, injection-moulded plastic, aluminium, 203 x 25 cm, Magis.
> Shelf material of any thickness can be accommodated by this unique shelving system which uses injection-moulded adjustable brackets. The brackets are fixed to a wall-mounted aluminium frame and can be moved up or down into any position.

3 Rasamny Chair, 1998–9, aluminium, teak wood, 81 x 53 x 50 cm, ICF.
> This classic chair is distinguished by its unobtrusive use of two very distinct materials. The two wooden frames are unconnected, so for its structural stability the chair relies on the strength of the three panels of clear, anodized aluminium.

4 Icon Work/Wall, 2001, coated sheet-metal boxes, plywood, 76 x 76 x 22 cm, Parallel Design Partnership.
> Icon is a partition wall-cum-storage space. It consists of a series of metal boxes which stack together creating walls; the shelves can be used as informal storage space for folders, CDs, documents and personal items.

1		
2	3	4

357

MACHINED ALUMINUM
LEGS

6"∅ PLYWOOD TUBE

ANODIZED ALUMINUM FOOT DETAIL?

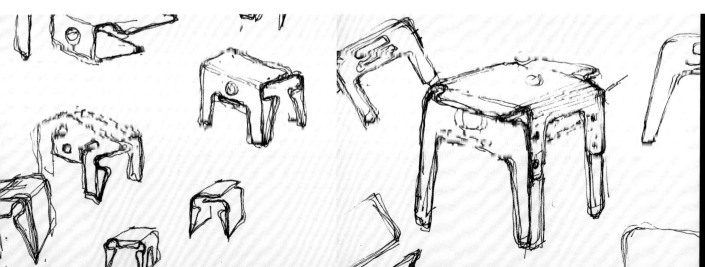

1 Elephant Table, 2001, glass, plywood, MDF, aluminium, 38 x 76 x 76 cm, Parallel Design Partnership.

3 The tabletop is supported by four ply-wood tubes. Each leg is identical and protrudes at an angle of 60 degrees. However, in the production of these tables, a computer has been randomly programmed to mill out the intersection of the top and the legs in countless different positions, thereby achieving a number of variations in this table design.

2 Roy's TV Table, 2001, anodized sheet aluminium, plywood, 50 x 63 x 40 cm, Parallel Design Partnership.

1 This television table is an exercise in the application of modern technology to design processes. The cutting patterns for all of the components are generated with a CAD (Computer Aided Design) pro-gramme and then e-mailed to the fabricator, who then generates the instructions for the cutter. A plywood chute at the rear is intended for the cable box.

1	2

Like many great product designers, Shuwa Tei is first and foremost an architect. After graduating in 1994 from the College of Art and Design, Musashino Art University in Tokyo, he established a design collective called Intentionallies Inc in 1996. Tei explains that the credo of the company is built into its name: 'We intend to transcend existing ideas by any means. We intend to design things people have never seen before. Everything is created with confidence and conviction, thus Intentionallies.'

Intentionallies has become a darling of the quick-spirited Tokyo design scene, and the city's thirst for consumerism has provided many opportunities for Tei and his colleagues. The collective has completed many small-scale architectural and interior design commissions since its inception, but the most interesting aspect of the work comes from Shuwa Tei's insistence that he be permitted to design site-specific furniture for each project. For example, he designed a wooden interior for Motion Element (2000), a clothes shop in a fashionable Tokyo district, and then went on to produce the ITL006 chair (2001) for the site. Exquisitely carved from a solid piece of mahogany, the chair is sculpted to enclose the sitter perfectly, encouraging them to adopt a relaxed and natural posture. The ITL006 marries a form drawn from traditional Japanese carpentry with contemporary detail. It is Tei's most cherished design to date, which he describes as the combination of 'the fruit of my thoughts and craftsmen's skill'.

The Atehaca home appliances range was designed (2001) for Toshiba. It represents Tei's first foray into mass production, and reflects his ambition to simplify the mechanics of everyday household items and to create a collection of functional design objects. With their simple lines and pared-down forms, the individual elements, including a rice cooker and microwave oven, are the sum of a shared aesthetic.

Tei revels in the diversity of the commissions and stresses that 'we create our vision only after we understand our client's demands. We always keep a serious attitude towards creating objects.' The Hanamiduki restaurant project (2000) provided Tei with a formula that he wishes to repeat. Intentionallies did all the architecture and interior design, right down to the flower displays and menu, and the restaurant is also managed by the group. The restaurant's second function is as a showroom. Guests can order furniture along with their dessert. It is a winning formula, which Tei hopes to take into the American market. LAURA HOUSELEY

1 ITL004, chair, 2000, beech wood, polyurethane finish, 75 x 42 x 47 cm, Hoshikame wood-processing plant.
> The seat of this chair, moulded out of a single piece of beech veneer, is both flexible and light, which provides a stark contrast to the solid, load-bearing base.

2 ITL005, lounge chair, 2000, walnut-oil finish, 69 x 86 x 61 cm, Hoshikame wood-processing plant.
> This lounge chair has elements of traditional Japanese design, though its wide carved seat was constructed using contemporary methods.

3 ITL003, sofa, 2000, beech wood, polyurethane finish, rattan peel, 75 x 130 x 60 cm, Hoshikame wood-processing plant.
> Together Tei and Intentionallies transformed this traditional design into a double seat. The middle leg evokes the original single-seat chair.

4 ITL007, chair, 2001, stainless steel, fabric or leather upholstery, 75.5 x 55 x 66.5 cm, OSK.
> Here Tei has moved away from traditional materials and forms. The chair has a steel base and the seat is flexible and can be reclined.

| 1 | 2 | 3 |
| | 4 | 4 |

360

1 View of the Motion Element pressroom furnished with Shuwa Tei's ITL006 chair.

2 ITL006, chair, 2001, mahogany-oil finish, 67 x 47 x 41 cm, Hoshikame wood-processing plant.
› Each Tei design is the product of a specific commission. This chair was for the pressroom of the fashion brand Motion Element, established in 2001. The design was realized by Isamu Hoshino, a highly skilled chair craftsman, who carved it out of solid wood. The chair weighs 10 kg.

3 Microwave Oven, 2001, ABS, 28.3 x 45 x 36 cm, Toshiba.
4 IH Rice Cooker, 2001, Lid PP, 22.9 x 26.4 x 26.1 cm, Toshiba.
5 Electric Pot, 2001, Lid PP, 30.2 x ø 24.3 cm, Toshiba.
› These kitchen appliances are part of the Atehaca Collection, a range of home wares designed by Intentionallies and Tycoon Graphics for Toshiba. Injection moulding gives these simple forms their uninterrupted lines. In old Japanese *atehaca* means elegant and beautiful.

1	2	3
		4
		5

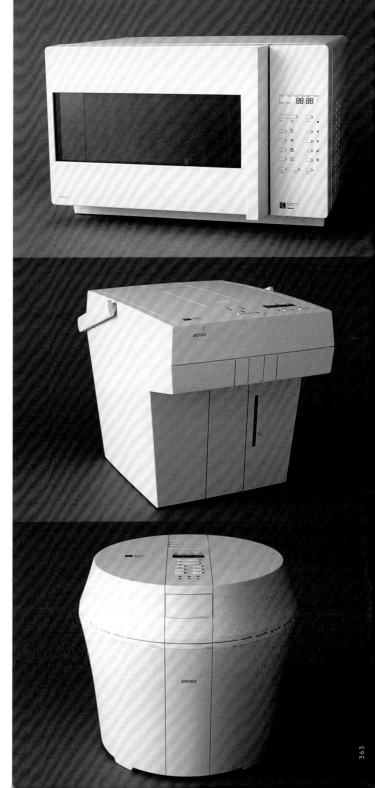

Kay Thoss has an impressive design pedigree. He studied first in Weimar before being invited by his tutor to study furniture design at the Polytechnic of Milan. His very first collection (2000) secured Thoss a deal with the Brazilian manufacturer Artificial, which still produces many of his designs while others are produced by Thoss himself.

The Compact (1999), a nest of tables initially produced by Kay Thoss and then manufactured by Artificial, makes full use of his favourite material, a flexible, Austrian laminate, which is sometimes called 'Max'. Made from cellulose layers glued together, it becomes incredibly flexible when heated, and can be used to produce a wrinkle-free curve. Only a handful of companies have the technology available to mould the material successfully, but when you find one, as Thoss did, the effects are spectacular. The design for Compact made full use of the sandwiched black cellulose at the centre of the laminate, using its contrast with the white outer layer to create a defined contour, emphasizing the curve of the tables. Compact has the additional feature of being modular, with separate elements that slot together.

When working with his graphic designer or assistant, Thoss' explanation of a new design is often deliberately obscure. He enjoys watching others work on the problems he creates and then he turns their mistakes into a design. Thoss also takes inspiration from existing pieces of furniture, focusing on a specific feature and then making it relevant to today's consumer. For example, the measurements for Compact were lifted directly from a set of teak nesting tables at his parents' home.

Bend (1998) is essentially the same design as Compact but using different materials. Dice (2000), a modern version of a wicker stool, is being mass-produced in Brazil. It is an example of Thoss' determination to combine 'the functional elements and formal features of a design'. He considers an object well designed if it is both innovative – either in terms of the production process or the use of materials – and it involves the user's mind.

Thoss is currently developing a carpet design. He is concentrating on patterns and colours rather than experimenting with new materials. Although he is not ready to give up on design yet, Thoss describes the contemporary scene as 'too much show, not enough income'. Perhaps this is why he is setting his sights on the fashion industry and even considering developing his own perfume. LAURA HOUSELEY

1 Coup, table, 2001, compact-forming laminate, 33.5 x ø 60 cm, Kay Thoss.
> This delicate side-table is an exercise in symmetry. It is constructed from two identically moulded halves.

2 Quartett, table, 2001, compact-forming laminate, 45 x 80 x 80 cm, Kay Thoss.
> With this table Thoss makes the most of the alucobond laminate material. The dark inner material sandwiched between white sheets of plastic provided a definite outline.

3 Delft, stool, 2000, compact-forming laminate, 42/84 x 42 x 42 cm, Kay Thoss.
> This pair of highly sculptural stools makes full use of the simplicity of the design; they can be turned upside down or angled to create a number of different effects.

4 Dice, stool, 2000, ash wood, rice straw, 41 x 41 x 41 cm, Kay Thoss.
> The inspiration for these stackable stools came from an old piece of furniture. A very contemporary cubic form is combined with a traditionally woven wicker top.

5 Wood Stools, 2000, wood, 42 x 42 x 42 cm, prototype.
> The design of this stool is closely linked to the design for Delft, although it predates it. It looks like a cube made out of a very soft, but sharp-edged, material.

1		4
	4	
2	3	5

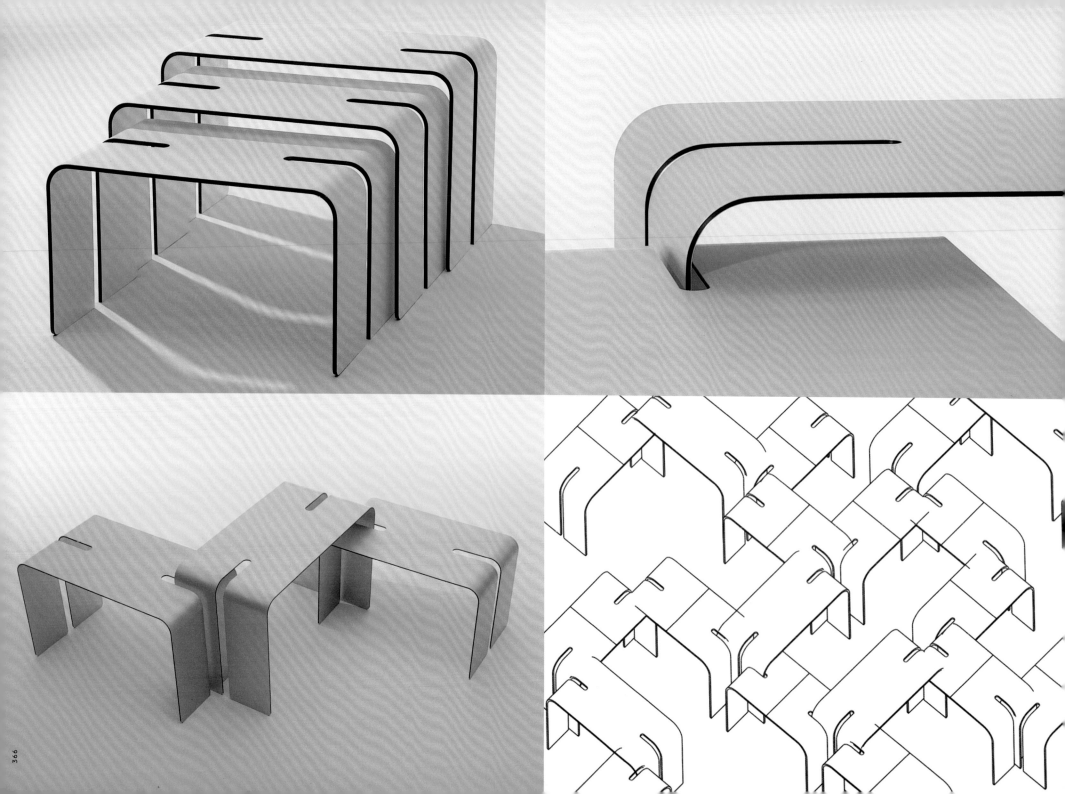

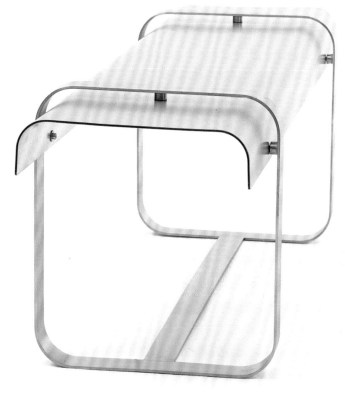

1	2	3
	3	

NOAM TORAN LONDON

Noam Toran creates objects and films that examine the messiness of the human condition: the realm of the emotions, irrationality, perversion, subversion. His work looks at our relationship with objects and how this relationship manipulates or informs our sense of identity. In almost all of his work there is a darkly humorous conflict between the objects and the user. Who is in control of this relationship? What types of identity do we project onto our objects? What does this reveal about us and the systems that organize our society?

Noam tends to develop fictional histories for his objects, deceitfully creating individuals and inventions as if they already existed and he merely discovered them. This gives the objects an illusive sense of weight and forces the viewer to question the absurdity of their function.

Objects for Lonely Men (2001) consists of a collection of eight products designed to alleviate loneliness after the departure or loss of a woman. The project was an attempt by the artist to understand what initiates loneliness: do we miss the individual or the generic traces they leave behind? One of the objects lets you share a cigarette and another steals the sheets by winding them up in a tube attached to the side of the bed.

Subliminal Furniture (2001) proposes a narrative in which objects become the protagonist, a physical form representing the subtleties of persuasion within human relationships. A fictional setting is fabricated, with all the conventions and conduct of present society, except that subliminal persuasion has been successfully relocated in the domestic arena. By taking a traditionally public and infamous form of influence and grafting it onto the private domain, a framework is provided to promote speculation and narrative. The installation consists of a group of technologically augmented objects and a film depicting their use in domestic circumstances. A message is typed into a secret keyboard located in the footrest of the reclining armchair. The message is then sent electronically to the lamp and radio, where it is converted into a subliminal format and transmitted, allowing the user a discreet method of influencing family members, guests and themselves.

The film is made up of two vignettes. In the first, a woman uses the subliminal furniture to influence her husband into having sex with her. In the second vignette, a woman uses the same furniture to exact revenge on an unfaithful husband. RON ARAD

1 **Object for Lonely Men**, camera shots from an 8-minute film, 2001.
› This film tells the story of a man so obsessed with Godard's *A Bout de Souffle* that he builds a tray which reflects the physical language of the film.

2 **Object for Lonely Men**, dinner tray, 2001, single sheet of vacuum-formed plastic, 140 x 60 cm.
› The tray serves as an outlet for man's desires; it allows him to channel his fantasies from the movie into physical action. It includes a mannequin head resembling Jean Seberg (the female lead), a gun, hat,

telephone, *Herald Tribune* newspaper, sunglasses, ashtray, steering wheel, rear-view mirror and a packet of Gitanes non-filtered cigarettes.

3 **Objects for Lonely Men**, series of products, 2001, laser-cut aluminium, plastic, electronics, heavy breather, 6 x 14-x 6 cm, shared cigarette, 6 x 14-x 6 cm, sheet thief, 180 x ø 10 cm, plate thrower, 6 x 30 x 30 cm, silhouette light, 6 x 16 x 6 cm, cold feet, 7 x 27 x 22 cm, chest-hair curler, 20 x 6 x 2.5 cm, hair alarm clock, 3 x 20 x 8 cm.
› This collection attempts to alleviate the loneliness after the departure of a woman. The project defines this as the loss of the generic physical sensations we experience with someone, rather than the loss of the person themselves.

1	
	3
2	

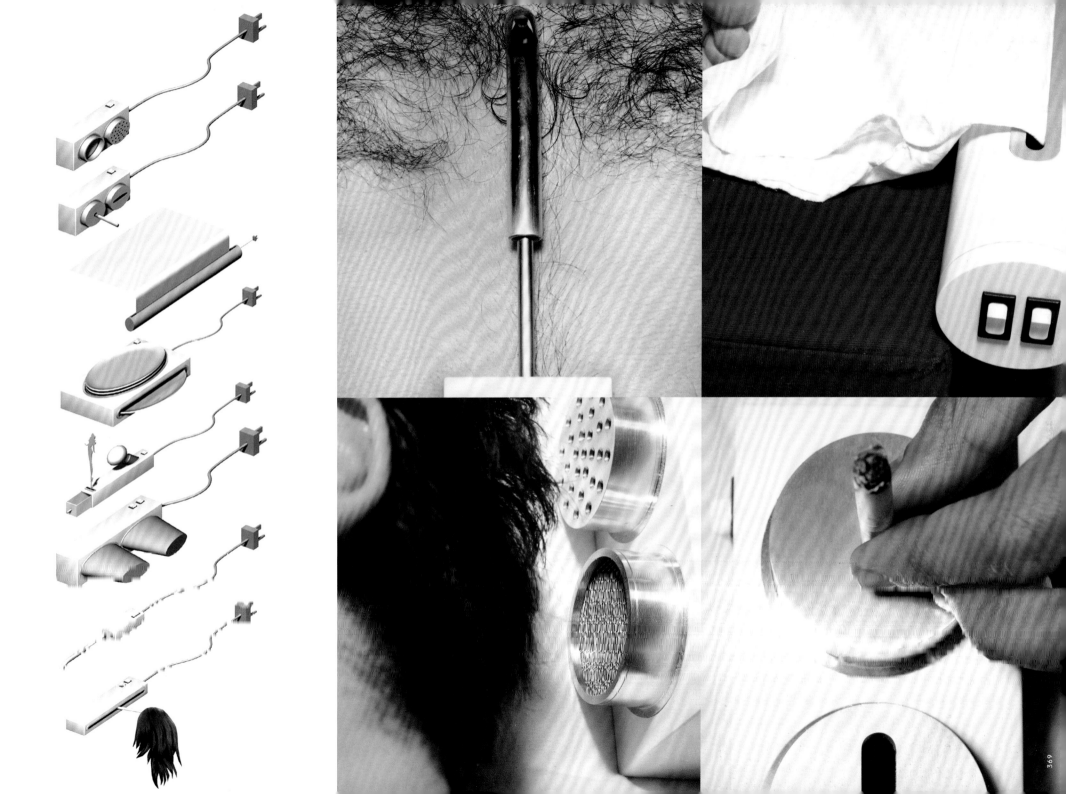

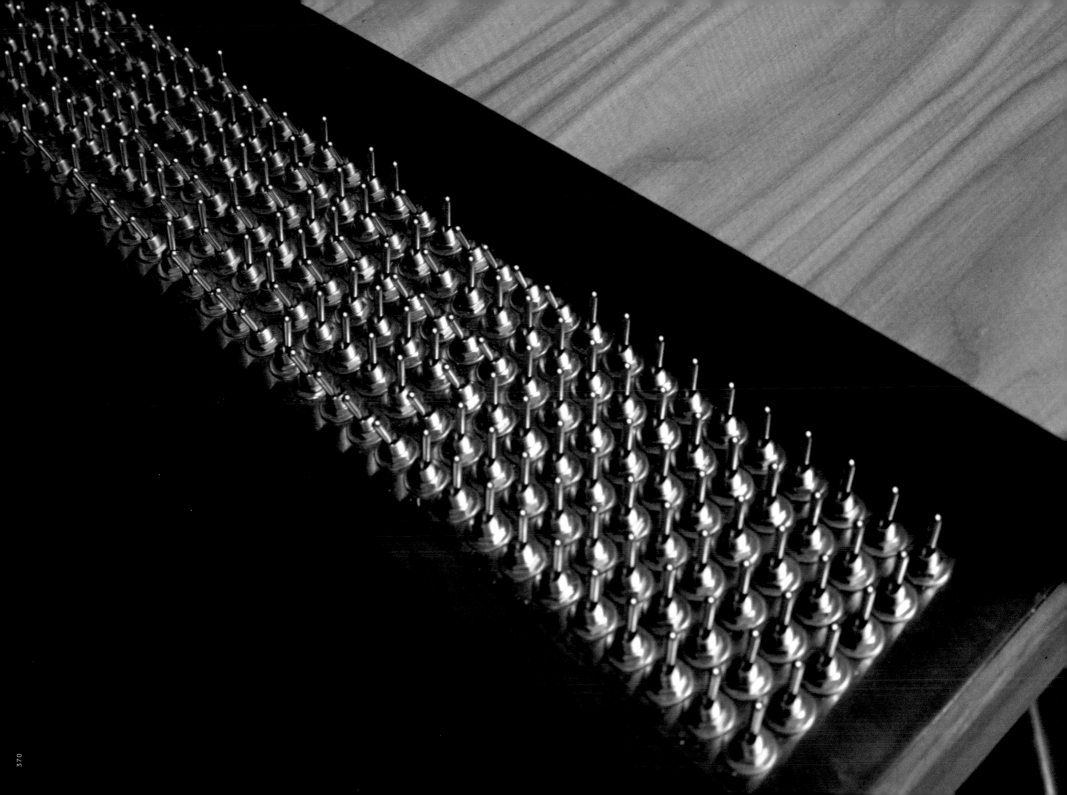

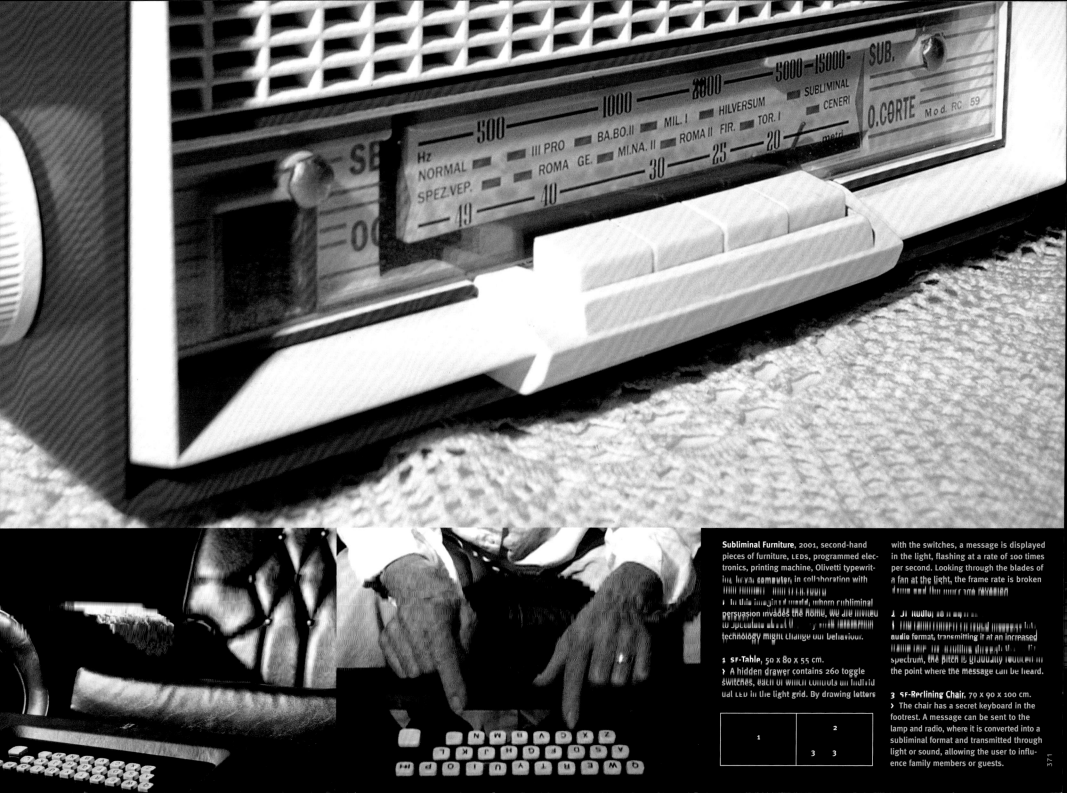

Subliminal Furniture, 2001, second-hand pieces of furniture, LEDs, programmed electronics, printing machine, Olivetti typewriting local computer, in collaboration with [illegible] and [illegible]

> In this imagined world, where subliminal persuasion invades the home, we are invited to speculate about the ways in which technology might change our behaviour.

1 SF-Table, 50 x 80 x 55 cm.
> A hidden drawer contains 260 toggle switches, each of which controls an individual LED in the light grid. By drawing letters

with the switches, a message is displayed in the light, flashing at a rate of 100 times per second. Looking through the blades of a fan at the light, the frame rate is broken down and the message revealed.

2 SF-Radio, [illegible]
> The radio converts a voice message into audio format, transmitting it at an increased [illegible] spectrum, the pitch is gradually reduced to the point where the message can be heard.

3 SF-Reclining Chair, 70 x 90 x 100 cm.
> The chair has a secret keyboard in the footrest. A message can be sent to the lamp and radio, where it is converted into a subliminal format and transmitted through light or sound, allowing the user to influence family members or guests.

1	2
	3 3

VALVOMO HELSINKI

Valvomo is the name of a group of young, Finnish designers and architects who share a studio in Helsinki. All the members of the studio (Teppo Asikainen, Vesa Hinkola, Markus Nevalainen, Kari Sivonen, Ilkka Terho, Jan Tromp, Rane Vaskivuori, Timo Vierros) are all in their thirties, and they all studied architecture at the University of Technology, Estoo. Although free to work independently, members of the group generally work as a team, designing both products and interiors.

Founded in 1993, Valvomo has become immensely popular over the last two or three years. Their success dates from 1997, when they organized 'Snowcrash', a legendary exhibition at the Salone del Mobile in Milan. The exhibition attracted the attention of the Trico Group, an entrepreneurial Swedish company that also owns and produces Artek Furniture. Under its umbrella, Snowcrash became the name of an immensely popular product line, and Valvomo was transformed into a well-known name in the avant-garde design business.

The blend of different skills in the Valvomo studio – product design, architecture and interior design – brings a unique character to their work. Above all, it is an organic approach to design and a tactile sensuality that create the hallmarks of what they do. The design of their chaise longue, the FRP, is a sensational example of their design. Globlow LED, a light looking like an inflated pillow (2000), is another successful product. As the light is switched on the pillow inflates accordingly. There is something intrinsically Finnish about the character of Valvomo's work. This is found above all in the marriage between high-tech materials and tactile, organic forms.

Valvomo are now enthusiastically engaged in designing e-3™, an IT communication system for public places. While the project focuses on the interface between architecture and design, Valvomo will also be called upon to tackle the issues arising from the placement of this product in the environment.

The group has also been working on café and restaurant interiors. Pravda, beside the Artek showroom in the centre of the Helsinki, is one such example. The walls are covered with their Soundwave panel (1999), a series of wave-shaped removable panels made from compressed fibres designed to absorb high levels of sound. Soundwave has been so successful that the panels are now generally available. RYU NIIMI

1 Globlow LED, lamp, 2000, transparent circuit board, microprocessor, LED, fan, ripstop nylon shade, 30 x 70 x 20 cm (switched on), 15 x 35 x 5 cm (packed), prototype for Snowcrash.
› This next generation 'living light' inflates when it is switched on. New microprocessor technology enables light sequences to be programmed or activated by different methods of wireless, remote control. LEDs are energy saving, lasting up to 100,000 hours.

2 Complement Colour Light, 2000, dichroic glass, 5 x 50 x 14 cm, prototype.
› Dichroic glass is a glass in which a very thin metal surface is embedded; a curious effect is created when white light shines through the gap between glass and metal. The complementary colour of the glass shade tints the surrounding surface. The light source is a short fluorescent tube and the structure is a laser-cut, bent metal sheet.

1	2

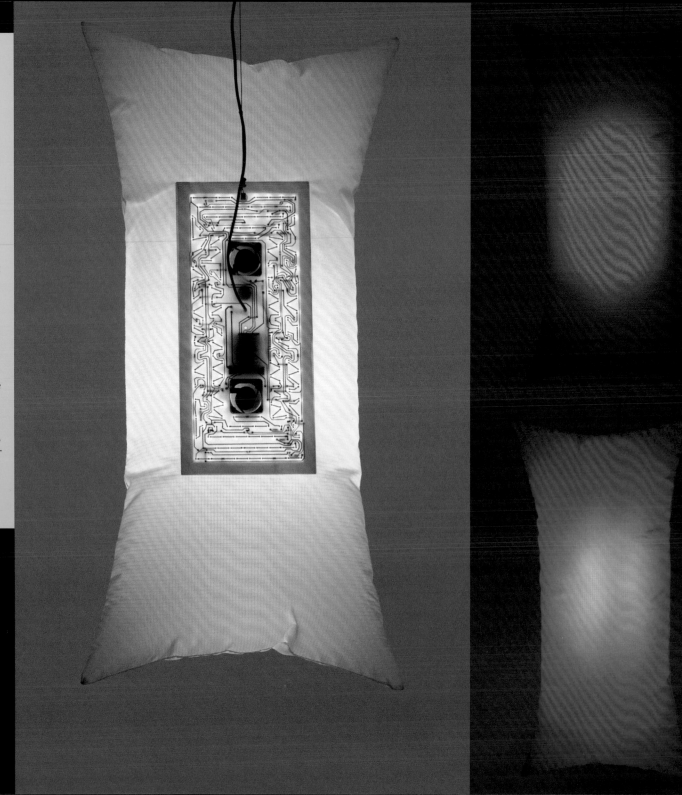

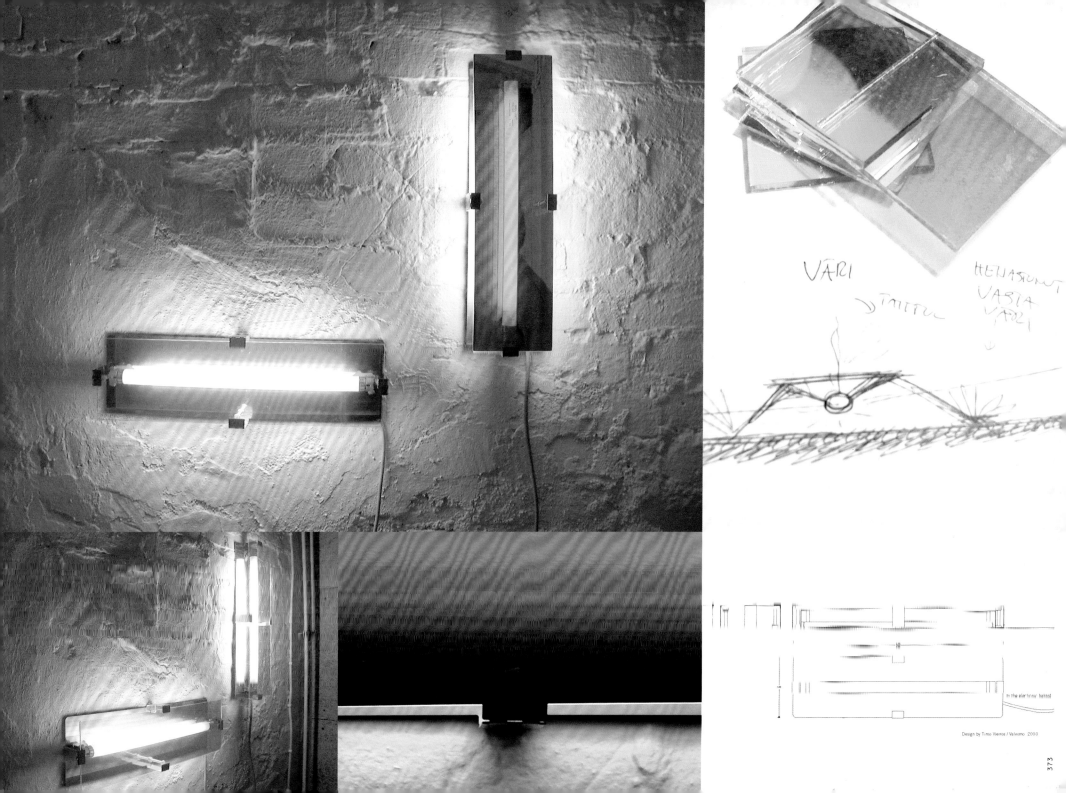

VÄRI

HEIJASTUNUT
VASTA
VÄRI

TAITTUI

In the electronic ballast

Design by Timo Vierros / Valvomo 2000

373

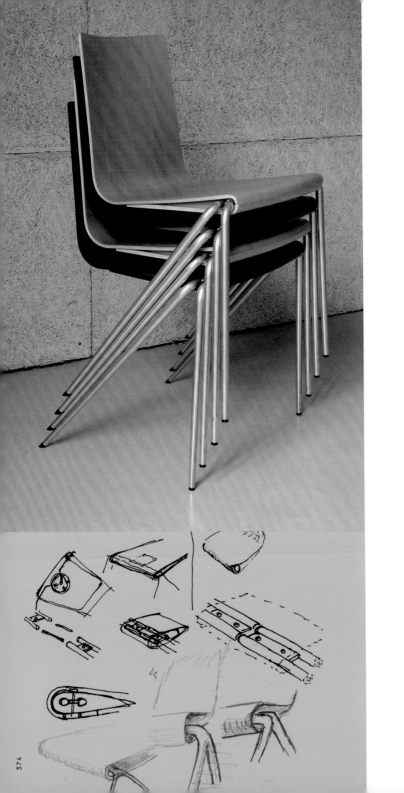

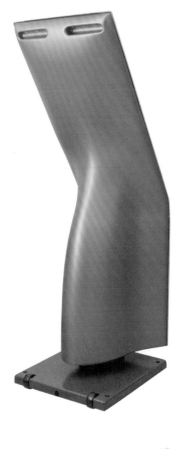

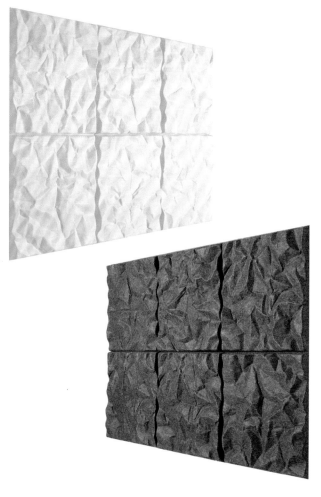

1 **Droppe**, chair, 2000, birchwood, steel, 77 x 50 x 44 cm, Snowcrash.
> At first glance, this chair appears to hover in the air. Its challenge gravity. Its sleek seat makes defying the law of gravity an exceptionally comfortable and easy event, and the dynamic legs are incorporated in a teardrop-shaped enclosure.

2 **e-3™** Internet Transaction Kiosk, 2000, thermo-moulded plastic, stainless steel, 158 x 50 x 56 cm, e-3 Solutions Oy.
> This freestanding communication centre was designed for electronic self-service e-distribution. The kiosk is equipped with touch screen, web cam, ticket printer, smart/magnetic cards reader, barcode reader, coin mechanism, motion detector and VOIP (voice over Internet protocol) handset.

3 **Soundwave**, soundproof panel, 1999, moulded polyester fibre, 58.5 x 58.5 x 4 cm, Snowcrash.
> Designed for a large restaurant in Helsinki, in order to keep the volume of noise within tolerance levels, the Soundwave is a 3-dimensional wallpaper. The different textures play with light and shadow and give the product character in addition to the technical acoustic capability.

| 1 | 2 | 3 |

375

MIGUEL VIEIRA BAPTISTA LISBON

In recent years, Miguel Vieira Baptista and a group of colleagues have established Portugal as a design nation and opened the doors of this country at the periphery of Europe to the wider design world. After training in Lisbon and at Glasgow School of Art, Vieira Baptista first attracted attention with his clever lamp design Ultra Luz at Frankfurt in 1995. He very quickly understood how the whole design scene works and forged connections with other young designers in Europe.

Portugal has a tradition of good craftsmanship but is not very technologically advanced in the design field. This has pushed Portuguese designers to be more inventive and in the last few years they have surprised the design world with their ingenious design solutions. Vieira Baptista's pen and pad Furo (2001) is typical of this phenomenon. Whereas other designers might have come up with some construction in metal or plastic to bring the pen and paper together, Vieira Baptista resolves the problem very simply by extending the paper pad in one corner and making a hole in which to rest the pen. This product is now being mass-produced. The philosophy of simple but clever solutions has been applied by Vieira Baptista to everything from trays to cutlery. But his products can also be very witty, such as the ceramic double lamp B (1997) made by the German company Authentics.

When considering Vieira Baptista's work, refreshing is the word that first comes to mind: in thought, colour and expression. He also uses exciting, new combinations of materials. He has produced a vase and a box (2002) that combine glass and ceramic. This is something which is very hard to do so that the two materials fit well together. But this is typical of the way he works – taking on interesting challenges and persevering and stuggling to find solutions.

Vieira Baptista has also established a reputation as an entrepreneur – not only developing his own products but also organizing exhibitions. He has been a wonderful design ambassador for Portugal, creating shows that display contemporary Portuguese design, such as glass design by young designers for the Portuguese company Atlantis. He has also done an exhibition (2001) on Dieter Rams, the German designer who has done such outstanding work for Braun and is a cult figure among younger designers. Rams was surprised that a young Portuguese designer put on this exhibition but very pleased with the result. STEFAN YTTERBORN

1 **Combine Collection**, 2002, porcelain, glass, vase, 2R x ø 11.5 cm, box, 11 x ø 17 cm, Vista Alegre.
› This design demonstrates the potential of using two incongruous materials in the same object. Both substances are able to exploit their finest natural characteristics; the porcelain can be modelled into an intricate and multifaceted shape, while the translucency of crystal benefits the other part.

2 **mvb**, cutlery, 2002, stainless steel, fork 2.4 x 19.6 x 2.4 cm, knife 0.8 x 23 x 2 cm, spoon 2.4 x 19.5 x 4 cm, Cutipol.

› The main aim in designing this range of cutlery was that it should reflect a sense of ease and should be truly ergonomic. Inspiration came from everyday objects such as a painting spatula and even Castiglioni's mayonnaise-jar spoon.

3 **Pile**, trays, 2001, plastic, 38 x 7 cm, Authentics.
› At first glance these stackable trays look too simple to be of interest, but they are in fact a very clever and functional design. The need for a perfect fit of the stackable parts has influenced the complex shapes and adjustments of the moulding tools.

1	2	3

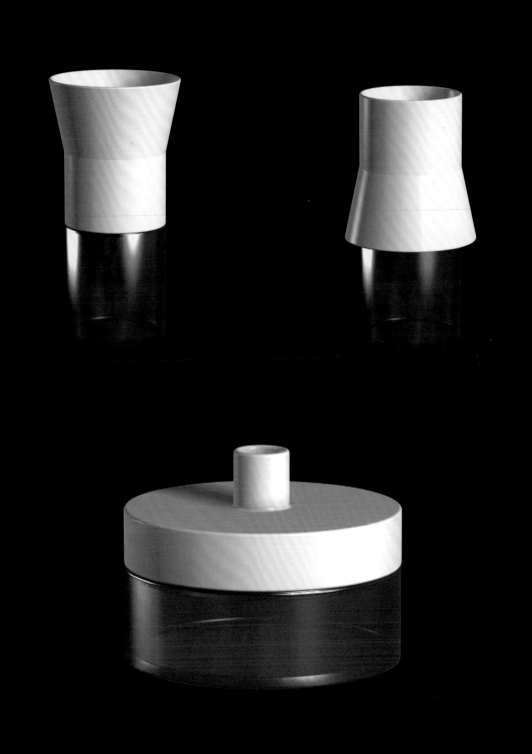

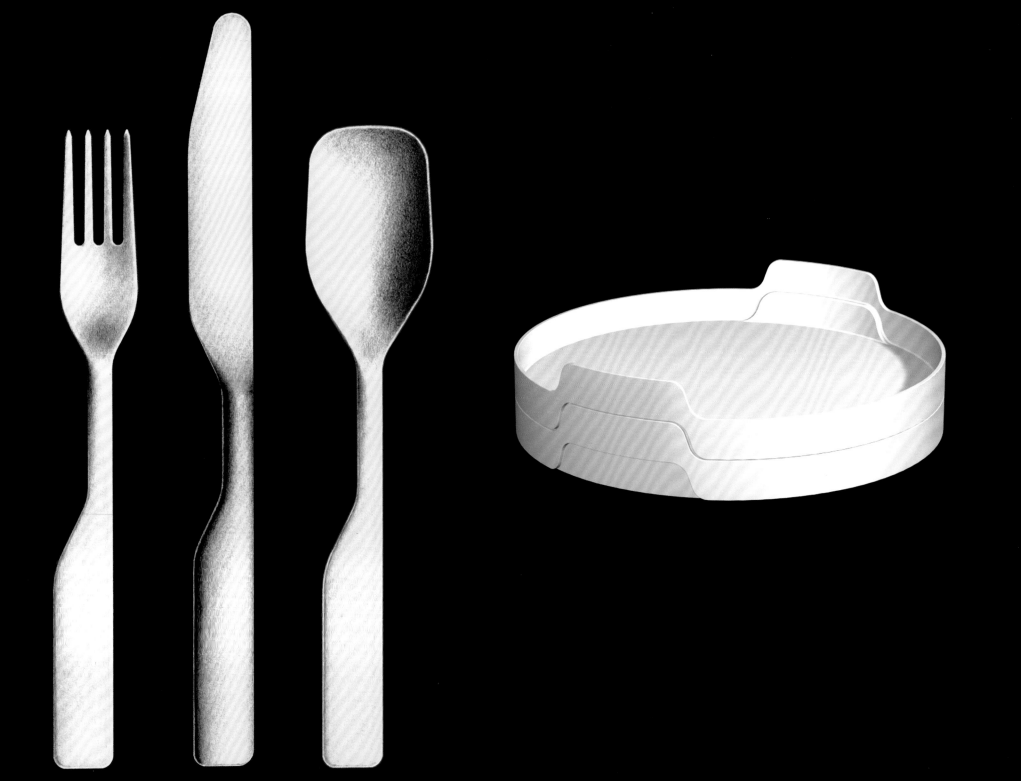

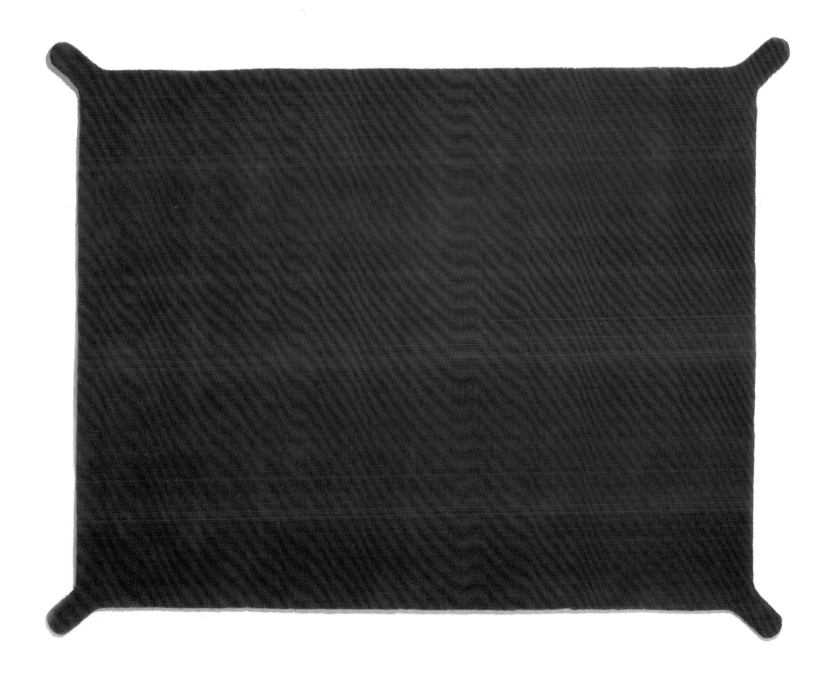

1 Handle It, rug, 2001, wool, various sizes, Asplund.
› The idea here was to explore the carpet as a dimensional object and to see it as more than a floor covering. By holding or grabbing the handles, people can move and touch the rug.

2 Furo, notebook, 2001, paper, 21 x 17 x 8 cm, Modal Lisboa.
› In this notebook the designer was keen to use the paper itself as a constructive material. The notebook has a hole that supports a pencil or pen, and the sheets

are torn along a standard perforation, allowing the hole to keep its shape.

3 Voyager, 2001, several materials, experimentadesign.
› Voyager, an exhibition space where temporary Portuguese creativity can be easily presented abroad, was commissioned by experimentadesign. Several modules support disciplines such as poetry, architecture, dance, graphics, new media and industrial design, mainly using video and audio systems. Flexibility in setting up Voyager is provided by six independent parts.

4 Double Lamp, 1997, porcelain, 11.5 x 25 x 11 cm, Authentics.
› This lamp was developed to a strict brief: it had to be functional, have a low production cost and be made only of ceramic.

	2	4
1		
	3	

VOGT + WEIZENEGGER BERLIN

Always curiously looking around, and always with surprising, brand-new information on their lips, Oliver Vogt and Hermann Weizenegger are constantly evolving new approaches to design and new ways of thinking that break through the boundaries of product design. In Vogt+Weizenegger's hands, designs develop naturally, easily and without affectation, and their originality is both authentic and demanding. What is most surprising, given that there is so much wit and innovation in their approach, is the sureness of their design and the simplicity of the concepts and the products that they have made to date.

The production process is as important to them as the product itself. Whenever they receive a new commission, they work with the company to develop the idea for production. This process has been responsible for products such as Pure Glass ® (1998). The aim here was to employ the thin, heat-resistant glass traditionally used in scientific laboratories for home and kitchen products. At the same time they researched the work of the Bauhaus designer Wilhelm Wagenfeld and the manufacturing process developed by the German manufacturer Jena Glass and came up with a design-based glass collection suited to fully automatic industrial production. In addition, they co-operated with a Chinese plastics manufacturer, which produced the requisite plastic accessories, such as lids. They managed the logistical problems of co-ordinating product solutions involving different parts and different materials over a distance of 7,000 miles. Pure Glass ® represents a complex design solution, which, thanks to its complexity, limits the possibility of it being copied by other manufacturers.

All of Vogt+Weizenegger's product lines have been conceived as an exhibition, an event or a performance. In this way they communicate directly with the consumer, and this exchange brings them information that would not be available through normal sales channels. In this respect the team benefits from Oliver Vogt's journalistic training. The presentation of information – the treatment of language and pictures – is an essential concern of these two designers. It is a way of bringing their design creations closer to the public.

Vogt+Weizenegger's product design occupies the spaces between vision, technology, research, resources and communication. They see hasty press reactions or short-term success as threats that can be controlled easily. Their interest in the socio-cultural impact of their work, 'acting within open boundaries' as they put it, often leads to surprises, and arouses great enthusiasm from anyone with a degree of curiosity. HANSJERG MAIER-AICHEN

1 123 Regalsystem, shelf system, 1997, birch plywood, aluminium, variable dimensions, Lichtung.
> This large shelving system consists of three components: aluminium legs, plywood boards, and screws that secure them all together. The unit has an open back, and can be used as a room division or propped up against a wall. The different sizes of the compartments make it a very versatile and functional piece of furniture.

2 Pure Glass®, 1998, borosilicate heat-resistant laboratory glass, various sizes, Authentics.
> Pure Glass® is a family of household objects for which the basic design ingredients are four sizes and an angle of ten degrees. The result is that these glass forms are stackable, standardized and also possess character.

3 Sir Lightwood, lamp, 1999, plywood, stainless steel, 75/106 x ø 25 cm, Babylon.
> As his names suggests, Sir Lightwood is a very upright fellow, yet doubles up as a distinctive standard lamp. It comes in two sizes: one is intended to be at eye-level when the user is slumped in a low arm chair, the other throws its light upwards. The lampshades are made out of curved plywood, which means that the light funnels out from the top and bottom.

1	2	3

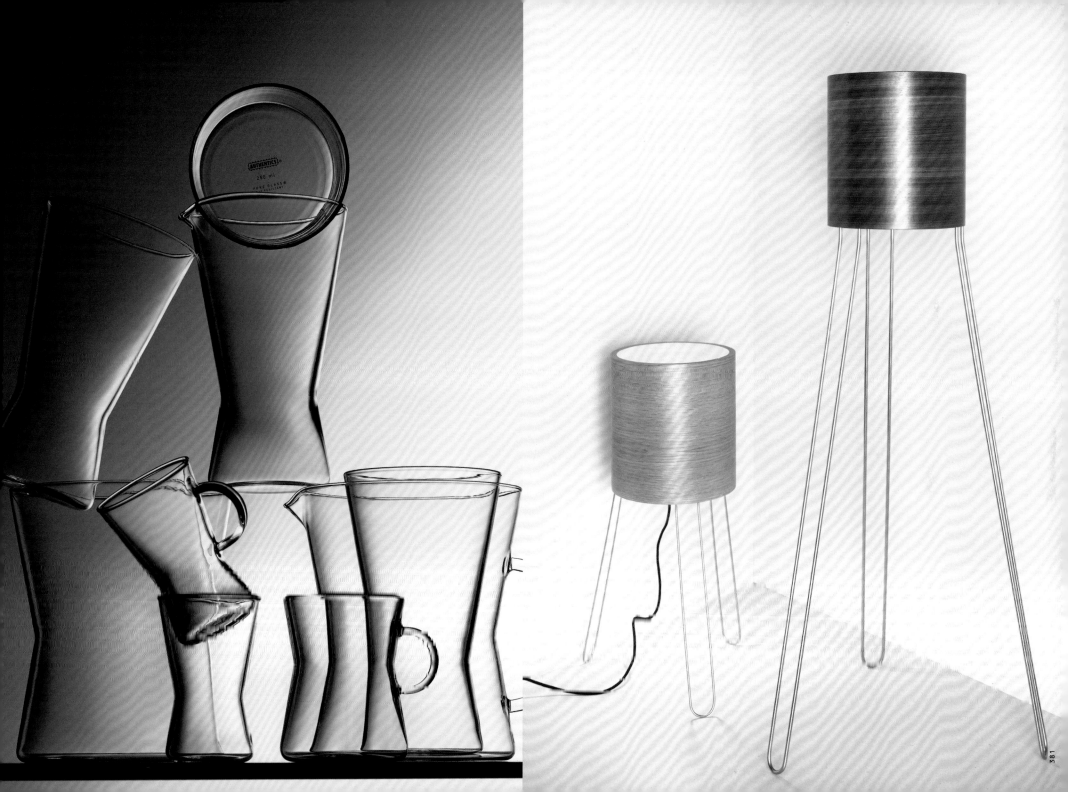

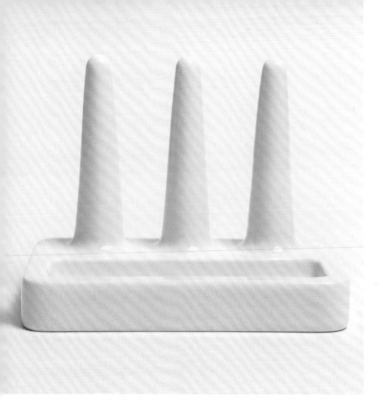

1 **Threesisters**, ring stand, 1999, porcelain, 15 x 12 x 9 cm, Moeve.
> This object is intended to stand in front of the mirror or above a basin, to hold valuable things that should be taken off while washing.

2 **Soft Bag**, 2001, PVC, 48 x 38 x 0.5 cm, Moeve.
> This transparent bag is intended to store bathroom accessories; the two suction cups enable it to be positioned anywhere.

3 **Sweet Bag**, 2000, neoprene, cotton terry towel, 45 x 35 x 15 cm, Moeve.

4 **Loop Bag**, 2000, neoprene, cotton terry towel, 80 x 35 x 8 cm, Moeve.
> The handle has been secured with a twist, making it both distinctive and easy to carry.

5 **Maxi Bag**, 2001, polypropylene, 25 x 22 x 9 cm, Authentics.
> This bag, suitable for the kitchen or bathroom, is sufficiently big to hold various bottles and tubes.

6 **Vital 42**, collage for Architektur + Wohnen.
> In this illustration the designers translate their fantasy world to paper.

7 **PULP**, soap dispenser, 2000, PVC, stainless steel, 22 x 9 x 9 cm, Moeve.
> This pear-shaped bulb is actually a soap dispenser!

1	3			7
			6	
2	4	5		

PIA WALLÉN STOCKHOLM

In the design industry we often talk about what makes relevant design. Ideally, it consists of three factors: consistency, continuity and clarity. And I cannot think of anybody whose work embodies these qualities better than Pia Wallén.

She originally trained as a fashion designer at Anders Beckman School of Design in Stockholm, graduating in 1983 and then in the mid-1980s began to design carpets. Made of hand-tufted wool, with large, clear, organic patterns, they were art works in their own right. In the early 1990s, Wallén started to experiment by cutting the wool of the carpets to create a 3-dimensional effect and this prompted her to move towards designing objects. The carpets left the floor and became baskets, slippers, pouffes and cushions.

Since that time Wallén has experimented with industrial felt with great success. You might almost call it a love affair with this material and she has investigated the use of felt as far afield as Iceland and Japan. She has led the development of its use in product design, which has gained followers around the world. Wallén found that the character of felt means that you can create structures that will hold their shape, such as baskets, bowls and even bags. It has proved to be a remarkably versatile material. In order to make a sphere, she used, after much experimentation, the 'tennis-ball-method', whereby two s-shaped sheets are joined. The felt products have an organic apperance and also work beautifully in two- or three-colour combinations. They have visible stitching, sometimes in another colour, making the method of assembly part of the design.

In spite of a great deal of international attention, Wallén has chosen to work on a small scale. After doing work with companies such as IKEA and Cappellini, she established her own company Pia Wallén AB in 2000 so she could go in the direction she wanted. She is greatly involved in everything concerning her enterprise, from product development to production and distribution. By maintaining such control, she can ensure high quality and continuously improve her products. The care, spontaneity and enthusiasm that she brought to her carpets is still there but now perhaps combined with a more rigorous approach. Her attitude of making sure that her products are long-lived is attractive. New objects appear in her relatively limited collection when they are ready. This is an outlook and a way of running a business that is highly commendable.

STEFAN YTTERBORN

1 Ring, 1999, sterling silver, industrial felt, diamonds, H 5 cm, Pia Wallén & Maria Elmqvist.
> This highly unconventional ring was inspired by the designers' exploration and experimentation with paradoxical materials and techniques. Free of restraining production demands, they combined silver, felt and diamonds.

2 Three Bowls, industrial felt, ø 25 cm, prototype.
> These striking white bowls show the variations that can be drawn out of the same material and the same product. The stitching is a very powerful decorative device.

3 3-Coloured Bowl, 1999, industrial felt, ø 45 cm, Pia Wallén.
> Seen from beneath, the derivation of this felt bowl from the tennis ball is overt. Pia Wallén very rarely sketches out her ideas. It is more common for products to emerge out of modelling, so for each new product she generates an enormous number of prototypes.

1	2	3

384

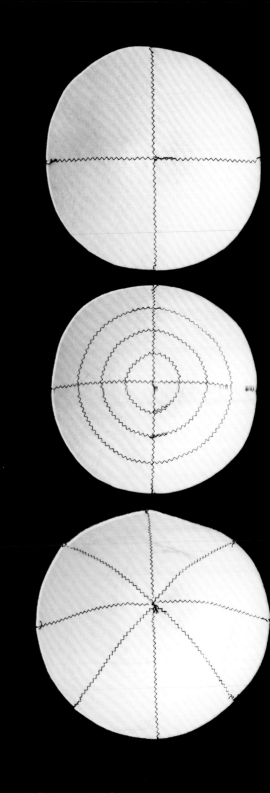

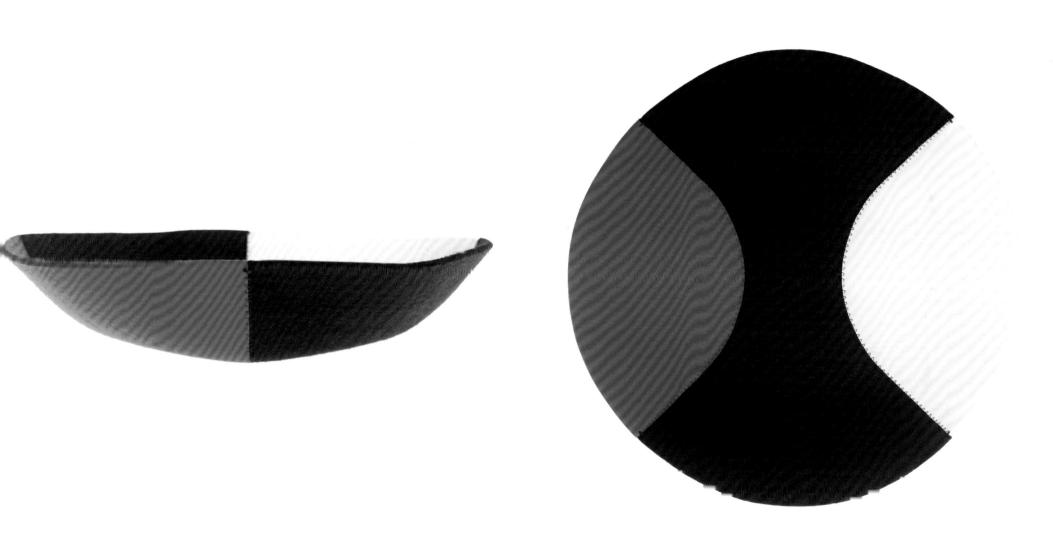

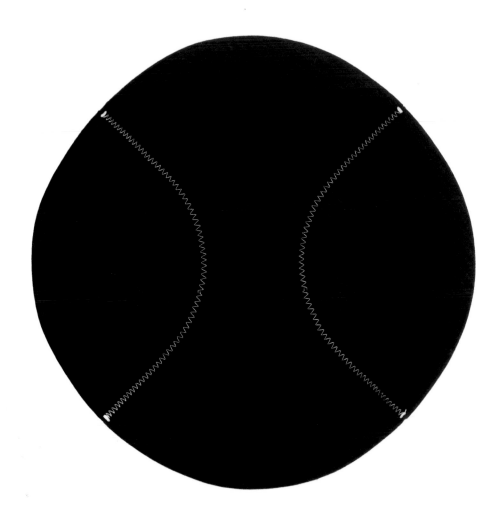

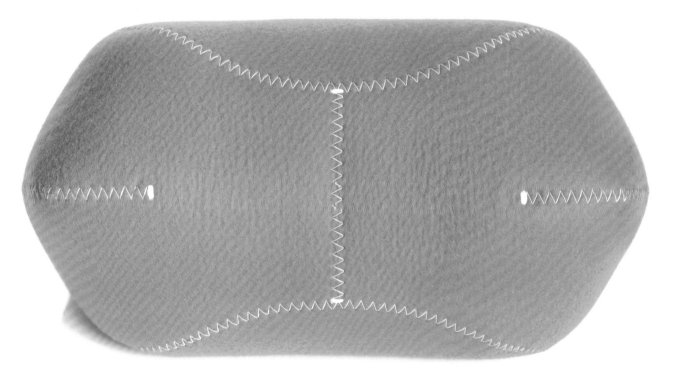

1 Black Bowl, 1995, industrial felt,
ø 45 cm, Pia Wallén.

2 Arm Ring, 1997, industrial felt, sterling
silver, 4 x ø 6 cm, Pia Wallén & Maria
Elmqvist.
› This was Wallén & Elmqvist's first project together, a partnership made famous
by their jewellery in totally contradictory
materials in this work: sterling silver is
coupled with industrial felt that would normally be used in the manufacture of, such as
the manufacture of cars and aeroplanes.

3 Bag in Green, 1999, industrial felt,
30 x 40 cm, Pia Wallén.
› Part of the Dot collection, this felt bag
has close links with the tennis-ball collection, but the felt here has been selected
in accommodating the dimensions of the bag

4 Bag in Black, 1999, industrial felt,
rubber sole, 30 x 40 cm, Pia Wallén.
› This bag is not only remarkable for its
highly stylized outline, but also because
it is constructed out of rubber-soled felt,
which was originally devised to improve
the grip and durability on the soles of
slippers.

| 1 | 2 | 3 | 4 |

MARCEL WANDERS AMSTERDAM

Marcel Wanders seems to have become an industrial designer almost by chance. Indeed, his first ventures into the world of products were more like those of an artist than a designer. For some years now he has been conducting a craftsman's experiments with materials, shapes and techniques, working out new forms and ideas. His craftsman's roots initially enabled him to create unique, one-off objects, which immediately provoked widespread interest, both among international critics and the leading design houses. The next challenge for the designer and those working with him was to turn these ideas into actual products.

Once his career as a designer was under way Wanders lost none of his innate curiosity about all that is innovative, unusual and striking. The unaccustomed has become the trademark of his products. Light, ironic, often deliberately out of scale, these objects have a powerful mood of their own and an irresistible appeal to the consumer, such as the vases designed on a 3-dimensional scan of an airborne piece of snot and finally produced using a digital prototyping technology (2001).

Wanders' designs reflect a continuous search for new and untried production methods, such as for the Sponge Vase (1997), made with a sponge impregnated with clay. He takes ideas from the artisan and the industrial traditions, using them to create both the rationale and the identity of his products. The material is the driving force behind the product, and the factor that determines its form. Wanders is always happy to embark on new projects, designing products, both large and small, that bear the stamp of his strong personality. His thinking as a designer shows clear references to historical archetypes, and while refreshing and updating them, he has no wish to erase or forget his cultural roots.

Marcel Wanders is an open, sociable person, and this is clearly reflected in the products that he creates, products that are not only useful, but also powerfully attractive. Many designers design primarily with their minds, but Wanders designs first and foremost from the heart, believing that creating objects is the best way of expressing his own ideas and individuality. Whether we like them or not, they affect and fascinate us, leaving us with an indelible mental image. Knotted Chair (1996) is perhaps Wanders' best-known and most admired object, and represents the essence of his approach to design. Very lightweight, it revolves around new forms and unusual materials, yet retains an appealing handcraft look. GIULIO CAPPELLINI

1 Knotted Chair, 1996, carbon, aramide, epoxy resin, 72 x 56 x 65 cm, Cappellini.
› Macramé meets high-tech: this light-weight chair is a surprising marriage of handcraft and industrial technology.

2 Knotted Table, 2001, parabeam, fibre-glass-reinforced fabric, carbon, aramide, epoxy resin, mirror, 52 x ø 90 cm, Cappellini.
› The tabletop is constructed out of a 3-dimensional fibreglass-reinforced fabric.

3 Fishnet Chair, 2001, net or rope, 67 x 81 x 77 cm, Cappellini.

› Although this chair was designed for industrial production, it is actually knotted by hand because of the low production numbers.

4 Sponge Vase, 1997, porcelain, 7 ø 10 cm, Moooi.
› A natural sponge is dipped and impregnated with liquid clay, then fired in a kiln.

5 Lace Table, 1997, Swiss lace, epoxy, glass, different sizes, Droog Design.
› This table is made of Swiss lace hardened by resin.

6 Airborne Snotty Vases: Coryza, Influenza, 2001, polyamide, 15 x 14 x 15 cm, Cappellini.

1	2		
3	4	5	6

1 **VIP**, chair, 2000, textile, metal,
78.5 x 62 x 53 cm, Moooi.
> Designed specifically for the Dutch Pavilion
at World Expo 2000 in Hanover, the woollen
felt like upholstery covering the legs of
these chairs hangs loosely like trouser
legs. Hidden wheels make it appear as if
the chair is floating above the ground.

2 **Lighting**, collection of lamps,
1997-2000, PVC/cotton laminate, metal,
Cappellini.
Big Shadows round, extra big 808 x ø 91 cm,
big 100 x ø 90 cm, little big 86 x ø 56.0 cm.

Panpipes, 2000, 110 ø 22 cm,
Set Up Round, 1998, 124 x ø 60 cm,
Set Up Square, 1997, 110 x 55 x 55 cm.
> This family of lights comprises a variety
of different shapes and colours, and is
intended to meet every lighting demand,
both in the living space and elsewhere.

3 **Birdhouse**, 1999, porcelain, recycled
plastic, 12 x 28 x 38 cm, DMD.
> This is a 5-star knockdown bird restaurant,
a project in co-operation with Frank
Tjepkema for DroomenLuM.

4 **BLO**, lamp, 2001, plastics, 18 x ø 12, HÖS.
> This lamp can be switched on or off by
blowing towards the light bulb. This function is assured by virtue of an acoustic
sensor.

		2	2	3
1	2			
		4	2	

The ceramics industry has always been a very distinct community within the design world. This goes back to the beginnings of the industry in the eighteenth century when fine china manufacturers such as Wedgwood or Sèvres engaged designers to work in an industrial way. Kennet Williamsson is part of that tradition and sees himself as an artist who works in ceramics. As for the work itself, it is not surprising to find that he greatly admires the Finn Kaj Franck, who transformed Scandinavian ceramic design after World War II, creating beautiful, simple and functional objects.

Williamsson's focus on ceramics began at an early age. He became fascinated by seeing a potter throwing a bowl on a wheel. By the age of 17 he had created his own studio, and at 19 bought the farm at Zinkgruvan where he still works today. Apart from two years working with Bertil Vallien, he is self-taught, which makes his achievement all the more remarkable. He works in a very slow, small-scale way, but is influential on the wider industry through his exploration of simplicity. And in a world which seems increasingly fragile and high tech the intimacy and care that is evident in his natural bowls and vases is very appealing.

The Excellent Swedish service of bowls and plates marked a new departure in Williamsson's work because these were not one-offs but produced in multiples. But although Williamsson's work is produced in only small series such as this, it is meant to be used. The service was launched in 1997 and enlarged in 2000. It is timeless but not anonymous. The objects are made of faience – earthenware covered in a smooth, shiny and opaque glaze. They are fresh and crisp in colour and semi-transparent so you can see their structure. For Williamsson, art – whether it is a cup or a sculpture (for he is also a sculptor) – is an opportunity to transform his feelings into a material object. He thinks that handmade ware created by someone who loves what he is doing will convey that feeling to the user through the lightness of a cup, the smoothness of the glaze or the pleasure of holding the handle. He feels that this very particular quality is hard to achieve in a factory and in this respect he considers himself to be anti-industrial. STEFAN YTTERBORN

1 **Blueberry Baskets**, 1997, faience, 25/18 x ø 18 cm, Kennet Williamsson.
› As a teacher, Williamsson's hope is that the authentic techniques of his handmade creations, and the intimacy and love he pours into them, will inspire his students to approach design with the same passion. The Blueberry Baskets are in the Röhsska Museum, Gothenburg.

2 **Snack Boxes**, 2001, faience, square 9.5 x 23 x 23 cm, rectangular 8.5 x 18 x 23 cm, Kennet Williamsson.

› The faience ware is redbrick clay covered in a smooth, shiny and opaque glaze, and then fired to 1080°c. As a teenager, Williamsson was fascinated by watching potters throwing bowls on the wheel. As a result, all his ware is first thrown on the wheel, and in this instance then formed into squares.

3 **Vodkabar**, pottery, 2002, stained and lacquered pinewood, faience, various sizes, Kennet and Simon Williamsson.
› Vodkabar is a family work: handmade pottery sits on top of a table built by Williamsson's son.

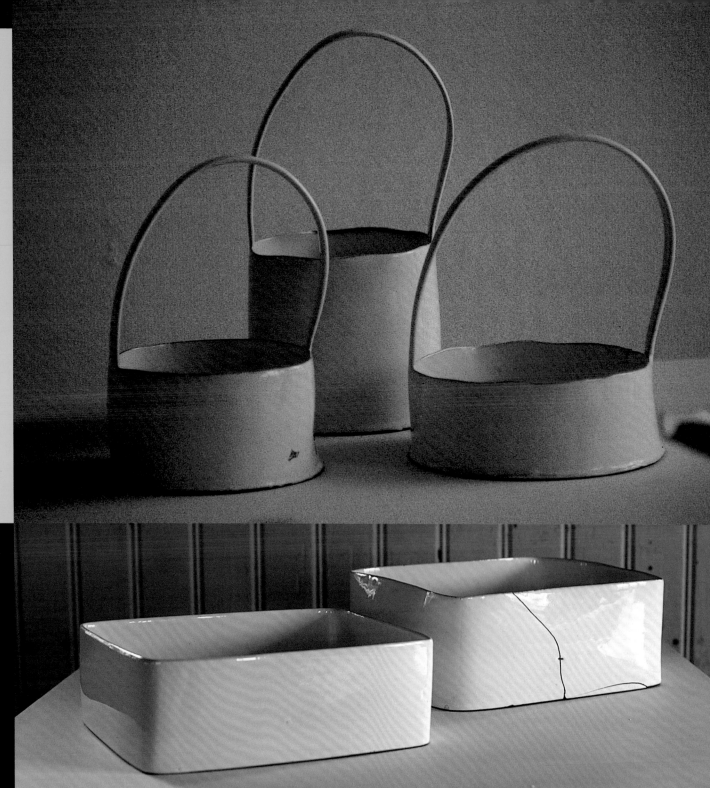

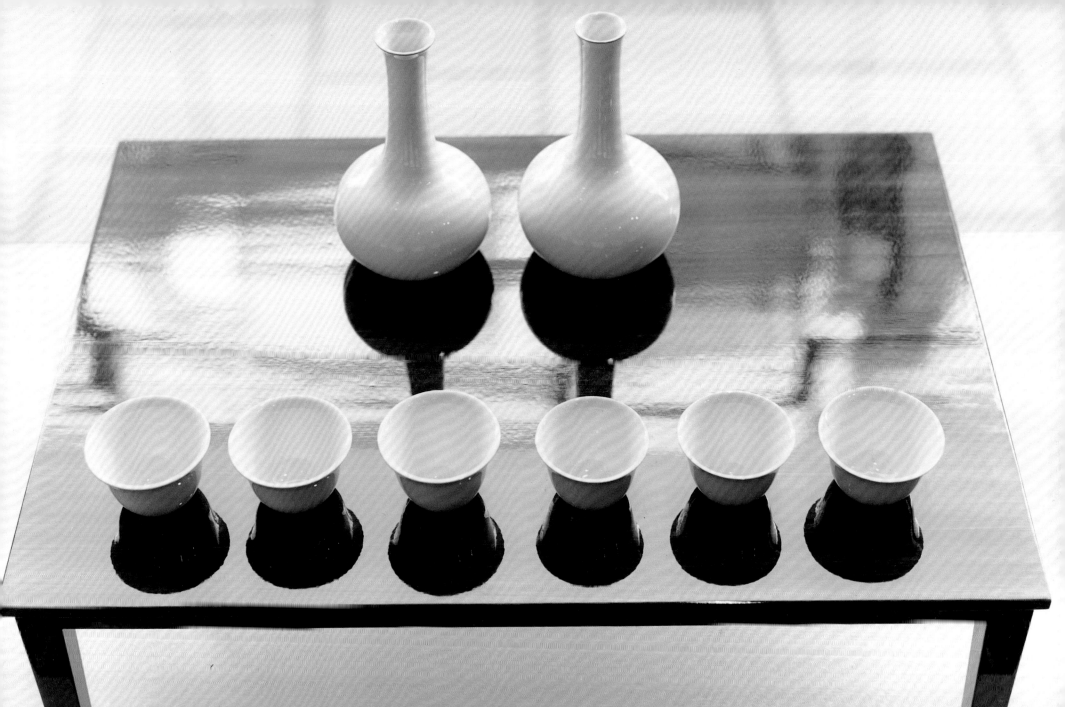

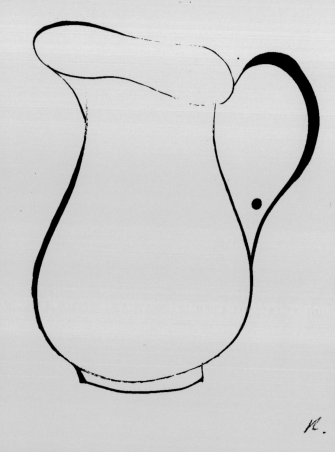

1 **Romantic Tableware**, 2001, faience, various sizes, Kennet Williamsson.
› The Romantic Collection was inspired by very mixed sources: Swedish rococo, Korean Yi dynastic style and early movies by Walt Disney.

2 **Fruitbowl**, 2003, faience, h 5 x ø 26 cm, Kennet Williamsson.
› This handsome bowl is the result of Williamsson's search into tradition and beauty.

3 **Safe Candleholder**, 1995–2002, faience, 5 x ø 14 cm, Kennet Williamsson.

› The Safe Candleholder epitomizes Williamsson's attitude towards design: it is elegant and functional.

4 **Wine Jugs**, 1997, faience, 10/13 x ø 35 cm, Kennet Williamsson.
5 **Yellow Self-Portrait, Blueberry Baskets, Wine Jugs**, 1997, faience, various sizes, Kennet Williamsson.
› The lightness and smoothness of the glaze, and the pleasure of holding hand made handles, is what Williamsson has excelled at, creating products by joyful manipulation of simple forms. Although they are rather exclusive and produced in small series, they are intended to be used, not simply exhibited.

6 **Sketch for Romantic Tableware Jug**, 2001.

1		4	6
2	3	5	

Ben Wilson has a passion for bicycles and motorbikes and an as yet unweaned addiction to skateboards. He has a passion for the way they are built, a passion for speeding along on them and a passion for their evolving appearance. This passion became manifest in a series of 'low-riders', such as the Low Rider Recumbent (1997), a series of somewhat retro hot rods, choppers or over-stylized bicycles with far too many spokes and exaggerated, easy-rider postures. His unique skill in controlling form and function runs through every project.

Ben's skill was harnessed to one of my favourite design projects in recent times: David's Hand-driven Trike (2001). For a whole year Ben worked with David, a 9-year-old boy paralyzed from the waist down. Together, they developed David's vehicle, with its chopper posture, bicycle wheels and skateboard steering. It is not very often that you come across a product that is all good, without 'ifs' or 'buts' – and David's Trike is one of them.

The video of David's first ride in his vehicle is my favourite video clip of all time. It is happiness on wheels, with a soundtrack by War called *Low Rider*. Until recently, this boy could only move in a wheelchair, and now he is the fastest boy on the block. The trike is powered by hand pedals, as is the braking system. The steering is done by shifting the bodyweight from one side to the other. This was a project done for one unique person, but now Ben is busy developing a more universal trike that could become a product for others too.

Ben's mastery of tubes and handlebars was recently channelled into a completely different realm. He constructed an experimental rig that enabled two digital video cameras to orbit around a helmet, for use when cycling or snowboarding. He also designed Wheel (2001) a camera-rig stabilizer to assist the experimental, pioneering film director Mike Figgis in his latest film, *Hotel*, and an inflatable camera-rig stabilizer (2001).

Ben's designs are not aspiring to be cultural comments or style statements. They sprout directly from his own culture. RON ARAD

1 **Low Rider Recumbent Bicycle**, 1997, steel, 61 x 183 x 91 cm, prototype.
> **This bicycle has been designed for easy riding, but it retains strong aesthetic qualities from 'low riding' history. It has been realized by assembling brazed chromed steel tubing with various ready-made components.**

| 1 | 1 |

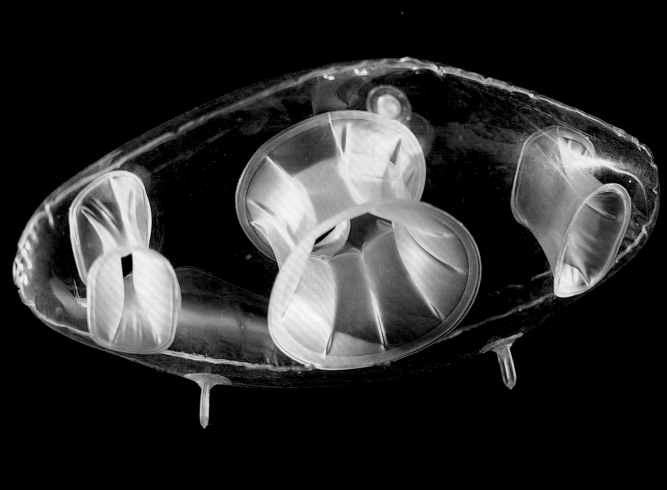

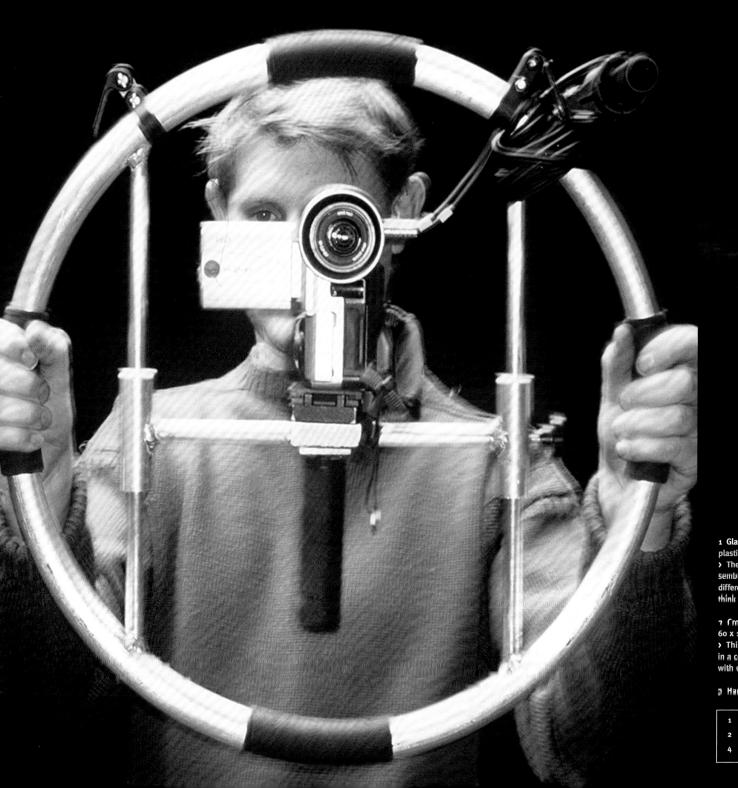

1 Glass Telephone, 2001, glass, metal, plastic, electronics, 15 x 20 x 20 cm.
› The traditional telephone has been disassembled and blown out of glass. It creates a different optic when ringing and makes you think twice about slamming the phone down.

2 Crochet Chair, 2001, cotton, resin, 60 x 150 x 80 cm.
› This chair has been crocheted by hand in a coarse-gauge natural cotton, saturated with epoxy resin

3 Hand-driven Trike, 2001, tube steel, camouflage paint, ready-made bicycle components, 50 x 120 x 60 cm, prototype.
› This tricycle has a hand-propelled front-wheel drive with an innovative steering mechanism for users with restricted lower-body mobility.

4 Inflatable Camera-Rig Stabilizer, 2001, PVC, 30 x 55 x 20 cm.
› The video camera is placed inside a plastic cushion, which when inflated creates an airbag that protects the contents from damage.

5 Wheel Camera-Rig Stabilizer, 2001, aluminium, ø 45 cm, in collaboration with Mike Figgis.
› The grips of this lightweight camera are placed shoulder-width apart, producing a steadier shot.

1		
2	4	5
4	3	

TOKUJIN YOSHIOKA TOKYO

Tokujin Yoshioka must be one of the most celebrated designers of recent times. The essence of his work comes from a determination to question stereotypes. He poses the question that should be asked by every designer: what does design offer beyond the harmonious use of materials, form and colour?

Yoshioka's products encapsulate both question and answer in their design. Whether it is an installation, an object or an interior, the end result is deceptively simple, and the conceptual nature of the design process is all but concealed. And sometimes he also designs or tries to design the material itself. If he cannot design the material then he wishes to make clear the relationship between the concept and the materials used.

A passion for aesthetics characterizes Yoshioka's products, and his work evokes memories of the Art Nouveau period, achieving the same astonishing marriage between function and aesthetic brilliance. Yoshioka recently designed a series of light fixtures that he named ToFU (2000). He could be cited as the first designer successfully to overcome the fatal division between the light source and the fixture. As a result, he was able to impose his design on light itself.

Yoshioka has executed numerous important designs for exhibitions and interiors. The influences that run right through the body of his work are those of Shiro Kuramata and Issey Miyake, two great masters with whom Yoshioka has collaborated over the years. Kuramata's lifelong passion for lightness and transparency finds its way into Yoshioka's work. It is especially apparent in his determination to hide physical structure and support systems in his furniture (see Tadashi Yokoyama, 'The Search for the Absolute Purity', catalogue of the Shiro Kuramata exhibition, Hara Museum of Contemporary Art, 1996). The most recent example of this technique is Yoshioka's Honey Pop Armchair (2001), inspired by Kuramata. Its dramatic elegance and organic sensuality put it on a par with the work of Frank Gehry, one of the greatest designers of the twentieth century.

Working with Bruce Mau in 2001, Yoshioka designed the breathtaking interior of Think Zone, the Tokyo lifestyle café, conceived as one vast single product. With Issey Miyake he designed a series of remarkable installations for exhibitions such as 'Making Things', and 'A-POC'. He also designed the interior of Miyake's boutique, also called A-POC. Here, we see two great designers working together to produce works that are both physically and intellectually democratic. RYU NIIMI

1 **Issey Miyake Concept Shop, A-POC,** 2001, Issey Miyake.
> The original and new concept for this shop is transparency. The venue is not composed merely from glass and acrylic furniture, but from the juxtaposition of transparent and opaque things. Wall lighting and fibre-optic cables give light to items such as display units.

2 **Honey Pop Armchair,** 2001, honeycomb sheets of paper, 81 x 85 x 80 cm, Tokujin Yoshioka Design.
> Honeycomb sheets of paper are rolled and piled up, and by following a procedure of cutting, unfolding and sitting a chair is created. Because of the honeycomb structure it has immense strength.

MIYAKE

| 1 | 2 |

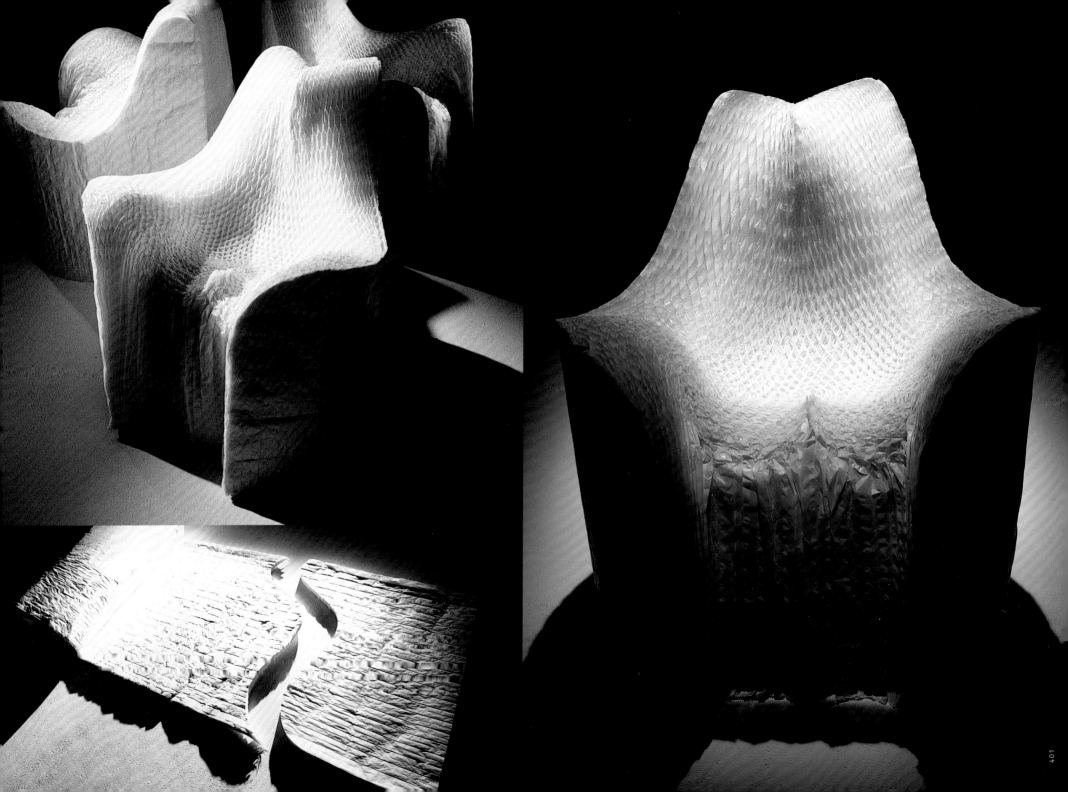

1 **ToFU**, lamp, 2000, plexiglass,
30 x 30 x 8 cm, Yamagiwa.
> While it takes a lot of work and much
attention to ingredients to make ToFU, the
resultant form is the paradigm of simplicity

MICHAEL YOUNG REYKJAVIK

In 1998, tired of the over-stimulation and constant distractions of London, Michael Young chose the isolated calm of Reykjavik in Iceland for his new home. It was a move that catapulted Young from moderate renown to international acclaim. Since his move, Young has been widely accepted as one of the most exciting architect-designers of his generation.

The move to Iceland was brilliantly timed. No sooner had he arrived than he was commissioned to design the Astro nightclub in an old Reykjavik industrial building. The design was a triumph, transforming a dour, industrial space into a fantasy inner-scape of colourful, airy, asymmetric volumes. It is this skilful use of volume, colour and asymmetry, combined with a certain wide-boy knowingness, that makes Young the product designer he is.

What is it about designing a chair that attracts architects and designers? Perhaps it is because good chairs take a fast track to design-icon status. Young's MY 068 chair, designed for Sawaya & Moroni (1998) is simple, functional, beautiful and notably successful. Avoiding the trap of being cute or clever, he allowed the curve of the chair to play against the horizontal elements and the splayed legs. It is humorous, but it demands to be taken seriously.

The Holey chair (2001), a stool designed for the Astro nightclub, is another success. Stools are daunting: if you decide on ones with legs, you are immediately up against Aalto. Go bentwood, and everyone thinks of Eames or Britain's Corin Mellor, whose one-piece bentwood stool is a masterpiece. Young's solution lay in the material. He chose a solid plastic from DuPont which gives weight to the stool and great flexibility in choice of colour. The stool is beautifully curved for comfort, yet solid and stable. Young's sense of humour, never far from the surface, comes out in the Braille-like holes that he drilled in the top. Is it a code? If so, good luck in trying to figure it out.

The Dog House (2001) for Magis seems trite or ephemeral when compared to Young's other work. It looks all right, and probably works well too, with little touches such as the step for puppies, or the double skin of the moulding process, which allows it to be insulated with injected foam. But it seems to contradict much of the rest of Young's career to date, which has been characterized by his work for companies with deep design roots and solid, even traditional, aesthetic judgements. But therein lies Young's charm. Quick to react, quick to lead, quick to turn his considerable talent to the job in hand, be it architecture, furniture, jewellery or dog kennels, Young will be sought after for a long time to come. ULTAN GUILFOYLE

1 **MY 068**, chair, 1998, wood, 80 x 38 x 52 cm, Sawaya Moroni.
> This chair is made entirely of wood, without even metal fixings.

2 **Lemonade Chair**, 2001, metal, bent ply, upholstery, 88 x 70 x 53 cm, Swedese.
> This design is Young's homage to Scandinavian design, which has always captured his imagination.

3 **Sticklight**, 1998, rotation-moulded polyethelene, 140 x ø 50 cm, Eurolounge.

> The Sticklight, created for the Astro nightclub, plays with the traditional neon tube.

4 **Wagon**, 2002, injection-moulded zylar, polyurethane, die-cast aluminium, 12 x 68 x 30 cm, Magis.
> This multi-directional wagon is a clever spin on the traditional children's cart. It is also a flexible storage system.

5 **Hringbol Post Computer Game**, 2000, blow-moulded plastic, ball ø 15 cm, bone 32 x ø 14 cm, sticks 25 x ø 10 cm, Magis.
> This game is based on a combination of baseball and the Icelandic form of stick and ball scurry. It is part of the Magis Post Computer Games, a collection aimed at creating new versions of the world's traditional games.

1		4
	3	
2		5

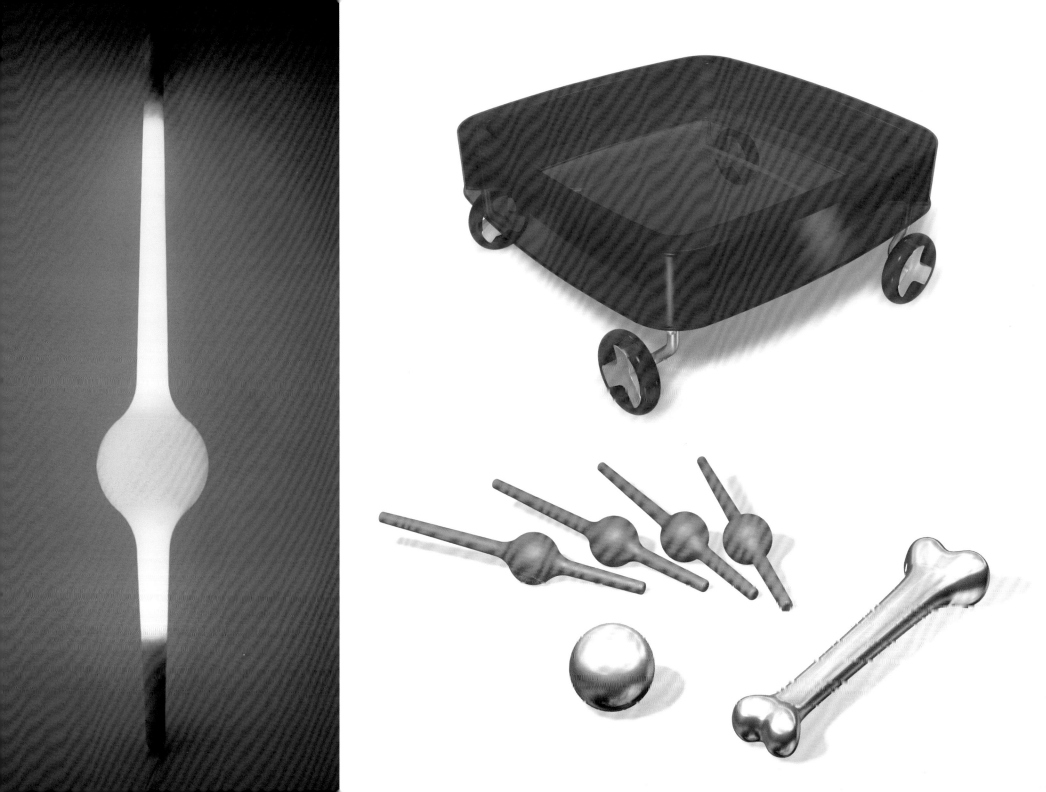

Dog Home

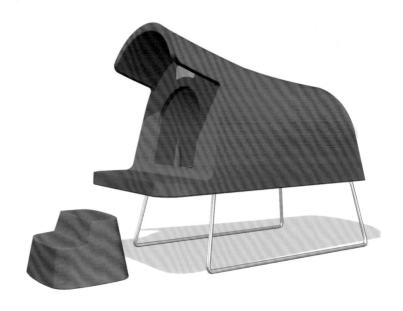

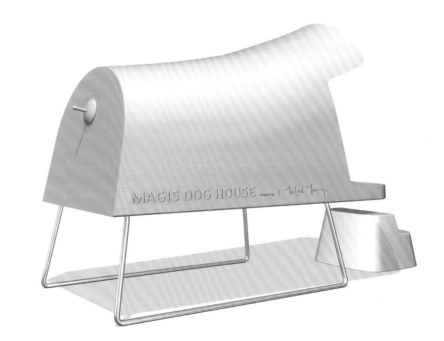

1 Dog House, 2001, rotation-moulded polyethelene, 75 x 48 x 32 cm, Magis.
› By a neat sleight of hand, Young manages to create a 3-dimensional cartoon of a dog. He also turns the most prosaic object imaginable into a thing of fun and beauty. The dimensions of the dog, think it, are about the same as that of a Cocker Spaniel, and the design includes a step-up for a Jack Russell or puppy.

2 Yogi Furniture, 2002, rotation-moulded polyethelene, seat 66 x 61 x 37 cm, bench 88 x 138 x 80 cm, table 25 x 0 00 cm, Magis.

› With these pieces of furniture Young hopes to induce a smile and to refresh the genre of garden furniture.

3 Red Tray MY 080, 2000, air-moulded plastic, steel, 24 x 38.5 x 66 cm, Magis.
› This red tray has folding legs and is stackable. It also has a locking system that ensures that the legs remain fixed and open during use.

4 Holey Chair, 2001, DuPont © Corian acrylic polymer, 59 x 59 x 59 cm, DuPont.
› Young used DuPont's solid polymer Corian for this gently curved and punctuated stool. It was made using CNC fabrication and it has a thermoformed seat.

1			
	1	3	4
2			

SPOON

Nominate my design classic? What does nominating a design classic mean? Is it something I like a lot, not only me but lots of other people too, and have done for a great number of years, and that I am guaranteed to go on liking for many years to come? Generally, I don't like design classics. They make themselves an easy choice for lazy minds – 'let's have Barcelona Chairs in our lounge', 'maybe even a fake Jacobsen will do'. They don't induce progress. They don't bring about change, even though their original *raison d'être* was change and progress. But I have been requested to choose a design classic for this book. So, the Goddess, or the Déesse, or the DS, Citroën DS, that is, 'the best car that has fallen from the sky', not my words of course and there's another problem – what can you write about the DS after Ronald Barthes (*Mythologies*, 1957) without stating the already stated? Just treat yourself to getting into one, start the engine, soar, turn the steering wheel and watch the beams of the headlights turning, watch (classic) French films and see the chasers favour the same car as the chased, think why Muhammad Ali chooses the Goddess for his epic trip in Africa (*When We Were Kings*). I always wanted a DS, still do, but I settled for a 1969 Fiat 500.

The New Citroën, by Roland Barthes 1957

I think that cars today are almost the exact equivalent of the great Gothic cathedrals: I mean the supreme creation of an era, conceived with passion by unknown artists, and consumed in image if not in usage by a whole population which appropriates them as a purely magical object.

It is obvious that the new Citroën has fallen from the sky inasmuch as it appears at first sight as a superlative *object*. We must not forget that an object is the best messenger of a world above that of nature: one can easily see in an object at once a perfection and an absence of origin, a closure and a brilliance, a transformation of life into matter (matter is much more magical than life), and in a word a *silence* which belongs to the realm of fairy-tales. The DS – the 'Goddess' – has all the features (or at least the public is unanimous in attributing them to it at first sight) of one of those objects from another universe which have supplied fuel for the neomania of the eighteenth century and that of our own science-fiction: the *Déesse* is *first and foremost* a new *Nautilus*.

This is why it excites interest less by its substance than by the junction of its components. It is well known that smoothness is always an attribute of perfection because its opposite reveals a technical and typically human operation of assembling: Christ's robe was seamless, just as the airships of science-fiction are made of unbroken metal. The DS 19 has no pretensions about being as smooth as cake-icing, although its general shape is very rounded; yet it is the dove-tailing of its sections which interest the public most: one keenly fingers the edges of the windows, one feels along the wide rubber grooves which link the back window to its metal surround. There are in the DS the beginnings of a new phenomenology of assembling, as if one progressed from a world where elements are welded to a world where they are juxtaposed and hold together by sole virtue of their wondrous shape, which of course is meant to prepare one for the idea of a more benign Nature. from *Mythologies* (Jonathan Cape, 1972)

Flaminio Bertoni
Citroën DS, 1955,
Citroën

147 cm

179 cm

147 cm

487 cm

Tavolo '64 was created in 1964 by the Milanese industrial designer AG Fronzoni. By eliminating all but the essential elements of the design, he created an object that was simple but not commonplace. It has proved to be one of the most influential design products of the twentieth century.

Tavolo '64 is a perfect example of both purity and vitality. It could be seen as an emblem of the minimalist movement in industrial design, a forerunner of the 'cult of simplicity' that flourished in the 1980s. It is also a perfect expression of AG Fronzoni's approach, an overall philosophy of design that continues to give inspiration to so many graphic and industrial designers today. The principles behind Fronzoni's designs were always the same. He unerringly focuses on what is essential, excluding superfluous effects and unnecessary decoration. He devises a basic structure around an underlying idea, and then develops concepts mathematically, avoiding waste or excess of any kind. He masters both gesture and thought, so that he can reveal them more clearly and uses geometrical forms as cultural elements. Fronzoni uses colour and shape only when they are essential to an understanding of the design. He chooses basic materials that will create harmony between the object, its immediate setting and its architectural environment. Tavolo '64 combines all the elements of Fronzoni's philosophy in a most remarkable way, and its simplicity is as striking as it is attractive.

Given his philosophy of design, Fronzoni must always create objects that are almost brutal in their honesty. By paring away all that is irrelevant, he must strive to communicate through content alone. The content is laid bare, and it must be powerful enough to work in isolation. Decoration is to be found only in the surrounding space. The richness of this space becomes apparent when compared to the space that envelopes 'saturated' objects, where form is a substitute for concept. At the same time, space can mean more than the mere representation of space.

Fronzoni lays claim to an interdisciplinary practice, refusing to define himself as an architect, a graphic artist, or a designer. He sees himself as the initiator of design projects conceived as solutions to design and communication problems of various kinds. His purely conceptual method of working enables him to take a consistent approach, whether the design is for a one- or two-dimensional object, on a large or small scale. Broadly speaking, it is openness before the object that is the most distinctive characteristic of Fronzoni's work. Nowhere else is the battle over 'modernity' fought out so intensely. Fronzoni exemplifies sobriety and the rejection of the aesthetic of excess that was so typical some decades ago.

When we consider Fronzoni's designs, we should not confuse space understood as an aesthetisizing element, a means of achieving beauty for its own sake, with the reasoned aesthetic he defends. His methods involve a process whereby perfection is destroyed before it becomes absolute, and the habitual is rendered slightly skewed. But destruction is never more than minimal. His use of black and white should not be seen as part of a current trend, but as a conscious decision, taken in order to make his message clear.

Media hype, the 'star system' that prevails in the world of applied art and the confusion between art and design all serve to make us forget the real functions of design. The situation is further confused by the artists who insist on considering architectural and industrial aesthetics in the same light as the vagaries of fashion. Fronzoni reminds us what design is for.

Tavolo '64 occupies a special place in the collective memory of many young designers. Taking this archetype as their starting-point, they create new forms for this basic piece of furniture. In the work of Ora-Ïto, Jean-Marie Massaud, Matali Crasset, Claesson Koivisto Rune and many other up-and-coming young designers, we find different variations on a single theme. All of them seek to create limpid, transparent objects which have an almost child-like quality. The great achievement of AG Fronzoni has been to teach all designers to work by subtraction rather than addition, a somewhat complex exercise, but one that is both formative and fascinating.

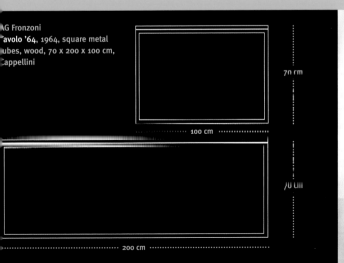

AG Fronzoni
Tavolo '64, 1964, square metal tubes, wood, 70 x 200 x 100 cm, Cappellini

70 cm

100 cm

70 cm

200 cm

Almost a century ago, Henry Ford understood the need for a practical and affordable means of transport to mobilize the working population of America. Ford's solution was the Model T. Nicknamed the 'Tin Lizzie', Ford's miraculous car quickly solved the problem of mass transport in urban America. Affordable? At a price of little more than six months' wages for the average blue-collar worker in America, it was certainly affordable. Practical? You only have to look at films of the period to see how ubiquitous the Model T became.

Now, jump forward to 1945 and the end of World War II. Pontedera is an Italian industrial town on the river Serchio, a short distance from Pisa in northern Tuscany, and one of the important manufacturing centres for the great Piaggio Corporation. Piaggio had been a jewel of Italian heavy industry, producing trains, ships and aeroplanes, but by 1945, the factories were in ruins, destroyed by Italy's defeat at the hands of the Allies. Enrico Piaggio was desperate to come up with a plan to save his family firm. He called in Corradino d'Ascanio, his star aviation designer, who is credited with designing the first Italian helicopter in the 1920s, sketched originally by Leonardo da Vinci, some 500 years earlier.

Piaggio's brief was almost socialist in its thinking. Taking inspiration from Henry Ford, he wanted to invent a mode of transport that would mobilize the working people of Italy during the terrible postwar period. Piaggio knew that cars would not do it, as they were not affordable for the average working-class European. The answer had to be a motorcycle of some sort.

As a prelude to his meeting with d'Ascanio, Piaggio had his engineers knock together a basic motorcycle, dubbed the MP5. D'Ascanio was not impressed, principally because he was not a motorcycle fan. He hated the uncompromising macho character of the average bike and rider. At that time, it was assumed you were part mechanic, part fanatic, if you rode a motorcycle at all. Bikes were filthy and unreliable. If the weather did not destroy the motorcycle's leather-wrapped rider, a manly man of course, then he would be defeated by the oil, which oozed relentlessly from every mechanical pore. What d'Ascanio wanted was a bike for all seasons and all kinds of riders: men, women and teenagers.

D'Ascanio's prototype was a perfect union of the mechanical with the aesthetic. Its small wheels, mounted on single sided, tubular arms, were borrowed directly from aviation. The wheels were interchangeable, and there was a spare tyre. The engine was directly connected to the rear wheel,

doing away with the chain, the oily bane of motorcycle riders since the earliest days. Most remarkably, the whole engine and transmission was concealed within an elegant sheet-metal enclosure – standard automobile practice – with a front leg shield to protect the rider from the weather. Simple, effective and original. The final touch was the riding position. Abandoning the horse saddle, which, in America and Europe, forced riders to sit astride their bikes, Corradino d'Ascanio provided a saddle that could be sat upon. Why, even a nun in full regalia could ride this kind of motorcycle.

When presented with the prototype by d'Ascanio, Enrico Piaggio's first words were 'Sembra una vespa!' (It looks like a wasp!). It was one of those historical accidents that could not have been scripted. The name stuck and the rest, as we say, is history.

Piaggio's success was due in part to fantastic marketing and the inspired introduction of hire purchase, a financing option borrowed from the car industry in America. In 1946, the first full year of production, Piaggio produced over 2,000 Vespas. The following year, the number jumped to over 10,000. From then on, sales increases were almost exponential. The public imagination was aflame. Production spread throughout Europe, even to Britain, which had its own thriving motorcycle industry.

Cultural commentators were quick to catch on to this pretty little wasp. The 1953 film *Roman Holiday*, starring Gregory Peck and Audrey Hepburn, sealed the deal. In the 1950s the Vespa was as essential an accessory as a fashionable handbag is today. The fact that it also got you to school or work was the key to the Vespa's success.

The model shown on these pages, the enlarged 150 cc Grand Sport of 1956, epitomizes both Vespa's technological achievement and its aesthetic development. It is no shame on Vespa to say that this is as good as the machine ever got. Nor is it fanciful to suggest that the Vespa is the inspiration for current retro car design, of which the re-designed VW Beetle is one of the best, and the Chrysler PT Cruiser the absolute nadir.

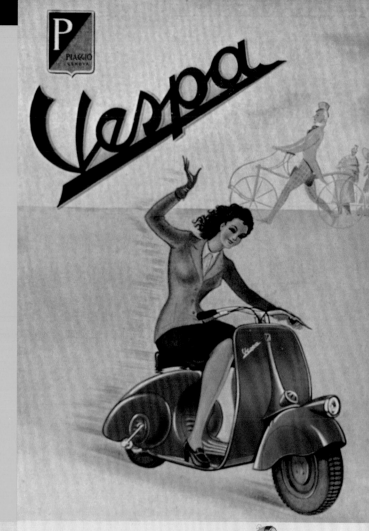

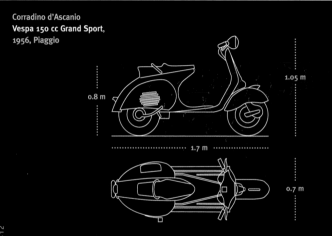

Corradino d'Ascanio
Vespa 150 cc Grand Sport,
1956, Piaggio

1.05 m

0.8 m

1.7 m

0.7 m

When I was first presented with the task of contributing to this volume on design, the assignment seemed relatively straightforward. I was asked to choose ten designers and one example of 'classic' design. Of these tasks, the selection of the 'classic' design was the most simple. The choice of ten designers that would encompass a range of approaches – for this was important to me – was another matter. As I began to put my list together, my own beliefs about design began to emerge, as did my own definition of what 'design' actually means. Sometimes, my reactions were sharply focused, accompanied, as it were, by the 'ah-ha' of discovery, at others, the vision seemed cloudy, as standard definitions of design expanded and work danced on the threshold of other territories.

'Design' is a difficult term, for it encompasses many different practices and a multiplicity of products. If it is to thrive, it is imperative that design is not pigeon-holed within one discipline or another. To remain vibrant, it must draw on other disciplines and, in return, it will give something back. This might be its production processes, technology, newly developed materials, or other, less predictable assets. Just as designers look to other realms, we must be willing to seek out design in unexpected places, and to allow it to enter new territories and institutions. Design is not simply a commercial endeavour; it can also be an art form, although it is rarely allowed to coexist with art in the hallowed halls of museums.

I identified my 'classic' design before I chose the ten designers. Nevertheless, the Superleggera Chair, designed by Gio Ponti in 1955, produced by Cassina from 1957 and still in production today, sits well beside the work of my chosen designers. Ponti is a designer who cannot be neatly fitted into one discipline or another. He was an architect who also worked as an industrial designer, a set designer, a fashion designer, a graphic designer – the list is endless. Through his holistic approach, he expanded the universe of design in a way that was quite remarkable, and his influence has been both far reaching and undeniable. The Superleggera was a classic almost from the moment it was designed. Its roots were clearly in traditional design, but its profile was modern. The chair's clean, elegant lines are timeless and its lightness, though sought after, has never been superseded.

Superleggera represents a legacy of modernism, and it soon became my *leitmotif* as the work on my ten designers progressed. Some of the designers on my list were raised – as I was – by parents with a predilection

for modern design. Others came of age at a time when mid-century modernism was again the focus of attention. Whatever the reason, all of the designers that I selected create work rooted in an awareness of the modernist legacy. They may use new technologies and materials, but the influence is clear. In some cases it is revealed in the clean, simple lines of their work – you'll find no baroque flourishes here. In others it is in the deeply felt imperative to produce good design at an affordable price. This is not to say that design has become derivative. All of the work is new in some way. Some of it is radical. I hope that it may, one day, be considered timeless.

Another common thread connecting some of the designers is their desire to establish an 'emotional' connection between product and the user. The desire for meaning, for association, is strong. In some cases this desire is more important than strict functionalism. In others, the two go hand in hand.

I was determined to select my designers from a variety of different areas. The field is vast and rich. Reiko Sudo, a textile designer, and Ted Muehling, a designer of exquisite jewellery and other objects, occupy one end of the spectrum. Both of them work in a very particular style. At the other end are J Mays, a designer in the motor industry, and Frank Nuovo, a designer of electronic objects for Nokia, whose work is produced for a vast public in enormous quantities. At the middle of the spectrum I selected designers whose work may appear 'conventional', because it falls into established product categories, although the production processes and personal vision of the designer may not. Perhaps surprisingly, several of these designers come from an architectural background. Somewhere, orbiting around the others, is Jorge Pardo, an artist – definitely an artist. While his work addresses design and is, in some cases, fabricated like design, it would not satisfy a strict definition of design. It is an example of 'cross-pollination', an increasingly important aspect of design in a world that has become larger, with boundaries that are more fluid.

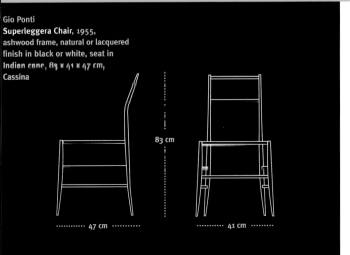

Gio Ponti
Superleggera Chair, 1955, ashwood frame, natural or lacquered finish in black or white, seat in Indian cane, 83 x 41 x 47 cm, Cassina

83 cm

47 cm 41 cm

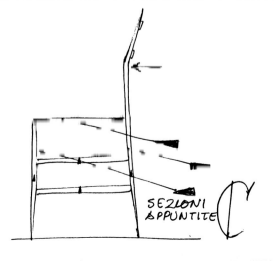

SEZIONI APPUNTITE

When asked to select a favourite iconic design, I struggled to choose something unexpected. There is little that did not pass over my desk in my years as design editor at *Wallpaper**, and while the amount of new products being designed and old designs being resurrected is formidable, I believe that there are still few pieces of really excellent, original craftsmanship. I love Gio Ponti, adore Jean Prouvé and would not say 'no' to any George Nelson piece, but I eventually settled on the Flag Halyard Lounge Chair (1950) by Hans Wegner.

The chair has a low-slung chromed steel frame and is upholstered with thick yarn. The natural materials are typical of Wegner and are evocative of the designer's heritage in Danish craftwork. The chair has great proportions: it allows you to sit comfortably and read, without nastily tipping you backwards as if you were in a dentist's chair. Wings instead of arms gently envelop you and usually the chair is decorated with a fur throw. The chair is the epitome of comfort and I like the fact that Wegner achieved this with rustic materials and construction methods. This is a piece that I would choose for my home and that, after all, is the reaction that every contemporary designer is trying to achieve. Few since Wegner have managed to create such a catalogue of original designs – each effortlessly elegant and timeless. His pieces sit happily alongside designs from any epoch and are clever in their sculptural forms and use of traditional materials. The thing I love most about Wegner is that he was really a humble craftsman at heart, and that was enough to propel him into the stratosphere of international design.

Our contemporary climate is beneficial to the people who spend their days giving form to the items that surround us. Never before have product designers enjoyed such a far-reaching influence. The media have developed a love affair with domestic design and by doing so have created a handful of celebrity designers and ensured that today's consumer is better educated in design then ever before. With education comes knowledge, and the more consumers learn about product design, the faster they absorb the information that is increasingly available on TV or in the printed press and the higher the demands on designers will be. This process has resulted in a renewed expectancy for high-quality craftsmanship. Shuwa Tei, a young Japanese designer, is among the group that I have selected for this book. He has chosen to combine modern design with traditional techniques. Similarly, Lena Bergström is a glass designer renowned for adapting traditional glass-blowing techniques to the production of thoroughly contemporary pieces.

Western society is defined by a 'keeping up with the Joneses' attitude to domestic purchases. Of course, economic success has always been measured by material possessions, but it is only recently that this attitude has become so widespread. The social hierarchy now takes into account not only our domestic appliances and cars, but also our sofas and dish-racks, creating an environment that is good news for designers in every area. The German designer Kay Thoss works in both Munich and Milan. Although the phrase 'urban nomad' has been used too frequently for my liking, it does go some way towards describing the transient nature of a lifestyle such as his. Lucky enough to earn almost immediate success with his first collection, Thoss has the rootless career typical of so many young designers today. And like so many of them, his work is international both in inspiration and appeal.

Todd Bracher and Johanna Grawunder are also among the group that I have selected. Their work reflects an amalgamation of influences, which they offer to like-minded consumers. It seems that product design has ingrained itself into the contemporary lifestyle in a way unique to this period.

Among the designers who cater directly for contemporary culture is Thorsten Franck, maker of mobile furniture for a mobile society. In a conscious effort to reflect the lifestyle of his contemporaries, Thorsten designed a furniture system that leans on the wall rather than being fixed to it. With so much competition out there, an original idea goes a long way. Then there is Norway Says, which is a unique collective of young Norwegians who rely on their inherent craftsmanship skills and good taste rather than gimmicks.

For those who live life on the fastest of tracks, Todd Bracher's innovative, dual-function seating and dining products have instant appeal. Bloom is a multi-functional seating system which has practical use and a sculptural quality that brings another purpose to the product when it is not in use. This kind of dual function is extremely attractive and it also sets the standard for an interesting career. Finally, Michael Anastassiades is a young British designer dedicated to invention and experimentation. His work consists of a collection of familiar objects that have an unusual task allotted to them. The alarm table is a prime example of a piece whose worth lies in its concept. Our current generation of designers face a far more critical reception than their predecessors ever did. They are judged not only against a vast number of contemporaries but also against their twentieth-century precursors and their increasingly respected legacies.

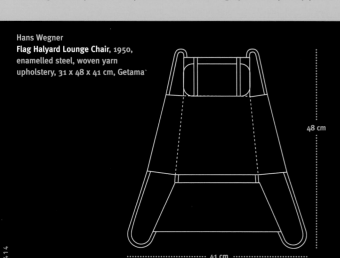

Hans Wegner
Flag Halyard Lounge Chair, 1950,
enamelled steel, woven yarn
upholstery, 31 x 48 x 41 cm, Getama

48 cm

41 cm

The search for an icon of contemporary design need extend no further than Wilhelm Wagenfeld's salt and pepper shakers, Max and Moritz, which were first produced in 1952. With them as an example, I would like to establish an intellectual connection between Wagenfeld's work and the efforts of a contemporary group of young international designers who are creating exemplary designs for industrial production.

My aim is to establish continuity between this example of 1950s design and the work of the designers I have chosen. Despite their varied origins and training, they have one thing in common: they all develop their ideas with a simple economy of means, they reduce their forms and materials, and make the most of modern technology and other resources. At the same time, their curiosity is always evident, introducing the necessary element of surprise and innovation in even the smallest products.

Wagenfeld was born in Bremen in 1900 and served his apprenticeship in a draftsman's office, attended the Kunstgewerbeschule in Bremen, and then became director of the metal workshop of the Weimar Bau-Hochschule, the institution that followed the Bauhaus. He began collaborating with industry in 1929, and his work put him in touch with major German companies such as the Jena glassworks and the Württemberger Metallwarenfabrik (WMF).

From the outset, Wagenfeld was concerned less with individual, finished pieces, and more with the intellectual connection between form and utility. He focused on designs that would remain contemporary in the long term, rather than obsessively following seasonal trends. Wagenfeld's universalism has always been connected with that of the Bauhaus, and he set himself subtly and radically apart from the provincialism of the simple life and the longing for the rustic roots of the primal form, thus creating a niche for the survival of 'good form' during the era of National Socialism. The example of Wagenfeld establishes a connection with some younger designers who are presented in this book. They are equally aware of how strong the influence of industry can be on the mass consumption of users. In an age of global conformity they also register the opportunities of providing authentic and long-lasting products, so-called archetypal design solutions, which clearly demonstrate the special quality of everyday objects.

Wagenfeld's salt and pepper shakers have been manufactured by WMF without interruption for 50 years. They are a perfect form, a true everyday icon and they have outsold all of this large company's other products, both in terms of overall profit and unit sales. The declared goal of industrial mass production has been perfectly realized through the combination of form and quality with a reasonable price.

Several factors combine to create an icon of design. First, the form cannot be categorized, either in terms of its style or its components. Every detail of Max and Moritz has been reduced to its essential form. The choice of materials, namely glass, with its austere clarity and transparency, and the matt sheen of high-grade steel, has been carefully considered. It is hard to identify any previous designer who would have risked clamping a high-grade steel cap to a fragile glass body without using a conventional screw or bayonet fitting. There is both a visual and a physical tension between the two materials, glass and steel. This is intensified by the unusual way in which the metal lid clicks on to the glass body. The unusually flexible, homogeneous and almost amorphous glass shape makes it the ideal utility product. When picked up, it practically melts into the hand. This unique design achievement is impossible to ignore. Regular, vertical incisions in the edge of the high-grade steel cap create a slightly springy effect, making the rigid material 'soft', a precondition that was necessary to make the simple clamping mechanism work. At the same time, the incisions create a profoundly simple form of elegance. Even today, we must admire this design solution, so obvious in its simplicity. Last but not least, there is not a single detail in this product that one could criticize on grounds of design, function or perception. How often do we experience such perfection In the field of design? All subsequent adaptations and variations on Max and Moritz have proved incapable of rivalling the original, perfect concept.

If we compare Max and Moritz with other designs, we are forced to acknowledge and applaud the product as a prime example of contemporary design – despite the passage of 50 years. This is proof that the design has the archetypal quality that makes an icon, combined with appropriate technology and the correct choice of materials.

There is a specific spirit of design, based on close observation of the needs of everyday life, that sooner or later leads to brilliant solutions. We must often wait for some time before this brilliance is properly acknowledged by users. A real icon of design will usually take even longer to be recognized.

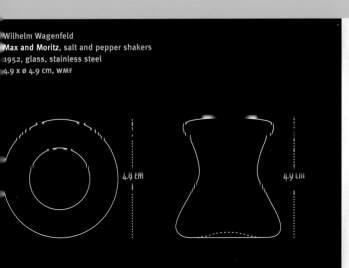

Wilhelm Wagenfeld
Max and Moritz, salt and pepper shakers
1952, glass, stainless steel
4.9 x ø 4.9 cm, WMF

4.9 cm   4.9 cm

The architecture and design of the 1950s has an enduring appeal. Today, we are as attracted to the organic, tactile characteristics of the buildings and products of the period as to their profoundly modern functionalism. Any discussion of the 1950s is bound to include Alvar Aalto (1898–1976), champion of the 'organic league' of designers. Born in the heavily forested landscape of Finland, Aalto took inspiration from the natural forms of plants, trees and the forest itself. He was also fascinated by the concept of transformation, whether applied to the materials that he used, or to the objects that he designed with them. Aalto's ideal – and his enduring legacy – was the concept of 'growing design'.

When the department of architecture and design at MoMA, New York, staged a retrospective at the end of the twentieth century, two architects were selected to form the focus of the exhibition. They were Frank Lloyd Wright and Alvar Aalto. I believe that time has proved the worth of these two talents. Both of them focused on a single aim: that of creating architectural spaces to mirror nature itself. Their work continues to serve as a treasure trove of ideas for designers and architects of the twenty-first century.

When the iittala Company launched a competition for the design of a new vase in 1936, Aalto's entry reflected his roots in the Finnish-Swedish architectural tradition. Entitled Skirt of the Eskimo Lady, the initial proposal was presented as a freehand drawing done in crayon and rough collage. The result looked very much like a real reindeer-skin skirt, flapping in the north winds of Lapland. When it was finally realized in glass, the vase had the sensuality of human flesh. It became a wonderful expression of the nuances of light and shade playing over the white birch forests and tranquil lakes of the Finnish landscape.

While I am always tempted to use Aalto's vase as a goldfish bowl, my daughter, who has recently started to learn Japanese flower arranging, is very against this idea. She says that the vase can be best appreciated when it is packed with 40 or 50 small, white tulips. They should be trimmed to exactly the same height, so that the flower heads are just visible above the rim of the vase.

Aalto's Finnish Pavilion at the 1939 World's Fair in New York caused a sensation. With its undulating, wooden walls and beautiful, coloured lights, it was compared to the aurora borealis. Like so many of the architectural spaces that Aalto created, it seemed to exude the air of nature itself.

I am often struck by the affinity between the Finns and the Japanese. We are equally aware of the immense resonance of nature's changing seasons. Thus, a feeling for the ephemeral is at the heart of our aesthetic sense. The designers of Finland and Japan could be said to share a common aim. They all set out to understand the essence of their materials, and then to find a form that will act as an expression of that understanding. This characteristic can be traced through the development of design and architecture in both countries.

To a certain extent, the futuristic attitude of Alvar Aalto and others of his generation was obscured by lack of materials and technology. This should not blind us, however, to their radical approach. Aalto's legacy can be seen in the work of many of the designers that I have chosen to write about. This link is expressed first and foremost by their desire to combine high-tech with an innate simplicity of form and materials. Aalto's influence is very obvious in the work of Valvomo – particularly in the Soundwave panel for Snowcrash. While it functions at a simple level as a piece of compressed fibre, the panel might be used to transform the whole wall or even the floor. This remarkable and inspiring panel is very similar to the round-edged brick invented by Aalto when he designed the House of Culture in Helsinki (1952–8).

The Finnish tradition of system-oriented organic design has developed to encompass form-oriented organic design as well. In this sense, Kawaguchi, another of my choices from Japan, is very compatible. She used traditional materials, such as bamboo, in designs for contemporary lighting fixtures. Her use of expanding and foldable materials to support wide surfaces is also reminiscent of Aalto. His influence can also be seen in the system that she developed for the Paulownia Collection. It all makes me wonder whether Alvar Aalto's use of space was actually inspired by the Japanese tradition.

Alvar Aalto
Savoy Vase, 1936, mouth-blown glass
and hand-finished lead-free crystal,
16 x 20.5 x 17.5 cm, 20 x 19 x 18.4 cm, iittala

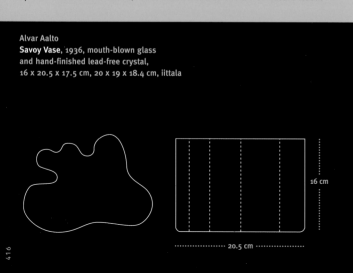

16 cm

······················ 20.5 cm ······················

There is no more significant endorsement of a design than the length of its useful life. Lluís Clotet and Óscar Tusquets have a lot to say on that score. When they graduated from the ETSAB School of Architecture in Barcelona they did not know much about industrial design, but they had lots of good ideas. As so often happens when you are young, they could find no one willing to produce them. They had no alternative but to opt for the role of designer-entrepreneur in order to make their ideas a reality. The company that Clotet and Tusquets set up in 1972 together with their colleagues at Studi Per was called Bd Ediciones de Diseño, and from it came such iconic pieces as the Catalano bench.

Clotet and Tusquets designed the Catalano at a time when street furniture had scarcely been invented. The secret of its success lies in its superbly ergonomic silhouette, the designers' inspired adaptation of the form Gaudí created for his famous ceramic-mosaic bench in Parque Güell, Barcelona. The choice of folded steel gives the bench transparency, ensuring that it does not steal the limelight from its surroundings, avoids the accumulation of rain-water and makes the seat warm in winter and cool in summer. With the passage of time, the Catalano has become a classic, and even now it is one of the most widely sold and copied examples of Spanish design.

A lot of people ask themselves what has happened to Spanish design. What has become of the great expectations generated during the boom years of the mid-1980s? The answer is simple. Thanks to such timely ideas as the Catalano, Spanish design was catapulted from obscurity. Members of the design community were as surprised as anyone else. A handful of pioneering designers had started to take an interest in industrial design in the 1960s and had spent long years wandering in the wilderness of Spanish industry, preaching their visionary ideas. All through the 1970s they tilled a virgin field that finally bore fruit in the 1980s. The first specialist magazines appeared, exhibitions were organized and they consolidated their position at trade fairs. Design hit the street, generating a wave of media attention. Those pioneers, spurned for so long by Spanish manufacturers, were eventually courted by leading European firms.

So, what happened next? Quite simply, Spain's industrial fabric does not have the potential that exists in countries such as Italy. Nor does the culture of design enjoy the institutional support to be found, for example, in the United Kingdom. Since that generation of very successful Spanish designers there has been something of a void. If manufacturers are not ready to back young talent, and institutions do not support them, the future of the thousands of design students is uncertain. Just like the veterans before them, they too have to make their way through the desert.

Although Spanish industry does not realize it yet, a change is already taking place. In 2000, when *Domus* magazine organized a competition to design the interior of the new Boeing business jet, the latest generation of 737-700s for private users, it attracted entries from such famous names as Richard Sapper and Toyo Ito. In the end, however, the competition was won by two unknowns, Ana Mir and Emili Padrós, a Valencian and a Catalan who had only just turned 30. They belong to a generation that no longer venerates the veterans, with the exception of one or two old masters such as Ron Arad or Ingo Maurer. They are the young talents that straddle different disciplines, such as graphics and digital design, who have clearly grasped the importance of promoting themselves, and respond to the indifference of industry by tirelessly publicizing their work in exhibitions and design magazines.

It was publicity that brought me into contact with the work of Ana Mir and Emili Padrós, Martín Ruiz de Azúa, and the extraordinary talent of Martí Guixé, an 'ex-designer', as he now likes to describe himself, capable of re-inventing the world and the design profession as well, by designing ideas rather than products. Some of these up-and-coming professionals, such as Héctor Serrano, have chosen to set up shop in London, knowing that you have to be in the right place at the right time in order to get yourself noticed. Others, like Candela Reymundo, Curro Claret and Joan Gaspar, respectively represent the most romantic, idealistic and technical facets of the profession. They have not yet learnt to promote their work, but they too have a place in a future that will always be open to ideas. And time will tell if those ideas last.

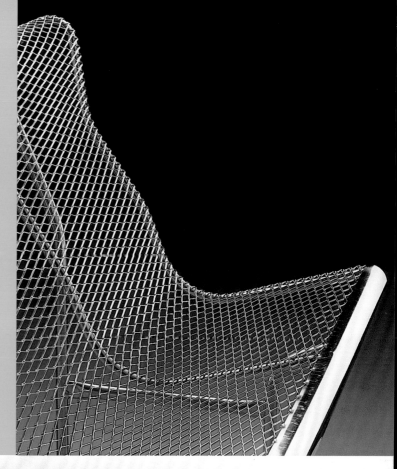

Lluís Clotet and Óscar Tusquets
Banco Catalano, 1974, legs in galvanized, hot-dipped or electro-polished stainless-steel tube, bench in deep galvanized tube; versions: galvanized and painted or hot dipped, 89 x 100 x 77 cm, Bd Ediciones de Diseño

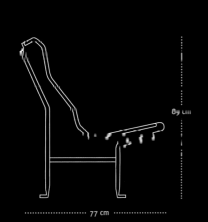

89 cm

77 cm

I object to objects. I am drawn to them by need or desire, but at the same time I often feel an overwhelming sense of responsibility. If I acquire an object, I must accept, and even condone, its function and aesthetics. I must also take on its entire life, from the harvesting of the raw materials from which it is made to the manufacturing process. I must accept the marketing strategies and ethical policy of the company that produces it, its packaging and even its final destiny, whether it is passed on, recycled or left in a landfill. The fairly straightforward question 'Do I really need this object?' has become a much more complex: 'Can I accept everything this object represents?'

I am sure that I am not alone. Even marketing experts are now sensitive to the conscious consumer. They tout wares produced and sold through fair trade, and offer objects made from bio-plastics or recycled materials. Fine examples of this phenomenon are Polartec fabric and the Furnature Company in the us. Polartec is made from 90 per cent post-consumer waste, endowing the ready-to-wear industry with increasingly noble qualities. The Furnature Company produces goods that look exactly the same as any other high-quality furniture, although they are made from wood and organic cotton, and are 100 per cent biodegradable.

Out of all the design classics, the one I find most touching is the Heineken WOBO. Short for WOrld BOttle, the WOBO never made it to the consumer. Nevertheless, it is a study in what can go wrong – and right – in producing an object that evolves from the environmental and social concerns of an individual.

In 1960, Alfred Heineken, the young president of the eponymous company, visited the former Dutch colony of Curaçao, which was part of the beer giant's export market. He was struck both by the deplorable living conditions in the shanty towns and the multitude of empty Heineken bottles that littered the island. From this experience the idea of a beer bottle that could be reused as a building block was born. The container would become more useful than its contents. The object would respond to the objections of shanty towns and rubbish heaps.

Never before had a company taken on the challenge to conceive, produce and market their containers for second use. Alfred Heineken chose a young architect called John Habraken to supervise the development of the product, and to design a house made from WOBOS. The plans had to be simple enough to fit on the bottle's label. Thus the quest for the bottle-brick/brick-bottle began. Some elements of the bottle were to serve both of its purposes: beer-drinking and house-building. Such dual-purpose features included the raised bumps on the bottle's surface, which improved the drinker's hold on the bottle and also provided the necessary rough surface for mortar to adhere to.

After much trial and error, the design for the WOBO was finished in 1963 and produced in 350 ml and 530 ml sizes. Masculine and monumental in shape, it had the allure of a beer bottle and the added intrigue of an architectural function. The home developed by Habraken resembled a timber-framed log cabin made from green bottle-bricks laid in horizontal rows, the neck of each bottle fitting the recess in the bottom of another bottle. Originally, the roof was to be made from the plastic pallets in which the bottles were shipped. However, the need for good ventilation between walls and roof in the tropical climate made it necessary to substitute a corrugated material.

Heineken manufactured 100,000 bottles, and 40 years later they are still in a warehouse in Rotterdam. The only WOBO house ever made stands in the grounds of Alfred Heineken's home near Amsterdam. The strength of Heineken's vision saw the WOBO through the concept, design and production stages. The vision folded, however, when the marketing stage was reached. The marketing department at Heineken predicted the downfall of the brewery itself if Alfred changed the traditional design of the bottle. The new WOBO, they reasoned, would damage Heineken's identity and put consumers off the beer. Unwilling to bring down the 150-year-old family business, Alfred reluctantly cancelled the operation.

Perhaps the urgency of recycling was not as deeply felt as it is today. Perhaps situations in far-flung areas of the world were not experienced as much as they are in our age of news 24-hours a day, seven days a week. Consumers in developed countries are increasingly aware of their responsibilities, not only to the earth, but also to its inhabitants. Today they would surely be pleased to participate in public-housing solutions for developing countries. The intentions of the WOBO would bring added value to both the beer and the brewery's image. Today the WOBO could still succeed, because even now shantytowns made from rotting materials and landfills composed of useless objects continue to exist, side by side, in abject, objectionable poverty.

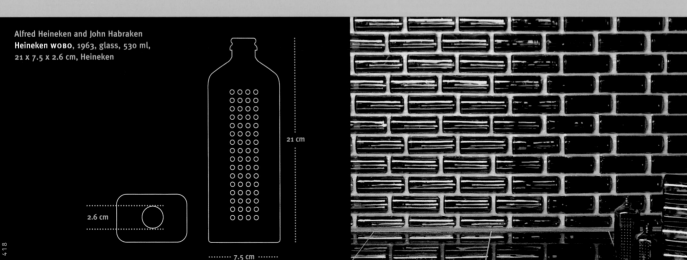

Alfred Heineken and John Habraken
Heineken WOBO, 1963, glass, 530 ml,
21 x 7.5 x 2.6 cm, Heineken

21 cm

2.6 cm

7.5 cm

To be defined as a 'classic', a product must be truly representative of its age in terms of intention, expression, technique and choice of material. When asked to choose such a design, I found it difficult not to look back – way back – in time. I came up with many products that met my criteria and yet which failed to arouse my unreserved passion. So, I turned things around and sought for a design that was imbued with a feeling of excellence and had aroused my most intense feelings. Suddenly, it was crystal clear – Apple's Sub-woofer, designed by Jonathan Ive and his team in collaboration with the sophisticated loudspeaker manufacturer Harman Kardon. What a revelation! It has integrity as well as a clear creative connection to the other Apple products by Ive and his team. In my view, it is not only an incredibly good-looking loudspeaker, but also one that breaks the mould of loudspeakers. Change of this kind rarely happens. Usually companies and designers reinvent or renew a product category by borrowing from another one. Therefore, we have kitchen equipment that looks like a hi-fi system or TV sets imitating baroque paintings with frames and so forth. But these products lack integrity, do not represent their time, will not affect future development and certainly will not become 'classics'. This loudspeaker is just the opposite. It flirts with no other designs and is wonderfully revolutionary and fresh. To me it is a true classic. Swift acceptance of a radical new design is rare. Ive and his team had already accomplished that with the iMac, but for me, this sideline is more powerful than anything else.

While seeking my 'classic', I had to consider the issue of 'good design'. Is there such a thing? I believe that there was a time when the notion of good design was valid. In perhaps more socially-minded times, it was thought that the 'good' product could deliver a better quality of life. For the most part I think that attitude is no longer valid, although there are some societies where good design is of vital importance in the context of development and democratization: for example, the production of cost-efficient but functional medical equipment for people in underdeveloped countries. It could also be said that all design not directly harmful to society can be considered good design. But in this context there is sometimes bad design, such as in the fashion industry, where raincoats are made that do not withstand rain.

That the notion of good design still holds true for so many individuals and groups within the design community is, in my opinion, a problem. It is a stumbling block to the development of design. We must stop lecturing, moralizing and preaching about what is good. Instead, we should embrace diversity, remembering that this is the starting point for what can be described as 'right design'. Not right design from our own subjective perspective as designers – but right design that takes into account the values and wishes of its recipients and users. To make the designer absolute judge over what constitutes good design feels very outdated. By accepting right design instead of good design we accept diversity and realize that there is not one path or solution. It is the recipient who decides – and we are all different.

I am convinced that the consumer's sympathy and liking, not only for the product but also for the company that produces it, will be deciding factors in the future. It will be a question of long-term relationships based on shared values. While our demands about our surroundings are becoming more sophisticated, we are also crying out for meaning, content and responsibility. So, I believe that neither the individual designer's dialogue with the marketplace nor the particular product or object are as significant as they once were. The complete picture has become the important thing, along with the organizations that want to start a dialogue with the consumer. What is decisive is how well these organizations understand their customers, how much they dare to surprise them, and how honest and relevant they are.

As for my choice of designers, it seemed natural to focus primarily on the geographical area where I live and work. Apart from Alfredo Häberli and Miguel Vieira Baptista, all those I have selected either work in or are from Sweden or Finland. And, interestingly, Portugal, where Miguel Vieira Baptista comes from, has some of the same characteristics of a country at the margins of Europe as Scandinavia. The people I have chosen are those that I respect. They are a diverse group yet they seem to share a common value system, contributing to society in a thoughtful way.

Apple Design Team
i.sub Sub-woofer, 1999, plastic,
26 x 23.2 cm, Apple

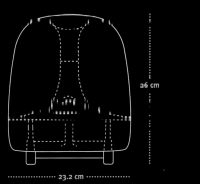

26 cm

23.2 cm

BIOGRAPHIES

A-POC

Issey Miyake's design engineer partner Dai Fujiwara
Born Tokyo, 1967. Lives and works in Tokyo
EDUCATION
1995 Tama Art University, Textile Design, Tokyo
PRACTICE
1997 A-POC Design Engineer, Miyake Design Studio, Tokyo
SELECTED PROJECTS
2002 A-POC Stretch T-shirt, Miyake Design Studio; Flat Jeans, Miyake Design Studio;
2001 One Piece, Miyake Design Studio; Zoo, Miyake Design Studio; Berlinewald,
Miyake Design Studio; Berlin District, Miyake Design Studio; **2000** Baguette, Miyake
Design Studio; Pain De Mie, Miyake Design Studio; Midas, Miyake Design Studio;
Caravan, Miyake Design Studio; **1999** King & Queen, Miyake Design Studio; Eskimo,
Miyake Design Studio; Alien, Miyake Design Studio
SELECTED BIBLIOGRAPHY
2001 *Radical Fashion*, London; *A-POC Making*, Berlin: Vitra Design Museum; *Beaux
Arts*, Hors-Serie, November, Paris; *MIT Thresholds*, no.22, Boston; *H O M E*, no.5,
Berlin; *Design Report*, no.6, Stuttgart; *Der Spiegel*, no.23, Hamburg; *TIP*, no.13,
Berlin; *Crafts Magazine*, no.173, London
SELECTED EXHIBITIONS
2001 'Radical Fashion', Victoria & Albert Museum, London; 'A-POC Making', Vitra
Design Museum, Berlin; **2000** 'Making Things', Tokyo Museum of Contemporary Art,
Tokyo; 'Making Things', Ace Gallery, New York; **1998** 'Making Things', Fondation Cartier,
Paris
AWARDS
2001 The 10th International Design Award, Osaka; **2000** Mainichi Fashion Grand Prix
Millennium Award, Tokyo; Good Design Award 2000 Grand Prix, Tokyo

VOLKER ALBUS

Born Frankfurt am Main, 1949. Lives and works in Frankfurt am Main
EDUCATION
1968–76 Architektur-Studium an der RWTH, Aachen
PRACTICE
1996 Co-editor of *formdiskurs*; **1994** Professor of Product Design, Staatlichen
Hochschule für Gestaltung, Karlsruhe; **1992–4** Member of Commission d'achat du
FNAC (Fondation National des Arts Contemporain), Paris, France; **1984 to present**
Writing for *Form, Design Report, Bauwelt, Hochparterre*; **1982 to present** Furniture
and interior designer
SELECTED PROJECTS
2001 Squarelight; **1999–2000** Downlight; **2000** Wicker Donut, DIM; Wonderbrush, DIM;
Glass Collection, Ritzenhoff; Exit, towel; Fleisch, towel, Moeve
SELECTED BIBLIOGRAPHY
2001 Volker Albus, Renate Goldmann, *Come-in*, Cologne; **2000** Member of editors'
board, *Design! Das 20. Jahrhundert*, Munich; **1999** Volker Albus, Michael Kriegeskorte
Kauf mich! Der Prominente als Message und Markenartikel, Cologne; **1997** *Der
Bookworm*, Frankfurt; **1996** Volker Albus, Klaus Klemp, *Lieber Gast*, Stuttgart
SELECTED EXHIBITIONS
2001 'Frankfurter Kreuz', Schirn Kunsthalle, Frankfurt am Main; **2000** '50 Jahre ital-
ienisches und deutsches Design', Kunst- und Ausstellungshalle der Bundesrepublik
Deutschland, Bonn; **1999** 'Das XX. Jahrhundert – ein Jahrhundert Kunst in Deutschland
– Form ohne Ornament?', Kunstgewerbemuseum, Berlin; **1996** 'Design og Identitet',
Louisiana Museum, Humlebaek
AWARDS
2001 Baden-Württemberg International Design Prize, Germany; **2000** Design Plus Award

MICHAEL ANASTASSIADES

Born Athens, 1967. Lives and works in London
EDUCATION
1991–3 Royal College of Art MDes Industrial Design, London; Imperial College
of Science, Technology and Medicine. DIC Industrial Design Engineering, London;
1988–91 Imperial College of Science, Technology and Medicine. BEng Civil
Engineering. Associateship of the City and Guilds of London Institute, London
PRACTICE
www.michael-anastassiades.com
1994–7 Visiting Tutor, BA Graphic Design, Camberwell College of Arts, London;
1995 Freelance design for Pentagram, London; Freelance design for Studio Brown,
Bath; **1994** Established his own Design Studio, London; Space Workshop, Tom Dixon,
furniture design and manufacture, London; **1993** Freelance design for Planet Design,
London; Freelance design for TKO, London; **1992** Toshiba Design Centre, Tokyo
SELECTED PROJECTS
2001 Corner Mirrors; Globe Vases, Babylon; Ball Vases, Babylon; Anti-social light;
Social light; **1999** Sitooteries, Fountain/Stool, Lamp-post, joint project with Wim de
Mul, English Heritage, Belsay Hall, Northumberland; Cola bottle opener, Coca Cola;
Mirror Vases, Babylon; **1998** Dining table, chair, light; Mirror chair; Pendant light,
Babylon; Box light, Babylon; Message cups, produced by designer; **1997** Laundry
basket, Mast; Mirror glasses, ice bucket, Babylon; Bedside table alarm clock;
Bedside table weekend 1-2; Table mirror; Thermometer table, produced by designer;
1996 Weeds, Aliens and Other Stories, joint project with designers Dunne & Raby
SELECTED BIBLIOGRAPHY
2002 *Wallpaper**, March, London; *New York Times*, 28 December, New York; **2001**
Independent, 2 April, London; *International Herald Tribune*, 9 January, Paris; **2000**
David Redhead, *Products of Our Time*, London; **1999** *Lost & Found, Critical Voices
in New British Design*, London; Claire Catteral, *Stealing Beauty*, exhibition catalogue,
ICA, London; *Numero*, November, Paris; **1998** Marco Suzani, *Weeds, Aliens and Other
Stories*, London; *Blueprint*, January, London; *Blueprint*, April, London; *Elle Decoration*,
July–August, London; *Blueprint*, October, London; **1997** *Monument*, July–August,
London; *Blueprint*, November, London; Katerina Gregos, *Intersection*, exhibition
catalogue, June, London
SELECTED EXHIBITIONS
2001 'Corner Mirrors', Applied Arts Agency, London; 'Living Britain', Tokyo Designers
Week; 'Global tools – spin off', Klaus Engelhorn Gallery, Vienna; 'Industry of one',
The Crafts Council, London; 'Home Sweet Home', The British Council, touring show;
2000–2003 'Coming to our senses', Craftspace, touring show; **2000–2002** 'Lost and
Found', British Council touring show; **1999** 'Sitooteries', Belsay Hall, Northumberland;
'Identity Crisis', Glasgow; 'Stealing Beauty. British Design Now', ICA, London; **1998**
'Dining Table, Chair, Light', Colette, Paris; 'Weeds, Aliens and Other Stories', touring
exhibition; '100% Design', London; 'No Picnic', Crafts Council, London; 'London,
Functional Art', Generous Miracles Gallery, New York; Sothebys, Contemporary
Decorative Arts exhibition, London
AWARDS
2001 Testing Ground, The Crafts Council, Architecture Foundation; research scholar-
ship, Royal Society of Art, London; **2000** Design Plus Award, Messe Frankfurt,
Frankfurt; **1999** Artist of the Year Award, The Hellenic Foundation, London

ED ANNINK

Born Utrecht, 1956. Lives and works in The Hague
EDUCATION
School for Gold and Silver smiths, Schoonhoven, The Netherlands;
Academy for Art and Design, The Hague
PRACTICE
www.ontwerpwerk.com
1987 to present Designer, The Hague
SELECTED PROJECTS
Design for a series of products for Driade (mirrors, cups and vases);
Widget (stool, wastepaper basket, laundry basket); Cleverline (coat hanger, garden
light, mouse mats); Authentics (ashtray, dish drainer)
SELECTED BIBLIOGRAPHY
2002 *Ed Annink Designer*, Rotterdam. His work has been published worldwide
AWARDS
1999 Design Plus Award, Frankfurt; **1997** Red Dot Award, Essen

APPLE DESIGN TEAM

PRACTICE
Apple Design Team, led by Jonathan Ive, is based in Cupertino, California and features
hand-picked talent from around the world
SELECTED PROJECTS
2002 iMac G4; Cinema Displays; **2001** Power Mac G4 Cube; Titanium PowerBook G4;
iBook; Titanium Power Mac G4; iPod MP3 player
SELECTED BIBLIOGRAPHY
2001 *Designing the 21st Century*, Cologne; *Business Week, Vogue, ID, The Face
Magazine*
SELECTED EXHIBITIONS
MoMA, New York, permanent collection
AWARDS
iMac, 'Best of Category', ID; Gold Award, British Design and Art Direction
'Object of the Year', *The Face*

MIDORI ARAKI

Born Fukuoka, Japan, 1966. Lives and works in Tokyo
EDUCATION
1987–90 Graphic Design Course, Tama Art University, Tokyo
PRACTICE
1999 to present Freelance; **1997–9** Editor in Chief *Gap*, Tokyo;
1991–6 Editor *Elle Décor*, Tokyo
SELECTED PROJECTS
2001 Urushi Steeple, stackable bowls, Abode; **2000** Stump Chair, E&Y; Junk Sweets,
cake sculpture art book, Aspect; **1999** Bottle Light, Abode; Church-less Chair, Abode;
Polar Bear Table, Abode
SELECTED BIBLIOGRAPHY
2002 *Axis*, no.95, Tokyo; *Casa Brutus*, no.23, Tokyo; *Nikei Woman*, January, Tokyo;
Jalouse, May, Paris; **2001** *Wallpaper**, July–August, London; *Interni* no.512, Milan;
Monument, no.42, Australia; *Mainichi Cyugakusei Shinbun*, 10 June, Tokyo; *Spur*,
September, Tokyo; *Elle Japon*, Tokyo; **2000** *Axis*, no.83, Tokyo; **1999** *Intramuros*,
no.87, Paris
SELECTED EXHIBITIONS
2001 'Junk Sweets', Graf Gallery, Osaka; 'Salone Off Site', Spazio Consolo, Milan;
'Japan Design Nouvelle Generation', VIA, Paris; 'News From Japan', P.S.1 Contemporary
Art Center, New York; **2000** Biennale International Design, Saint-Etienne;
1999 'Happening 1999–2000 Abode', Tokyo; 'Off Site', New York

MIKI ASTORI

Born Milan, 1965. Lives and works in Milan
EDUCATION
1991 Architecture degree, Polytechnic, Milan
PRACTICE
1995 to present Own interior design studio in Milan; **1993–4** Collaboration with
Philippe Starck Design Studio; **1992** Collaboration with Antonia Astori Architectural
Studio, Milan
SELECTED PROJECTS
2001 Thali, tables, Driade; **2000** Nantuk, bed, Driade; Hako, cabinets, Driade; On
Land, table, Driade; Bento, containers, Driade; **1999** Libeccio, hood, Driade; Twister,

hood, Driade; Bacello, sofa, Driade; Fucina, kitchen unit, Driade; **1998** Wok, kitchen tools, Driade; Olek, tables and benches, Driade; Galoppino, trolley, Driade; Alchemilla, chair, Driade; Mirto, side-table, Driade; Satori, lamp/shelf, Driade; **1997** Plug In Kit, kitchen accessories, Driade; Mumdesk, trays, Driade; Soundtrack, CD holder, Driade

SELECTED BIBLIOGRAPHY
2001 *Living Design*, no.15, Tokyo; **1999** *Supplemento di Antiquariato*, June, Milan; *Carnet*, no.5, Italy; **1998** *Giornale dell'arredamento*, 9 September, Milan; **1997** *Ideales Heim*, 6, June; **1996** *Abitare*, no.344, Milan

AWARDS
1999 Special Mention for 'Concorso young and design', Milan; **1997** Special Mention for 'Concorso young and design', Milan

ASYMPTOTE

Hani Rashid, Lise Anne Couture live and work in New York; Hani Rashid, born Cairo, 1958; Lise Anne Couture, born Montreal, 1959

EDUCATION
Hani Rashid and Lise Anne Couture: **1986** MA, Architecture, Yale University, New Haven; **1983** Bachelor of Architecture, Carleton University, Ottawa

PRACTICE
www.asymptote.net
1988 to present Hani Rashid + Lise Anne Couture / Principals of Asymptote, New York

SELECTED PROJECTS
2001 Flux 3.0 Motionscapes; **2000** New York Stock Exchange, 3D Trading Floor; Flux 2.0 representing the United States at the Venice Biennale; **1999** New York Stock Exchange Advanced Trading Floor Operations Center; Guggenheim Virtual Museum

SELECTED BIBLIOGRAPHY
2002 Asymptote, Hani Rashid and Lise Anne Couture, *Asymptote FLUX*, London; **2001** *Architecture*, July; **1999** *A+U, Architecture and Urbanism*, no.344 *Architectural Record*, no.12, New York

SELECTED EXHIBITIONS
2002 'Flux 3.0 Motionscapes', Documenta 11, Kassel; **2001** 'Flux 3.0 Motionscapes', ICA, Philadelphia; '010101', San Francisco Museum of Modern Art; **2000** 'Fluxspace 2.0', Venice Biennale; **1999** 'OffsideOn', Henry Urbach Gallery, New York

AWARDS
2001 National Design Awards finalist, New York; **1999** Emerging Voices Architecture League of New York; **1996** Annual Building Prize, Univers Theater, Aarhus

JAMES AUGER

Born Burton, 1970. Lives and works in London
EDUCATION
2001 Royal College of Art, London; **1995** Glasgow School of Art, Glasgow
PRACTICE
2002 Research associate, Media Lab Europe (MIT), Dublin; **2001-2** Freelance designer; also working on design proposals in collaboration with Jimmy Loizeau; **2001** Design intern at IDEO, San Francisco; **1995-9** Model-making and special effects for television and film, London and Munich; **1990** 3d finite element stress analysis technician for Rolls-Royce aero division, Derby

SELECTED PROJECTS
2001 Social Tele-presence, exploring the use of the Audio Tooth Implant in a social context, RCA; **2000-1** Audio Tooth Implant, RCA; **2000** Artificial Horizon, an aid for sea-sickness, RCA

SELECTED BIBLIOGRAPHY
2001 *Axis*, no.93, October, Tokyo; *Blueprint*, no.188, London; *Domus*, no.841, Milan; Dunne & Raby, *Design Noir*, London; James Auger, *Augmented Animals*, self-publication, June, London

SELECTED EXHIBITIONS
2002 'Future products', Science Museum, London; **2001** '6 Visions', MDSG, Tokyo;

'Global Tools', Vienna; 'Don't tempt me', ICA, touring exhibition; 'Graphic Architecture', RIBA, London

AWARDS
2001 Talking points, Science Museum, London; Design for our future selves, Helen Hamlyn Award, London

MASAYO AVE

Born Tokyo, 1962. Lives and works in Milan
EDUCATION
1990 MA Industrial Design, Domus Academy, Milan; **1983-7** Graduate degree in architecture from the engineering department, Hosei University, Tokyo
PRACTICE
www.macreation.org
2000 Established her own collection, MasayoAve creation, Milan/Tokyo; **1993-4** Stardust textile colour tendance book (as colour and image researcher), Milan-Como; **1992** Established her own studio, Ave Design Corporation, Milan/Tokyo; **1991** Design studio Dante Donegani, Milan; **1985-9** Ichiro Ebihara Architect and Associates, Tokyo

SELECTED PROJECTS
2001 Sahara, la mia Africa, wall carpet, MasayoAve creation; Corian Beauties, table décor, MasayoAve creation; Cosmos, set of containers, Colombostile; **2000** Genesi, table wall light, MasayoAve creation; Block and Cool, modular sofas and cushion, MasayoAve creation; Arca, Duet magazine rack, Duet tray; Triplet, felt baskets, tray, table mat, MasayoAve creation; **1999** Candle Bar, Authentics; Vis a Vis, bath mat, Authentics; **1998** Tip Tap, bottle keeper, Authentics; Ad Hook family, series of suction pads, Authentics

SELECTED BIBLIOGRAPHY
2001 *ARC design*, no.18, São Paulo; **2000** Jennifer Hudson, *International Design Yearbook*, London; *Interni*, no.513, Milan; *Rikuyoska*, June, Tokyo; *Gap*, November, Tokyo; *Four Rooms*, no.10, Moscow; *annabelle creation*, no.10, Zurich; Linda Hales, *Washington Post*, 27 May, New York; *Domus*, no.832, Milan; **1997** Philippe Starck, *International Design Yearbook*, London; **1996** Alessandro Mendini, *International Design Yearbook*, London; *Ideales Heim*, nos.7-8, Zurich; Jeremy Myerson, *The International Lighting Design*, London

SELECTED EXHIBITIONS
2002 'World Wide', Salon du Meuble, Paris; **2001** 'FILZ', Museum Bellerive, Zurich; 'MasayoAve creation', Salone del Mobile, Salone Satellite, Milan; 'Japan design nouvelle generation', VIA, Paris; **2000** 'MasayoAve creation', Biennale International Design, Saint-Etienne; **1999** 'Masayo Ave "Sound of material"', Chisato Tsumori, Tokyo; **1998** 'Labyrinths of light', Palazzo dell'Arengario, Milan

AWARDS
2000 ICFF 2000 Editor's Award, New York; **1996** Paris EMBALLAGE 96, packaging competition, Top 10, Paris, France; **1991** Napoleon Bullukian textile competition First Prize, Lyon; **1989** Honeymoon Miranda project – costume design competition Second Prize, Tokyo; **1987** Roof top design competition First Prize, Tokyo

SHIN + TOMOKO AZUMI

Shin Azumi, Tomoko Azumi live and work in London; Shin Azumi born Osaka, 1965; Tomoko Azumi born Hiroshima, 1966
EDUCATION
Shin Azumi: **1994** MA, Industrial Design, Royal College of Art, London; **1989** BA, Product Design, Kyoto City University of Art; Tomoko Azumi: **1995** MA, Furniture Design, Royal College of Art, London; **1989** BA, Environmental Design, Kyoto City University of Art
PRACTICE
www.azumi.co.uk
1995 Founded Azumi, London; Shin Azumi: **1989** Nec Design Centre, Toyko; Tomoko Azumi: **1990-2** Toda Construction Corporation, Japan; **1989-90** Kazuhiro Ishii Architect & Associates

SELECTED PROJECTS
2001 Wire Frame Chair and Stool, Meshman; Nw11, light, Mathmos; One Side, armchair E&Y; Strata, chaise longue, E&Y; hm30, sofa, Hitch Mylius; **2000** Lem, barstool, La Palma; Nyota, coat hanger, Habitat; Big Arm, armchair, Brühl & Sippold; Snowman Salt & Pepper Shaker, Authentics; **1999** H-1, H-2, directional speaker, Toa; **1998** St300, St301, coathanger, clock, shelf, La Palma

SELECTED BIBLIOGRAPHY
2001 Peter & Charlotte Fiell, *Designing the 21st Century*, Cologne; Penny Sparke, *Design Direction: Great Britain*, London; **2000** *Tectonic*, exhibition catalogue, London; **1999** Alexander Payne, *Ideas=book: Azumi*, London; *Creator's File for Living*, Tokyo; **1998** Peta Levi, *New British Design*, London; **1997** Sylvia Katz; *Studio Living*, London

SELECTED EXHIBITIONS
2002 Window Gallery, British Council, Prague; **2001** Design Now-London, Design Museum, London; Functionality, Un Cafe Garden, Tokyo; **2000** Tectonic, Crafts Council, London; Personal Space, British Council, New York; **1999** Azumi Solo Exhibition, Lighthouse, Glasgow; Stealing Beauty, ICA, London; **1998** Sinn & Forml, International Design Zentrum, Berlin; Powerhouse UK, Horse Guards Parade, London; **1997** Flexible Furniture, Crafts Council, London

AWARDS
2001 Furniture of The Year, by Fx International Design Awards, London; **2000** Product of The Year, by Fx International Design Awards, London; Good Design Award, by JIDPO, Tokyo; Good Design Award, by JIDPO, Tokyo; **1999** Peugeot Design Awards, London; Good Design Award, by JIDPO, Tokyo; Furniture Futures, by *Design Week* Magazine, London

BARBER OSGERBY

Edward Barber, Jay Osgerby live and work in London; Edward Barber, born Shrewsbury, 1969; Jay Osgerby, born Oxford, 1969
EDUCATION
1992-4 Royal College of Art, London
Edward Barber: **1988-91** MA, Architecture & Interior, Leeds Polytechnic, BA, Interior Design, Leeds, UK; Jay Osgerby: **1989-92** Ravensbourne College of Design and Communication, BA, Furniture and Related Products, London
PRACTICE
www.barberosgerby.com
1996 to present Barber Osgerby, London

SELECTED PROJECTS
2002 Stencilscreen, Cappellini; Aerial Table, Offecct; Choir stalls, Portsmouth Cathedral; Stools and salad spoons, Sotheby's project in support of South African communities; **2001** Shirt & Trouser Hangers, Levi Strauss; Concept for the interior of the Boeing 747-400 for the executive traveller, International airline; The Cross Bathmodule, concept bathroom, Dornbracht; Shell table, Cappellini; **2000** Hula Stool, Cappellini; Superlight, Cappellini; Home table, Isokon Plus; Loop bed, Cappellini; **1999** Loop bench, chaise longue, desk, Cappellini; Pilot table, Cappellini; **1997** Loop table, Cappellini and Isokon Plus; Flight stool, Isokon Plus

SELECTED BIBLIOGRAPHY
2002 Antonio G Gardoni, *Food by Design*, London; Ross Lovegrove, *International Design Yearbook*, London; *Architektur & Wohnen*, March, Germany; *Ideales Heim*, March, Zurich; *Frame*, no.25, Amsterdam; *FX Design*, January, London; **2001** Michele De Lucchi, *International Design Yearbook*, London; Paola Antonelli, *Workspheres: Design*, New York; *In Design*, no.7, Australia; *Frame*, no.22, Amsterdam; *Design Report*, September, Stuttgart; *Blueprint*, no.185, London; **2000** Jeremy Myerson, *International Interiors 7*, London; **1999** Sebastian Conran and Mark Bond, *Furniture*, London; Jasper Morrison, *International Design Yearbook*, London; **1998** Petra Levi, *New British Design 1998*, London

SELECTED EXHIBITIONS
2002 'Spot on Exhibition', Haute Definition, Paris; 'Au vestiaire, une histoire de cintres'

Musée des Arts Décoratifs, Paris; 'LOSA (London – South Africa)', Sotheby's, London; **2001** 'Home Sweet Home', The British Council, Stockholm; 'Great Expectations', Design Council, Britain, New York (and touring North America, Asia and the Pacific); 'The Evolution of British Design', Tempio di Adriano, Rome; **2000** 'Creative Britain – Stars of the Millennium', British European Design Group, Berlin, Milan, Rome; '100 pieces of modern design, Jasper Morrison curator', Museum für Angewandte Kunst, Cologne; 'Woody', Contemporary Applied Arts, London; **1998** 'Living Rooms. Installation design together with Jasper Morrison, Marc Newson, Michael Young and Michael Marriot', Atlantis Gallery, London

AWARDS

2001 Home Table, Judges' Prize, Victoria & Albert Classic Design Awards, London; Best Piece of Furniture, *FX/Blueprint* Design Awards, London; **1998** Best New Designer, ICFF, New York

SEBASTIAN BERGNE

Born Tehran, 1966. Lives and works in London and Bologna

EDUCATION

1988–90 MA, Industrial Design, Royal College of Art, London; **1985–8** BA, Industrial Design (Engineering), Central School of Art & Design, London; **1984–85** Central School of Art & Design, Foundation Course, London

PRACTICE

1990 to present Bergne: design for manufacture, London

SELECTED PROJECTS

2002 Spin, laundry drying stand, Magis; **2000** Slot, chair and side table, View; **1999** Dr Spock, lamp, Oluce; Kult, stainless steel and lead crystal breakfast range, WMF; One Ceramic, vase family, Driade; IXIX, table, Vitra; **1998** Candloop, candlestick, Wireworks; **1997** Lid, lamp, Oluce; Leg Over, stacking stool, Authentics; Sip, tasting spoon, Authentics; **1997** Torso, lamp, Protodesign

SELECTED BIBLIOGRAPHY

2001 Charlotte & Peter Fiell, *Designing the 21st Century*, Cologne; **1999** Catherine McDermott, *The Product Book*, Rotovision; Catherine McDermott, *C20 Design*, Carlton; Sebastian Conran & Mark Bond, *Contemporary Lighting*, Conran Octopus; *Abitare*, nos.398, 375, 372, 366, 357, 350, 340, Milan; *ARC design*, no.12, São Paulo; **1998** Peta Levi, *New British Design*, London; *Design Report*, no.5, Frankfurt; *ID*, January/February, New York; **1997** *Interni*, nos.515, 510, 474, Milan; **1997, 1999, 2000** *International Design Yearbook*, London

SELECTED EXHIBITIONS

2001 'Workspheres', MoMA, New York; **2000** 'Freeze Frame', Museum of Modern Art, Lisbon; **1999** 'Zuppa Inglese', A *Blueprint* and British Council touring exhibition and film, Milan; **1998** 'Street of young designers', solo presentation, Interieur 98 Bienal, Kortrijk, Belgium; **1997** 'Intramuros presents Sebastian Bergne', ICFF – special solo presentation, New York; **1996** 'Mutant Material in Contemporary Design', MoMA, New York

AWARDS

2001, 2000, 1999, 1998, 1993 Design Plus Award, Frankfurt; **1999, 1993** Red Dot Award, Essen; **1999** IF Design Award, Industrie Forum Design, Hanover; **1994** Gold Medal – German Designers Club, Germany

LENA BERGSTRÖM

Born Umea, Sweden, 1961. Lives and works in Stockholm

EDUCATION

1991 Design Studies and Apprenticeship (carpets), Japan; **1989** Studies of computer-aided textile production, Sophis System, Belgium; University of Art and Design, Helsinki; **1988, 1986** Workshop Ann Sutton, UK

PRACTICE

1994 to present Designer, Orrefors; **1988 to present** Freelance designer, Designers Eye (textiles)

SELECTED PROJECTS

2002 Planets, bowls, Pastill, bowl, Cyclop, vase, Flovers, vase, Orrefors; Wall, screen, Designers Eye; **2001** Paper Bag, Designers Eye; **2000** Squeeze Black, vase, Orrefors; Saab Car Blanket, Saab; Cutted Cross, room divider, Designers Eye; **1999** Cyrano, vase, Orrefors; **1998** Slitz, vase, Orrefors; Roll, quilted roll, Designers Eye.

SELECTED BIBLIOGRAPHY

2000 Susanne Helgesson, *Svenska Former*, Stockholm; **1998** Kerstin Wickman, Orrefors, *A Century of Swedish Glassmaking*, Stockholm

SELECTED EXHIBITIONS

2002 'New Works Limited Edition', Orrefors and Kosta Boda, Stockholm; 'Contemporary Glass and Furniture', Orrefors and Kosta Boda, Stockholm; **2001** 'The Bombay Sapphire Blue Room', 100% Design, London; Studiohaus Rosenthal, Nuremberg, Germany; **2000** 'Glas, Dagens konstnärer möter Historika', Museum of National Antiquities, Stockholm; 'Glas, Vetro', Italienska Kulturinstitutet, Stockholm; **1999** Scandinavian Gallery, São Paulo; 'Swedish Style in Tokyo', IDEE, Tokyo; 'Slitz', Nordiska Kristallmagasinet, Stockholm; **1998** Galleri Orrefors Kosta Boda, New York; 'Orrefors 100 Years', Nationalmuseum, Stockholm

AWARDS

2001 The Formidable Design Prize; **1996–2001, 1992–3**, Excellent Swedish Design

JEFFREY BERNETT

Born Champaign, Illinois, 1964. Lives and works in New York

EDUCATION

1993–4 Parnham College, Dorset, UK; **1988–9** University of Minnesota, Minneapolis; **1984–8** Northeastern University, Boston

PRACTICE

1995 Established Studio B, New York

SELECTED PROJECTS

2002 First class in-flight airline seating program, Northwest Airlines; Glow, floor lamp, Ligne Roset; 100% Design, desk, Ligne Roset; Quad, Bathroom sink, Boffi; **2001** Freelance, seating collection, Hidden; Academy, storage unit, Hidden; Glow, table light, Ligne Roset; Monza Soft, upholstered chair, Cappellini; Urban, folding table, Cappellini; Box, bathroom sink, Boffi; Landscape, chaise longue, B&B; **2000**; Proggetto Oggetto, object collection, Cappellini; Monza light, plexiglass chair, Cappellini; Tulip, chair, B&B; **1999** Monza, metal chair, Cappellini

SELECTED BIBLIOGRAPHY

2001 *Surface*, October, San Francisco; *Box*, September, Milan; *Intramuros*, September, Paris; *Interni*, April, Milan; *Vogue*, April, Hamburg; **2000** *International Design Yearbook*, London; *Ottagono*, August–September, Milan; *New York Times*, October, New York, NY; **1998** *Elle Décor*, December–January, New York

SELECTED EXHIBITIONS

1996 'Ideas for Production', ICFF, New York

AWARDS

2002 Young Designer of the Year, Cologne; **2001** Tokyo Designer's Block Best of Show, Covo, Tokyo; ICFF Editor's Award Best of Show, Dune, New York; **1996** ICFF Editor's Award Best of Show in category, New York

THOMAS BERNSTRAND

Born Stockholm, 1965. Lives and works in Stockholm

EDUCATION

1994–9 Konstfack, University of Arts, Crafts and Design, Stockholm; **1996** Danmarks Designskole, Industrial design, Copenhagen

PRACTICE

www.bernstrand.com

Bernstrand & Co, own practice, Stockholm

SELECTED PROJECTS

2001 Sluk, coat hanger, Bernstrand & Co; Boxer, armchair, Södebergs Möbler;

Olympic, bench, Nola Industrier; Flop Table; **1999** Flop Chair; Flop Bench, ikea; Wembley Sofa; Wembley Park, Nola Industrier; Tablelighttable; Sugar Ray, lamp; Do Swing, lamp, Kressels Kramers

SELECTED BIBLIOGRAPHY

2002 *Architektur & Wohnen*, no.3, Germany; *Metropolis*, May, USA; **2001** *Case da Abitare*, October, Milan; Paola Antonelli, *Workspheres*, New York; Michele De Lucchi, *International Design Yearbook*, London; **2000** *Interni*, no.505, Milan; *Vogue*, November, Germany

SELECTED EXHIBITIONS

2002 'Design X two', Instituto Europeo di Design, Milan; **2001** ICFF Furniture Fair, New York; 'Swedish style in Tokyo', Tokyo; 'Upplyst', Svensk Form, Stockholm; Salone Satellite, Salone del Mobile, Milan; 'Workspheres', MoMA, New York; '3D+', touring exhibition; **2001–2000** 'Do + Droog Design = do create', touring exhibition; 'Bernstrand & Co', AGATA, Stockholm; 'Generation X', Scandinavian House, touring exhibition; 'Design for Everybody', Object Galleries, touring exhibition; **1999** 'Forum För Form', Temporary Design Museum, Stockholm

AWARDS

2002 Konstnärsnämndens Workgrant, Sweden; **2000** Excellent Swedish Design, Sweden; Young & Design, Italy; **1999** Light of the Year, *Design* Magazine Sköna Hem, Sweden; **1998** Young Swedish Design Award, Sweden; Estrid Ericson Grant, Sweden; **1997–8** Gustav och Ida Unman Grant, Sweden

JURGEN BEY

Born Soest, The Netherlands, 1965. Lives and works in Rotterdam

EDUCATION

1984–9 Design Academy, Eindhoven; Department of the Environment, Eindhoven

PRACTICE

2000–2 Teaching at the Design Academy, Eindhoven, MA Industrial Design; **1999–2000** Teaching at the Design Academy, Eindhoven, Department Het Atelier; **1998–9** Teaching at the Design Academy, Eindhoven, Department Interactivity; **1998 to present** Jurgen Bey, Rotterdam; **1990–8**, Konings + Bey, Rotterdam

SELECTED PROJECTS

2000 do-add, chairs collection, Droog Design for Do (Kessels Kramer), Jurgen Bey; Healing, chair-toy, table-stove, cupboard-storage, Jurgen Bey; **1999** Broken family, tea set, Jurgen Bey; Lightshade-shade, lamps, Droog Design collection, Shade Lamps collection, Moooi; Kokon furniture, Droog Design collection, Jurgen Bey; Treetrunk-bench, Droog Design collection, Jurgen Bey; Gardening-bench, Droog Design collection, Jurgen Bey

SELECTED EXHIBITIONS

2001 'Home Made Holland', Crafts Council, London; 'Designprice Rotterdam 2001', Boymans van Beuningen Museum, Rotterdam; 'Jurgen Bey + Hella Jongerius', ICA, Philadelphia ; **2000** 'Design World 2000', Taideteollisuusmuseo, Museum of Arts and Design, Helsinki; **1999** 'A Grand Design', Victoria & Albert Museum, London; 'Couleur Locale', Oranienbaum, Germany

BIGERT + BERGSTRÖM

Mats Bigert, Lars Bergström live and work in Stockholm

EDUCATION

1985–90 Royal Academy of Fine Arts, Stockholm

PRACTICE

1990–2000 Artists, Stockholm

SELECTED PROJECTS

2001 Coldfront Glass and Hotfront Mug, Immaterial; **2000** Egg carpet, Asplund, Stockholm

SELECTED BIBLIOGRAPHY

2001 *Zoo*, October, London; *Bon*, no.4, Stockholm; **2000** *Flashart*, Summer, Milan; **1999** *Neue Bildende Kunst*, no.3, Berlin; *Metropolis*, New York; **1998** *Kunstforum*,

no.140, Germany; **1996** *Purple Prose*, no.11, Paris
SELECTED EXHIBITIONS
2002 'The Waiting Room', Zinc Gallery, Stockholm; **2001** 'Mega-Wave', Yokohama Triennale, Japan; **2000** 'Man and Space', Kwangju Biennale, South Korea; **1999** 'Peptalk', Galerie Barbara Thumm, Berlin; **1998** 'Climatic Chambers', Swedish pavilion, Expo 98, Lisbon, **1996** 'Interpol', Färgfabriken, Stockholm;

BLU DOT

Charles Lazor, Maurice Blanks, John Christakos live and work in Minneapolis and Los Angeles; Charles Lazor: born Morristown, New Jersey, 1964; Maurice Blanks: born Midland, Texas, 1965; John Christakos: born New York, 1964
EDUCATION
Charles Lazor: **1993** MA, Architecture, Yale School of Architecture, New Haven, Connecticut; **1988–9** School of Visual Arts, New York; **1987** BA, Williams College, Williamstown, Massachusetts; Maurice Blanks: **1991** MA, Architecture, University of Illinois at Chicago; **1987** BA, Williams College, Williamstown, Massachusetts; John Christakos: **1991–3** MA, Northwestern University Kellogg School of Management, Evanston, Illinois; **1983–7** BA, Studio Art and Economics, Williams College, Williamstown, Massachusetts
PRACTICE
www.bludot.com
1996 to present Blu Dot, Minneapolis; Charles Lazor: **1995–6** Architect, Roth & Moore Architects, New Haven, Connecticut; **1994–5** Architect, Gray Organschi Architects, New Haven, Connecticut; **1989** Architecture Intern – Michelle Franck Architecture, New York; Maurice Blanks: **2001 to present** Television design show host – Style Network, Los Angeles; **1996** Co-founder, Blu Dot Design, Minneapolis; **1996–2002**, Architect; Maurice Blanks Architects, Chicago; **1993–6** Architect, Hartshorne & Plunkard, Chicago; **1991** Architect, Tigerman McCurry, Chicago; John Christakos: **1996** Co-founder, Blu Dot Design, Minneapolis; **1993–6** Core Group, Marketing Consultant, Minneapolis; **1988–91** Bain & Company, Management Consultant, Boston
SELECTED PROJECTS
1996 to present Blu Dot product line, affordable furniture using modern materials and methods, Blu Dot; **2001** Design submission to Herman Miller home office brief, Blu Dot; **2000** Furniture for Target, Blu Dot
SELECTED BIBLIOGRAPHY
2002 *Skin: Surface and Substance in Contemporary Design*, Smithsonian; *ID*, August; **2001** *Workspheres*, New York; **2000** *New American Contemporary Furniture*, Rizzoli, Milan; *Metropolis*, October; numerous articles in different magazines and newspapers: *Newsweek, Domus, Abitare, House & Garden, 10x10, The New York Times, San Francisco Examiner, Washington Post, Chicago Tribune, The Wall Street Journal*
SELECTED EXHIBITIONS
2002 'Mood River', Wexner Art Center, Columbus, Ohio; 'Skin: Surface and Substance in Contemporary Design', Cooper Hewitt Design Museum, New York; **2001** 'New Blue': selected work by graduates of Yale School of Architecture; 'Here by Design', Goldstein Museum of Design, University of Minnesota at St Paul; 'Workspheres', MoMA, New York
AWARDS
2001, 2000 Chicago Atheneum Good Design Award; **1998** Best Collection, Accent on Design, New York Gift Show

TORD BOONTJE

Born Enschede, The Netherlands, 1968. Lives and works in London
EDUCATION
1992–4 MA, Industrial Design, Royal College of Art, London; **1986–91** BA, Design Academy, Eindhoven
PRACTICE
2000–2 Tutor, Royal College of Art, Design Products, London;
1994 to present Tord Boontje studio, London

SELECTED PROJECTS
2002 Inflorescence, computer generated floral drawings and out put; Graland Light, Habitat; Chandelier, Swarovski; **2001** Wednesday, collection of products and furniture, Tord Boontje; Product design for Alexander McQueen; Collection of tableware, based on the Wednesday pieces, Dartington Crystal; Glass products, tranSglass; **1998–9** Rough-and-Ready, furniture collection, Tord Boontje
SELECTED BIBLIOGRAPHY
2001 Boris Groys, *Home, Homeless*, Malmö; Emma Dexter, *Century City, Art and Culture in the Modern Metropolis*, London; **1999** Claire Catterall, *Stealing Beauty*, London; Nick Barley, *Critical Voices in New British Design*, London; **1998** Martina Margets, *No Picnic*, London
SELECTED EXHIBITIONS
2002 'Milan in a Van', Victoria & Albert Museum, London; 'Crystal Palace', Swarovski Milan; **2001** 'The Unexpected', Sotheby's, New York; 'Global Tools', Kunstlerhaus, Vienna; 'Wednesday', Applied Arts Agency, London and The British Council Window Gallery, Prague; 'Home, Homeless', Boo1, Malmö; 'Century City, Art and Culture in the Modern Metropolis', Tate Modern, London; 'Dead', The Roundhouse, London; 'Industry of One', Crafts Council, London; **2000** 'Salviati meets London', Vessel, London; **1999** 'Stealing Beauty, British Design Now', ICA, London; 'Lost and Found: Critical Voices in New British Design', British Council, touring exhibition; 'Designers Block', London; **1998** '100% Design', London; 'No Picnic', Crafts Council, London

FABIO BORTOLANI

Born Spilamberto, Modena, Italy, 1957. Lives and works in Spilamberto, Modena, Italy
EDUCATION
1977–85 Università degli studi di Firenze Facoltà di Architettura, Florence
PRACTICE
1983–5 Architect Cesare Leonardi Studio, Modena
SELECTED PROJECTS
2001 Professional, combs, Crena, mirror with towel holder, Linea, bath accessories, Flipper, bath (tub), Interrasse, tiles, Colours, soap dispenser, Virtuallydesign.com; **2000** Comic, bath accessories, Authentics; Flower Vase, Oil and vinegar set, Tray, Cappellini; Bottle Rack, Seccose; Staccami, plate, Pandora; Bucatini **2000**, Agape; **1999** Face, mirror, Triangle, candle, Authentics; Salt and pepper, Cappellini; **1998** Ball point, memo pin with magnet, Tube, toothbrush, Authentics; Bucatini, bath accessories, Multiplo, paper roll holder, Gerba, liquid soap holder, Agape; Opus, small table, La Palma; **1997** Note book, note book with handle, Authentics
SELECTED BIBLIOGRAPHY
2001 *Abitare*, no.411, November, Milan; **2000** *Aperto Vetro*, Venice; *Abitare*, April, Milan; **1999** *Design Lexikon Italy*, Cologne; **1998** *Around Photography*, no.4, Paris/Milan; **1997** *Abitare*, no.366, Milan; *Domus*, no.799, Milan
SELECTED EXHIBITIONS
2001 'Virtuallydesign.com', Galleria Belvedere, Milan; **2000** 'Clandestino', Opos, Milan; 'Aperto vetro', Museo Correr, Venice; 'Usa e getta', Inter-Nos, Milan; **1998** 'Around Photography', Fondazione Jaqueline Vodoz Bruno Danese, Milan
AWARDS
2001 Selezione Compasso d'oro, Milan; **1997** Design Plus, Frankfurt

RONAN + ERWAN BOUROULLEC

Ronan and Erwan Bouroullec live and work in Paris; Ronan Bouroullec: born Quimper, France, 1971; Erwan Bouroullec: born Quimper, France, 1976
EDUCATION
Ronan Bouroullec: **1997** Ecole nationale des arts décoratifs, Paris; Erwan Bouroullec: **1995–96** Ecole nationale d'arts de Cergy, France; **1994–95** Ecole des beaux arts de Quimper, France
PRACTICE
Ronan Bouroullec: Furniture designer, Paris; Architect of interior, Paris; Design tutor at

Ecole cantonale d'art de Lausanne, Switzerland; Erwan Bouroullec: Furniture designer, Paris; Architect of interior, Paris
SELECTED PROJECTS
2001 Square Vase, Cabane, Hut, Parasol Lumineux, Grape Carpet, Honda Vase, Galerie Kréo; **2000** Hole Chair, Lit Clos, bed, Cappellini; **1999** Objets Lumineux, 3 lights, Spring Chair, Cappellini; Safe Rest, daybed, Domeau et Pérès
SELECTED BIBLIOGRAPHY
2002 *The World of Interiors*, February, London; **2001** Laurence Salmon, *Ronan et Erwan Bouroullec*, MDSGallery, Tokyo; Charlotte and Peter Fiell, *Designing the 21st Century*, Cologne; *The Guardian*, 5 April, London; *Axis*, no.90, Tokyo; *Domus*, no.840, Milan; **2000** Mel Byars, *50 Beds, Innovations In Design and Materials*, New York; **1999** Jasper Morrison, *International Design Yearbook*, London; Brigitte Fitoussi, *Bouroullec à Vallauris*, Nice; *Bouroullec-ECAL 1-1*, Lausanne; *Intramuros*, no.82, Paris; **1998** *Le Monde*, 13 November, Paris
SELECTED EXHIBITIONS
2002 'Ronan and Erwan Bouroullec', Design Museum, London; **2001** 'Ronan and Erwan Bouroullec', Miyake Design Studio Gallery, Tokyo; 'Ronan and Erwan Bouroullec', Galerie Kréo, Paris; **1999** 'A grand design', Victoria & Albert Museum, London; **1997** 'Vases combinatoires', Galerie Néotu, Paris; 'Made in France', Musée national d'art moderne Centre Georges Pompidou, Paris
AWARDS
2001 Compasso d'oro, ADI; **1999** New Designer Award, International Contemporary Furniture Fair, New York; **1998** Grand Prix de la Critique de la Presse Internationale, Salon du Meuble de Paris; Grand Prix du Design de la Ville de Paris

BOYM PARTNERS

Constantin Boym, Laurene Leon Boym live and work in New York; Constantin Boym, born Moscow, 1955; Laurene Leon Boym, born New York, 1964
EDUCATION
Constantin Boym: **1988**, Becomes US registered Architect Undergraduate, Moscow Architectural Institute, Moscow; **1984–85** MA, Domus Academy, Milan; Laurene Leon Boym: **1993** MA, Pratt Institute, Brooklyn; **1985** BA, School of Visual Arts, New York
PRACTICE
www.boym.com
1994 Laurene Leon Boym joins Boym Design Studio as partner, New York;
1986 Constantin Boym establishes Boym Design Studio, New York
SELECTED PROJECTS
2002 So Droog, Dated Collection, objects, Droog Design; Ceramics, Moooi; **2001–2** Untitled, children's floor lighting collection, Flos; The Menagerie, children's rugs and pillows, Handy; **2001** Grid, stationery, writing instruments and neckware collection, Acme Studios, Glowrug, rug collection, Handy; Snail Mailbox, Urbanmailbox, Pure Design; webchair, Ultra Light, lounge chair, Vitra; **2000** Stationery Collection, desktop accessories, MoMA; Less is More, shelving system, Pure Design
SELECTED BIBLIOGRAPHY
2002 Peter Hall, *Curious Boym*, December, New York: Princeton Architectural Press; **2001** *Dwell*, no.4, San Francisco; **2000** Albrecht, Lupton, Holt, *Design Culture Now: National Design Triennal*, New York: Princeton Architectural Press; *ID*, no.5, USA; **1999** David Redhead, *Products of Our Time*, Basel; *Wallpaper**, no.22, London; **1997** *Domus*, no.799, Milan
SELECTED EXHIBITIONS
2002 'US Design 1975–2000', The Denver Art Museum, Colorado; **2000** 'National Design Triennal', Cooper Hewitt, National Design Museum, New York; 'The American Century, Part 2', Whitney Museum of American Art, New York; **1996** 'Missing Monuments', VI International Architectural Biennale, Venice
AWARDS
2000 *ID* Annual Design Award, Best of Category, New York; **1999** The George Nelson Award from *Interiors* Magazine, New York; **1997** *ID* Annual Design Award, New York

TODD BRACHER

Born New York, 1974. Lives and works in Milan

EDUCATION

1998–2000 Danmarks Designskole, Copenhagen; 1992–6 Pratt Institute, Brooklyn

PRACTICE

/go.to/toddbracher

2001-2 Senior Design Consultant for Studio Giorgio Marianelli, Milan; 1999–2001 Consultant for Thomas Damgård Arkitekten, Copenhagen; 1996–00 Consultant for Bosman Collegiate Bookstores, New York; 1996–99 Consultant for Quattrocchio, Manufacturer, Alessandria; 1996–9 Consultant for Studio DDL, D'Pas, D'Urbino, Lomazzi, Milan; 1994–9 Consultant for Zero US Corp, New York; 1994–2000 Consultant for TZ Design, New York

SELECTED PROJECTS

2002 Freud, sofa, Zanotta; Eyelash, Scribble, Compliment, rugs, Urban Outfitters; Bowl Table; Bent Lamp; Floppy, hanging lampshade, Urban Outfitters; Sun Lamp, To22; 2001 Bloom, café seating, IDEE; The Chairing Project, experimental dining project; Open Privacy, café/dining table, Zanotta; 1998 Penumbra, lamp

SELECTED BIBLIOGRAPHY

2001 ID, no.47, New York; Michele De Lucchi, International Design Yearbook, London; Frame, July–August, Amsterdam; Wallpaper*, no.37, London; Intramuros, no.93, Paris; *Surface no.27, San Francisco; 2000 Elle Décor, no.9, Milan; Wallpaper*, no.29, London; Zoo, no.6, London; 1999 Wohnen & Design, no.9, Vienna; Abitare, no.384, Milan; 1998 New York Times, September, New York

SELECTED EXHIBITIONS

2002 'Continuous Connection', Felissimo & UNESCO Headquarters, New York, Paris; 2000, 2001 Tokyo's Designers Block, Tokyo; 2001 Stockholm Furniture Fair, Stockholm; 2000 Salone del Mobile, Milan; 1999 Scandinavian Furniture Fair, Copenhagen; 1998, 1997 ICFF, New York

AWARDS

2002 UNESCO Design 21 International Award, New York, Paris; 2000, 2001 IDEE Design Award, Tokyo; 2000 Promosedia Design Award, Udine; 2001, 2000 ID Design Award, New York

HUMBERTO + FERNANDO CAMPANA

Humberto and Fernando Campana live and work in São Paulo; Humberto Campana: born Rio Claro, São Paulo, 1953; Fernando Campana: born Brotas, São Paulo, 1961

EDUCATION

Fernando Campana: 1979–84 BA, Architecture, Faculty of Decorative Arts, São Paulo; Humberto Campana: 1972–7 BA, Law, University of São Paulo

PRACTICE

1999–2000 Teachers at MUBE (Brazilian Museum of Sculpture), São Paulo; 1998 Teachers of Industrial Design at the Fundação Armando Alvares Penteado, São Paulo

SELECTED PROJECTS

2002 Project of chairs and tables, L'est Parisienne bar, Paris; 2001 Collections of jewellery, H Stern; Anemona Chair and Cardboard Furniture, Edra; Bambu Metal Chair, Hidden; Batuque Vase, Cappellini; Collection of pens, ACME; 2000 Bambu Lamp, Plastic Lamp, Tattoo Table, Fontana Arte; Inflating Table, MoMA, New York; Eva Desk organizer, MoMA, New York; 1999 Cone Chair, Zig Zag Benches, Edra; 1998 Cotton String Chairs, Edra; 1997 Estela Lamp, Oluce

SELECTED BIBLIOGRAPHY

2002 Jenette Hahn, At Your Space: Decorating Your Home and Office, New York; 2001 Designing the 21st Century, Cologne; Paola Antonelli, WORKSPHERES, New York; 2000 Kirk Varnedoe, Paola Antonelli, Joshua Siegel, Modern Contemporary Art at MoMA since 1980, New York; Ingo Maurer, International Design Yearbook, London; Sarah Nichols, Aluminium by Design, Carnegie Museum of Art; Design 1950–2000, Musée des Arts Decoratifs de Montreal; Wallpaper*, March, London; Nuevo Estilo, no.264, Spain; Metropolis, January, USA; 1999 Mel Byars, 50 Products Innovations in Design and Materials, New York; 1998 Cristina Morozzi, Oggetti risorti: quando i rifiuti prendono forma, Genova; Elle Decoration, May–June, Germany; Interiors, May, USA; Interni, July-August, Milan; Intramuros, February-March, Paris; 1997 Philippe Starck, International Design Yearbook, London; Mel Byars, 50 Chairs Innovations in Design and Materials, New York; Mel Byars, 50 Tables Innovations in Design and Materials, New York

SELECTED EXHIBITIONS

2001 'On Paper, New Paper Art', Crafts Council Gallery, London; 'Blow Up', Vitra Design Museum, Berlin; 'Abitare il Tempo, Beyond European Design, projects from around the world', Verona; 2000 'Entre o Design e a Arte', Museum of Modern Art, São Paulo; 1999 'Numeros', Brazilian Museum of Sculpture, São Paulo; 'Retrospective Campana', Casa França Brasil, Rio de Janeiro; 'Matérias, Materiais', Bahia Museum of Modern Art, Salvador, Brazil; 1998 Campana, Ingo Maurer', MoMA, New York

AWARDS

2001 Special Prize, Museu da Casa Brasileira, São Paulo; 1999 George Nelson Design Award, USA; 1997 First Prize, Residential Furniture category, Museu da Casa Brasileira, São Paulo; 1996 First Prize, Design category, XXI Salão de Arte de Ribeirão Preto (cardboard side chair), Brazil

CLAESSON KOIVISTO RUNE

Claesson Koivisto Rune live and work in Stockholm; Mårten Claesson, born Lidingö, Sweden, 1970; Eero Koivisto, born Karlstad, Sweden, 1958; Ola Rune, born Lycksele, Sweden, 1963

EDUCATION

Claesson Koivisto Rune: 1994 Konstfack, University College of Arts, Crafts and Design, Stockholm; Claesson, Koivisto: 1992 Parsons School of Design, Department of Architecture; Department of Product Design, New York; Koivisto: 1993–5 University of Art & Design, Architecture & Furniture Design; Design Leadership, Helsinki; Rune: 1992 The Royal Academy of Art, Interior and Furniture Design, Copenhagen

PRACTICE

1995 Founded Claesson Koivisto Rune, Stockholm

SELECTED PROJECTS

2001 Pebbles, sofa, Criss Cross, coffee table, Cappellini; Scoop, easy chair, sofa, daybed and coffee table, Living Divani; Cornflake, chairs and tables, Swoop, swivel chair, Orbit, seating system, Offecct; Omni, armchair, Swedese; 2000 Arc, table, Asplund; Berlin, table and floor lamps, Ateljé Lyktan; Mood, bathtub, Boffi; Fruit Basket, Cappellini; Bend, chair and table, Swedese; Vibe, vases, David Design; 1999 Berliner, sofas, armchair and tables, Swedese; Hockney, sofa system, David Design; 1998 Bowie, lounge chair, footrest and table, Camp, wall clock, David Design; Golden Section, carpet, Asplund; Tinto, low chair and tables, Offecct

SELECTED BIBLIOGRAPHY

2001 Terence Riley, Piero Lissoni, Alberto Campo Baeza, Claesson Koivisto Rune, Barcelona; FX, no.85, April, London; 2000 Susanne Helgeson, Svenska former, Stockholm; Azure, September–October, Toronto; Architecture & Urbanism, no.359, Tokyo; 1999 Jasper Morrison, International Design Yearbook, London; Bernd Polster, Design Lexicon, Scandinavia, Bonn; Uta Abendroth, Karin Beate Phillips, Christian Pixis, World Design, 1 Century 400 Designers, 1000 Objects, London; Frame, no.8, Amsterdam; 1998 Interni, no.482, Milan

SELECTED EXHIBITIONS

2002 'Totem', New York; 2001 'Swedish Style', Tokyo; Strictly Swedish, Washington, DC; 1999–2002 'Angles Suédois', touring exhibition; 1990–2001 More than 60 exhibitions in Sweden and abroad

AWARDS

2000, 1999, 1998, 1996, Excellent Swedish Design, the annual Swedish design award; 2000 The Golden Chair, the Association of Swedish Interior Architects' (SIR) award for the best interior project, Sweden; The Future of Wood In Our Homes, The jury's Special Award for a housing project 'QBKL' for the B001 building fair in Malmö

CURRO CLARET

Born Barcelona, 1968. Lives and works in Barcelona

EDUCATION

1993–5 Industrial Design, Central Saint Martins College of Art & Design, London; 1987–92 Industrial Design, Escola Superior de Disseny Elisava, Barcelona

PRACTICE

1997 to present Freelance designer, Barcelona; Teaching in different schools of design and architecture: IDEP, LAI, Elisava, EINA, Ramon Llull, La Salle, Barcelona; 1993–7 HTT Arquitectes, Barcelona; 1989 Jordi Busquets industrial design, Barcelona; 1988 B&R Graphic Design, Barcelona

SELECTED PROJECTS

2001 Recycled porexpan lighting, lamps; Recycled pen, Pro Carton; 2000 Orange mesh fruitbowl; 1999 Raining water pot, to collect rainwater; Chestnuts paper container for eating chestnuts in the street; Cigarette pack, redesigning a pack of cigarettes in order to accommodate butts when smokers are outside; Cleaning shoe box, Luis Montesinos

SELECTED BIBLIOGRAPHY

2001 Ottagono, no.144; Ramon Prat, Barcelona +, Barcelona; 1999 Joan Reera Devall, Joan Vinyets, Ecodisseny I Ecoproductes, Barcelona; Abitare, no.389, Milan; Domus, no.820, Milan; Experimenta, no.27; 1998 Mel Byars, 50 Products; Diseño Interior, no.69; 1997 Abitare, no.365, Milan; 1996 Domus, no.787, Milan

SELECTED EXHIBITIONS

2002 'Limites Borrosos 1:1', Ministerio de Fomento, Madrid; 2001 'Felissimo', New York; 'Clandestino', OPOS, Milan; 1999 'Italia-Europa: Scenari del giovane design', Abitare il Tempo, Verona; 1998 Biennale International Design, Saint-Etienne

AWARDS

2001 Accessit, Concurso del mueble Manacor, Spain; 2000 Second prize, Nuevos envases, a, embalajes y aplicaciones Pro-Carton, Barcelona; Mentien, International Furniture Festival, Valencia; 1996 Second Prize, Premio Internacional Jóvenes Diseñadores Diseño Interior, Madrid

CLAUDIO COLUCCI

Born Locarno, Switzerland, 1965. Lives and works in Paris and Tokyo

EDUCATION

1991 Scholarship exchange, Kingston Polytechnic; 1988–1992 Ecole Nationale Superieur de Création Industrielle, Paris; 1984–8 Ecole des Arts Décoratifs, Geneva

PRACTICE

www.colucci-design.com

1998 Assistant to Philippe Starck for the project 7/eleven, 'Tomorrow will be less', Tokyo; 1997–8 Designer for IDEE, Tokyo; 1995 Designer at Thomson Multimedia under the leadership of Philippe Starck, Paris; 1994 Co-founder of the group Radi Designers; 1993 Designer at Pascal Mourgue, Paris; 1992 Work experience at Niegel Coates Architect, London; 1992 Work experience at Ron Arad, London

SELECTED PROJECTS

2002 Sumo, ton table/shelf, Claudio Colucci Design Duo+Solo, Sambu, Sambu, Sambu; 2001 Tento-Mushi, tile carpet, Tarkett Sommer. Waves, cabinet, Time & Style; Wok, Suzi-wan; Glass Jug, Vine jug, Sentou; 2000 Fisholino, toilet brush, Marna; Duo+Solo, sofa bed, Habitat; 1997, Dada, Mini Dada, IDEE; Dolce Vita, chair, Joli Cœur, chair, IDEE

SELECTED BIBLIOGRAPHY

2001 Interni, July-August, Milan; L'œil, November, Paris; 2000 Creators file, Tokyo; 2001 London Marie Claire Maison, December, Paris; 1999 Radi Designers, réalité fabriquée, Fondation Cartier pour l'Art contemporain; Creators file 1, Tokyo; Frame, December, Amsterdam; Anne Bony, Les années 90, France; 1998 Mel Byars, 50 Products, Roto Vision; 1996 Les Villages Fonction et Fiction, Paris: Les Industries Françaises de l'ameublements; Arlette Barre-Despond, Dictionnaire International des Arts Appliqués et du Design, Paris

SELECTED EXHIBITIONS

2001 'Supreme love by Claudio Colucci', Off Gallery, Tokyo; **2000** 'Claudio Colucci', Sentou Gallery, Paris; **1999** 'Fantasizing', Cartier Foundation, Paris; **1998**, 'Radi', Emmanuel Perrotin Gallery, Paris; **1997** 'Claudio Colucci', IDEE Gallery, Tokyo

AWARDS

2000 Salon du meuble de Paris, Paris; **1999** *Architektur & Wohnen* magazine, Hamburg; **1999** AFAA Paris; **1995** 7th Osaka International Design competition

MATALI CRASSET

Born Chalons-en-Champagne, France, 1965. Lives and works in Paris

EDUCATION

1991 Les Ateliers, Ecole Nationale Supérieure de Création Industrielle, Paris

PRACTICE

2002 Creation of the society Matali Crasset Productions, Paris; **1998** Creation of own studio, Paris; **1994–7** Responsible for Tim Thom design centre de Thomson Multimédia, Paris; **1993–7** Agence Philippe Starck; **1992** Studio Denis Santachiara, Milan

SELECTED PROJECTS

2002 Update, bath projects, Dornbracht; Glass collection, Cristal Saint-Louis; **2001** Ierace, ceiling lamp, Artemide; **2000** Digestion, furniture collection with manufactured objects, Edra; **1997** Toothbrush cup, Authentics; Quand Jim monte à Paris, hospitality column; Parici, alarm radio-clock, Lexon Design Concept/Spirix; **1996** The empathic chair, Sandberg Institute, Amsterdam

SELECTED BIBLIOGRAPHY

2001 *IM/Identity*, no.4, Amsterdam; *Atrium*, no.5, Zürich; *Du* no.38, Brussels; **2000** *Designnet*, no.37, Seul; *H O M E* no.9, Berlin; *Architektur & Wohnen*, no.3, Hamburg; *Elle*, no.3, Hamburg; *Libération*, no.5805, Paris; **1998** *Interni*, no.482, Milan; **1997** *Domus*, no.796, Milan; *L'architecture d'aujourd'hui*, no.310, Paris

SELECTED EXHIBITIONS

2002 'First restrospective exhibition', Musée du design et des arts appliqués, Lausanne; **2001** 'Polarisation' Espace Paul Bert, Nontron, France; **2000** 'Flat-flat', Biennale Interieur, Kortrijk, Belgium; **1999** 'Looking for chlorophyll', Authentics Gallery-Shop, Berlin; **1998** 'Matali in Colette', Colette, Paris

AWARDS

2000 Etoile de l'Observeur du design, Paris; **1999** Grand Prix de la Presse Internationale de la Critique du Meuble Contemporain, Paris; **1996** Grand Prix du design de la Ville de Paris, Paris; **1994** Sandberg Instituut & Gerrit Rietveld Academie, 'Young designer grant', Amsterdam

D TEC

Dainese Technology Center constituted of technicians, engineers, modellists, designers, headed by Lino Dainese, Molvena, Italy

PRACTICE

www.dainese.com
1993 Established D-TEC

SELECTED PROJECTS

2001–2 D-Air, electronic airbag for motorcyclist, Dainese; **1999** D-Axial Boots, Dainese; **1998** Pro Com, electronic leathers equipped with sensors that measure biomedical data of the human, Dainese; **1997** Safety Jacket, Dainese, **1993** Full Pro Gloves, innovative gloves equipped with rigid Kevlar carbon, Dainese

SELECTED BIBLIOGRAPHY

2001 *Moto Revue*, no.3476, France; *Motorrad*, no.16, Germany; **2000** *Il Sole-24 Ore*, December, Italy; **1999** *Class*, no.5, Italy; **1997** *VTT Magazine*, no.89, France; *Motor Week*, February, Belgium; *Motor Rijder*, no.12, Belgium; *Option Moto*, no.18, France; **1996** Terence Conran, *Terence Conran on Design*, UK; *Intramuros*, no.67, Paris

SELECTED EXHIBITIONS

2001 'Sensible Objects', Paris; 'Mostra del XIX Premio Compasso d'Oro ADI', Palazzo dell'Arte, Milan; 'La città del design', Triennale di Milano; **2000** 'Körper, Hüllen,

---

Oberflächen', Museum für Kunst und Gewerbe, Hamburg; **1996–9** 'Design and Identity, Aspects of European Design', touring exhibition; 'Photographier l'Objet', Musée des Arts Décoratifs, Paris

AWARDS

2001 XIX Premio Compasso d'Oro, ADI, Milan

LORENZO DAMIANI

Born Lissone, Milan, 1972. Lives and works in Lissone, Milan

EDUCATION

1998 Architecture Degree, Polytechnic, Milan

SELECTED PROJECTS

2001 Mirror Table; Shelf-Salver, shelf-tray; Filocontinuo, lamp; Flex, CD stand, Montina International; W Doppio, tray box, Bianca, lamp; **1999** Tavolante, table; **1996** Packlight; **1998** Scomposto, panel, Cappellini

SELECTED BIBLIOGRAPHY

2001 *Interior & Design Magazine*, no.6/53, Mosca; *Interni*, no.510, Milan; Stefano Maffei, *Opos 1991–2000*, Milan; *Metropolis*, July, New York; *Abitare*, no.411, Milan; Michele De Lucchi, *International Design Yearbook*, London; **2000** *Domus*, no.822, Milan; *Abitare*, no.396, Milan; *Interni*, no.506, Milan; **1999** *Axis*, no.78, Tokyo; Giuliana Gramigna, Paola Biondi, *Il Design in Italia*, Milan; **1998** *Abitare*, no.375, Milan; **1997** *Abitare*, no.365, Milan

SELECTED EXHIBITIONS

2002 'Good Design Show 2001', Chicago Athenaeum; **2001** 'XIX Compasso D'Oro', Triennale, Milan; **2001, 2002** 'Salone Satellite', Salone del Mobile, Milan; **2000** 'Italia', Biennale International Design, Saint-Etienne; **1999** 'Pluri-Existenzen', Designer Saturday, Dusseldorf; 'Biennale dei Giovani Artisti dell'Europa e del Mediterraneo', Ex mattatoio, Rome; **1998** 'XVIII Compasso d'Oro', Palazzo della Triennale, Milan; 'Intorno alla Fotografia: 37 Cornici per 37 Fotografi', Associazione Jacqueline Vodoz e Bruno Danese, Milan; 'Design for Europe', Interieur, Kortrijk; 'Ambulanti', Nuovo Spazio Opos, Milan; 'XVIII Compasso D'Oro', Triennale, Milan; **1996, 1997, 1999, 2000, 2001** 'Under 35', Spazio Opos, Milan

AWARDS

2001 Young & Design Competition: First prize, Milan; Chicago Athenaeum – Museum of Architecture and Design: Good Design Award; **2000** Koizumi Lighting Design Competition: Special Prize, Tokyo; **1998** XVIII Premio Compasso d'Oro ADI: Progetto Giovane, Milan; **1996** Concorso Osram: Verso una Nuova Ecologia della Luce: First Prize, Milan

WILLIE G DAVIDSON

Willie G Davidson, Head of V-Rod Design Team composed of Louie Netz, Director, Styling; Ray Drea, Manager, Styling; Kirk Rasmussen, Industrial Designer/Stylist; Frank Savage, Industrial Designer/Stylist. A team of engineers was responsible for the engineering.
Willie G Davidson, born USA, 1933. Lives and works in Milwaukee, Wisconsin

EDUCATION

1957 Art Center College of Design, Pasadena, California

PRACTICE

1963 to present Harley-Davidson Motor Co, Milwaukee, Wisconsin
1957–63 Brooks Stevens Associates, Milwaukee, Wisconsin

SELECTED EXHIBITIONS

1997–2002 'The Art of the Motorcycle', Guggenheim Museum, New York, Bilbao, Las Vegas

DUNNE + RABY

Anthony Dunne, Fiona Raby live and work in London;
Anthony Dunne, born London, 1964; Fiona Raby, born Singapore, 1963

EDUCATION

Anthony Dunne: **1997** PhD Computer Related Design, Royal College of Art, London;

1988 MA, Industrial Design, Royal College of Art, London; **1986** BA, Industrial Design, National College of Art & Design, Dublin; Fiona Raby: **1995** MPhil, Computer Related Design, Royal College of Art, London; **1988** MA, Architecture, RIBA part II, Royal College of Art, London; **1986** BA, Architecture, RIBA part I, Birmingham School of Architecture

PRACTICE

Anthony Dunne: **1999 to present** Senior Research Fellow, Computer Related Design, Royal College of Art, London; **1998 to present** Part-time Senior Tutor, Design Products, Royal College of Art, London; **1994–1999** Research Fellow, Computer Related Design, Royal College of Art, London; **1992 to present** Partner, Dunne & Raby, London; **1989–90** Designer, Sony Design Centre, Tokyo; Fiona Raby: **1999 to present** Senior Research Fellow, Computer Related Design, Royal College of Art, London; **1995** Unit Tutor, Architecture and Interior Design, Royal College of Art, London; **1995** Research Fellow, Computer Related Design, Royal College of Art, London; **1992 to present** Partner, Dunne & Raby, London; **1991–3** Independent Designer, working freelance with Pierre d'Avoine Architects, London; **1989–91** Architectural Designer – Kei'ichi Irie Architects and Associates, Tokyo,

SELECTED PROJECTS

2000–1 Placebo Project, collection of furniture, RCA; M-Set, location-based services for 3G mobile phones, Philips Research Labs; Park Interactives, adult garden furniture, Academie de France, Villa Medici, Rome; **1998–2000** Flirt, location-based WAP services, European Union; **1998–9** Presence, investigating uses of electronic media for elderly people, European Union; **1995–9** Weeds, Aliens & Other Stories, psychological furniture for the home and garden (with Michael Anastassiades), British Council

SELECTED BIBLIOGRAPHY

2001 Anthony Dunne and Fiona Raby, *Design Noir*, London; *Weekend FT*, May, London; *Independent on Sunday*, February, London; *Design News*, no.256, Tokyo; Jonathan Hill, *Architecture – the subject is matter*, London; *The Sunday Times*, March, Ireland; **2000** Fiona Raby, *Project #26765 – FLIRT*, London; *Domus*, no.825, Milan; *Independent on Sunday*, April; **1999** Anthony Dunne, *Hertzian Tales*, London; **1997** *Blueprint*, October, London

SELECTED EXHIBITIONS

2001 'Placebo Project', Victoria & Albert Museum, London; 'Great Expectations', Grand Central Station, New York; 'Global Tools Spin Off', Klaus Engelhorn22, Vienna; **1999–2001** 'Lost and Found', British Council touring exhibition; **1999** 'Stealing Beauty', Institute of Contemporary Art, London; **1998** 'Weeds, Aliens & Other Stories', British Council, Prague

AWARDS

2001 Designers in Residence, Victoria & Albert Museum, London; **2000** Nominated for the Perrier-Jouët Selfridges Design Prize, London; Honorary Professorship, Central Saint Martins College of Art & Design, London (Anthony Dunne)

EL ULTIMO GRITO

Roberto Feo, Rosario Hurtado live and work in London; Roberto Feo, born London, 1964; Rosario Hurtado, born Madrid, 1966

EDUCATION

Roberto Feo: **1997** Royal College of Art, London; **1995** London Guildhall University; Rosario Hurtado: **1998** Kingston University, London; **1995** London Guildhall University

PRACTICE

1997 to present studio El Ultimo Grito, London; Roberto Feo: **1999 to present** Tutor at Design Products, Royal College of Art, London; Rosario Hurtado: **1999 to present** Tutor at Design Department, Goldsmith University, London

SELECTED PROJECTS

2002 The New Collection, chair and sofa, tables and lighting, Touch; **2001** Ego Club, disco for one person, Bloomberg; Us Open, paper game; Funktion object, modular unit, Anura Living; SE 15, lamp, Mathmos; What goes down must come up, laundry basket, Hidden; Marilyn I can see your knickers, chairs, Hidden; Bathroom Collection, plastic accessories for bathrooms, Orden en Casa; **2000** Lavazza Coffee Corner, ortable cafeteria, Lavazza; The Evolution will not be Televised, T-shirt, Trico ternational; **1999** La Lu, lamp, EUG; Mind the gap, table, Punt Mobles

ELECTED BIBLIOGRAPHY

001 Charlotte and Peter Fiell, *Designing the 21st Century*, Cologne; *On Diseño*, .221, Barcelona; David Redhead, *Industry of One*, London; *Independent on Sunday*, ne, London; *Frame*, July–August, Amsterdam; **2000** Guy Beggs and Kate Holmes, *6M ix Moments*, London; Virginio Briatore, *Restyling*, Rome; *ID*, January– February, USA; 999 *Lost and Found, Critical Voices in New British Design*, London; Claire Catterall, *tealing Beauty, British Design Now*, London; *BIG* Magazine, Spain, New York; 998 *Domus*, no.803, Milan; *Design News*, no.224, Japan

ELECTED EXHIBITIONS

001 'El Ultimo Grito: 2001 una odisea en el espacio', Elba Benitez Galeria, Madrid; l Ultimo Grito: Me, You, Us, Them', Bloomberg, London; 'Home Sweet Home', touring xhibition, British Council; 'Great Expectations', New York Festival at Grand Central tation, 2000 'Six Moments', Design Museum, London; **1999** 'Stealing Beauty', stitute of Contemporary Art, London

WARDS

999 Peugeot Design Award for Furniture, London; **1999, 1998, 1997** *Blueprint*/100% esign Award, London

CAMILA FIX
orn Brazil, 1969. Lives and works in São Paulo

DUCATION

988–92 BA, Architecture, Mackenzie University, São Paulo

PRACTICE

995 to present Fix Design, enterprise for creation and development of object and urniture designs, São Paulo; **1994** Docent at the museum: Graphic Design and Art useum Studies, São Paulo; **1993–4** Museu de Arte Contemporânea of São Paulo niversity, co-ordination in the Design Department

ELECTED PROJECTS

002 Orla Table, Tigre; **2001** Rio Line, Fix Design; Macao Tray, Fix Design; **2000–1** ipa Furniture, Fix Design; **2000** Rótula Table, Fix Design; Magnético Bench, Fix Design; slo Tray, Fix Design; Meta Bench Azurra Móveis; **1999** Ripa; Fix Design; **1998** Fanny all Ranger, Fix Design; Pino Magazine Corner, Fix Design; **1997** Poli Jug, Polimold

ELECTED BIBLIOGRAPHY

001 *Arc Design*, no.18, São Paulo; *Casa & Jardim*, no.559, August, São Paulo; entras, no.4, Vilnius; **2000** *Azimuts*, nos.18–19, Saint-Étienne, **1999** *Casa Claudia*, o.10, São Paulo

ELECTED EXHIBITIONS

002 'Singular e Plural, 50 anos de design', Instituto Tomie Ohtake, São Paulo; 001 'Expo Universo Brasil, Itáli', Triennale, Milan; **2000** 'Brasil Faz Design', Salone el Mobile, Milan; 'Biennale Internationale Design, Saint-Étienne'; '500 Anos Design, bjeto Brasil', Pinacoteca do Estado de São Paulo; **1998** 'Brazilina Design', Forum dustri, Hannover

WARDS

997 Museo da Casa Brasileira, São Paulo

JOZEPH FORAKIS
orn New York, 1962. Lives and works in Milan and New York

DUCATION

992 Domus Academy, Milan; **1984–5** Rhode Island School of Design, Providence

PRACTICE

993 to present Jozeph Forakis Design Direction, Milan/New York; **1999–2002** otorola Inc, Milan; **1993–7** Domus Academy Research Centre, Milan

ELECTED PROJECTS

002 Ballo and Vela, Objects for home and home/office in collaboration with Jim annon-Tan, Elysha Huntington, Georgiana VanWalsum, Magis; v.70, mobile phone,

---

in collaboration with Iulius Lucaci and Vitor Medeiros; **2000–01** Future Wearability Concepts, research for a new generation of wearable communication experiences and products, in collaboration with Marco Susani, Lorna Ross, Matthias Richter, Robert Gelick, Roberto Tagliabue, Motorola; **2000** Talk, watch-phone, in collaboration with Elysha Huntington, Deoksan Lee, Roberto Tagliabue, Swatch; **1998** Irony Scuba 200, watch and packaging design in collaboration with Deoksan Lee, Swatch; **1996** Logitech Cordless Mouseman Pro, cordless computer mouse

SELECTED BIBLIOGRAPHY

2001 *Les Vif/L'Express*, Winter 2001–02, Brussels; *FT Creative Business*, 9 January; *Wallpaper**, no.37, London; *Knaack Weekend*, 10 October, Brussel; **2000** *Abitare Daily*, no.394, Milan; **1998** *Binyan Vedivr Magazine*, Israel; **1997** Mel Byers, *50 Lights-Innovations in Design and Materials*, UK

SELECTED EXHIBITIONS

2001 'Workspheres', MoMA, New York; **1999** 'Dopo Domus', Calvin Klein Showroom, Milan; **1996** 'Mutant Materials in Contemporary Design', MoMA, New York; 'Design for New Future Aged Society', Tokyo Gas Showroom, Tokyo

AWARDS

1997 IF Design Award, Hanover

FRANCÈS + POLICAR
Elsa Francès, Jean-Michel Policar live and work in Paris;
Elsa Francès, born Paris, 1966; Jean-Michel Policar, born Versailles, 1970

EDUCATION

Elsa Francès: **1991** Diplôme: Ecole Nationale Supérieur de Création Industrielle, Les Ateliers Saint Sabin, Paris; **1985** Diplôme: Beaux Arts de Versailles, Paris; Jean-Michel Policar: **1993** Diplome National Supérieur d'Arts Appliqués, Ecole Supérieur des Arts Appliqués et de Métieres d'Art, Paris; **1990** B.T.S. esthétique industrielle, Ecole Supérieur des Arts Appliqués et de Métieres d'Art, Paris;

PRACTICE

1998 to present Francès + Policar, Paris; Elsa Francès **2001** Worldwide strategic design manager In Tim Thom, Worldwide Design organization of Thomson Multimedia, Boulogne, France; **1993** to present Engaged by Philippe Starck to be member of the Tim Thom (Thomson Multimedia design team), Boulogne, France; **1992** Associated designers, Barcelona; **1991–3** Guliver Design, Paris; Jean-Michel Policar: **2001** World-wide Colours and Materials design manager, Tim Thom, Worldwide Design organization of Thomson Multimedia, Boulogne, France; **1993** to present Engaged by Philippe Starck to be member of the Tim Thom, Thomson Multimedia design team, Paris

SELECTED PROJECTS

2002 La Conic, lamp, So Watt, lamp, Ligne Roset; **2001** On air; Videosender, transmitter, receiver, Thomson; **1999** De-Lumineux, table-lamp, Ligne Roset; Smiling Orange, portable TV, 36 cm, **1998** Radio Porcelaine, Thomson

SELECTED BIBLIOGRAPHY

2002 *Marie-Claire Maison*, April, Paris; *Intramuros*, no.100, Paris; **2001** Lionel Blaisse, François Gaillard, *Temps denses*, Paris; Mel Byars, *On Off*, New York; *IT Magazine*, Paris; **2000** Christine Collin, *Design et Utopie* (interview E Francès only), Les Villages, Dijon; **1999** *Interior View*, Paris; Laurence Picot, *Portraits* (E Francès only), Paris

SELECTED EXHIBITIONS

2002, 2001, 1998 'VIA', Salone del Mobile, Milan; 'VIA', International Furniture Fair of Paris; **2000** 'Les sapins de Noël des Créateurs', Centre Georges Pompidou, Paris

AWARDS

1998 'Prix special du jury de la presse internationale de la critique de meuble contemporain', Paris

THORSTEN FRANCK
Born Hamburg, 1970. Lives and works in Munich

EDUCATION

1998–2000 MA, Design Products, Royal College of Art, London;

1993–8 Fachhochschule for product, Hildesheim, Germany

PRACTICE

2001 to present Thorsten Franck Studio for Product Design, Munich; **2000–1** Thorsten Franck Studio for Product Design, London; **1998–2000** Working for different design studios, London; **1990–3** Self-employed doing furniture one-offs, Hamburg; **1991–2** Furniture one-offs in the workshop from E Brüggemann, Winsen, Germany

SELECTED PROJECTS

2001 Folding Furniture, Habitat; Tisch und Stuhl, bent wood chairs and table, Thonet; Ein Tisch, table; Build in a Minute, furniture, Möbelbau Kaether&Weise; **2000** Domestic Accessories, functions off the wall, Moormann; Ply Wood, furniture, self production; **1999** Chair Family, Race; **1998** Office for the Future, office furniture, Gesika; **1997** Folding, folding furniture, self production

SELECTED BIBLIOGRAPHY

2002 *Art*, no.3, Hamburg; **2001**, The poetry of the functional, Chemnitz; **2000** *Wallpaper**, no.31, London; **1996** *z.b. eiche*, Hamburg

SELECTED EXHIBITIONS

2002 'Talents', Ambiente, Frankfurt; 'Salone satellite', Salone del Mobile, Milan; 'Red Dot Award', Essen; **2001** '100% design', London; **1998** 'Talents '98', 50. Internationale Handweksmesse, Munich; 'Designale', Heim+Handwerk, Munich; **1996** 'z.b. eiche', Museum für Kunst und Gewerbe, Hamburg

AWARDS

2002 Red Dot Award, Essen; **2000** Marianne-Brandt-Contest, Chemnitz, Germany; **1998** 'Office for the Future', Second Prize, Gesika, Hildesheim, Germany; First Prize 'Alles Klappt', folding table for the new collection, Munich

JOAN GASPAR
Born Barcelona 1966. Lives and works in Barcelona

EDUCATION

1987–92 Escuela De Artes Y Oficios (Llotja), Barcelona

SELECTED PROJECTS

2001 Flash, wall and ceiling lamp, Olivia, pendant lamp, Marset; **1999** Sydney, table; Atlas, spot light, Marset; **1998** Atila, task lamp, Marset; **1997** TV, wall and ceiling lamp, Marset; **1996** Sac, wall lamp, Marset; **1994** Bloc, shelf lamp, Blux

SELECTED BIBLIOGRAPHY

2001 *International Design Yearbook*, London; **1999** Ramón Ubeda, *Diseño Interior*, Barcelona; **1998** *International Design Yearbook*, London

AWARDS

2000 Delta De Plata Adi Fad, Barcelona; **1999** Concurso Feria Del Mueble De Valencia, First Prize, Valencia; **1992** Concurso Diseño Del Mueble, Comunidad Autónoma Castilla La Mancha, First Prize, Toledo

JOHANNA GRAWUNDER
Born San Diego, 1961. Lives and works in Milan and San Francisco

EDUCATION

1983–4 California Polytechnic State University, Florence;
1979–83 California Polytechnic State University, San Luis Obispo, USA

PRACTICE

2001 to present Studio Johanna Grawunder, San Francisco; **1995** to present Studio Johanna Grawunder, Milan; **1985–2001** Architect and Partner with Studio Sottsass Associati, Milan; **1984–5** Architect in Studio Toraldo di Francia, Florence

SELECTED PROJECTS

2002 Jazz and Generation, collections of cut crystal tableware, J G Durand; Pillow Talk, lamps and furniture, Design Gallery, Milan; Grid To Blob, with Karim Rashid, ceramics, Galleria Giustini; **2001** Ultralight, Furniture Co, New York; Poetic Expressions in Glass, with Ingo Mauer, Ted Muehling, handblown glass pieces, Salviati; **1999** Fractals, collection of lights, Post Design Gallery, Milan; Memes, 35 unique glass pieces, Gallery Mourmans; **1997** Lighting Management, collection of architectural light elements,

Post Design Gallery, Milan
SELECTED BIBLIOGRAPHY
2001 *Chicago Tribune*, May; H O M E, no.4, Berlin; *Beaux Arts*, no.8147, Paris; **2000** *Johanna Grawunder*, Beijing; *Abitare*, no.398, Milan; **1999** Barbara Radice, *Johanna Grawunder and Modernity*, Milan; **1996** *Modo*, no.170, Milan
SELECTED EXHIBITIONS
2001 'Lowrider', Post Design Gallery, Milan, Italy; 'Ultralight', Furniture Co, New York; **2000** 'Aperto Vetro', Museo Copper, Venice; **1999** 'Fractals', Post Design Gallery, Milan; 'Transparent Technology', Museo d'Arte Contemporanea, Prato, Italy; **1997** 'Lighting Management', Post Design Gallery, Milan; 'Fase Alternative', Abitare Il Tempo, Verona

KONSTANTIN GRCIC
Born Munich, 1965. Lives and works in Munich
EDUCATION
1988–90 Royal College of Art, London
1985–7 The John Makepeace School for Craftsmen in Wood, Parnham, England;
PRACTICE
www.konstantin-grcic.com
1991 to present Konstantin Grcic Industrial Design, Munich
SELECTED PROJECTS
2001 Chaos, chair, Classicon; Sky Cab, conceptual study for a vertical car, Drive-In; **2000** Chef Macrowave, conceptual study for a microwave oven, Whirlpool; Magnum and Hertz, spot light systems, Flos; Scolaro, stool/table, Montina **1999** Six Public Clocks, installation in a public square in Canary Wharf, London; Relations 1, glasses, iittala; Belle & Bon, egg-cup and spoon, Nymphenburg; **1998** Mayday, portable lamp, Flos; Boxer, lamp, Flos; Kehrschaufel, dust pan and brush, Authentics; **1997** H2O, bucket, Techno, tray, Authentics; Mania, chest of drawers, Classicon
SELECTED BIBLIOGRAPHY
2001 *Designing the 21st Century*, Cologne; *Le Design, BeauxArts Magazine*, special issue, May, Paris; *Workspheres*, MoMA, New York; *Mut Zur Lücke/Daring the Gap*, Stuttgart-London; *Axis*, no.1, Japan; **2000** *Goethe-Grcic*, Milan; *Interieur 2000*, Ludion, Ghent-Amsterdam; *Frame*, September–October, Amsterdam; **1999** *Domus*, no.820, Milan
SELECTED EXHIBITIONS
2001 'Vous Aimez Les Objets...?' Dunkirk, France; **2000** 'Guest of Honour' Interieur Biennal 2000, Kortrijk, Belgium; 4:3 'Fifty Years of Italian and German Design', Kunst-und Ausstellungshalle der Bundesrepublik Deutschland, Bonn
AWARDS
2001 XIX. Premio Compasso d'Oro, ADI FAD, Milan; **2000** Guest of Honour, Interieur Biennial, Kortrijk, Belgium; **1999** Modernism Award For Young Designers, Brooklyn Museum of Art; **1997** Young Designer of The Year Award, nominated by Achille Castiglioni, *Architektur & Wohnen*, Hamburg,

MARTÍ GUIXÉ
Born Barcelona, 1964. Lives and works in Barcelona
EDUCATION
1986–7 Industrial design studies, Polytechnic, Milan
1983–5 Interior design studies in Elisava, Barcelona
PRACTICE
www.guixe.com
Present, Working as Techno-Gastrosof, Tapaist and Designer for Camper, Authentics, Alessi, Droog Design, Chupa Chups, Vitra and others, Barcelona and Berlin;
1994–6 Design Consultant of KIDP, Seoul
SELECTED PROJECTS
2001 Beach towel, Moeve; Concept book for office pets, Vitra; Concept for a long drink, Kessel Kramer; **2000** Spamt, Kids' toolkit, H2O; H2O chair, H2O; Food Pack concept, El Sindicato Agency; DIM (Die Imaginäre Manufaktur), project; Bag Collection, Authentics; Do Create, project, Droog Design; **1999** Autoband, toy, H2O;

Oranienbaum, project, Droog Design; Apron collection, Authentics;
1998 Flamp, Phosphor lamp, H2o
SELECTED BIBLIOGRAPHY
2001 Paola Antonelli, *Workspheres*, New York; *Monument*, no.39, Australia; *New York Times*, 9 February, New York; *Frame*, no.20, Amsterdam; *Experimenta*, no.34, Madrid; *Domus*, no.839, Milan; *Interior and Design*, no.7, Moscow; *Axis*, no.91, Tokyo; *Azure*, July–August, Toronto; **2000** *El Pais*, 1 February; *Domus*, no. 828, Milan; *Independent on Sunday*, 9 July, London; *Aximuts*, no.17, Saint-Etienne; *Intramuros*, no.90, Paris; **1999** *Coleur Locale*, Rotterdam; Claire Catteral, *Food: Design and Culture*, Glasgow; *Intramuros*, no.83, Paris; *Liberation*, no.6, October, France; **1998** *El Mundo*, no.21.6, Madrid; **1997** *Domus*, no.799, Milan; *El Pais*, 3 March, Madrid
SELECTED EXHIBITIONS
2001 'Martí Guixé retrospective', La Fondation pour l'Architecture, Brussels; 'Do Droog Design in the AA', London; 'Workspheres', MoMA, New York; **2000** 'H2o Exhibition', H2o Gallery, Barcelona; 'Martí Guixé by Ingo Maurer', Krizia, Milan; 'Urban Post-It Exhibition', Gallery SSK, Berlin; 'Do for Droog Design', touring show; 'Presentation of the football tape', Biennale International Design, Saint-Etienne; **1999** 'Autoband presentation', H2o Gallery, Barcelona; 'Spamt Factory by Transversal 10', La Virreina, Barcelona; 'Futur Compost', La Virreina, Barcelona; 'Coleur Locale', Droog Design for Oranienbaum, touring show; **1998** 'Fish Futures Exhibition', H2o Gallery, Barcelona; **1997** 'Techno-Tapas SPAMT Bar', La Sala Vinçon, Barcelona
AWARDS
1999 Ciutat de Barcelona Design Prize, Barcelona; **1985** INFAD medal of interior design, Barcelona

ALFREDO HÄBERLI
Born Buenos Aires, 1964. Lives and works in Zurich
EDUCATION
1986–91 Degree in Industrial Design at the Hohere Schule für Gestaltung, Zurich
PRACTICE
2000 Established Alfredo Häberli Design Development Atelier;
1989 Practical experience at Siemens, New York; Product Development, Roericht, Ulm
SELECTED PROJECTS
2001 Solitaire, low chair with table, Offecct; LegnoLetto, modular wooden bed, Alias; Doppio Appendiabiti, double wardrobe, Cappellini; Ueli, paper and wastebasket, Trunz Collection; **2000** Move Away, moveable stool, Cappellini; Origo, table service, Rorstrand; Ginger, barstool; **1999** Wing, daybed, sofa and table, Edra; Zurigo, armchair and sofa, Zanotta; Mirabelle, flowerpot, Eternit; **1998** Sirio, table, Zanotta; CD Rack, CD holder, Authentics; Matabre, bed and sofa and moveable table, VIA; S 175, bookshelf, S 1062, table, Thonet; Currently involved in numerous projects including assignments for Absolut Vodka, Alias, Asplund, Cappellini, Hackmann, Littala, Leitner, Luceplan, Magis, Offecct, Rorstrand, Samplicitas, Trunz, Zanotta
SELECTED BIBLIOGRAPHY
2001 *Heim*, April; *Abitare*, no.405, Milan; *Frame*, no.23, Amsterdam; **2000** *Abitare*, no.394, Milan; *Frame*, no.17, Amsterdam; **1999** *Frame*, no.6, Amsterdam; *Items*, no.3; **1998** *Abitare*, no.375, Milan; *Domus*, no.809, Milan; **1997** *Design Report*, May, Germany; *Intramuros*, no.71, Paris; *Interni*, no.473, Milan; *Abitare*, no.366, Milan
SELECTED EXHIBITIONS
2002 'Sketching my own Landscape', Asplund, Stockholm; **2001** 'Skin & Soul', 3rd Design and Architecture Symposium and Exhibition, Jyväskylä, Finland; **2000** 'Hothouse', Biennale Interieur, Kortijk, Belgium; **1999** 'Experimenta', Essential De Luxe, Lisbon; **1998** 'Street of Young Designer', Interieur 98, Kortijk, Belgium
AWARDS
Since 1992 Several international prizes in Europe and America; **1998** Grant Carte Blanche, Industries Françaises de l'Ameublement, VIA, Paris; **1994** Achievement Prize of the Hochschule fur Gestaltung, Zurich

THOMAS HEATHERWICK
Born UK, 1970. Lives and works in London
EDUCATION
1992–4 MA, Royal College of Art, London; **1989–92** BA, Three Dimensional Design, Manchester Polytechnic; **1987–9** Kingsway Princeton College, BTEC National Diploma in Art and Design, London
PRACTICE
1994 to present Design Director, Thomas Heatherwick Studio, London
SELECTED PROJECTS
2002 Blue Carpet, design of new urban public square, Newcastle City Council; A13 Roundabouts, competition-winning design for two roundabouts; **2001** Mailbox Circuit, street furniture design, Birmingham; Rolling Bridge, Berkshire; **2000** Plank, stool, Keen; **1999** Identity Crisis, design exhibition, Glasgow; **1998** Materials House, design exhibition, Science Museum, London; **1997** Autumn Intrusion, sculptural installation, Harvey Nichols, London
SELECTED BIBLIOGRAPHY
2002 *Independent*, January, UK; *Sunday Times*, April, UK **2001** *Architect's Journal*, no.28, UK; *Domus*, no.833, Milan; *Design Week*, April, UK; **2000** *Frame*, no.19, Amsterdam; *Blueprint*, no.178, London; *Evening Standard*, October, London; *Sunday Times*, October, UK; *The Times*, October, UK; *Independent*, September, UK
SELECTED EXHIBITIONS
2000 'Tectonic' (retrospective), Crafts Council, London; **1999** 'Royal Academy Summer Exhibition', London; 'Blue Carpet', Laing Art Gallery, Newcastle
AWARDS
2001 *Design Week* Best Temporary Exhibition, UK; **1998** British Design & Art Direction Gold, UK; **1995** Crafts Council Setting-up Award, UK; **1994** Edward Marshall Prize

SAM HECHT
Born London, 1969. Lives and works in London
EDUCATION
1993 Royal College of Art, London; **1991** Central Saint Martins College of Art & Design, London; **1987** Hornsey School of Art, London
PRACTICE
2002 to present Sam Hecht Studio, London; **1999** Head of Industrial Design IDEO London, London; **1996** Design partner with Naoto Fukasawa, IDEO Japan, Tokyo **1994** Designer, IDEO San Francisco, San Francisco; **1993** Design Partner, Studio, Tel-Aviv; **1992** Designer, David Chipperfield, London
SELECTED PROJECTS
2002 Prada Staff Products, Prada; **2001** Fabrications, a set of products that involve intelligent fabric, Eleksen; Airbus A380, Economy Class Cabin Interior, Airbus Industrie; Remote Controls, Netgem; Bellagio Kitchen appliances, LG; **1999** Domestic cooking tools, Matsushita; Tile collection, a set of objects for the bathroom, INAX; Printables, colour printers, Epson; **1997** Whitebox, computer, NEC
SELECTED BIBLIOGRAPHY
2002 Diane Strong, *International Architecture*, Australia; Kim Colin, *Instructions*, London; **2001** *Le Design, Beaux Arts*, Paris; Liz Brown, *zoo*, London; Paola Antonelli, *Workspheres*, London; Kim Colin, *Fabrications*, London; Kim Colin, *Working Lunch*, Strafor; **2000** *Matsushita Design Monograph*, Tokyo; Jeremy Myerson, *International Design Book*, London; Sam Hecht, *Under a Fiver*, London; Jeremy Myerson, *The Creative Office*, London; **1998** Sam Hecht, *Printables*, Tokyo
SELECTED EXHIBITIONS
2002 'Skin: Surface, Substance and Design', Cooper-Hewitt, New York; **2001** 'Workspheres', MoMA, New York; **2000** 'Young Emerging Architecture', Danish Design Centre, Copenhagen; 'Under a Fiver', Design Museum, London; **1999** 'Identity Crisis', Glasgow Lighthouse
AWARDS
2002 IF International Forum design, Hanover; **2001** Museum of Modern Art Permanent

ollection, New York; **2000** AR+D Young Emerging Architecture, Copenhagen, enmark; **2000** D&AD, London, England

RICHARD HUTTEN

orn Zwollerkerspel, The Netherlands, 1967. Lives and works in Rotterdam

DUCATION

986–91 Design Academy, Eindhoven

PRACTICE

www.richardhutten.com

991 to present Designer at Studio Richard Hutten, Rotterdam

ELECTED PROJECTS

001 Back-up, ratan chair, Sputnik; Coattrunk, coat hanger, Pure-design; **2000** What appened?, mouth-blown Murano glass, Covo; One of a Kind, furniture, Hidden; Sexy-alaxy, chair E&Y; **1999** Table-sofa, Sawaya & Moroni; **1998** The Switch, lamp, E&Y; ings, SMAK; **1996** 3 minus 1 desk, Richard Hutten Studio Collection

ELECTED BIBLIOGRAPHY

002 Ed van Hinte, *Richard Hutten – Taking Form, Making Form*, Rotterdam; **1996** enny Ramakers, *Droog Design, Spirit of the Nineties*, Rotterdam; Ida Van Zijl, *Droog Design 1993–1996*, Utrecht: Centraal Museum; *Design Report*, Germany; *New York Times*, USA; *Domus*, Milan; *Interni*, Milan; *Blueprint*, London; *ID Magazine*; *Surface*; *Wallpaper**, London

ELECTED EXHIBITIONS

998 'Do Normal', San Francisco Museum of Modern Art; 'No Sign of Design', &Y Gallery, Tokyo and Osaka; **1996** 'Threshold, Contemporary Design from he Netherlands', MoMA, New York

AWARDS

000 Ko Liang le award co/ Droog Design, The Netherlands; **1997** Red Dot, Essen **996**, **1992** Dutch furniture award, The Netherlands

HISAE IGARASHI

orn Tokyo 1964. Lives and works in Tokyo

DUCATION

985 Graduated from Kuwasawa Institute of Design, Tokyo

PRACTICE

993 Established Igarashi Design Studio, Tokyo; **1991** Freelance, Tokyo; **986–91** Kuramata Design Office, Tokyo

ELECTED PROJECTS

001 Sunny Side Up, chair, Ishimaru Co; **2000** Massage Chair, Yudai Tachikawa; **998** Ecco Furniture development project in Miyakonojyo Miyazaki, Hashizume; **999** Pure+Pure, display shelves, Pure; **1997** Astral M1, mirror, Matsunaga Co; Modern Times, Igarashi Design Studio; Tango Chest and Cabinet, Horizumi Co

ELECTED BIBLIOGRAPHY

001 *Japan Design To The New Generation*, Tokyo; **2000** Shu Haginara, Yudai achikawa, *Creator's File for Living*, vol.2, October, Tokyo; **1999** Shu Haginara, udai Tachikawa, *Creator's File for Living*, vol.1, October, Tokyo,

ELECTED EXHIBITIONS

001 'Japan Design, nouvelle génération', VIA, Paris; **2001** Skill and Soul, Jyvaskyla, inland; **1999** 'Miyazaki Ecco Furniture IFFT 99', Tokyo Big Sight, Tokyo; **1998** Miyazaki Ecco Furniture IFFT 98', Tokyo Big Sight, Tokyo; **1997** 'Shizuoka Dynamics', xis Gallery, Tokyo

AWARDS

994 25 Design Prize, Gold Prize, Salt de Paris exhibition, Tokyo

HELLA JONGERIUS

orn De Meern, The Netherlands, 1963. Lives and works in Rotterdam

EDUCATION

988–93 Design Academy, Eindhoven

PRACTICE

www.jongeriuslab.com

2000 Established the company JongeriusLab

SELECTED PROJECTS

2002 Chandelier, Swarovski; Silk Project, Hermes; **2001** Delfts Blue, Gemeente-museum, The Hague; My Soft Office, MoMA, New York; **2000** Groove and Long Neck Bottles, JongeriusLab; Giant Prince, stoneware and cotton, JongeriusLab; Embroidered Tablecloth, JongeriusLab; **1999** Kasese Chair, Cappellini; Felt Stool, Cappellini, JongeriusLab; **1998** B-service, Koninklijke Tichelaar Makkum; **1997** Porcelain Stool, Rosenthal, Droog Design

SELECTED BIBLIOGRAPHY

2001 *New York Times*, March, New York; *Case da Abitare*, April, Milan; *Design Report*, June, Germany; **2000** *View on Colour*; **1999** *Harper's Bazaar*, New York; **1998** *Spirit of the Nineties, Droog Design*, Rotterdam; **1998**, **1996**, **1995** *International Design Yearbook*, London

SELECTED EXHIBITIONS

2001 'Delft in Detail', Gemeentemuseum, The Hague; 'Workspheres', MoMA, New York; **2000** 'Pseudofamilies', Institute of Contemporary Art, Philadelphia; 'Design World 2000', Museum of Art and Design, Helsinki; **1999** 'Oranienbaum', exhibition with Droog Design, Milan; **1997** '5 years Droog Design', Centraal Museum, Utrecht; **1993–2002** participation in several international exhibitions of Droog Design

AWARDS

2000 AVA Ceramic Award, The Netherlands;

1999 World Technology Award for Design, World Technology Network, London;

1997 Incentive Award Industrial Design, Amsterdam Foundation of Art

TOSHIKO KAWAGUCHI

Born Niigata Prefecture, Japan, 1956. Lives and works in Tokyo

EDUCATION

1982 Graduated School of Nihon University, Tokyo

PRACTICE

1993 Established Archistudio Kawaguchi Co, Tokyo; **1989** Established Archistudio OZONE, Tokyo; **1987–8** Worked for Hans Hollein, Vienna; **1983–6** Worked at Tohata Architects & Associates, qualification First Degree Architect, Tokyo

SELECTED PROJECTS

2001 Washi fittings and partition, Adachi Shiki Kogyo; **2000** Paulownia Chest, cabinet, Kiriya Tanaka; **1999** Paulownia Chair, Kiriya Tanaka; **1998** Paulownia Furniture, beyond the tradition, Kiriya Tanaka, Kuriyama Bussan, BC Koubou; Bamboo Light, Kingiri Kogei; **1996** Easy Chair, Marco, Minerva; **1994** Bridal Furniture, YOS

SELECTED BIBLIOGRAPHY

2000 *Jt*, no.123, Tokyo; *Shitsunai*, no.548, Tokyo; **1999** *Jt*, no.114, Tokyo; *Shitsunai*, no.531, Tokyo; *Box*, no.5, Milan; *Modern Living*, no.126, Tokyo; **1997** *Shitsunai*, no.516, Tokyo; **1996** *Shitsunai*, no.501, Tokyo

SELECTED EXHIBITIONS

2002 'Kaminoshigoto, Living Design Centre Ozone, Tokyo; 'Eco Products', Living Design Centre Ozone, Tokyo; **2001** 'Human Products', Living Design Centre Ozone, Tokyo; 'Flying Coffer', Ginza Matsuya Season Studio, Tokyo; **1999** 'Toshiko Kawaguchi Living Space of 21st Century', Yamato Plaza, Tokyo; 'Toshiko Kawagudhi, Beyond the Tradition', Arte Giappone, Milan

ARASH KAYNAMA

Born Tehran, 1973. Lives and works in London

EDUCATION

1999 BA, Royal College of Art, London; **1997** BA, Industrial Design, Central Saint Martins College of Art & Design, London; **1994** BEng Mechanical Engineering, University of Manchester, Institute of Science and Technology

---

PRACTICE

2000 Part-time lecturer, Foundation Studies in Art and Design, Kingston University, Kingston upon Thames, UK

SELECTED PROJECTS

2001 Off the Wall, furniture series; **2000** The Empire Strikes Back, flag; Euro Bowls; **1999** Big candle lighter, Big clip, hanger; God Light; Genius, table, Hidden; **1998** Home from home, container; Loving McDonalds, container; **1997** Lemon Squeezer

SELECTED BIBLIOGRAPHY

1999 *Blueprint*, no.164, London; *Axis*, vol.81, Tokyo

SELECTED EXHIBITIONS

2001 'Helen Hamlyn Research Centre Show', Royal College of Art, London; 'Village Fête', Victoria & Albert Museum, London; 'Contemporary Decorative Arts Exhibition', Sotheby's, London; **2000** 'Rest and Play', 100% Design, London

AWARDS

1999 Winner, Victoria & Albert Museum Hoarding competition, London;

1998 Commendation, Driade Lemon Squeezer competition, Milan

HELEN KERR

Born Montreal, 1959. Lives and works in Toronto

EDUCATION

1985–8 Ontario College of Art & Design, AOCAD, Toronto; University of Waterloo, Canada

PRACTICE

1988 to present Designer, Kerr & Co, Toronto

SELECTED PROJECTS

2002 SynapTek Surface, Teknion Furniture System; **2001** Cuisipro Café Line, Browne & Co; Balance Flatware, Gourmet Settings; Domo Laundry Hamper, Umbra; Plato Dishrack, Umbra; **2000** Tempo Tools, Browne & Co

SELECTED BIBLIOGRAPHY

2001 *Metropolis*, no.3, New York; *Knopf Canada*, September, Toronto; **2000** *Azure*, March–April, Toronto; **1999** *Azure*, March–April, Toronto; **1997** *ID*, June, New York

SELECTED EXHIBITIONS

2002–3 'Habitat: Canadian Design Now', touring exhibition; **2002** 'New Landscape: Design Transforms Canadian Furniture', DX-The Design Exchange, Toronto; **1999** 'Objects for Life, Case Study', Harbourfront Centre Gallery, Toronto

AWARDS

1999 IIDEX NeoCon Silver Award, Tradeshow Booth Design, Toronto; **1999** IIDEX NeoCon Bronze Award, Textile Colour Palette, Toronto; Virtu 12 Gourmet Settings, Toronto; **1997** IDSA Bronze Medal, USA

HARRI KOSKINEN

Born Karstula, Finland, 1970. Lives and works in Helsinki

EDUCATION

1994–8 University of Art and Design, Helsinki;

1989–93 Lahti Design Institute, Lahti, Finland

PRACTICE

2001 to present Friends of Industry Ltd (own company), Helsinki;

1998 2001 designer, iittala, Finland

SELECTED PROJECTS

2002 6040A, speaker, Genelec; Lumieres d'issey, summer concept, Issey Miyake; Folded, carpet, Asplund; **2001** Ali, containers, Arabia; Halo, candleholder, iittala; **2000** Outdoor Cooking, kitchen utensils, Hackman; Muotka, vase, iittala; **1999** Relations Koskinen, lantern; Aluo, glass object; Klubi, barware, iittala; **1998** Block, glass lamp, Design house Stockholm; Pick up, rack, Källemo; Fatty-containers, birch plywood containers, Schmidinger Modul; **1996** Atlas, candleholder, iittala

SELECTED BIBLIOGRAPHY

2002, *Repères 2002*, Paris; **2001** *Designing the 21st Century*, Cologne; **2001** *Interni*, no.513, Milan; *Abitare*, no.405, Milan; *Designers' Workshop*, no.114, Japan;

2000 *Form Function* Finland, no.79-80, Helsinki; *Design World 2000, Harri Koskinen*, Taideteollisuusmuseo Helsinki; *Interni*, no.500, Milan; **1999** *Axis*, no.9–10, Japan; *Blueprint*, no.160, London

SELECTED EXHIBITIONS

2002 'Harri Koskinen', Finnish Institut in Germany, Berlin; 'World wide', Salon de meuble, Paris; **2001** 'Young designer of the year', Koskinen and Suppanen, Design Forum Finland, Helsinki; 'Harri Koskinen hos Asplund', Stockholm; **2000** 'Privacy', Harri Koskinen, Miyake Design Studio-Gallery, Tokyo

AWARDS

2002, 1999 Design Plus Award, Frankfurt; **2001** Red Dot Award, Essen; **2000** Young Designer of the Year, Helsinki; **2000** Good design, Chicago; **1999** Accent, New York

TSUTOMU KUROKAWA

Born Tokai-Shi Aichi, Japan, 1962. Lives and works in Tokyo

EDUCATION

1986 Tokyo Designer Gakuin College, Nagoya, Aichi, Japan

PRACTICE

www.outdesign.com

2000 Established OUT.DeSIGN, Tokyo; **1992** H Design Associates, Tokyo; **1987** Super Potato Co, Tokyo; **1986** ICS, Aichi, Japan

SELECTED PROJECTS

2001 Papina, chair, Kalfa, chair, Maty, led lamp, OUT.DeSIGN; **2000** Mapell, chair, Fal, chair, Olberi, table, OUT.DeSIGN; **1998** Quit, TV stand, Flow, lamp, OUT.DeSIGN

SELECTED BIBLIOGRAPHY

2002 *Power Shop*, The Netherlands; **2001** *Creators File for Living*, vol.2, Tokyo; Michele De Lucchi, *International Design Yearbook*, London; Akari Matsuura, *Japan Design to the New Generation*, Tokyo; Ando Koichi, *New Blood*, Tokyo; *Frame*, no.24, Amsterdam; **2000** *Interni*, nos.499, 492, Milan; *Frame*, no. 10, Amsterdam; *Creators File For Living*, Tokyo; **1998** *Frame*, no.5, Amsterdam

SELECTED EXHIBITIONS

2001 'OUT.deSIGN Po1DB*T', Batsu Art Gallery, Tokyo Designers Block, Tokyo; **2000** 'OUT.deSIGN', Salon du Meuble de Paris, Design Lab, Paris; 'OUT.deSIGN PooDB&T', Hilside Terrace, Tokyo Designers Block; **1999** 'H Design Associates', Salone Satellite, Salone del Mobile, Milan; 'H Design Products', Kiss Build, Tokyo

AWARDS

2001 Frame Award, Tokyo Designers Block, Tokyo

MARTIN LOTTI

Born Fribourg, Switzerland, 1974. Lives and works in Portland, Oregon

EDUCATION

1995–97 BA, Science Degree with Honors in Industrial Design, Art Center College of Design, Pasadena, California; **1994–95** Art Center College of Design (Europe), Vevey, Switzerland

PRACTICE

2001 to present Nike, Creative Director, Women's Footwear Division, Beaverton, Oregon; **1997–2001** Nike, Senior Designer, Footwear Design, Beaverton, Oregon

SELECTED PROJECTS

2002 The Kyoto, women's footwear, Nike; **2001** Air Visi Havoc, women's footwear, Nike; Air Max Craze, women's footwear, Nike; Air Max Specter, footwear, Nike; **2000** Ovidian, reversible shoe, Nike; **1997** Fun Sound, educational kid's toy, concept project; Track Ball Digital watch, Timex

SELECTED BIBLIOGRAPHY

2002 *Time Magazine*, March, New York; **2001** *Surface Magazine*, no.29, San Francisco; *Teen Vogue*, Spring, New York; *Facts*, July, Zurich; *New York Magazine*, February, New York; *Vogue*, February, Milan; **2000** *New York Times,* September, New York; *Le Figaro*, June, Paris; *Black Book Magazine*, Autumn, New York; **1997** *ID*, July, New York; *Metropolis*, January, New York

SELECTED EXHIBITIONS

2000 'Design Afoot: Athletic Shoes, 1995–2000', San Francisco Museum of Modern Art; **1997** 'ID Best of Design', AIGA Gallery, New York

AWARDS

2002, 1997 ID Magazine Annual Design Review, Honorable Mention; **2001** Nike: Innovation of the Year, Beaverton, Oregon

JEAN-MARIE MASSAUD

Born Toulouse, 1966. Lives and works in Paris

EDUCATION

1985–90 Les Ateliers, ENSCI Paris

PRACTICE

www.massaud.com

1996 Established Studio Massaud, Paris; **1993–6** Associated with Marc Berthier in Design Plan Studio, Paris; **1992–3** Works for Marc Berthier, Paris; **1990–1** Lives and works for himself in Hong Kong

SELECTED PROJECTS

2001 Outline and Inout, Cappellini; Pipe Line Light, Tronconi; **2000** Net, Liv'it; Paradoxe, Baccarat; **1999** Luxlab prototype, Horizontal Chair, Heaven; Dark Light, Ligne Roset; **1998** Nemo perfume, Cacharell; Ness Collection (clocks, calculators, pens), Back; **1997** Tohot Salt and Pepper Shakers, Hooky home accessories, Authentics; **1996** Lift Tennis Raquette, Mizuno; O'Hazard Chair, Magis

SELECTED BIBLIOGRAPHY

2001 Marie-Laure Jousset, *La Collection de Design du Centre Georges Pompidou*, France; Jean-Claude Maugirard, *L'école française*, IFA, France; *New York Times* 24 May, USA; **2000** Raymond Guidot, *Histoire du Design 1940–2000*, Hazan, France; *L'Œil*, no.574, France; *Idéat*, January, France; **1999** *Figaro*, no.169, Japan; *Le Monde*, 11 March, France; *Vogue*, September, France; *Libération*, 19 January, France; *Maison Française*, no.500, France; *Intramuros*, no.83, Paris; **1998** Mel Bryars, *50 products, 50 lights*, USA

SELECTED EXHIBITIONS

2002 'Mood River', The Wexner Center for Arts, Columbus, Ohio, USA; 'Carrefour de la Création', Centre Georges Pompidou, Paris; **2001** 'La fin du livre?', Institut franco-japonais de Tokyo; 'Génération France', VIA Paris, France–Washington; 'Designers au tapis', Musée du feutre, Mouzon, France; 'Paris–New York', The Conrad Shop, New York; 'Offect', Totem Gallery, New York; 'Salon France–Chine', APCI, Beijing; **2000** 'Design Design', Villa de Nouailles, Hyères, France; 'Les petits enfants de Starck?', Boulogne-Billancourt, France; 'Siège Social', VIA Paris; **1999** 'Think Horizontal', Musée des Arts Décoratifs, Paris; **1998** 'La nature du futur, une nature apprivoisée', VIA Paris

AWARDS

2001 Ness Collection, Séphora Blanc architecture: Etoiles APCI Observeur du Design, France; **2000** Best Design, Norvège; **1999** Nombre d'Or, Salon du Meuble de Paris; **1996** O'Hazard: Chair of the Year (Promosedia dell'Anno), Italy; The National Product Design Award, Australia; Prize FORM, Germany; Grand Prix de la Presse Internationale et de la Critique du Meuble Contemporain; First Prize Maquill'Art, Paris

MAT STUDIO

Antonio Brizzi, born Florence, 1960; Babette Riefenstahl, born Berlin, 1967; Carla M Crosina, born Merano, 1961; Marco Bellomo, born Rome, 1961

EDUCATION

Antonio Brizzi: **1980** Attainment of High-school scientific degree, Florence; Babette Riefenstahl: **1996** Graduated in industrial-design at the I.S.I.A. of Florence; Carla M Crosina: **1995** Graduated in architecture, Florence; Marco Bellomo: **1999** Graduated in architecture, Florence

PRACTICE

2001 Mat Studio established in Milan; Antonio Brizzi: **1981–98** Collaborations with several architecture studios, furniture shops and other, Italy; Babette Riefenstahl:

1998–2000 Working in different furniture shops as consultant, Milan; **1996–8** Working as garden-planner in different gardening companies, Perugia; **1995** Working in different studios of architecture, Florence; Carla M Crosina: **1995–8** Collaboration as interior designer, Rome; **1984–95** Collaboration with several architecture studios, Florence; Marco Bellomo: **1981–98** Collaboration with several architecture studios

SELECTED PROJECTS

2001 Extra, shelf system, Sink, Soft Bathtub, Cappellini; **2000** Bathroom-line Navilio, sink uno, Habitat; **1999** Ovalotto, fruit-bowl, Dovetusai, Milan; **1997** Kimo, Dilmos; Tania, table-mats, Dovetusai, Milan; Samadhi-gel, carpets, Kundalini, Milan

SELECTED BIBLIOGRAPHY

2001 *Gap Casa*, December–January, Milan; *Wired*, January, San Francisco; *Design Report*, June, July–August, Stuttgart; *Abitare*, no.407, Milan; *Casa Claudia*, May, São Paulo; *Wallpaper**, July–August, London; *Intramuros*, July, Paris; *HOME*, April, Hamburg; *DDN*, September, Milan; **2000** *Interni Annual*, October, Milan; *DDN*, September, Milan; *Elle Décor*, July–August, September, Milan; *Paris Match*, May, Paris; *Ottagono*, June–July, Milan; *Modo*, November, Milan; *Vogue*, September, Paris; *Wallpaper**, July–August, London; *Intramuros*, September, Paris; **1999** *Süddeutsche Zeitung*, April, Munich; *Abitare*, September, Milan; *DDN*, September, Milan; *Vogue*, July, Milan; **1998** *Interni*, May, Milan; *DDN*, May, Milan

SELECTED EXHIBITIONS

2001, 2000 'Salone satellite', Salone del Mobile, Milan; 'Now', Maison & Objet, Paris; **2000** 'Bagno senza confini', Quid Cersaie, Bologna

AWARDS

2001, 2000 Design-Report Award during the Salone Satellite, selected project, Salone del Mobile, Milan

J MAYS

Born Pauls Valley, Oklahoma, 1954. Lives and works in Dearborn, Michigan

EDUCATION

1976–80 Bachelor of Science, Art Center College of Design, Pasadena, California; **1972–6** Journalism, University of Oklahoma

PRACTICE

1997 to present Ford Motor Company, Vice-President Global Design, Dearborn, Michigan; **1995–7** SHR Perceptual Management, Vice-President Design Development, Scottsdale, Arizona; **1993–4** Audi AG, Design Director, Ingolstadt, Germany; **1989–93** Volkswagen of America Design Center, Chief Designer, Simi Valley, California; **1984–9** Audi/EDM, Senior Designer, Munich; **1983–4** BMW AG, Designer, Munich; **1980–3** Audi AG, Designer, Ingolstadt, Germany

SELECTED PROJECTS

2002 GT 40, concept (2001) to production vehicle, Thunderbird, concept (1999) to production vehicle (2002), Fusion, concept (2001) to production vehicle (Europe), Ford Motor Co; **2001** Fiesta, production vehicle (Europe), Ford 49, concept vehicle, **2000** 24.7, concept vehicle, Mondeo, production vehicle (Europe), Ford Motor Co; **1999** O21C, concept vehicle with Marc Newson, Ford Motor Co; **1997** Audi A6, production vehicle, Audi AG; **1994** VW concept 1 (new Beetle), concept vehicle, VW

SELECTED BIBLIOGRAPHY

2002 *Vanity Fair*, February; *Blueprint*, no.192, London, February; **2001** *New York Times*, August; Charlotte and Peter Fiell, *Designing the 21st Century*, Cologne; **1999** Time.com, no.9

SELECTED EXHIBITIONS

2002–3 'Retrofuturism: the car design of J Mays' (working title), The Museum of Contemporary Art, Los Angeles; **2002** 'Autoemotive: The Design Work of J Mays', Gund Hall Gallery, Harvard University Graduate School of Design, Cambridge, Massachusetts

AWARDS

2002 Excellence in Design Award, Harvard University Graduate School of Design, Cambridge, Massachusetts; **2001** Honorary Doctorate, Art Center College of Design, Pasadena, California

THOMAS MEYERHOFFER

Born Stockholm, 1965. Lives and works in Montara, California
EDUCATION
1989–91 Art Center College of Design, (Europe), Vevey
PRACTICE
www.meyerhoffer.com
1999 to present Meyerhoffer Studios, Montara, California; 1995–8 Designer, Apple Computers, Cupertino, California; 1993–5 Designer, IDEO, Palo Alto, San Francisco; 1992 Designer, Porsche, Stuttgart; 1991 Designer, Julian Brown, London
SELECTED PROJECTS
2002 Swell, bowl, Danese; 2001 Smith Warp, ski goggle, Smith; 2000 MO3, wearable concept, Ericsson; 1998 Apple Studio Display, monitor, Apple; 1997 Apple Emate, translucent computer, Apple; 1996 NEC Monitor, monitor, Ideo
SELECTED BIBLIOGRAPHY
2002 International Design Yearbook, London; 1999 International Design Yearbook, London; 1998 Domus, no.801, Milan; 1997 ID, Annual Design Review; Business Week, Annual Design Issue; International Design Yearbook, London
SELECTED EXHIBITIONS
2000 'New Scandinavian', Die Neue Sammlung, Munich, Germany; 1999 'Permanent Collection', San Francisco Museum of Modern Art
AWARDS
1997 D&AD Silver Award for most outstanding product design, London; ID Magazine Annual Design Review 97, Best of Category, USA; IF Awards, Germany; IDSA/Business Week Silver Award, USA

ANA MIR

Born Valencia, 1969. Lives and works in Barcelona
EDUCATION
1992–4 MA, Central Saint Martins School of Art & Design, London;
1987–92 Fine Arts degree, Universidad Politecnica de Bellas Artes de Valencia
PRACTICE
www.emilianadesign.com
2002 Established Emiliana Design Studio with Emili Padrós, Barcelona;
1996–2002 Freelance designer, Barcelona; 1996–9 Industrial designer at Óscar Tusquets design and architecture studio, Barcelona;
1995 Freelance designer, Valencia
SELECTED PROJECTS
2001 Panama, tablemat, Cha-Cha; Chocolate Accents, chocolates for champagne glass, Xocolater; 1999 Gelapeutic Bath; Pillows Play, pillows made of one piece of fabric; 1997 Porno Wedding Dress
SELECTED BIBLIOGRAPHY
2001 El Pais, October, Barcelona; El Periodico, October, Barcelona; South China Morning Post, April, Hong Kong; Barcelona + Barcelona, Barcelona; El Pais Semanal, April, Madrid; Beaux Arts, special Maji Paris; AIT + Architektur & Wohnen, special December–January, Hamburg; 2000 Intramuros, no.87, Paris; Merian, March, Hamburg; Domus, no.827, Milan; 1999 Domus, no.820, 814, Milan; Intramuros, no.81, Paris
SELECTED EXHIBITIONS
2001–2 'Past Future Visions', Kunst Halle Krems, Austria; 2001 'Shock Design', H2O Gallery, Barcelona; 'Dirty Washing', Design Museum, London; 'Clandestino', Opos Gallery, Milan; 'Ahora Diseño', Sala Amadis, Madrid; 2000 'Opos Under 35', Opos Gallery, Milan; 'Now! Design Avivre-Recherche Futur', Salon du Meuble, Paris; 1999 'Futur Compost', Palau De La Virreina, Barcelona
AWARDS
2001 Fad Prize of Architecture, Barcelona; 2000 First Prize Domus, BBJ New Ideas for Boeing Business Jet Interior Design, Milan; 1999 Ciutat de Barcelona Design Prize, Barcelona

MARRE MOEREL

Born Breda, The Netherlands, 1966. Lives and works in New York
EDUCATION
1989–91 Furniture MFA, Royal College of Art, London; 1987–9 Sculpture BA, Exeter College of Art and Design, Exeter, UK; 1985–7 Akademie v. Beeldende Kunsten, Rotterdam, The Netherlands; 1984–5 Kunstakademie St Joost, Breda, The Netherlands
PRACTICE
1997 to present Designer; 1991–6 Artist, sculptor
SELECTED PROJECTS
2001 Chair, Offect; Lighting design for W Hotel, Chicago; Watch, Ozone; Lighting design for Fiorucci store, New York; 2000 Biology + Barnacle Series, ceramic lighting and tiles, Cappellini; Smash, Anatomy Series, Murano glassware and porcelain, Covo; 1999 Soft Box series, ceramic lighting, Cappellini; Century Collection and Millennium Collection, laminate designs, Wilsonart International; Surface Form Collection, Furniture, Inside Design and Wilsonart International; 1998 Office desk and storage unit, Jodi Harrow Design
SELECTED BIBLIOGRAPHY
2001 Avenue no. 1, December–January; Case da abitare, July–August; Elle Decoration, April, UK; 2000 Black + White, no.48; New York Times, September; Frame, September–October, Amsterdam; Elle Décor, no.11, Milan, Italy; Vogue, no.8, Munich; M Bartolucci and Cathy Lang Ho, American Contemporary Furniture, New York; Ingo Maurer, International Design Yearbook, London; Tina Skinner, Lighting 2000: a Guide to the Best in Contemporary Lighting Design, Atglen: Schiffer; Surface Supplement, April, San Francisco; 1999 Harper's Bazaar, September; Interni, no.492, Milan; Elle Décor, August, Japan; Eigen Huis & Interieur, no.1, Haarlem
SELECTED EXHIBITIONS
2001 'Hall 01', 100 Lafayette, New York; 'Design 21', Felissimo, New York; Cappellini, Superstudio, Milan; 'Smash', Covo, Milan, touring exhibition; 2000 'Fresh Produce', Charas/El Bohio, New York; 'The Erotic Lives of Women', Zao, New York; 1999 'ICFF', Wilsonart International; 1998 'WAH', Vibrant, New York; 'csv Open Studios', csv Center, New York; 'International Contemporary Furniture Fair', Javits Center, New York; 'Hot House', Aronson Galleries, New York
AWARDS
2001 Best New Collection, Smash glass collection for Covo, Tokyo Designers Block, Japan; Furniture, Millennium Collection, I.D. Annual Design Review, USA;
1999 Best of ICFF Show, Design Journal, New York; Best Body of Work for Wilsonart International, ICFF, New York

TED MUEHLING

Born Passaic, New Jersey, 1953. Lives and works in New York
EDUCATION
1972–5 Pratt Institute, Brooklyn, New York
PRACTICE
1990 Established store-atelier, New York; 1976 Independent design and manufacture of jewellery and decorative metalwork
SELECTED PROJECTS
Ongoing design for independent small-scale production; 2000 Salviati;
1999 Nymphenburg Porzellan manufaktur
SELECTED BIBLIOGRAPHY
2001 Vogue, November, Germany; 2000 Casa Vogue, October; House & Garden, May; Architektur & Wohnen, April; Elle Décor, April; Paper Magazine, March; Marie Claire, February–March; 1999 Paper Magazine, March; Town & Country, January; 1997 Beate Wedekind, New York Interiors, New York; New York Times Magazine, December; Paper Magazine, October; ID, January–February; 1996 House & Garden, December
SELECTED EXHIBITIONS
2000 'Design Matters', Miami Museum of Contemporary Art, Miami; 'Drawn by the Sea', Glenn Horowitz, East Hampton, New York; 'White Gold', Moss, New York;

'Souvenir de Yue', Joyce: Jardins du Palais Royal, Paris
AWARDS
2000 Cooper-Hewitt National Design Award Finalist; Chrysler Design Award

YUGO NAKAMURA

Born Nara, Japan, 1970. Lives and works in Tokyo
EDUCATION
1994 Graduate School of Tokyo University, Engineering Dept, Tokyo;
1992 Tokyo University, Engineering Dept, Tokyo
PRACTICE
www.yugop.com
2000 to present Programmer / Designer / Art Director at Business Architects, Tokyo
SELECTED PROJECTS
2001 Sony Connected_Identity, website for new corporate identity for Sony, Sony Corporation; NTT DATA website, corporate website, NTT DATA Corporation; Matsushita website, corporate website, Matsushita Electric Industrial;
1996 to present MONO*CRAFTS, a series of experiments on the web
SELECTED BIBLIOGRAPHY
2001 DGV, 72dpi, Germany; Friends of ED, New Master of Flash, UK; Matt Woolman, Moving Type: Designing for Time and Space, UK; New Craftsmanship, UK; Web Design Now, no.48, Japan; 2000 Gasbook, no.8, Japan; 1999 Big, no.26, December, USA
SELECTED EXHIBITIONS
2002 'Web Wizards Exhibition', Design Museum, London; 2001 'Movement', Sendai Mediateque, Sendai, Japan

MARC NEWSON

Born Sydney, 1963. Lives and works in London
EDUCATION
1984 Graduation from Sydney College of the Arts, Sydney
PRACTICE
www.marc-newson.com
2001 Curator of the Conran Foundation Collection, Design Museum, London; Adjunct Professor in Design at Sydney College of the Arts; 1997 Established Marc Newson Ltd with Benjamin De Haan, London; 1991 Established own studio in Paris, formed the joint venture Ikepod Watch Company, Paris; 1987–91 Designer at IDEE, Tokyo
SELECTED PROJECTS
2000 Bicycle MN01, Biomega; Door Handles, Erreti; Manatee, watch, Ikepod Watch; Tourbillon, watch, Ikepod Watch; 1999 021 C Concept Car, Ford Motor Company; Hair Care Appliances, Vidal Sassoon; 1998 Dassault Falcon 900 B, airplane; Io Table, B&B; David Gill, chair, B&B; 1997 Dish Doctor, dish drainer, Magis; Apollo Torch, Flos
SELECTED BIBLIOGRAPHY
2001 Miller's Collecting Modern Design, Reed; Designing the 21st Century, Cologne; Imagination, London; Ar, September, Germany; Die WeltWoche, November, Switzerland; Architecture y Diseño, no.16, Spain; Blueprint, October, London; New York Times Magazine, March 11; Intramuros, April–May, Paris; 2000 Der Spiegel-Kultur, December, Germany; Sputnik, October, Japan; Interior & Design Russia, July; Automotive Engineering International, July; Brutus, February, Japan; Interni, February, Milan; 1999 Marc Newson, Booth Clibborn Editions; Catherine McDermott, The Product Book, D&AD; Jasper Morrison, International Design Yearbook, London; Wallpaper*, November, London; Domus, May, Milan; 1998 Abitare, November, Milan; ID, December, UK; Wallpaper*, September, London; Blueprint, June, London; Abitare, April, Milan
SELECTED EXHIBITIONS
Permanent collection: Design Museum, London; MoMA, New York; Musée des Arts Décoratifs, Paris
2001–2 'Personal Retrospective', Powerhouse Museum, Sydney; 2001 'Aluminium by Design: Jewellery to Jets', Carnegie Museum of Art, Pittsburgh; 1999 'Marc Newson'

McLellan Gallery, UK; **1998** Boymans van Beuningen Museum, Rotterdam
AWARDS
1984 Australian Crafts Council among many others

SHIN NISHIBORI

Born Japan, 1966. Lives and works in Kyoto
EDUCATION
1985–9 Musashino Art University, Tokyo
PRACTICE
www.shinproducts.com
1999 to present Shin Products, President, Kyoto;
1989–98 Inhouse designer at Matsushita Electric Industrial Co, Osaka
SELECTED PROJECTS
2002 Hanaiki, ashtray; Amida, Japanese towel; Cokmok, kitchen ware, Covo; CB lamp, Inax; **2000** Kutsunugi, chair and table, Japan; Ringring, tableware, Ricordi & Sfela; **1999** Sponge Chair, Sogo; Kunkun, speaker, Shin Products; Kyorokyoro, speakers, Shin Products; Tongpoo, carpet, Shin Products; **1996** p-case, portable CD tuner system, Panasonic
SELECTED EXHIBITIONS
2002 'Shin Nishibori Exhibition', One's room, Tokyo, Japan;
2001 'Toilet exhibition', Matsuya Gallery, Tokyo
AWARDS
1987 Good Design and Some, Japan, Tokyo and Osaka

PATRICK NORGUET

Born Tours, France, 1969. Lives and works in Paris
EDUCATION
1996 Ecole supérieure de design industriel, Paris
PRACTICE
1997 Head of Visual Identity Louis Vuitton, Decorator Louis Vuitton, Paris; **1995** Collaboration with Hilton McConnico, Paris; **1995** Collaboration Studio Naço, Paris
SELECTED PROJECTS
2001 Furniture Emilio Pucci, Cappellini; Furniture, Artifor; Ceramic Objects, Artoria; Limoges, Artoria; Furniture, Moroso; Luminaire, Tronconi; Commercial Architecture, Renault car; **2000** Furniture, Milan, Cappellini
SELECTED BIBLIOGRAPHY
2001 WWD, October, Tokyo; Vogue, December, Germany; Daily Design, September, Tokyo; Paris Match, no.2533, Paris; ID, June; DS, no.49, Paris; **2000** Elle Decoration, no.101, Paris; Maison Française, no.505, Paris; Ottagono no.138, Milan
SELECTED EXHIBITIONS
2002 'Personal Exhibition', Moscow; **2001** Group exhibition 'ICFF Felissimo design 21', New York; 'Furniture Cappellini', Salone del Mobile, Milan, 'Off' Events, Milan; 'Furniture Cappellini / Emilio Pucci', Pucci store, Milan; **2000** Group exhibition, Paris Furniture Fair, Paris; Permanent collection of the MoMA, New York; Exhibition in the Museum of Modern Art of Miami; **1999** 'VIA Permanent Calls', VIA, Paris

NORWAY SAYS

Torbjørn Anderssen, Tore Borgersen, Andreas Engesvik, Frode Myhr, Espen Voll, live and work in Oslo and Bergen; Torbjørn Anderssen, born Bergen, Norway, 1976; Tore Borgersen, born Tønsberg, Norway, 1966; Andreas Engesvik, born Svolvaer, Norway, 1970; Frode Myhr, born Tromso, Norway, 1974; Espen Voll, born Trondheim, Norway, 1965
EDUCATION
Torbjørn Anderssen: **1997–2002** BA, National College of Art and Design, Bergen; Tore Borgersen: **1993–8** National College of Art and Design, Oslo; **1995** Royal College of Art, London; **1990–2** Carpenter education at Sandar VGS, Sandefjord, Norway; Andreas Engesvik: **1995–2000** BA, National College of Art and Design, Bergen; **1998** Erasmus scholarship, Denmark Design School, Copenhagen; **1991–5** University of

Bergen and Oslo; Frode Myhr: **1991–5** Education as an Electrician, Group L, Honefoss, Norway; Espen Voll: **1993** Rietveld Academy, Department of Interior, Architecture and Furniture Design, Amsterdam; **1989–7** National College of Art and Design, Department of Interior and Furniture Design, Oslo; **1984–6** Technical University, VGS, Architect, Trondheim, Norway
PRACTICE
www.norwaysays.com
2000 to present Norway Says; Tore Borgersen: **1998** Started his own company after college; Andreas Engesvik: **2000 to present** Andreas Engesvik Design; Frode Myhr: **1990–8** Freebased furniture reproduction, Honefoss; **1995–8** working as an Electrician at a paper factory, Honefoss; Espen Voll: **1998 to present** own practice, Oslo; **1986** Voll Architects, Trondheim
SELECTED PROJECTS
2001 The Konrad Chair, Playmo, coffee table; Hiawatha, furniture system; Chocco, chair; Crème, table, Norway Says; **2000** A large cupboard, a wedding present from the Norwegian Government to Prince Haakon and Princess Mette Marit; Dock, chair, Globe; Hole, side table; Backyard Accessory, chair, Norway Says
SELECTED BIBLIOGRAPHY
2001 Wallpaper*, July–August, December, London; Domus, September, Milan; Abitare October, Milan; Atrium, November–December, Germany; Frame, July–August, Amsterdam; Axis, July, Japan; Form, June, Sweden; Totem Magazine, May, New York; Surface, March–April, USA; Elle Decoration, May, Japan; **2000** Monitor, December, Moscow; New York Times, October, New York, USA; DDN, no.7, Italy; Wallpaper*, June, London; Elle Interior, no.3, Norway; Designweek, no.8, UK
SELECTED EXHIBITIONS
2002 'Norway Says', Stockholm International Furniture Fair; **2002, 2001, 2000** 'Norway Says', Salone Satellite, Salone del Mobile, Milan; **2001, 2000** 'Norway Says', Designers Block, London;
AWARDS
2000 Norwegian Design Council, 'Design of the Best Make', Oslo

FABIO NOVEMBRE

Born Lecce, Italy, 1966. Lives and works in Milan
EDUCATION
1992 Degree in Architecture, Polytechnic, Milan
PRACTICE
www.novembre.it
SELECTED PROJECTS
2002 AND, sofa, Cappellini; **2001** NET, carpet, ORG, table, Cappellini; **1995** Shot, bottle, prototype for Uliveto; **1991** Mediterranea, chaise longue, Pierantonio Bonacina; **1988** Honlywood, folding chair, B&B Italia
SELECTED BIBLIOGRAPHY
2001 Leo Gullbring, Fabio Novembre, Amsterdam; Fabio Novembre, Be Your Own Messiah, Milan; Escala, no.1, Rio de Janeiro; De Architect Interieur, no.6, The Hague; Casa Brutus, no.19, Tokyo; Playboy, July, Lubljana; **2000** Abitare, no.401, Milan; Interiors, no.159, New York; Diseño Interior, no.97, Madrid; **1999** Frame, no.9, Amsterdam; Virus, no.7, Milan; **1998** Domus, no.809, Milan
AWARDS
1990 Chairman's Special Award, International Furniture Design Competition, Asahikawa, Japan; **1988** First Prize 'Young & Design', Milan

FRANK NUOVO

Born Monterey, California, 1961. Lives and works in Los Angeles
EDUCATION
1986 Art Center College of Design, Pasadena, California
PRACTICE
1998 to present Vertu, Creative Director and Designer, Los Angeles;

1995 to present Nokia Design, VP Chief Designer, Los Angeles; **1986** Designworks USA/BMW Design Director, Newberry Park, California
SELECTED PROJECTS
2002 Vertu, mobile phone, Vertu; **1998** Nokia 8810, mobile phone; Nokia 5100 Series Global, mobile phones, Nokia; **1994** Nokia 232 Global, mobile phone; Nokia 2100 Series Global, mobile phones, Nokia
SELECTED BIBLIOGRAPHY
2002 The Peak, no.3, Singapore; GQ, March, UK; **2001** New Yorker, November, USA; **2000** Financial Times, June, UK-US Edition; Fortune, May, USA; Vogue, April, USA; Axis, January–February, Japan; Form, January–February, Germany; GQ, March, Germany; **1999** New York Times, December, USA; **1998** Harper's Bazaar, December, Australia; **1997** The Business Times, November, Singapore
SELECTED EXHIBITIONS
2001 'Workspheres', MoMA, New York; Neues Museum, Nuremberg, Germany
AWARDS
2000 Wired, USA; **1999** Design of the Decade, USA; **1999** IDSA, USA; **1997, 1995** Industry Form, Germany

ORA-ÏTO

Born Paris, 1977. Lives and works in Paris
EDUCATION
1996 Ecole Supérieure de Design Industriel (EDSI), Paris
PRACTICE
1998 Established a design brand and a communication studio named ORA-ÏTO, Paris
SELECTED PROJECTS
2002 Tetris, carpet, Tarkett Sommer; Absynthe, perfume bottle and merchandising products, Coty Lancaster; Paco, beer bottle and merchandising products, Heineken; **2001** Automotive, advertising campaign, Pechiney; Eggo, cellular phone prototype, Bouygues Telecom; Rouge Alfa, merchandising product of the car ALFA 147, Alfa-Romeo; Advent Calendar, temporary façade for a store in Osaka, Cartier; Urban-Chic, spray bottle, L'Oreal; **2000** Adrenaline, perfume bottle and merchandising products, Adidas; Cappellini family, advertising campaign, Cappellini; **1999** Secret, design of watches, Swatch
SELECTED BIBLIOGRAPHY
2002 Design Illustrated, January, Moscow; **2001** Interni, April, Milan; Design Week, December, London; **2000** Intramuros, special issue, February, Paris; The Face, no.39, London; The Financial Times, April, London; **1999** Casa Vogue, March, São Paulo; DDN, April, Milan; **2000** Neue Zurcher Zeitung, August, Zurich; Elle, March, Paris; Libération, March, Paris; Le Monde, January, Paris
SELECTED EXHIBITIONS
2002 'Camouflage', Musée du Design, Lausanne; 'Please Be', Gallery Eric Dupont, Paris; **2001** 'Motifs', Union Centrale des Arts Décoratifs, Paris; 'ORA-ÏTO', E&Y Gallery, Osaka; 'Paris 2010', Colette, Paris; **2000** 'L'art dans la Pub', Musée de la Pub, Paris; **1999** 'Ideal Room', Gallery Patricia Dorfmann, Paris; **1998** 'Nature Vive', Modem Gallery, Paris
AWARDS
2001 Dazed & Confused, award of the best designed website, London, France

EMILI PADRÓS

Born Barcelona, 1969. Lives and works in Barcelona
EDUCATION
1992–94 Central Saint Martins College of Art & Design, MA in Industrial Design, London; **1987–91** Industrial Design Degree, Elisava School of Design, Barcelona
PRACTICE
www.emilianadesign.com
2002 Founder, with Ana Mir, of Emiliana Design Studio, Barcelona; Since **1995** Teaching at Elisava School of Design, Barcelona; **1996–2001** Co-ordinator of 3rd and 4th Year at Elisava School of Design, Barcelona; **1995** Freelance designer, Barcelona

SELECTED PROJECTS
2001 Anónimo Family, objects for the bathroom; **1999** Measuring Drink and Food, 2 fingerprints on a glass, 10cm on a plate; NSS's, Non Stop Shoes, concept for energy collector shoes; TOU Soft Portable Computer, concept for a portable computer; **1997** Vespa Cavallet, seat
SELECTED BIBLIOGRAPHY
2001 *South China Morning Post*, April, Hong Kong; *El País* Semanal, April, Madrid; *Barcelona + Barcelona*, Barcelona; *Architektur & Wohnen*, February–March, Hamburg; **2000** *Domus*, no.822, Milan; *Intramuros*, no.87, Paris; *Design Week*, no.42, London; *Azimuts*, no.17, Saint-Etienne; *FX Design, Business & Society*, no.81, London; *Neo 2*, no.14, Madrid; **1999** *Domus*, no.820, Milan; **1997** *Experimenta*, no.16, Madrid
SELECTED EXHIBITIONS
2002 'Recollections', H2o Gallery, Barcelona; **2001–2** 'Past Future Visions', Kunst Halle Krems, Austria; **2001** 'Now! Design A Vivre-Recherche Futur', Salon du Meuble, Paris; 'Ahora Diseño', Sala Amadis, Madrid; **2000** 'Smart Futures', Netherlands Design Institute, Amsterdam; **1999** 'Futur Compost', Palau de la Virreina, Barcelona
AWARDS
2001 Fad Prize of Architecture, Barcelona; **2000** 1st Prize *Domus* BBJ, New Ideas for Boeing Business Jet Interior Design, Milan; **1999** Ciutat de Barcelona Design Prize

SATYENDRA PAKHALÉ
Born Washim, India, 1967. Lives and works in Amsterdam
EDUCATION
1992–4 Art Center College of Design (Europe), Vevey, Switzerland; **1989–91** Industrial Design Centre, Indian Institute of Technology, Bombay; **1985–9** Visvesvaraya College of Engineering Design, Nagpur, India
PRACTICE
www.satyendra-pakhale.com
1998 to present Designer, Atelier Satyendra Pakhalé, Amsterdam; **1995–8** Senior Product Designer, New Business Creation Team, Philips Design, Eindhoven; **1993** Junior Product Designer, Frogdesign, Altenstig, Germany; **1992** Industrial Designer, Bajaj Auto, Pune, India
SELECTED PROJECTS
2002–3 Objects, Furnishing For Young Urban Living, Deslato; Me Too, children's furniture system, Post Computer Games, Magis; Bell Metal Objects, Cappellini; Calender with Sundial, Danese; Spectacles, Cottet; **2002** Kalpa = Vase + Bowl, Cor-Unum; Hanger, Atelier SP; **2001–3** Computer Desk-mat, Magis; Nature & Beyond Bamboo, in collaboration with the Philippine Department of Trade & Industry, Material Connexion; China Project, range of objects, Atelier SP; **2001–2** Steel Vase, Alessi; **2001** Horse Chair and Horse Chair Family, Cappellini
SELECTED BIBLIOGRAPHY
2002 *Créatures*, no.33, Paris; *Repères 2002*, no.6, Paris; **2001** Michele de Lucchi, *International Design Yearbook*, London; *Intramuros*, no.95, Paris; **2000** *Domus*, no.832, Milan; *Case da Abitare*, no.38, Milan; *Casa Vogue*, no.604, Milan; *Interni*, nos.497–498, Milan; Paola Antonelli, Giulio Cappellini, Vanni Pasca, *Abitare Il Tempo – Beyond European Design, Projects from around the world*, Paris; *Design A*, no.96, Taipei; **1998** *Pangéa – Connected Wheels-Transport, digital technology and the sustainable society*, Eindhoven
SELECTED EXHIBITIONS
2002 'Wet Design', EKWC NL', Spazio Consolo, Milan; Galerie Binnen, Amsterdam; 'Clay & Beyond', Galleria Contemporanea, Milan; 'Off-Scale', Moroso-Showroom, Milan; 'River Deep, Mountain High', The Glass House Amstel Park, Amsterdam; 'World-Wide', Salon du Meuble de Paris; **2001** 'Tout Simplement Design', Atelier Renault Champs Elysees, Paris; 'Cappellini', Studio Super Piú, Milan; **2000** 'Beyond European Design', Abitare Il Tempo, Verona, Italy; 'Cultural Nomad – Satyendra Pakhalé', Alterpoint, Milan

AWARDS
1999, 1998, 1994 International Design Distinction Award, *ID* Magazine, New York; **1993** Goldstar Design Award, Goldstar Co, Seoul, Korea

JORGE PARDO
Born Havana, Cuba, 1963. Lives and works in Los Angeles
EDUCATION
BFA Art Center College of Design, Pasadena, California; University of Illinois at Chicago
SELECTED PROJECTS
2001 Copia: The American Center for Food, Wine and the Arts, Napa; Bar, Centre for Contemporary Art, Glasgow; Lamps, Sotheby's, New York; **2000** Project, Dia Center for the Arts, New York; Autobahn-Raststatte, Pratteln; **1999** Fabric Workshop & Museum, Philadelphia; **1998** Jorge Pardo 4166 Sea View Lane, Los Angeles; **1997** Pier, Muenster; Tomatensuppe, Cologne; Lighthouse, Boymans van Beuningen Museum Rotterdam; Clock, clock, clock, clock, clock (you have to say it fast), Stuttgart
SELECTED BIBLIOGRAPHY
2002 *Frieze*, no.86; *No Return*, Sammlung Haubrok, Städtliches Museum Abteiberg, Mönchengladbach; *ArtNexus*, nos.40, 43; **2001** *Tema Celeste* nos.85, 89; *SOMA* vol. 15.10; Cosima Von Bonin, *Bruder Poul Sticht In See*, Cologne; *ARTnews*, December; *Flash Art*, October; *New York Times*, 2 November; *Art in America*, November; *Artforum*, September, October; Burkhard Riemschneider and Uta Grosenick, *Icons, Art Now*, Cologne; *Artweek*, 12 July; *Metropolis*, May; *Flash Art International*, March–April; *New York Times*, 2 February; *Parkett, Collaborations & Editions Since 1984*, MoMA, New York; *Frame*, no.18, Amsterdam; Howard Singerman, *Jorge Pardo, Public Offerings*; **2000** *Artforum*, May, December; *Frieze*, November–December; *Against Design*, Institute of Contemporary Art, University of Pennsylvania; *New York Times*, February 3; **1999** *Artforum*, November, December; *Parkett*, no.56; Jan Tumlir, *Jorge Pardo Untitled*, The Royal Festival Hall, London; *Art Issues*, no.57; *Bauen+Wohnen*, no.3; **1998** *Art at the turn of the Millennium*, Taschen; Carlos Basualdo, *Cream Contemporary Art in Culture*, London; *New York Times*, January; *Flash Art*, no.199; *Artforum*, November, December; *Art in America*, December; *Frankfurter Allgemeine Zeitung*, 10 August
SELECTED EXHIBITIONS
2001 Montblanc Kulturstiftung, Hamburg; Friedrich Petzel Gallery, New York; **2000** Dia Art Foundation, New York; Kunsthalle Basel; **1999** The Fabric Workshop, Philadelphia; Royal Festival Hall, London; 'Swish I'm a Fish', Museum Abteiberg. Mönchengladbach; **1998** 'Jorge Pardo. 4166 Sea View Lane', Museum of Contemporary Art, Los Angeles; Patrick Painter, Santa Monica; 'Wool, Cotton, Latex, Wax & Steel', Friedrich Petzel Gallery, New York; Kunstverein Ludwigsburg, Villa Franck, Ludwigsburg
AWARDS
Smithsonian American Art Museum Lucelia Award; The Louis Comfort Tiffany Foundation

STEPHEN PEART
Born Durham, 1958. Lives and works in Campbell, California
SELECTED PROJECTS
1999 Panel Floor System, Knoll; **1998** Persona, answering machine, Sun Microsystem; **1996** Computer Cap, Virtual Vision; Shoe of the Future, Reebok; Keyboard/Scanner, Compaq; Papermax Scanner, Visioneer; Adjustable Keyboard, Apple; **1994** Surf Computer Accessories: Mouse Pad, Keyboard Wrist Rest, Lumbar Support, Knoll; **1990** Animal Wetsuit, O'Neill
SELECTED EXHIBITIONS
MoMA New York, Cooper-Hewitt, National Design Museum, Smithsonian Institution, New York, permanent collections
AWARDS
2000 National Design Triennial, Design Culture Now; Cooper-Hewitt, National Design Museum; **1997** Industrial Design Excellence Awards; **1996** Good Design Award, Chicago Athenaeum; **1994** BBC Design Awards, London; Red Dot Award, Essen

OLIVIER PEYRICOT
Born Lyon, 1969. Lives and works in Paris
EDUCATION
1989–94 Ecole Supérieure de Design Industriel (ESDI), Paris
PRACTICE
2002 Design Consulting for Renault, Guyancourt, France; **2001 to present** Teacher at l'Ecole Supérieure d'Art et de Design (ESAD), Reims, France; **2000–1** Teacher at Camondo, Paris; **1999–2000** Teacher at ENSCI, Les Ateliers, Paris; **1998 to present** Editor of *Revue Mobile*, Paris; **1996 to present** Manager of Idsland, Paris
SELECTED PROJECTS
2002 Frozen, new typology of cosmetics containers, Le Cercle; **2000** Pioneer Wagon, Slow Rider, Idsland; **1998 to present** *Revue Mobile*, experimental and thematic design review; **2001** Kléber, tyres, Michelin; Carrying, Planting, Growing, temporary shop, Mandarina Duck; Body Props, morphologic comfort pillow, Edra; **1999** Salière, Axis; Double Siége, chair, Idsland; **1998** Verre Poisson Rouge, glass, Axis
SELECTED BIBLIOGRAPHY
1999 *Surface*, no.17, New York; **1998** *Interior View*, no.11, Paris; **1997** *Intramuros*, special, January, Paris; **1995** *Modo*, no.166, Milan
SELECTED EXHIBITIONS
2001 'Idsland at IFA Futur design, Qualité photo', IFA Institut Français d'Architecture, Paris; **2000** 'Slow rider', Drive in at Cologne Messe, **1999–2000** 'Glassex/Glassexchange Glassextension', Glassbox Gallery, Salone satellite, Salone del Mobile, Milan; **1997** 'Arsenal', Salon du Meuble, Paris; **1995** 'Stratégies individuelles', Gallery Néotu, Paris
AWARDS
2001 Second Prize, Concours 'profession plastique', Paris; **2000** Lauréat du concours 'exercice de style', APCI, Paris; **1998** Lauréat bourse FIACRE à l'Edition, Ministère de la Culture, Paris; **1995** Lauréat bourse FIACRE à la Création, Ministère de la Culture, Paris

CHRISTOPHE PILLET
Born 1959. Lives and works in Paris
EDUCATION
1986 Domus Academy, Milan; **1985** Decorative Arts School, Nice
PRACTICE
1993 to present Freelance; **1988–93** Worked with Philippe Starck, Paris; **1986–8** Worked with Martin Bedin, Milan
SELECTED PROJECTS
2001 Mobilier, Liv'it; Bottle, Perrier; Sofas, Edra; Bed and console, Mobileffe; Table, Ceccotti; Table, Schopenhauer; **2000** Kitchen scales, Tanita; Lamp, Tronconi; Table, Magis; Tables and chairs, Hidden; Sofa, bedside tables, bed and screen, Domeau & Pérès; Wooden chair, Dornbracht; Table, Fiam; Lamp, Mazzega; Lamp, Fontana Arte; Household appliances, Whirlpool; Armchair, Dornbracht; Sofa, Artelano; **1999** Armchair, sofa, Domeau & Pérès; Ashtray, Get 27; Armchair, Bally; Glass table, Schopenhauer; Glassware, Daum; **1998** Furniture, Cambrai Chrome; Urban furniture, JC Decaux; Sofa, Domeau & Pérès; Table, Lema; Plastic Furniture, Magis
SELECTED BIBLIOGRAPHY
Articles in *Intramuros*, *Elle*, *Elle Décor*, *Vogue Décor*, *Vogue Homme*, *Maison Française*, *Maisons et Jardins*, *Glamour*, *Le Figaro*, *Figaro Magazine*, *Le Monde*, *Marie Claire Maison*, *Actel*, *Figaro Madame*, *International Design Yearbooks* (1990–93), *View on Colour*, *Beaux Arts*, *Casa Vogue*, *Domus*, *Interni*, *Modo*, *Abitare*, *Elle Décor*, *Elle Deco* (Japan), *Axis*, *Design Week*, *Wallpaper**, *Blueprint*, *Architektur & Wohnen*, *Raum & Wohnen*, *Design Report* (Germany), *Metropolitan Home*, *Washington Post*, *New York Times*, *Architectural Digest*, *House and Garden* (USA), *Vogue* (Brazil), *Casa* (Brazil)
SELECTED EXHIBITIONS
2000 Centre culturel de St Raphaël, Var, France; Forum, Paris; **1999** Galerie Peyroulet, Paris; 'Ecole français un siècle de design', Paris; 'Designers' Week', VIA, Tokyo, Japan;

'Deluxe', Experimanta Design, Lisbon, Portugal; 'Doposcuola', Domus Academy, Milan; **1998** E&Y, Osaka, Japan; 'Oggetti Resorti', Milan, Tokyo; Centre Culturel Français, Damascus; 'Trophée pour l'an 2000', Milan; 'New Kids in Town', Tokyo; 'Oggetti Onesti', Milan; 'Café – café', VIA, Paris; **1997** 'Parismix 10', Osaka, Japan; **1997** '10 ans du grand prix', VIA, Paris; 'Oggetti Discreti', Milan; '20 aus de création en France', Centre Georges Pompidou, Paris

AWARDS

1994 Créateur de l'année

CANDELA REYMUNDO

Born Córdoba, 1966. Lives and works in Barcelona

EDUCATION

1992 Escola Massana, Barcelona; **1987** E.A.A.O.A.-Mateo Inurria, Córdoba

PRACTICE

1995 Teacher, Escola Massana, Barcelona; **1993 to present** Freelance, industrial and graphic design, Barcelona

SELECTED PROJECTS

2002 EH, WC brush, Bd ediciones de diseño; **2001** Ven-imán, cupping glass for publicity in stores; **2000** Guayaba, electronic scale; **1999** Candela, lamp; **1998** Iota, clothes rack; **1997** Solaris, bath accessories, Nito Arredamenti; **1996** Iolaluna, scale, Rapsel; Señalex, sistem signals, XATRAC; Pacosol, kettle

SELECTED BIBLIOGRAPHY

1999 *Maison Française*, June-July; **1998** *Wallpaper**, September-October, London

SELECTED EXHIBITIONS

1998 'Delta award', Casa Caritat, CCCB, Barcelona; **1996** 'De Jacobsen a Siza Vieira: los maestros en el baño', Casa Battlló, Barcelona

AWARDS

1992 Special mention, Moulinex, Barcelona

DAVID ROBB

Born Arlington, Massachusetts, 1955. Lives and works in Munich

EDUCATION

1976–9 Art Center College of Design, Pasadena, California; **1973** South Grand Prairie High School, Grand Prairie, Texas

PRACTICE

1997 to present Vice-President BMW Motorcycle Design, Munich; **1993–7** Chief Designer BMW Motorcycle, Munich; **1984–93** BMW Design (Automobile), Exterior Design, Exterior Design Studio Chief, Munich; **1980–4** Audi Design, exterior, interior and advanced design, Ingolstadt, Germany; **1979–80** Chrysler Advanced Design, Farmington Hills/Highland Park, Michigan; **1978–9** Freelance work, among others, illustration work with Raymond Loewy, Los Angeles, California

SELECTED PROJECTS

2002 F 650 CS, R 1150 GS Adventure, BMW; **2001** R 1150 RT, BMW; **2000** R 1150 R, R 1150 GS, F 650 GS, F 650 GS Dakar, C-1, BMW; **1998** K 1200 LT, R 1100 S, BMW; **1997** R 1200 C, BMW; **1996** K 1200 RS, BMW

SELECTED EXHIBITIONS

1997–2002 'The Art of the Motorcycle', Guggenheim Museum, New York, Bilbao, Las Vegas

AWARDS

2002, 2001, 2000, 1999, 1998, 1997 Red Dot Award, Essen; **2002** Designpreis der Bundesrepublik Deutschland, Frankfurt; **2001** IF Product Design Award, Industrieforum Design Hanover; **2000, 1999** IDSA Gold Award, USA; **2000** Design Sense, Design Museum, London; **1997** IF Design Award, Industrieforum Design Hanover; **1997** Outstanding Design Styling, *Motor Cycle News*, UK

MARTÍN RUIZ DE AZÚA

Born Basque Country, 1965. Lives and works in Barcelona

EDUCATION

1996 Post graduate studies in Architecture and the Design of Ephemeral Constructions, University Politécnica de Barcelona; **1995** Graduated from the University of Barcelona with a degree in Fine Arts, specializing in Design

PRACTICE

1997 to present Freelance designer, teaching at different schools of design and architecture, Barcelona

SELECTED PROJECTS

2001 Interaction cushions, Päi-Thio; Universal-dish, Päi-Thio; **2000** Summer Rebolijo, jug, Aguadé Ceramica; **1999** Tache-naturelle, ceramic vases, Workshop, Ecole des Beaux Arts de Saint-Etienne; Basic House, Päi-Thio; Armchair-screen, Casas

SELECTED BIBLIOGRAPHY

2001 Phyllis Richardson, *xs Big Ideas Small Buildings*, London; Tulya Beyerle, *Global Tools*, Vienna; Chantal Prod'Hom, *Air en Forme*, Lausanne; **2000** Ramou Prat, *Barcelona + Barcelona*; *Domus*, no.832, 822, Milan; *Abitare*, no.405, Milan; *The World of Interiors*, July, London

SELECTED EXHIBITIONS

2001 'Living in Motion', Vitra Design Museum, Germany; 'Global Tools', Kunsthaus, Vienna; **2000** 'Blow Up', Vitra Design Museum, Germany; 'Air en forme', Design Museum, Lausanne; 'Recherche-futur', Nao, Paris; **1999** 'Futur Compost', Palau de la Virreina, Barcelona

AWARDS

2000 Ciutat de Barcelona Design Prize, Barcelona; **2000** Menliou/International Furniture Festival, Valencia; **1999, 1998** Premio Expo-Hogar, Barcelona

TIMO SALLI

Born Porvoo, Finland, 1963. Lives and works in Helsinki

EDUCATION

1996 MA, Craft and Design Program, University of Art and Design, Helsinki; **1992** BA, Furniture Design, Lahti Design Institute, Lahti, Finland

PRACTICE

1993 to present Muotoilutoimisto Salli, Helsinki; **1990–2** Stefan Lindfors design and interior architectural studio, Helsinki; **1990** Avarte Oy, Furniture Company, Helsinki

SELECTED PROJECTS

2002 Pairbag, bags, SITRA; Firebox-long, Muotoilutoimisto Salli; **2001** Firecase, fireplace, prototype, Snowcrash; Lamplamp, mirror lamp, Muotoilutoimisto Salli; Workshop, experimental plywood furniture, Huonekalutehdas Korhonen oy; Design Innovation Forum, exhibition architecture, Designium; **1999** Timotimo-lamp, prototype, Snowcrash

SELECTED BIBLIOGRAPHY

2002 *Repères*, Paris; **2001** *Designing the 21st Century*, Cologne; *Daring the Gap*, Cologne; *Zoo*, no.8, London; *Intramuros*, no.94, Paris; **2000**; *Objects-Concepts*, Helsinki; **1999** *Design-Directory Scandinavia*, Bonn; *Axis*, no.80, Tokyo; *Interiör*, no.4, Stockholm; **1998** *Design Report*, no.9, Hamburg; **1997** *Domus*, no.799, Milan

SELECTED EXHIBITIONS

2002 'Worldwide', Salon du Meuble, Paris; **2001** 'Daring the Gap', Rendel & Spitz, Cologne; 'SE', Life Space', Kunstindustimuseet, Copenhagen; **2000** '100', Railway storehouses, Helsinki; **1999** 'Taivas kattona', Street art happening, Tampere, Finland; **1997** 'Snowcrash', Facsimile, Milan

AWARDS

1999–2000 3-year State Grand, Taideteollisuus Toimikunta, Helsinki; **1998** Young Designer Prize by Ingo Maurer (for Snowcrash), *Architektur & Wohnen* magazine, Hamburg; **1997** Young Finland Prize, Taideteollisuus Toimikunta, Helsinki

KAZUYO SEJIMA

Born Ibaraki Prefecture, Japan, 1956. Lives and works in Tokyo

EDUCATION

1981 Graduated from Japan Women's University with Master Architecture Degree, Tokyo

PRACTICE

2001 Professor at Keio University, Tokyo, Visiting Lecturer at Tokyo University, Tokyo; **2000–1** Visiting Professor at ETH, Zurich; **2000** Visiting Professor at Harvard University Graduate School of Design, Cambridge; **1995** Established SANAA with Ryue Nishizawa, Tokyo; **1987** Established Kazuyo Sejima & Associates, Tokyo

SELECTED PROJECTS

2001 Flower Chair, IDEF; **2000** Hanahana, flower holder, Driade; Marumaru, chair Driade; **1998** Café Chair, Device Co; **1990** Floor Stand Light, Nippon Electricglass

SELECTED BIBLIOGRAPHY

2000 *Kazuyo Sejima + Ryue Nishizawa 1995–2000*, El Croquis, no.99, Spain; **1999** *Kazuyo Sejima 1987–1999 / Kazuyo Sejima + Ryue Nishizawa 1995–1999*, JA, vol.35, Japan; **1998** GA *Sejima Kazuyo Dokuhon*, Japan; **1996** Kenchiku Bunka, *Kazuyo Sejima & Associates: 1987–1996*, no.591, Japan; **1996** *Kazuyo Sejima 1988–1996*, El Croquis, no.77, Spain

SELECTED EXHIBITIONS

2001 'Breeze of Air', Witte de With, Rotterdam; **2000** Exhibition 'Kazuyo Sejima + Ryue Nishizawa 6 projects', Aedes Gallery, Berlin / NAI, Rotterdam, / Ministerior de Fomento, Madrid; **2000** Exhibition design for 'La Biennale di Venezia', Japanese Pavilion, Venice; **1999** Participation in exhibition 'The Un-Private House', New York; **1998** 'Kazuyo Sejima + Ryue Nishizawa', GA Gallery, Tokyo; **1997** Participation in the exhibition 'The Virtual Architecture', Tokyo University Digital Museum, Tokyo

AWARDS

2002 Arnold W Brunner Memorial Prize in Architecture, American Academy of Arts & Letters, New York; **2002** Architecture Award of Salzburg Vincenzo Scamozzi, Salzburg; **2000** Erich Schelling Architekturpreis, Karlsruhe; **1998** The Prize of Architectural Institute of Japan for Multi-media Workshop, Tokyo

HÉCTOR SERRANO

Born Valencia, 1974. Lives and works in London

EDUCATION

1998–2000 Royal College of Art, London; **1992–8** ESDI Ceu, Valencia

PRACTICE

www.hectorserrano.com

2001–2 Product design tutor at Ravensbourne College of Design and Communication, London; **2000–2** Started own studio, London; **2000** Designer at IDEO, London

SELECTED PROJECTS

2002 Inquieta, fashion catwalk, Fundacion Murcia XXI, Diseño y moda; **2001** Manolo is gonna have fun; Playboy, lamp; **2000** Superpatata, lamp, Droog Design Collection; Top Secret, lamp; **1999** La Siesta, bottle, in collaboration with Alberto Martinez, Raky Martinez, La Mediterranea; Aiberia, table, in collaboration with Alberto Martinez, Raky Martinez

SELECTED BIBLIOGRAPHY

2002 *Frame*, no.24, Amsterdam; *B-guided*, no.10, winter, Barcelona; **2001** *Un Móvil en la Patera*, *Diseñando el Siglo XXI*, Spain; *¡Ahora Diseño!*, Madrid; *Situaciones*, Spain; *Independent*, January, London; **2000** *Guardian*, July, London; *New Design*, no.8, London; *El Pais de las Tentaciones*, no.358, Madrid; *Experimenta*, no.33, Madrid; *NEO2*, November–December, Madrid; *Axis*, November–December, Tokyo

SELECTED EXHIBITIONS

2002 'Skin: Surface and Structure in Contemporary Design', Cooper-Hewitt, National Design Museum, New York; **2001** 'Great Expectations Exhibition', UK in NY Festival in Grand Central Terminal, New York; 'Re: Living Britain', Ozone Gallery, Tokyo; 'Un Móvil en la Patera, Diseñando el Siglo XXI', Espai D'Art Contemporary de Castelló, Castellón, Spain; 'New Designs', Droog Design, Milan; **1999** 'FIM', IVAM, Valencia

AWARDS

2002 Premio Nacional de Diseños no aburridos, Fundacion Murcia XXI, Diseño y Moda, Murcia, Spain; **2000** Peugeot Design Award, London

CARINA SETH ANDERSSON

Born Stockholm, 1965. Lives and works in Stockholm

EDUCATION

1989–93 National College of Art and Design, Konstfack, Stockholm; 1986 Orrefors glass school, Orrefors, Sweden

PRACTICE

1987–9 Working for Andes Wingårdh in his glass studio, Baskemölla, Sweden

SELECTED PROJECTS

2001 Arla milk glass, industrial press glass, for school in Sweden, Arla; 1999 Relation, glass bowl, iittala; 1997–8 Salad bowl, salad set, Hackman; 1996 csa 1 and csa 2, glass cylinders, cbi

SELECTED BIBLIOGRAPHY

2001 Swedish Architecture and Design Yearbook, Sweden; 2000 Susanne Helgesson, Svenska Former, Sweden; 1999, 1998 International Design Yearbook, London

SELECTED EXHIBITIONS

1999–2001 'Glas', Galleri Ingermolin, Stockholm; 1997 Victoria & Albert Museum, London; 1996 'Glass and Light', Form Design Center, Malmö; Röhsska Museet, Göteborg; 'Not so Simple', ICSS, New York; 1994 'Triennale di Milano', Milan

AWARDS

2000 Good Design, Chicago; 1998–9 Utmärkt svensk form, Stockholm; Design Plus Award, Frankfurt

MATT SINDALL

Born 1950. Lives and works in Paris

EDUCATION

BA Kingston Polytechnic

PRACTICE

www.mattsindall.com

1995 Freelance designer; Design Professor at LESAD, Reims; 1990–5 Jean-Michel Wilmotte, Function Chief Designer, Paris; 1988 Furniture and Office accessories, Product File International; 1985–90 Met Studio, Function Chief Designer, London; 1983–5 BBC Television; 1982–3 Wrightson & Raymond

SELECTED PROJECTS

2001 Niels, sofa, Sawaya & Moroni; Shark Christmas Tree; Nearly, chair; 2000 Chromatic Chair; Red Bed/Black Bed; Chair under the Influence, Street Lamp; Little Light Reading; Scarabé, table/bench; AAAAA, carpet; 1999 Klingon, vase; 1998 Whole, table; Ounze, stool/table

SELECTED EXHIBITIONS

2002 'Cité Radieuse de Le Corbusier', Briey, France; 2001 'Design Lab', Salon de Meuble Paris; 'Les Appelles Permenant' pour le VIA, Salon de Meuble, Paris; 2000, 'Biennale Internationale Design' St Etienne, member of Workshop; 'Déviation', St Etienne; 1999 'Détournement et Récupération', Paris, 1998 'Justin Petite Chaise' Paris, Rennes et Reims; 'La Vie En Rose', Fondation Cartier, Paris

JOB SMEETS

Born Hamont, Belgium, 1969. Lives and works in Eindhoven and Antwerp

EDUCATION

1990–5 Design Academy, Eindhoven

PRACTICE

www.studiojob.nl

1997 to present Head of design Studio Job, Eindhoven; 1997 to present Lectures in various companies, Foundations, Art Academies, University Faculties; 1995–7 Initiator, co-designer Oval, Eindhoven; 1994 Internship Premier Vision, Paris; Internship Studio Edelkoort, Paris; Internship Ravage, Paris

SELECTED PROJECTS

2001 to present Moving Sculpture, NPS/VARA-building mediapark Hilversum in co-oper-ation with Kunst en Bedrijf; 2001 Craft, Studio Job, Collection Groninger Museum; Toy

Time Tool, Studio Job; Be Furniture, Collection Centraal Museum; 2000–1 Cocoons, School de Boemerang in co-operation with Kunst en Bedrijf; 2000 Modular Cabinet, Studio Job; 1999–2000 Hall Cabinet, audiovisual 25kV-building Rotterdam; Communication Unit, audiovisual 25kV-building, Rotterdam; 2000 Curved Sofa, collection Galerie Binnen, Amsterdam; 1999 Moulding Grey, audio-equipment, Collection Marantz-Audio; 1999 Curved Cabinet; 1998 to present Curved Chair, collection Museum Boymans Van Beuningen, Rotterdam

SELECTED BIBLIOGRAPHY

2002 View on Colour, Paris; Spur, February, Tokyo; Zoo, no.12, London; Frame, Amsterdam; 2001 Interni, no.511, Milan; Wallpaper*, no.36, London; Surface, no.31, San Francisco; AMC, no.119, Paris; Zoo no.9, no.10, London; Metropolis M, no.2, Amsterdam; 2000 INView, no.16, Paris; Form, no.171, Frankfurt; 1999 Items, no.5, Amsterdam; Design Report, no.10, Munich; 1998 Paola Antonelli, Gijs Bakker, Renny Ramakers, Spirit of the Nineties, Rotterdam; 1997 Jennifer Hudson, International Design Yearbook, London; 1996 View on Colour, no.8, Paris; Domus, no.784, Milan

SELECTED EXHIBITIONS

2002 'Job at Viafarini', Salone del Mobile, Milan; 'Hand Made Holland', Crafts Council, London; 'Characters', Groninger Museum; 2001 'Rapids', Groninger Museum; 'Job', Exhibition KunstRAI Art Amsterdam; 'Solitary', Salone del Mobile, Milan; 2000–1 'Pleidooi voor intuïtie', Metropolitan Museum, The Hague; 2000 'Exhibition Elements', Gallery, The Apartment, New York; 'Job', Galerie Binnen, Amsterdam; 'Room with a View', Salone del Mobile, Milan; 1999 'Moulding Grey', Dutch Individuals, Salone del Mobile, Milan; 1996 'From the Netherlands', MoMA, New York; 'Plastic Now, Ironi', Droog Design, Salone del Mobile, Milan

AWARDS

2001 Nomination Communication Unit and Hall Cabinet for the Rotterdam Design Prize, Rotterdam; 2000 Nomination Dutch Culture Prize, Amsterdam; 1996 Nomination for best exam of the year, Renee Smeets Prize, Design Academy, Eindhoven

REIKO SUDO

Born Niihari, Ibaragi, Japan. Lives and works in Tokyo

PRACTICE

www.nuno.com

1989 to present Director, NUNO Corporation / Lecturer, Faculty of Textiles, Musashino Art University, Tokyo; 1984–9 Textile Designer, NUNO Corporation, Tokyo; 1977–84 Freelance textile designer, contracts with Kanebo, Nishikawa and others, Tokyo; 1975–7 Assistant to Professor Hideho Tanaka, Faculty of Textiles, Musashino Art University, Tokyo

SELECTED EXHIBITIONS

2001 'Structure and Surface: Contemporary Japanese Textiles', Museum für Angewandte Kunst, Frankfurt; 2000 'NUNO: Contemporary Japanese Textiles', Anna Leonowens Gallery, Nova Scotia College of Art and Design; 1999–2000 'Structure and Surface: Contemporary Japanese Textiles', touring exhibition

AWARDS

1999 JID Award; 1994, 1993 Roscoe Award; 1991 Roscoe Award finalist, Cooper-Hewitt Museum and Interior Design Magazine, New York

ILKKA SUPPANEN

Born Kotka, Finland, 1968. Lives and works in Helsinki

EDUCATION

1992–3 Gerrit Rietveldt Academy, Amsterdam; 1989 Studies in Design: University of Art and Design Helsinki; 1988 Studies in Architecture: Technical University of Helsinki

PRACTICE

2000–1 Creative Director of Snowcrash company, Stockholm; 1996 Snowcrash, Founding member, Helsinki; 1995 Studio Ilkka Suppanen founded, Helsinki

SELECTED PROJECTS

2001 Table, prototype; 2000 Fair stand, commercial space design, Artek Oy; 1999 Game, shelf; 1998 Hiwave, lamp, Snowcrash; Concept for Saab 93 convertible, Saab Automobiles; Virtual Fireplace, research and development, Nokia; 1997 Flying Carpet, furniture, Cappellini; Frozen Light; Nomad Chair; Airbag, chair, Snowcrash

SELECTED BIBLIOGRAPHY Interieur; New Scandinavian Design; Empty Spaces; Interni; Modern Scandinavian Design; International Design Yearbook; Furniture Design; Designing the 21st Century

SELECTED EXHIBITIONS

2001 'Workspheres', MoMA, New York; 2000 'Hothouse', Interieur 2001, Kortrijk, Belgium; 1999 'New Scandinavian Design', Museum für Angewandte Kunst, Cologne; 1998 'Modern Finnish Design', Bart Graduate Center, New York; 1997 'Snowcrash exhibition', Facsimile gallery, Milan

AWARDS

2001 Young Designer of the Year, Design Forum Finland, Helsinki; 1998 Young Suomi Prize, Helsinki; 1997 Young Designer Award, nominated by Ingo Mauer, for Snowcrash group, Hamburg; 1995 Habitare Prize, Nominated by Alessandro Mendini, Helsinki

TARTARINI DESIGN TEAM

PRACTICE

Originally associated with Ducati, Leopoldo Tartarini's career has been dominated by his work at Italjet, the company he founded. Now Alessandro has joined the company, pushing forward with the designs of a range of new motorcycles and scooters.

SELECTED EXHIBITIONS

2002 'Motorcycles at the Rockefeller Center', Rockefeller Centre, New York; 1997–2002 'The Art of the Motorcycle', Guggenheim Museum, New York, Bilbao, Las Vegas

AWARDS

1998 'Scooter of the Year' Italjet Formula 50, Italy, Germany, Spain

BIBLIOGRAPHY

1997 'The Art of the Motorcycle', Exhibition Catalogue, Guggenheim Museum, New York

ALI TAYAR

Born Istanbul, 1959. Lives and works in New York

EDUCATION

1983–6, MA, Science in Architecture Studies, MIT, Cambridge; 1978–83 University of Stuttgart, Diplom Ingenieur

PRACTICE

1991 to present Principal, Parallel Design Partnership, New York; 1988–91 Project Architect, FTL Associates, New York; 1986–8 Architect, Lev Zetlin Associates, New York

SELECTED PROJECTS

2001 Spider Shelving System, Magis; Elephant Table, Parallel Design Partnership; Roy's TV Table, Parallel Design Partnership; Icon Work/Wall, Parallel Design Partnership; 1998–9 Rasamny Chair Series, ICF; 1994 Ellen's Brackets, shelving system, Parallel Design Partnership;

SELECTED BIBLIOGRAPHY

2001 Graphis, no.329, New York; 1999 ID, September, New York; ID, June, New York; The New York Observer, 28 June – 5 July, New York; Abitare, no.384, Milan; New York Times, 20 May, New York; 1997 ID, October, New York; New York, 24 March, New York; 1996 Elle Décor, November, New York

SELECTED EXHIBITIONS

2002 'US Design', Denver Art Museum; 2001 'Workspheres', MoMA, New York; 2000 'Aluminum by Design', Carnegie Museum of Art, Pittsburgh; 1999 'On the Table', Wexner Center for the Arts, Columbus, Ohio

AWARDS

2002 Emerging Voices, The Architectural League of New York; 2000 Good Design Award, Chicago Athenaeum; 1995 Individual Grant, National Endowment for the Arts, Washington; 1994 Design Distinction Award, ID Magazine, New York

SHUWA TEI

Born Yokohama, Japan, 1968. Lives and works in Tokyo

EDUCATION
1994 Degree in Architecture, Musashino Art University School of Art and Design, Tokyo

PRACTICE
www.intentionallies.co.jp
1996 Established Intentionallies with two other partners; **1995** Established a label called Intentionallies, a creative force through architecture, with several other architects; **1994–5** Attended several projects as an architect at various architects' studios

SELECTED PROJECTS
2001 ITL006, chair, ITL007, lounge chair, Hoshikame wood processing plant; Atehaca Home Appliances Project, product design of home appliances, Toshiba Co Ltd; **2000** ITL003, lounge chair, ITL004, chair, ITL005, lounge chair, Hoshikame wood processing plant; Superv Interior Project, interior design of a pressroom of a clothing store, Superv Co; **1999** Hanamiduki Interior Project, interior design of a restaurant, Intentionallies

SELECTED BIBLIOGRAPHY
2002 Casa Brutus, no.23, Tokyo; **2001** Confort, no.102 Tokyo; Wallpaper*, September, October, London; **2000** Monument 43, Australia; **2000** Creator's File for Living, vol.2, Tokyo; **1999** Creator's File for Living, Tokyo; **1998** Frame, no.2, Amsterdam

SELECTED EXHIBITIONS
2001 Tokyo Designer's Week, Version Gallery; **2000** 'Designer's Block', St Pancras Chambers, King's Cross, London; 'Tokyo Designer's Block', IDEE; **1998–2000** 'Happening', Hanamiduki/United Arrows, Soph, Tokyo; **1997** 'Definition of Intentionallies', Art Laboratory Gallery Rocket, Tokyo

KAY THOSS

Born Mannheim, 1962. Lives and works in Münster and Milan

EDUCATION
1996–7 Studies in Interior Design, Polytechnic, Milan; **1995–6** Bauhaus University, Weimar, Studies in Product Design, Weimar; **1984–94** Studies in History of Art, Munich, Paris, Münster

PRACTICE
www.kaythoss.com
1998 to present Designer, Milan and Münster

SELECTED PROJECTS
2001 Luck, Quartett, table, Coup, compact forming laminate, own distribution; **2000** Delft, stool and barstool, Dice, stools, Fly, bookshelf, own distribution; **1999** Spring, bench, own distribution; String, armchair, Tok-Stok; Compact, nest of tables, Artificial; **1998** Bend, nest of tables, Artificial

SELECTED BIBLIOGRAPHY
2001 Madame Figaro, October, Athens; Modern Living, November, Hamburg; Vizyon/Dekorasyon, January, Istanbul; **2000** Interieur & Design, September, Moscow; **1999** Wallpaper*, August, London

SELECTED EXHIBITIONS
2002 'Spin-Off, Designed for Industry', Furniture Fair, Cologne; **2001** 'ICFF, Connected', The Apartment, New York; **2000** 'Tokyo Designers' Block'; **1998** 'Ambiente, Tendenze', At the Artificial Stand, Frankfurt; 'Salone Satellite', Salone del Mobile, Milan

NOAM TORAN

Born Las Cruces, USA, 1975. Lives and works in London

EDUCATION
1999–2001 Royal College of Art, London; **1993–7** University of California, Santa Cruz

PRACTICE
2001 Researcher, Interaction Design Institute Ivrea, Italy; Designer and Videographer, IDEO, San Francisco; **2000** Graphic Designer, Quintet Publishing Company, London; **1997–9** Designer, Gensler and Associate Architects, San Francisco

SELECTED PROJECTS
2001 Subliminal Furniture, installation and short film, in collaboration with Tom Hulbert and Stijn Ossevoort, Interactive Design Institute Ivrea; Palmistry, palm reading software, IDEO; Objects for Lonely Men, short film exhibited at Miyake Design Gallery, Tokyo and Global Tools, Künstlerhaus, Vienna; Objects for Lonely Men Collection, collection of conceptual products, exhibited at Miyake Design Gallery, Tokyo; Suicide Helmet, conceptual; Perpetual Motion Machine (Failed); **2000** Eye Contact Machines, exhibited at the Museum of London; Reverse Periscope, exhibited in the oxo Gallery, London; Rematerializing the Video Player, conceptual project

SELECTED BIBLIOGRAPHY
2002 So-En, January, Tokyo; **2001** Tony Dunne and Fiona Raby, Design Noir, Basel; Domus, no.841, Milan; Axis, no.93, Tokyo; FX, September, London; The Independent, July, London

SELECTED EXHIBITIONS
2001 'Six Visions', Miyake Design Studio Gallery, Tokyo; 'Mixed Realities', Interaction Design Institute Ivrea, Italy; 'Global Tools', Künstlerhaus, Vienna; 'Orange at Home', Orange House of the Future, Hatfield; **2000** 'The Unknown', The Museum Of... Fall Exhibition, London; 'Day Out', oxo Gallery, London; 'Recent Work', Stables Gallery, London; **1999** 'Room 13, Recent Work', Phoenix Hotel, San Francisco

AWARDS
2001 Orange at Home Award, London

VALVOMO

Teppo Asikainen, Vesa Hinkola, Markus Nevalainen, Kari Sivonen, Ilkka Terho, Jan Tromp, Rane Vaskivuori, Timo Vierros live and work in Helsinki

EDUCATION
1989 Architecture Faculty, University of Technology, Estoo, Finland

PRACTICE
www.valvomo.com
1993 to present Valvomo Architecture Studio, Helsinki

SELECTED PROJECTS
2001 e-3™ Internet Transaction Kiosk, e-3 Solutions; **2000** Soundwave, acoustic panel system, Snowcrash; Globlow Led, lamp, Snowcrash; Complement Colour Light, Droppe Chair, Snowcrash; **1996** Globlow, inflating lamp, Snowcrash; Chip, Floor Divan, Snowcrash; **1995** Netsurfer, Computer Divan, Snowcrash

SELECTED BIBLIOGRAPHY
1999 Axis, July–August, Tokyo; **1997** Frame, December, Amsterdam; Domus, December, Milan; Wallpaper*, September–October, London; Wallpaper*, July–August, London

SELECTED EXHIBITIONS
2001 'Workspheres', MoMA, New York; **1997** 'Snowcrash', Salone del Mobile, Milan

AWARDS
1997 Finnish National Award for Young Art, Finnish Ministry of Education, Helsinki, Finland; **1997** Architektur & Wohnen Young Designer of the Year, Hamburg

MIGUEL VIEIRA BAPTISTA

Born Lisbon, 1968. Lives and works in Lisbon

EDUCATION
1993 Glasgow School of Art, Product Design post-graduation, Lisbon, Glasgow; **1990** IADE, Industrial Design course, Lisbon

PRACTICE
1991 Henrik Tengler design office, Copenhagen

SELECTED PROJECTS
2002, Vase, combine collection, Box, combine collection, Vista Alegre; **2001** Pile, stackable tray, Authentics, Furo, notebook, ModaLisboa design; Voyager, exhibition design, travelling exhibition presented in Milan, London and Lisbon, experimentadesign; **2000** Handle it, carpet, Asplund; mvb, cutlery range, Cutipol; **1997** Terra, project co-ordination, ceramic lamps, Protodesign, later in 1999, produced by Authentics

SELECTED BIBLIOGRAPHY
2002 Homme no.3, Paris; **2001** Intramuros, no.97, Paris; Frame, no.23, Amsterdam; DDN, no.92, Milan; Interni, no.517, Milan; **2000** Interni, no.507, Milan; **1999** Jasper Morrison, International Design Yearbook, London; Form, no.170, Frankfurt; Wallpaper*, no.20, London; **1998** Domus, no.801, Milan; **1997** Design Report, no.11, November, Hamburg

SELECTED EXHIBITIONS
2002 'Project 01', La Pelota Fuori Salone, Milan; **2001** 'Sinne + 5', Stilwerk, Berlin; 'Vibration Européene', Now! design a vivre, Paris; 'Voyager', Atlantis Gallery, London; **2000** 'Portuguese Design Milan 2000', Superstudio Più, Fuori Salone, Milan; **1999** 'Design Clinic', Fashion Clinic shop, Lisbon; **1997** 'Terra', Ozone Living Design Gallery, Tokyo

AWARDS
1998 Prix d'excellence, Marie Claire Maison, Paris

VOGT + WEIZENEGGER

Oliver Vogt, Hermann Weizenegger live and work in Berlin; Oliver Vogt: born Essen, 1966; Hermann Weizenegger: born Kempten, Allgäu, Germany, 1963

EDUCATION
Oliver Vogt: **1986** Studium Industriedesign an der Hochschule der Bildenden Künste, Berlin, Germany

PRACTICE
www.vogtweizenegger.de
1996 Lecturers at Hochschule der Künste, Berlin; **1993** Established Vogt + Weizenegger, Designbüro, Berlin

SELECTED PROJECTS
2001 Soft Bag, Moeve; **2000** Sweet Bag, Loop Bag, Pulp, soap dispenser, Moeve; **1999** Lightwood Family, lamps, Babylon; Threesisters, ring holder, Moeve; **1997** 123 Regalsystem, shelf system, Lichtung; **1996** Mono Bags, Authentics

SELECTED BIBLIOGRAPHY
2001 art, no.2, Hamburg; Intramuros, no.93, Paris; Design News, no.243, Japan; **2000** Architektur & Wohnen, June–July, Germany; Vogue, November, Germany; Designers' Workshop, October, Japan; **1999** Gap, September, Japan; Domus, no.819, October, Milan; Bewußt, Einfach – Das Entstehen einer alternativen Produktkultur, Stuttgart; Nikkei Design, September, Japan

SELECTED EXHIBITIONS
2001 'Vogt + Weizenegger – Plan A', Galerie Schipper & Krome, Berlin; **2000** 'Going to the beach...', Stilwerk, Berlin; **1999** 'Ambiente', Die Imaginäre Manufaktur, touring exhibition; **1998** 'Blindenanstalt von Berlin, Die Imaginäre Manufaktur', Berlin; 'The Jekyll and Hide Cabinet', a project in collaboration with Andrea Zittel, Los Angeles, Berlin; **1997** 'Zuhause Wohnen: Wohnen in der Zukunft, Passagen', Imhoff-Stollwerk-Museum, Cologne; 'Volles Haus', Galerie Schipper & Krome, Berlin

AWARDS
1999 Design Plus Award, Frankfurt; Frame, Tokyo; IF Preis, Award for Design Excellence, Industrie Forum Design Hanover; **1998, 1996** Red Dot Award, Essen

PIA WALLÉN

Born Umeå, Sweden, 1957. Lives and works in Stockholm

EDUCATION
1980–3 Anders Beckman School of Design, Stockholm

SELECTED PROJECTS
1997 Curtains for the cinema at the Museum of Modern Art, Stockholm, Swedish Art Council; Curtains for the auditorium at the Museum of Architecture, Stockholm, Swedish Art Council; **1995** Carpet collection, Asplund; PS collection, glassware, IKEA

SELECTED BIBLIOGRAPHY
2001 Charlotte Fiell, Peter Fiell, Designing the 21st Century, Cologne; Denise Hagströmer, Swedish Design, Stockholm; Harper's Bazaar, October, Tokyo; Time Magazine, August,

London, 2000 *Stockholm New*, no.5, Stockholm; **1998** *Eigen Huis*, no.11; *ID*, January-February, New York

SELECTED EXHIBITIONS

2002 'Routsi, Finland', Artek, Helsinki; **2001** 'Carrefour de la creation', Centre de Georges Pompidou, Paris; '3D+ Swedish design on stage', touring exhibition; **2000** 'Stockholm – New York', Altman building, New York; **1999** 'New Scandinavia', Museum für Angewandte Kunst, Cologne; 'Swedish Style in Tokyo', Swedish Embassy in Tokyo

AWARDS

1993 The Swedish Artist's Board, 10 years work grant, Stockholm; **1992** Excellent Swedish Design, Honorary mention, Stockholm

MARCEL WANDERS

Born Boxtel, The Netherlands, 1963. Lives and works in Amsterdam

EDUCATION

1985–8 Hogeschool voor de Kunsten, Arnhem, The Netherlands; **1983–5** Academie voor Schone Kunsten, Hasselt, Belgium

PRACTICE

www.marcelwanders.nl

2001 to present Director of Marcel Wanders studio; Art-director of Moooi, Amsterdam; **1995 to present** Independent industrial product designer, Amsterdam; **1995–2001** Director of Wanders Wonders, Amsterdam; **1992–5** Partner in WAAC's Design & Consults, Rotterdam; **1990–2** Industrial product designer in Landmark Design & Consult, Rotterdam

SELECTED PROJECTS

2001 Fishnet Chair, Knotted Table, Airborne snotty vases: Coryza, Influenza, Ozaena, Pollinosis and Sinusitis, Stone Chair, Cappellini; BLO, lamp, Flos; Flower Chair, Moooi; Gwapa Chair, VIP Chair & Flower Coffee Table, Moooi; **2000** Crochet Table, Henna Table, Smoke, glass table, Cappellini; Pebbles, low stool, Magis; **1999** Lucy, candlestick, Goods; Birdhouse, project in co-operation with Droog Design, DMD; Nomad Carpet, Lighting Collection Shadows, Cappellini, **1997** Eggvases, porcelain vases, Sponge Vase and Foam bowl, Moooi; Lace Table, Droog Design; **1996** Knotted Chair, a project in co-operation with Droog Design, Cappellini

SELECTED BIBLIOGRAPHY

2001 *Surface*, October, San Francisco; Charlotte and Peter Fiell, *Designing the 21st Century*, Cologne; *Nylon*, September; *Wohnrevue*, no.8, Switzerland; *Wallpaper**, Fall, London; *Plus*, Fall, London; *het Parool*, 7 April, Amsterdam; **2000** *ID* Magazine, March-April, New York; *Frame*, no.17, The Netherlands; **1999** *Man*, June, Amsterdam

SELECTED EXHIBITIONS

2001 'Salone del Mobile Marcel Wanders, Moooi in Amstelveen' Milan; **2000** 'Dutch Design', Ozone, Living Design Centre, Tokyo; 'Wanders Wanted expo', Gallery Material Connection, New York; 'Design World' Taideteollisuusmuseo, Helsinki; 'Droog design exhibition' travelling through USA; **1999** 'Wanders Wonders, design for a new age', Museum het Kruithuis, Den Bosch, The Netherlands; 'Droog in Oranienbaum, Germany'

AWARDS

2001 Nominated for Designer of the Year category in Wired Magazine's *Wired* Rave Awards, San Francisco; **2000** Nomination Rotterdam Design Prize; **2000** George Nelson Award, *Interiors* Magazine; Alterpoint Design Award, Milan; **1999** Double nomination for Rotterdam Design Prize; **1998** Winner of the 'Woonbeurspin', Amsterdam; **1998** Honorable mention in the 'Compasso d'Oro', Italy

KENNET WILLIAMSSON

Born Ostansjo, Sweden, 1951. Lives and works in Zinkgruvan, Sweden

EDUCATION

Among others, worked with glass designer Bertil Vallien and Ulrica Hydman-Vallien, and basically self-taught, Sweden

PRACTICE

1966 to present Potter, Sweden

SELECTED PROJECTS

2002 Vodka Bar, bowls and bottles; Fruitbowl; **2001** Romantic Tableware; Snack Boxes; **1997** Blueberry Baskets; Wine Jugs; **1995–2002** Safe Candleholders

SELECTED BIBLIOGRAPHY

Several articles in books and magazines about craft and design and art magazines

SELECTED EXHIBITIONS

2002 Art Industrial Museum, Helsinki; **2000** 'The excellent Swedish set of china in light blue colour by Kennet Williamsson', Gallery Inger Molin, Stockholm. Different museums and galleries in Scandinavia and Europe: Contemporary Applied Arts, London, Royal College of Art, London and the Swedish National Museum, Stockholm

AWARDS

Since **1992** lifetime grant from the Swedish Cultural Department and other arts and crafts awards, Stockholm

BEN WILSON

Born London, 1976. Lives and works in London

EDUCATION

1999–2001 MA Design Product, Royal College of Art, London; **1995–8** MA 3D Design, Manchester; **1993–5** Barnet College, London

PRACTICE

2001–2 Designer Research Fellowship Helen Hamlyn, Royal College of Art, London; **2000** Designer, Creaneau, Hassult, Belgium; Consultant, McCann Ericson, London

SELECTED PROJECTS

2001–2 Suspension lights, Artemide; Cypress low, lowrider bicycle for Cypress Hill, Columbia Music, Sony; Circular Cam Rig, camera rig stabilizer, Mike Figgis, Red Mullet; **2001** Inflatable Cam Rig, protective inflatable cam rig; Crochet chair, RCA; **1999–2002** Tilt Trike, Hand powered trike, Wizzkidz; **1999** Pull Along, device for transporting children, Ron Arad Associates; **1998** Scooter, adult push scooter, Downlow; **1997–8** DLPT1, Lowrider recumbent bicycle, Downlow

SELECTED BIBLIOGRAPHY

2001 *Domus*, no.841, Milan; *Axis*, no.93, Tokyo; *ID*, September, New York; *Blueprint*, no.187, London; Laurance Remila, *Agency Business*, no.7, London; **1999** *Independent Magazine*, January, London; *Esquire*, February, London; *Lowdown*, no.3, March, London; Jez Ford, *Times*, May, London; *ID*, no.188, New York; *HPV*, August, London; **1998** *FX*, August, London; *Total Bike*, May, London

SELECTED EXHIBITIONS

2001 'Six Visions MDSG', Issey Miyake Gallery, Tokyo; 'Adorn Equip', The City Gallery, Leicester, UK; **2000–2001** 'Journey Zone', Millennium Dome, London; **2000** 'Mi Carizon', Brick Lane, London; 'Twisted Levis', Interjeans, Cologne; **1999** 'Winning The Design Of Sport', McLellan Galleries, Glasgow

AWARDS

2001 Lord Snowdon Prize, London; Design For Our Future Selfs, HHRC, London; **1999** Shortlisted Peugeot Design Awards, London

TOKUJIN YOSHIOKA

Born Saga, Japan, 1967. Lives and works in Tokyo

EDUCATION

1986 Kuwasawa Design School, Tokyo

PRACTICE

www.tokujin.com

2000 Established Tokujin Yoshioka Design, Tokyo; **1992** Started activity as a freelance designer, Tokyo; **1988 to present** Miyake Design Office, Tokyo; **1987–** Office of the late Shiro Kuramata, Tokyo

SELECTED PROJECTS

2002 Tokyo Pop, seats, Driade; **2001** Honey-pop, chair; Issey Miyake shop, Issey Miyake; **2000** ToFU, lamp, Yamagiwa; Nissan Project Plan, Nissan; **1999–2000** A House Moving Project; **1999** Window Display for Issey Miyake, Issey Miyake;

1998 BMW Window display for BMW's new model at the Oremachi Showroom, BMW

SELECTED BIBLIOGRAPHY

2002 *Axis*, no.95, Japan; **2001** *Abitare*, no.402, Milan; *Interni*, no.517, Milan; *Architektur & Wohnen*, March, Germany; *Axis*, no.93, Japan; **2000** *Designers' Workshop*, no.108, Japan; *Elle Décor*, no.50, Japan; **1999** *Frame*, November, Amsterdam; *Axis*, no.80, Japan

SELECTED EXHIBITIONS

2001 'Tokujin Yoshioka Design Exhibition-Xperiment', Axis Gallery, Tokyo

AWARDS

2001 The A&W Award, The Coming Designer for The Future, Germany; The Mainichi Design Award, Tokyo; **2001, 2000** The Award of Excellence, *ID* Annual Design Review, USA; **1997** The Award of Excellence, JDC Design, Tokyo

MICHAEL YOUNG

Born Sunderland, UK, 1966. Lives and works in London and Reykjavik

EDUCATION

1989–92 Kingston Polytechnic, Kingston, UK

PRACTICE

www.michael-young.com

2000 Established MY Studio in Reykjavik; **1992–4** Design Driver at Space Tom Dixon, London, UK

SELECTED PROJECTS

2002 Lemonade Chair, Swedese; Dog House, Post Computer Games, Hringbol, Wheel Table, Yogi Family, furniture, Magis; **2001** Ashtray, Self Cooling Glass, Ice Bucket, Rosenthal; Breakfast Set, Nikko, Mud; Bedtray, Magis; Pearl Necklace, concept, Golay Buchel; Holey Chair, Corian; Glass Tables, Barstools, Twenty Twentyone; **2000** Trestle Table, Magis; **1999** Champagne Glass, Laurent Perrier; Tablelight, IDEE; **1998** Candlesticks, Silver Vase, Sawaya & Moroni; Necklace, Smak; Sticklight, Eurolounge; Armed Chair, Michael Young; **1997** Wood Table and Chair, Sawaya & Moroni

SELECTED BIBLIOGRAPHY

2002 Bethan Ryder, *Bar & Club Design*, London; *Bar & Restaurants*, HBI; **2001** *Designing the 21st Century*, Cologne; *Black and White*, no.9; *Monitor*, no.1; **2000** *Frame*, no.1, Amsterdam; *Domus*, no.829, Milan

SELECTED EXHIBITIONS

2002 'Guest of Honour', Kortrijk, Interiur, Belgium; **1998** 'Michael Young, Marc Newson, Jasper Morrison', Icelandic Museum of Modern Art, Reykjavik

AWARDS

1995 Talente 95, Germany

Abode
www.abode.co.jp

Adachi Shiki Kogyo
www.adachishiki.co.jp

Agape
www.agapedesign.it

Aguadé Ceramica
www.aguade.com

Alias
www.aliasdesign.it

Anura Living
www.anuradesign.com

Apple
www.apple.com

Arabia
www.arabia.fi

Artificial
www.artificial.de

Artifort
www.artifort.com

Artoria
www.artoria.fr

Aspect
www.aspect.co.jp

Asplund
Sibyllegatan 31
114 42 Stockholm

Atelier Satyendra Pakhalé
www.satyendra-pakhale.com

Authentics
www.authentics.de

Axis
www.axis-paris.com

Azumi
www.azumi.co.uk

B&B Italia
www.bebitalia.it

Babylon Design
www.babylonlondon.com

BC Koubou
3-1-25 Jingumae, Shibuya-ku
Tokyo

Bd ediciones de diseño
www.bdbarcelona.com

Bernstrand & Co
www.bernstrand.com

Biomega
www.biomega.dk

Blu Dot
www.bludot.com

BMW
www.bmw.com

Browne & Co
www.browneco.com

Camper
www.camper.com

Cappellini
www.cappellini.it

Cassina
www.cassina.it

Citroën
www.citroen.com

ClassiCon
www.classicon.com

Claudio Colucci Design
www.colucci-design.com

Cleverline
www.cleverline.nl

Covo
www.covo.it

Cutipol
www.cutipol.com

Dainese
www.dainese.com

Danese
www.danesemilano.com

David Design
www.david.se

Designers eye
www.designerseye.se

Design House Stockholm
www.designhouse.se

De Vecchi
www.devecchi.com

Dilmos Edizioni
www.dilmos.it

DIM
www.blindenanstalt.de

Domeau & Pérès
www.domeauperes.com

Dornbracht
www.dornbracht.com

Dovetusai
www.dovetusai.it

Driade
www.driade.com

Droog Design
www.droogdesign.nl

Du Pont
www.dupont.com

e-3™ Solutions
www.e3solutions.fi

E&Y
www.eandy.com

Edra
www.edra.com

ElekSen
www.eleksen.com

Ericsson
www.ericsson.com

EUG (El Ultimo Grito)
4 Peacock Yard, Iliffe Street
London SE17 3LH

Eurolounge
www.eurolounge.co.uk

Fiam
www.fiamitalia.it

Fix Design
Rua Decio Reis 202
CEP 05446-010
São Paolo

Flos
www.flos.net

FontanaArte
www.fontanaarte.it

Ford Motor Company
www.ford.com

Galería H2O
Verdi 152
08012 Barcelona

Galerie Kréo
www.galeriekreo.com

Genelec
www.genelec.com

Getama
Holmmarksvej 22
4300 Holbaek, Denmark

Gilles Peyroulet & Cie
80 rue Quincampoix
75003 Paris

Globe
www.globefurniture.net

Gourmet Settings
www.gourmetsettings.com

Habitat
www.habitat.co.uk

Hackman
www.hackman.fi

Handy
55-59 Chrystie Street
#14, New York, NY 10002

Harley Davidson
www.harley-davidson.com

Hashizume
204-3 Hayasuzu-cho
Miyakonojyo-shi
Miyazaki, Japan

Heineken
www.heineken.com

Herman Miller
www.hermanmiller.com

Hidden
www.hidden.nl

Hitch Mylius
www.hitchmylius.co.uk

Horizumi
www.horizumi.co.jp

Hoshikame wood
processing plant
986 Nakagawa Omiya-city
Saitama 330-0831
Japan

Richard Hutten Studio
www.richardhutten.com

ICF
www.icfgroup.com

IDÉE
www.idee.co.jp

Idsland
www.idsland.com

Igarashi Design Studio
R.G.S. 3B 7-44-6 Takinogawa
kita-ku, Tokyo

iittala
www.iittala.fi

Ishimaru Co Ltd
7-3-24 Roppongi, Minato-ku
Tokyo

Isokon Plus
www.isokonplus.com

Italjet Moto
www.italjet.com

JongeriusLab
www.jongeriuslab.com

Keen
www.ke-en.com

Kingiri Kogei
6-16 Akifusa
Kamo-Shi, Niigata-ken

Kamo
Knoll International
www.knoll.com

Kundalini
www.kundalinidesign.com

Kuriyama Bussan
Shimohonai kamata
Sanjyou-shi
Nigata-ken, Tokyo

La Mediterranea
www.lamediterranea.es

La Palma
www.lapalma.it

Levi Strauss
www.levis.com

Ligne Roset
www.ligneroset.fr

Living Divani
www.livingdivani.it

Liv'it
www.livit.it

Magis
www.magisdesign.com

Marna Co
www.marna-inc.co.jp

Marset
www.marset.com

MasayoAve Creation
www.macreation.org

Matsunaga Co
www.matsunagakagu.co.jp

Matsushita
www.national.co.jp

Meshman
www.meshman.com

Miyake Design Studio
www.isseymiyake.com

Möbelbau Kaether & Weise
www.kaetherundweise.de

modalisboa
www.assoc-modalisboa.pt

Moeve
www.moeve.de

Montina
www.montina.it

Moooi
www.moooi.com

Nils Holger Moormann
www.moormann.de

Moroso
www.moroso.it

Motorola
www.motorola.com

Ted Muehling
27 Howard Street
New York, NY 10012

Muotoilutoimisto Salli
Meritullinkatu 11
00170 Helsinki,
Finland

Nike
www.nike.com

Nippon Electric Glass
www.neg.co.jp

Nokia
www.nokia.com

Nola
www.nola.se

Norway Says
www.norwaysays.com

NUNO Corporation
www.nuno.com

Nymphenburg
www.nymphenburg-porzel-
lan.com

Offecct
www.offecct.se

Oluce
www.oluce.com

Ontwerpwerk
www.ontwerpwerk.com

Orangina
www.orangina.fr

Orrefors
www.orrefors.se

OUT.DeSIGN
www.outdesign.com

Paï Thio
www.paithio.com

Panasonic
www.panasonic.com

Pandora
www.pandoradesign.it

Parallel Design
416 West 13th Street
New York, NY 10014

Philips
www.philips.com

Piaggio
www.piaggio.com

Polimold
www.polimold.com.br

Post Design Gallery
Via Moscova 27, Milan

Prada
www.prada.com

Punt Mobles
www.puntmobles.com

Pure Design
www.pure-design.com

Rapsel
www.rapsel.com

Richter Spielgeräte
www.spielgeraete-richter.de

Rörstrand
www.rorstrand.com

Enric Rovira
www.enricrovira.com

Salviati
www.salviati.com

Sawaya & Moroni
www.sawayamoroni.com

Shin Products
www.shinproducts.com

Skruf Svenska glasbruk
www.svenskaglasbruk.se

Smith Sports Inc.
www.smithsports.com

Snowcrash
www.snowcrash.se

Sogo Concept
3-17-37, kamicho hirano-ku
Osaka, Japan

Steelcase Strafor
www.steelcase-strafor.com

Studio Ilkka Suppanen
www.suppanen.com

Studio Job
www.studiojob.nl

Sun Microsystems
www.sun.com

Swatch
www.swatch.com

Swedese
www.swedese.se

Thomson Multimédia
www.thomson-
multimedia.com

Kay Thoss
www.kaythoss.com

Toshiba
www.atehaca.com

tranSglass
www.transglass.co.uk

VIA
www.via.asso.fr

Vidal Sassoon
www.vidalsassoon.com

View
www.viewonline.it

Virtuallydesign.com
www.virtuallydesign.com

Vista Alegre
www.vistaalegre.pt

Pia Wallén
www.piawallen.se

Whirlpool
www.whirlpool.com

WMF
www.wmf.de

Yamagiwa
www.yamagiwa.co.jp

Yos Collection
www.yos-collection.com

Yoshioka Design
www.tokujin.com

Yudai Tachikawa
3-5-5 Kakinokizaka
Meguroku
Tokyo 152-0022

Zanotta
www.zanotta.it

INDEX